Red Hat RHCSA™ 9 Cert Guide

EX200

Sander van Vugt

Red Hat RHCSA™ 9 Cert Guide: EX200

ISBN-13: 978-0-13-809627-4

ISBN-10: 0-13-809627-9

Library of Congress Cataloging-in-Publication Data Is On File

10 2024

Trademarks

All terms mentioned in this book that are known to be trademarks or service marks have been appropriately capitalized. Pearson IT Certification cannot attest to the accuracy of this information. Use of a term in this book should not be regarded as affecting the validity of any trademark or service mark.

Red Hat and RHCSA are registered trademarks of Red Hat, Inc. in the United States and other countries.

Pearson IT Certification and Sander van Vugt have no affiliation with Red Hat, Inc. The RED HAT and RHCSA trademarks are used for identification purposes only and are not intended to indicate affiliation with or approval by Red Hat, Inc.

Warning and Disclaimer

Every effort has been made to make this book as complete and as accurate as possible, but no warranty or fitness is implied. The information provided is on an "as is" basis. The author and the publisher shall have neither liability nor responsibility to any person or entity with respect to any loss or damages arising from the information contained in this book.

Special Sales

For information about buying this title in bulk quantities, or for special sales opportunities (which may include electronic versions; custom cover designs; and content particular to your business, training goals, marketing focus, or branding interests), please contact our corporate sales department at corpsales@pearsoned.com or (800) 382-3419.

For government sales inquiries, please contact governmentsales@pearsoned.com.

For questions about sales outside the U.S., please contact intlcs@pearson.com.

Vice President, IT Professional
Mark Taub

Acquisitions Editors
Harry Misthos
Denise Lincoln

Development Editor
Ellie Bru

Managing Editor
Sandra Schroeder

Senior Project Editor
Tonya Simpson

Copy Editor
Bill McManus

Indexer
Erika Millen

Proofreader
Jen Hinchliffe

Technical Editors
John McDonough
William "Bo" Rothwell

Publishing Coordinator
Cindy Teeters

Cover Designer
Chuti Prasertsith

Compositor
codeMantra

Pearson's Commitment to Diversity, Equity, and Inclusion

Pearson is dedicated to creating bias-free content that reflects the diversity of all learners. We embrace the many dimensions of diversity, including but not limited to race, ethnicity, gender, socioeconomic status, ability, age, sexual orientation, and religious or political beliefs.

Education is a powerful force for equity and change in our world. It has the potential to deliver opportunities that improve lives and enable economic mobility. As we work with authors to create content for every product and service, we acknowledge our responsibility to demonstrate inclusivity and incorporate diverse scholarship so that everyone can achieve their potential through learning. As the world's leading learning company, we have a duty to help drive change and live up to our purpose to help more people create a better life for themselves and to create a better world.

Our ambition is to purposefully contribute to a world where

- Everyone has an equitable and lifelong opportunity to succeed through learning
- Our educational products and services are inclusive and represent the rich diversity of learners
- Our educational content accurately reflects the histories and experiences of the learners we serve
- Our educational content prompts deeper discussions with learners and motivates them to expand their own learning (and worldview)

While we work hard to present unbiased content, we want to hear from you about any concerns or needs with this Pearson product so that we can investigate and address them.

Please contact us with concerns about any potential bias at https://www.pearson.com/report-bias.html.

Contents at a Glance

Introduction xxx

Part I Performing Basic System Management Tasks

CHAPTER 1 Installing Red Hat Enterprise Linux 3

CHAPTER 2 Using Essential Tools 27

CHAPTER 3 Essential File Management Tools 53

CHAPTER 4 Working with Text Files 81

CHAPTER 5 Connecting to Red Hat Enterprise Linux 9 101

CHAPTER 6 User and Group Management 121

CHAPTER 7 Permissions Management 145

CHAPTER 8 Configuring Networking 167

Part II Operating Running Systems

CHAPTER 9 Managing Software 195

CHAPTER 10 Managing Processes 231

CHAPTER 11 Working with Systemd 253

CHAPTER 12 Scheduling Tasks 271

CHAPTER 13 Configuring Logging 287

CHAPTER 14 Managing Storage 311

CHAPTER 15 Managing Advanced Storage 343

Part III Performing Advanced System Administration Tasks

CHAPTER 16 Basic Kernel Management 369

CHAPTER 17 Managing and Understanding the Boot Procedure 387

CHAPTER 18 Essential Troubleshooting Skills 403

CHAPTER 19 An Introduction to Automation with Bash Shell Scripting 421

Part IV Managing Network Services

CHAPTER 20 Configuring SSH 439

CHAPTER 21 Managing Apache HTTP Services 453

CHAPTER 22 Managing SELinux 469

CHAPTER 23 Configuring a Firewall 495

CHAPTER 24 Accessing Network Storage 509

CHAPTER 25 Configuring Time Services 523

CHAPTER 26 Managing Containers 539

CHAPTER 27 Final Preparation 573

CHAPTER 28 Theoretical Pre-Assessment Exam 579

Part V RHCSA 9 Practice Exams

RHCSA Practice Exam A 581

RHCSA Practice Exam B 583

APPENDIX A: Answers to the "Do I Know This Already?" Quizzes and Review Questions 585

APPENDIX B: *Red Hat RHCSA 9 Cert Guide: EX200* Exam Updates 617

Glossary 619

Index 641

Online Elements

RHCSA Practice Exam C

RHCSA Practice Exam D

APPENDIX C: Memory Tables

APPENDIX D: Memory Tables Answer Key

APPENDIX E: Study Planner

Glossary

Table of Contents

Introduction xxx

Part I Performing Basic System Management Tasks

Chapter 1 Installing Red Hat Enterprise Linux 3

"Do I Know This Already?" Quiz 3

Foundation Topics 6

Preparing to Install Red Hat Enterprise Linux 6

What Is Red Hat Enterprise Linux 9 Server? 6

Getting the Software 7

Using Red Hat Enterprise Linux 7

Using CentOS Stream 7

Other Distributions 8

Understanding Access to Repositories 8

Setup Requirements 9

Cert Guide Environment Description 9

Performing an Installation 10

Summary 22

Exam Preparation Tasks 23

Review All Key Topics 23

Define Key Terms 23

Review Questions 23

End-of-Chapter Lab 24

Lab 1.1 24

Chapter 2 Using Essential Tools 27

"Do I Know This Already?" Quiz 27

Foundation Topics 30

Basic Shell Skills 30

Understanding Commands 30

Executing Commands 30

I/O Redirection 32

Using Pipes 34

History 35

Bash Completion 37

Editing Files with vim 37
Understanding the Shell Environment 40
Understanding Variables 40
Recognizing Environment Configuration Files 41
Using /etc/motd and /etc/issue 42
Finding Help 43
Using --help 43
Using man 43
Finding the Right man Page 44
Updating mandb 46
Using info 47
Using /usr/share/doc Documentation Files 48
Summary 49
Exam Preparation Tasks 49
Review All Key Topics 49
Complete Tables and Lists from Memory 49
Define Key Terms 50
Review Questions 50
End-of-Chapter Lab 51
Lab 2.1 51
Chapter 3 Essential File Management Tools 53
"Do I Know This Already?" Quiz 53
Foundation Topics 56
Working with the File System Hierarchy 56
Defining the File System Hierarchy 56
Understanding Mounts 57
Managing Files 61
Working with Wildcards 61
Managing and Working with Directories 61
Working with Absolute and Relative Pathnames 62
Listing Files and Directories 64
Copying Files and Directories 64
Moving Files and Directories 65
Deleting Files and Directories 66

Using Links 68
Understanding Hard Links 68
Understanding Symbolic Links 69
Creating Links 69
Removing Links 70
Working with Archives and Compressed Files 71
Managing Archives with tar 72
Creating Archives with tar 72
Monitoring and Extracting tar Files 73
Using Compression 74
Summary 75
Exam Preparation Tasks 76
Review All Key Topics 76
Complete Tables and Lists from Memory 76
Define Key Terms 76
Review Questions 77
End-of-Chapter Lab 77
Lab 3.1 77
Chapter 4 Working with Text Files 81
"Do I Know This Already?" Quiz 81
Foundation Topics 84
Using Common Text File–Related Tools 84
Doing More with less 84
Showing File Contents with cat 85
Displaying the First or Last Lines of a File with head and tail 86
Filtering Specific Columns with cut 87
Sorting File Contents and Output with sort 87
Counting Lines, Words, and Characters with wc 88
A Primer to Using Regular Expressions 89
Using Line Anchors 90
Using Escaping in Regular Expressions 91
Using Wildcards and Multipliers 91
Using Extended Regular Expressions 91
Using grep to Analyze Text 93
Working with Other Useful Text Processing Utilities 94

Summary 96
Exam Preparation Tasks 96
Review All Key Topics 96
Complete Tables and Lists from Memory 96
Define Key Terms 97
Review Questions 97
End-of-Chapter Lab 98
Lab 4.1 98

Chapter 5 Connecting to Red Hat Enterprise Linux 9 101

"Do I Know This Already?" Quiz 101
Foundation Topics 104
Working on Local Consoles 104
  Logging In to a Local Console 104
  Switching Between Terminals in a Graphical Environment 105
  Working with Multiple Terminals in a Nongraphical Environment 107
  Understanding Pseudo Terminal Devices 108
  Booting, Rebooting, and Shutting Down Systems 109
Using SSH and Related Utilities 110
  Accessing Remote Systems Using SSH 110
  Using Graphical Applications in an SSH Environment 113
  Securely Transferring Files Between Systems 114
  Using scp to Securely Copy Files 114
  Using sftp to Securely Transfer Files 115
  Using rsync to Synchronize Files 115
  Configuring Key-Based Authentication for SSH 116
  Using Passphrases or Not? 116
Summary 117
Exam Preparation Tasks 118
Review All Key Topics 118
Complete Tables and Lists from Memory 118
Define Key Terms 118
Review Questions 118
End-of-Chapter Labs 119
Lab 5.1 119
Lab 5.2 119

Chapter 6 User and Group Management 121

"Do I Know This Already?" Quiz 121

Foundation Topics 124

Understanding Different User Types 124

Users on Linux 124

Working as Root 124

Using su 125

sudo 126

PolicyKit 127

Creating and Managing User Accounts 129

System Accounts and Normal Accounts 129

Creating Users 132

Modifying the Configuration Files 132

Using useradd 133

Home Directories 133

Default Shell 133

Managing User Properties 134

Configuration Files for User Management Defaults 134

Managing Password Properties 135

Creating a User Environment 135

Creating and Managing Group Accounts 137

Understanding Linux Groups 137

Creating Groups 137

Creating Groups with vigr 137

Using groupadd to Create Groups 138

Managing Group Properties 138

Summary 139

Exam Preparation Tasks 140

Review All Key Topics 140

Complete Tables and Lists from Memory 140

Define Key Terms 140

Review Questions 141

End-of-Chapter Labs 141

Lab 6.1 141

Lab 6.2 142

Chapter 7 Permissions Management 145

"Do I Know This Already?" Quiz 145

Foundation Topics 148

Managing File Ownership 148

Displaying Ownership 148

Changing User Ownership 149

Changing Group Ownership 150

Understanding Default Ownership 150

Managing Basic Permissions 151

Understanding Read, Write, and Execute Permissions 152

Applying Read, Write, and Execute Permissions 153

Managing Advanced Permissions 155

Understanding Advanced Permissions 155

Applying Advanced Permissions 157

Setting Default Permissions with umask 159

Working with User-Extended Attributes 160

Summary 162

Exam Preparation Tasks 162

Review All Key Topics 162

Complete Tables and Lists from Memory 162

Define Key Terms 163

Review Questions 163

End-of-Chapter Lab 164

Lab 7.1 164

Chapter 8 Configuring Networking 167

"Do I Know This Already?" Quiz 167

Foundation Topics 170

Networking Fundamentals 170

IP Addresses 170

IPv6 Addresses 171

IPv4 Network Masks 171

Binary Notation 172

MAC Addresses 173

Protocol and Ports 173

Managing Network Addresses and Interfaces 174
Validating Network Configuration 175
Validating Network Address Configuration 175
Validating Routing 178
Validating the Availability of Ports and Services 179
Managing Network Configuration with nmtui and nmcli 180
Required Permissions to Change Network Configuration 181
Configuring the Network with nmcli 182
Configuring the Network with nmtui 184
Working on Network Configuration Files 186
Setting Up Hostname and Name Resolution 187
Hostnames 187
DNS Name Resolution 189
Summary 191
Exam Preparation Tasks 191
Review All Key Topics 191
Complete Tables and Lists from Memory 192
Define Key Terms 192
Review Questions 192
End-of-Chapter Lab 193
Lab 8.1 193

Part II Operating Running Systems

Chapter 9 Managing Software 195
"Do I Know This Already?" Quiz 195
Foundation Topics 198
Managing Software Packages with dnf 198
Understanding the Role of Repositories 198
Registering Red Hat Enterprise Linux for Support 199
Managing Subscriptions 200
Specifying Which Repository to Use 200
Understanding Repository Security 203
Creating Your Own Repository 204
Using dnf 206
Using dnf to Find Software Packages 206

Getting More Information About Packages 208

Installing and Removing Software Packages 209

Showing Lists of Packages 211

Updating Packages 213

Working with dnf Package Groups 214

Using dnf History 216

Managing Package Modules 217

Understanding dnf Modules 218

Managing Modules 218

Managing Software Packages with rpm 221

Understanding RPM Filenames 222

Querying the RPM Database 222

Querying RPM Package Files 223

Using repoquery 224

Summary 226

Exam Preparation Tasks 226

Review All Key Topics 226

Complete Tables and Lists from Memory 226

Define Key Terms 226

Review Questions 227

End-of-Chapter Labs 227

Lab 9.1 228

Chapter 10 Managing Processes 231

"Do I Know This Already?" Quiz 231

Foundation Topics 234

Introduction to Process Management 234

Managing Shell Jobs 234

Running Jobs in the Foreground and Background 234

Managing Shell Jobs 235

Understanding Parent–Child Relations 237

Using Common Command-Line Tools for Process Management 237

Understanding Processes and Threads 238

Using ps to Get Process Information 239

Understanding Process Priorities 241

Exploring Relations Between Slices 241

Managing Process Priorities 242
Sending Signals to Processes with kill, killall, and pkill 243
Killing Zombies 245
Using top to Manage Processes 246
Using tuned to Optimize Performance 248
Summary 250
Exam Preparation Tasks 250
Review All Key Topics 250
Complete Tables and Lists from Memory 250
Define Key Terms 250
Review Questions 251
End-of-Chapter Lab 251
Lab 10.1 251

Chapter 11 Working with Systemd 253
"Do I Know This Already?" Quiz 253
Foundation Topics 256
Understanding Systemd 256
Understanding Systemd Unit Locations 256
Understanding Systemd Service Units 257
Understanding Systemd Mount Units 258
Understanding Systemd Socket Units 259
Understanding Systemd Target Units 260
Managing Units Through Systemd 261
Managing Dependencies 263
Managing Unit Options 265
Summary 267
Exam Preparation Tasks 267
Review All Key Topics 267
Complete Tables and Lists from Memory 267
Define Key Terms 268
Review Questions 268
End-of-Chapter Lab 268
Lab 11.1 268

Chapter 12 Scheduling Tasks 271

"Do I Know This Already?" Quiz 271

Foundation Topics 274

Understanding Task Scheduling Options in RHEL 274

Using Systemd Timers 274

Configuring cron to Automate Recurring Tasks 276

Managing the crond Service 276

Understanding cron Timing 278

Managing cron Configuration Files 278

Understanding the Purpose of anacron 281

Managing cron Security 282

Configuring at to Schedule Future Tasks 282

Summary 283

Exam Preparation Tasks 284

Review All Key Topics 284

Define Key Terms 284

Review Questions 284

End-of-Chapter Lab 285

Lab 12.1 285

Chapter 13 Configuring Logging 287

"Do I Know This Already?" Quiz 287

Foundation Topics 290

Understanding System Logging 290

Understanding the Role of systemd-journald and rsyslogd 290

Reading Log Files 292

Understanding Log File Contents 293

Live Log File Monitoring 294

Using logger 294

Working with systemd-journald 295

Using journalctl to Find Events 295

Preserving the Systemd Journal 298

Configuring rsyslogd 300

Understanding rsyslogd Configuration Files 300

Understanding rsyslog.conf Sections 300

Understanding Facilities, Priorities, and Log Destinations 301
Rotating Log Files 304
Summary 306
Exam Preparation Tasks 306
Review All Key Topics 306
Complete Tables and Lists from Memory 307
Define Key Terms 307
Review Questions 307
End-of-Chapter Lab 308
Lab 13.1 308
Chapter 14 Managing Storage 311
"Do I Know This Already?" Quiz 311
Foundation Topics 314
Understanding MBR and GPT Partitions 314
Understanding the MBR Partitioning Scheme 314
Understanding the Need for GPT Partitioning 315
Understanding Storage Measurement Units 316
Managing Partitions and File Systems 317
Creating MBR Partitions with fdisk 318
Using Extended and Logical Partitions on MBR 320
Creating GPT Partitions with gdisk 322
Creating GPT Partitions with parted 327
Creating File Systems 328
Changing File System Properties 329
Managing Ext4 File System Properties 329
Managing XFS File System Properties 331
Adding Swap Partitions 332
Adding Swap Files 333
Mounting File Systems 333
Manually Mounting File Systems 334
Using Device Names, UUIDs, or Disk Labels 334
Automating File System Mounts Through /etc/fstab 335
Using Systemd Mounts 338
Summary 339

Exam Preparation Tasks 340
Review All Key Topics 340
Complete Tables and Lists from Memory 340
Define Key Terms 340
Review Questions 341
End-of-Chapter Lab 341
Lab 14.1 341

Chapter 15 Managing Advanced Storage 343

"Do I Know This Already?" Quiz 343
Foundation Topics 346
Understanding LVM 346
  LVM Architecture 346
  LVM Features 347
Creating LVM Logical Volumes 348
  Creating the Physical Volumes 350
  Creating the Volume Groups 353
  Creating the Logical Volumes and File Systems 355
  Understanding LVM Device Naming 355
Resizing LVM Logical Volumes 358
  Resizing Volume Groups 358
  Resizing Logical Volumes and File Systems 358
  Reducing Volume Groups 360
Configuring Stratis 361
  Understanding Stratis Architecture 362
  Creating Stratis Storage 362
  Managing Stratis 363
Summary 365
Exam Preparation Tasks 365
Review All Key Topics 365
Complete Tables and Lists from Memory 365
Define Key Terms 365
Review Questions 366
End-of-Chapter Labs 366
Lab 15.1 366
Lab 15.2 367

Part III Performing Advanced System Administration Tasks

Chapter 16 Basic Kernel Management 369

"Do I Know This Already?" Quiz 369
Foundation Topics 372
Understanding the Role of the Linux Kernel 372
Understanding the Use of Kernel Threads and Drivers 372
Analyzing What the Kernel Is Doing 373
Working with Kernel Modules 375
Understanding Hardware Initialization 376
Managing Kernel Modules 378
Checking Driver Availability for Hardware Devices 381
Managing Kernel Module Parameters 382
Upgrading the Linux Kernel 383
Summary 383
Exam Preparation Tasks 384
Review All Key Topics 384
Complete Tables and Lists from Memory 384
Define Key Terms 384
Review Questions 384
End-of-Chapter Lab 385
Lab 16.1 385

Chapter 17 Managing and Understanding the Boot Procedure 387

"Do I Know This Already?" Quiz 387
Foundation Topics 390
Managing Systemd Targets 390
Understanding Systemd Targets 390
Working with Targets 390
Understanding Target Units 391
Understanding Wants 392
Managing Systemd Targets 392
Isolating Targets 393
Setting the Default Target 396
Working with GRUB 2 396
Understanding GRUB 2 396

Understanding GRUB 2 Configuration Files 397
Modifying Default GRUB 2 Boot Options 398
Summary 399
Exam Preparation Tasks 399
Review All Key Topics 399
Define Key Terms 400
Review Questions 400
End-of-Chapter Labs 401
Lab 17.1 401
Lab 17.2 401

Chapter 18 Essential Troubleshooting Skills 403

"Do I Know This Already?" Quiz 403
Foundation Topics 406
Understanding the RHEL 9 Boot Procedure 406
Passing Kernel Boot Arguments 408
Accessing the Boot Prompt 408
Starting a Troubleshooting Target 409
Using a Rescue Disk 410
Restoring System Access Using a Rescue Disk 411
Reinstalling GRUB Using a Rescue Disk 413
Re-creating the Initramfs Using a Rescue Disk 413
Fixing Common Issues 414
Reinstalling GRUB 2 414
Fixing the Initramfs 415
Recovering from File System Issues 415
Resetting the Root Password 416
Summary 417
Exam Preparation Tasks 417
Review All Key Topics 418
Complete Tables and Lists from Memory 418
Define Key Terms 418
Review Questions 418
End-of-Chapter Lab 419
Lab 18.1 419

Chapter 19 An Introduction to Automation with Bash Shell Scripting 421

"Do I Know This Already?" Quiz 421

Foundation Topics 424

Understanding Shell Scripting Core Elements 424

Using Variables and Input 426

Using Positional Parameters 426

Working with Variables 427

Using Conditional Loops 429

Working with if ... then ... else 430

Using || and && 431

Applying for 431

Understanding while and until 432

Understanding case 434

Bash Shell Script Debugging 435

Summary 435

Exam Preparation Tasks 436

Review All Key Topics 436

Define Key Terms 436

Review Questions 436

End-of-Chapter Lab 437

Lab 19.1 437

Part IV Managing Network Services

Chapter 20 Configuring SSH 439

"Do I Know This Already?" Quiz 439

Foundation Topics 442

Hardening the SSH Server 442

Limiting Root Access 442

Configuring Alternative Ports 443

Modifying SELinux to Allow for Port Changes 443

Limiting User Access 444

Using Other Useful sshd Options 445

Session Options 446

Connection Keepalive Options 446

Configuring Key-Based Authentication with Passphrases 447

Summary 448
Exam Preparation Tasks 448
Review All Key Topics 448
Complete Tables and Lists from Memory 449
Define Key Terms 449
Review Questions 449
End-of-Chapter Lab 450
Lab 20.1 450

Chapter 21 Managing Apache HTTP Services 453

"Do I Know This Already?" Quiz 453
Foundation Topics 456
Configuring a Basic Apache Server 456
  Installing the Required Software 456
  Identifying the Main Configuration File 456
  Creating Web Server Content 459
Understanding Apache Configuration Files 460
Creating Apache Virtual Hosts 462
Summary 464
Exam Preparation Tasks 464
Review All Key Topics 464
Define Key Terms 465
Review Questions 465
End-of-Chapter Lab 466
Lab 21.1 466

Chapter 22 Managing SELinux 469

"Do I Know This Already?" Quiz 470
Foundation Topics 473
Understanding SELinux Working Modes 473
Understanding Context Settings and the Policy 477
  Monitoring Current Context Labels 477
  Setting Context Types 479
  Finding the Context Type You Need 482
Restoring Default File Contexts 483
Managing Port Access 484

Using Boolean Settings to Modify SELinux Settings 485
Diagnosing and Addressing SELinux Policy Violations 487
Making SELinux Analyzing Easier 489
Summary 490
Exam Preparation Tasks 491
Review All Key Topics 491
Complete Tables and Lists from Memory 491
Define Key Terms 491
Review Questions 491
End-of-Chapter Lab 492
Lab 22.1 492

Chapter 23 Configuring a Firewall 495

"Do I Know This Already?" Quiz 495
Foundation Topics 498
Understanding Linux Firewalling 498
Understanding Previous Solutions 498
Understanding Firewalld 498
Understanding Firewalld Zones 499
Understanding Firewalld Services 500
Working with Firewalld 501
Summary 504
Exam Preparation Tasks 504
Review All Key Topics 505
Complete Tables and Lists from Memory 505
Define Key Terms 505
Review Questions 505
End-of-Chapter Lab 506
Lab 23.1 506

Chapter 24 Accessing Network Storage 509

"Do I Know This Already?" Quiz 509
Foundation Topics 512
Using NFS Services 512
Understanding NFS Security 512
RHEL NFS Versions 512

Setting Up NFS 513

Mounting the NFS Share 514

Mounting Remote File Systems Through fstab 515

Mounting NFS Shares Through fstab 515

Using Automount to Mount Remote File Systems 516

Understanding Automount 516

Defining Mounts in Automount 516

Configuring Automount for NFS 517

Using Wildcards in Automount 517

Summary 518

Exam Preparation Tasks 518

Review All Key Topics 519

Define Key Terms 519

Review Questions 519

End-of-Chapter Lab 520

Lab 24.1 520

Chapter 25 Configuring Time Services 523

"Do I Know This Already?" Quiz 523

Foundation Topics 526

Understanding Local Time 526

Using Network Time Protocol 527

Managing Time on Red Hat Enterprise Linux 527

Using date 528

Using hwclock 528

Using timedatectl 529

Managing Time Zone Settings 531

Configuring Time Service Clients 533

Summary 534

Exam Preparation Tasks 535

Review All Key Topics 535

Complete Tables and Lists from Memory 535

Define Key Terms 535

Review Questions 536
End-of-Chapter Lab 536
Lab 25.1 536
Chapter 26 Managing Containers 539
"Do I Know This Already?" Quiz 539
Foundation Topics 542
Understanding Containers 542
    Container Host Requirements 543
    Containers on RHEL 9 544
    Container Orchestration 545
Running a Container 545
Working with Container Images 550
    Using Registries 550
    Finding Images 552
    Inspecting Images 553
    Performing Image Housekeeping 556
    Building Images from a Containerfile 556
Managing Containers 558
    Managing Container Status 558
    Running Commands in a Container 559
    Managing Container Ports 561
    Managing Container Environment Variables 562
Managing Container Storage 563
Running Containers as Systemd Services 566
Summary 568
Exam Preparation Tasks 569
Review All Key Topics 569
Complete Tables and Lists from Memory 569
Define Key Terms 569
Review Questions 569
End-of-Chapter Lab 570
Lab 26.1 570

Chapter 27 Final Preparation 573

General Tips 573

Verifying Your Readiness 573

Registering for the Exam 573

On Exam Day 574

During the Exam 575

The Nondisclosure Agreement 576

Chapter 28 Theoretical Pre-Assessment Exam 579

Part V RHCSA 9 Practice Exams

RHCSA Practice Exam A 581

RHCSA Practice Exam B 583

Appendix A: Answers to the "Do I Know This Already?" Quizzes and Review Questions 585

Appendix B: *Red Hat RHCSA 9 Cert Guide: EX200* Exam Updates 617

Glossary 619

Index 641

Online Elements:

RHCSA Practice Exam C

RHCSA Practice Exam D

Appendix C: Memory Tables

Appendix D: Memory Tables Answer Key

Appendix E: Study Planner

Glossary

About the Author

Sander van Vugt is an independent Linux trainer, author, and consultant living in the Netherlands. Sander is the author of the best-selling *Red Hat Certified System Administrator (RHCSA) Complete Video Course* and the *Red Hat Certified Engineer (RHCE) Complete Video Course*. He has also written numerous books about different Linux-related topics and many articles for Linux publications around the world. Sander has been teaching Red Hat, Linux+, and LFCS classes since 1994. As a consultant, he specializes in Linux high-availability solutions and performance optimization. You can find more information about Sander on his website at https://www.sandervanvugt.com.

For more information about RHCSA certification and additional resources, visit the author's Red Hat Certification page at https://www.rhatcert.com/.

Acknowledgments

This book could not have been written without the help of all the people who contributed to it. I want to thank the people at Pearson, Denise Lincoln, Harry Misthos, and Ellie Bru in particular. We've worked a lot together over the years, and this book is another milestone on our road to success!

About the Technical Reviewers

John McDonough is a cloud architect/cloud DevOps engineer at Fortinet, delivering innovative cloud deployment and automation solutions to global customers. Prior to Fortinet, John was a Developer Advocate for Cisco Systems' DevNet. During his almost 35-year career, John has contributed to open source projects, Ansible, and OpenStack, has been a distinguished speaker at more than 20 Cisco Live events, and has spoken about open source contribution and data center and cloud automation at many industry events, including HashiConf, SXSW, Devopsdays, Cisco Live, Apidays, and more.

William "Bo" Rothwell, at the impressionable age of 14, crossed paths with a TRS-80 Micro Computer System (affectionately known as a Trash 80). Soon after, the adults responsible for Bo made the mistake of leaving him alone with the TRS-80. He immediately dismantled it and held his first computer class, showing his friends what made this "computer thing" work.

Since this experience, Bo's passion for understanding how computers work and sharing this knowledge with others has resulted in a rewarding career in IT training. His experience includes Linux, Unix, IT security, DevOps, and programming languages such as Perl, Python, Tcl, and Bash. Bo is the founder and lead instructor of One Course Source, an IT training organization.

Bo is an author of several books, including *Linux for Developers: Jumpstart Your Linux Programming Skills*, *Linux Essentials for Cybersecurity*, and *LPIC-2 Cert Guide*. He can be reached on LinkedIn: https://www.linkedin.com/in/bo-rothwell/.

We Want to Hear from You!

As the reader of this book, *you* are our most important critic and commentator. We value your opinion and want to know what we're doing right, what we could do better, what areas you'd like to see us publish in, and any other words of wisdom you're willing to pass our way.

We welcome your comments. You can email or write to let us know what you did or didn't like about this book—as well as what we can do to make our books better.

Please note that we cannot help you with technical problems related to the topic of this book.

When you write, please be sure to include this book's title and author as well as your name and email address. We will carefully review your comments and share them with the author and editors who worked on the book.

Email: community@informit.com

Reader Services

Register your copy of *Red Hat RHCSA 9 Cert Guide: EX200* at www.pearsonitcertification.com for convenient access to downloads, updates, and corrections as they become available. To start the registration process, go to www.pearsonitcertification.com/register and log in or create an account*. Enter the product ISBN 9780138096274 and click Submit. When the process is complete, you will find any available bonus content under Registered Products.

*Be sure to check the box that you would like to hear from us to receive exclusive discounts on future editions of this product.

Introduction

Welcome to the *Red Hat RHCSA 9 Cert Guide: EX200*. The Red Hat exams are some of the toughest in the business, and this guide will be an essential tool in helping you prepare to take the Red Hat Certified System Administrator (RHCSA) exam.

As an instructor with more than 20 years of experience teaching Red Hat Enterprise Linux, I have taken the RHCSA exam (and the RHCE exam) numerous times so that I can keep current on the progression of the exam, what is new, and what is different. I share my knowledge with you in this comprehensive Cert Guide so that you get the guidance you need to pass the RHCSA exam.

This book contains everything you need to know to pass the 2022 version of the RHCSA exam. As you will see, the Cert Guide covers every objective in the exam and comprises 28 chapters, more than 80 exercises, 4 practice exams, an extensive glossary, and hours of video training. This Cert Guide is the best resource you can get to prepare for and pass the RHCSA exam.

Goals and Methods

To learn the topics described in this book, it is recommended that you create your own testing environment. You cannot become an RHCSA without practicing a lot. Within the exercises included in every chapter of the book, you will find all the examples you need to understand what is on the exam and thoroughly learn the material needed to pass it. The exercises in the chapters provide step-by-step procedures that you can follow to find working solutions so that you can get real experience before taking the exam.

Each chapter also includes one or more end-of-chapter labs. These labs ask questions that are similar to the questions that you might encounter on the exam. Solutions are not provided for these labs, and that is on purpose, because you need to train yourself to verify your work before you take the exam. On the exam, you also have to be able to verify for yourself whether the solution is working as expected. Please be sure to also go to this book's companion website, which provides additional practice exams, appendixes, and video training—all key components to studying for and passing the exam.

To make working with the assignments in this book as easy as possible, the complete lab environment is Bring Your Own. In Chapter 1 you'll learn how to install Red Hat Enterprise Linux 9 in a virtual machine, and that is all that is required to go through the labs.

This book contains everything you need to pass the exam, but if you want more guidance and practice, I have a number of video training titles available to help you study, including the following:

- *Linux Fundamentals*, Second Edition
- *Red Hat Certified System Administrator (RHCSA) RHEL 9*

Apart from these products, you might also appreciate my website, https://rhatcert.com. Through this website, I provide updates on anything that is useful to exam candidates. I recommend that you register on the website so that I can send you messages about important updates that I've made available. Also, you'll find occasional video updates on my YouTube channel, rhatcert. I hope that all these resources provide you with everything you need to pass the Red Hat Certified System Administrator exam in an affordable way. Good luck!

Who Should Read This Book?

This book is written as an RHCSA exam preparation guide. That means that you should read it if you want to increase your chances of passing the RHCSA exam. A secondary use of this book is as a reference guide for Red Hat system administrators. As an administrator, you'll like the explanations and procedures that describe how to get things done on Red Hat Enterprise Linux.

So, why should you consider passing the RHCSA exam? That question is simple to answer: Linux has become a very important operating system, and qualified professionals are in demand all over the world. If you want to work as a Linux professional and prove your skills, the RHCSA certificate really helps and is one of the most sought-after certificates in IT. Having this certificate dramatically increases your chances of becoming hired as a Linux professional.

How This Book Is Organized

This book is organized as a reference guide to help you prepare for the RHCSA exam. If you're new to the topics, you can just read it cover to cover. You can also read the individual chapters that you need to fine-tune your skills in this book. Every chapter starts with a "Do I Know This Already?" quiz that asks questions about ten topics that are covered in that chapter and provides a simple tool to check whether you're already familiar with the topics covered in the chapter.

The book also provides two RHCSA practice exams; these are an essential part of readying yourself for the real exam experience. You might be able to provide the right answer to the multiple-choice chapter questions, but that doesn't mean that you can create the configurations when you take the exam. The companion website includes two extra practice exams, two hours of video from the *Red Hat Certified System Administrator (RHCSA) RHEL 9*, and additional appendixes. The following outline describes the topics that are covered in the chapters:

Part I: Performing Basic System Management Tasks

- **Chapter 1: Installing Red Hat Enterprise Linux:** In this chapter, you learn how to install Red Hat Enterprise Linux Server (RHEL). It also shows how to set up an environment that can be used for working on the labs and exercises in this book.
- **Chapter 2: Using Essential Tools:** This chapter covers some of the Linux basics, including working with the shell and Linux commands. This chapter is particularly important if you're new to working with Linux.
- **Chapter 3: Essential File Management Tools:** In this chapter, you learn how to work with tools to manage the Linux file system. This is an important skill because everything on Linux is very file system oriented.
- **Chapter 4: Working with Text Files:** In this chapter, you learn how to work with text files. The chapter teaches you how to create text files, but also how to look for specific content in the different text files.
- **Chapter 5: Connecting to Red Hat Enterprise Linux 9:** This chapter describes the different methods that can be used to connect to RHEL 9. It explains both local login and remote login and the different terminal types used for this purpose.
- **Chapter 6: User and Group Management:** On Linux, users are entities that can be used by people or processes that need access to specific resources. This chapter explains how to create users and make user management easier by working with groups.
- **Chapter 7: Permissions Management:** In this chapter, you learn how to manage Linux permissions through the basic read, write, and execute permissions, but also through the special permissions and access control lists.
- **Chapter 8: Configuring Networking:** A server is useless if it isn't connected to a network. In this chapter, you learn the essential skills required for managing network connections.

Part II: Operating Running Systems

- **Chapter 9: Managing Software:** Red Hat offers an advanced system for managing software packages. This chapter teaches you how it works.
- **Chapter 10: Managing Processes:** As an administrator, you need to know how to work with the different tasks that can be running on Linux. This

chapter shows how to do this, by sending signals to processes and by changing process priority.

- **Chapter 11: Working with Systemd:** Systemd is the standard manager of services and more in RHEL 9. In this chapter, you learn how to manage services using Systemd.
- **Chapter 12: Scheduling Tasks:** In this chapter, you learn how to schedule a task for execution at a time that fits you best.
- **Chapter 13: Configuring Logging:** As an administrator, you need to know what's happening on your server. The rsyslogd and systemd-journald services are used for this purpose. This chapter explains how to work with them.
- **Chapter 14: Managing Storage:** Storage management is an important skill to master as a Linux administrator. This chapter explains how hard disks can be organized in partitions and how these partitions can be mounted in the file system.
- **Chapter 15: Managing Advanced Storage:** Dividing disks in partitions isn't very flexible. If you need optimal flexibility, you need LVM logical volumes, which are used by default while you're installing Red Hat Enterprise Linux. This chapter shows how to manage those logical volumes. You'll also learn how to work with the Stratis and VDO storage techniques.

Part III: Performing Advanced System Administration Tasks

- **Chapter 16: Basic Kernel Management:** The kernel is the part of the operating system that takes care of handling hardware. This chapter explains how that works and what an administrator can do to analyze the current configuration and manage hardware devices in case the automated procedure doesn't work well.
- **Chapter 17: Managing and Understanding the Boot Procedure:** Many things are happening when a Linux server boots. This chapter describes the boot procedure in detail and zooms in on vital aspects of the boot procedure, including the GRUB 2 boot loader and the Systemd service manager.
- **Chapter 18: Essential Troubleshooting Skills:** Sometimes a misconfiguration can cause your server to no longer boot properly. This chapter teaches you some of the techniques that can be applied when normal server startup is no longer possible.
- **Chapter 19: An Introduction to Automation with Bash Shell Scripting:** Some tasks are complex and need to be performed repeatedly. Such tasks are ideal candidates for optimization through shell scripts. In this chapter, you learn how to use conditional structures in shell scripts to automate tasks efficiently.

Part IV: Managing Network Services

- **Chapter 20: Configuring SSH:** Secure Shell (SSH) is one of the fundamental services that is enabled on RHEL 9 by default. Using SSH allows you to connect to a server remotely. In this chapter, you learn how to set up an SSH server.
- **Chapter 21: Managing Apache HTTP Services:** Apache is the most commonly used service on Linux. This chapter shows how to set up Apache web services, including the configuration of Apache virtual hosts.
- **Chapter 22: Managing SELinux:** Many Linux administrators only know how to switch off SELinux, because SELinux is hard to manage and is often why services cannot be accessed. In this chapter, you learn how SELinux works and what to do to configure it so that your services are still working and will be much better protected against possible abuse.
- **Chapter 23: Configuring a Firewall:** Apart from SELinux, RHEL 9 comes with a firewall as one of the main security measures, which is implemented by the firewalld service. In this chapter, you learn how this service is organized and what you can do to block or enable access to specific services.
- **Chapter 24: Accessing Network Storage:** While you're working in a server environment, managing remote mounts is an important skill. A remote mount allows a client computer to access a file system offered through a remote server. These remote mounts can be made through a persistent mount in /etc/fstab, or by using the automount service. This chapter teaches how to set up either of them and shows how to configure an FTP server.
- **Chapter 25: Configuring Time Services:** For many services, such as databases and Kerberos, it is essential to have the right time. That's why as an administrator you need to be able to manage time on Linux. This chapter teaches you how.
- **Chapter 26: Managing Containers:** Containers have revolutionized datacenter IT. Where services not so long ago were running directly on top of the server operating system, nowadays services are often offered as containers. Red Hat Enterprise Linux 9 includes a complete platform to run containers. In this chapter, you learn how to work with it.
- **Chapter 27: Final Preparation:** In this chapter, you get some final exam preparation tasks. It contains many tips that help you maximize your chances of passing the RHCSA exam.
- **Chapter 28: Theoretical Pre-Assessment Exam:** This chapter provides an RHCSA theoretical pre-assessment exam to help you assess your skills and determine the best route forward for studying for the exam.

Part V: RHCSA 9 Practice Exams

This part supplies two RHCSA practice exams so that you can test your knowledge and skills further before taking the exams. Two additional exams are on the companion website.

How to Use This Book

To help you customize your study time using this book, the core chapters have several features that help you make the best use of your time:

- **"Do I Know This Already?" Quizzes:** Each chapter begins with a quiz that helps you determine the amount of time you need to spend studying that chapter and the specific topics that you need to focus on.
- **Foundation Topics:** These are the core sections of each chapter. They explain the protocols, concepts, and configuration for the topics in that chapter.
- **Exam Preparation Tasks:** Following the "Foundation Topics" section of each chapter, the "Exam Preparation Tasks" section lists a series of study activities that you should complete. Each chapter includes the activities that make the most sense for studying the topics in that chapter. The activities include the following:
  - **Review All Key Topics:** The Key Topic icon is shown next to the most important items in the "Foundation Topics" section of the chapter. The Review All Key Topics activity lists the key topics from the chapter and their corresponding page numbers. Although the contents of the entire chapter could be on the exam, you should definitely know the information listed in each key topic.
  - **Complete Tables and Lists from Memory:** To help you exercise your memory and memorize some facts, many of the more important lists and tables from the chapter are included in a document on the companion website. This document offers only partial information, allowing you to complete the table or list.
  - **Define Key Terms:** This section lists the most important terms from the chapter, asking you to write a short definition and compare your answer to the glossary at the end of this book.
- **Review Questions:** These questions at the end of each chapter measure insight into the topics that were discussed in the chapter.
- **End-of-Chapter Labs:** Real labs give you the right impression of what an exam assignment looks like. The end-of-chapter labs are your first step in finding out what the exam tasks really look like.

Other Features

In addition to the features in each of the core chapters, this book, as a whole, has additional study resources on the companion website, including the following:

- **Two practice exams:** *Red Hat RHCSA 9 Cert Guide: EX200* comes with four practice exams. You will find two in the book and two additional exams on the companion website; these are provided as PDFs so you can get extra practice testing your skills before taking the exam in the testing facility.
- **More than an hour of video training:** The companion website contains more than an hour of instruction from the best-selling *Red Hat Certified System Administrator (RHCSA) RHEL 9 Complete Video Course*.

Exam Objective to Chapter Mapping

Table 1 details where every objective in the RHCSA exam is covered in this book so that you can more easily create a successful plan for passing the exam.

Table 1 Coverage of RHCSA Objectives

Objective	Chapter Title	Chapter
Understand and use essential tools		
Access a shell prompt and issue commands with correct syntax	Using Essential Tools	2
Use input-output redirection (>, >>, |, 2>, etc.)	Using Essential Tools	2
Use grep and regular expressions to analyze text	Working with Text Files	4
Access remote systems using SSH	Connecting to Red Hat Enterprise Linux 9	5
Log in and switch users in multiuser targets	Connecting to Red Hat Enterprise Linux 9	5
Archive, compress, unpack, and uncompress files using tar, star, gzip, and bzip2	Essential File Management Tools	3
Create and edit text files	Working with Text Files	4
Create, delete, copy, and move files and directories	Essential File Management Tools	3
Create hard and soft links	Essential File Management Tools	3
List, set, and change standard ugo/rwx permissions	Permissions Management	7
Locate, read, and use system documentation including man, info, and files in /usr/share/doc	Using Essential Tools	2

Objective	Chapter Title	Chapter
Create simple shell scripts		
Conditionally execute code (use of: if, test, [], etc.)	An Introduction to Automation with Bash Shell Scripting	19
Use Looping constructs (for, etc.) to process file, command line input	An Introduction to Automation with Bash Shell Scripting	19
Process script inputs ($1, $2, etc.)	An Introduction to Automation with Bash Shell Scripting	19
Processing output of shell commands within a script	An Introduction to Automation with Bash Shell Scripting	19
Operate running systems		
Boot, reboot, and shut down a system normally	Connecting to Red Hat Enterprise Linux 9	5
Boot systems into different targets manually	Essential Troubleshooting Skills	18
Interrupt the boot process in order to gain access to a system	Essential Troubleshooting Skills	18
Identify CPU/memory intensive processes and kill processes	Managing Processes	10
Adjust process scheduling	Managing Processes	10
Manage tuning profiles	Managing Processes	10
Locate and interpret system log files and journals	Configuring Logging	13
Preserve system journals	Configuring Logging	13
Start, stop, and check the status of network services	Configuring Networking	8
Securely transfer files between systems	Connecting to Red Hat Enterprise Linux 9	5
Configure local storage		
List, create, and delete partitions on MBR and GPT disks	Managing Storage	14
Create and remove physical volumes	Managing Advanced Storage	15
Assign physical volumes to volume groups	Managing Advanced Storage	15
Create and delete logical volumes	Managing Advanced Storage	15
Configure systems to mount file systems at boot by universally unique ID (UUID) or label	Managing Storage	14
Add new partitions and logical volumes, and swap to a system nondestructively	Managing Storage	14

Objective	Chapter Title	Chapter
Create and configure file systems		
Create, mount, unmount, and use vfat, ext4, and xfs file systems	Managing Storage	14
Mount and unmount network file systems using NFS	Accessing Network Storage	24
Configure autofs	Accessing Network Storage	24
Extend existing logical volumes	Managing Advanced Storage	15
Create and configure set-GID directories for collaboration	Permissions Management	7
Diagnose and correct file permission problems	Permissions Management	7
Deploy, configure, and maintain systems		
Schedule tasks using at and cron	Scheduling Tasks	12
Start and stop services and configure services to start automatically at boot	Working with Systemd	11
Configure systems to boot into a specific target automatically	Managing and Understanding the Boot Procedure	17
Configure time service clients	Configuring Time Services	25
Install and update software packages from Red Hat Network, a remote repository, or from the local file system	Managing Software	9
Modify the system bootloader	Managing and Understanding the Boot Procedure	17
Manage basic networking		
Configure IPv4 and IPv6 addresses	Configuring Networking	8
Configure hostname resolution	Configuring Networking	8
Configure network services to start automatically at boot	Configuring Networking	8
Restrict network access using firewall-cmd/firewall	Configuring a Firewall	23
Manage users and groups		
Create, delete, and modify local user accounts	User and Group Management	6
Change passwords and adjust password aging for local user accounts	User and Group Management	6

Objective	Chapter Title	Chapter
Create, delete, and modify local groups and group memberships	User and Group Management	6
Configure superuser access	User and Group Management	6
Manage security		
Configure firewall settings using firewall-cmd/firewalld	Configuring a Firewall	23
Manage default file permissions		
Configure key-based authentication for SSH	Configuring SSH	20
Set enforcing and permissive modes for SELinux	Managing SELinux	22
List and identify SELinux file and process context	Managing SELinux	22
Restore default file contexts	Managing SELinux	22
Manage SELinux port labels		
Use Boolean settings to modify system SELinux settings	Managing SELinux	22
Diagnose and address routine SELinux policy violations	Managing SELinux	22
Manage containers		
Find and retrieve container images from a remote registry	Managing Containers	26
Inspect container images	Managing Containers	26
Perform container management using commands such as podman and skopeo	Managing Containers	26
Build a container from a Containerfile	Managing Containers	26
Perform basic container management such as running, starting, stopping, and listing running containers	Managing Containers	26
Run a service inside a container	Managing Containers	26
Configure a container to start automatically as a systemd service	Managing Containers	26
Attach persistent storage to a container	Managing Containers	26

Where Are the Companion Content Files?

Register this print version of *Red Hat RHCSA 9 Cert Guide: EX200* to access the bonus content online.

This print version of this title comes with a website of companion content. You have online access to these files by following these steps:

1. Go to www.pearsonitcertification.com/register and log in or create a new account.
2. Enter the ISBN: **9780138096274**.
3. Answer the challenge question as proof of purchase.
4. Click the **Access Bonus Content** link in the Registered Products section of your account page to be taken to the page where your downloadable content is available.

Please note that many of the companion content files can be very large, especially image and video files.

If you are unable to locate the files for this title by following the steps, please visit www.pearsonitcertification.com/contact and select the Site Problems/Comments option. A customer service representative will assist you.

This book also includes an exclusive offer for 70 percent off the *Red Hat Certified System Administrator (RHCSA) RHEL 9 Complete Video Course*.

Figure Credits

Cover image: eniegoite/Shutterstock

Figure 1-1 through Figure 1-12, Figure 5-1, Figure 5-2, Figure 8-1, Figure 8-2, Figure 8-4, Figure 8-5, Figure 10-1, Figure 18-1 through Figure 18-5: Red Hat, Inc

Figure 8-3: GNOME Project

The following topics are covered in this chapter:

- Preparing to Install Red Hat Enterprise Linux
- Performing an Installation

This chapter covers no exam objectives.

CHAPTER 1

Installing Red Hat Enterprise Linux

To learn how to work with Red Hat Enterprise Linux (RHEL) as an administrator, you first need to install it. This chapter teaches you how to set up an environment in which you can perform all exercises in this book.

On the Red Hat Certified System Administrator (RHCSA) exam, you do not need to install Red Hat Enterprise Linux. However, because you need to install an environment that allows you to test all items discussed in this book, you start by installing Red Hat Enterprise Linux in this chapter. This chapter describes all steps that you will encounter while performing an installation of RHEL 9. It also discusses how to set up an environment in which you can perform all exercises in this book.

"Do I Know This Already?" Quiz

The "Do I Know This Already?" quiz enables you to assess whether you should read this entire chapter thoroughly or jump to the "Exam Preparation Tasks" section. If you are in doubt about your answers to these questions or your own assessment of your knowledge of the topics, read the entire chapter. Table 1-1 lists the major headings in this chapter and their corresponding "Do I Know This Already?" quiz questions. You can find the answers in Appendix A, "Answers to the 'Do I Know This Already?' Quizzes and Review Questions."

Table 1-1 "Do I Know This Already?" Section-to-Question Mapping

Foundation Topics Section	Questions
Preparing to Install Red Hat Enterprise Linux	1, 2, 6
Performing an Installation	3–5, 7–10

1. You want to install a test environment to practice for the RHCSA exam. Which of the following distributions should you avoid?
   a. The most recent Fedora version
   b. CentOS Stream
   c. AlmaLinux
   d. Rocky Linux

2. Which of the following features is available in both RHEL and CentOS Stream?
   a. Hardware certification
   b. Software certification
   c. The right to make support calls
   d. Software updates

3. Why should you install the server with a GUI installation pattern?
   a. To prepare for RHCSA, you need some tools that run in a GUI only.
   b. The minimal installation is incomplete.
   c. If you do not install a GUI immediately, it is hard to add it later.
   d. The Server with GUI is the default installation that is recommended by Red Hat.

4. Which is the default file system that is used in RHEL 9?
   a. Ext3
   b. Ext4
   c. XFS
   d. Btrfs

5. Which feature is supported in Ext4 but not in XFS?
   a. The ability to shrink the file system
   b. Snapshots
   c. File system quota
   d. A maximum size that goes beyond 2 TB

6. Which of the following is not a reason why Fedora should be avoided?
   a. Fedora contains features that may or may not be available in future RHEL releases.
   b. Fedora distributions show a much later state of development than RHEL.
   c. Fedora software is not stable.
   d. Software in Fedora may differ from the same software in RHEL.

7. Which of the following options is not available from the Installation Summary screen?
   a. Time & Date
   b. Keyboard
   c. Language Support
   d. Troubleshoot an Existing Installation

8. After setting the root password that you want to use, you cannot proceed in the installation. What is the most likely reason?
   a. The password is unsecure, and unsecure passwords are not accepted.
   b. The password does not meet requirements in the password policy.
   c. You also need to create a user.
   d. If an unsecure password is used, you need to click Done twice.

9. Which statement about the system language is *not* true?
   a. You can change the system language from the Installation Summary screen.
   b. You can change the system language directly after booting from the installation media.
   c. When setting the installation language, you can also select a keyboard layout.
   d. After installation, you cannot change the language settings.

10. When installing a server that uses LVM logical volumes, you'll get at least three storage volumes (partitions or LVM). Which of the following is not part of them?
    a. /boot
    b. /var
    c. /
    d. swap

Foundation Topics

Preparing to Install Red Hat Enterprise Linux

Before you start installing Red Hat Enterprise Linux, a bit of preparation is helpful, as discussed in this section. You first learn what exactly Red Hat Enterprise Linux is. Then you learn how you can get access to the software. We then discuss the setup requirements. After you know all about these, you move on to the next section, where you learn how to install Red Hat Enterprise Linux.

What Is Red Hat Enterprise Linux 9 Server?

RHEL 9 is a Linux ***distribution***. As you probably know, ***Linux*** is a free operating system. That means that the source code of all programs is available for free. However, some enterprise Linux distributions are sold as commercial products, with bundled support and maintenance, which is the case for RHEL 9. To use RHEL 9 for free you can register for a free Red Hat developer subscription at https://developers.redhat.com. With this subscription, you can run up to 16 unsupported instances of RHEL in any environment you'd like.

To use RHEL 9, you need a subscription. Only if you use a valid subscription can you get access to free patches and updates. When you pay for Red Hat Enterprise Linux, ***Red Hat*** offers you a supported Enterprise Linux operating system, which has some key benefits that are a normal requirement in corporate environments:

- Monitored updates and patches that have gone through a thorough testing procedure
- Different levels of support and help, depending on which type of subscription you have purchased
- A certified operating system that is guaranteed to run and to be supported on specific hardware models
- A certified platform for running enterprise applications such as SAP middleware, Oracle Database, and many more
- Access to the Red Hat Customer Portal at https://access.redhat.com, where you can find much detailed documentation that is available to customers only

Red Hat understands that not all potential customers are interested in these enterprise features. That is why Red Hat is involved in two free alternatives also:

- CentOS Stream
- Fedora

Apart from these, there are also two community initiatives to provide free alternatives to RHEL, which contain the same software but without the Red Hat branding:

- Rocky Linux
- AlmaLinux

You learn more about these free alternatives in the upcoming sections of this chapter.

Getting the Software

There are different ways to get the software required to perform all exercises in this book. In this section, you learn what your options are.

Using Red Hat Enterprise Linux

If you want to learn how to work with the different programs, tools, and services that are provided in Red Hat Enterprise Linux 9, the easiest way is to use the developer program that Red Hat offers. Go to https://developers.redhat.com to register for the free developer program. This program gives you access to Red Hat Enterprise Linux for free, which allows you to work with RHEL in your own test environment without having to purchase it.

The most important thing that you get in the official RHEL 9 Server release is access to the Red Hat Customer Portal. Through this portal, you have access to a wide variety of information regarding RHEL, in addition to updates provided through Red Hat Network (RHN). In particular, the Red Hat knowledge base is invaluable; you can use it to find answers to many common problems that have been posted there by Red Hat consultants.

Using CentOS Stream

CentOS is the Community Enterprise Operating System. CentOS started as a recompiled version of RHEL, with all items that were not available for free removed from the RHEL software. Basically, just the name was changed and the Red Hat logo (which is proprietary) was removed from all the CentOS software packages. Before 2020, CentOS provided a good and completely free alternative to RHEL.

In the past years, Red Hat has acquired CentOS and changed its policy. Nowadays CentOS is provided as CentOS Stream. CentOS Stream is a Linux distribution where new features that will be released in the next version of RHEL are introduced. In the RHEL development cycle, new features are introduced in Fedora. After testing in Fedora, some features are introduced in CentOS Stream, which is used as the last testing platform before the features are included in RHEL.

New features are continuously integrated in CentOS Stream, and for that reason, it doesn't know any sub-versions such as RHEL 9.1. This makes CentOS Stream not a good candidate for production environments.

Other Distributions

Another Linux distribution closely related to Red Hat Enterprise Linux is ***Fedora***, a completely open source Linux distribution that is available for free. Red Hat has a lot of staff dedicated to contributing to the Fedora project, because Red Hat uses Fedora as the development platform for RHEL. The result is that Fedora offers access to the latest and greatest software, which in most cases is much more recent than the thoroughly tested software components of RHEL (which is why you should not use Fedora to prepare for the RHCSA exam). Fedora is also used by Red Hat as a testing ground for new features that might or might not be included in future RHEL releases. If you were to choose Fedora, you would be working with items that are not available in RHEL, which means that you would have to do things differently on the exam. So, don't use it!

AlmaLinux and ***Rocky Linux*** are community distributions that provide the same software as in RHEL, but without any license restrictions or support. These distributions are independently developed and in no way supervised by Red Hat. If you want to use a 100 percent compatible alternative for RHEL without being bound by any license conditions, both AlmaLinux and Rocky Linux are good alternatives.

Understanding Access to Repositories

An important difference between RHEL and the other distributions is the access to repositories. A *repository* is the installation source used for installing software. If you are using free software such as AlmaLinux, correct repositories are automatically set up, and no further action is required. If you are using Red Hat Enterprise Linux with a subscription, you'll need to use the Subscription Manager software to get access to repositories.

TIP If you install Red Hat from the RHEL 9 installation disc but do not register it, you will not have access to a repository, which is why you need to know how to set up a repository access manually. Manually setting up a repository is a key skill that you should master on the exam. In Chapter 9, "Managing Software," you learn how to do this.

Setup Requirements

RHEL 9 can be installed on physical hardware and on virtual hardware. For the availability of specific features, it does not really matter which type of hardware is used, as long as the following minimal conditions are met:

- 1 GiB of RAM
- A 10-GiB hard disk
- A network card

TIP One GB is 1000 × 1000 × 1000 bytes. With hardware vendors it is common to work with multiples of 1000; however, that doesn't correspond with how a computer works, which is why most computer software works with KiB, MiB, and GiB instead. In this context, one GiB is 1024 × 1024 × 1024 bytes (which is 1.07 GB).

The preceding requirements allow you to run a minimal installation of RHEL, but if you want to create an environment that enables you to perform all exercises described in this book, make sure to meet the following minimal requirements:

- 64-bit platform support, either Intel based or ARM
- 2 GiB of RAM
- A 20-GiB hard disk
- A DVD drive, either virtual or physical
- A network card

NOTE Some resources on the Internet mention different minimal requirements. This is not a big deal for the RHCSA exam.

Cert Guide Environment Description

To set up an environment to work your way through this book, I suggest you start by installing one RHEL 9 server, following the instructions in the next section. For the chapters in Part IV, "Managing Network Services," it is useful if you have a second server as well. This second server doesn't have any specific requirements.

To set up the Cert Guide environment, I recommend that you use a solution for desktop virtualization, such as VMware Workstation (or VMware Fusion if you are on Mac), Microsoft Hyper-V, or Oracle VM VirtualBox. Using one of these solutions has the benefit that you can use snapshots, which enables you to easily revert to a previous state of the configuration. Other virtualization solutions, such as KVM, are supported as well, but because KVM runs on Linux, you'll need to have some Linux knowledge already if you'd like to start with KVM. You can also install on real hardware, but that solution will be less flexible.

TIP In all chapters, you'll find step-by-step exercises that tell you exactly what to do to configure specific services. At the end of all chapters, you'll find end-of-chapter labs that provide assignments that are very similar to the types of assignments that you will encounter on the exam. To get the most out of the end-of-chapter labs, it is a good idea to start from a clean environment. The most efficient way to do this is by creating snapshots of the state of your virtual machines when you are starting the chapter. This allows you to revert to the state your virtual machines were in when you started working on the chapter, while still keeping all the work that you have done in previous chapters.

Performing an Installation

Even if RHEL 9 can be installed from other media such as an installation server or a USB key, the most common installation starts from the installation DVD or, when you are working in a virtual machine, from the installation DVD ISO file. So, take your installation DVD (or its ISO) and boot the computer on which you want to install the software. The following steps describe how to proceed from the moment you see the installation DVD boot screen:

Step 1. After booting from DVD, you'll see the RHEL 9 boot menu. From this menu, you can choose from different options:

- **Install Red Hat Enterprise Linux 9.0:** Choose this for a normal installation.
- **Test This Media & Install Red Hat Enterprise Linux 9.0:** Select this if before installing you want to test the installation media. Note that testing will take a significant amount of time and should not be necessary in most cases.
- **Troubleshooting:** Select this option for some troubleshooting options. This option is useful if you cannot boot normally from your computer's hard drive after RHEL has been installed on it.

When the installation program starts, you can pass boot options to the kernel to enable or disable specific features. To get access to the prompt where you can add these options, press Tab from the installation menu. This shows you the kernel boot line that will be used and offers an option to change boot parameters.

Step 2. To start a normal installation, select the **Install Red Hat Enterprise Linux 9.0** boot option (see Figure 1-1). Note that the exact sub-version will change if you install a later version of RHEL 9.

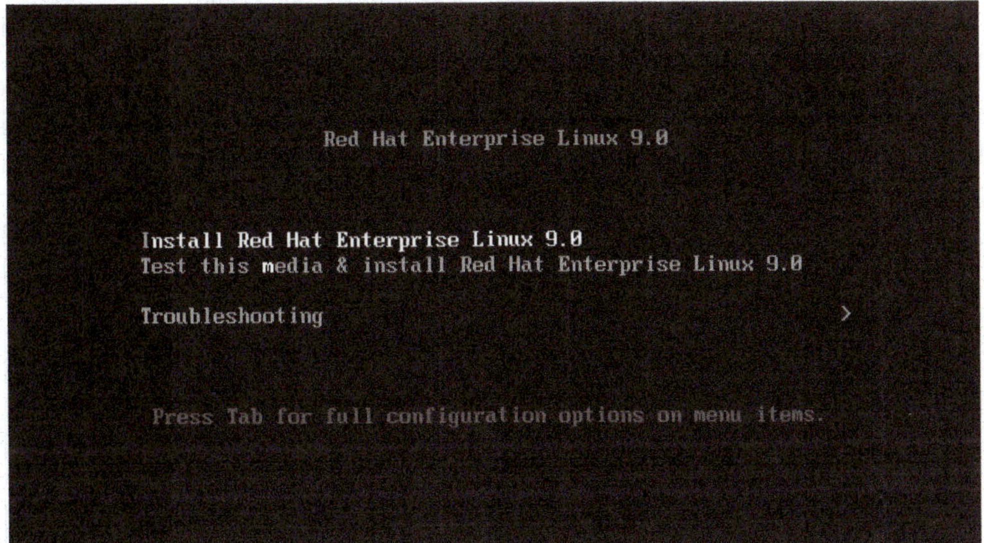

Figure 1-1 Select Install Red Hat Enterprise Linux 9.0 to Start the Installation

Step 3. Once the base system from which you will perform the installation has loaded, you see the Welcome to Red Hat Enterprise Linux 9.0 screen. From this screen, you can select the language and the keyboard setting. For the RHCSA exam, it makes no sense to choose anything but English. If you are working on a non-U.S. keyboard, from this screen you can select the keyboard setting. Make sure to select the appropriate keyboard setting, after which you click **Continue** to proceed (see Figure 1-2).

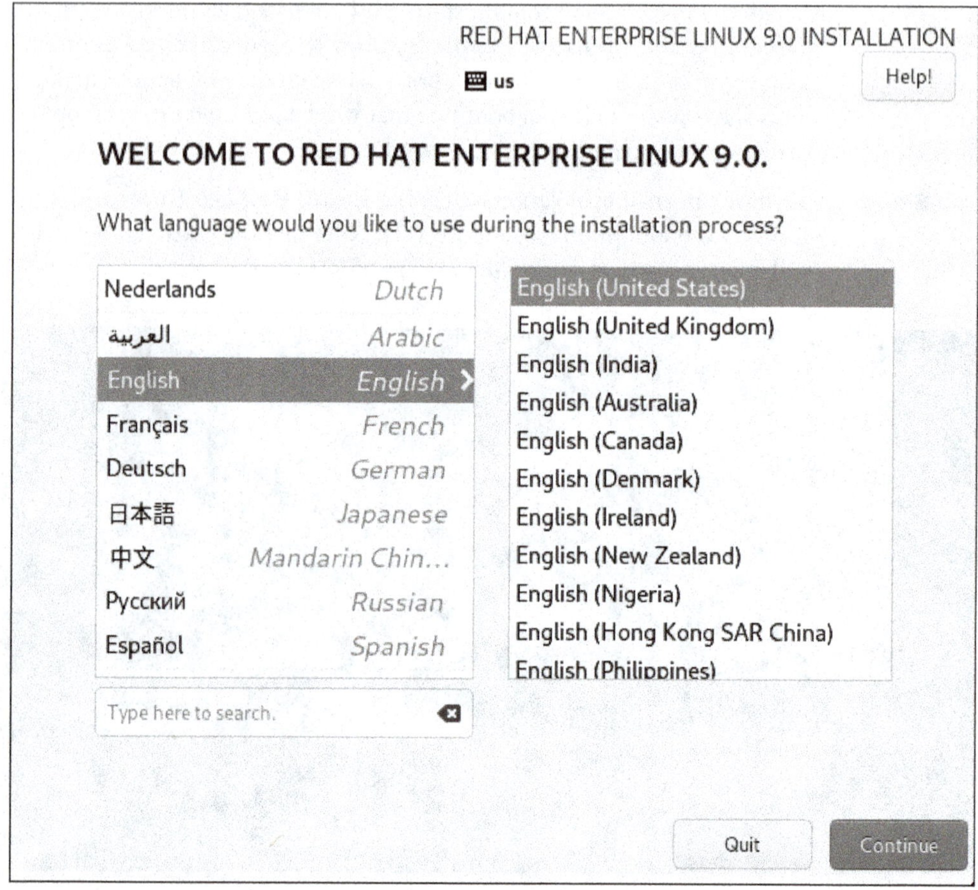

Figure 1-2 Select the Appropriate Language and Keyboard Setting Before Continuing

Step 4. After selecting the keyboard and language settings, you'll see the Installation Summary screen (see Figure 1-3). From this screen, you specify all settings you want to use. On this screen, you have several different options:

- **Keyboard:** Used to change the keyboard disposition.
- **Language Support:** Used to add support for additional languages.
- **Time & Date:** Used to specify the current time and date, as well as the time zone.
- **Root Password:** Used to enable or disable the root user, and if this user is enabled, to set a password.

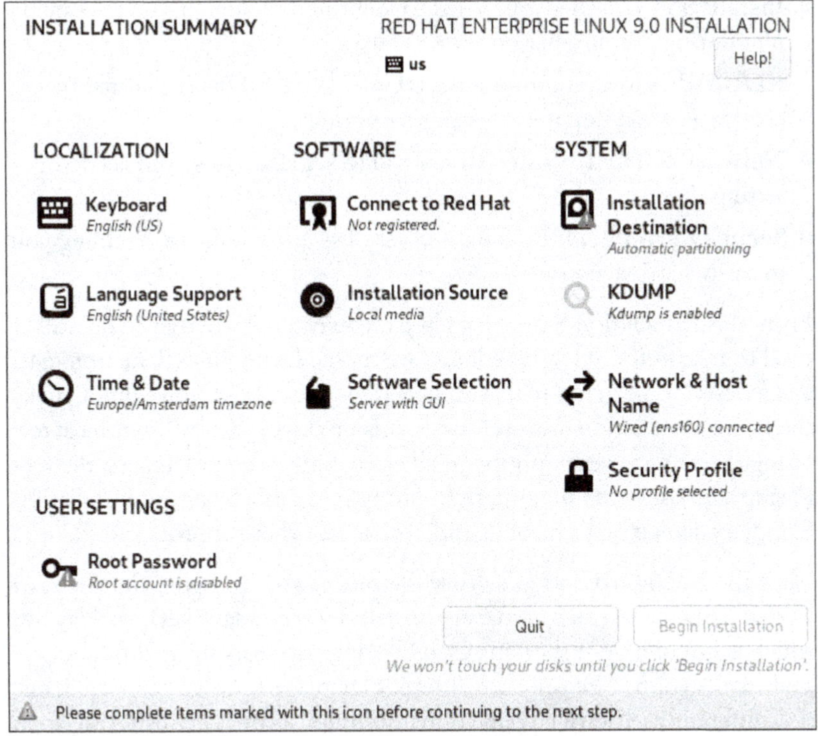

Figure 1-3 Specify the Complete Configuration of Your Server from the Installation Summary Screen

- **User Creation:** Used to create a non-root user account and, optionally, mark this user as an administrator.
- **Connect to Red Hat:** Used to register your system with Red Hat before starting the installation. Notice that all exercises in this book assume that your system is not installed with Red Hat!
- **Installation Source:** Used to specify where to install from. Typically, you'll install from the installation DVD, which is referred to as Local Media.
- **Software Selection:** Offers different installation patterns, to easily install a default set of packages.

- **Installation Destination:** Used to identify to which disk(s) to copy the files during the installation.
- **KDUMP:** Allows you to use a KDUMP kernel. This is a kernel that creates a core dump if anything goes wrong.
- **Network & Host Name:** Allows you to set IP address and related settings here.
- **Security Profile:** Offers a limited set of security policies, enabling you to easily harden a server.

From this Installation Summary screen, you can see whether items still need to be configured—these items are marked with an exclamation mark and a description in red text. As long as any issues exist, you cannot click the Begin Installation button (that is, it is disabled). You will not have to change settings for each option in all cases, but for completeness, the following steps describe the different settings available from the Installation Summary screen, with recommended changes where appropriate.

Step 5. Click the **Keyboard** option to view the settings to configure the keyboard layout. From this screen, you can also select a secondary keyboard layout, which is useful if your server is used by administrators using different keyboard layouts. Not only are different language settings supported, but also different hardware layouts. If many administrators are using an Apple Mac computer, for instance, you can select the standard keyboard layout for Mac in the appropriate region.

After adding another keyboard layout, you can also configure layout switching options. This is a key sequence that is used to switch between different kinds of layout. Select **Options** to specify the key combination you want to use for this purpose. After specifying the configuration you want to use, click **Done** to return to the Installation Summary screen.

Step 6. The Language Support option on the Installation Summary screen is the same as the Language Support option that you used in step 3 of this procedure. If you've already configured the language settings to be used, you do not need to change anything here.

Step 7. Click **Time & Date** to see a map of the world on which you can easily click the time zone that you are in (see Figure 1-4). Alternatively, you can select the region and city you are in from the corresponding drop-down list boxes. You can also set the current date and time, and after setting the network, you can specify the Network Time Protocol (NTP) to be used to synchronize time with time servers on the Internet. This option is not accessible if the network is not accessible—you'll have to set up your network connection first to access this option. When using network time, you can add the network time servers to be used by clicking the configuration icon in the upper-right part of the screen. After specifying the settings you want to use, click **Done** in the upper-left corner of the screen to write the settings.

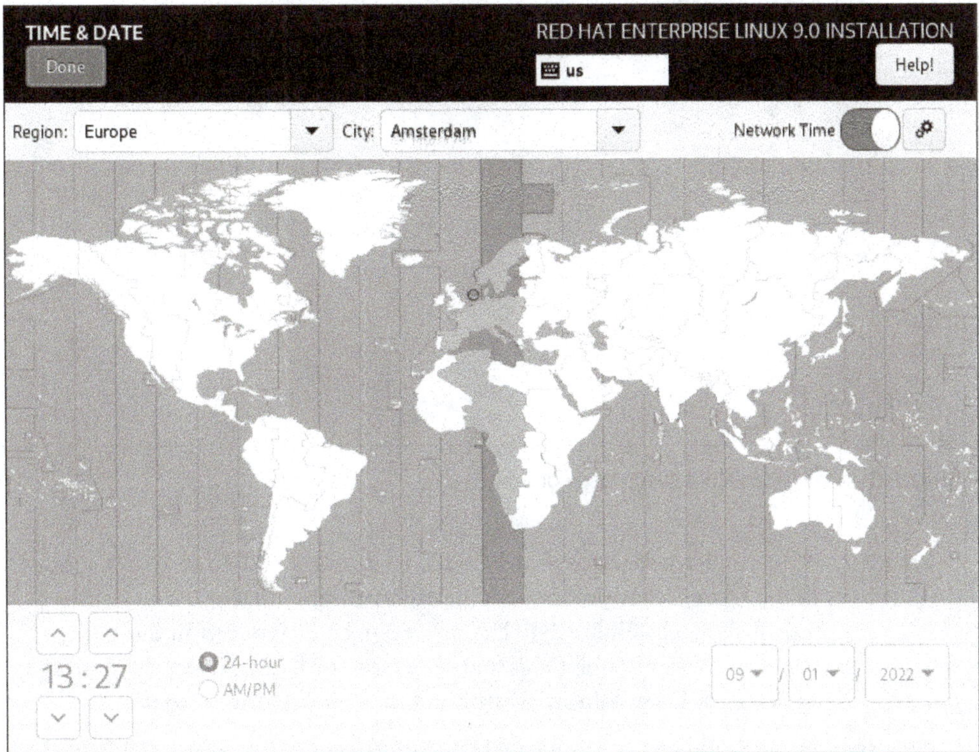

Figure 1-4 Selecting Time & Date Settings

Step 8. In the User Settings section, select **Root Password**. This opens the screen that you can see in Figure 1-5. By default, the root user account is disabled. If you want to be able to work as root, you need to set a password here. Enter the same password twice, and next click **Done** to continue.

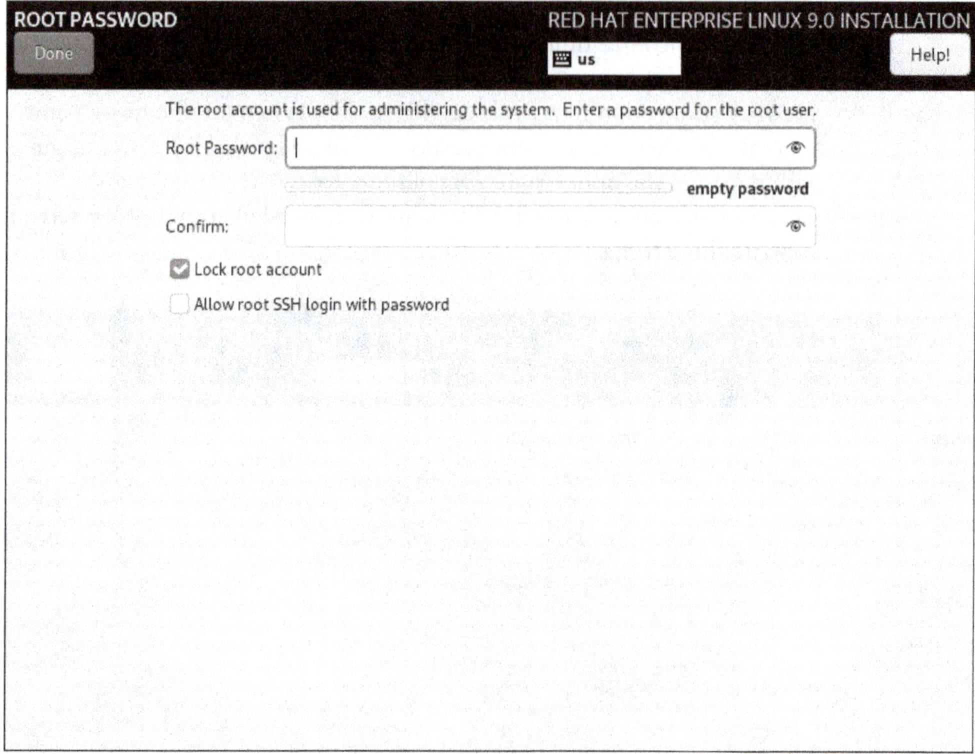

Figure 1-5 Setting the Root User Password

Step 9. After you have set a password for the root user, scroll down to get access to the **User Creation** option. Click to open it, so that you can see the screen shown in Figure 1-6. In this screen, enter **student** in the Full Name and User Name fields and set a password. Also, select the option **Make This User Administrator** and then click **Done** to continue.

Step 10. In the Software section of the Installation Summary screen, click **Installation Source** to see the screen shown in Figure 1-7. If you have booted from a regular installation disc, there is nothing to specify. If you have booted from a minimal boot environment, you can specify the network URL where additional packages are available, as well as additional repositories that need to be used. You do not have to do this for the RHCSA exam, but if ever you are setting up an installation server, it is useful to know that this option exists. Click **Done**.

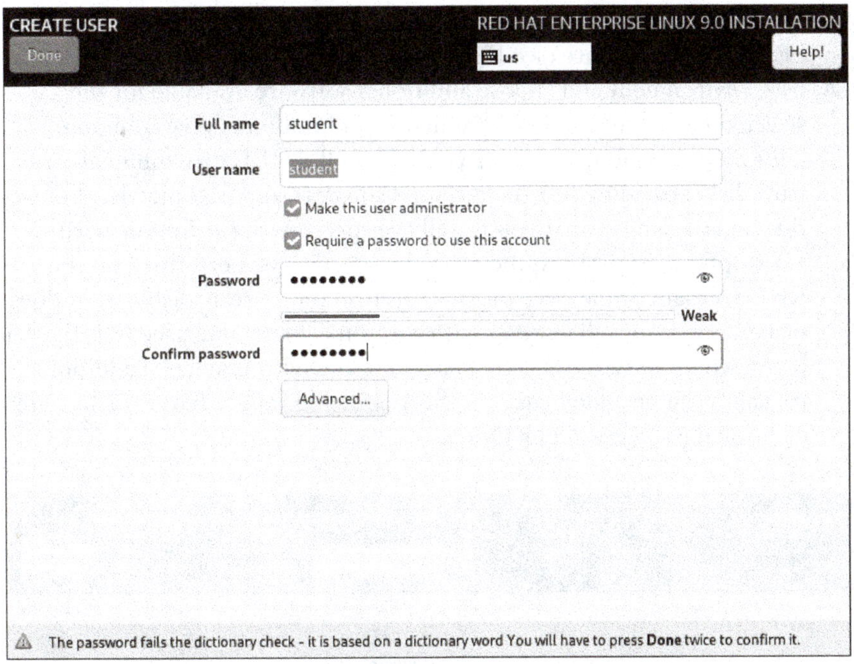

Figure 1-6 Creating an Administrator User

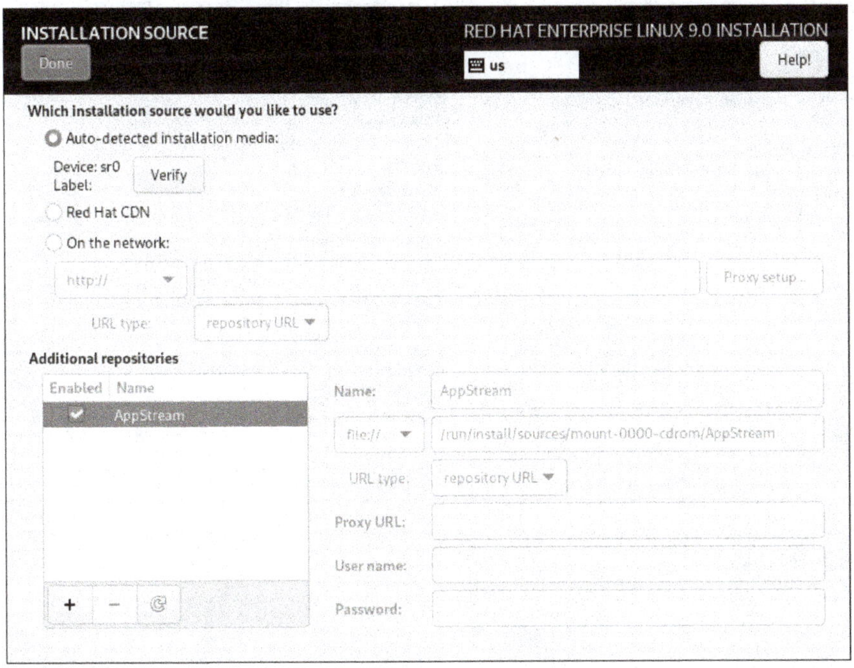

Figure 1-7 Selecting the Installation Source

Step 11. Click **Software Selection** to access an important part of the installation procedure (see Figure 1-8). From here, you select the base environment and choose additional software available for the selected environment. The Minimal Install option is very common. This base environment allows you to install RHEL on a minimal-size hard disk, providing just the essential software and nothing else. For this book, I assume that you install the server with the **Server with GUI** option. To perform the tasks that need to be performed on the RHCSA exam, some easy-to-use graphical tools are available, so it does make sense to install a server with a graphical user interface (GUI), even if you would never do this in a production environment. All additional packages can be added later. At this point, you do not have to select any additional packages. Click **Done**.

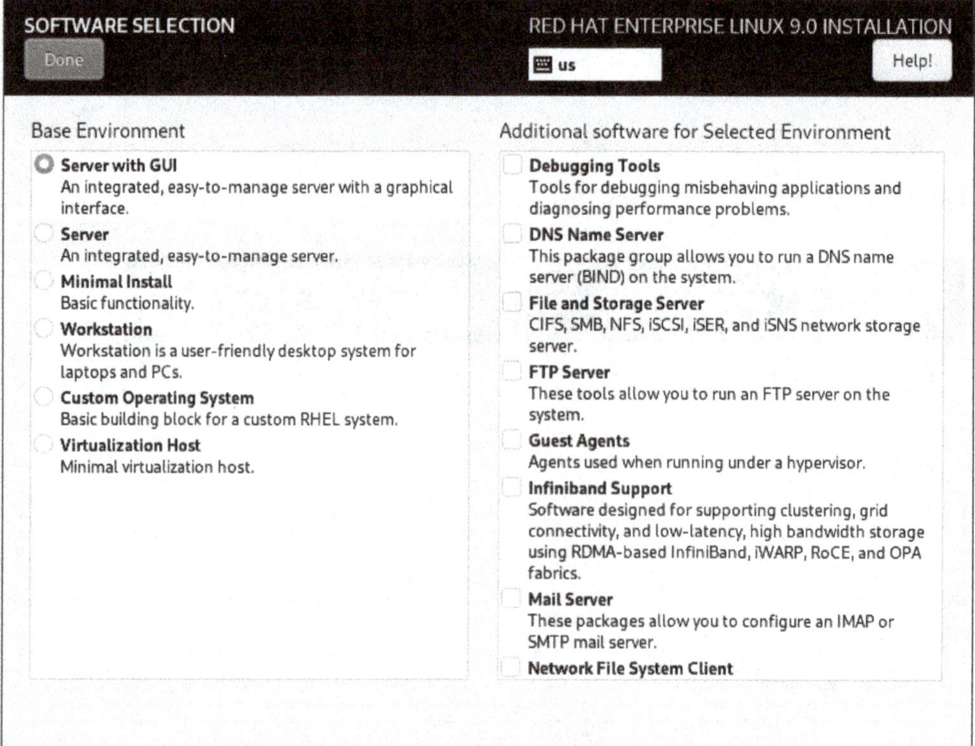

Figure 1-8 Make Sure You Select Server with GUI for Every Server You Are Going to Use for the Exercises in This Book

NOTE Some people say that *real* administrators do not use the Server with GUI installation pattern. Preparing for the RHCSA exam is not about being a real administrator. The big advantage of using the Server with GUI installation pattern is that it provides an easy-to-use interface. Some tools discussed in this book only run on a GUI. Also, when using a server with a GUI, you can use multiple terminal windows simultaneously, and that makes working with the RHEL command line really easy!

Step 12. After installing the software, you need to specify where you want to install to. Click **Installation Destination** on the Installation Summary screen. By default, automatic partitioning is selected, and you only need to approve the disk device you want to use for automatic partitioning (see Figure 1-9). Many advanced options are available as well. You can install using the Automatic option under Storage Configuration to ensure that no matter how your server is started, everything is configured to have it boot correctly and your file systems are configured with the default XFS file system.

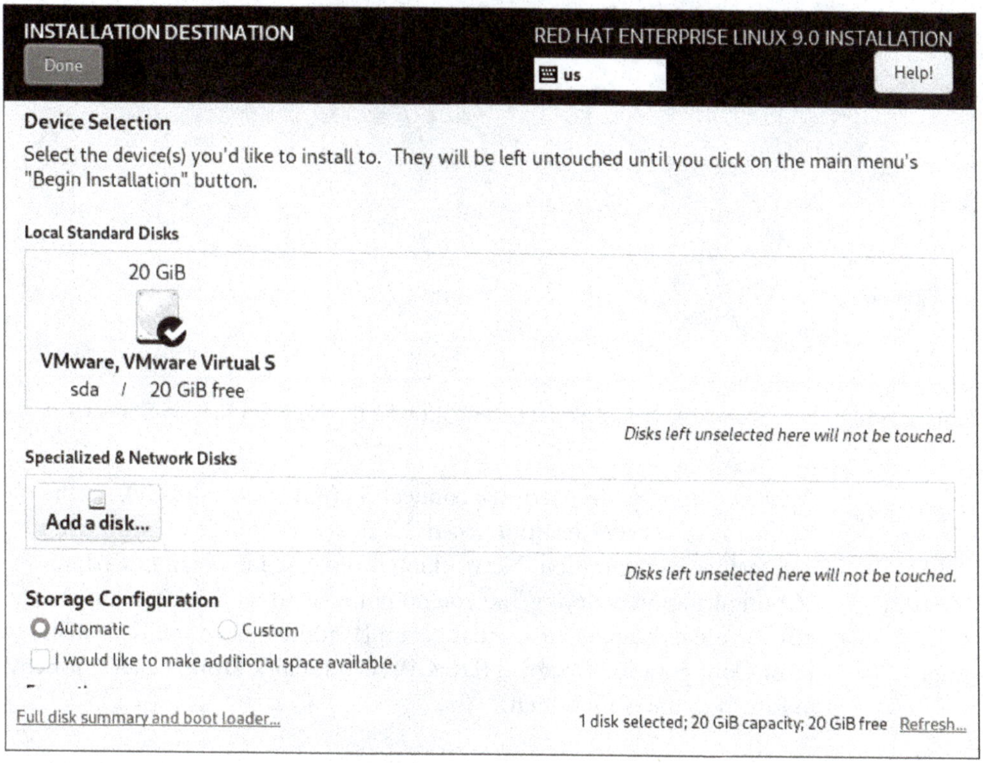

Figure 1-9 Click Done to Proceed and Automatically Create the Storage Configuration

Step 13. The next part of the Installation Summary screen enables you to set up networking. Notice that you must configure something. If you do not do anything, your server might not be able to connect to any network. Click **Network & Host Name** to set up networking. This opens the screen that you see in Figure 1-10.

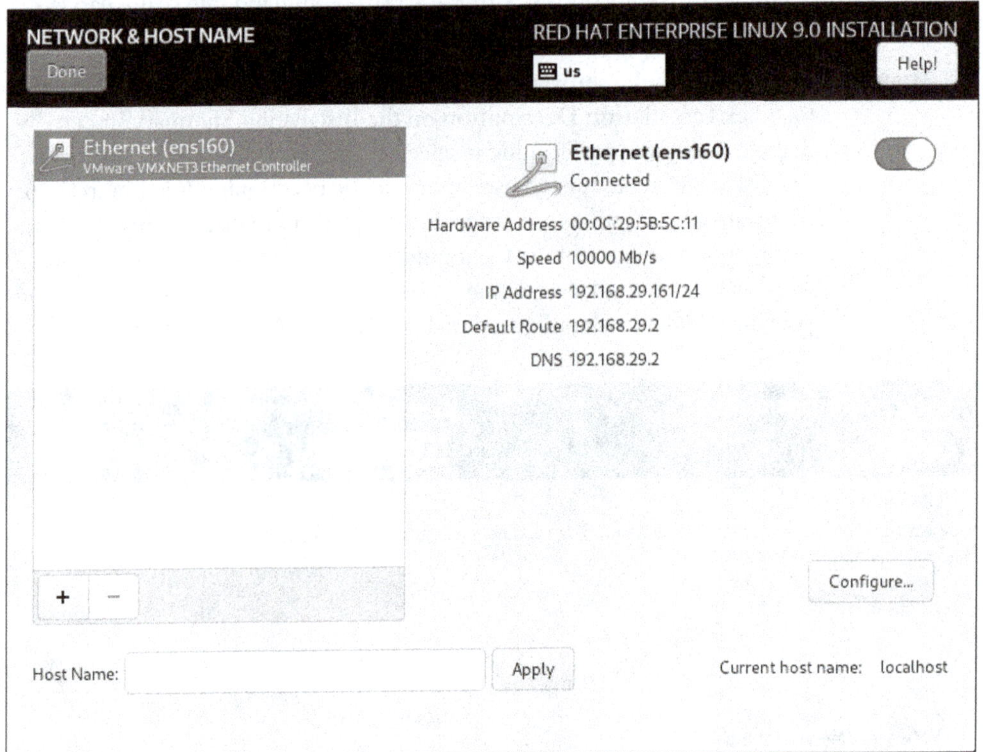

Figure 1-10 On the Network & Host Name Screen, Ensure the Network Card Is Connected

After switching on the network connection (if it wasn't already), set the hostname to **server1.example.com**. Next, you could click **Configure** to add further configuration. Networking is discussed in detail in Chapter 8, "Configuring Networking," so you do not have to do that now and can just leave the default settings that get an IP address from the Dynamic Host Configuration Protocol (DHCP) server. Click **Done** when finished to return to the main screen.

Step 14. The Security Profile option does not need any change.

Step 15. After specifying all settings from the Installation Summary screen options, you can click **Begin Installation** to start the installation. This immediately starts the installation procedure and displays the screen shown in Figure 1-11.

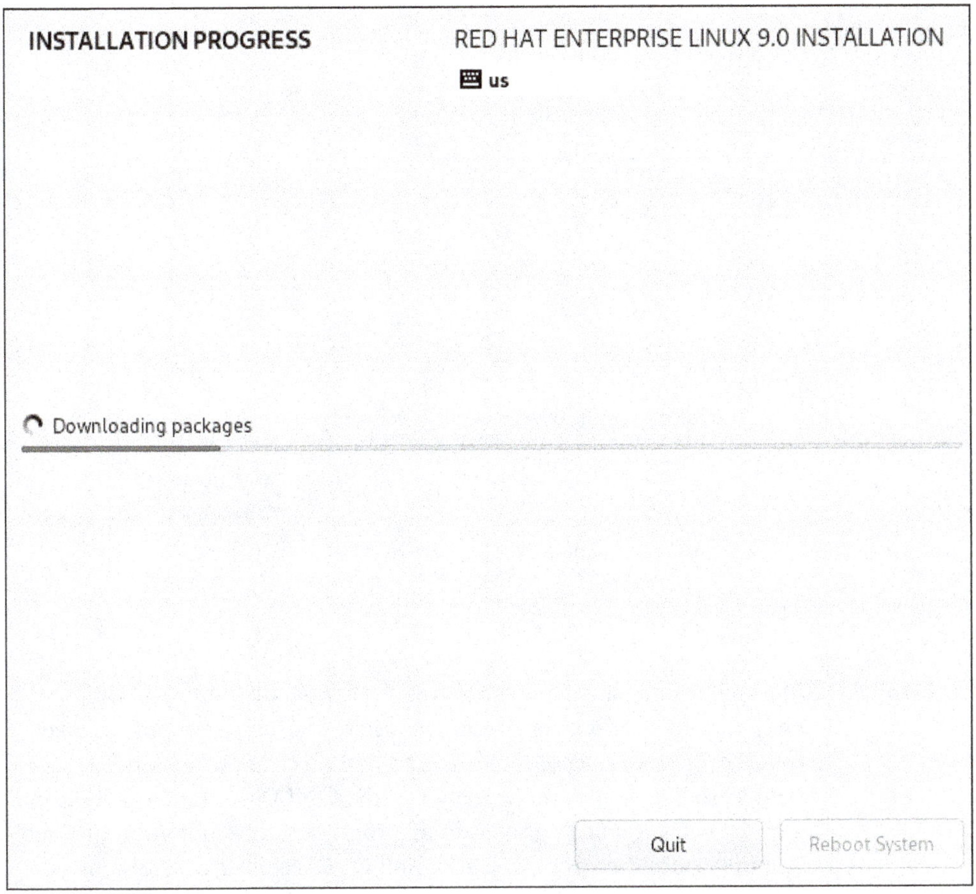

Figure 1-11 Starting the Installation

Step 16. When the installation has completed, you'll see the screen shown in Figure 1-12. You'll now need to click **Reboot System** to restart the computer and finalize the installation.

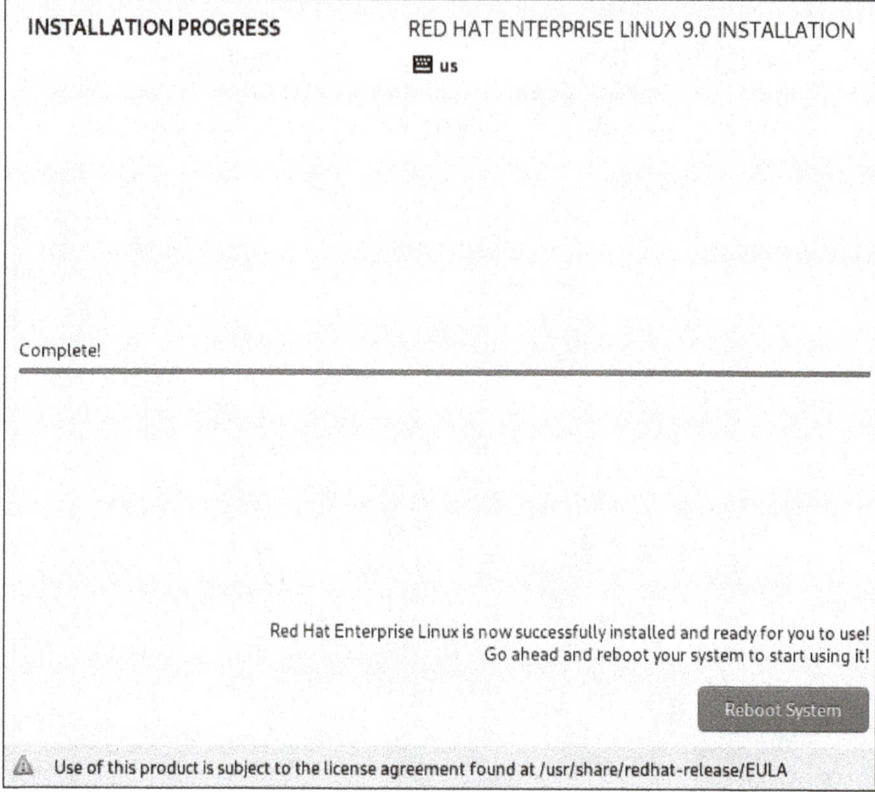

Figure 1-12 Reboot to Finalize the Installation

Step 17. After rebooting, you have to go through a couple of additional setup steps to set up your user environment. First, you'll be prompted to take a tour. Feel free to select No Thanks to skip this tour, which otherwise would introduce you to the workings of the GNOME graphical desktop. Next you will see a prompt mentioning that your system is not registered. Click to dismiss this prompt; you should NOT register your system at this moment because that will complicate all the exercises about repository management that you'll find in Chapter 9.

Summary

In this chapter, you learned what Red Hat Enterprise Linux is and how it relates to some other Linux distributions. You also learned how to install Red Hat Enterprise Linux 9. You are now ready to set up a basic environment that you can use to work on all the exercises in this book.

Exam Preparation Tasks

As mentioned in the section "How to Use This Book" in the Introduction, you have several choices for exam preparation: the end-of-chapter labs; the memory tables in Appendix C; Chapter 27, "Final Preparation"; and the practice exams.

Review All Key Topics

Review the most important topics in the chapter, noted with the Key Topic icon in the margin of the page. Table 1-2 lists a reference of these key topics and the page number on which each is found.

Table 1-2 Key Topics for Chapter 1

Key Topic Element	Description	Page
List	How to perform a RHEL 9 installation	10

Define Key Terms

Define the following key terms from this chapter and check your answers in the glossary:

distribution, Linux, Red Hat, CentOS, Fedora, AlmaLinux, Rocky Linux

Review Questions

The questions that follow are meant to help you test your knowledge of concepts and terminology and the breadth of your knowledge. You can find the answers to these questions in Appendix A.

1. You do not want to buy a RHEL license, but you want to create an environment to practice for the exam. Which distribution should you use?
2. What happens to the network configuration if you don't specify anything during the installation?
3. You want to install a minimal system. How much RAM do you need?
4. Why is it a good idea to have Internet access on all servers you are installing?
5. You want to install a virtual machine on a computer that does not have an optical disk drive. What is the easiest alternative to perform the installation?
6. Why is it a good idea to install a GUI?

7. What is the default file system on RHEL 9?
8. Can you install RHEL if you do not have Internet access?
9. What is the most important benefit of using Subscription Manager to register your RHEL 9 installation?
10. Which installation pattern should you use if you have a very limited amount of disk space available?

End-of-Chapter Lab

In this chapter, you learned how to set up Red Hat Enterprise Linux. At this point, you should have one server up and running. For exercises in later chapters in this book, one additional server is needed.

Lab 1.1

Repeat the procedure "Performing an Installation" to install one more server. Details about the additional configuration on this server follow in exercises in later chapters. For now, it is sufficient to ensure that the following conditions are met:

- Use the server name server2.example.com.
- Set the network configuration to obtain an IP address automatically.
- Install this server using the Minimal Installation pattern.

The following topics are covered in this chapter:

- Basic Shell Skills
- Editing Files with **vim**
- Understanding the Shell Environment
- Finding Help

The following RHCSA exam objectives are covered in this chapter:

- Use input-output redirection (>, >>, |, 2>, etc.)
- Access a shell prompt and issue commands with correct syntax
- Create and edit text files
- Locate, read, and use system documentation including man, info, and files in /usr/share/doc

CHAPTER 2

Using Essential Tools

This chapter is dedicated to coverage of the basic Linux skills that everyone should have before attempting to take the RHCSA exam.

"Do I Know This Already?" Quiz

The "Do I Know This Already?" quiz enables you to assess whether you should read this entire chapter thoroughly or jump to the "Exam Preparation Tasks" section. If you are in doubt about your answers to these questions or your own assessment of your knowledge of the topics, read the entire chapter. Table 2-1 lists the major headings in this chapter and their corresponding "Do I Know This Already?" quiz questions. You can find the answers in Appendix A, "Answers to the 'Do I Know This Already?' Quizzes and Review Questions."

Table 2-1 "Do I Know This Already?" Section-to-Question Mapping

Foundation Topics Section	Questions
Basic Shell Skills	1, 3–7
Editing Files with **vim**	8
Understanding the Shell Environment	2, 9
Finding Help	10

1. Which of the following commands enables you to redirect standard output as well as standard error to a file?

    a. **1&2> file**

    b. **> file 2>&1**

    c. **>1&2 file**

    d. **1>2& file**

2. You want to set a local variable that will be available for every user in every shell. Which of the following files should you use?
   a. /etc/profile
   b. /etc/bashrc
   c. ~/.bash_profile
   d. ~/.bashrc

3. A user has created a script with the name myscript. The user tries to run the script using the command **myscript**, but it is not started. The user has verified that the script permissions are set as executable. Which of the following is the most likely explanation?
   a. An internal command is preventing the startup of the script.
   b. Users are not allowed to run scripts.
   c. The directory that contains the script is not in the **$PATH** variable.
   d. The script does not have appropriate permissions.

4. You need the output of the command **ls** to be used as input for the **less** command. Which of the following examples will do that for you?
   a. **ls > less**
   b. **ls >> less**
   c. **ls >| less**
   d. **ls | less**

5. A user by accident has typed a password, which now shows as item 299 in history. Which of the following do you recommend to ensure the password is not stored in history?
   a. Remove the ~/.bash_history file and type **history -c**.
   b. Type **history -c**.
   c. Remove the ~/.bash_history file.
   d. Type **history -d 299**.

6. Which of the following is *not* a valid method to repeat a command from history?
   a. Press Ctrl-r and start typing a part of the command.
   b. Type **!** followed by the first letters in the command.

   c. Type ! followed by the number of the command as listed in history.
   d. Press Ctrl-x followed by the number in history.

7. For which of the following items can Bash completion be used?
   a. Commands
   b. Files
   c. Variables
   d. All of the above

8. Which of the following commands enables you to replace every occurrence of *old* with *new* in a text file that is opened with **vim**?
   a. **:%s/old/new/g**
   b. **:%r/old/new/**
   c. **:%s/old/new/**
   d. **r:/old/new**

9. Which approach works best if during the login process you want to show a message to all users who have just logged in to a shell session on your server?
   a. Put the message in /etc/issue.
   b. Put the message in /etc/motd.
   c. Put the message in /etc/profile.
   d. Put the message in /etc/bashrc.

10. You are using **man -k user**, but you get the message "nothing appropriate." Which of the following solutions is most likely to fix this for you?
    a. Type **sudo updatedb** to update the mandb database.
    b. Type **sudo makewhatis** to update the mandb database.
    c. Type **sudo mandb** to update the mandb database.
    d. Use **man -K**, not **man -k**.

Foundation Topics

Basic Shell Skills

The **shell** is the default working environment for a Linux administrator. It is the environment where users and administrators enter commands that are executed by the operating system. Different shells for Linux are available, but Bash is the most common shell. So, when we are talking about "the shell" in this book, we are actually talking about the **Bash** shell. This chapter provides an overview of some of the items that you will encounter when working with the shell.

Understanding Commands

Working with the shell is all about working with command syntax. Typically, command syntax has three basic parts: the command, its options, and its arguments.

The command is the command itself, such as **ls**. This command shows a list of files in the current directory. To modify the behavior of the command, you can use *options*. Options are a part of the program code, and they modify what the command is doing. For instance, when you use the **-l** (lowercase letter *l*, not number 1) option with the **ls** command, a long listing of filenames and properties is displayed.

The word *argument* is a bit confusing. Generally speaking, it refers to anything that the command addresses, so anything you put after the command is an argument (including the options). Apart from the options that can be used as an argument, commands can have other arguments as well, which serve as a target to the command.

Let's have a look at an example: the command **ls -l /etc**. This command has two different arguments: **-l** and **/etc**. The first argument is an option, modifying the behavior of the command. The second argument is a target, specifying where the command should do its work. You'll find these three elements in nearly all commands you work with in a Linux environment.

Executing Commands

The purpose of the Linux shell is to provide an environment in which commands can be executed. The shell takes care of interpreting the command that a user has entered correctly. To do this, the shell makes a distinction between three kinds of commands:

- Aliases
- Internal commands
- External commands

An *alias* is a command that a user can define as needed. Some aliases are provided by default; type **alias** on the command line to get an overview. To define an alias, use **alias newcommand='oldcommand'** (as in the default alias **ll='ls -l --color=auto'** that has already been created on your system). Aliases are executed before anything else. So, if you have an alias with the name **ll** but also a command with the name **ll**, the alias will always take precedence for the command, unless a complete pathname like /usr/bin/ls is used.

An ***internal command*** is a command that is a part of the shell itself and, as such, doesn't have to be loaded from disk separately. An ***external command*** is a command that exists as an executable file on the disk of the computer. Because it has to be read from disk the first time it is used, it is a bit slower. When a user executes a command, the shell first looks to determine whether it is an internal command; if it is not, it looks for an executable file with a name that matches the command on disk. To find out whether a command is a Bash internal command or an executable file on disk, you can use the **type** command. Use for instance **type pwd** to find out that the **pwd** command that will be executed is really an alias.

To change how external commands are found by the shell, use the ***$PATH*** variable. This variable defines a list of directories that is searched for a matching filename when a user enters a command. To find out which exact command the shell will be using, you can use the **which** command. For instance, type **which ls** to find out where the shell will get the **ls** command from. An even stronger command is **type**, which will also work on internal commands and aliases.

You should notice that, for security reasons, the current directory is not in the **$PATH** variable and Linux does not look in the current directory to see whether a specific command is available from that directory. That is why you need to start a command that is in the current directory but nowhere in the **$PATH** by including ./ in front of it. The dot stands for the current directory, and by running it as ./, you tell Bash to look for the command in the current directory. Although running commands this way is not very common, you will have to do it to run scripts that you've created in your current directory.

The **$PATH** variable can be set for specific users, but in general, most users will be using the same **$PATH** variable. The only exception to this is the user root, who needs access to specific administration commands. In Exercise 2-1, you learn some of the basics about working with commands.

Exercise 2-1 Using Internal and External Commands from the Shell

1. Authenticate on the server1 server that you created in Chapter 1, "Installing Red Hat Enterprise Linux," as the user that you also created in Chapter 1 when installing your server.
2. Click **Activities**. In the Search bar that appears, type **term** and click the terminal icon that shows to open a terminal. All exercises in this book are intended to be executed in a terminal.
3. Type **time ls**. This executes the **ls** command where the Bash internal **time** shows information about the time it took to complete this command.
4. Type **which time**. This shows the filename /usr/bin/time that was found in the **$PATH** variable.
5. **Type time**, which shows that **time** is a shell keyword.
6. Type **echo $PATH** to show the contents of the **$PATH** variable. You can see that /usr/bin is included in the list, but because there also is an internal command **time**, the **time** command from the path will not be executed unless you tell the shell specifically to do so—the command in step 3 has executed the internal command for you because of command precedence.
7. Type **/usr/bin/time ls** to run the **/usr/bin/time** command when executing **ls**. You'll notice that the output differs completely. Ignore the meaning of the output; we get back to that later. What matters for now is that you realize that these are really two different commands.

I/O Redirection

By default, when a command is executed, it shows its results on the screen of the computer you are working on. The computer monitor is used as the standard destination for output, which is also referred to as STDOUT. The shell also has default standard destinations to send error messages to (STDERR) and to accept input (STDIN). Table 2-2 gives an overview of all three.

Table 2-2 Standard Input, Output, and Error Overview

Name	Default Destination	Use in Redirection	File Descriptor Number
STDIN	Computer keyboard	< (same as 0<)	0
STDOUT	Computer monitor	> (same as 1>)	1
STDERR	Computer monitor	2>	2

So if you run a command, that command would expect input from the keyboard, and it would normally send its output to the monitor of your computer without making a distinction between normal output and errors. Some commands, however, are started in the background and not from a current terminal session, so these commands do not have a monitor or console session to send their output to, and they do not listen to keyboard input to accept their standard input. That is where redirection comes in handy. ***Redirection*** is also useful if you want to work with input from an alternative location, such as a file.

Programs started from the command line have no idea what they are reading from or writing to. They just read from what the Linux kernel calls file descriptor 0 if they want to read from standard input, and they write to file descriptor number 1 to display non-error output (also known as "standard output") and to file descriptor 2 if they have error messages to be output. By default, these ***file descriptors*** are connected to the keyboard and the screen. If you use redirection symbols such as <, >, and |, the shell connects the file descriptors to files or other commands. Let's first look at the redirectors < and >. Later we discuss pipes (the | symbol). Table 2-3 shows the most common redirectors that are used from the Bash shell.

Table 2-3 Common Bash Redirectors

Redirector	Explanation
> (same as 1>)	Redirects STDOUT. If redirection is to a file, the current contents of that file are overwritten.
>> (same as 1>>)	Redirects STDOUT in append mode. If output is written to a file, the output is appended to that file.
2>	Redirects STDERR.
2>&1	Redirects STDERR to the same destination as STDOUT. Notice that this has to be used in combination with normal output redirection, as in **ls whuhiu > errout 2>&1**.
< (same as 0<)	Redirects STDIN.

In I/O redirection, files can be used to replace the default STDIN, STDOUT, and STDERR. You can also redirect to ***device files***. A device file on Linux is a file that is used to access specific hardware. Your hard disk, for instance, can be referred to as /dev/sda in most cases, the console of your server is known as /dev/console or /dev/tty1, and if you want to discard a command's output, you can redirect to /dev/null. Note that to access most device files, you need to have root privileges.

Using Pipes

Whereas an I/O redirector is used as an alternative for a keyboard and computer monitor, a ***pipe*** can be used to catch the output of one command and use that as input for a second command. If a user runs the command **ls**, for instance, the output of the command is shown onscreen, because the screen is the default STDOUT. If the user uses **ls | less**, the commands **ls** and **less** are started in parallel. The standard output of the **ls** command is connected to the standard input of **less**. Everything that **ls** writes to the standard output will become available for reading from standard input in **less**. The result is that the output of **ls** is shown in the **less** pager, where the user can browse up and down through the results easily.

As a Linux administrator, you will use pipes a lot. Using pipes makes Linux a flexible operating system; by combining multiple commands using pipes, you can create "super" commands that make almost anything possible. In Exercise 2-2, you use I/O redirectors and pipes.

Exercise 2-2 Using I/O Redirection and Pipes

1. Open a shell as user **student** and type **cd** without any arguments. This ensures that the home directory of this user is the current directory while working on this exercise. Type **pwd** to verify this.
2. Type **ls**. You'll see the **ls** command output onscreen.
3. Type **ls > /dev/null**. This redirects STDOUT to the null device, with the result that you will not see it.
4. Type **ls ilwehgi > /dev/null**. This command shows a "no such file or directory" message onscreen. You see the message because it is not STDOUT, but rather an error message that is written to STDERR.
5. Type **ls ilwehgi 2> /dev/null**. Now you will no longer see the error message.
6. Type **ls ilwehgi /etc 2> /dev/null**. This shows the contents of the /etc folder while hiding the error message.
7. Type **ls ilwehgi /etc 2> /dev/null > output**. In this command, you still write the error message to /dev/null while sending STDOUT to a file with the name output that will be created in your home directory.
8. Type **cat output** to show the contents of this file.
9. Type **echo hello > output**. This overwrites the contents of the output file. Verify this by using **cat output** again.

10. Type **ls >> output**. This appends the result of the **ls** command to the output file. Type **cat output** to verify.
11. Type **ls -R /**. This shows a long list of files and folders scrolling over your computer monitor. (You might want to press Ctrl-C to stop [or wait some time]).
12. Type **ls -R /. | less**. This shows the same result, but in the **less** pager, where you can scroll up and down using the arrow keys on your keyboard.
13. Type **q** to close **less**. This will also end the **ls** program.
14. Type **ls > /dev/tty1**. This gives an error message because you are executing the command as an ordinary user, and ordinary users cannot address device files directly (unless you were logged in to tty1). Only the user root has permission to write to device files directly.

History

A convenient feature of the Bash shell is the Bash history. Bash is configured by default to keep the last 1,000 commands a user used. When a shell session is closed, the history of that session is updated to the history file. The name of this file is .bash_history and it is created in the home directory of the user who started a specific shell session. Notice that the history file is written to only when the shell session is closed; until that moment, all commands in the history are kept in memory.

The history feature makes it easy to repeat complex commands. There are several ways of working with history:

- Type **history** to show a list of all commands in the Bash history.
- Press Ctrl-r to open the prompt from which you can do backward searches in commands that you have previously used. Just type a string and Bash will look backward in the command history for any command containing that string as the command name or one of its arguments. Press Ctrl-r again to repeat the last backward search.
- Type **!number** to execute a command with a specific number from history.
- Use **history -d number** to delete a specific command from history. Notice that this command will renumber all other lines in history: if you've removed line 31, the line previously numbered as line 32 will now be line 31.
- Type **!sometext** to execute the last command that starts with *sometext*. Notice that this is a potentially dangerous command because the command that was found is executed immediately!

In some cases it might be necessary to wipe the Bash history. This capability is useful, for instance, if you've typed a password in clear text by accident. If that happens, you can type **history -c** to clear the current history. Commands from this session won't be written to the history file when you exit the current session. If you want to remove both the current history and the contents of the .bash_history file, then type **history -w** immediately after running the **history -c** command. Alternatively, use **history -d number** to remove a specific command from history.

Exercise 2-3 guides you through some history features.

Exercise 2-3 Working with History

1. Make sure that you have opened a shell as user **student**.
2. Type **history** to get an overview of commands that you have previously used.
3. Type some commands, such as the following:

   ```
   ls
   pwd
   cat /etc/hosts
   ls -l
   ```

   The goal is to fill the history a bit.
4. Open a second terminal on your server. To do so, click **Activities** in the upper-left corner, and in the Search bar, type **term**. Next, click the terminal window to start it.
5. Type **history** from this second terminal window. Notice that you do not see the commands that you just typed in the other terminal. The reason is that the history file has not been updated yet.
6. From the first terminal session, press Ctrl-r. From the prompt that opens now, type **ls**. You'll see the last **ls** command you used. Press Ctrl-r again. You'll now see that you are looking backward and that the previous **ls** command is highlighted. Press Enter to execute it.
7. Type **history | grep cat**. The **grep** command searches the history output for any commands that contain the text *cat*. Note the command number of one of the **cat** commands you have previously used.
8. Type **!nn**, where *nn* is replaced by the number you noted in step 7. You'll see that the last **cat** command is repeated.
9. Close this terminal by typing **exit**.

10. From the remaining terminal window, type **history -c**. This wipes all history that is currently in memory. Close this terminal session as well.
11. Open a new terminal session and type **history**. The result may be a bit unexpected, but you'll see a list of commands anyway. The reason is that **history -c** clears the in-memory history, but it does not remove the .bash_history file in your home directory.

Bash Completion

Another useful feature of the Bash shell is command-line completion. This feature helps you to find the command that you need, and it also works on variables and filenames.

Bash completion is useful when you're working with commands. Just type the beginning of a command and press the Tab key. If there is only one option for completion, Bash will complete the command automatically for you. If there are several options, you need to press Tab once more to get an overview of all the available options. In Exercise 2-4, you learn how to work with these great features.

Exercise 2-4 Using Bash Completion

1. Still from a user shell, type **gd** and press Tab. You'll see that nothing happens.
2. Press Tab again. Bash now shows a short list of all commands that start with the letters *gd*.
3. To make it clear to Bash what you want, type **i** (so that your prompt at this point shows the command **gdi**). Press Tab again. Bash now completes the command to **gdisk**. Press Enter to launch it, and press Enter again to close it.
4. Use **cd /etc** to go to the /etc directory.
5. Type **cat pas** and press Tab. Because there is one file only that starts with *pas*, Bash knows what to do and automatically completes the filename to passwd. Press Enter to execute the command.

Editing Files with vim

Managing Linux often means working with files. Most things that are configured on Linux are configured through files. To complete administrative tasks, you often need to change the contents of a configuration file with a text editor.

Over the years, many text editors have been created for Linux. One editor really matters, though, and that is **vi**. Even if some other text editors are easier to use, **vi** is the only text editor that is always available. That is why as a Linux administrator you need to know how to work with **vi**. One common alternative is **vim**, or "**vi** improved"; it is a complete rewrite of **vi** with a lot of enhancements that make working with **vi** easier, such as syntax highlighting for many configuration files, which makes it easy to recognize typing errors that you have made. Everything that you learn in this section about **vim** works on **vi** as well.

An important concept when working with **vim** is that it uses different modes. Two of them are particularly important: *command mode* and *input mode*. These modes often cause confusion because in command mode you can just enter a command and you cannot edit the contents of a text file. To change the contents of a text file, you need to get to input mode.

The challenge when working with **vim** is the vast number of commands that are available. Some people have even produced **vim** cheat sheets, listing all available commands. Do not use them. Instead, focus on the minimal number of commands that are really important. Table 2-4 summarizes the most essential **vim** commands. Use these (and only these) and you'll do fine on the RHCSA exam.

TIP Do *not* try to work with as many commands as possible when working with **vim**. Just use a minimal set of commands and use them often. You'll see; you'll get used to these commands and remember them on the exam. Also, you may like the **vimtutor** command. (You may have to use **dnf install vim-enhanced** to install it; Chapter 9, "Managing Software," provides more details about software installation.) This command opens a **vim** tutorial that has you work through some nice additional exercises.

Table 2-4 vim Essential Commands

vim Command	Explanation
Esc	Switches from input mode to command mode. Press this key before typing any command.
i, a	Switches from command mode to input mode at (**i**) or after (**a**) the current cursor position.
o	Opens a new line below the current cursor position and goes to input mode.
:wq	Writes the current file and quits.
:q!	Quits the file without applying any changes. The **!** forces the command to do its work. Add the **!** only if you really know what you are doing.

:w filename	Writes the current file with a new filename.
dd	Deletes the current line and places the contents of the deleted line into memory.
yy	Copies the current line.
p	Pastes the contents that have been cut or copied into memory.
v	Enters visual mode, which allows you to select a block of text using the arrow keys. Use **d** to cut the selection or **y** to copy it.
u	Undoes the last command. Repeat as often as necessary.
Ctrl-r	Redoes the last undo. (Cannot be repeated more than once.)
gg	Goes to the first line in the document.
G	Goes to the last line in the document.
/text	Searches for *text* from the current cursor position forward.
?text	Searches for *text* from the current cursor position backward.
^	Goes to the first position in the current line.
$	Goes to the last position in the current line.
!ls	Adds the output of **ls** (or any other command) in the current file.
:%s/old/new/g	Replaces all occurrences of *old* with *new*.

Now you know the most essential commands for working with **vim**. Exercise 2-5 gives you the opportunity to test them.

Exercise 2-5 vim Practice

1. Type **vim ~/testfile**. This starts **vim** and opens a file with the name testfile in ~, which represents your current home directory.
2. Type **i** to enter input mode and then type the following text:

```
cow
sheep
ox
chicken
snake
fish
oxygen
```

3. Press Esc to get back to command mode and type **:w** to write the file using the same filename.
4. Type **:3** to go to line number 3.
5. Type **dd** to delete this line.
6. Type **dd** again to delete another line.
7. Type **u** to undo the last deletion.
8. Type **o** to open a new line.
9. Enter some more text at the current cursor position:

```
tree
farm
```

10. Press Esc to get back into command mode.
11. Type **:%s/ox/OX/g** and note the changes to the line that contained ox.
12. Type **:wq** to write the file and quit. If for some reason that does not work, use **:wq!**

Understanding the Shell Environment

When you are working from a shell, an ***environment*** is created to ensure that all that is happening is happening the right way. This environment consists of variables that define the user environment, such as the **$PATH** variable discussed earlier. In this section, you get a brief overview of the shell environment and how it is created.

Understanding Variables

The Linux shell environment consists of many variables. ***Variables*** are fixed names that can be assigned dynamic values. An example of a variable is **$LANG**, which in my shell is set to **en_US.UTF-8**. This value (which may differ on your system) ensures that I can work in the English language using settings that are common in the English language (think of how date and time are displayed).

The advantage of working with variables for scripts and programs is that the program only has to use the name of the variable without taking interest in the specific value that is assigned to the variable. Because different users have different needs, the variables that are set in a user environment will differ. To get an overview of the current variables defined in your shell environment, type the **env** command, which will show environment variables that are used to set important system settings. Example 2-1 shows some lines of the output of this command.

Example 2-1 Displaying the Current Environment

```
[user@server1 ~]$ env
MAIL=/var/spool/mail/user
PATH=/usr/local/bin:/bin:/usr/bin:/usr/local/sbin:/usr/sbin:/home/
user/.local/bin:/home/user/bin
PWD=/home/user
LANG=en_US.UTF-8
HISTCONTROL=ignoredups
SHLVL=1
HOME=/home/user
LOGNAME=user
LESSOPEN=||/usr/bin/lesspipe.sh %s
_=/bin/env
OLDPWD=/etc
```

As you can see from Example 2-1, to define a variable, you type the name of the variable, followed by an equal sign (=) and the value that is assigned to the specific variable. To read the value of a variable, you can use the **echo** command (among others), followed by the name of the variable, as in **echo $PATH**, which reads the current value of the **$PATH** variable and prints that to STDOUT. For now, you do not have to know much more about variables. You can read about more advanced use of variables in Chapter 19, "An Introduction to Automation with Bash Shell Scripting."

Recognizing Environment Configuration Files

When a user logs in, an environment is created for that user automatically. This happens based on the following four configuration files, where some script code can be specified and where variables can be defined:

- **/etc/profile:** This is the generic file that is processed by all users upon login.
- **/etc/bashrc:** This file is processed when subshells are started.
- **~/.bash_profile:** In this file, user-specific login shell variables can be defined.
- **~/.bashrc:** In this user-specific file, subshell variables can be defined.

As you have seen, in these files a distinction is made between a ***login shell*** and a ***subshell***. A login shell is the first shell that is opened for a user after the user has logged in. From the login shell, a user may run scripts, which will start a subshell of that login shell. Bash allows for the creation of a different environment in the login shell and in the subshell, but to make sure the same settings are used in all shells, it's a good idea to include subshell settings in the login shell as well.

Using /etc/motd and /etc/issue

To display messages during the login process, Bash uses the /etc/motd and the /etc/issue files. Messages in /etc/motd display after a user has successfully logged in to a shell. (Note that users in a graphical environment do not see its contents after a graphical login.) Using /etc/motd can be a convenient way for system administrators to inform users about an issue or a security policy, for example.

Another way to send information to users is by using /etc/issue. The contents of this file display before the user logs in from a text-based console interface. Using this file provides an excellent means of specifying login instructions to users who are not logged in yet.

In Exercise 2-6, you can practice the topics that have been discussed in this section.

Exercise 2-6 Managing the Shell Environment

1. Open a shell in which you are user **student**.
2. Type **echo $LANG** to show the contents of the variable that sets your system keyboard and language settings.
3. Type **ls --help**. You'll see that help about the **ls** command is displayed in the current language settings of your computer.
4. Type **LANG=es_ES.UTF-8**. This temporarily sets the language variable to Spanish. Type **ls --help** again to verify.
5. Type **exit** to close your terminal window. Because you have not changed the contents of any of the previously mentioned files, when you open a new shell, the original value of the **LANG** variable will be used.
6. Open a shell as **user** again.
7. Verify the current value of the **LANG** variable by typing **echo $LANG**.
8. Type **vim .bashrc** to open the .bashrc configuration file.
9. In this file, add the line **COLOR=red** to set a variable with the name **COLOR** and assign it the value **red**. Notice that this variable doesn't really change anything on your system; it just sets a variable.

10. Close the user shell and open a new user shell.
11. Verify that the variable **COLOR** has been set, by using **echo $COLOR**. Because the .bashrc file is included in the login procedure, the variable is set after logging in.

Finding Help

On an average Linux system, hundreds of commands are available—way too many to ever be able to remember all of them, which is why using the help resources on your computer is so very important. The **man** command is the most important resource for getting help about command syntax and usage. Apart from that, you can show a compact list of command options by using **command --help**.

Using --help

The quickest way to get an overview of how to use a command is by running the command with the **--help** option. Nearly all commands will display a usage summary when using this option. In this summary you'll see all options that can be used with the command. Notice that there is no strict order for the options; you can use them in any order you'd like.

The list of options that is shown in this way is of use mainly when you already have a generic understanding of how to use the command and need a quick overview of options available with the command—it doesn't give detailed information that will help users who don't know the command yet.

TIP Nearly all commands provide a short overview of help when the option **--help** is used. Some commands do not honor that option and consider it erroneous. Fortunately, these commands will be so friendly as to show an error message, displaying valid options with the command, which effectively means that you'll get what you needed anyway.

Using man

When using the Linux command line, you will at some point consult man pages. The **man** command is what makes working from the command line doable. If you do not know how a command is used, the man page of that command will provide valuable insight. This section covers a few **man** essentials.

To start with, the most important parts of the man page in general are at the bottom of the man page. Here you'll find two important sections: In many cases there are examples; if there are no examples, there is always a "See Also" section. The topics you find here are related man pages, which is useful if you have just not hit the right man page. To get to the bottom of the man page as fast as possible, use the **G** command. You can also type **/example** to search the man page for any examples. Figure 2-1 shows what the end of a man page may look like.

```
File  Edit  View  Search  Terminal  Help
       Create a 1TiB thin LV, first creating a new thin pool for it, where the thin pool has 100MiB of space,  uses  2  stripes,  has  a
       64KiB stripe size, and 256KiB chunk size.
       lvcreate --type thin --name mylv --thinpool mypool
              -V 1t -L 100m -i 2 -I 64 -c 256 vg00

       Create a thin snapshot of a thin LV (the size option must not be used, otherwise a copy-on-write snapshot would be created).
       lvcreate --snapshot --name mysnap vg00/thinvol

       Create a thin snapshot of the read-only inactive LV named "origin" which becomes an external origin for the thin snapshot LV.
       lvcreate --snapshot --name mysnap --thinpool mypool vg00/origin

       Create a cache pool from a fast physical device. The cache pool can then be used to cache an LV.
       lvcreate --type cache-pool -L 1G -n my_cpool vg00 /dev/fast1

       Create  a  cache  LV, first creating a new origin LV on a slow physical device, then combining the new origin LV with an existing
       cache pool.
       lvcreate --type cache --cachepool my_cpool
              -L 100G -n mylv vg00 /dev/slow1

SEE ALSO
       lvm(8) lvm.conf(5) lvmconfig(8)

       pvchange(8) pvck(8) pvcreate(8) pvdisplay(8) pvmove(8) pvremove(8) pvresize(8) pvs(8) pvscan(8)

       vgcfgbackup(8) vgcfgrestore(8) vgchange(8) vgck(8) vgcreate(8)  vgconvert(8)  vgdisplay(8)  vgexport(8)  vgextend(8)  vgimport(8)
       vgimportclone(8) vgmerge(8) vgmknodes(8) vgreduce(8) vgremove(8) vgrename(8) vgs(8) vgscan(8) vgsplit(8)

       lvcreate(8) lvchange(8) lvconvert(8) lvdisplay(8) lvextend(8) lvreduce(8) lvremove(8) lvrename(8) lvresize(8) lvs(8) lvscan(8)

       lvm-fullreport(8) lvm-lvpoll(8) lvm2-activation-generator(8) blkdeactivate(8) lvmdump(8)

       dmeventd(8) lvmetad(8) lvmpolld(8) lvmlockd(8) lvmlockctl(8) clvmd(8) cmirrord(8) lvmdbusd(8)

       lvmsystemid(7) lvmreport(7) lvmraid(7) lvmthin(7) lvmcache(7)

Red Hat, Inc.                           LVM TOOLS 2.03.00(2) (2018-10-10)                                          LVCREATE(8)
 Manual page lvcreate(8) line 1910/1945 (END) (press h for help or q to quit)
```

Figure 2-1 Sample man Page Contents

Finding the Right man Page

To find information in man pages, you can search the mandb database by using **apropos** or **man -k**. If the database is current, getting access to the information you need is easy. Just type **man -k**, followed by the keyword you want to search for. This command looks in the summary of all man pages that are stored in the mandb database. If you get "nothing appropriate" when running this command, consult the section "Updating mandb" later in this chapter. Example 2-2 shows a partial result of this command.

Example 2-2 Searching man Pages with **man -k**

```
[root@server1 ~]# man -k partition
addpart (8)          - simple wrapper around the "add partition" ioctl
cfdisk (8)           - display or manipulate disk partition table
cgdisk (8)           - Curses-based GUID partition table (GPT)
manipulator
delpart (8)          - simple wrapper around the "del partition" ioctl
fdisk (8)            - manipulate disk partition table
fixparts (8)          - MBR partition table repair utility
gdisk (8)            - Interactive GUID partition table (GPT)
manipulator
iostat (1)           - Report Central Processing Unit (CPU) statistics
and in...
kpartx (8)           - Create device maps from partition tables
mpartition (1)         - partition an MSDOS hard disk
os-prober (1)          - Discover bootable partitions on the local
system
partprobe (8)          - inform the OS of partition table changes
partx (8)            - tell the Linux kernel about the presence and
numbering...
pvcreate (8)          - initialize a disk or partition for use by LVM
pvresize (8)          - resize a disk or partition in use by LVM2
resizepart (8)         - simple wrapper around the "resize partition"
ioctl
sfdisk (8)           - partition table manipulator for Linux
sgdisk             (- Command-line GUID partition table (GPT)
manipulator fo...
systemd-efi-boot-generator (8) - Generator for automatically mounting
the EFI...
systemd-gpt-auto-generator (8) - Generator for automatically
discovering and ..
```

Based on the information that **man -k** is giving you, you can probably identify the man page that you need to access to do whatever you want to accomplish. Be aware, however, that **man -k** is not perfect; it searches only the short summary of each command that is installed. If your keyword is not in the summary, you'll find nothing and get a "nothing appropriate" error message.

TIP Instead of using **man -k**, you can use the **apropos** command, which is equivalent to **man -k**.

When using **man -k** to find specific information from the man pages, you'll sometimes get a load of information. If that happens, it might help to filter down the results a bit by using the **grep** command. But if you want to do that, it is important that you know what you are looking for.

Man pages are categorized in different sections. The most relevant sections for system administrators are as follows:

- **1:** Executable programs or shell commands
- **5:** File formats and conventions
- **8:** System administration commands

There are also sections that provide in-depth details about your Linux system, such as the sections about system calls and library calls. When using **man -k**, you'll get results from all of these sections. To limit the results that display, it makes sense to use **grep** to show only those sections that are relevant for what you need. So, if you are looking for the configuration file that has something to do with passwords, use **man -k password | grep 5**, or if you are looking for the command that an administrator would use to create partitions, use **man -k partition | grep 8**.

Another useful man option is **-f**. The command **man -f <somecommand>** displays a short description of the item as found in the mandb database. This description may help you when deciding whether this man page contains the information you are looking for.

Updating mandb

As previously mentioned, when you use the **man -k** command, the mandb database is consulted. This database is automatically created through a scheduled job. Occasionally, you might look for something that should obviously be documented, but all you get is the message "nothing appropriate." If that happens, you might need to update the mandb database manually. Doing that is easy: Just run the **mandb** command as root without any arguments. It will see whether new man pages have been installed and update the mandb database accordingly.

> **TIP** Do not try to memorize all the commands that you need to accomplish specific tasks. Instead, memorize how to find these commands and find which man page to read to get more information about the command. In Exercise 2-7, you see how that works.

Assume that you are looking for a command, using **man -k**, but all you get is the message "nothing appropriate" and you do not remember how to fix it. Exercise 2-7 shows what you can do in such cases.

Exercise 2-7 Using man -k

1. Make sure you are logged in as the **student** account.
2. Because **man -k** does not give the expected result, it makes sense to look in the man page for the **man** command for additional information about **man -k**. Type **man man** to open the man page of **man**. Once in the man page, type **/-k** to look for a description of the **-k** option. Type **n** a few times until you get to the line that describes the option. You'll see that **man -k** is equivalent to **apropos** and that you can read the man page of **apropos** for more details. So type **q** to exit this man page.
3. Type **man apropos** and read the first paragraphs of the description. You'll see that the database searched by **apropos** is updated by the **mandb** program.
4. Type **man mandb**. This man page explains how to run **mandb** to update the mandb database. As you'll read, all you need to do is type **mandb**, which does the work for you.
5. Type **sudo mandb** to update the mandb database. Notice that you won't see many man pages being added if the mandb database was already up to date.

Using info

Apart from the information that you'll find in man pages, another system provides help about command usage. This is the info system. Most commands are documented in man pages, but some commands have their main documentation in the info system and only show a short usage summary in the man page. If that is the case, the "See Also" section of the man page of that command will tell you that "The full documentation for…is maintained as a Texinfo manual." You then can read the info page using the command **pinfo** or **info**. Both commands work, but in **pinfo**, special items such as menu items are clearly indicated, which is why using **pinfo** is easier.

When working with **info**, take a look at the top line of the viewer. This shows the current position in the info document. Particularly interesting are the Up, Next, and Previous indicators, which tell you how to navigate. Info pages are organized like web pages, which means that they are organized in a hierarchical way. To browse through that hierarchy, type **n** to go to the next page, **p** to go to the previous page, or **u** to move up in the hierarchy.

In an info page, you'll also find menus. Each item that is marked with an asterisk (*) is a menu item. Use the arrow keys to select a specific menu item. This brings you down one level. To get back up again, type **u**. This brings you back to the original starting point in the **pinfo** hierarchy. Figure 2-2 shows what an info page looks like.

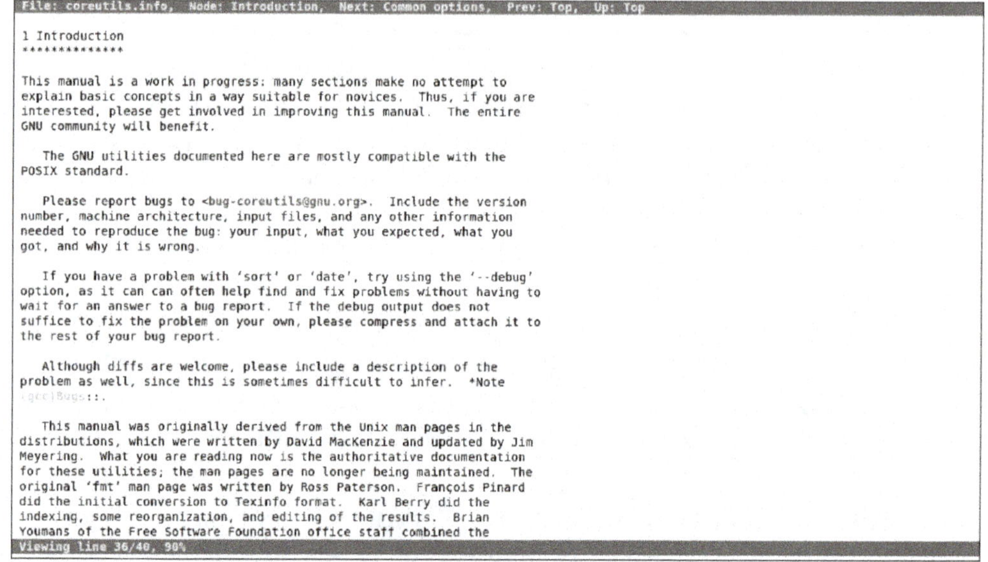

```
File: coreutils.info,  Node: Introduction,  Next: Common options,  Prev: Top,  Up: Top

1 Introduction
**************

This manual is a work in progress: many sections make no attempt to
explain basic concepts in a way suitable for novices.  Thus, if you are
interested, please get involved in improving this manual.  The entire
GNU community will benefit.

   The GNU utilities documented here are mostly compatible with the
POSIX standard.

   Please report bugs to <bug-coreutils@gnu.org>.  Include the version
number, machine architecture, input files, and any other information
needed to reproduce the bug: your input, what you expected, what you
got, and why it is wrong.

   If you have a problem with 'sort' or 'date', try using the '--debug'
option, as it can can often help find and fix problems without having to
wait for an answer to a bug report.  If the debug output does not
suffice to fix the problem on your own, please compress and attach it to
the rest of your bug report.

   Although diffs are welcome, please include a description of the
problem as well, since this is sometimes difficult to infer.  *Note
(gcc)Bugs::.

   This manual was originally derived from the Unix man pages in the
distributions, which were written by David MacKenzie and updated by Jim
Meyering.  What you are reading now is the authoritative documentation
for these utilities; the man pages are no longer being maintained.  The
original 'fmt' man page was written by Ross Paterson.  François Pinard
did the initial conversion to Texinfo format.  Karl Berry did the
indexing, some reorganization, and editing of the results.  Brian
Youmans of the Free Software Foundation office staff combined the
Viewing line 36/40, 90%
```

Figure 2-2 Getting More Command Usage Information Using **pinfo**

Exercise 2-8 shows an example of such a command, and in this exercise you learn how to get the information out of the info page.

Exercise 2-8 Using info

1. Type **man ls**. Type **G** to go to the end of the man page and look at the "See Also" section. It tells you that the full documentation for **ls** is maintained as a Texinfo manual that can be shown with the **info** command. Quit the man page by pressing **q**.
2. Type **pinfo '(coreutils) ls invocation'**. This shows the information about **ls** usage in the **pinfo** page. Read through it and press **q** when done. Alternatively, you can use the **info** command, but **pinfo** shows nicer formatting.

Using /usr/share/doc Documentation Files

A third source of information consists of files that are sometimes copied to the /usr/share/doc directory. These files are available in particular for services and larger systems that are a bit more complicated. You will not typically find much information about a command like **ls**, but some services do provide useful information in /usr/share/doc.

Some services store very useful information in this directory, like rsyslog, bind, Kerberos, and OpenSSL. For some services, even sample files are included.

Summary

In this chapter, you read about essential Linux administration tasks. You learned about some of the important shell basics, such as redirecting I/O, working with history, and managing the environment. You also learned how to edit text files with the **vim** editor. In the last part of this chapter, you learned how to find information using **man** and related commands.

Exam Preparation Tasks

As mentioned in the section "How to Use This Book" in the Introduction, you have several choices for exam preparation: the end-of-chapter labs; the memory tables in Appendix C; Chapter 27, "Final Preparation"; and the practice exams.

Review All Key Topics

Review the most important topics in the chapter, noted with the Key Topic icon in the margin of the page. Table 2-5 lists a reference of these key topics and the page number on which each is found.

Table 2-5 Key Topics for Chapter 2

Key Topic Element	Description	Page
Table 2-4	**vim** Essential Commands	38
List	Significant sections in **man**	46

Complete Tables and Lists from Memory

Print a copy of Appendix C, "Memory Tables" (found on the companion website), or at least the section for this chapter, and complete the tables and lists from memory. Appendix D, "Memory Tables Answer Key," includes completed tables and lists to check your work.

Define Key Terms

Define the following key terms from this chapter and check your answers in the glossary:

shell, Bash, internal command, external command, $PATH, STDIN, STDOUT, STDERR, redirection, file descriptor, device file, pipe, environment, variable, login shell, subshell

Review Questions

The questions that follow are meant to help you test your knowledge of concepts and terminology and the breadth of your knowledge. You can find the answers to these questions in Appendix A.

1. What is a variable?
2. Which command enables you to find the correct man page based on keyword usage?
3. Which file do you need to change if you want a variable to be set for user bob when this user logs in?
4. When analyzing how to use a command, you read that the documentation is maintained with the Techinfo system. How can you read the information?
5. What is the name of the file where Bash stores its history?
6. Which command enables you to update the database that contains man keywords?
7. How can you undo the last modification you have applied in **vim**?
8. What can you add to a command to make sure that it does not show an error message, assuming that you do not care about the information that is in the error messages either?
9. How do you read the current contents of the **$PATH** variable?
10. How do you repeat the last command you used that contains the string *dog* somewhere in the command?

End-of-Chapter Lab

You have now learned about some of the most important basic skills that a Linux administrator should have. Apply these skills by doing the following end-of-chapter lab. End-of-chapter labs have no solutions; you should be able to complete the end-of-chapter labs without any additional help.

Lab 2.1

1. Modify your shell environment so that on every subshell that is started, a variable is set. The name of the variable should be **COLOR**, and the value should be set to **red**. Verify that it is working.
2. Use the appropriate tools to find the command that you can use to change a user password. Do you need root permissions to use this command?
3. From your home directory, type the command **ls -al wergihl** * and ensure that errors as well as regular output are redirected to a file with the name /tmp/lsoutput.

The following topics are covered in this chapter:

- Working with the File System Hierarchy
- Managing Files
- Using Links
- Working with Archives and Compressed Files

The following RHCSA exam objectives are covered in this chapter:

- Create, delete, copy, and move files and directories
- Archive, compress, unpack, and uncompress files using **tar, star, gzip,** and **bzip2**
- Create hard and soft links

CHAPTER 3

Essential File Management Tools

Linux is a file-oriented operating system. That means that many things an administrator has to do on Linux can be traced down to managing files on the Linux operating system. Also, when using hardware devices, files are involved. This chapter introduces you to essential file management skills. You learn how the Linux file system is organized and how you can work with files and directories. You also learn how to manage links and compressed or uncompressed archives.

"Do I Know This Already?" Quiz

The "Do I Know This Already?" quiz enables you to assess whether you should read this entire chapter thoroughly or jump to the "Exam Preparation Tasks" section. If you are in doubt about your answers to these questions or your own assessment of your knowledge of the topics, read the entire chapter. Table 3-1 lists the major headings in this chapter and their corresponding "Do I Know This Already?" quiz questions. You can find the answers in Appendix A, "Answers to the 'Do I Know This Already?' Quizzes and Review Questions."

Table 3-1 "Do I Know This Already?" Section-to-Question Mapping

Foundation Topics Section	Questions
Working with the File System Hierarchy	1–4
Managing Files	5–7
Using Links	8–9
Working with Archives and Compressed Files	10

1. Under which directory would you expect to find temporary files that have been dynamically created since the last time you've booted?
   a. /boot
   b. /bin
   c. /sbin
   d. /run

2. Under which directory would you expect to find log files?
   a. /proc
   b. /run
   c. /var
   d. /usr

3. When /home is mounted on a different device, additional mount options can be provided to enhance security. Which of the following are examples of these options?
   a. **ro**
   b. **nodev**
   c. **noexec**
   d. **nosuid**

4. Which of the following commands would give the most accurate overview of mounted disk devices (without showing much information about mounted system devices as well)?
   a. **mount**
   b. **mount -a**
   c. **df -hT**
   d. **du -h**

5. Which command enables you to show all files in the current directory so that the newest files are listed last?
   a. **ls -lRt**
   b. **ls -lrt**
   c. **mls -alrt**
   d. **ls -alr**

6. Which command enables you to copy hidden files as well as regular files from /home/$USER to the current directory?
   a. **cp -a /home/$USER**
   b. **cp -a /home/$USER/***
   c. **cp -a /home/$USER/.**
   d. **cp -a home/$USER.**

7. Which command enables you to rename the file myfile to mynewfile?
   a. **mv myfile mynewfile**
   b. **rm myfile mynewfile**
   c. **rn myfile mynewfile**
   d. **ren myfile mynewfile**

8. Which statement about hard links is *not* true?
   a. Hard links cannot be created to directories.
   b. Hard links cannot refer to files on other devices.
   c. The inode keeps a hard link counter.
   d. If the original hard link is removed, all other hard links become invalid.

9. Which command creates a symbolic link to the directory /home in the directory /tmp?
   a. **ln /tmp /home**
   b. **ln /home /tmp**
   c. **ln -s /home /tmp**
   d. **ln -s /tmp /home**

10. Which **tar** option enables you to update an existing tar archive?
    a. **-a**
    b. **-A**
    c. **-r**
    d. **-u**

Foundation Topics

Working with the File System Hierarchy

To manage a Linux system, you should be familiar with the default directories that exist on almost all Linux systems. This section describes these directories and explains how mounts are used to compose the file system hierarchy.

Defining the File System Hierarchy

The file system on most Linux systems is organized in a similar way. The layout of the Linux file system is defined in the ***Filesystem Hierarchy Standard (FHS)***, and this file system hierarchy is described in **man 7 file-hierarchy**. Table 3-2 shows an overview of the most significant directories that you'll encounter on a Red Hat Enterprise Linux (RHEL) system, as specified by the FHS.

Table 3-2 FHS Overview

Directory	Use
/	Specifies the root directory. This is where the file system tree starts.
/boot	Contains all files and directories that are needed to boot the Linux kernel.
/dev	Contains device files that are used for accessing physical devices. This directory is essential during boot.
/etc	Contains configuration files that are used by programs and services on your server. This directory is essential during boot.
/home	Used for local user home directories.
/media, /mnt	Contain directories that are used for mounting devices in the file system tree.
/opt	Used for optional packages that may be installed on your server.
/proc	Used by the proc file system. This is a file system structure that gives access to kernel information.
/root	Specifies the home directory of the root user.
/run	Contains process and user-specific information that has been created since the last boot.
/srv	May be used for data by services like NFS, FTP, and HTTP.
/sys	Used as an interface to different hardware devices that are managed by the Linux kernel and associated processes.

Directory	Use
/tmp	Contains temporary files that may be deleted without any warning during boot.
/usr	Contains subdirectories with program files, libraries for these program files, and documentation about them.
/var	Contains files that may change in size dynamically, such as log files, mail boxes, and spool files.

Understanding Mounts

To understand the organization of the Linux file system, you need to understand the important concept of mounting. A ***mount*** is a connection between a device and a directory. A Linux file system is presented as one hierarchy, with the ***root directory*** (/) as its starting point. This hierarchy may be distributed over different devices and even computer systems that are mounted into the root directory.

In the process of mounting, a ***device*** is connected to a specific directory, such that after a successful mount this directory gives access to the device contents.

Mounting devices makes it possible to organize the Linux file system in a flexible way. There are several disadvantages to storing all files in just one file system, which gives several good reasons to work with multiple mounts:

- High activity in one area may fill up the entire file system, which will negatively impact services running on the server.
- If all files are on the same device, it is difficult to secure access and distinguish between different areas of the file system with different security needs. By mounting a separate file system, you can add mount options to meet specific security needs.
- If a one-device file system is completely filled, it may be difficult to make additional storage space available.

To avoid these pitfalls, it is common to organize Linux file systems in different devices (and even shares on other computer systems), such as disk partitions and logical volumes, and mount these devices into the file system hierarchy. By configuring a device as a dedicated mount, you also are able to use specific mount options that can restrict access to the device. Some directories are commonly mounted on dedicated devices:

- **/boot:** This directory is often mounted on a separate device because it requires essential information your computer needs to boot. Because the root directory (/) is often on a Logical Volume Manager (LVM) logical volume, from which

Linux cannot boot by default, the kernel and associated files need to be stored separately on a dedicated /boot device.

- **/boot/EFI:** If a system uses Extensible Firmware Interface (EFI) for booting, a dedicated mount is required, giving access to all files required in the earliest stage of the boot procedure.
- **/var:** This directory is often on a dedicated device because it grows in a dynamic and uncontrolled way (for example, because of the log files that are written to /var/log). By putting it on a dedicated device, you can ensure that it will not fill up all storage on your server.
- **/home:** This directory often is on a dedicated device for security reasons. By putting it on a dedicated device, you can mount it with specific options, such as **noexec** and **nodev**, to enhance the security of the server. When you are reinstalling the operating system, it is an advantage to have home directories in a separate file system. The home directories can then survive the system reinstall.
- **/usr:** This directory contains operating system files only, to which normal users normally do not need any write access. Putting this directory on a dedicated device allows administrators to configure it as a read-only mount.

Apart from these directories, you may find servers that have other directories that are mounted on dedicated partitions or volumes also. After all, it is up to the discretion of the administrator to decide which directories get their own dedicated devices.

To get an overview of all devices and their mount points, you can use different commands:

- The **mount** command gives an overview of all mounted devices. To get this information, the /proc/mounts file is read, where the kernel keeps information about all current mounts. It shows kernel interfaces also, which may lead to a long list of mounted devices being displayed. Example 3-1 shows sample output of this command.

Example 3-1 Partial **mount** Command Output

```
[root@server1 ~]# mount
sysfs on /sys type sysfs (rw,nosuid,nodev,noexec,relatime,seclabel)
proc on /proc type proc (rw,nosuid,nodev,noexec,relatime)
devtmpfs on /dev type devtmpfs (rw,nosuid,seclabel,size=909060k,
  nr_inodes=227265,mode=755)
```

```
securityfs on /sys/kernel/security type securityfs (rw,nosuid,nodev,
  noexec,relatime)
tmpfs on /dev/shm type tmpfs (rw,nosuid,nodev,seclabel)
devpts on /dev/pts type devpts (rw,nosuid,noexec,relatime,seclabel,
   gid=5,mode=620,ptmxmode=000)
tmpfs on /run type tmpfs (rw,nosuid,nodev,seclabel,mode=755)
tmpfs on /sys/fs/cgroup type tmpfs (ro,nosuid,nodev,noexec,seclabel,
  mode=755)
...
/dev/nvme0n1p1 on /boot type xfs (rw,relatime,seclabel,attr2,inode64
,  noquota)
sunrpc on /var/lib/nfs/rpc_pipefs type rpc_pipefs (rw,relatime)
tmpfs on /run/user/42 type tmpfs (rw,nosuid,nodev,relatime,seclabel,
  size=184968k,mode=700,uid=42,gid=42)
tmpfs on /run/user/1000 type tmpfs (rw,nosuid,nodev,relatime,seclabel,
  size=184968k,mode=700,uid=1000,gid=1000)
gvfsd-fuse on /run/user/1000/gvfs type fuse.gvfsd-fuse
  (rw,nosuid,nodev,relatime,user_id=1000,group_id=1000)
/dev/sr0 on /run/media/student/RHEL-9-0-BaseOS-x86_64 type iso9660
(ro,nosuid,nodev,relatime,nojoliet,check=s,map=n,blocksize=2048,
  uid=1000,gid=1000,dmode=500,fmode=400,uhelper=udisks2)
tmpfs on /run/user/0 type tmpfs (rw,nosuid,nodev,relatime,seclabel,
  size=184968k,mode=700))
```

- The **df -Th** command was designed to show available disk space on mounted devices; it includes most of the system mounts. Because it will look on all mounted file systems, it is a convenient command to use to get an overview of current system mounts. The **-h** option summarizes the output of the command in a human-readable way, and the **-T** option shows which file system type is used on the different mounts.
- The **findmnt** command shows mounts and the relationship that exists between the different mounts. Because the output of the **mount** command is a bit overwhelming, you may like the output of **findmnt**. Notice that because of width limitations of the book page, the output that belongs in the OPTIONS column appears on the left side of the page.

In Exercise 3-1, you use different commands to get an overview of currently mounted devices.

Exercise 3-1 Getting an Overview of Current Mounts

1. Log in as the **student** user and type **mount**. Notice that the output of the command is quite overwhelming. If you read carefully, though, you'll see a few directories from the Linux directory structure and their corresponding mounts.
2. Type **df -hT**. Notice that a lot fewer devices are shown. An example of the output of this command is shown in Example 3-2.

Example 3-2 df -hT Sample Output

```
[root@server1 ~]# df -hT
    Filesystem           Type         Size   Used Avail Use%   Mounted on
    /dev/mapper/centos-root xfs        5.9G   3.9G   2.1G   66%   /
    devtmpfs            devtmpfs     908M       0        908M    0%    /dev
    tmpfs               tmpfs      918M   144K   917M     1%    /dev/shm
    tmpfs               tmpfs      918M    21M   897M     3%    /run
    tmpfs               tmpfs      918M      0         918M    0%    /sys/fs/
cgroup
    /dev/sda1              xfs              197M   131M    67M   67%    /boot
```

Now that you have entered the **mount** and **df** commands, let's have a closer look at the output of the **df -hT** command in Example 3-2.

The output of **df** is shown in seven columns:

- **Filesystem:** The name of the device file that interacts with the disk device that is used. The real devices in the output start with /dev (which refers to the directory that is used to store device files). You can also see a couple of tmpfs devices. These are kernel devices that are used to create a temporary file system in RAM.
- **Type:** The type of file system that was used.
- **Size:** The size of the mounted device.
- **Used:** The amount of disk space the device has in use.
- **Avail:** The amount of unused disk space.
- **Use%:** The percentage of the device that currently is in use.
- **Mounted on:** The directory the device currently is mounted on.

Note that when you use the **df** command, the sizes are reported in kibibytes. The option **-m** will display these in mebibytes, and using **-h** will display a human-readable format in KiB, MiB, GiB, TiB, or PiB.

Managing Files

As an administrator, you need to be able to perform common file management tasks. These tasks include the following:

- Working with wildcards
- Managing and working with directories
- Working with absolute and relative pathnames
- Listing files and directories
- Copying files and directories
- Moving files and directories
- Deleting files and directories

The following subsections explain how to perform these tasks.

Working with Wildcards

When you're working with files, using wildcards can make your work a lot easier. A wildcard is a shell feature that helps you refer to multiple files in an easy way. Table 3-3 gives an overview.

Table 3-3 Wildcard Overview

Wildcard	Use
*	Refers to an unlimited number of any characters. **ls ***, for instance, shows all files in the current directory (except those that have a name starting with a dot).
?	Used to refer to one specific character that can be any character. **ls c?t** would match *cat* as well as *cut*.
[auo]	Refers to one character that may be selected from the range that is specified between square brackets. **ls c[auo]t** would match *cat*, *cut*, and *cot*.

Managing and Working with Directories

To organize files, Linux works with ***directories*** (also referred to as ***folders***). You have already read about some default directories as defined by the FHS. When users start creating files and storing them on a server, it makes sense to provide a directory structure as well. As an administrator, you have to be able to walk through the directory structure. Exercise 3-2 gives you practice working with directories.

Exercise 3-2 Working with Directories

1. Open a shell as the **student** user. Type **cd**. Next, type **pwd**, which stands for *print working directory*. You'll see that you are currently in your home directory; that is, name /home/<username>.
2. Type **touch file1**. This command creates an empty file with the name file1 on your server. Because you currently are in your home directory, you can create any file you want to.
3. Type **cd /**. This changes the current directory to the root (/) directory. Type **touch file2**. You'll see a "permission denied" message. Ordinary users can create files only in directories where they have the permissions needed for this.
4. Type **cd /tmp**. This brings you to the /tmp directory, where all users have write permissions. Again, type **touch file2**. You'll see that you can create items in the /tmp directory (unless there is already a file2 that is owned by somebody else).
5. Type **cd** without any arguments. This command brings you back to your home directory.
6. Type **mkdir files**. This creates a directory with the name files in the current directory. The **mkdir** command uses the name of the directory that needs to be created as a relative pathname; it is relative to the position you are currently in.
7. Type **mkdir /home/$USER/files**. In this command, you are using the variable **$USER**, which is substituted with your current username. The complete argument of **mkdir** is an absolute filename to the files directory that you are trying to create. Because this directory already exists, you'll get a "file exists" error message.
8. Type **rmdir files** to remove the files directory that you have just created. The **rmdir** command enables you to remove directories, but it works only if the directory is empty and does not contain any files.

Working with Absolute and Relative Pathnames

In the previous section, you worked with the commands **cd** and **mkdir**. You used these commands to browse through the directory structure. You also worked with a relative filename and an absolute filename.

An ***absolute filename***, or *absolute pathname*, is a complete ***path*** reference to the file or directory you want to work with. This pathname starts with the root directory, followed by all subdirectories up to the actual filename. No matter what your current directory is, absolute filenames will always work. An example of an absolute filename is /home/lisa/file1.

A ***relative filename*** is relative to the current directory as shown with the **pwd** command. It contains only the elements that are required to get from the current directory up to the item you need. Suppose that your current directory is /home (as shown by the **pwd** command). When you refer to the relative filename lisa/file1, you are referring to the absolute filename /home/lisa/file1.

When working with relative filenames, it is sometimes useful to move up one level in the hierarchy. Imagine you are logged in as root and you want to copy the file /home/lisa/file1 to the directory /home/lara. A few solutions would work:

- Use **cp /home/lisa/file1 /home/lara**. Because in this command you are using absolute pathnames, this command will work at all times.
- Make sure your current directory is /home and use **cp lisa/file1 lara**. Notice that both the source file and the destination file are referred to as relative filenames and for that reason do *not* start with a /. There is a risk though: if the directory lara in this example doesn't exist, the **cp** command creates a file with the name lara. If you want to make sure it copies to a directory, and generates an error message if the directory doesn't exist, use **cp lisa/file1 lara/**.
- If the current directory is set to /home/lisa, you could also use **cp file1 ../lara**. In this command, the name of the target file uses .., which means go up one level. The .. is followed by /lara, so the total name of the target file would be interpreted as "go up one level" (so you would be in /home), and from there, look for the /lara subdirectory.

TIP If you are new to working with Linux, understanding relative filenames is not always easy. There is an easy workaround, though. Just make sure that you always work with absolute pathnames. Using absolute pathnames involves more typing, but it is easier, so you'll make fewer mistakes.

In Chapter 2, "Using Essential Tools," you learned how you can use Bash completion via the Tab key to complete commands. Using Bash completion makes it a lot easier to work with long commands. Bash completion works on filenames, too. If you have a long filename, like my-long-file-name, try typing **my-** and pressing the Tab key. If in the current directory, just one file has a name starting with my-, the filename will automatically be completed. If there are more files that have a name starting with my-, you have to press the Tab key twice to see a list of all available filenames.

Listing Files and Directories

While working with files and directories, it is useful to show the contents of the current directory. For this purpose, you can use the **ls** command. If used without arguments, **ls** shows the contents of the current directory. Some common arguments make working with **ls** easier. Table 3-4 gives an overview.

Table 3-4 **ls** Common Command-Line Options

Command	Use
ls -l	Shows a long listing, which includes information about file properties, such as creation date and permissions.
ls -a	Shows all files, including hidden files.
ls -lrt	The **-t** option shows commands sorted based on modification date. You'll see the most recently modified files last in the list because of the **-r** option. This is a very useful command.
ls -d	Shows the names of directories, not the contents of all directories that match the wildcards that have been used with the **ls** command.
ls -R	Shows the contents of the current directory, in addition to all of its subdirectories; that is, it **R**ecursively descends all subdirectories.

TIP A hidden file on Linux is a file that has a name that starts with a dot. Try the following: **touch .hidden**. Next, type **ls**. You will not see the file. Then type **ls -a**. You'll see it.

When using **ls** and **ls -l**, you'll see that files are color-coded. The different colors that are used for different file types make it easier to distinguish between different kinds of files. Do not focus too much on them, though, because the colors that are used are the result of a variable setting that might be different in other Linux shells or on other Linux servers.

Copying Files and Directories

To organize files on your server, you'll often copy files. The **cp** command helps you do so. Copying a single file is not difficult: just use **cp /<path to file> /<path to destination>**. To copy the file /etc/hosts to the directory /tmp, for instance, use **cp /etc/hosts /tmp**. This results in the file hosts being written to /tmp.

> **TIP** If you copy a file to a directory but the target directory does not exist, a file will be created with the name of the alleged target directory. In many cases, that's not the best solution and it would be better to just get an error message instead. You can accomplish this by placing a / after the directory name, so use **cp /etc/hosts /tmp/** and not **cp /etc/hosts /tmp**.

With the **cp** command, you can also copy an entire subdirectory, with its contents and everything beneath it. To do so, use the option **-R**, which stands for recursive. (You'll see the option **-R** with many other Linux commands also.) For example, to copy the directory /etc and everything in it to the directory /tmp, you would use the command **cp -R /etc /tmp**.

While using the **cp** command, you need to consider permissions and other properties of the files. Without extra options, you risk these properties not being copied. If you want to make sure that you keep the current permissions, use the **-a** option, which has **cp** work in archive mode. This option ensures that permissions and all other file properties will be kept while copying. So, to copy an exact state of your home directory and everything within it to the /tmp directory, use **cp -a ~ /tmp**.

A special case when working with **cp** is hidden files. By default, hidden files are not copied over. There are three solutions to copy hidden files as well:

- **cp /somedir/.* /tmp** This copies all files that have a name starting with a dot (the hidden files, that is) to /tmp. It gives an error message for directories whose name starts with a dot in /somedir, because the **-R** option was not used.
- **cp -a /somedir/ .** This copies the entire directory /somedir, including its contents, to the current directory. So, as a result, a subdirectory somedir will be created in the current directory.
- **cp -a /somedir/. .** This copies all files, regular and hidden, to the current directory (notice the space between the two dots at the end of this command).

Moving Files and Directories

To move files and directories, you use the **mv** command. This command removes the file from its current location and puts it in the new location. You can also use it to rename a file (which, in fact, is nothing else than copying and deleting the original file anyway). Let's take a look at some examples:

- **mv myfile /tmp** Moves the file myfile from the current directory to /tmp.

- **mkdir somefiles; mv somefiles /tmp** First creates a directory with the name somefiles and then moves this directory to /tmp. Notice that this also works if the directory contains files.
- **mv myfile mynewfile** Renames the file myfile to a new file with the name mynewfile.

Deleting Files and Directories

The last common file administration task is file deletion. To delete files and directories, you use the **rm** command. When this command is used on a single file, the single file is removed. You can also use it on directories that contain files. To do so, include the **-r** option, which again stands for recursive.

NOTE Many commands have an option that creates recursive behavior. On some commands you use the option **-R**, and on other commands you use the option **-r**. That is confusing, but it is just the way it is.

On RHEL 9, if you use the **rm** command as root, it prompts for confirmation. The reason is that through /root/.bashrc, **rm** is defined as an alias to **rm -i**. If you do not like that, you can use the **-f** option or remove the alias from /root/.bashrc. Make sure that you know what you are doing after removing this safety feature, because you'll never be warned anymore while removing files.

In Exercise 3-3, you work with the common file management utilities.

NOTE In this exercise dots are important and used as a part of the commands. To avoid confusion, if normally a dot would be used to indicate the end of a sentence, in this exercise I've left it out if it immediately follows a command.

Exercise 3-3 Working with Files

Figure 3-1 provides an overview of the directory structure you are working with in this exercise.

1. Open a shell as an ordinary user.
2. Type **pwd**

   You should be in the directory /home/$USER.

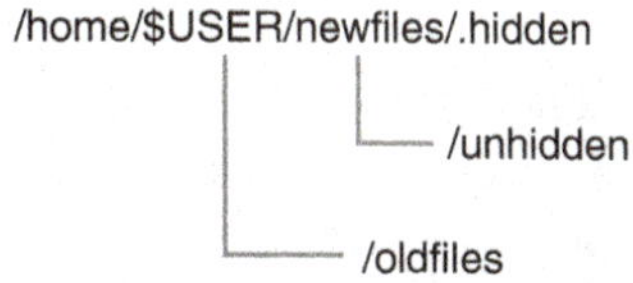

Figure 3-1 Sample Directory Structure Overview

3. Type **mkdir newfiles oldfiles**

   Type **ls**

   You'll see the two directories you have just created, as well as some other directories that already existed in the user home directory.

4. Type **touch newfiles/.hidden; touch newfiles/unhidden**

   This creates two files in the directory newfiles.

5. Type **cd oldfiles**

6. Type **ls -al**

   This shows two items only: ., which refers to the current directory; and .., which refers to the item above this (the parent directory).

7. Type **ls -al ../newfiles**

   In this command, you are using a relative pathname to refer to the contents of the /home/$USER/newfiles directory.

8. Use the command **cp -a ../newfiles/ .** (notice the space between the / and the . at the end of the command).

9. Type **ls -a**

   You see that you have created the subdirectory newfiles into the directory oldfiles.

10. Make sure that you are still in /home/$USER/oldfiles, and type **rm -rf newfiles**

11. Now use the command **cp -a ../newfiles/* .** (notice the space between the * and .). Type **ls -al** to see what has been copied now. You'll see that the hidden file has not been copied.

12. To make sure that you copy hidden files as well as regular files, use **cp -a ../newfiles/. .**

13. Verify the command worked this time, using **ls -al**

    You'll notice that the hidden files as well as the regular files have been successfully copied.

Using Links

Links on Linux are like aliases that are assigned to a file. There are symbolic links, and there are hard links. To understand a link, you need to know a bit about how the Linux file system uses inodes for file system administration.

Understanding Hard Links

Linux stores administrative data about files in ***inodes***. The inode is used to store all administrative data about files. Every file on Linux has an inode, and in the inode, important information about the file is stored:

- The data block where the file contents are stored
- The creation, access, and modification date
- Permissions
- File owners

Just one important piece of information is not stored in the inode: the name of the file. Names are stored in the directory, and each filename knows which inode it has to address to access further file information. It is interesting to know that an inode does not know which name it has; it just knows how many names are associated with the inode. These names are referred to as ***hard links***. So every file always has one hard link to start with, which is the name of the file.

When you create a file, you give it a name. Basically, this name is a hard link. On a Linux file system, multiple hard links can be created to a file. This is useful if a file with the same contents needs to be available at multiple locations, and you need an easy solution to keep the contents the same. If a change is applied to any one of the hard links, it will show in all other hard links as well, as all hard links point to the same data blocks. Some restrictions apply to hard links, though:

- Hard links must exist all on the same device (partition, logical volume, etc).
- You cannot create hard links to directories.
- When the last name (hard link) to a file is removed, access to the file's data is also removed.

The nice thing about hard links is that no difference exists between the first hard link and the second hard link. They are both just hard links, and if the first hard link that ever existed for a file is removed, that does not impact the other hard links that still exist. The Linux operating system uses links on many locations to make files more accessible.

Understanding Symbolic Links

A ***symbolic link*** (also referred to as a *soft link*) does not link directly to the inode but to the name of the file. This makes symbolic links much more flexible, but it also has some disadvantages. The advantage of symbolic links is that they can link to files on other devices, as well as on directories. The major disadvantage is that when the original file is removed, the symbolic link becomes invalid and does not work any longer.

Figure 3-2 gives a schematic overview of how inodes, hard links, and symbolic links relate to one another.

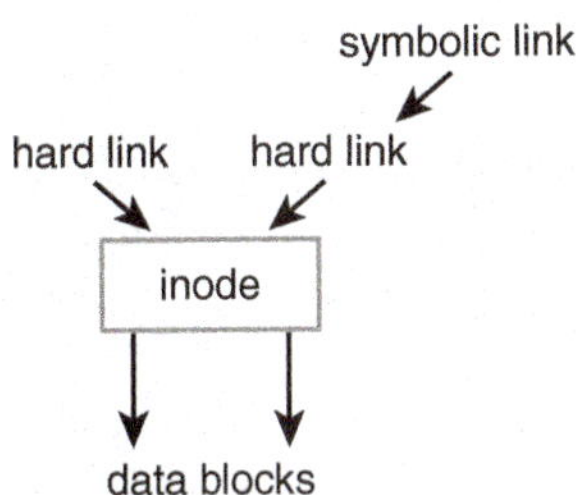

Figure 3-2 Links and Inodes Overview

Creating Links

Use the **ln** command to create links. It uses the same order of parameters as **cp** and **mv**; first you mention the source name, followed by the destination name. If you want to create a symbolic link, you use the option **-s**, and then you specify the source and target file or directory. One important restriction applies: to be able to create hard links, you must be the owner of the item that you want to link to.

Table 3-5 shows some examples.

Table 3-5 **ln** Usage Examples

Command	Explanation
ln /etc/hosts .	Creates a link to the file /etc/hosts in the current directory
ln -s /etc/hosts .	Creates a symbolic link to the file /etc/hosts in the current directory
ln -s /home /tmp	Creates a symbolic link to the directory /home in the directory /tmp

The **ls** command will reveal whether a file is a link:

- In the output of the **ls -l** command, the first character is an l if the file is a symbolic link.
- If a file is a symbolic link, the output of **ls -l** shows the name of the item it links to after the filename.

- If a file is a hard link, **ls -l** shows the hard link counter. In the output in Example 3-3, this is the number 3 that is right before root root for the hosts file.

Example 3-3 Showing Link Properties with **ls -l**

```
[root@localhost tmp]# \ls -l
total 3
lrwxrwxrwx. 1 root root 5 Jan 19 04:38 home -> /home
-rw-r--r--. 3 root root 158 Jun 7 2013 hosts
```

NOTE In Example 3-3, the command used is **\ls -l**, not **ls -l**. The **ls** command by default is an alias, which takes care of using the different colors when showing **ls** output; the \ in front of the command causes the alias not to be used.

Removing Links

Removing links can be dangerous. To show you why, let's consider the following procedure.

1. Make a directory named test in your home directory: **mkdir ~/test**
2. Copy all files that have a name starting with a, b, c, d, or e from /etc to this directory: **cp /etc/[a-e]* ~/test**
3. Type **ls -l ~/test/** to verify the contents of the test directory.
4. Make sure that you are in your home directory, by using **cd** without arguments.
5. Type **ln -s test link**
6. Type **rm link**. This removes the symbolic link. (Do *not* use **-r** or **-f** to remove symbolic links, even if they are subdirectories.)
7. Type **ls -l**. You'll see that the symbolic link has been removed.
8. Let's do it again. Type **ln -s test link** to create the link again.
9. Type **rm -rf link/** (which is what you would get by using Bash command-line completion).
10. Type **ls**. You'll see that the directory link still exists.
11. Type **ls test/**. You'll see the directory test is now empty.

In Exercise 3-4, you learn how to work with symbolic links and hard links.

Exercise 3-4 Working with Symbolic Links and Hard Links

NOTE In this exercise dots are important and used as a part of the commands. To avoid confusion, if normally a dot would be used to indicate the end of a sentence, in this exercise I've left it out if it immediately follows a command.

1. Open a shell as the **student** user.
2. From your home directory, type **ln /etc/passwd .** (Make sure that the command ends with a dot that has a space before it!) This command gives you an "operation not permitted" error because you are not the owner of /etc/passwd.
3. Type **ln -s /etc/passwd .** (Again, make sure that the command ends with a space and a dot!) This works; you do not have to be the owner to create a symbolic link.
4. Type **ln -s /etc/hosts** (this time with no dot at the end of the command). You'll notice this command also works. If the target is not specified, the link is created in the current directory.
5. Type **touch newfile** and create a hard link to this file by using **ln newfile linkedfile**
6. Type **ls -l** and notice the link counter for newfile and linkedfile, which is currently set to 2.
7. Type **ln -s newfile symlinkfile** to create a symbolic link to newfile.
8. Type **rm newfile**
9. Type **cat symlinkfile.** You will get a "no such file or directory" error message because the original file could not be found.
10. Type **cat linkedfile.** This gives no problem.
11. Type **ls -l** and look at the way the symlinkfile is displayed. Also look at linkedfile, which now has the link counter set to 1.
12. Type **ln linkedfile newfile**
13. Type **ls -l** again. You'll see that the original situation has been restored.

Working with Archives and Compressed Files

Another important file-related task is managing archives and compressed files. To create an archive of files on a Linux computer, you often use ***tar*** command. This command was originally designed to stream files to a tape without any compression of the files, and it still doesn't compress anything by default. If you want to compress files as well, you have to either use a specific compression tool or specify an option that compresses the archive while it is created. In this section, you learn how to work with archives and compressed files.

Managing Archives with tar

The Tape ARchiver (**tar**) utility is used to archive files. Although originally designed to stream files to a backup tape, in its current use **tar** is used mostly to write files to an archive file. You have to be able to perform four important tasks with **tar** on the RHCSA exam:

- Create an archive
- List the contents of an archive
- Extract an archive
- Compress and uncompress archives

Creating Archives with tar

To create an archive, you use the following syntax: **tar -cf archivename.tar /files-you-want-to-archive**. If you want to see what is happening, use the **-v** option as well. To put files in an archive, you need at least read permissions to the file and execute permissions on the directory the file resides in. Use **tar -cvf /root/homes.tar /home** as user root to write the contents of the /home directory and everything below it to the file homes.tar in the directory /root. Notice the options that are used; the order in these options is important.

Originally, **tar** did not use the dash (-) in front of its options. Modern **tar** implementations use that dash, as do all other Linux programs, but they still allow the old usage without a dash for backward compatibility. For a complete overview of relevant options used, see Table 3-6 in the next section.

While you're managing archives with **tar**, it is also possible to add a file to an existing archive or to update an archive. To add a file to an archive, you use the **-r** options. Use, for instance, **tar -rvf /root/homes.tar /etc/hosts** to add the /etc/hosts file to the archive.

To update a currently existing archive file, you can use the **-u** option. So, use **tar -uvf /root/homes.tar /home** to write newer versions of all files in /home to the archive.

Monitoring and Extracting tar Files

Before you extract a file, it is good to know what might be expected. The option **-t** can be used to find out. Type, for instance, **tar -tvf /root/homes.tar** to see the contents of the tar archive.

TIP It is good practice to create archive files with an extension such as .tar or .tgz so that they can be easily recognized, but not everyone does that. If you think that a file is a tar archive but you are not sure, use the **file** command. If you type file somefile, **for instance**, the **file** command analyzes its contents and shows on the command line what type of file it is.

To extract the contents of an archive, use **tar -xvf /archivename.tar**. This extracts the archive in the *current* directory. That means that if you are in /root when typing **tar -xvf /root/homes.tar**, and the file contains a directory /home, after extracting you'll have a new directory /root/home that contains the entire contents of the file. This might not be what you wanted to accomplish. There are two solutions to put the extracted contents right where you want to have them:

- Before extracting the archive file, use the **cd** command to get into the directory where you want to extract the file.
- Use the option **-C /targetdir** to specify the target directory where you want to extract the file to. If you want to put the contents of the file /root/homes.tar in the directory /tmp, for instance, you can use **tar -xvf homes.tar -C /tmp**.

NOTE The RHCSA objectives mention that you need to know how to work with **star** as well. The ***star*** utility was designed to offer support for archiving nondefault file attributes, such as access control lists (see Chapter 7, "Permissions Management") or SELinux file context (see Chapter 22, "Managing SELinux"). In its current release, **tar** offers this functionality also, so there is no real need to use **star** anymore. You'll also notice that it isn't even included in the default installation patterns.

Apart from extracting an entire archive file, it is also possible to extract one file out of the archive. To do so, use **tar -xvf /archivename.tar file-you-want-to-extract**. If your archive etc.tar contains the file /etc/hosts that you want to extract, for instance, use **tar -xvf /root/etc.tar etc/hosts**.

Using Compression

Many files contain a lot of redundancy. ***Compression*** programs allow you to make files take less disk space by taking out that redundancy. If there is no redundancy, you won't gain much by using compression. In all examples of the **tar** command that you have seen so far, not a single byte has been compressed. Originally, after you created the archive, it had to be compressed with a separate compression utility, such as ***gzip*** or ***bzip2***. After having created home.tar, you can compress it with **gzip home.tar**. **gzip** replaces home.tar with its compressed version, home.tar.gz, which takes significantly less space.

As an alternative to using **gzip**, you can use the **bzip2** utility. Originally, **bzip2** used a more efficient encryption algorithm, which resulted in smaller file sizes, but currently hardly any difference in file size exists between the result of **bzip2** and the result of **gzip**. Another alternative for compressing files, is the ***xz*** utility, which has recently been introduced.

To decompress files that have been compressed with **gzip** or **bzip2**, you can use the **gunzip** and **bunzip2** utilities; you work with some examples of this command in Exercise 3-5.

As an alternative to using these utilities from the command line, you can include the **-z (gzip)**, **-J (xz)**, or **-j (bzip2)** option while creating the archive with **tar**. This will immediately compress the archive while it is created. There is no need to use this option while extracting. The **tar** utility will recognize the compressed content and automatically decompress it for you. In Exercise 3-5, you apply the newly acquired **tar** skills. Table 3-6 gives an overview of the most significant **tar** options.

Table 3-6 Overview of **tar** Options

Option	Use
c	Creates an archive.
v	Shows verbose output while **tar** is working.
t	Shows the contents of an archive.
z	Compresses/decompresses the archive while creating it, by using **gzip**.
j	Compresses/decompresses the archive by using **bzip2**.
J	Compresses/decompresses the archive using **xz**.
x	Extracts an archive.
u	Updates an archive; only newer files will be written to the archive.
C	Changes the working directory before performing the command.
r	Appends files to an archive.

Exercise 3-5 Using tar

1. Open a root shell on your server. When you log in, the home directory of user root will become the current directory, so all relative filenames used in this exercise refer to /root/.
2. Type **tar cvf etc.tar /etc** to archive the contents of the /etc directory.
3. Type **file etc.tar** and read the information that is provided by the command. This should look like the following:

   ```
   [root@server1 ~]# file etc.tartar: POSIX tar archive (GNU)
   ```

4. Type **gzip etc.tar** to compress the tar file, which packages it into the file etc.tar.gz.
5. Type **tar tvf etc.tar.gz** Notice that the **tar** command has no issues reading from a **gzip** compressed file. Also notice that the archive content consists of all relative filenames.
6. Type **tar xvf etc.tar.gz etc/hosts**
7. Type **ls -R** Notice that a subdirectory etc has been created in the current directory. In this subdirectory, the file hosts has been restored.
8. Type **gunzip etc.tar.gz** This decompresses the compressed file but does not change anything else with regard to the **tar** command.
9. Type **tar xvf etc.tar -C /tmp etc/passwd** This extracts the password file including its relative pathname to the /tmp directory. Use **ls -l /tmp/etc/passwd** to verify.
10. Type **tar cjvf homes.tar /home** This creates a compressed archive of the home directory to the home directory of user root.
11. Type **rm -f *gz *tar** to remove all files resulting from exercises in this chapter from the home directory of /root.

Summary

In this chapter, you learned how to work with essential file management tools. You learned how the Linux directory structure is organized by default, and you learned what file types to expect in which directories. You also learned how to find your way in the directory structure and to work with files.

Exam Preparation Tasks

As mentioned in the section "How to Use This Book" in the Introduction, you have several choices for exam preparation: the end-of-chapter labs; the memory tables in Appendix C; Chapter 27, "Final Preparation"; and the practice exams.

Review All Key Topics

Review the most important topics in the chapter, noted with the Key Topic icon in the margin of the page. Table 3-7 lists a reference for these key topics and the page number on which each is found.

Table 3-7 Key Topics for Chapter 3

Key Topic Element	Description	Page
Table 3-2	FHS Overview	56
Table 3-3	Wildcard Overview	61
Paragraph	Definition of an absolute filename	63
Paragraph	Definition of a relative filename	63
Table 3-4	**ls** Common Command-Line Options	64
Paragraph	Definition of an inode	68
Table 3-5	**ln** Usage Examples	69
Table 3-6	Overview of **tar** Options	74

Complete Tables and Lists from Memory

Print a copy of Appendix C, "Memory Tables" (found on the companion website), or at least the section for this chapter, and complete the tables and lists from memory. Appendix D, "Memory Tables Answer Key," includes completed tables and lists to check your work.

Define Key Terms

Define the following key terms from this chapter and check your answers in the glossary:

File System Hierarchy Standard (FHS), mount, root directory, device, directory, folder, absolute filename, path, relative filename, inode, hard link, symbolic link, **tar**, **star**, compression, **gzip**, **bzip2**, **xz**

Review Questions

The questions that follow are meant to help you test your knowledge of concepts and terminology and the breadth of your knowledge. You can find the answers to these questions in Appendix A.

1. Which directory would you go to if you were looking for configuration files?
2. Which command enables you to display a list of current directory contents, with the newest files listed first?
3. Which command enables you to rename the file myfile to yourfile?
4. Which command enables you to wipe an entire directory structure, including all of its contents?
5. How do you create a link to the directory /tmp in your home directory?
6. How would you copy all files that have a name that starts with a, b, or c from the directory /etc to your current directory?
7. Which command enables you to create a link to the directory /etc in your home directory?
8. What is the safe option to remove a symbolic link to a directory?
9. How do you create a compressed archive of the directories /etc and /home and write that archive to /tmp/etchome.tgz?
10. How would you extract the file /etc/passwd from /tmp/etchome.tgz that you have created in the previous step?

End-of-Chapter Lab

In this chapter, you learned how to perform basic file management tasks. Managing files is an essential task for a Linux administrator. This end-of-chapter lab enables you to practice these skills and make sure that you master them before taking the RHCSA exam.

Lab 3.1

1. Log in as user **student** and use **sudo -i** to open a root shell. In the home directory of root, create one archive file that contains the contents of the /home directory and the /etc directory. Use the name /root/essentials.tar for the archive file.
2. Copy this archive to the /tmp directory. Also create a hard link to this file in the / directory.

3. Rename the file /essentials.tar to **/archive.tar**.
4. Create a symbolic link in the home directory of the user root that refers to /archive.tar. Use the name **link.tar** for the symbolic link.
5. Remove the file /archive.tar and see what happened to the symbolic link. Remove the symbolic link also.
6. Compress the /root/essentials.tar file.

The following topics are covered in this chapter:

- Using Common Text File–Related Tools
- A Primer to Using Regular Expressions
- Using **grep** to Analyze Text
- Working with Other Useful Text Processing Utilities

The following RHCSA exam objectives are covered in this chapter:

- Use **grep** and regular expressions to analyze text
- Create and edit text files

CHAPTER 4

Working with Text Files

Since the early days of UNIX, working with text files has been an important administrator skill. Even on modern Linux versions such as Red Hat Enterprise Linux 9, working with text files is still an important skill, as everything you do on Linux is stored as a text file. By applying the correct tools, you'll easily find and modify the configuration of everything. This chapter is about these tools. Make sure that you master them well, because good knowledge of these tools really will make your work as a Linux administrator a lot easier. At the same time, it will increase your chances of passing the RHCSA exam.

"Do I Know This Already?" Quiz

The "Do I Know This Already?" quiz enables you to assess whether you should read this entire chapter thoroughly or jump to the "Exam Preparation Tasks" section. If you are in doubt about your answers to these questions or your own assessment of your knowledge of the topics, read the entire chapter. Table 4-1 lists the major headings in this chapter and their corresponding "Do I Know This Already?" quiz questions. You can find the answers in Appendix A, "Answers to the 'Do I Know This Already?' Quizzes and Review Questions."

Table 4-1 "Do I Know This Already?" Section-to-Question Mapping

Foundation Topics Section	Questions
Using Common Text File–Related Tools	1–5
A Primer to Using Regular Expressions	6–8
Using **grep** to Analyze Text	10
Working with Other Useful Text Processing Utilities	9

1. Which command was developed to show only the first ten lines in a text file?
   a. **head**
   b. **top**
   c. **first**
   d. **cat**

2. Which command enables you to count the number of words in a text file?
   a. **count**
   b. **list**
   c. **ls -l**
   d. **wc**

3. Which key on your keyboard do you use in **less** to go to the last line of the current text file?
   a. End
   b. Page Down
   c. q
   d. G

4. Which option is missing (...) from the following command, assuming that you want to filter the first field out of the /etc/passwd file and assuming that the character that is used as the field delimiter is a :?

   ```
   cut ... : -f 1 /etc/passwd
   ```

   a. **-d**
   b. **-c**
   c. **-t**
   d. **-x**

5. Which option is missing (...) if you want to sort the third column of the output of the command **ps aux**?

   ```
   ps aux | sort ...
   ```

   a. **-k3**
   b. **-s3**
   c. **-k f 3**
   d. **-f 3**

6. Which of the following commands would only show lines in the file /etc/passwd that start with the text *anna*?
   a. **grep anna /etc/passwd**
   b. **grep -v anna /etc/passwd**
   c. **grep $anna /etc/passwd**
   d. **grep ^anna /etc/passwd**

7. Which regular expression do you use to make the previous character optional?

   a. ?

   b. .

   c. *

   d. &

8. Which regular expression do you use if you want the preceding character to occur at least one time?

   a. ?

   b. .

   c. *

   d. +

9. Assuming that the field delimiter : is used, which command prints the fourth field of a line in the /etc/passwd file if the text *user* occurs in that line?

   a. **awk '/user/ { print $4 }' /etc/passwd**

   b. **awk -d : '/user/ { print $4 }' /etc/passwd**

   c. **awk -F : '/user/ $4' /etc/passwd**

   d. **awk -F : '/user/ { print $4 }' /etc/passwd**

10. Which option would you use with **grep** to show only lines that do *not* contain the regular expression that was used?

    a. **-x**

    b. **-v**

    c. **-u**

    d. **-q**

Foundation Topics

Using Common Text File–Related Tools

Before we start talking about the best possible way to find text files containing specific text, let's take a look at how you can display text files in an efficient way. Table 4-2 provides an overview of some common commands often used for this purpose.

Table 4-2 Essential Tools for Managing Text File Contents

Command	Explanation
less	Opens the text file in a pager, which allows for easy reading
cat	Dumps the contents of the text file on the screen
head	Shows the top of the text file
tail	Shows the bottom of the text file
cut	Used to filter specific columns or characters from a text file
sort	Sorts the contents of a text file
wc	Counts the number of lines, words, and characters in a text file

Apart from their use on a text file, these commands may also prove very useful when used with pipes. You can use the command **less /etc/passwd**, for example, to open the contents of the /etc/passwd file in the **less** ***pager***, but you can also use the command **ps aux | less**, which sends the output of the command **ps aux** to the **less** pager to allow for easy reading.

Doing More with less

In many cases, as a Linux administrator you'll need to read the contents of text files. The **less** utility offers a convenient way to do so. To open the contents of a text file in **less**, just type **less** followed by the name of the file you want to see, as in **less /etc/passwd**.

From **less**, you can use the Page Up and Page Down keys on your keyboard to browse through the file contents. Seen enough? Then you can press **q** to quit **less**. Also very useful is that you can easily search for specific contents in **less** using **/sometext** for a forward search and **?sometext** for a backward search. Repeat the last search by using **n**.

If you think this sounds familiar, it should. You have seen similar behavior in **vim** and **man**. The reason is that all of these commands are based on the same code.

NOTE Once upon a time, **less** was developed because it offered more features than the classical UNIX tool **more,** which was developed to go through file contents page by page. So, the idea was to do more with **less.** Developers did not like that, so they enhanced the features of the **more** command as well. The result is that both **more** and **less** offer many features that are similar, and which tool you use doesn't really matter that much anymore. There is one significant difference, though, and that is the **more** utility ends if the end of the file is reached. To prevent this behavior, you can start **more** with the **-p** option. Another difference is that the **more** tool is a standard part of any Linux and UNIX installation. This is not the case for **less**, which may have to be installed separately.

In Exercise 4-1, you apply some basic **less** skills to work with file contents and command output.

Exercise 4-1 Applying Basic less Skills

1. From a terminal, type **less /etc/passwd**. This opens the /etc/passwd file in the **less** pager.
2. Type **/root** to look for the text *root*. You'll see that all occurrences of the text *root* are highlighted.
3. Press **G** to go to the last line in the file.
4. Press **q** to quit **less**.
5. Type **ps aux | less.** This sends the output of the **ps aux** command (which shows a listing of all processes) to **less**. Browse through the list.
6. Press **q** to quit **less**.

Showing File Contents with cat

The **less** utility is useful to read long text files. If a text file is not that long, you are probably better off using **cat**, which just dumps the contents of the text file on the terminal it was started from. This is convenient if the text file is short. If the text file is long, however, you'll see all contents scrolling by on the screen, and only the lines that fit on the terminal screen are displayed. Using **cat** is simple. Just type **cat** followed by the name of the file you want to see. For instance, use **cat /etc/passwd** to show the contents of this file on your computer screen.

TIP The **cat** utility dumps the contents of a file to the screen from the beginning to the end, which means that for a long file you'll see the last lines of the file only. If you are interested in the first lines, you can use the **tac** utility, which gives the inversed result of **cat**.

Displaying the First or Last Lines of a File with head and tail

If a text file contains much information, it can be useful to filter the output a bit. You can use the **head** and **tail** utilities to do that. Using **head** on a text file will show by default the first ten lines of that file. Using **tail** on a text file shows the last ten lines by default. You can adjust the number of lines that are shown by adding **-n** followed by the number you want to see. So, **tail -n 5 /etc/passwd** shows the last five lines of the /etc/passwd file.

TIP With older versions of **head** and **tail**, you had to use the **-n** option to specify the number of lines you wanted to see. With current versions of both utilities, you may also omit the **-n** option. So, using either **tail -5 /etc/passwd** or **tail -n 5 /etc/passwd** gives you the exact same results.

Another useful option that you can use with **tail** is **-f**. This option starts by showing you the last ten lines of the file you've specified, but it refreshes the display as new lines are added to the file. This is convenient for monitoring log files. The command **tail -f /var/log/messages** (which has to be run as the root user) is a common command to show in real time messages that are written to the main log file /var/log/messages. To end this command, press Ctrl-C.

By combining **tail** and **head**, you can do smart things as well. Suppose, for instance, that you want to see line number 11 of the /etc/passwd file. To do that, use **head -n 11 /etc/passwd | tail -n 1**. The command before the pipe shows the first 11 lines from the file. The result is sent to the pipe, and on that result **tail -n 1** is used, which leads to only line number 11 being displayed. In Exercise 4-2, you apply some basic **head** and **tail** operations to get the exact results that you want.

Exercise 4-2 Using Basic head and tail Operations

1. From a root shell, type **tail -f /var/log/messages**. You'll see the last lines of /var/log/messages being displayed. The file doesn't close automatically.
2. Press Ctrl-C to quit the previous command.
3. Type **head -n 5 /etc/passwd** to show the first five lines in /etc/passwd.
4. Type **tail -n 2 /etc/passwd** to show the last two lines of /etc/passwd.
5. Type **head -n 5 /etc/passwd | tail -n 1** to show only line number 5 of the /etc/passwd file.

Filtering Specific Columns with cut

When you're working with text files, it can be useful to filter out specific fields. Imagine that you need to see a list of all users in the /etc/passwd file. In this file, several fields are defined, of which the first contains the name of the users who are defined. To filter out a specific field, the **cut** command is useful. To do this, use the **-d** option to specify the field delimiter followed by **-f** with the number of the specific field you want to filter out. So, the complete command is **cut -d : -f 1 /etc/passwd** if you want to filter out the first field of the /etc/passwd file. You can see the result in Example 4-1.

Example 4-1 Filtering Specific Fields with **cut**

```
[root@localhost ~]# cut -d : -f 1 /etc/passwd
root
bin
daemon
adm
lp
sync
shutdown
halt
...
```

Sorting File Contents and Output with sort

Another very useful command to use on text files is **sort**. As you can probably guess, this command sorts text. If you type **sort /etc/passwd**, for instance, the content of the /etc/passwd file is sorted in byte order. You can use the **sort** command on the output of a command also, as in **cut -f 1 -d : /etc/passwd | sort**, which sorts the contents of the first column in the /etc/passwd file.

By default, the **sort** command sorts in byte order, which is the order in which the characters appear in the ASCII text table. Notice that this looks like alphabetical order, but it is not, as all capital letters are shown before lowercase letters. So *Zoo* would be listed before *apple*. In some cases, that is not convenient because the content that needs sorting may be numeric or in another format. The **sort** command offers different options to help sorting these specific types of data. Type, for instance, **cut -f 3 -d : /etc/passwd | sort -n** to sort the third field of the /etc/passwd file in numeric order. It can be useful also to sort in reverse order; if you use the command **du -h | sort -rn**, you get a list of files sorted with the biggest file in that directory listed first.

You can also use the **sort** command and specify which column you want to sort. To do this, use **sort -k3 -t : /etc/passwd**, for instance, which uses the field separator : to sort the third column of the /etc/passwd file. Add **-n** to the command to sort in a numeric order, and not in an alphabetic order.

Another example is shown in Example 4-2, where the output of the **ps aux** command is sorted. This command gives an overview of processes running on a Linux system. The fourth column indicates memory usage, and by applying a numeric sort to the output of the command, you can see that the processes are sorted by memory usage, such that the process that consumes the most memory is listed last.

Example 4-2 Using **ps aux** to Find the Busiest Processes on a Linux Server

```
[root@localhost ~]# ps aux | sort -k 4 -n
root          897  0.3  1.1 348584 42200 ?        Ssl  08:12   0:00
  /usr/bin/python3 -s /usr/sbin/firewalld --nofork --nopid
student      2657  1.0  1.1 2936188 45200 ?       Ssl  08:14   0:00
  /usr/bin/gjs /usr/share/org.gnome.Characters/org.gnome.Characters.
  BackgroundService
student      2465  0.3  1.3 143976 52644 ?        S    08:14   0:00
  /usr/bin/Xwayland :0 -rootless -noreset -accessx -core -auth /
  run/user/1000/.mutter-Xwaylandauth.OSRUV1 -listenfd 4 -listenfd 5
  -displayfd 6 -initfd 7
student      2660  1.9  1.4 780200 53412 ?        Ssl  08:14   0:00
  /usr/libexec/gnome-terminal-server
root         2480  2.1  1.6 379000 61568 ?        Ssl  08:14   0:00
  /usr/bin/python3 /usr/libexec/rhsm-service
student      2368  0.9  1.6 1057048 61096 ?       Sl   08:14   0:00
  /usr/libexec/evolution-data-server/evolution-alarm-notify
root         1536  0.6  1.8 555908 69916 ?        Ssl  08:12   0:00
  /usr/libexec/packagekitd
student      2518  0.6  1.8 789408 70336 ?        Ssl  08:14   0:00
  /usr/libexec/gsd-xsettings
student      2540  0.5  1.8 641720 68828 ?        Sl   08:14   0:00
  /usr/libexec/ibus-x11 --kill-daemon
student      2381  4.7  1.9 1393476 74756 ?       Sl   08:14   0:00
  /usr/bin/gnome-software --gapplication-service
student      2000 16.0  7.8 3926096 295276 ?      Ssl  08:14   0:03
  /usr/bin/gnome-shell
```

Counting Lines, Words, and Characters with wc

When working with text files, you sometimes get a large amount of output. Before deciding which approach to handling the large amount of output works best in a specific case, you might want to have an idea about the amount of text you are dealing with. In that case, the **wc** command is useful. In its output, this command gives three different results: the number of lines, the number of words, and the number of characters.

Consider, for example, the **ps aux** command. When executed as root, this command gives a list of all processes running on a server. One solution to count how many processes there are exactly is to pipe the output of **ps aux** through **wc**, as in **ps aux | wc**. You can see the result of the command in Example 4-3, which shows that the total number of lines is 90 and that there are 1,045 words and 7,583 characters in the command output.

Example 4-3 Counting the Number of Lines, Words, and Characters with **wc**

```
[root@localhost ~]# ps aux | wc
     90     1045    7583
```

A Primer to Using Regular Expressions

Working with text files is an important skill for a Linux administrator. You must know not only how to create and modify existing text files, but also how to find the text file that contains specific text.

It will be clear sometimes which specific text you are looking for. Other times, it might not. For example, are you looking for *color* or *colour*? Both spellings might give a match. This is just one example of why using flexible patterns while looking for text can prove useful. In Linux these flexible patterns are known as ***regular expressions***, often also referred to as *regex*.

To understand regular expressions a bit better, let's take a look at a text file example, shown in Example 4-4. This file contains the last six lines from the /etc/passwd file. (This file is used for storing Linux accounts; see Chapter 6, "User and Group Management," for more details.)

Example 4-4 Sample Lines from **/etc/passwd**

```
[root@localhost ~]# tail -n 6 /etc/passwd
anna:x:1000:1000::/home/anna:/bin/bash
rihanna:x:1001:1001::/home/rihanna:/bin/bash
annabel:x:1002:1002::/home/annabel:/bin/bash
anand:x:1003:1003::/home/anand:/bin/bash
joanna:x:1004:1004::/home/joanna:/bin/bash
joana:x:1005:1005::/home/joana:/bin/bash
```

Now suppose that you are looking for the user anna. In that case, you could use the general regular expression parser **grep** to look for that specific string in the file /etc/passwd by using the command **grep anna /etc/passwd**. Example 4-5 shows the results of that command, and as you can see, way too many results are shown.

Example 4-5 Example of Why You Need to Know About Regular Expressions

```
[root@localhost ~]# grep anna /etc/passwd
anna:x:1000:1000::/home/anna:/bin/bash
rihanna:x:1001:1001::/home/rihanna:/bin/bash
annabel:x:1002:1002::/home/annabel:/bin/bash
joanna:x:1004:1004::/home/joanna:/bin/bash
```

A regular expression is a search pattern that allows you to look for specific text in an advanced and flexible way.

Using Line Anchors

In Example 4-5, suppose that you wanted to specify that you are looking for lines that start with the text *anna*. The type of regular expression that specifies where in a line of output the result is expected is known as a ***line anchor***.

To show only lines that start with the text you are looking for, you can use the regular expression ^ (in this case, to indicate that you are looking only for lines where *anna* is at the beginning of the line; see Example 4-6).

Example 4-6 Looking for Lines Starting with a Specific Pattern

```
[root@localhost ~]# grep ^anna /etc/passwd
anna:x:1000:1000::/home/anna:/bin/bash
annabel:x:1002:1002::/home/annabel:/bin/bash
```

Another regular expression that relates to the position of specific text in a specific line is $, which states that the line ends with some text. For instance, the command **grep ash$ /etc/passwd** shows all lines in the /etc/passwd file that end with the text *ash*. This command shows all accounts that have a shell and are able to log in (see Chapter 6 for more details).

Using Escaping in Regular Expressions

Although not mandatory, when you're using regular expressions, it is a good idea to use ***escaping*** to prevent regular expressions from being interpreted by the shell. When a command line is entered, the Bash shell parses the command line, looking for any special characters like *, $, and ?. It will next interpret these characters. The point is that regular expressions use some of these characters as well, and to make sure the Bash shell doesn't interpret them, you should use escaping.

In many cases, it is not really necessary to use escaping; in some cases, the regular expression fails without escaping. To prevent this from ever happening, it is a good idea to put the regular expression between quotes. So, instead of typing **grep ^anna /etc/passwd**, it is better to use **grep '^anna' /etc/passwd**, even if in this case both examples work.

Using Wildcards and Multipliers

In some cases, you might know which text you are looking for, but you might not know how the specific text is written. Or you might just want to use one regular expression to match different patterns. In those cases, wildcards and multipliers come in handy.

To start with, there is the dot (.) regular expression. This is used as a ***wildcard*** character to look for one specific character. So, the regular expression **r.t** would match the strings *rat*, *rot*, and *rut*.

In some cases, you might want to be more specific about the characters you are looking for. If that is the case, you can specify a range of characters that you are looking for. For instance, the regular expression **r[aou]t** matches the strings *rat*, *rot*, and *rut* but it wouldn't match *rit* and *ret*.

Another useful regular expression is the ***multiplier*** *. This matches zero or more of the previous character. That does not seem to be very useful, but indeed it is, as you will see in the examples at the end of this section.

If you know exactly how many of the previous character you are looking for, you can specify a number also, as in **re\{2\}d**, which would match *reed*, but not *red*. The last regular expression that is useful to know about is ?, which matches zero or one of the previous character. Table 4-3 provides an overview of the most important regular expressions.

Using Extended Regular Expressions

What makes regular expressions sometimes a bit hard to understand is the fact that there are different sets of regular expressions. The base regular expressions as discussed so far are supported by tools like **grep**. There is also a set of extended regular expressions, which is not supported by default. When used with **grep**, you'll have to add the **-E** option to indicate it is an extended regular expression. The + can be used to indicate that a character should occur one or more times, and the ? is used to indicate that a character should occur zero or one times. When used in **grep**, don't forget to use **grep -E** to ensure that these are interpreted as extended regular expressions!

Key Topic

Table 4-3 Most Significant Regular Expressions

Regular Expression	**Use**
^text	Matches line that starts with specified text.
text$	Matches line that ends with specified text.
.	Wildcard. (Matches any single character.)
[abc]	Matches *a*, *b*, or *c*.
?	Extended regular expression that matches zero or one of the preceding character.
+	Extended regular expression that matches one or more of the preceding character.
*	Matches zero to an infinite number of the previous character.
\{2\}	Matches exactly two of the previous character.
\{1,3\}	Matches a minimum of one and a maximum of three of the previous character.
colou?r	Matches zero or one of the previous character. This makes the previous character optional, which in this example would match both *color* and *colour*.
(...)	Used to group multiple characters so that the regular expression can be applied to the group.

Let's take a look at an example of a regular expression that comes from the man page semanage-fcontext and relates to managing SELinux (see Chapter 22, "Managing SELinux"). The sample line contains the following regular expression:

```
"/web(/.*)?"
```

In this regular expression, the text */web* is referred to. This text string can be followed by the regular expression (/.*)?. To understand the regular expression, start with the ?, which refers to the part between braces and indicates that the part between braces may occur zero times or one time. Within the braces, the pattern starts with a slash, which is just a slash, followed by zero or more characters. So this means that just the directory name gives a match, but also the directory name followed by just a slash, or a slash that is followed by a filename.

What makes regular expressions difficult is that there is not just one set of regular expressions; there are also extended regular expressions. And to make the concept more complex, the extended regular expressions need specific commands. The well-known command **grep** (covered next) by default deals with base regular expressions. If you want to use extended regular expressions, you need **grep -E** or **egrep**.

Two common extended regular expressions are + and ?. The + will look for a pattern where the preceding character occurs one or more times, and the ? looks for a pattern where the preceding character does not occur or occurs one time. Use the following procedure to find out how these extended regular expressions can be confusing:

Step 1. Create a text file with the name **regex.txt** and the following contents:

```
bat
boot
boat
bt
```

Step 2. Use **grep 'b.*t' regex.txt** to see any line that starts with a *b* and ends with a *t*.

Step 3. Use **grep 'b.+t' regex.txt**. You might expect to see only lines that have at least three characters, but you don't, because you are using an extended regular expression, and without using any additional options, **grep** doesn't recognize the extended regular expression.

Step 4. Use **grep -E 'b.+t' regex.txt**. Now you see that the extended regular expression does work as expected.

Using grep to Analyze Text

The ultimate utility to work with regular expressions is **grep**, which stands for "general regular expression parser." Quite a few examples that you have seen already were based on the **grep** command. The **grep** command has a couple of useful options to make it even more efficient. Table 4-4 describes some of the most useful options.

Table 4-4 Most Useful **grep** Options

Option	Use
-i	Matches upper- and lowercase letters (i.e., not case sensitive).
-v	Shows only lines that do *not* contain the regular expression.
-r	Searches files in the current directory and all subdirectories.
-e	Searches for lines matching more than one regular expression. Use **-e** before each regular expression you want to use.
-E	Interprets the search pattern as an extended regular expression.
-A <number>	Shows <number> of lines after the matching regular expression.
-B <number>	Shows <number> of lines before the matching regular expression.

In Exercise 4-3, you work through some examples using these **grep** options.

Exercise 4-3 Using Common grep Options

1. Type **grep ' #'/etc/services.** This shows that the file /etc/services contains a number of lines that start with the comment sign, #.
2. To view the configuration lines that really matter, type **grep -v '^#' /etc/ services.** This shows only lines that do not start with a #.
3. Type **grep -v '^#' /etc/services -B 5**. This shows lines that do not start with a # sign but also the five lines that are directly before each of those lines, which is useful because in the preceding lines you'll typically find comments on how to use the specific parameters. However, you'll also see that many blank lines are displayed.
4. Type **grep -v -e '^#' -e '^$'/etc/services.** This excludes all blank lines and lines that start with #.

Working with Other Useful Text Processing Utilities

The **grep** utility is a powerful utility that allows you to work with regular expressions. It is not the only utility, though. Some even more powerful utilities exist, like **awk** and **sed**, both of which are extremely rich and merit a book by themselves. The utilities were developed in the time that computers did not commonly have screens attached, and for that reason they do a good job of treating text files in a scripted way.

As a Linux administrator in the twenty-first century, you do not have to be a specialist in using these utilities anymore. It does make sense, however, to know how to perform some common tasks using these utilities. The most useful use cases are summarized in the following examples.

This command shows the fourth field from /etc/passwd:

```
awk -F :    '{ print $4 }'   /etc/passwd
```

This is something that can be done by using the **cut** utility as well, but the **awk** utility is more successful in distinguishing the fields that are used in command output of files. The bottom line is that if **cut** does not work, you should try the **awk** utility.

You can also use the **awk** utility to do tasks that you might be used to using **grep** for. Consider the following example:

```
awk -F : '/user/ { print $4 }' /etc/passwd
```

This command searches the /etc/passwd file for the text *user* and will print the fourth field of any matching line.

In this example, the "stream editor" **sed** is used to print the fifth line from the /etc/passwd file:

```
sed -n 5p /etc/passwd
```

The **sed** utility is a very powerful utility for filtering text from text files (like **grep**), but it has the benefit that it also allows you to apply modifications to text files, as shown in the following example:

```
sed -i s/old-text/new-text/g ~/myfile
```

In this example, the **sed** utility is used to search for the text *old-text* in ~/myfile and replace all occurrences with the text *new-text*. Notice that the default **sed** behavior is to write the output to STDOUT, but the option **-i** will write the result directly to the file. Make sure that you know what you are doing before using this command, because it might be difficult to revert file modifications that are applied in this way.

You'll like the following example if you've ever had a utility containing a specific line in a file that was erroneous:

```
sed -i -e '2d' ~/myfile
```

With this command, you can delete a line based on a specific line number. You can also make more complicated references to line numbers. Use, for instance, **sed -i -e '2d;20,25d' ~/myfile** to delete lines 2 and 20 through 25 in the file ~/myfile.

TIP Do not focus on **awk** and **sed** too much. These are amazing utilities, but many of the things that can be accomplished using them can be done using other tools as well. The **awk** and **sed** tools are very rich, and you can easily get lost in them if you are trying to dig too deep.

Summary

In this chapter, you learned how to work with text files. You acquired some important skills like searching text files with **grep** and displaying text files or part of them with different utilities. You also learned how regular expressions can be used to make the search results more specific. Finally, you learned about the very sophisticated utilities **awk** and **sed**, which allow you to perform more advanced operations on text files.

Exam Preparation Tasks

As mentioned in the section "How to Use This Book" in the Introduction, you have several choices for exam preparation: the end-of-chapter labs; the memory tables in Appendix C; Chapter 27, "Final Preparation"; and the practice exams.

Review All Key Topics

Review the most important topics in the chapter, noted with the Key Topic icon in the margin of the page. Table 4-5 lists a reference for these key topics and the page number on which each is found.

Table 4-5 Key Topics for Chapter 4

Key Topic Element	Description	Page
Table 4-2	Essential Tools for Managing Text File Contents	84
Paragraph	Definition of a regular expression	90
Table 4-3	Most Significant Regular Expressions	92
Table 4-4	Most Useful **grep** Options	94

Complete Tables and Lists from Memory

Print a copy of Appendix C, "Memory Tables" (found on the companion website), or at least the section for this chapter, and complete the tables and lists from memory.

Appendix D, "Memory Tables Answer Key," includes completed tables and lists to check your work.

Define Key Terms

Define the following key terms from this chapter and check your answers in the glossary:

pager, regular expression, line anchor, escaping, wildcard, multiplier

Review Questions

The questions that follow are meant to help you test your knowledge of concepts and terminology and the breadth of your knowledge. You can find the answers to these questions in Appendix A.

1. Which command enables you to see the results of the **ps aux** command in a way that you can easily browse up and down in the results?
2. Which command enables you to show the last five lines from ~/samplefile?
3. Which command do you use if you want to know how many words are in ~/samplefile?
4. After opening command output using **tail -f ~/mylogfile**, how do you stop showing output?
5. Which **grep** option do you use to exclude all lines that start with either a # or a ;?
6. Which regular expression do you use to match one or more of the preceding characters?
7. Which **grep** command enables you to see *text* as well as *TEXT* in a file?
8. Which **grep** command enables you to show all lines starting with *PATH*, as well as the five lines just before that line?
9. Which **sed** command do you use to show line 9 from ~/samplefile?
10. Which command enables you to replace all occurrences of the word *user* with the word *users* in ~/samplefile?

End-of-Chapter Lab

In this end-of-chapter lab, you work with some of the most significant text processing utilities.

Lab 4.1

1. Describe two ways to show line 5 from the /etc/passwd file.
2. How would you locate all text files on your server that contain the current IP address? Do you need a regular expression to do this?
3. You have just used the **sed** command that replaces all occurrences of the text *Administrator* with *root*. Your Windows administrators do not like that very much. How do you revert?
4. Assuming that in the **ps aux** command the fifth line contains information about memory utilization, how would you process the output of that command to show the process that has the heaviest memory utilization first in the results list?
5. Which command enables you to filter the sixth column of **ps aux** output?
6. How do you delete the sixth line from the file ~/myfile?

The following topics are covered in this chapter:

- Working on Local Consoles
- Using SSH and Related Utilities

The following RHCSA exam objectives are covered in this chapter:

- Access remote systems using SSH
- Log in and switch users in multiuser targets
- Boot, reboot, and shut down a system normally
- Securely transfer files between systems
- Configure key-based authentication for SSH

CHAPTER 5

Connecting to Red Hat Enterprise Linux 9

You have already learned how to log in on Linux from a graphical environment. In this chapter, you learn about some other methods to access a Linux shell and start working. You learn how to work from local consoles and from Secure Shell (SSH) to connect to Linux. You also learn how to perform some basic tasks from these environments.

"Do I Know This Already?" Quiz

The "Do I Know This Already?" quiz enables you to assess whether you should read this entire chapter thoroughly or jump to the "Exam Preparation Tasks" section. If you are in doubt about your answers to these questions or your own assessment of your knowledge of the topics, read the entire chapter. Table 5-1 lists the major headings in this chapter and their corresponding "Do I Know This Already?" quiz questions. You can find the answers in Appendix A, "Answers to the 'Do I Know This Already?' Quizzes and Review Questions."

Table 5-1 "Do I Know This Already?" Section-to-Question Mapping

Foundation Topics Section	Questions
Working on Local Consoles	1–6
Using SSH and Related Utilities	7–10

1. Which is the correct term for the description here?

   "Used to refer to the physical screen you are currently looking at as a user"

   a. Terminal

   b. Console

   c. Shell

   d. Interface

2. Which is the correct term for the description here?

   "The environment from which a shell is used where users can enter their commands"

   a. Terminal
   b. Console
   c. Shell
   d. Interface

3. Which is the correct term for the description here?

   "The environment that offers a command line on which users type the commands they want to use"

   a. Terminal
   b. Console
   c. Shell
   d. Interface

4. Which device file is associated with the virtual console that is opened after using the Alt-F6 key sequence?

   a. /dev/console6
   b. /dev/tty6
   c. /dev/vty6
   d. /dev/pts/6

5. Which of the following methods will open a pseudo terminal device? (Choose two)

   a. Log in using an SSH session
   b. Press Alt-F2 to open a new nongraphical login
   c. Type **terminal** in the search menu and open it
   d. Enter your username and password on a nongraphical console

6. Sometimes a server reboot may be necessary to accomplish a task. Which of the following is *not* typically one of them?

   a. To recover from serious problems such as server hangs and kernel panics
   b. To apply kernel updates
   c. To apply changes to kernel modules that are being used currently and therefore cannot be reloaded easily
   d. To apply changes to the network configuration

7. Which of the following is true about remote access to Linux servers from a Windows environment?

    a. Open a shell terminal on Windows and type **ssh** to access Linux servers remotely. The **ssh** command is available as a default part of the Windows operating system.

    b. Configure Remote Access on Windows if you want to access Linux servers running the sshd process.

    c. Install the PuTTY program on Windows to access sshd services on Linux from Windows.

    d. You cannot remotely access Linux machines from Windows.

8. What is the name of the file in which the public key fingerprint of the SSH servers you have connected to in the past are stored?

    a. /etc/ssh/remote_hosts

    b. /etc/ssh/known_hosts

    c. ~/.ssh/remote_hosts

    d. ~/.ssh/known_hosts

9. To allow graphical applications to be used through an SSH session, you can set a parameter in the /etc/ssh/ssh_config file. Using this parameter makes it unnecessary to use the **-X** command-line option each time an SSH session is initiated. Which of the following parameters should be used?

    a. **Host ***

    b. **TunnelX11 yes**

    c. **ForwardX11 yes**

    d. **Xclient yes**

10. Which of the following statements about key-based SSH authentication is true?

    a. After creating the key pair, you need to copy the private key to the remote server.

    b. Use **scp** to copy the public key to the remote server.

    c. Use **ssh-copy-id** to copy the public key to the remote server.

    d. Use **ssh-keygen** on the server to generate a key pair that matches the client keys.

Foundation Topics

Working on Local Consoles

You have already learned how to log in on Linux by using a graphical console. In this section, you learn some more about the possibilities you have while working from either a graphical Linux console or a text-based Linux console.

Before we get into details, it makes sense to highlight the difference between the words ***console*** and ***terminal***. In this book, I follow the common notion of a console as the environment the user is looking at. That means that the console is basically what you see when you are looking at your computer screen.

A terminal is an environment that is opened on the console and provides access to a nongraphical shell, typically Bash. This is the command-line environment that can be used to type commands. A terminal can be offered through a window while using a graphical console, but it can also be opened as the only thing that you see in a textual console. You can also open a remote terminal, using SSH.

This means that in a textual environment, the words *console* and *terminal* are more or less equivalent. In a graphical environment, they are not. Think of it like this: You can have multiple terminals open on a console, but you cannot have multiple consoles open in one terminal.

Logging In to a Local Console

Roughly, there are two ways to make yourself known to a Linux server. Sometimes you just sit at the Linux console and interactively log in from the login prompt that is presented. In other cases, a remote connection is established. The second part of this chapter is about logging in from a remote session; in this part, you learn how to work from a local console.

If a Linux server boots with a graphical environment (the so-called graphical target), you see a login prompt requesting you to select a username and enter a password. Many Linux servers do not use a graphical environment at all, though, and just present a text-based console, as shown in Figure 5-1.

```
Red Hat Enterprise Linux 9.0 (Plow)
Kernel 5.14.0-70.13.1.el9_0.x86_64 on an x86_64

Activate the web console with: systemctl enable --now cockpit.socket

localhost login:
```

Figure 5-1 Logging In from a Text Console

To log in from a text console, you need to know which user account you should use. On many installations, the unrestricted system administrator user root is available, but using this account to do your work typically is not a good idea. The user root has no limitations to access the system and can therefore do a lot of damage. A small mistake can have a huge impact. On older versions of RHEL, the user root was enabled by default. On RHEL 9, you can indicate while installing if the root user should have a password or not. If the root user doesn't get a password, you'll only be able to log in with an administrator user. This is a user that will only obtain root superpowers while using the **sudo** command.

If the root user, is enabled, you shouldn't use it. Typically, it is a better idea to log in as one of the locally defined users, and there are many reasons to do so, including the following:

- Logging in this way will make it more difficult to make critical errors.
- On many occasions, you will not need root permissions anyway.
- If you only allow access to normal users and not to root, it will force an attacker to guess two different things: the name of that specific user as well as the password of that user.
- If you do need root access anyway, you can use the **sudo -i** command from the local user environment to open a root shell. Note that you are allowed to do this only if you have **sudo** privileges, and you'll have to type your current user password after using the command.
- If you know the root user password, use **su -** to open a root shell. This command will prompt for the root user password, and you'll be able to work as root until you type **exit**. Notice that the **sudo -i** command only works for authorized users and doesn't require the user to enter the root password, and for that reason is considered more secure.
- Use **sudo** to configure specific administration tasks for specific users only. See Chapter 6, "User and Group Management," for more information.

Switching Between Terminals in a Graphical Environment

When you're working in a graphical environment, it is relatively easy to open several different working environments, such as different terminal windows in which you can work from a shell. In the upper-left part of the graphical interface, click Activities, and in the Search bar that appears, type **term**, which presents an icon to open a terminal. Because terminals are opened as a ***subshell***, you do not have to log in to each terminal again, and will get access as the same user account that was originally used to log in to the graphical environment (see Figure 5-2).

Figure 5-2 Using Different Terminal Windows from the Graphical Environment

Working from a graphical environment is convenient. As an administrator, you can open several terminal windows, and in each terminal window you can use the **su -** command to open a shell in which you can work with a different user identity, or use **sudo -i** to open a root shell. This allows you to easily test features and see the results of these tests immediately. Exercise 5-1 guides you through a common scenario where you can do this and see how testing things from one terminal window while monitoring from another terminal window can be convenient.

Exercise 5-1 Working from Several Terminal Windows Simultaneously

1. Start your computer and make sure to log in as a non-root user account from the graphical login window that is presented. You should have a local user with the name *student* and the password *password* that you can use for this purpose.
2. Click **Activities**, and type **term**. Next, click the terminal icon to open a new terminal window.
3. From the Terminal menu on the top of your screen, select **New Window**.
4. From one of the terminal windows, type the command **sudo -i** and enter the password of the student user. Then, type **tail -f /var/log/secure**. This opens a trace on the file /var/log/secure, where you can monitor security events in real time.
5. From the other terminal windows, type **su -**. When asked for a password, you normally enter the password for the user root. Enter a wrong password.
6. Now look at the terminal where the trace on /var/log/secure is still open. You will see that an error message has been written to this file.
7. Press Ctrl-C to close the **tail -f** session on the /var/log/secure file.

Working with Multiple Terminals in a Nongraphical Environment

In the previous section, you learned how to work with multiple terminals in a graphical environment. This is relatively easy because you just have to open a new terminal window. In a nongraphical environment, you have only one terminal interface that is available, and that makes working in different user shell environments a bit more difficult.

To offer an option that makes working from several consoles on the same server possible, Linux uses the concept of a *virtual terminal*. This feature allows you to open six different terminal windows from the same console at the same time and use key sequences to navigate between them. To open these terminal windows, you can use the key sequences Alt-F1 through Alt-F6. The following virtual consoles are available:

- **F1:** Gives access to the GNOME Display Manager (GDM) graphical login
- **F2:** Provides access to the current graphical console
- **F3:** Gives access back to the current graphical session
- **F4–F6:** Gives access to nongraphical consoles

TIP A convenient alternative to using the Alt-Function key sequences is offered by the **chvt** command. This command enables you to switch to a different virtual environment directly from the current environment. If you are in a graphical console right now, open a terminal and type **chvt 4**. This brings you to a login prompt on virtual terminal 4. Switch back to the graphical environment using the **chvt 3** command, or use **chvt 1** to switch back to a graphical login prompt.

Of these virtual consoles, the first one is used as the default console. It is commonly known as the *virtual console tty1*, and it has a corresponding device file in the /dev directory that has the name /dev/tty1. The other virtual consoles also have corresponding device files, which are numbered /dev/tty1 through /dev/tty6.

When you're working from a graphical environment, it is also possible to open different virtual consoles. Because the combinations between the Alt key and the Function keys typically already have a meaning in the graphical environment, you need to use a Ctrl-Alt-Function key instead. So, do not use Alt-F4 to open /dev/tty4 from a graphical environment, but instead use Ctrl-Alt-F4. To get back to the graphical console, you can use the Alt-F3 key sequence. The Alt-F6 and Ctrl-Alt-F6 key sequences are essentially the same. It is important to use the Ctrl key as well when going from a GUI to a text environment. To go back from the text environment to the GUI environment, using the Ctrl key is optional.

NOTE A long time ago, big central computers were used, to which dumb terminal devices were connected. These dumb terminal devices consisted of nothing more than a monitor and keyboard attached to it. From each of these dumb terminal devices, a console session to the operating system could be started. On a modern Linux server, no dumb terminals are attached. They have been replaced with the virtual terminals described here.

Understanding Pseudo Terminal Devices

Every terminal used in a Linux environment has a device file associated with it. You've just learned that terminals that are started in a nongraphical environment are typically referred to through the devices /dev/tty1 through /dev/tty6.

For terminal windows that are started from a graphical environment, pseudo terminals are started. These pseudo terminals are referred to using numbers in the /dev/pts directory. So, the first terminal window that is started from a graphical environment appears as /dev/pts/1, the second terminal window appears as /dev/pts/2, and so on. In Exercise 5-2, you learn how to work with these pseudo terminal devices and see which user is active on which pseudo terminal.

NOTE On earlier versions of Linux, pseudo terminals were seen as pty devices. These types of terminals are now deprecated and replaced with the pts terminal types, as described before.

Exercise 5-2 Working with Pseudo Terminals

1. Log in to the graphical console, using a non-root user account.
2. Open a terminal window.
3. From the terminal window, type **w**. This will give an overview of all users who are currently logged in. Notice the column that mentions the tty the users are on, in which you see tty2 that refers to the terminal window.
4. Open another graphical terminal window. Type **su -** to become root.
5. Type **w** to display once more an overview of all users who are currently logged in. Notice that the second **su -** session doesn't show as an additional user account because both have been started from the graphical interface, which is tty2.

At this point, you know how to work with the console, terminals, virtual terminals, and pseudo terminals. In the section "Using SSH and Related Utilities" later in this chapter, you use SSH to open terminal sessions to your server. These sessions show as pseudo terminals as well.

Booting, Rebooting, and Shutting Down Systems

As an administrator of a Linux server, you occasionally have to ***reboot*** the Linux server. Rebooting a server is not often a requirement, but it can make your work a lot easier because it will make sure that all processes and tasks that were running on your server have reread their configurations and initialized properly.

> **TIP** Rebooting a Linux server is an important task on the RHCSA exam. Everything you have configured should still be working after the server has rebooted. So, make sure that you reboot at least once during the exam, but also after making critical modifications to the server configuration. If your server cannot reboot anymore after applying critical modifications to your server's configuration, at least you know where to look to fix the issues.

For an administrator who really knows Linux very thoroughly, rebooting a server is seldom necessary. Experienced administrators can often trigger the right parameter to force a process to reread its configurations. There are some scenarios, though, in which even experienced Linux administrators have to reboot:

- To recover from serious problems such as server hangs and kernel panics
- To apply kernel updates
- To apply changes to kernel modules that are being used currently and therefore cannot be reloaded easily

When a server is rebooted, all processes that are running need to shut down properly. If the server is just stopped by pulling the power plug, much data will typically be lost. The reason is that processes that have written data do not typically write that data directly to disk, but instead store it in memory buffers (a cache) from where it is committed to disk when it is convenient for the operating system.

To issue a proper reboot, you have to alert the Systemd process. The ***Systemd*** process is the first process that was started when the server was started, and it is responsible for managing all other processes, directly or indirectly. As a result, on system reboots or halts, the Systemd process needs to make sure that all these processes are stopped. To tell the Systemd process this has to happen, you can use a few commands:

- **systemctl reboot** or **reboot**
- **systemctl halt** or **halt**
- **systemctl poweroff** or **poweroff**

When stopping a machine, you can use the **systemctl halt** command or the **systemctl poweroff** command. The difference between these two commands is that the **systemctl poweroff** command talks to power management on the machine to shut off power on the machine. This often does not happen when using **systemctl halt**.

NOTE Using the methods that have just been described will normally reboot or stop your machine. In some cases, these commands might not work. For such scenarios, there is an emergency reset option as well. Using this option may prove useful if the machine is not physically accessible. To force a machine to reset, from a root shell you can type **echo b > /proc/sysrq-trigger**. This command immediately resets the machine without saving anything. Notice that this command should be used only if there are no other options!

Using SSH and Related Utilities

In the previous sections in this chapter, you learned how to access a terminal if you have direct access to the server console. Many administrators work with servers that are not physically accessible. To manage these servers, Secure Shell (SSH) is normally used. In this section, you learn how to work with SSH.

On modern Linux distributions, Secure Shell is the common method to gain access to other machines over the network. In SSH, cryptography is used to ensure that you are connecting to the intended server. Also, traffic is encrypted while being transmitted.

Accessing Remote Systems Using SSH

To access a server using SSH, you need the sshd server process, as well as an SSH client. On the remote server that you want to access, the sshd service must be running and offering services, which it does at its default port 22, and it should not be blocked by the firewall. After installation, Red Hat Enterprise Linux starts the sshd process automatically, and by default it is not blocked by the firewall.

If the SSH port is open, you can access it using the **ssh** command from the command line. The **ssh** command by default tries to reach the sshd process on the server port 22. If you have configured the sshd process to offer its services on a different port, use **ssh -p** followed by the port number you want to connect to.

The **ssh** command is available on all Linux distributions, and on Apple Mac computers as well, where it can be launched from a Mac terminal.

If you have a Windows version that does not have the Windows subsystem for Linux, the **ssh** command is not a native part of the Windows operating system. If you want to access Linux servers through SSH from a Windows computer, you need to install an SSH client like PuTTY on Windows. From PuTTY, different types of remote sessions can be established with Linux machines. Alternative SSH clients for Windows are available as well, such as MobaXterm, KiTTY, mRemoteNG, Bitvise, and Xshell.

Accessing another Linux machine from a Linux terminal is relatively easy. Just type **ssh** followed by the name or IP address of the other Linux machine. After connecting, you will be prompted for a password if a default configuration is used. This is the password of a user account with the same name as your current user account, but who should exist on the remote machine.

When remotely connecting to a Linux server, the SSH client tries to do that as the user account you are currently logged in with on the local machine. If you want to connect using a different user account, you can specify the name of this user on the command line, in the user@server format. If, for instance, you want to establish an SSH session as user root to a remote server, type **ssh root@remoteserver**. In Exercise 5-3, you learn how to log in to a remote server using SSH.

Exercise 5-3 Using SSH to Log In to a Remote Server

This exercise assumes that a remote server is available and reachable. In this exercise, server1 is used as the local server, and server2 is the remote server on which the sshd process should be up and running. If you cannot access a remote server to perform the steps in the exercise, you might alternatively replace server2 with localhost. It is obvious that by doing so you will not log in to a remote server, but you still use the **ssh** command to connect to an sshd process, and you'll get the full experience of working with **ssh**.

1. Open a root shell on server2. Type **systemctl status sshd**. This should show you that the sshd process is currently up and running.
2. Type **ip a | grep 'inet '**. (Notice the space between **inet** and the closing quote mark.) Notice the IPv4 address your server is currently using. In the rest of this exercise, it is assumed that server2 is using IP address 192.168.4.220. Replace that address with the address that you have found here.

3. Open a shell as a nonprivileged user on server1.
4. On server1, type **ssh root@192.168.4.220**. This connects to the sshd process on server2 and opens a root shell.
5. Before being prompted for a password, you see a message indicating that the authenticity of host 192.168.4.220 cannot be established (see Example 5-1). This message is shown because the host you are connecting to is not yet known on your current host, which might involve a security risk. Type **yes** to continue.
6. When prompted, enter the root password. After entering it, you now are logged in to server2.
7. Type **w**. Notice that the SSH session you have just opened shows as just another pseudo terminal session, but you'll see the source IP address in the FROM column.
8. Type **exit** to close the SSH session.

Example 5-1 Security Message Displayed When Logging In to a Remote Server for the First Time

```
[student@localhost ~]$ ssh root@192.168.29.161
The authenticity of host '192.168.29.161 (192.168.29.161)' can't be
  established.
ED25519 key fingerprint is SHA256:+1vqdHo9iV/
  RNOq26LHsgcASPPW1ga6kxEVjYyAKWIk.
This key is not known by any other names
Are you sure you want to continue connecting (yes/no/[fingerprint])? y
```

NOTE On some occasions, using **ssh** to get access to a server will be slow. If you want to know why, use the **-v** option with the **ssh** command. This will start SSH in verbose mode and show all the individual components that are contacted. By doing so, you might get an indication why your server is being slow.

The security message in Example 5-1 is displayed because the remote server has never been contacted before and therefore there is no way to verify the identity of the remote server. After you connect to the remote server, a public key fingerprint is stored in the file ~/.ssh/known_hosts.

The next time you connect to the same server, this fingerprint is checked with the encryption key that was sent over by the remote server to initialize contact. If the fingerprint matches, you will not see this message anymore.

In some cases, the remote host key fingerprint does not match the key fingerprint that is stored locally. That is a potentially dangerous situation. Instead of being connected to the intended server, you might be connected to the server of an evildoer. It does, however, also happen if you are connecting to an IP address that you have been connected to before but that is now in use by a different server, or if the sshd service has been deleted and reinstalled.

If you encounter such a mismatch between the host key that is presented and the one that you've cached, you just have to remove the key fingerprint from the ~/.ssh/known_hosts file on the client computer. You can easily do so, using **sed**. For instance, use **sed -i -e '25d' ~/.ssh/known_hosts** to remove line 25 from the known_hosts file (assuming that is the line containing the erroneous key).

Using Graphical Applications in an SSH Environment

From an SSH session, by default you cannot start graphical applications. That is because of security; a remote host cannot display screens on your computer without specific permission to do that. There are two requirements for starting graphical applications through an SSH connection:

- An X server must be running on the client computer. The X server is the software component that creates the graphical screens.
- The remote host must be allowed to display screens on the local computer.

The easiest way to allow the remote host to display graphical screens on your computer is by adding the **-Y** option to the **ssh** command. So, use **ssh -Y linda@server2** if you want to connect as linda to server2, and also be able to start graphical applications.

As you have noticed, the **ssh** command gives you a few options. Table 5-2 shows some of the most common options available.

Table 5-2 Common **ssh** Options

Option	Use
-v	Verbose; shows in detail what is happening while establishing the connection
-Y	Enables support for graphical applications
-p <PORT>	Used to connect to an SSH service that is not listening on the default port 22

As an administrator, you can also create a systemwide configuration that allows you to use *X forwarding*, which is starting graphical applications through an SSH session. As root, open the configuration file /etc/ssh/ssh_config and make sure it includes the following line:

```
ForwardX11 yes
```

The next time you use the **ssh** command, X forwarding will be available by default.

Securely Transferring Files Between Systems

If a host is running the sshd service, that service can also be used to securely transfer files between systems. To do that, you can use the **scp** command if you want the file to be copied, or **rsync** if you want to synchronize the file. Also, the **sftp** command is a part of the SSH solution and enables users to use an FTP command-line syntax to transfer files using sshd.

Using scp to Securely Copy Files

The **scp** command is similar to the **cp** command, which is used to copy local files, but it also includes an option that enables it to work with remote hosts. You can use **scp** to copy files and subdirectories to and from remote hosts. To copy, for instance, the /etc/hosts file to the /tmp directory on server2 using your current user account, use the following command:

```
scp /etc/hosts server2:/tmp
```

If you want to connect to server2 as user root to copy the /etc/passwd file to your home directory, you use the following command:

```
scp root@server2:/etc/passwd ~
```

You can also use **scp** to copy an entire subdirectory structure. To do so, use the **-r** option, as in the following command:

```
scp -r server2:/etc/ /tmp
```

Notice that the **scp** command can be configured to connect to a nondefault SSH port also. It is a bit confusing, but to do this with the **scp** command, you need the **-P** option followed by the port number you want to connect to. Notice that **ssh** uses **-p** (lowercase) to specify the port it needs to connect to; the **scp** command uses an uppercase **-P**.

Using sftp to Securely Transfer Files

The **sftp** command provides an alternative to securely transfer files. Whereas the **scp** command provides an interface that is very similar to the **cp** command, the **sftp** command provides an FTP-like interface. Because even modern FTP servers are still transferring passwords and other sensitive data without using encryption, **sftp** should be considered as an alternative.

When working with **sftp**, you open an FTP client session to the remote server, where the only requirement on the remote server is that it should be running the sshd process. From the FTP client session, you use typical FTP client commands, like **put** to upload a file or **get** to download a file.

Notice that when working with **sftp**, the local directory is important, even if after opening the FTP session you only see the remote directory on the server. When you're downloading a file using the **get** command, the file will be stored in the current local directory, and when you're uploading a file using **put**, the file will be searched for in the local directory. Exercise 5-4 gives you a guided tour through using the **sftp** command and the **rsync** command, discussed next.

Using rsync to Synchronize Files

The **rsync** command uses SSH to synchronize files between a remote directory and a local directory. The advantage of synchronizing files is that only differences need to be considered. So, for example, if you synchronize a 100-MiB file in which only a few blocks have changed since the previous sync, only the changed blocks will be synchronized. This approach is also known as a delta sync.

When you use the **rsync** command, multiple options are available. Table 5-3 provides an overview.

Table 5-3 Common **rsync** Options

Option	Use
-r	Synchronizes the entire directory tree
-l	Copies symbolic links as symbolic links
-p	Preserves permissions
-n	Performs only a dry run, not actually synchronizing anything
-a	Uses archive mode, thus ensuring that entire subdirectory trees and all file properties will be synchronized
-A	Uses archive mode, and in addition synchronizes ACLs
-X	Synchronizes SELinux context as well

Exercise 5-4 Using SFTP to Manage Files on a Remote Server

1. From a sudo shell, add a line that matches the server2 IP address to the hostname server2.
2. From a terminal, type **sftp student@server2**. This gives you access to an SFTP prompt that is opened on server2.
3. Type **ls**. You'll see files in the current working directory on the remote server.
4. Type **pwd**. This shows the current directory on the remote server.
5. Type **lpwd**. This shows your local current directory.
6. Type **lcd /tmp**. This changes the local current directory to /tmp.
7. Type **put /etc/hosts**. This file will upload the /etc/hosts file from server1 to the user student home directory on server2.
8. Type **exit** to close your SFTP session.

Configuring Key-Based Authentication for SSH

If SSH is used on the Internet, it might not be a good idea to allow password logins. SSH is more secure when using public/private keys for authentication. This authentication method is normally enabled by default because it is more secure than password-based authentication. Only if that is not possible is a password login used. The only thing you need to do to enable ***key-based login*** is to create a key pair; everything else is organized by default already.

When using public/private key-based authentication, the user who wants to connect to a server generates a public/private key pair. The private key needs to be kept private and will never be distributed. The ***public key*** is stored in the home directory of the target user on the SSH server in the file .ssh/authorized_keys.

When authenticating using key pairs, the user generates a hash derived from the ***private key***. This hash is sent to the server, and if on the server it proves to match the public key that is stored on the server, the user is authenticated.

Using Passphrases or Not?

When creating a public/private key pair, you are prompted for a passphrase. If you want maximal security, you should enter a passphrase. You are prompted for that passphrase each time that you are using the private key to authenticate to a remote host. That is very secure, but it is not very convenient. To create a configuration that allows for maximal convenience, you can just press the Enter key twice when generating the public/private key pair to confirm that you do not want to set a passphrase. This is a typical configuration that is used for authentication between servers in a trusted environment where no outside access is possible anyway.

To create a key pair, use the **ssh-keygen** command. Next, use the **ssh-copy-id** command to copy the public key over to the target server. In Exercise 5-5, you create a public/private key pair to log in to the server2 host. (If no remote host is available, you can use localhost as an alternative to verify the procedure.)

Exercise 5-5 Connecting to a Remote Server with Public/Private Keys

1. On server1, open a root shell.
2. Type **ssh-keygen**.
3. When asked for the filename in which to store the (private) key, accept the default filename ~/.ssh/id_rsa.
4. When asked to enter a passphrase, press Enter twice.
5. The private key now is written to the ~/.ssh/id_rsa file and the public key is written to the ~/.ssh/id_rsa.pub file.
6. Use **ssh-copy-id server2** to copy to server2 the public key you have just created. You are then asked for the password on the remote server one last time.
7. After copying the public key, verify that it can actually be used for authentication. To do this, type **ssh server2**. You should now authenticate without having to enter the password for the remote user account.

After you copy the public key to the remote host, it will be written to the ~/.ssh/authorized_keys file on that host. Notice that if multiple users are using keys to log in with that specific account, the authorized_keys file may contain a lot of public keys. Make sure never to overwrite it because that will wipe all keys that are used by other users as well!

Summary

In this chapter, you learned how to connect to Red Hat Enterprise Linux 9. You learned the difference between consoles, terminals, and shells, and you learned how to set up terminal sessions locally as well as remotely. You also learned how to use SSH to connect to a remote server and how to securely copy files between servers.

Exam Preparation Tasks

As mentioned in the section "How to Use This Book" in the Introduction, you have several choices for exam preparation: the end-of-chapter labs; the memory tables in Appendix C; Chapter 27, "Final Preparation"; and the practice exams.

Review All Key Topics

Review the most important topics in the chapter, noted with the Key Topic icon in the margin of the page. Table 5-4 lists a reference for these key topics and the page number on which each is found.

Table 5-4 Key Topics for Chapter 5

Key Topic Element	Description	Page
Paragraph	Definitions of the words *console* and *terminal*	104
List	Situations that typically require a server reboot	109
Table 5-2	Common **ssh** Options	113

Complete Tables and Lists from Memory

Print a copy of Appendix C, "Memory Tables" (found on the companion website), or at least the section for this chapter, and complete the tables and lists from memory. Appendix D, "Memory Tables Answer Key," includes completed tables and lists to check your work.

Define Key Terms

Define the following key terms from this chapter and check your answers in the glossary:

console, terminal, subshell, reboot, Systemd, key-based login, public key, private key

Review Questions

The questions that follow use an open-ended format that is meant to help you test your knowledge of concepts and terminology and the breadth of your knowledge. You can find the answers to these questions in Appendix A.

1. What is the console?

2. On a server that currently has an operational graphical interface, you are at a text-based login prompt. Which key sequence do you use to switch back to your current work on the graphical interface?
3. Which command(s) show(s) all users that currently have a terminal session open to a Linux server?
4. On a server where no GUI is operational, what would you expect to be the device name that is used by the first SSH session that is opened to that server?
5. Which command would you use to get detailed information on what SSH is doing while logging in?
6. How do you initiate an SSH session with support for graphical applications?
7. What is the name of the configuration file that needs to be edited to modify SSH client settings?
8. How do you copy the /etc/hosts file to the directory /tmp on server2 using the username lisa?
9. What is the name of the file in which public keys are stored for remote users who want to log in to this machine using key-based authentication?
10. Which command enables you to generate an SSH public/private key pair?

End-of-Chapter Labs

The end-of-chapter labs help you practice what you learned throughout the chapter. The first lab is about connecting to RHEL 9 locally, and the second lab is about using SSH to log in to a remote server.

Lab 5.1

1. Log in to the local console on server1. Make sure that server1 does *not* show a graphical interface anymore, but just a text-based login prompt.
2. Log in from that environment and activate tty6. From tty6, switch back on the graphical interface and use the correct key sequence to go to the graphical interface.

Lab 5.2

1. Set up SSH-based authentication. From server2, use SSH to connect to server1.
2. Make sure that graphical applications are supported through the SSH session. Also set up key-based authentication so that no password has to be entered while connecting to the remote server.

The following topics are covered in this chapter:

- Understanding Different User Types
- Creating and Managing User Accounts
- Creating and Managing Group Accounts

The following RHCSA exam objectives are covered in this chapter:

- Create, delete, and modify local user accounts
- Change passwords and adjust password aging for local user accounts
- Create, delete, and modify local groups and group memberships
- Configure superuser access

User and Group Management

On a Linux system, various processes are normally being used. These processes need access to specific resources on the Linux system. To determine how these resources can be accessed, a distinction is made between processes that run in kernel mode and processes that run without full permissions to the operating system. In the latter case user accounts are needed, not only to grant the required permissions to processes, but also to make sure that people can do their work. This chapter explains how to set up user and group accounts.

"Do I Know This Already?" Quiz

The "Do I Know This Already?" quiz enables you to assess whether you should read this entire chapter thoroughly or jump to the "Exam Preparation Tasks" section. If you are in doubt about your answers to these questions or your own assessment of your knowledge of the topics, read the entire chapter. Table 6-1 lists the major headings in this chapter and their corresponding "Do I Know This Already?" quiz questions. You can find the answers in Appendix A, "Answers to the 'Do I Know This Already?' Quizzes and Review Questions."

Table 6-1 "Do I Know This Already?" Section-to-Question Mapping

Foundation Topics Section	Questions
Understanding Different User Types	1–4
Creating and Managing User Accounts	3–6
Creating and Managing Group Accounts	7–10

1. What should you do with the root user account to enhance system security?
   a. Don't set a password.
   b. Allow password-less **sudo**.
   c. Delete the root user.
   d. Disable SSH login for the root user.

2. On a default installation of an RHEL 9 server, which group does the user typically need to be a member of to be able to use **sudo** to run all administration commands?

   a. admin
   b. root
   c. sys
   d. wheel

3. Which of the following **sudo** configurations allows user amy to change passwords for all users, but not root?

   a. **amy ALL=! /usr/bin/passwd root, /usr/bin/passwd**
   b. **amy ALL=/usr/bin/passwd, ! /usr/bin/passwd root**
   c. **amy ALL=passwd, ! passwd root**
   d. **amy ALL=! passwd root, passwd**

4. Which of the following commands shows correct syntax for using a command with a pipe in a **sudo** environment?

   a. **sudo -c "cat /etc/passwd | grep root"**
   b. **sudo "cat /etc/passwd | grep root"**
   c. **sudo sh -c "cat /etc/passwd | grep root"**
   d. **sudo cat /etc/passwd | grep root**

5. Which configuration file should you change to set the default location for all new user home directories?

   a. /etc/login.defaults
   b. /etc/login.defs
   c. /etc/default/useradd
   d. /etc/default/login.defs

6. Which command enables you to get information about password properties such as password expiry?

   a. **chage -l**
   b. **usermod --show**
   c. **passwd -l**
   d. **chage --show**

7. Which of the following files is not processed when a user starts a login shell?
   a. /etc/profile
   b. /etc/.profile
   c. ~/.bashrc
   d. ~/.bash_profile

8. Which of the following offers the best option to modify user group membership?
   a. **vigr**
   b. **vipw**
   c. **vipasswd**
   d. **usermod**

9. Which command can be used to list all the groups a user is a member of?
   a. **userlist**
   b. **grouplist**
   c. **id**
   d. **groups**

10. What can you do to ensure that no users, except for the user root, can log in temporarily?
    a. Set the default shell to /usr/sbin/nologin.
    b. Set the default shell to /bin/false.
    c. Create a file with the name /etc/nologin.
    d. Create a file with the name /etc/nologin.txt.

Foundation Topics

Understanding Different User Types

In this chapter, you learn how to create and manage ***user*** accounts. Before diving into the details of user management, you learn how users are used in a Linux environment.

Users on Linux

On Linux, there are two ways to look at system security. There are ***privileged users***, and there are ***unprivileged users***. The default privileged user is ***root***. This user account has full access to everything on a Linux server and is allowed to work in system space without restrictions. The root user account is meant to perform system administration tasks and should be used for that only. For all other tasks, an unprivileged user account should be used.

On modern Linux distributions like RHEL 9, the root user account is often disabled. While installing RHEL 9, you have a choice of what to do with the root user. If you create a regular user and choose the option Make This User Administrator, you don't have to set a root ***password*** and you'll be able to use **sudo** when administrator privileges are needed. If you want to be able to log in as root directly, you can set a password for the root user.

To get information about a user account, you can use the **id** command. When using this command from the command line, you can see details about the current user. You can also use it on other user accounts to get details about those accounts. Example 6-1 shows an example of the output of the command.

Example 6-1 Getting More Information About Users with **id**

```
[root@localhost ~]# id linda
uid=1001(linda) gid=1001(linda) groups=1001(linda)
```

Working as Root

On all Linux systems, by default there is the user root, also known as the superuser. This account is used for managing Linux and has no restrictions at all. Root, for instance, can create other user accounts on the system. For some tasks, root privileges are required. Some examples are installing software, managing users, and creating partitions on disk devices. Generally speaking, all tasks that involve direct access to devices need root permissions.

Because the root account is so useful for managing a Linux environment, some people make a habit of logging in as root directly. That is not recommended, especially not when you are logging in to a graphical environment. When you log in as root in a graphical environment, all tasks that are executed run as root as well, and that involves an unnecessary security risk. Therefore, you should instead use one of the alternative methods described in Table 6-2.

Table 6-2 Methods to Run Tasks with Elevated Permissions

Method	Description
su	Opens a subshell as a different user, with the advantage that commands are executed as root only in the subshell
sudo	Allows authorized users to work with administrator privileges
PolicyKit	Enables you to set up graphical utilities to run with administrative privileges

Using su

From a terminal window, you can use the **su** command to start a subshell in which you have another identity. To perform administrative tasks, for instance, you can log in with a normal user account and type **su** to open a root shell. The benefit is that root privileges are used only in the root shell. You do need to enter the root password though, which is best practice from a security perspective.

If you type just the command **su**, the username root is implied. But **su** can be used to run tasks as another user as well. Type **su linda** to open a subshell as the user linda, for example. When using **su** as an ordinary user, you are prompted for a password, and after entering that, you acquire the credentials of the target user:

```
[linda@localhost ~]$ su
Password:
[root@localhost linda]#
```

The subshell that is started when using **su** is an environment where you are able to work as the target user account, but environment settings for that user account have not been set. If you need complete access to the entire environment of the user account, you can use **su -** to start a login shell. If you start a login shell, all scripts that make up the user environment are processed, which makes you work in an environment that is exactly the same as when logging in as that user.

TIP If you want to use **su**, using **su -** is better than using **su**. When the **-** is used, a login shell is started; without the **-**, some variables may not be set correctly. So, you are better off using **su -** immediately. But don't forget that for running tasks with administrator privileges, you're better off using **sudo**.

In Exercise 6-1, you practice switching user accounts.

Exercise 6-1 Switching User Accounts

1. Log in to your system as a nonprivileged user and open a terminal.
2. Type **whoami** to see which user account you are currently using. Type **id** as well, and notice that you get more detail about your current credentials when using **id**.
3. Type **su -**. When prompted for a password, enter the root password. Type **id** again. You see that you are currently root.
4. Type **useradd bob** to create a user that you can use for testing purposes.
5. Still from the root shell, use **su - bob** and confirm that you can log in without entering a password. Notice that user bob doesn't even have a password that is currently set.
6. Type **exit** to exit from the user bob shell. Type **exit** again to exit from the root shell and return to the ordinary user shell.

sudo

If a non-root user needs to perform a specific system administration task, the user does not need root access; instead, the system administrator can configure **sudo** to give that user administrator permissions to perform the specific task. The user then carries out the task by starting the command with **sudo** (and entering the user's password when prompted). So, instead of using commands like **useradd** as the root user, you can use a **sudo**-enabled user account and type **sudo useradd.** This approach is definitely more secure because you will have administrator permissions only while running this specific command.

When creating a Linux user during the installation process as described in Chapter 1, "Installing Red Hat Enterprise Linux," you can select to grant administrator permissions to that specific user. If you select to do so, the user will be able to use all administrator commands using **sudo**. It is also possible to set up **sudo** privileges after installation by making the user a member of the group wheel. To do that in a very easy way, use this simple two-step procedure:

1. Make the administrative user account a member of the group wheel by using **usermod -aG wheel user**.
2. Type **visudo** and make sure the line %wheel ALL=(ALL) ALL is included.

Apart from this method, which would give a user access to all administrative commands, you can use **visudo** to edit the /etc/sudoers configuration file and give user access to specific commands only. For example, if you included the line **linda ALL=/usr/bin/useradd, /usr/bin/passwd** in this file, that would allow user linda to run only the commands **useradd** and **passwd** with administrative privileges.

TIP While using **sudo**, you are prompted to enter a password. Based on this password a token is generated, which allows you to run new **sudo** commands without having to enter the password again. However, this token is valid for only five minutes. It is possible to extend the lifetime of the token: include the following in /etc/sudoers (using **visudo**) to extend the token lifetime to 240 minutes:

```
Defaults timestamp_timeout=240
```

If you want to set up users with specific **sudo** privileges, be careful with the **passwd** command. If a user has **sudo** privileges on the **passwd** command, that would allow the user to set or change the password for the root user as well. This can be easily prevented, though, by adding an exception. Just include the line **linda ALL=/usr/bin/useradd, /usr/bin/passwd, ! /usr/bin/passwd root**. This would allow user linda to change the password for all users, but not for root.

To assign **sudo** privileges to individual users or groups of users, you can change the contents of /etc/sudoers using **visudo**. A better practice is to create a drop-in file in the directory /etc/sudoers.d. This drop-in file would have the exact same contents as the modification you would make to /etc/sudoers, with the benefit that the custom configuration is separated from the standard configuration that was created while installing Linux. Files in /etc/sudoers.d are always included while using **sudo**.

TIP It's convenient to be able to use pipes in **sudo** commands. By default, this is not allowed, but if you use **sudo sh -c**, you can use any command containing a pipe as its argument. For example, use **sudo sh -c "rpm -qa | grep ssh"** to get a list of all packages that have the string "ssh" in their name.

PolicyKit

Most administration programs with a graphical user interface use PolicyKit to authenticate as the root user. If a normal user who is not a member of the group wheel accesses such an application, that user will be prompted for authentication. If a user who is a member of the group wheel opens a PolicyKit application, that user will have to enter their own password. For the RHCSA exam, you do not have to know the details of PolicyKit, but it is good to know that you can use the

pkexec command as an alternative to **sudo** in case you ever completely lose **sudo** access to a system. In that case, just use **pkexec visudo** to be able to repair the **sudo** configuration.

In Exercise 6-2, you practice working with **sudo**.

Exercise 6-2 Switching User Accounts

1. Log in to your system as the **student** user and open a terminal.
2. Type **sudo -i** to open a sudo root shell. When prompted for a password, enter the password assigned to user student.
3. Use **useradd betty; useradd amy** to create two users.
4. Type **echo password | passwd --stdin betty; echo password | passwd --stdin amy** to set the password for these two users. Type **exit** to return to the user student shell.
5. Use **su - betty** to open a shell as user betty. When prompted for a password, enter the password you've just assigned for user betty.
6. Type **sudo ls /root**, enter the user betty password and notice the error message.
7. Type **exit** to return to the shell in which you are user student. Use **whoami** to verify the current user ID.
8. Type **sudo sh -c 'echo "betty ALL=(ALL) ALL" > /etc/sudoers.d/betty'** to allow full **sudo** access for betty.
9. Use **su - betty** to open a shell as betty and enter the password of this user when prompted.
10. Use **sudo ls -l /root** to verify that **sudo** access is working. The /root directory can only be viewed by the root user due to the permissions on that directory.
11. Use **sudo sh -c ' echo "amy ALL=/usr/sbin/useradd, /usr/bin/passwd, ! /usr/bin/passwd root" > /etc/sudoers.d/amy'** to allow user amy to create users and reset user passwords, but not for root.
12. Type **su - amy** and enter user amy's password when prompted.
13. Use **sudo passwd betty** to verify that you can change the password as user amy.
14. Use **sudo passwd root** to verify that changing the root user password is not allowed.
15. Type **exit** and **exit** to return to the user student shell. Use **whoami** to verify that you're in the right shell.

Creating and Managing User Accounts

Now that you know how to perform tasks as either an administrative user or a non-administrative user, it is time to learn how to manage user accounts on Linux. In this section, you learn what is involved.

System Accounts and Normal Accounts

A typical Linux environment has two kinds of user accounts. There are normal user accounts for the people who need to work on a server and who need limited access to the resources on that server. These user accounts typically have a password that is used for authenticating the user to the system. There are also system accounts that are used by the services the server is offering. Both types of user accounts share common properties, which are kept in the files /etc/passwd and /etc/shadow. Example 6-2 shows a part of the contents of the /etc/passwd file.

Example 6-2 Partial Contents of the /etc/passwd User Configuration File

```
ntp:x:38:38::/etc/ntp:/sbin/nologin
chrony:x:994:993::/var/lib/chrony:/sbin/nologin
abrt:x:173:173::/etc/abrt:/sbin/nologin
pulse:x:171:171:PulseAudio System Daemon:/var/run/pulse:/sbin/nologin
gdm:x:42:42::/var/lib/gdm:/sbin/nologin
gnome-initial-setup:x:993:991::/run/gnome-initial-setup/:/sbin/nologin
postfix:x:89:89::/var/spool/postfix:/sbin/nologin
sshd:x:74:74:Privilege-separated SSH:/var/empty/sshd:/sbin/nologin
tcpdump:x:72:72::/:/sbin/nologin
user:x:1000:1000:user:/home/user:/bin/bash
```

NOTE On many Linux servers, hardly any user accounts are used by people. Many Linux servers are installed to run a specific service, and if people interact with that service, they will authenticate within the service.

As you can see in Example 6-2, to define a user account, different fields are used in /etc/passwd. The fields are separated from each other by a colon. The following is a summary of these fields, followed by a short description of their purpose.

- **Username:** This is a unique name for the user. Usernames are important to match a user to their password, which is stored separately in /etc/shadow (see next bullet). On Linux, there can be no spaces in the username, and in general it's a good idea to specify usernames in all lowercase letters.

- **Password:** In the old days, the second field of /etc/passwd was used to store the hashed password of the user. Because the /etc/passwd file is readable by all users, this poses a security threat, and for that reason on current Linux systems the hashed passwords are stored in /etc/shadow (discussed in the next section).

- **UID:** Each user has a unique user ID (UID). This is a numeric ID. It is the UID that really determines what a user can do. When permissions are set for a user, the UID (and not the username) is stored in the file metadata. UID 0 is reserved for root, the unrestricted user account. The lower UIDs (typically up to 999) are used for system accounts, and the higher UIDs (from 1000 on by default) are reserved for people who need to connect a directory to the server. The range of UIDs that are used to create regular user accounts is set in /etc/login.defs.

- **GID:** On Linux, each user is a member of at least one group. This group is referred to as the *primary group*, and this group plays a central role in permissions management, as discussed later in this chapter. Users can be a member of additional groups, which are administered in the file /etc/group.

- **Comment field:** The Comment field, as you can guess, is used to add comments for user accounts. This field is optional, but it can be used to describe what a user account is created for. Some utilities, such as the obsolete **finger** utility, can be used to get information from this field. The field is also referred to as the ***GECOS*** field, which stands for General Electric Comprehensive Operating System and had a specific purpose for identifying jobs in the early 1970s when General Electric was still an important manufacturer of servers.

- **Directory:** This is the initial directory where the user is placed after logging in, also referred to as the *home directory*. If the user account is used by a person, this is where the person would store their personal files and programs. For a system user account, this is the environment where the service can store files it needs while operating.

- **Shell:** This is the program that is started after the user has successfully connected to a server. For most users this will be **/bin/bash**, the default Linux shell. For system user accounts, it will typically be a shell like **/sbin/nologin**. The **/sbin/nologin** command is a specific command that silently denies access to users (to ensure that if by accident an intruder logs in to the server, the intruder cannot get any shell access). Optionally, you can create an /etc/nologin.txt file, in which case only root will be able to log in but other users will see the contents of this file when their logins are denied.

A part of the user properties is stored in /etc/passwd, which was just discussed. Another part of the configuration of user properties is stored in the /etc/shadow file. The settings in this file are used to set properties of the password. Only the user root and processes running as root have access to /etc/shadow. Example 6-3 shows /etc/shadow contents.

Example 6-3 Sample Content from /etc/shadow

```
[root@localhost ~]# tail -n 10 /etc/shadow
ntp:!!:16420::::::
chrony:!!:16420::::::
abrt:!!:16420::::::
pulse:!!:16420::::::
gdm:!!:16420::::::
gnome-initial-setup:!!:16420::::::
postfix:!!:16420::::::
sshd:!!:16420::::::
tcpdump:!!:16420::::::
user:$6$3VZbGx1djo6FfyZo$/Trg7Q.3foIsIFYxBm6UnHuxxBrxQxHDnDuZxgS.
We/MAuHn8HboBZzpaMD8gfm.fmlB/ML9LnuaT7CbwVXx31:16420:0:99999:7:::
```

The following fields are included in /etc/shadow:

- **Login name:** Notice that /etc/shadow does not contain any UIDs, but usernames only. This opens up a possibility for multiple users using the same UID but different passwords (which, by the way, is not recommended).
- **Encrypted password:** This field contains all that is needed to store the password in a secure way. If the field is empty, no password is set and the user cannot log in. If the field starts with an exclamation mark, login for this account currently is disabled.
- **Days since Jan. 1, 1970, that the password was last changed:** Many things on Linux refer to this date, which on Linux is considered the beginning of time. It is also referred to as *epoch*.
- **Days before password may be changed:** This allows system administrators to use a stricter password policy, where it is not possible to change back to the original password immediately after a password has been changed. Typically this field is set to the value 0.
- **Days after which password must be changed:** This field contains the maximal validity period of passwords. Notice in the last line of Example 6-3 that it is set to 99,999 (about 274 years), which is the default.
- **Days before password is to expire that user is warned:** This field is used to warn a user when a forced password change is upcoming. Notice in the last line of Example 6-3 that it is set to 7 days, which is the default (even if the password validity is set to 99,999 days).

- **Days after password expires that account is disabled:** Use this field to enforce a password change. After password expiry, the user no longer can log in. After the account has reached the maximum validity period, the account is locked out. This field allows for a grace period in which the user can change her password, but only during the login process. This field is set in days and is unset by default.
- **Days since Jan. 1, 1970, that account is disabled:** An administrator can set this field to disable an account on a specific date. This is typically a better approach than removing an account, as all associated properties and files of the account will be kept, but the account no longer can be used to authenticate on your server. Note that this field does not have a default value.
- **A reserved field, which was once added "for future use":** This field was reserved a long time ago; it will probably never be used.

Most of the password properties can be managed with the **passwd** or **chage** command, which are discussed later in this chapter.

Creating Users

There are many solutions for creating users on a Linux server. To start, you can edit the contents of the /etc/passwd and /etc/shadow configuration files directly in an editor, using the **vipw** command (with the risk of making an error that could make logging in impossible to anyone). Another option is to use **useradd**, which is the utility that you should use for creating users. To remove users, you can use the **userdel** command. Use **userdel -r** to remove a user and the complete user environment.

Modifying the Configuration Files

Creating a user account by modifying the configuration files simply requires adding one line to /etc/passwd and another line to /etc/shadow, in which the user account and all of its properties are defined. This method of creating users is not recommended, though. If you make an error, you might mess up the consistency of the file and make logging in completely impossible to anyone. Also, you might encounter locking problems if one administrator is trying to modify the file contents directly while another administrator wants to write a modification with some tool.

If you insist on modifying the configuration files directly, you should use **vipw**. This command opens an editor interface on your configuration files, and more important, it sets the appropriate locks on the configuration files to prevent corruption. It does *not* check syntax, however, so make sure that you know what you are doing, because making even one typo might still severely mess up your server. If you want to use this tool to modify the /etc/shadow file, use **vipw -s**. To edit the contents of the

/etc/group file where groups are defined, you can use a similar command with the name **vigr**.

> **NOTE** It is nice to know that **vipw** and **vigr** exist, but it is better not to use these utilities or anything else that opens the user and group configuration files directly. Instead, use tools like **useradd** and **groupmod**.

Using useradd

The **useradd** utility is probably the most common tool on Linux for adding users. It allows you to add a user account from the command line by using many of its parameters. Use, for instance, the command **useradd -m -u 1201 -G sales,ops linda** to create a user linda who is a member of the secondary groups sales and ops with UID 1201 and add a home directory to the user account as well. (Secondary groups are explained in the section "Understanding Linux Groups," later in the chapter.)

Home Directories

All normal users will have a home directory. For people, the home directory is the directory where personal files can be stored. For system accounts, the home directory often contains the working environment for the service account.

As an administrator, you normally will not change home directory–related settings for system accounts because they are created automatically from the RPM post-installation scripts when installing the related software packages. If you have people who need user accounts, you probably do want to manage home directory contents a bit.

When creating home directories (which happens by default while you're creating users), the content of the "skeleton" directory is copied to the user home directory. The skeleton directory is /etc/skel, and it contains files that are copied to the user home directory at the moment this directory is created. These files will also get the appropriate permissions to ensure that the new user can use and access them.

By default, the skeleton directory contains mostly configuration files that determine how the user environment is set up. If in your environment specific files need to be present in the home directories of all users, you take care of that by adding the files to the skeleton directory.

Default Shell

Most regular users normally have a default shell. This is the program that is started after successful authentication. For most users, this shell is set to /bin/bash. System users should not have an interactive shell as the default shell. For most system users this shell is set to /sbin/nologin. To set or change the default shell using **useradd** or

usermod, use the **-s** option. Use for instance **useradd caroline -s /sbin/nologin** to make sure this user will not be allowed to log in.

Managing User Properties

For changing user properties, the same rules apply as for creating user accounts. You can either work directly in the configuration files using **vipw** or use command-line tools.

The ultimate command-line utility for modifying user properties is **usermod**. It can be used to set all properties of users as stored in /etc/passwd and /etc/shadow, plus some additional tasks, such as managing group membership. There is just one task it does not do well: setting passwords. Although **usermod** has an option **-p** that tells you to "use encrypted password for the new password," it expects you to do the password encryption before adding the user account. That does not make it particularly useful. If as root you want to change the user password, you'd use the **passwd** command.

Configuration Files for User Management Defaults

When you're working with tools such as **useradd**, some default values are assumed. These default values are set in two configuration files: /etc/login.defs and /etc/default/useradd. Example 6-4 shows the contents of /etc/default/useradd.

Example 6-4 useradd Defaults in /etc/default/useradd

```
[root@localhost skel]# cat /etc/default/useradd
# useradd defaults file
GROUP=100
HOME=/home
INACTIVE=-1
EXPIRE=
SHELL=/bin/bash
SKEL=/etc/skel
CREATE_MAIL_SPOOL=yes
```

As shown in Example 6-4, the /etc/default/useradd file contains some default values that are applied when using **useradd**.

In the file /etc/login.defs, different login-related variables are set. This file is used by different commands, and it relates to setting up the appropriate environment for new users. Here is a list of some of the most significant properties that can be set from /etc/login.defs:

- **MOTD_FILE:** Defines the file that is used as the "message of the day" file. In this file, you can include messages to be displayed after the user has successfully logged in to the server.

- **ENV_PATH:** Defines the $PATH variable, a list of directories that should be searched for executable files after logging in.
- **PASS_MAX_DAYS, PASS_MIN_DAYS, and PASS_WARN_AGE:** Define the default password expiration properties when creating new users.
- **UID_MIN:** Indicates the first UID to use when creating new users.
- **CREATE_HOME:** Indicates whether or not to create a home directory for new users.

Managing Password Properties

You learned about the password properties that can be set in /etc/shadow. You can use two commands to change these properties for users: **chage** and **passwd**. The commands are rather straightforward, as long as you know what the options are used for. For instance, the command **passwd -n 30 -w 3 -x 90 linda** sets the password for user linda to a minimal usage period of 30 days and an expiry after 90 days, where a warning is generated 3 days before expiry.

Many of the tasks that can be accomplished with **passwd** can be done with **chage** also. For instance, use **chage -E 2025-12-31 bob** to have the account for user bob expire on December 31, 2025. To see current password management settings, use **chage -l** (see Example 6-5). The **chage** command also has an interactive mode; if you type **chage anna**, for instance, the command will prompt for all the password properties you want to set interactively.

Example 6-5 Showing Password Expiry Information with **chage -l**

```
linux:~ # chage -l linda
Last password change                                    : Apr 11, 2020
Password expires                                        : never
Password inactive                                       : never
Account expires                                         : never
Minimum number of days between password change          : 0
Maximum number of days between password change          : 99999
Number of days of warning before password expir         : 7
```

Creating a User Environment

When a user logs in, an environment is created. The environment consists of some variables that determine how the user is working. One such variable, for instance, is $PATH, which defines a list of directories that should be searched when a user types a command.

To construct the user environment, a few files play a role:

- **/etc/profile:** Used for default settings for all users when starting a login shell
- **/etc/bashrc:** Used to define defaults for all users when starting a subshell
- **~/.profile:** Specific settings for one user applied when starting a login shell
- **~/.bashrc:** Specific settings for one user applied when starting a subshell

When you log in, the files are read in this order, and variables and other settings that are defined in these files are applied. If a variable or setting occurs in more than one file, the last one wins.

In Exercise 6-3, you apply common solutions to create user accounts.

Exercise 6-3 Creating User Accounts

1. From a sudo shell, type **vim /etc/login.defs** to open the configuration file /etc/login.defs and the PASS_MAX_DAYS to use the value 99 before you start creating users. Look for the parameter **CREATE_HOME** and make sure it is set to "yes."
2. Use **cd /etc/skel** to go to the /etc/skel directory. Type **mkdir fotos** and **mkdir files** to add two default directories to all user home directories. Also change the contents of the file .bashrc to include the line **export EDITOR=/usr/bin/vim**, which sets the default editor for tools that need to modify text files.
3. Type **useradd linda** to create an account for user linda. Then, type **id linda** to verify that linda is a member of a group with the name linda and nothing else. Also verify that the directories Pictures and Documents have been created in user linda's home directory.
4. Use **passwd linda** to set a password for the user you have just created. Use the password **password**.
5. Type **passwd -n 30 -w 3 -x 90 linda** to change the password properties. This has the password expire after 90 days (**-x 90**). Three days before expiry, the user will get a warning (**-w 3**), and the password has to be used for at least 30 days before (**-n 30**) it can be changed.
6. Create a few more users: lucy, lori, and bob, using **for i in lucy lori bob; do useradd $i; done**. You may get an error message stating the user already exists. This message can be safely ignored.
7. Use **grep lori /etc/passwd /etc/shadow /etc/group**. This shows the user lori created in all three critical files and confirms they have been set up correctly.

Creating and Managing Group Accounts

Every Linux user has to be a member of at least one group. In this section, you learn how to manage settings for Linux group accounts.

Understanding Linux Groups

Linux users can be a member of two different kinds of ***groups***. First, there is the ***primary group***. Every user must be a member of the primary group, and a user has only one primary group. When a user creates a file, the user's primary group becomes the group owner of the file. (File ownership is discussed in detail in Chapter 7, "Permissions Management.") Users can also access all files their primary group has access to. The user's primary group membership is defined in /etc/passwd; the group itself is stored in the /etc/group configuration file.

Besides the mandatory primary group, users can be a member of one or more secondary groups as well. A user can be a member of a ***secondary group*** in addition to the primary group. Secondary groups are important to get access to files. If the group a user is a member of has access to specific files, the user will get access to those files also. Working with secondary groups is important, in particular in environments where Linux is used as a file server to allow people working for different departments to share files with one another. You have also seen how secondary group membership can be used to enable user administrative privileges through **sudo**, by making the user a member of the group wheel.

Creating Groups

As is the case for creating users, there are also different options for creating groups. The group configuration files can be modified directly using **vigr** or the command-line utility **groupadd**.

Creating Groups with vigr

With the **vigr** command, you open an editor interface directly on the /etc/group configuration file. In this file, groups are defined in four fields per group (see Example 6-6).

Example 6-6 Sample /etc/group Content

```
kvm:x:36:qemu
qemu:x:107:
libstoragemgmt:x:994:
rpc:x:32:
rpcuser:x:29:
"/etc/group.edit" 65L, 870C
```

The following fields are used in /etc/group:

- **Group name:** As is suggested by the name of the field, it contains the name of the group.
- **Group password:** Where applicable, this field contains a group password, a feature that is hardly used anymore. A group password can be used by users who want to join the group on a temporary basis, so that access to files the group has access to is allowed. If a group password is used, it is stored in the /etc/gshadow file, as that file is root accessible only.
- **Group ID:** This field contains a unique numeric group identification number.
- **Members:** Here you find the names of users who are a member of this group as a secondary group. Note that this field does not show users who are a member of this group as their primary group.

As mentioned, in addition to /etc/group, there is the /etc/gshadow file. This file is not commonly used to store group passwords (because hardly anyone still uses them), but it does have a cool feature. In the third field of this file you can list administrators. This is a comma-separated list of users that can change passwords for group members, which are listed in the fourth field of this file. Note that specifying group members here is optional, but if it is done, the group member names must be the same as the group members in /etc/group.

Using groupadd to Create Groups

Another method to create new groups is by using the **groupadd** command. This command is easy to use. Just use **groupadd** followed by the name of the group you want to add. There are some advanced options; the only significant one is **-g**, which allows you to specify a group ID when creating the group.

Managing Group Properties

To manage group properties, **groupmod** is available. You can use this command to change the name or group ID of the group, but it does not allow you to add group members. Notice that it may be a bad idea to change either of these properties, as it can affect group-owned files that already exist. To do this, you use **usermod**. As discussed before, **usermod -aG** will add users to new groups that will be used as their secondary group. Because a group does not have many properties, it is quite common that group properties are managed directly in the /etc/group file by using the **vigr** command.

To see which users are a member of a group, use the **lid** command. For example, use **lid -g sales** to check which users are a member of the group sales.

In Exercise 6-4, you create two groups and add some users as members to these groups.

TIP Because a user's group membership is defined in two different locations, it can be difficult to find out which groups exactly a user is a member of. A convenient command to check this is **groupmems**. Use, for example, the command **groupmems -g sales -l** to see which users are a member of the group sales. This shows users who are a member of this group as a secondary group assignment, but also users who are a member of this group as the primary group assignment.

Exercise 6-4 Working with Groups

1. Open a **sudo** shell and type **groupadd sales** followed by **groupadd account** to add groups with the names sales and account.
2. Use **usermod** to add users linda and laura to the group sales, and lori and bob to the sales group account:

```
usermod -aG sales linda
usermod -aG sales lucy
usermod -aG account lori
usermod -aG account bob
linux:~ # id linda
```

3. Type **id linda** to verify that user linda has correctly been added to the group sales. In the results of this command, you see that linda is assigned to a group with the name linda. This is user linda's primary group and is indicated with the gid option. The **groups** parameter shows all groups user linda currently is a member of, which includes the primary group as well as the secondary group sales that the user has just been assigned to.

```
uid=1000(linda) gid=1000(linda) groups=1000(linda),1001(sales)
```

Summary

In this chapter, you learned how to create and manage users and groups. You learned which configuration files are used to store users and groups, and you learned which properties are used in these files. You also learned which utilities are available to manage user and group accounts.

Exam Preparation Tasks

As mentioned in the section "How to Use This Book" in the Introduction, you have a couple of choices for exam preparation: the end-of-chapter labs; the memory tables in Appendix C; Chapter 27, "Final Preparation"; and the practice exams.

Review All Key Topics

Review the most important topics in the chapter, noted with the Key Topic icon in the margin of the page. Table 6-3 lists a reference for these key topics and the page number on which each is found.

Table 6-3 Key Topics for Chapter 6

Key Topic Element	Description	Page
Section	Users on Linux	124
Table 6-2	Methods to Run Tasks with Elevated Permissions	125
List	Description of user account fields in /etc/passwd	129
List	Description of password property fields in /etc/shadow	131
List	Significant properties that can be set from /etc/login.defs	134
List	Files that play a role in constructing the user environment	136

Complete Tables and Lists from Memory

Print a copy of Appendix C, "Memory Tables" (found on the companion website), or at least the section for this chapter, and complete the tables and lists from memory. Appendix D, "Memory Tables Answer Key," includes completed tables and lists to check your work.

Define Key Terms

Define the following key terms from this chapter and check your answers in the glossary:

user, privileged user, unprivileged user, root, password, GECOS, group, primary group, secondary group

Review Questions

The questions that follow are meant to help you test your knowledge of concepts and terminology and the breadth of your knowledge. You can find the answers to these questions in Appendix A.

1. What is the name of the default parameter that you can change to expand the lifetime of the **sudo** token that is generated after entering the **sudo** password?
2. What is the configuration file in which **sudo** is defined?
3. Which command should you use to modify a **sudo** configuration?
4. What can you do if you've made an error to the **sudo** configuration and because of this error **sudo** no longer works, assuming that the root user does not have a password set?
5. How many groups can you assign to a user account in /etc/passwd?
6. If you want to grant a user access to all admin commands through **sudo**, which group should you make that user a member of?
7. Which command should you use to modify the /etc/group file manually?
8. Which two commands can you use to change user password information?
9. What is the name of the file where user passwords are stored?
10. What is the name of the file where group accounts are stored?

End-of-Chapter Labs

You have now learned how to set up an environment where user accounts can log in to your server and access resources on your server. In these end-of-chapter labs, you learn how to configure an environment for users and groups.

Lab 6.1

Set up a shared group environment that meets the following requirements:

- Create two groups: sales and account.
- Create users joana, john, laura, and beatrix. Make sure they have their primary group set to a private group that has the name of the user.

- Make joanna and john members of the group sales, and laura and beatrix members of the group account.
- Set a password policy that requires users to change their password every 90 days.

Lab 6.2

Create a **sudo** configuration that allows user bill to manage user properties and passwords, but which does not allow this user to change the password for the root user.

The following topics are covered in this chapter:

- Managing File Ownership
- Managing Basic Permissions
- Managing Advanced Permissions
- Setting Default Permissions with **umask**
- Working with User-Extended Attributes

The following RHCSA exam objectives are covered in this chapter:

- Manage default permissions
- List, set, and change standard ugo/rwx permissions
- Create and configure set-GID directories for collaboration
- Diagnose and correct file permission problems

Permissions Management

To get access to files on Linux, you use permissions. These permissions are assigned to three entities: the file owner, the group owner, and the others entity (which is everybody else). In this chapter, you learn how to apply permissions. The chapter starts with an overview of the basic permissions, after which the special permissions are discussed. At the end of this chapter, you learn how to set default permissions through the **umask** and how to manage user-extended attributes.

"Do I Know This Already?" Quiz

The "Do I Know This Already?" quiz enables you to assess whether you should read this entire chapter thoroughly or jump to the "Exam Preparation Tasks" section. If you are in doubt about your answers to these questions or your own assessment of your knowledge of the topics, read the entire chapter. Table 7-1 lists the major headings in this chapter and their corresponding "Do I Know This Already?" quiz questions. You can find the answers in Appendix A, "Answers to the 'Do I Know This Already?' Quizzes and Review Questions."

Table 7-1 "Do I Know This Already?" Section-to-Question Mapping

Foundation Topics Section	Questions
Managing File Ownership	1–3
Managing Basic Permissions	4–5
Managing Advanced Permissions	6–7
Setting Default Permissions with **umask**	8–9
Working with User-Extended Attributes	10

1. A user needs to work in a session where all new files that the user creates will be group-owned by the group sales, until the session is closed. Which command would do that?
    a. **chgrp sales**
    b. **setgid sales**
    c. **newgrp sales**
    d. **setgroup sales**

2. Which command enables you to find all files on a system that are owned by user linda?
   a. **find / -user linda**
   b. **find / -uid linda**
   c. **ls -l | grep linda**
   d. **ls -R | find linda**

3. Which command does not set group ownership to the group sales for the file myfile?
   a. **chgrp sales myfile**
   b. **chown .sales myfile**
   c. **chgrp myfile sales**
   d. **chown :sales myfile**

4. Which command would be used to allow read and write permissions to the user and group owners and no permissions at all to anyone else?
   a. **chown 007 filename**
   b. **chmod 077 filename**
   c. **chmod 660 filename**
   d. **chmod 770 filename**

5. You want to apply the execute permission recursively, such that only all subdirectories and not the files in these directories will get the execute permission assigned. How can you do this?
   a. Use **chmod +x */**
   b. Use **chmod +X ***
   c. Use **umask 444**, and then use **chmod +x ***
   d. Use **umask 444**, and next use **chmod +X ***

6. Which command enables you to set the SGID permission on a directory?
   a. **chmod u+s /dir**
   b. **chmod g-s /dir**
   c. **chmod g+s /dir**
   d. **chmod 1770 /dir**

7. While observing current permission settings, you notice that the **passwd** program file has the execute permission set. What should you do?
   a. Run a security scan on your system, because something obviously is wrong.
   b. Check the system logs to find out who has wrongly applied this permission.
   c. Check whether the execute permission is also set. If that is not the case, it's not a big deal.
   d. Nothing, because the **passwd** program file needs the SUID permission to be able to update passwords in the secured /etc/shadow file.

8. How can you make sure that the root user has a different **umask** than ordinary users?
   a. You don't have to do anything; this happens by default.
   b. Set the default **umask** in /etc/login.defs.
   c. Set a specific **umask** for the root user in the ~/bash_profile file.
   d. Use an **if** statement to apply a specific **umask** for the root user in the /etc/profile file.

9. Which of the following **umask** settings meets the following requirements?
   - Grants all permissions to the owner of the file
   - Grants read permissions to the group owner of the file
   - Grants no permissions to others

   a. 740
   b. 750
   c. 027
   d. 047

10. Which command enables you to check all attributes that are currently set on myfile?
    a. **ls --attr myfile**
    b. **getattr myfile**
    c. **lsattr myfile**
    d. **listattr myfile**

Foundation Topics

Managing File Ownership

Before we discuss permissions, you need to understand the role of file and directory ***ownership***. File and directory ownership are vital for working with permissions. In this section, you first learn how you can see ownership. Then you learn how to change user and group ownership for files and directories.

Displaying Ownership

On Linux, every file and every directory has two owners: a user owner and a group owner. Apart from that, there is the "others" entity, which also is considered to be an entity to determine the permissions a user has. Collectively, the user, group, and others (ugo) owners are shown when listing permissions with the **ls -l** command.

These owners are set when a file or directory is created. On creation, the user who creates the file becomes the user owner, and the primary group of that user becomes the group owner. To determine whether you as a user have permissions to a file or a directory, the shell checks ownership. This happens in the following order:

1. The shell checks whether you are the user owner of the file you want to access, which is also referred to as the user of the file. If you are the user, you get the permissions that are set for the user, and the shell looks no further.
2. If you are not the user owner, the shell checks whether you are a member of the group owner, which is also referred to as the group of the file. If you are a member of the group, you get access to the file with the permissions of the group, and the shell looks no further.
3. If you are neither the user owner nor the group owner and have not obtained permissions through access control lists (ACLs), you get the permissions of the others entity.

To see current ownership assignments, you can use the **ls -l** command. This command shows the user owner and the group owner. In Example 7-1, you can see the ownership settings for directories in the directory /home.

Example 7-1 Displaying Current File Ownership

```
[root@server1 home]# ls -l
total 8
drwx------. 3 bob bob                74 Feb 6 10:13 bob
drwx------. 3 caroline caroline      74 Feb 6 10:13 caroline
drwx------. 3 fozia fozia            74 Feb 6 10:13 fozia
drwx------. 3 lara lara              74 Feb 6 10:13 lara
drwx------. 5 lisa lisa              4096 Feb 6 10:12 lisa
drwx------. 14 user user             4096 Feb 5 10:35 user
```

Using the **ls** command, you can display ownership for files in a given directory. It may on occasion be useful to get a list of all files on the system that have a given user or group as owner. To do this, you may use **find** with the argument **-user**. For instance, the following command shows all files that have user linda as their owner:

```
find / -user linda
```

You can also use **find** to search for files that have a specific group as their owner. For instance, the following command searches all files that are owned by the group users:

```
find / -group users
```

Changing User Ownership

To apply appropriate permissions, the first thing to consider is ownership. To do this, you can use the **chown** command. The syntax of this command is not hard to understand:

```
chown who what
```

For instance, the following command changes ownership for the file files to user linda:

```
chown linda files
```

The **chown** command has a few options, of which one is particularly useful: **-R**. You might guess what it does, because this option is available for many other commands as well. It allows you to set ownership recursively, which allows you to set ownership of the current directory and everything below. The following command changes ownership for the directory /files and everything beneath it to user linda:

```
chown -R linda /files
```

Changing Group Ownership

There are actually two ways to change group ownership. You can do it using **chown**, but there is also a specific command with the name **chgrp** that does the job. If you want to use the **chown** command, use a **.** or **:** in front of the group name. The following changes the group owner of directory /home/account to the group account:

```
chown .account /home/account
```

You can use **chown** to change user and/or group ownership in a number of ways, an overview of which follows:

- **chown lisa myfile** Sets user lisa as the owner of myfile
- **chown lisa.sales myfile** Sets user lisa as user owner and group sales as group owner of myfile
- **chown lisa:sales myfile** Sets user lisa as user owner and group sales as group owner of myfile
- **chown .sales myfile** Sets group sales as group owner of myfile without changing the user owner
- **chown :sales myfile** Sets group sales as group owner of myfile without changing the user owner

You can also use the **chgrp** command to change group ownership. Consider the following example, where you can use **chgrp** to set group ownership for the directory /home/account to the group account:

```
chgrp account /home/account
```

As is the case for **chown**, you can use the option **-R** with **chgrp** as well to change group ownership recursively.

Understanding Default Ownership

You might have noticed that when a user creates a file, default ownership is applied. The user who creates the file automatically becomes user owner, and the primary group of that user automatically becomes group owner. Normally, this is the group that is set in the /etc/passwd file as the user's primary group. If the user is a member of more groups, however, the user can use the **newgrp** command to change the effective primary group so that new files will get the new primary group as group owner.

To show the current primary group, a user can use the **groups** command. Of the groups listed, the primary group is the first name after the : character:

```
[root@server1 ~]# groups lisa
lisa : lisa account sales
```

If the current user linda wants to change the effective primary group, user linda can use the **newgrp** command, followed by the name of the group that user linda wants to set as the new effective primary group. This will open a new shell, in which the new temporary primary group is set. This group will continue to be used as the effective primary group until user linda uses the **exit** command or logs out. Example 7-2 shows how user linda uses this command to make sales her effective primary group.

Example 7-2 Using **newgrp** to Change the Effective Primary Group

```
[lisa@server1 ~]$ groups
lisa account sales
[lisa@server1 ~]$ newgrp sales
[lisa@server1 ~]$ groups
sales lisa account
[lisa@server1 ~]$ touch file1
[lisa@server1 ~]$ ls -l
total 0
-rw-r--r--. 1 lisa sales 0 Feb 6 10:06 file1
```

After you change the effective primary group, all new files that the user creates will get this group as their group owner. To return to the original primary group setting, use **exit**.

To be able to use the **newgrp** command, a user has to be a member of that group. Alternatively, a group password can be set for the group using the **gpasswd** command, but that is uncommonly used. If a user uses the **newgrp** command but is not a member of the target group, the shell prompts for the group password. After the user enters the correct group password, the new effective primary group is set.

Managing Basic Permissions

The Linux permissions system was invented in the 1970s. Because computing needs were limited in those years, the basic permission system that was created was rather limited as well. This basic permission system uses three permissions that can be applied to files and directories. In this section, you learn how the system works and how to modify these permissions.

Understanding Read, Write, and Execute Permissions

The three basic ***permissions*** allow users to read, write, and execute files. The effect of these permissions differs when applied to files or directories. If applied to a file, the read permission gives the right to open the file for viewing. Therefore, you can read its contents, but it also means that your computer can open the file to do something with it. A program file that needs access to a library needs, for example, read access to that library. From that follows that the read permission is the most basic permission you need to work with files.

If applied to a directory, read allows you to list the contents of that directory. You should be aware that this permission does not allow you to read files in the directory as well. The Linux permission system does not know ***inheritance***, and the only way to read a file is by using the read permissions on that file. To open a file for reading, however, it is required to have read as well as execute permissions to the directory because you would not see the file otherwise.

As you can probably guess, the write permission, if applied to a file, allows you to modify the contents of the file. Stated otherwise, write allows you to modify the contents of existing files. It does not, however, allow you to create or delete new files. To do that, you need write permission on the directory where you want to create the file. To modify the permissions on a file, you don't need permissions on the file; you just have to be owner, or root. On directories, this permission also allows you to create and remove new subdirectories.

The execute permission is what you need to run a program file. Also, you need the execute permission on a directory if you want to do anything in that directory. The execute permission will never be set by default, which makes Linux almost completely immune to viruses. Only the user owner and the root user can apply the execute permission.

Whereas having the execute permission on files means that you are allowed to run a program file, if applied to a directory it means that you are allowed to use the **cd** command to enter that directory. This means that execute is an important permission for directories, and you will see that it is normally applied as the default permission to directories. Without it, there is no way to change to that directory! Table 7-2 summarizes the use of the basic permissions.

Table 7-2 Use of Read, Write, and Execute Permissions

Permission	Applied to Files	Applied to Directories
Read	View file content	List contents of directory
Write	Change contents of a file	Create and delete files and subdirectories
Execute	Run a program file	Change to the directory

Applying Read, Write, and Execute Permissions

To apply permissions, you use the **chmod** command. When using **chmod**, you can set permissions for user, group, and others. You can use this command in two modes: the relative mode and the absolute mode. In absolute mode, three digits are used to set the basic permissions. The three digits apply to user, group, and others, respectively. Table 7-3 provides an overview of the permissions and their numeric representation.

Table 7-3 Numeric Representation of Permissions

Permission	Numeric Representation
Read	4
Write	2
Execute	1

When setting permissions, calculate the value that you need. If you want to set read, write, and execute for the user, read and execute for the group, and read and execute for others on the file /somefile, for example, you use the following **chmod** command:

```
chmod 755 /somefile
```

When you use **chmod** in this way, all current permissions are replaced by the permissions you set. If you want to modify permissions relative to the current permissions, you can use **chmod** in relative mode. When using **chmod** in relative mode, you work with three indicators to specify what you want to do:

- First, you specify for whom you want to change permissions. To do this, you can choose between user (**u**), group (**g**), others (**o**), and all (**a**).
- Then, you use an operator to add or remove permissions from the current mode, or set them in an absolute way.
- At the end, you use **r**, **w**, and **x** to specify what permissions you want to set.

When changing permissions in relative mode, you may omit the "to whom" part to add or remove a permission for all entities. For instance, the following adds the execute permission for all users:

```
chmod +x somefile
```

When working in relative mode, you may use more complex commands as well. For instance, the following adds the write permission to the group and removes read for others:

```
chmod g+w,o-r somefile
```

When applied in recursive mode, the execute permission needs special attention. In the following procedure you can find out why:

1. Open a root shell and type **mkdir ~/files**
2. Use **cp /etc/[a-e]* ~/files**. Ignore the errors and warnings that you see.
3. Type **ls -l ~/files/*** and observe the permissions that are set on the files.
4. Use **chmod -R a+x ~/files**
5. Type **ls -l ~/files/*** again. You'll notice that all files have become executable as well.

Files becoming executable in an uncontrolled way are a major security issue. For that reason, if you want to apply the execute permission in a recursive way, you should apply it as X, not x. So instead of using **chmod -R a+x files**, use **chmod -R a+X files**. This ensures that subdirectories will obtain the execute permission but the execute permission is not applied to any files.

In Exercise 7-1, you learn how to work with basic permissions by creating a directory structure for the groups that you created earlier. You also assign the correct permissions to these directories.

Exercise 7-1 Managing Basic Permissions

1. From a root shell, type **mkdir -p /data/sales /data/account**.
2. Before setting the permissions, change the owners of these directories using **chown linda.sales /data/sales** and **chown linda.account /data/account**.
3. Set the permissions to enable the user and group owners to write files to these directories, and deny all access for all others: **chmod 770 /data/sales**, and next **chmod 770 /data/account**.
4. Use **su - laura** to become user laura and change into the directory /data/account. Use **touch emptyfile** to create a file in this directory. Does this work? Type **groups** to figure out why.
5. Still as user laura, use **cd /data/sales** and use **touch emptyfile** to create a file in this directory. Does this work? Type **groups** to figure out why.

Managing Advanced Permissions

Apart from the basic permissions that you have just read about, Linux has a set of advanced permissions as well. These are not permissions that you would set by default, but they sometimes provide a useful addition to realize more advanced scenarios. In this section, you learn what they are and how to set them.

Understanding Advanced Permissions

There are three advanced permissions. The first of them is the set user ID (SUID) permission. On some very specific occasions, you may want to apply this permission to executable files. By default, a user who runs an executable file runs this file with their own permissions. For normal users, that usually means that the use of the program is restricted. In some cases, however, the user needs special permissions, just for the execution of a certain task.

Consider, for example, the situation where a user needs to change their password. To do this, the user needs to write their new password to the /etc/shadow file. This file, however, is not writeable for users who do not have root permissions:

```
[root@hnl ~]# ls -l /etc/shadow
----------. 1 root root 1184 Apr 30 16:54 /etc/shadow
```

The SUID permission offers a solution for this problem. On the /usr/bin/passwd utility, this permission is applied by default. That means that when a user is changing their password, the user temporarily has root permissions because the /usr/bin/passwd utility is owned by the root user, which allows the user to write to the /etc/shadow file. You can see the SUID permission with **ls -l** as an **s** at the position where normally you would expect to see the **x** for the user permissions (the lowercase **s** means that both SUID and execute are set, whereas an uppercase **S** would mean that only SUID is set):

```
[root@hnl ~]# ls -l /usr/bin/passwd
-rwsr-xr-x. 1 root root 32680 Jan 28 2010 /usr/bin/passwd
```

The SUID permission may look useful (and it is in some cases), but at the same time, it is potentially dangerous. If it is applied wrongly, you may give away root permissions by accident. I therefore recommend using it with the greatest care only, or better yet: don't apply it to any files at all. It is set on some operating system files and should stay there, but there really is no good reason to set it on files ever.

The second special permission is set group ID (SGID). This permission has two effects. If applied on an executable file, it gives the user who executes the file the permissions of the group owner of that file. So, SGID can accomplish more or less the same thing that SUID does. For this purpose, however, SGID is hardly used.

As is the case for the SUID permission, SGID is applied to some system files as a default setting.

When applied to a directory, SGID may be useful, because you can use it to set default group ownership on files and subdirectories created in that directory. By default, when a user creates a file, the user's effective primary group is set as the group owner for that file. That is not always very useful, especially because on Red Hat Enterprise Linux, users have their primary group set to a group with the same name as the user, and of which the user is the only member. So by default, files that a user creates will be group shared with nobody else.

Imagine a situation where users linda and lori work for the accounting department and are both members of the group account. By default, these users are members of the private group of which they are the only member. Both users, however, are members of the accounting group as well but as a secondary group setting.

The default situation is that when either of these users creates a file, the primary group becomes owner. So by default, user linda cannot access the files that user lori has created and vice versa. However, if you create a shared group directory (say, /groups/account) and make sure that the SGID permission is applied to that directory, and that the group account is set as the group owner for that directory, all files created in this directory and all its subdirectories also get the group accounting as the default group owner. For that reason, the SGID permission is a very useful permission to set on shared group directories.

The SGID permission shows in the output of **ls -l** as an **s** at the position where you normally find the group execute permission (a lowercase **s** indicates that both SGID and execute are set, whereas an uppercase **S** means that only SGID is set):

```
[root@hnl data]# ls -ld account
drwxr-sr-x. 2 root account 4096 Apr 30 21:28 account
```

The third of the special permissions is sticky bit. This permission is useful to protect files against accidental deletion in an environment where multiple users have write permissions in the same directory. If sticky bit is applied, a user may delete a file only if they are the user owner of the file or of the directory that contains the file. It is for that reason that sticky bit is applied as a default permission to the /tmp directory, and it can be useful on shared group directories as well.

Without sticky bit, if a user can create files in a directory, the user can also delete files from that directory. In a shared group environment, this may be annoying. Imagine users linda and lori again, who both have write permissions to the directory /data/account and get these permissions because of their membership in the group accounting. Therefore, user linda can delete files that user lori has created and vice versa.

When you apply sticky bit, a user can delete files only if one of the following is true:

- The user has root access.
- The user is owner of the file.
- The user is owner of the directory where the file exists.

When using **ls -l**, you can see sticky bit as a **T** at the position where you normally see the execute permission for others (a lowercase **t** indicates that sticky bit as well as the execute permission for the others entity are set, whereas uppercase **T** indicates that only sticky bit is set):

```
[root@hnl data]# ls -ld account/
drwxr-sr-T 2 root account 4096 Apr 30 21:28 account/
```

TIP Make sure that you know how to manage these advanced permissions. The RHCSA objectives specifically mention that you need to be able to use SGID to create a shared group directory.

Applying Advanced Permissions

To apply SUID, SGID, and sticky bit, you can use **chmod** as well. SUID has numeric value 4, SGID has numeric value 2, and sticky bit has numeric value 1. If you want to apply these permissions, you need to add a four-digit argument to **chmod**, of which the first digit refers to the special permissions. The following line would, for example, add the SGID permission to a directory and set rwx for user and rx for group and others:

```
chmod 2755 /somedir
```

It is rather impractical if you have to look up the current permissions that are set before working with **chmod** in absolute mode. (You risk overwriting permissions if you do not.) Therefore, I recommend working in relative mode if you need to apply any of the special permissions:

- For SUID, use **chmod u+s**
- For SGID, use **chmod g+s**
- For sticky bit, use **chmod +t**, followed by the name of the file or the directory that you want to set the permissions on

Table 7-4 summarizes all that is important to know about managing special permissions.

Table 7-4 Working with SUID, SGID, and Sticky Bit

Permission	Numeric Value	Relative Value	On Files	On Directories
SUID	4	u+s	User executes file with permissions of file owner.	No meaning.
SGID	2	g+s	User executes file with permissions of group owner.	Files created in directory get the same group owner.
Sticky bit	1	+t	No meaning.	Prevents users from deleting files from other users.

In Exercise 7-2, you use special permissions to make it easier for members of a group to share files in a shared group directory. Make sure you have finished Exercise 7-1 before starting this exercise. You assign the set group ID bit and sticky bit and see that after setting these, features are added that make it easier for group members to work together.

Exercise 7-2 Working with Special Permissions

1. Start this exercise from a root shell.
2. Use **su - linda** to open a terminal in which you are user linda.
3. Use **cd /data/sales** to go to the sales directory. Use **touch linda1** and **touch linda2** to create two files of which linda is the owner.
4. Type **exit** to go back to a root shell, and next use **su - laura** to switch the current user identity to user laura, who also is a member of the sales group.
5. Use **cd /data/sales** again, and from that directory, use **ls -l**. You'll see the two files that were created by user linda that are group-owned by the group linda. Use **rm -f linda***. This will remove both files.
6. Use the commands **touch laura1 laura2** to create two files that are owned by user laura.
7. Use **su -** to escalate your current permissions to root level.
8. Use **chmod g+s,o+t /data/sales** to set the group ID bit as well as sticky bit on the shared group directory.

9. Use **su - linda** and type **cd /data/sales**. First, use **touch linda3 linda4**. You should now see that the two files you have created are owned by the group sales, which is group owner of the directory /data/sales.
10. Use **rm -rd laura***. Normally, sticky bit prevents you from doing so, but because user linda is the owner of the directory that contains the files, you are allowed to do it anyway!

Setting Default Permissions with umask

To set default permissions, you use either file ACLs or **umask**. ACLs were within the scope of previous versions of the RHCSA exam, but you don't have to know about them for the RHCSA 9 exam. In this section, you learn how to modify default permissions using **umask**.

You have probably noticed that when creating a new file, some default permissions are set. These permissions are determined by the **umask** setting. This shell setting is applied to all users when logging in to the system. In the **umask** setting, a numeric value is used that is subtracted from the maximum permissions that can be set automatically to a file; the maximum setting for files is 666, and for directories is 777.

Of the digits used in the **umask**, like with the numeric arguments for the **chmod** command, the first digit refers to user permissions, the second digit refers to the group permissions, and the last refers to default permissions set for others. The default **umask** setting of 022 gives 644 for all new files and 755 for all new directories that are created on your server. A complete overview of all **umask** numeric values and their result is shown in Table 7-5.

Table 7-5 **umask** Values and Their Result

Value	Applied to Files	Applied to Directories
0	Read and write	Everything
1	Read and write	Read and write
2	Read	Read and execute
3	Read	Read
4	Write	Write and execute
5	Write	Write
6	Nothing	Execute
7	Nothing	Nothing

An easy way to see how the **umask** setting works is as follows: Start with the default permissions for a file set to 666 and subtract the **umask** to get the effective permissions. For a directory, start with its default permissions that are set to 777 and subtract the **umask** to get the effective permissions.

There are two ways to change the **umask** setting: for all users and for individual users. If you want to set the **umask** for all users, you must make sure the **umask** setting is considered when starting the shell environment files as directed by /etc/profile. The right approach is to create a shell script with the name umask.sh in the /etc/profile.d directory and specify the **umask** you want to use in that shell script. If the **umask** is changed in this file, it applies to all users after logging in to your server.

An alternative to setting the **umask** through /etc/profile and related files where it is applied to all users logging in to the system is to change the **umask** settings in a file with the name .profile, which is created in the home directory of an individual user. Settings applied in this file are applied for the individual user only; therefore, this is a nice method if you need more granularity. I personally like this feature to change the default **umask** for user root to 027, whereas normal users work with the default **umask** 022.

Working with User-Extended Attributes

When you work with permissions, a relationship always exists between a user or group object and the permissions these user or group objects have on a file or directory. An alternative method of securing files on a Linux server is by working with attributes. ***Attributes*** do their work regardless of the user who accesses the file.

Many attributes are documented. Some attributes are available but not yet implemented. Do not use them; they bring you nothing. Following are the most useful attributes that you can apply:

- **A** This attribute ensures that the file access time of the file is not modified. Normally, every time a file is opened, the file access time must be written to the file's metadata. This affects performance in a negative way; therefore, on files that are accessed on a regular basis, the **A** attribute can be used to disable this feature.
- **a** This attribute allows a file to be added to but not to be removed.
- **c** If you are using a file system where volume-level compression is supported, this file attribute makes sure that the file is compressed the first time the compression engine becomes active.

- **D** This attribute makes sure that changes to files are written to disk immediately, and not to cache first. This is a useful attribute on important database files to make sure that they do not get lost between file cache and hard disk.
- **d** This attribute makes sure the file is not backed up in backups where the legacy **dump** utility is used.
- **I** This attribute enables indexing for the directory where it is enabled.
- **i** This attribute makes the file immutable. Therefore, no changes can be made to the file at all, which is useful for files that need a bit of extra protection.
- **s** This attribute overwrites the blocks where the file was stored with 0s after the file has been deleted. This makes sure that recovery of the file is not possible after it has been deleted.
- **u** This attribute saves undelete information. This allows a utility to be developed that works with that information to salvage deleted files.

NOTE Although quite a few attributes can be used, be aware that most attributes are rather experimental and are only of any use if an application is used that can work with the given attribute. For example, it does not make sense to apply the **u** attribute if no application has been developed that can use this attribute to recover deleted files.

If you want to apply attributes, you can use the **chattr** command. For example, use **chattr +s somefile** to apply the attributes to somefile. Need to remove the attribute again? Then use **chattr -s somefile** and it will be removed. You should try this to find out how attributes are one of the rare cases where you can even block access to the root user:

Step 1. Open a root shell.

Step 2. Create a file named **touch /root/myfile**

Step 3. Set the immutable permission to **chattr +i /root/myfile**

Step 4. Try to remove the file: **rm -f /root/myfile**. You can't!

Step 5. Remove the attribute again: **chattr -i /root/myfile**

To get an overview of all attributes that are currently applied, use the **lsattr** command.

Summary

In this chapter, you learned how to work with permissions. You read about the three basic permissions as well as the advanced permissions. You also learned how to use the **umask** setting to apply default permissions. Toward the end of this chapter, you learned how to use user-extended attributes to apply an additional level of file system security.

Exam Preparation Tasks

As mentioned in the section "How to Use This Book" in the Introduction, you have several choices for exam preparation: the end-of-chapter labs; the memory tables in Appendix C; Chapter 27, "Final Preparation"; and the practice exams.

Review All Key Topics

Review the most important topics in the chapter, noted with the Key Topic icon in the margin of the page. Table 7-6 lists a reference for these key topics and the page number on which each is found.

Table 7-6 Key Topics for Chapter 7

Key Topic Element	Description	Page
Table 7-2	Use of Read, Write, and Execute Permissions	152
Table 7-3	Numeric Representation of Permissions	153
Table 7-4	Working with SUID, SGID, and Sticky Bit	158
Table 7-5	**umask** Values and Their Result	159

Complete Tables and Lists from Memory

Print a copy of Appendix C, "Memory Tables" (found on the companion website), or at least the section for this chapter, and complete the tables and lists from memory. Appendix D, "Memory Tables Answer Key," includes completed tables and lists to check your work.

Define Key Terms

Define the following key terms from this chapter and check your answers in the glossary:

ownership, permissions, inheritance, attribute

Review Questions

The questions that follow use an open-ended format that is meant to help you test your knowledge of the concepts and terminology and the breadth of your knowledge. You can find the answers to these questions in Appendix A.

1. How do you use **chown** to set the group owner to a file?
2. Which command finds all files that are owned by a specific user?
3. How would you apply read, write, and execute permissions to all files in /data for the user and group owners while setting no permissions for others?
4. Which command enables you in relative permission mode to add the execute permission to a file that you want to make executable?
5. Which command enables you to ensure that group ownership of all new files that will be created in a directory is set to the group owner of that directory?
6. You want to ensure that users can only delete files of which they are the owner, or files that are in a directory of which they are the owner. Which command will do that for you?
7. Which **umask** do you need to set if you never want "others" to get any permissions on new files?
8. Which command ensures that nobody can delete myfile by accident?
9. How can you search for all files that have the SUID permission set?
10. Which command do you use to check if any attributes have been applied?

End-of-Chapter Lab

In Chapter 6, "User and Group Management," you created some users and groups. These users and groups are needed to perform the exercises in this lab.

Lab 7.1

1. Set up a shared group environment. If you haven't created these directories in a previous exercise yet, create two directories: /data/account and /data/sales. Make the group sales the owner of the directory sales, and make the group account the owner of the directory account.
2. Configure the permissions so that the user owner (which must be root) and group owner have full access to the directory. There should be no permissions assigned to the others entity.
3. Ensure that all new files in both directories inherit the group owner of their respective directory. This means that all files that will be created in /data/sales will be owned by the group sales, and all files in /data/account will be owned by the group account.
4. Ensure that users are only allowed to remove files of which they are the owner.

The following topics are covered in this chapter:

- Networking Fundamentals
- Managing Network Addresses and Interfaces
- Validating Network Configuration
- Managing Network Configuration with nmtui and nmcli
- Setting Up Hostname and Name Resolution

The following RHCSA exam objectives are covered in this chapter:

- Configure IPv4 and IPv6 addresses
- Configure hostname resolution

Configuring Networking

Networking is one of the most essential items on a modern server. On RHEL 9, networking is managed by the NetworkManager service. The old network service doesn't exist anymore, and that means that modern NetworkManager-related tools like **nmcli** and **nmtui** are the only way to manage network settings.

"Do I Know This Already?" Quiz

The "Do I Know This Already?" quiz enables you to assess whether you should read this entire chapter thoroughly or jump to the "Exam Preparation Tasks" section. If you are in doubt about your answers to these questions or your own assessment of your knowledge of the topics, read the entire chapter. Table 8-1 lists the major headings in this chapter and their corresponding "Do I Know This Already?" quiz questions. You can find the answers in Appendix A, "Answers to the 'Do I Know This Already?' Quizzes and Review Questions."

Table 8-1 "Do I Know This Already?" Section-to-Question Mapping

Foundation Topics Section	Questions
Networking Fundamentals	1–2
Managing Network Addresses and Interfaces	3
Validating Network Configuration	4
Managing Network Configuration with **nmtui** and **nmcli**	5–8
Setting Up Hostname and Name Resolution	9–10

1. Which of the following IP addresses belong to the same network?

   I. 192.168.4.17/26

   II. 192.168.4.94/26

   III. 192.168.4.97/26

   IV. 192.168.4.120/26

   a. I and II

   b. II and III

   c. III and IV

   d. II, III, and IV

2. Which of the following is *not* a private IP address?

   a. 10.10.10.10

   b. 169.254.11.23

   c. 172.19.18.17

   d. 192.168.192.192

3. Which of the following could be the network interface name on a RHEL 9 system?

   a. p6p1

   b. eth0

   c. eno1677783

   d. e0

4. Which command shows the recommended way to display information about the network interface as well as its IP configuration?

   a. **ifconfig -all**

   b. **ipconfig**

   c. **ip link show**

   d. **ip addr show**

5. Which statement about NetworkManager is *not* true?

   a. It is safe to disable NetworkManager and work with the network service instead.

   b. NetworkManager manages network connections that are applied to network interfaces.

   c. NetworkManager has a text-based user interface with the name **nmtui**

   d. NetworkManager is the default service to manage networking in RHEL 9.

6. Which man page contains excellent examples on **nmcli** usage?

   a. nmcli

   b. nmcli-examples

   c. nm-config

   d. nm-tools

7. Which of the following is the name of the text user interface to specify network connection properties?
   a. system-config-network
   b. system-config-networkmanager
   c. nmtui
   d. nmcli

8. Which of the following commands shows correct syntax to set a fixed IP address to a connection using **nmcli**?
   a. **nmcli con add con-name "static" ifname eth0 autoconnect no type ethernet ipv4 10.0.0.10/24 gw4 10.0.0.1**
   b. **nmcli con add con-name "static" ifname eth0 autoconnect no type ethernet ipv4 10.0.0.10/24 gwv4 10.0.0.1**
   c. **nmcli con add con-name "static" ifname eth0 type ethernet ipv4 10.0.0.10/24 gw4 10.0.0.1**
   d. **nmcli con add con-name "static" ifname eth0 autoconnect no type ethernet ip4 10.0.0.10/24 gw4 10.0.0.1**

9. Which of the following is *not* a recommended way to specify which DNS servers to use?
   a. Edit /etc/resolv.conf.
   b. Set the DNS options in /etc/sysconfig/network-scripts/ifcfg-<ID>.
   c. Set the DNS server names using **nmcli**.
   d. Use **nmtui** to set the DNS server names.

10. In which configuration file would you set the hostname?
    a. /etc/sysconfig/network
    b. /etc/sysconfig/hostname
    c. /etc/hostname
    d. /etc/defaults/hostname

Foundation Topics

Networking Fundamentals

To set up networking on a server, your server needs a unique address on the network. For this purpose, ***Internet Protocol (IP)*** addresses are used. Currently, two versions of IP addresses are relevant:

- ***IPv4* addresses:** These are based on 32-bit addresses and have four octets, separated by dots, such as 192.168.10.100.
- ***IPv6* addresses:** These are based on 128-bit addresses and are written in eight groups of hexadecimal numbers that are 16 bits each and separated by colons. An IPv6 address may look like fe80:badb:abe01:45bc:34ad:1313:6723:8798.

In this chapter, you learn how to work with IPv4 addresses. IPv6 addresses are described only briefly (but in enough detail to deal with it on the exam), as IPv4 is still the protocol used by most administrators.

IP Addresses

Originally, IP addresses were assigned to computers and routers. Nowadays, many other devices also need IP addresses to communicate, such as smartphones, industrial equipment, and almost all other devices that are connected to the Internet. This chapter refers to all of those devices by using the word *node*. You'll also occasionally encounter the word *host*. A host is typically a server providing services on the network.

To make it easier for computers to communicate with one another, every IP address belongs to a specific network, and to communicate with computers on another network, a router is used. A router is a machine (often dedicated hardware that has been created for that purpose) that connects networks to one another.

To communicate on the Internet, every computer needs a worldwide unique IP address. These addresses are scarce; a theoretical maximum of four billion IP addresses is available, and that is not enough to provide every device on the planet with an IP address. IPv6 is the ultimate solution for that problem, because a very large number of IP addresses can be created in IPv6. Because many networks still work with IPv4, though, another solution exists: private network addresses.

Private network addresses are addresses that are for use in internal networks only. Some specific IP network addresses have been reserved for this purpose:

- 10.0.0.0/8 (a single Class A network)

- 172.16.0.0/12 (16 Class B networks)
- 192.168.0.0/16 (256 Class C networks)

When private addresses are used, the nodes that are using them cannot access the Internet directly, and nodes from the Internet cannot easily access them. Because that is not very convenient, Network Address Translation (NAT) is commonly used on the router that connects the private network to the Internet. In NAT, the nodes use a private IP address, but when accessing the Internet, this private IP address is replaced with the IP address of the NAT router. Hence, nodes on the Internet think that they are communicating with the NAT router, and not with the individual hosts.

The NAT router in its turn uses tables to keep track of all connections that currently exist for the hosts in the network. Based on this table, the NAT router helps make it possible for computers with a private IP address to connect to hosts on the Internet anyway. The use of NAT is very common; it is embedded in most routers that are used in home and small business networks to connect computers and other devices in those networks to the Internet.

IPv6 Addresses

Let's look at a valid IPv6 address, such as 02fb:0000:0000:0000:90ff:fe23:8998:1234. In this address, you can see that a long range of zeros occurs. To make IPv6 addresses more readable, you can replace one range of zeros with :: instead. Also, if an IPv6 address starts with a leading zero, you can omit it. So the previously mentioned IPv6 address can be rewritten as 2fb::90ff:fe23:8998:1234.

IPv4 Network Masks

To know to which network a computer belongs, a subnet mask is used with every IP address. The ***subnet mask*** defines which part of the network address indicates the network and which part indicates the node. Subnet masks may be written in the Classless Inter-Domain Routing (CIDR) notation, which indicates the number of bits in the subnet mask, or in the classical notation, and they always need to be specified with the network address. Examples include 192.168.10.100/24 (CIDR notation), which indicates that a 24-bit network address is used, and 192.168.10.100/255.255.255.0 (classical notation), which indicates exactly the same.

Often, network masks use multiple bytes. In the example using 192.168.10.100/24, the first 3 bytes (the 192.168.10 part) form the network part, and the last byte (the number 100) is the host part on that network.

When talking about network addresses, you use a 4-byte number, as well, in which the node address is set to 0. So in the example of 192.168.10.100/24, the network address is 192.168.10.0. In IPv4 networks, there is also always a *broadcast address*. This is the address that can be used to address all nodes in the network. In the broadcast address, all node bits are set to 1, which makes for the decimal number 255 if an entire byte is referred to. So in the example of the address 192.168.10.100/24, the broadcast address is 192.168.10.255.

Binary Notation

Because the number of IPv4 addresses is limited, in modern IPv4 networks variable-length network masks are used. These are network masks such as 212.209.113.33/27. In a variable-length subnet mask, only a part of the byte is used for addressing nodes, and another part is used for addressing the network. In the subnet mask /27, the first 3 bits of the last byte are used to address the network, and the last 5 bits are used for addressing nodes. This becomes clearer if you write down the address in a binary notation:

IP address:

```
212.209.113.33 = 11010100.11010001.00001010.00100001
```

Subnet mask:

```
/27 = 11111111.11111111.11111111.11100000
```

When applying the subnet mask to the IP address, you can see that the first 3 bits of the IP address belong to the network, so the network is 00100000. And if you use a binary calculator, you can see that it corresponds with the decimal IP address 32. Using the /27 subnet mask allows for the creation of multiple networks. Table 8-2 gives an overview.

Table 8-2 Binary-Decimal Conversion Overview

Binary Value	Decimal Value
00000000	0
00100000	32
01000000	64
01100000	96
10000000	128
10100000	160
11000000	192
11100000	224

So, based on this information, if you consider the IP address 212.209.113.33/27 again, you can see that it belongs to the network 212.209.113.32/27, and that in this network the broadcast address (which has the node part of the IP address set to all 1s) is 212.209.113.63; therefore, with a /27 subnet mask, 30 nodes can be addressed per network. You'll get 32 IP addresses, but 2 of them are the network address and the broadcast address, which cannot be used as a host IP address.

EXAM TIP You do not need to make this kind of calculation on the RHCSA exam, but it helps in understanding how IP network addressing works.

MAC Addresses

IP addresses are the addresses that allow nodes to communicate to any other node on the Internet. They are not the only addresses in use though. Each network card also has a 12-byte MAC address. MAC addresses are for use on the local network (that is, the local physical network or local WLAN, just up to the first router that is encountered); they cannot be used for communications between nodes that are on different networks. MAC addresses are important, though, because they help computers find the specific network card that an IP address belongs to.

An example of a MAC address is 00:0c:29:7d:9b:17. Notice that each MAC address consists of two parts. The first 6 bytes is the vendor ID, and the second 6 bytes is the unique node ID. Vendor IDs are registered, and by using registered vendor IDs, it is possible to allocate unique MAC addresses.

Protocol and Ports

In the previous section you learned how to use IP addresses to identify individual nodes. On these nodes, you will typically be running services, like a web server or an FTP server. To identify these services, ***port*** addresses are used. Every service has a specific port address, such as port 80 for Hypertext Transfer Protocol (HTTP) or port 22 for a Secure Shell (SSH) server, and in network communication, the sender and the receiver are using port addresses. So, there is a destination port address as well as a source port address involved in network communications.

Because not all services are addressed in a similar way, a specific ***protocol*** is used between the IP address and the port address, such as Transfer Control Protocol (TCP), User Datagram Protocol (UDP), or Internet Control Message Protocol (ICMP). Every protocol has specific properties: TCP is typically used when the network communication must be reliable and delivery must be guaranteed; UDP is used when it must be fast and guaranteed delivery is not necessary.

Managing Network Addresses and Interfaces

As a Linux server administrator, you need to manage network addresses and network ***interfaces***. The network addresses can be assigned in two ways:

- **Fixed IP addresses:** Useful for servers and other computers that always need to be available at the same IP address.
- **Dynamically assigned IP addresses:** Useful for end users' devices, and for instances in a cloud environment. To dynamically assign IP addresses, you usually use a ***Dynamic Host Configuration Protocol (DHCP)*** server.

For a long time, network cards in Linux have had default names, such as eth0, eth1, and eth2. This naming is assigned based on the order of detection of the network card. So, eth0 is the first network card that is detected, eth1 the second, and so on. This works well in an environment where a node has one or two network cards only. If a node has multiple network cards that need to be dynamically added and removed, however, this approach does not work so well because it is very hard to identify which physical network card is using which name.

In RHEL 9, the default names for network cards are based on firmware, device topology, and device types. This leads to network card names that always consist of the following parts:

- Ethernet interfaces begin with *en*, WLAN interfaces begin with *wl*, and WWAN interfaces begin with *ww*.
- The next part of the name represents the type of adapter. An *o* is used for onboard, *s* is for a hotplug slot, and *p* is for a PCI location. Administrators can also use *x* to create a device name that is based on the MAC address of the network card.
- Then follows a number, which is used to represent an index, ID, or port.
- If the fixed name cannot be determined, traditional names such as eth0 are used.

Based on this information, device names such as eno16777734 can be used, which stands for an onboard Ethernet device, with its unique index number.

Apart from this default device naming, network cards can be named based on the BIOS device name as well. In this naming scheme, names such as em1 (embedded network card 1) or p4p1 (which is PCI slot 4, port 1) can be used.

Validating Network Configuration

Before you can learn how to set network information, you must know how to verify current network information. In this section, you learn how to do that, and you learn how to check the following networking items:

- IP address and subnet mask
- Routing
- Availability of ports and services

Validating Network Address Configuration

To verify the configuration of the network address, you need to use the **ip** utility. The **ip** utility is a modern utility that can consider advanced networking features that have been introduced in the past decades. With the **ip** utility, you can monitor many aspects of networking:

- Use **ip addr** to configure and monitor network addresses.
- Use **ip route** to configure and monitor routing information.
- Use **ip link** to configure and monitor network link state.

Apart from these items, the **ip** utility can manage many other aspects of networking, but you do not need to know about them for the RHCSA exam.

WARNING In earlier Linux versions and some other UNIX-like operating systems, the **ifconfig** utility was and is used for validating network configuration. Do not use this utility on modern Linux distributions. Because Linux has become an important player in cloud computing, networking has evolved a lot to match cloud computing requirements, and many new features have been added to Linux networking. With the **ifconfig** utility, you cannot manage or validate these concepts. Even if **ifconfig** is still the default tool on some operating systems (like macOS, for instance), you should never use it anymore on Linux!

To show current network settings, you can use the **ip addr show** command (which can be abbreviated as **ip a s** or even as **ip a**). The **ip** command is relatively smart and does not always require you to type the complete option.

The result of the **ip addr show** command looks like Example 8-1.

Example 8-1 Monitoring Current Network Configuration with **ip addr show**

```
[root@server1 ~]# ip addr show
1: lo: <LOOPBACK,UP,LOWER_UP> mtu 65536 qdisc noqueue state UNKNOWN
  group default qlen 1000
    link/loopback 00:00:00:00:00:00 brd 00:00:00:00:00:00
    inet 127.0.0.1/8 scope host lo
       valid_lft forever preferred_lft forever
    inet6 ::1/128 scope host
       valid_lft forever preferred_lft forever
2: ens33: <BROADCAST,MULTICAST,UP,LOWER_UP> mtu 1500 qdisc fq_codel
  state UP group default qlen 1000
    link/ether 00:0c:29:50:9e:c9 brd ff:ff:ff:ff:ff:ff
    inet 192.168.4.210/24 brd 192.168.4.255 scope global dynamic
      noprefixroute ens33
       valid_lft 1370sec preferred_lft 1370sec
    inet6 fe80::959:3b1a:9607:8928/64 scope link noprefixroute
       valid_lft forever preferred_lft forever
```

In the result of this command, you see a listing of all network interfaces in your computer. You'll normally see at least two interfaces, but on specific configurations, there can be many more interfaces. In Example 8-1, two interfaces are shown: the loopback interface lo and the onboard Ethernet card ens33.

The loopback interface is used for communication between processes. Some processes use the IP protocol for internal communications. For that reason, you'll always find a loopback interface, and the IP address of the loopback interface is always set to 127.0.0.1. The important part of the output of the command is for the onboard Ethernet card. The command shows the following items about its current status:

- **Current state:** The most important part of this line is the text state UP, which shows that this network card is currently up and available.
- **MAC address configuration:** This is the unique MAC address that is set for every network card. You can see the MAC address itself (00:0c:29:50:9e:c9), as well as the corresponding broadcast address.
- **IPv4 configuration:** This line shows the IP address that is currently set, as well as the subnet mask that is used. You can also see the broadcast address that is used for this network configuration. Notice that on some interfaces you may find multiple IPv4 addresses.

- **IPv6 configuration:** This line shows the current IPv6 address and its configuration. Even if you haven't configured anything, every interface automatically gets an IPv6 address, which can be used for communication on the local network only.

If you are just interested in the link state of the network interfaces, you can use the **ip link show** command. This command (of which you can see the output in Example 8-2) repeats the link state information of the **ip addr show** command. If you add the option **-s**, you can also see current link statistics, which gives information about packets transmitted and received, as well as an overview of errors that have occurred during packet transmission.

Example 8-2 ip link show Output

```
[root@server1 ~]# ip -s link show
1: lo: <LOOPBACK,UP,LOWER_UP> mtu 65536 qdisc noqueue state UNKNOWN
  mode DEFAULT group default qlen 1000
    link/loopback 00:00:00:00:00:00 brd 00:00:00:00:00:00
    RX: bytes  packets  errors   dropped overrun mcast
    0          0        0        0       0       0
    TX: bytes  packets  errors   dropped carrier collsns
    0          0        0        0       0       0
2: ens33: <BROADCAST,MULTICAST,UP,LOWER_UP> mtu 1500 qdisc fq_codel
   state UP mode DEFAULT group default qlen 1000
    link/ether 00:0c:29:50:9e:c9 brd ff:ff:ff:ff:ff:ff
    RX: bytes  packets  errors   dropped overrun  mcast
    143349     564      0        0       0        0
    TX: bytes  packets  errors   dropped carrier  collsns
    133129     541      0        0       0        0
```

In case the **ip link show** command shows the current link state as down, you can temporarily bring it up again by using **ip link set**, which is followed by **dev devicename** and **up** (for example, **ip link set dev ens33 up**).

In Exercise 8-1, you learn how to manage and monitor networking with the **ip** utility and other utilities.

Exercise 8-1 Validating Network Configuration

1. Open a root shell.
2. Type **ip -s link show**. This shows all existing network connections, in addition to statistics about the number of packets that have been sent and associated error messages.
3. Type **ip addr show**. You'll see the current address assignments for network interfaces on your server.

Validating Routing

One important aspect of networking is routing. On every network that needs to communicate to nodes on other networks, routing is a requirement. Every network has, at least, a default router (also called the default gateway) that is set, and you can see which router is used as the default router by using the command **ip route show** (see Example 8-3). You should always perform one quick check to verify that your router is set correctly: the default router at all times must be on the same network as the local IP address that your network card is using.

Example 8-3 ip route show Output

```
[root@server1 ~]# ip route show
default via 192.168.4.2 dev ens33 proto dhcp metric 100
192.168.4.0/24 dev ens33 proto kernel scope link src 192.168.4.210
  metric 100
192.168.122.0/24 dev virbr0 proto kernel scope link src 192.168.122.1
  linkdown
```

In Example 8-3, the most important part is the first line. It shows that the default route goes through ("via") IP address 192.168.4.2, and also shows that network interface ens33 must be used to address that IP address. The line shows that this default route was assigned by a DHCP server. The metric is used in case multiple routes are available to the same destination. In that case, the route with the lowest metric will be used. This is something important on router devices, but on computers that are not a router, the metric doesn't really matter.

Next you can see lines that identify the local connected networks. When you're booting, an entry is added for each local network as well, and in this example this applies to the networks 192.168.4.0 and 192.168.122.0. These routes are automatically generated and do not need to be managed.

Validating the Availability of Ports and Services

Network problems can be related to the local IP address and router settings but can also be related to network ports that are not available on your server or on a remote server. To verify availability of ports on your server, you can use the **netstat** command or the newer **ss** command, which provides the same functionality. Exercise 8-2 shows how to verify network settings. By typing **ss -lt**, you'll see all listening TCP ports on the local system (see Example 8-4).

Example 8-4 Using **ss -lt** to Display All Listening Ports on the Local System

```
[root@server1 ~]# ss -lt
State        Recv-Q       Send-Q       Local Address:Port         Peer
   Address:Port
LISTEN       0            32           192.168.122.1:domain       0.0.0.0:*
LISTEN       0            128          0.0.0.0:ssh                0.0.0.0:*
LISTEN       0            5            127.0.0.1:ipp              0.0.0.0:*
LISTEN       0            128          0.0.0.0:sunrpc             0.0.0.0:*
LISTEN       0            128          [::]:ssh                   [::]:*
LISTEN       0            5            [::1]:ipp                  [::]:*
LISTEN       0            128          [::]:sunrpc                [::]:*
```

Notice where the port is listening on. Some ports are only listening on the IPv4 loopback address 127.0.0.1 or the IPv6 loopback address ::1, which means that they are locally accessible only and cannot be reached from external machines. Other ports are listening on *, which stands for all IPv4 addresses, or on :::*, which represents all ports on all IPv6 addresses.

Exercise 8-2 Verifying Network Settings

1. Open a root shell to your server and type **ip addr show**. This shows the current network configuration. Note the IPv4 address that is used and the network device names that are used; you need these later in this exercise.
2. Type **ip route show** to verify routing configuration.

3. If your computer is connected to the Internet, you can now use the **ping** command to verify the connection to the Internet is working properly. Type **ping -c 4 8.8.8.8**, for instance, to send four packets to IP address 8.8.8.8. If your Internet connection is up and running, you should get "echo reply" answers.
4. Type **ip addr add 10.0.0.10/24 dev <yourdevicename>**. This will temporarily set a new IP address.
5. Type **ip addr show**. You'll see the newly set IP address, in addition to the IP address that was already in use.
6. Type **ifconfig**. Notice that you do not see the newly set IP address (and there are no options with the **ifconfig** command that allow you to see it). This is one example of why you should not use the **ifconfig** command anymore.
7. Type **ss -tul**. You'll now see a list of all UDP and TCP ports that are listening on your server.

Managing Network Configuration with nmtui and nmcli

As mentioned earlier in this chapter, networking on RHEL 9 is managed by the NetworkManager service. You can use the **systemctl status NetworkManager** command to verify its current status. When NetworkManager comes up, it reads the network card configuration scripts, which are in /etc/NetworkManager/system-connections and have a name that starts with the name of the network interface the configuration applies to, like ens160.nmconnection.

When working with network configuration in RHEL 9, you should know the difference between a device and a connection:

- A device is a network interface card.
- A ***connection*** is the configuration that is used on a device.

In RHEL 9, you can create multiple connections for a device. This makes sense on mobile computers, for example, to differentiate between settings that are used to connect to the home network and settings that are used to connect to the corporate network. Switching between connections on devices is common on end-user computers but not so common on servers. To manage the network connections that you want to assign to devices, you use the **nmtui** command or the **nmcli** command.

> **EXAM TIP** The **nmcli** tool is cool and very powerful, but it's not the easiest tool available. To change network configurations fast and efficiently, you should use the menu-driven **nmtui** utility. It may not be as cool as **nmcli**, but it allows you to do what you need to do in less than a minute, after which you can continue with the other tasks.

Required Permissions to Change Network Configuration

Obviously, the root user can make modifications to current networking. However, if an ordinary user is logged in to the local console, this user is able to make changes to the network configuration as well. As long as the user is using the system keyboard to enter either a graphical console or a text-based console, these permissions are granted. The reason is that users are supposed to be able to connect their local system to a network. Notice that regular users who have used **ssh** to connect to a server are not allowed to change the network configuration. To check your current permissions, use the **nmcli general permissions** command, as shown in Figure 8-1.

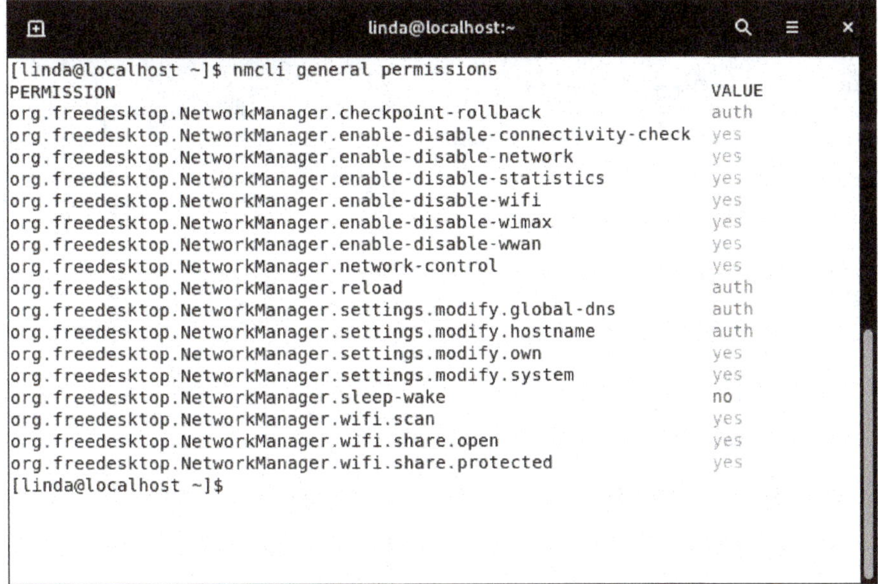

Figure 8-1 Verifying Current Permissions to Change Network Configuration

Configuring the Network with nmcli

Earlier in this chapter, you learned how to use **ip** to verify network configuration. You have also applied the **ip addr add** command to temporarily set an IP address on a network interface. Everything you do with the **ip** command, though, is nonpersistent. If you want to make your configuration persistent, use **nmtui** or **nmcli**.

A good start is to use **nmcli** to show all connections. This shows active *and* inactive connections. You can easily see the difference because inactive connections are not currently assigned to a device (see Example 8-5).

Example 8-5 Showing Current Connection Status

```
[root@server1 ~]# nmcli con show
NAME    UUID                                  TYPE      DEVICE
ens33   db6f53bd-654e-45dd-97ef-224514f8050a  ethernet  ens33
```

After finding the name of the connection, you can use **nmcli con show** followed by the name of the connection to see all properties of the connection. Notice that this command shows many properties. Example 8-6 shows the partial output of this command.

Example 8-6 Displaying Connection Properties

```
[root@server1 ~]# nmcli con show ens33
connection.id:                          ens33
connection.uuid:                        db6f53bd-654e-45dd-97ef-
                                          224514f8050a
connection.stable-id:                   --
connection.type:                        802-3-ethernet
connection.interface-name:              ens33
connection.autoconnect:                 yes
connection.autoconnect-priority:        0
connection.autoconnect-retries:         -1 (default)
connection.multi-connect:               0 (default)
...
DHCP4.OPTION[21]:                       requested_wpad = 1
DHCP4.OPTION[22]:                       routers = 192.168.4.2
DHCP4.OPTION[23]:                       subnet_mask = 255.255.255.0
IP6.ADDRESS[1]:                         fe80::959:3b1a:9607:8928/64
IP6.GATEWAY:                            --
IP6.ROUTE[1]:                           dst = fe80::/64, nh = ::,
                                          mt = 100
IP6.ROUTE[2]:                           dst = ff00::/8, nh = ::,
                                          mt = 256, table=255
```

To find out what exactly these settings are doing, execute **man 5 nm-settings**. You can also use **nmcli** to show an overview of currently configured devices and the status of these devices. Type, for instance, the **nmcli dev status** command to show a list of all devices, and **nmcli dev show <devicename>** to show settings for a specific device.

TIP Using **nmcli** might seem difficult. It's not, because it offers excellent command-line completion features—just make sure that the **bash-completion** package has been installed. Try it by typing **nmcli**, but don't press Enter! Instead, press the Tab key twice—you will see all available options that **nmcli** expects at this moment. Choose an option, such as **connection**, and press the Tab key twice. Using this approach helps you to compose long commands without the need to memorize anything!

In Exercise 8-3, you learn how to create connections and switch between connections using the **nmcli** command.

Exercise 8-3 Managing Network Connections with nmcli

In this exercise you create a new connection and manage its status. This connection needs to be connected to a network device. In this exercise the device ens33 is used. If necessary, change this to the name of the network device in use on your computer. Run this exercise from a console session, not using an SSH connection.

1. Create a new network connection by typing **nmcli con add con-name dhcp type ethernet ifname ens33 ipv4.method auto**.
2. Create a connection with the name *static* to define a static IP address and gateway: **nmcli con add con-name static ifname ens33 autoconnect no type ethernet ip4 10.0.0.10/24 gw4 10.0.0.1 ipv4.method manual**. The gateway might not exist in your configuration, but that does not matter.
3. Type **nmcli con show** to show the connections, and use **nmcli con up static** to activate the static connection. Switch back to the DHCP connection using **nmcli con up dhcp**.

In this exercise, you created network connections using **nmcli con add**. You can also change current connection properties by using **nmcli con mod**.

In Exercise 8-4, you learn how to change connection parameters with **nmcli**.

Exercise 8-4 Changing Connection Parameters with nmcli

1. Make sure that the static connection does not connect automatically by using **nmcli con mod static connection.autoconnect no**.
2. Add a DNS server to the static connection by using **nmcli con mod static ipv4.dns 10.0.0.10**. Notice that while adding a network connection, you use **ip4**, but while modifying parameters for an existing connection, you often use **ipv4** instead. This is not a typo; it is just how it works.
3. To add a second item for the same parameters, use a + sign. Test this by adding a second DNS server, using **nmcli con mod static +ipv4.dns 8.8.8.8**.
4. Using **nmcli con mod**, you can also change parameters such as the existing IP address. Try this by using **nmcli con mod static ipv4.addresses 10.0.0.100/24**.
5. And to add a second IP address, you use the + sign again: **nmcli con mod static +ipv4.addresses 10.20.30.40/16**.
6. After changing connection properties, you need to activate them. To do that, you can use **nmcli con up static**.

This is all you need to know about **nmcli** for the RHCSA exam. As you've noticed, **nmcli** is a very rich command. The exact syntax of this command may be hard to remember. Fortunately, though, there is an excellent man page with examples. Type **man nmcli-examples** to show this man page; you'll notice that if you can find this man page, you can do almost anything with **nmcli**. Also, don't forget to use Tab completion while working with **nmcli**.

Configuring the Network with nmtui

If you do not like the complicated syntax of the **nmcli** command line, you might like **nmtui**. This is a text user interface that allows you to create network connections easily. Figure 8-2 shows what the **nmtui** interface looks like.

The **nmtui** interface consists of three menu options:

- **Edit a Connection:** Use this option to create new connections or edit existing connections.
- **Activate a Connection:** Use this to (re)activate a connection.
- **Set System Hostname:** Use this to set the hostname of your computer.

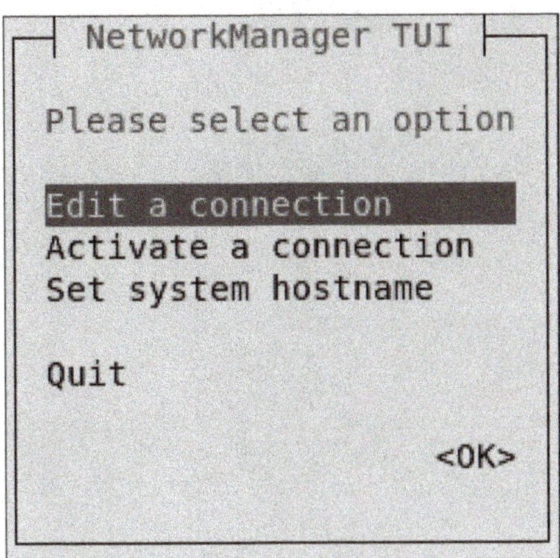

Figure 8-2 The **nmtui** Interface

The option to edit a connection offers almost all the features that you might ever need while working on network connections. It sure allows you to do anything you need to be doing on the RHCSA exam. You can use it to add any type of connection—not just Ethernet connections, but also advanced connection types such as network bridges and teamed network drivers are supported.

When you select the option Edit a Connection, you get access to a rich interface that allows you to edit most properties of network connections. After editing the connection, you need to deactivate it and activate it again.

TIP If you like graphical user interface (GUI) tools, you are lucky. Use nm-connection-editor instead of **nmtui**, but be prepared that this interface offers a relatively restricted option set. It does not contain advanced options such as the options to create network team interfaces and manage network bridge interfaces. It does, however, offer all you need to manage address configuration on a network connection. Start it by using the **nm-connection-editor** command or by using the applet in the GNOME graphical interface. Figure 8-3 shows what the default interface of this tool looks like.

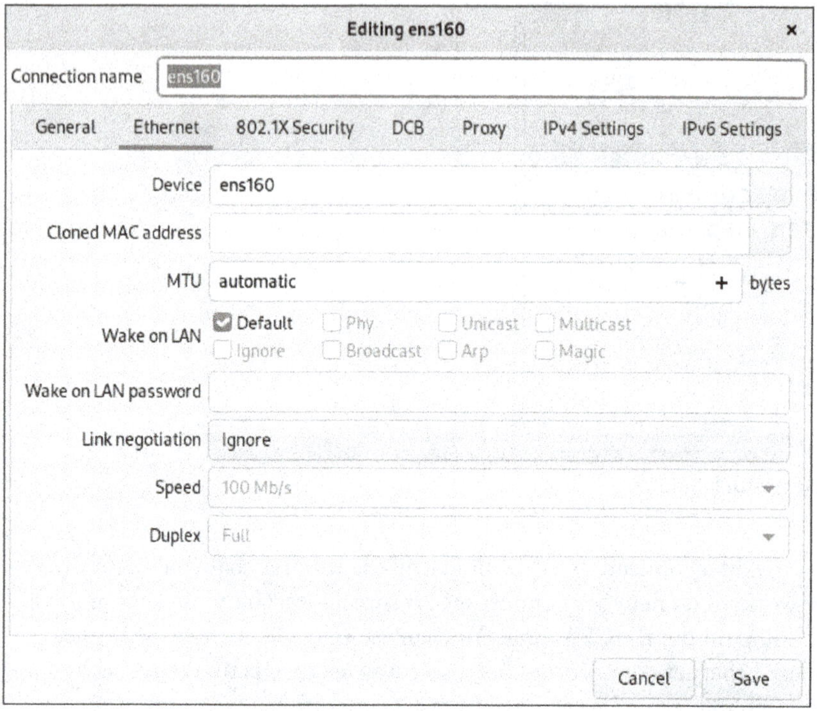

Figure 8-3 The nm-connection-editor Interface

Working on Network Configuration Files

Every connection that you create is stored as a configuration file in the directory /etc/NetworkManager/system-connections. The name of the configuration files starts with the name of the connection, followed by .nmconnection. In Example 8-7, you can see what such a configuration file looks like.

In previous versions of RHEL, network connections were stored in the /etc/sysconfig/network-scripts directory. If NetworkManager finds legacy connection scripts in this directory, they will still be used, but NetworkManager connection scripts are no longer stored by default at this location.

Example 8-7 Example of a NetworkManager Connection File

```
[root@server1 ~]# cat /etc/NetworkManager/system-connections/
  ens160.nmconnection
[connection]
id=ens160
uuid=5e4ddb28-2a00-3c27-9ba6-c773de3d7bcb
```

```
type=ethernet
autoconnect-priority=-999
interface-name=ens160
timestamp=1663070258

[ethernet]

[ipv4]
address1=192.168.29.5/24,192.168.29.2
dns=8.8.8.8;8.8.4.4;
method=manual

[ipv6]
addr-gen-mode=eui64
method=auto
```

Setting Up Hostname and Name Resolution

To communicate with other hosts, hostnames are used. As an administrator, you must know how to set the hostname. You also need to make sure that hosts can contact one another based on hostnames by setting up hostname resolution. In this section, you learn how to do that.

Hostnames

Because hostnames are used to access servers and the services they're offering, it is important to know how to set the system hostname. A hostname typically consists of different parts. These are the name of the host and the ***Domain Name System (DNS)*** domain in which the host resides. These two parts together make up the ***fully qualified domain name (FQDN)***, which looks like server1.example.com. It is good practice to always specify an FQDN, and not just the hostname, because the FQDN provides a unique identity on the Internet. There are different ways to change the hostname:

- Use **nmtui** and select the option **Change Hostname**.
- Use **hostnamectl set-hostname**.
- Edit the contents of the configuration file /etc/hostname.

To configure the hostname with **hostnamectl**, you can use a command like **hostnamectl set-hostname myhost.example.com**. After setting the hostname, you can use **hostnamectl status** to show the current hostname. Example 8-8 shows the output of this command.

Example 8-8 Showing Current Hostname Configuration

```
[root@server1 ~]# hostnamectl status
   Static hostname  : server1.example.com
         Icon name  : computer-vm
           Chassis  : vm
        Machine ID  : 5aa095b495ed458d934c54a88078c165
           Boot ID. : 5fdef4be9cab48c59873af505d778761
    Virtualization  : vmware
  Operating System  : Red Hat Enterprise Linux 9.0 (Ootpa)
       CPE OS Name  : cpe:/o:redhat:enterprise_linux:9.0:GA
            Kernel  : Linux 4.18.0-80.el9.x86_64
      Architecture  : x86-64
```

When using **hostnamectl status**, you see not only information about the hostname but also information about the Linux kernel, virtualization type, and much more.

Alternatively, you can set the hostname using the **nmtui** interface. Figure 8-4 shows the screen from which this can be done.

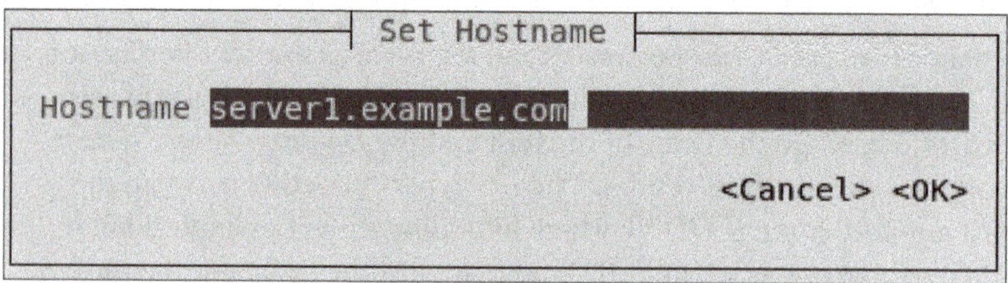

Figure 8-4 Changing the Hostname Using **nmtui**

To set hostname resolution, you typically use DNS. Configuring a DNS server is not an RHCSA objective, but you need to know how to configure your server to use an existing DNS server for hostname resolution. Apart from DNS, you can configure hostname resolution in the /etc/hosts file. Example 8-9 shows the contents of an /etc/hosts file as it generated by default after installation.

Example 8-9 /etc/hosts Sample Contents

```
[root@server1 ~]# cat /etc/hosts
127.0.0.1     localhost localhost.localdomain localhost4
  localhost4.  localdomain4
::1            localhost localhost.localdomain localhost6
  localhost6.  localdomain6
```

All hostname–IP address definitions as set in /etc/hosts will be applied before the hostname in DNS is used. This is configured as a default in the hosts line in /etc/nsswitch.conf, which by default looks like this:

```
hosts: files dns myhostname
```

Setting up an /etc/hosts file is easy; just make sure that it contains at least two columns. The first column has the IP address of the specific host, and the second column specifies the hostname. The hostname can be provided as a short name (like server1) or as an FQDN. In an FQDN, the hostname as well as the complete DNS name are included, as in server1.example.com.

If a host has more than one name, like a short name and a fully qualified DNS name, you can specify both of them in /etc/hosts. In that case, the second column must contain the FQDN, and the third column can contain the alias. Example 8-10 shows a hostname configuration example.

Example 8-10 /etc/hosts Configuration Example

```
[root@server2 ~]# cat /etc/hosts
127.0.0.1     localhost localhost.localdomain localhost4
  localhost4.  localdomain4
::1            localhost localhost.localdomain localhost6
  localhost6.  localdomain6
10.0.0.10      server1.example.com server1
10.0.0.20      server2.example.com server2
```

DNS Name Resolution

Just using an /etc/hosts file is not enough for name resolution if you want to be able to communicate with other hosts on the Internet. You should use DNS, too. To specify which DNS server should be used, set the DNS server using **nmcli** or **nmtui** as previously discussed. The NetworkManager configuration stores the DNS information in the configuration file for the network connection, which is in /etc/sysconfig/network-scripts, and from there pushes the configuration to the /etc/resolv.conf file, which is used for DNS name server resolving. Do not edit /etc/resolv.conf directly, as it will be overwritten the next time you restart NetworkManager.

It is recommended to always set up at least two DNS name servers to be contacted. If the first name server does not answer, the second name server is contacted. To specify which DNS name servers you want to use, you have a few different options:

- Use **nmtui** to set the DNS name servers. Figure 8-5 shows the interface from which you can do this.
- Use a DHCP server that is configured to hand out the address of the DNS name server.
- Use **nmcli con mod <connection-id> [+]ipv4.dns <ip-of-dns>**.

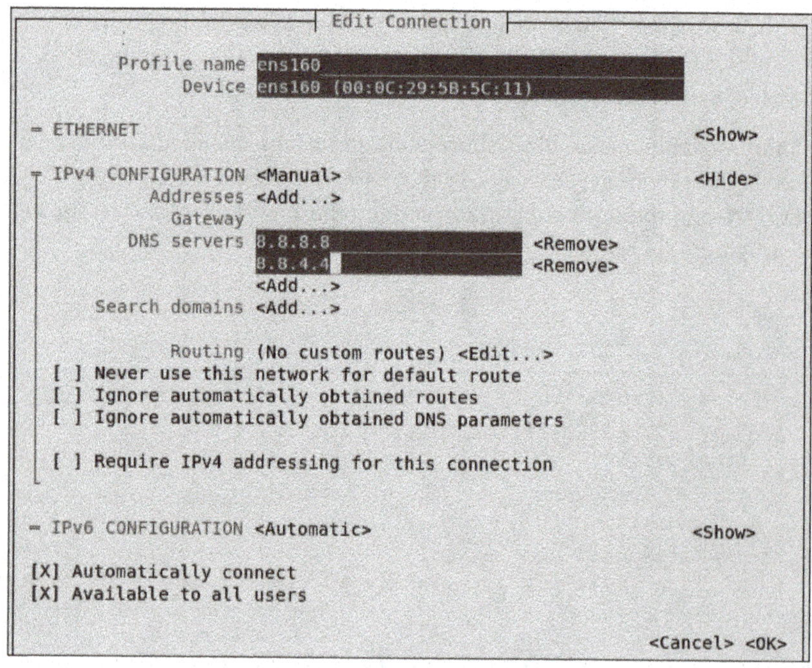

Figure 8-5 Setting DNS Servers from the **nmtui** Interface

Notice that if your computer is configured to get the network configuration from a DHCP server, the DNS server is also set via the DHCP server. If you do not want this to happen, use the following command: **nmcli con mod <con-name> ipv4.ignore-auto-dns yes**.

To verify hostname resolution, you can use the **getent hosts <servername>** command. This command searches in both /etc/hosts and DNS to resolve the hostname that has been specified.

EXAM TIP Do *not* specify the DNS servers directly in /etc/resolv.conf. They will be overwritten by NetworkManager when it is (re)started.

Summary

In this chapter, you learned how to configure networking in RHEL 9. First you read how the IP protocol is used to connect computers, and then you read which techniques are used to make services between hosts accessible. Next you read how to verify the network configuration using the **ip** utility and some related utilities. In the last part of this chapter, you read how to set IP addresses and other host configurations in a permanent way by using either the **nmcli** or the **nmtui** utility.

Exam Preparation Tasks

As mentioned in the section "How to Use This Book" in the Introduction, you have several choices for exam preparation: the end-of-chapter labs; the memory tables in Appendix C; Chapter 27, "Final Preparation"; and the practice exams.

Review All Key Topics

Review the most important topics in the chapter, noted with the Key Topic icon in the margin of the page. Table 8-3 lists a reference for these key topics and the page number on which each is found.

Table 8-3 Key Topics for Chapter 8

Key Topic Element	Description	Page
List	IPv4 and IPv6 short descriptions	170
List	Private network addresses	170
Table 8-2	Binary-Decimal Conversion Overview	172
List	IP address types	174

Complete Tables and Lists from Memory

Print a copy of Appendix C, "Memory Tables" (found on the companion website), or at least the section for this chapter, and complete the tables and lists from memory. Appendix D, "Memory Tables Answer Key," includes completed tables and lists to check your work.

Define Key Terms

Define the following key terms from this chapter and check your answers in the glossary:

Internet Protocol (IP), IPv4, IPv6, subnet mask, port, protocol, interface, Dynamic Host Configuration Protocol (DHCP), connection, Domain Name System (DNS), fully qualified domain name (FQDN)

Review Questions

The questions that follow are meant to help you test your knowledge of concepts and terminology and the breadth of your knowledge. You can find the answers to these questions in Appendix A.

1. What is the network address in the address 213.214.215.99/29?
2. Which command only shows link status and not the IP address?
3. You have manually edited the /etc/resolv.conf file to include DNS servers. After a restart your modifications have disappeared. What is happening?
4. Which file contains the hostname in RHEL 9?
5. Which command enables you to set the hostname in an easy way?
6. Where does NetworkManager store the configuration that it generates?
7. Which configuration file can you change to enable hostname resolution for a specific IP address?
8. Is a non-administrator user allowed to change NetworkManager connections?
9. How do you verify the current status of the NetworkManager service?
10. Which command enables you to change the current IP address and default gateway on your network connection?

End-of-Chapter Lab

For exercises in later chapters in this book, it is recommended to have a test environment in which at least two servers are present. To do the exercises in this lab, make sure that you have a second server installed.

Lab 8.1

1. If you didn't do so earlier, set up the first server to use the FQDN **server1.example.com**. Set up the second server to use **server2.example.com**.
2. On server1.example.com, use **nmtui** and configure your primary network card to automatically get an IP address through DHCP. Also set a fixed IP address to **192.168.4.210**. On server2, set the fixed IP address to **192.168.4.220**.
3. Make sure that from server1 you can ping server2, and vice versa.
4. To allow you to access servers on the Internet, make sure that your local DHCP server provides the default router and DNS servers.

The following topics are covered in this chapter:

- Managing Software Packages with **dnf**
- Using **dnf**
- Managing Package Modules
- Managing Software Packages with **rpm**

The following RHCSA exam objective is covered in this chapter:

- Install and update software packages from Red Hat Network, a remote repository, or from the local file system

CHAPTER 9

Managing Software

Managing software packages is an important task for an administrator of Red Hat Enterprise Linux. In this chapter, you learn how to manage software packages from the command line by using the **dnf** utility. You also learn which role repositories play in software management with **dnf**. Next, we cover working with Package Modules, a solution that makes it possible to work with the specific version packages that you need in your environment. In the last part of this chapter, you learn how to manage software with the **rpm** command, which is useful to query new and installed software packages.

"Do I Know This Already?" Quiz

The "Do I Know This Already?" quiz enables you to assess whether you should read this entire chapter thoroughly or jump to the "Exam Preparation Tasks" section. If you are in doubt about your answers to these questions or your own assessment of your knowledge of the topics, read the entire chapter. Table 9-1 lists the major headings in this chapter and their corresponding "Do I Know This Already?" quiz questions. You can find the answers in Appendix A, "Answers to the 'Do I Know This Already?' Quizzes and Review Questions."

Table 9-1 "Do I Know This Already?" Section-to-Question Mapping

Foundation Topics Section	Questions
Managing Software Packages with **dnf**	1–4
Using **dnf**	5
Managing Package Modules	6–7
Managing Software Packages with **rpm**	8–10

1. Which of the following is *not* a mandatory component in a .repo file that is used to indicate which repositories should be used?
   a. [label]
   b. name=
   c. baseurl=
   d. gpgcheck=

2. Which installation source is used on RHEL if a server is not registered with Red Hat?
   a. The installation medium is used.
   b. No installation source is used.
   c. The base Red Hat repository is used, without updates.
   d. You have full access to Red Hat repositories, but the software you are using is not supported.

3. Which of the following should be used in the .repo file to refer to a repository that is in the directory /repo on the local file system?
   a. file=/repo
   b. baseurl=file://repo
   c. baseurl=file:///repo
   d. file=http:///repo

4. Which of the following is true about GPG-based repository security?
   a. If packages in the repository have been signed, you need to import the GPG key while installing packages from the repository for the first time.
   b. GPG package signing is mandatory.
   c. GPG package signatures prevent packages in a repository from being changed.
   d. GPG package signing is recommended on Internet repositories but not required on local repositories that are for internal use only.

5. Which command enables you to search the package that contains the file semanage?
   a. **dnf search seinfo**
   b. **dnf search all seinfo**
   c. **dnf provides seinfo**
   d. **dnf whatprovides */seinfo**

6. Which **dnf** module component allows you to work with different versions side by side?
   a. Application profile
   b. Application stream
   c. Module version
   d. RPM group

7. Which of the following commands allows you to install the devel profile of the PHP 8.1 application stream?
   a. **dnf module install php:8.1 devel**
   b. **dnf module install php:8.1 --devel**
   c. **dnf module install php:8.1/devel**
   d. **dnf module install php:8.1@devel**

8. Which command should you use to install an RPM file that has been downloaded to your computer?
   a. **dnf install**
   b. **dnf localinstall**
   c. **rpm -ivh**
   d. **rpm -Uvh**

9. Which command enables you to find the RPM package a specific file belongs to?
   a. **rpm -ql /my/file**
   b. **rpm -qlf /my/file**
   c. **rpm -qf /my/file**
   d. **rom -qa /my/file**

10. Which command enables you to analyze whether there are scripts in an RPM package file that you have just downloaded?
   a. **rpm -qs packagename.rpm**
   b. **rpm -qps packagename.rpm**
   c. **rpm -qp --scripts packagename.rpm**
   d. **rpm -q --scripts packagename.rpm**

Foundation Topics

Managing Software Packages with dnf

The default utility used to manage software ***packages*** on Red Hat Enterprise Linux is **dnf**. ***dnf*** is designed to work with repositories, which are online depots of available software packages. In this section, you learn how to create and manage repositories and how to manage software packages based on the contents of the repositories.

Understanding the Role of Repositories

Software on Red Hat Enterprise Linux is provided in the ***Red Hat Package Manager (RPM)*** format. This is a specific format used to archive the package and provide package metadata as well.

When you are working with software in RHEL, ***repositories*** play a key role. Working with repositories makes it easy to keep your server current: The maintainer of the repository publishes updated packages in the repository, and the result is that whenever you use the **dnf** command to install software, the most recent version of the software is automatically used.

Another major benefit of working with **dnf** is the way that package dependencies are dealt with. On Linux (as on most other modern operating systems), software packages have dependencies. This means that to be able to use one package, other packages may have to be present as well. Without using repositories, that would mean that these packages have to be installed manually.

The repository system takes care of resolving dependencies automatically. If a package is going to be installed, it contains information about the required dependencies. The **dnf** command then looks in the repositories configured on this system to fetch the dependencies automatically. If all goes well, the installer just sees a short list of the dependencies that will be installed as a ***dependency*** to install the package. If you are using RHEL with the repositories that are provided for registered installations of RHEL, there is no reason why this procedure should not work, and the attempts to install software will usually succeed.

While installing RHEL 9, it asks you to register with the Red Hat Customer Portal, which provides different repositories. After registering, you can install software packages that are verified by Red Hat automatically. If you choose to install RHEL without registration, it cannot get in touch with the Red Hat repositories, and you end up with no repositories at all. In that case, you have to be able to configure a repository client to specify yourself which repository you want to use.

Note that repositories are specific to an operating system. Therefore, if you are using RHEL, you should use RHEL repositories only. Do not try, for instance, to add CentOS repositories to a RHEL server. If you want to provide additional software from the Fedora project to a RHEL server (which for support reasons is not recommended), you can consider adding the EPEL (Extra Packages for Enterprise Linux) repositories. See https://fedoraproject.org/wiki/EPEL for more information, including information on how to configure your system to use EPEL repositories.

WARNING Before adding the EPEL repository to RHEL, make sure that it doesn't break your current support status. EPEL packages are not managed by Red Hat, and adding them may break supported Red Hat packages.

Registering Red Hat Enterprise Linux for Support

Red Hat Enterprise Linux is a supported Linux operating system that requires you to register. To register RHEL, you need a valid entitlement. This entitlement is associated to your account on the Red Hat Customer Portal. You can obtain an entitlement by purchasing a subscription for RHEL or by joining the Red Hat Developer program, which gives access to the no-cost Red Hat Enterprise Developer subscription. With a developer subscription you are allowed to install a maximum of 16 RHEL systems. You won't get any support on these systems, but you will be able to access the Red Hat repositories and receive updates. You can sign up for the Red Hat Developer subscription at https://developers.redhat.com.

After obtaining a valid subscription for Red Hat Enterprise Linux, you can use the Red Hat Subscription Management (RHSM) tools to manage your entitlement. Managing an entitlement involves four basic tasks:

- **Register:** While registering a subscription, you connect it to your current Red Hat account. As a result, the **subscription-manager** tool can inventory the system. If a system is no longer used, it can also be unregistered.
- **Subscribe:** Subscribing a system gives it access to updates for Red Hat products that your subscription is entitled to. Also, by subscribing, you'll get access to the support level that is associated with your account.
- **Enable repositories:** After subscribing a system, you'll get access to a default set of repositories. Some repositories by default are disabled but can be enabled after subscribing your system.
- **Review and track:** You can review and track current subscriptions that are in use.

Managing Subscriptions

You can manage subscriptions either from the GNOME graphical interface or from the command line. The **subscription-manager** tool is used for managing subscriptions from the command line. You can use it in the following ways:

- **Register a system:** Type **subscription-manager register** to register. It will prompt for the name of your Red Hat user account as well as your password, and after you enter these, your RHEL server will be registered.
- **List available subscriptions:** Each account has access to specific subscriptions. Type **subscription-manager list --available** to see what your account is entitled to.
- **Automatically attach a subscription:** Registering a server is not enough to get access to the repositories. Use **subscription-manager attach --auto** to automatically attach your subscription to the repositories that are available.
- **Get an overview:** To see which subscriptions you're currently using, type **subscription-manager list --consumed**.
- **Unregister:** If you're going to deprovision a system, use **subscription-manager unregister**. If you have access to a limited number of registered systems only, unregistering is important to ensure that you don't run out of available licenses.

After you register and attach a subscription, entitlement certificates are written to the /etc/pki directory. In /etc/pki/product, stored certificates indicate which Red Hat products are installed on this system. In /etc/pki/consumer, stored certificates identify the Red Hat account to which the system is registered, and the /etc/pki/entitlement directory contains information about the subscriptions that are attached to this system.

Specifying Which Repository to Use

On most occasions, after the installation of your server has finished, it is configured with a list of repositories that should be used. You sometimes have to tell your server which repositories should be; for example, if:

- You want to distribute nondefault software packages through repositories.
- You are installing Red Hat Enterprise Linux without registering it.

Telling your server which repository to use is not difficult, but it is important that you know how to do it (for the RHCSA exam, too).

IMPORTANT! To learn how to work with repositories and software packages, do *not* use the repositories that are provided by default. So if you have installed RHEL, do *not* register using **subscription-manager**, and if you have installed CentOS, remove all files from /etc/yum.repos.d. If you overlooked this requirement while installing earlier, you can use **subscription-manager unregister** to remove all registration.

To tell your server which repository to use, you need to create a file with a name that ends in .repo in the directory /etc/yum.repos.d. The following parameters are commonly used:

- **[label]** The .repo file can contain different repositories, each section starting with a label that identifies the specific repository.
- **name=** Use this to specify the name of the repository you want to use.
- **baseurl=** This option contains the URL that points to the specific repository location.
- **gpgcheck=** Use this option to specify if a GNU Privacy Guard (GPG) key validity check should be used to verify that packages have not been tampered with.

In older versions of RHEL you needed to memorize how to create a repository client file. In RHEL 9, the **dnf config-manager** tool is available, even in a minimal installation, to create the repository client file for you. To easily generate the repository client file, use **dnf config-manager --add-repo=http://reposerver.example.com/BaseOS**. Just make sure to replace the URL in this example with the correct URI that points to the location of the repository that you want to use. If for instance you have copied the contents of the RHEL 9 installation disk to the /repo directory, you would be using a file:// URI. In that case, the following command would add the BaseOS repository: **dnf config-manager --add-repo=file:///repo/BaseOS**.

If you're using the **dnf config-manager** tool to add repositories, you need to edit the repository file in /etc/yum.conf.d after adding it, so that it includes the line **gpgcheck=0**. Without that option the **dnf** tool wants to do a GPG check on incoming packages, which requires additional complex configuration that is not needed on the RHCSA exam. In Example 9-1 you can see what the resulting repository file would look like. In Exercise 9-1 you will find all the instructions that are needed to set up your own repository and configure access to it.

Example 9-1 Repository File Example

```
[root@server1 ~]# cat /etc/yum.repos.d/repo_BaseOS.repo
[repo_BaseOS]
name=created by dnf config-manager from file:///repo/BaseOS
baseurl=file:///repo/BaseOS
enabled=1
gpgcheck=0
```

In the repository configuration files, several options can be used. Table 9-2 summarizes some of the most common options.

Table 9-2 Key Options in .repo Files

Option	Explanation
[label]	Contains the label used as an identifier in the repository file.
name=	Mandatory option that specifies the name of the repository.
mirrorlist=	Optional parameter that refers to a URL where information about mirror servers for this server can be obtained. Typically used for big online repositories only.
baseurl=	Mandatory option that refers to the base URL where the RPM packages are found.
gpgcheck=	Set to 1 if a GNU Privacy Guard (GPG) integrity check needs to be performed on the packages. If set to 1, a GPG key is required.
gpgkey=	Specifies the location of the GPG key that is used to check package integrity.

When you're creating a repository file, the baseurl parameter is the most important because it tells your server where to find the files that are to be installed. The baseurl takes as its argument the URL where files need to be installed from. This will often be an HTTP or FTP URL, but it can be a file-based URL as well.

When you use a URL, two components are included. First, the URL identifies the protocol to be used and is in the format protocol://, such as http://, ftp://, or file://. Following the URL is the exact location on that URL. That can be the name of a web server or an FTP server, including the subdirectory where the files are found. If the URL is file based, the location on the file system starts with a / as well.

Therefore, for a file system-based URL, there will be three slashes in the baseurl, such as baseurl:///repo, which refers to the directory /repo on the local file system.

Understanding Repository Security

Using repositories allows you to transparently install software packages from the Internet. This capability is convenient, but it also involves a security risk. When installing RPM packages, you do that with root permissions, and if in the RPM package script code is executed (which is common), it is executed as root as well. For that reason, you need to make sure that you can trust the software packages you are trying to install. This is why repositories in general use keys for package signing. This is also why on Red Hat Enterprise Linux it is a good idea to use trusted repositories only.

To secure packages in a repository, these packages are often signed with a GPG key. This makes it possible to check whether packages have been changed since the owner of the repository provided them. The GPG key used to sign the software packages is typically made available through the repository as well. The users of the repository can download that key and store it locally so that the package signature check can be performed automatically each time a package is downloaded from the repository.

If repository security is compromised and an intruder manages to hack the repository server and put some fake packages on it, the GPG key signature will not match, and the **dnf** command will complain while installing new packages. This is why it is highly recommended to use GPG keys when using Internet repositories.

If you are using a repository where GPG package signing has been used, on first contact with that repository, the **dnf** command will propose to download the key that was used for package signing (see Example 9-2). This is a transparent procedure that requires no further action. The GPG keys that were used for package signing are installed to the /etc/pki/rpm-gpg directory by default.

TIP For using internal repositories, the security risks are not that high. For that reason, you do not have to know how to work with GPG-signed packages on the RHCSA exam.

Example 9-2 On First Contact with a Repository, the GPG Key Is Downloaded

```
[
[root@localhost ~]# dnf install nmap
Updating Subscription Management repositories.
Red Hat Enterprise Linux 9 for x86_64 - AppStream (RPMs)
10 MB/s | 9.3 MB     00:00
Red Hat Enterprise Linux 9 for x86_64 - BaseOS (RPMs)
4.0 MB/s | 3.6 MB     00:00
```

```
Dependencies resolved.
 Package                    Architecture                       Version
Repository                                                     Size
================================================================================
Installing:
 nmap                            x86_64                    3:7.91-10.el9
rhel-9-for-x86_64-appstream-rpms                           5.6 M

Transaction Summary
================================================================================
Install  1 Package
Total download size: 5.6 M
Installed size: 24 M
Is this ok [y/N]: y
Downloading Packages:
nmap-7.91-10.el9.x86_64.rpm
9.8 MB/s | 5.6 MB     00:00
Total
9.8 MB/s | 5.6 MB     00:00
================================================================================
Red Hat Enterprise Linux 9 for x86_64 - AppStream (RPMs)
3.5 MB/s | 3.6 kB     00:00
Importing GPG key 0xFD431D51:
 Userid     : "Red Hat, Inc. (release key 2) <security@redhat.com>"
 Fingerprint: 567E 347A D004 4ADE 55BA 8A5F 199E 2F91 FD43 1D51
 From       : /etc/pki/rpm-gpg/RPM-GPG-KEY-redhat-release
Is this ok [y/N]:
```

Creating Your Own Repository

Creating your own repository is not a requirement for the RHCSA exam, but knowing how to do so is useful if you want to test setting up and working with repositories. Also, if you're using a RHEL system that is not connected to the Red Hat repositories, it's the only way you can install packages.

The procedure itself is not hard to summarize. You need to make sure all RPM packages are available in the directory that you want to use as a repository, and after doing that, you need to use the **createrepo** command to generate the metadata that enables you to use that directory as a repository. If you're using the RHEL 9 installation disk, the procedure is even easier, as you don't have to generate the repository metadata. Exercise 9-1 describes how to create your own repository using the RHEL 9 installation disk.

Exercise 9-1 Creating Your Own Repository

To perform this exercise, you need to have access to the RHEL or CentOS installation disk or ISO file.

1. Insert the installation disk in your virtual machine and make sure it is attached and available.
2. Open a root shell and type **mkdir /repo** so that you have a mount point where you can mount the ISO file.
3. Add the following line to the end of the /etc/fstab configuration file: **/dev/sr0 /repo iso9660 defaults 0 0**
4. Type **mount -a**, followed by **mount | grep sr0**. You should now see that the optical device is mounted on the directory /repo. At this point, the directory /repo can be used as a repository.
5. Now, two subdirectories are available through the /repo directory. The BaseOS repository provides access to the base packages, and the ***Application Stream (AppStream)*** repository provides access to application streams (these repositories are described in more detail in the "Managing Package Module Streams" section later in this chapter). To make them accessible, you need to add two files to the /etc/yum.repos.d directory. Start with the file BaseOS.repo. You can generate this file using **dnf config-manager --add-repo=file:///repo/BaseOS**
6. Add the file /etc/yum.repos.d/AppStream.repo using the following command: **dnf config-manager --add-repo=file:///repo/AppStream**
7. Type **ls /etc/yum.repos.d/**. This will show you two new files: repo_BaseOS.repo and repo_AppStream.repo. Add the following line to the end of both files: **gpgcheck=0**
8. Type **dnf repolist** to verify the availability of the newly created repository. It should show the name of both repositories, including the number of packages offered through this repository (see Example 9-3). Notice that if you're doing this on RHEL, you'll also see a message that this system is not registered with an entitlement server. You can safely ignore that message.

Example 9-3 Verifying Repository Availability with **dnf repolist**

```
[root@server1 ~]# dnf repolist
Updating Subscription Management repositories.
Unable to read consumer identity
```

```
This system is not registered with an entitlement server. You can use
  subscription-manager to register.
repo id                                              repo name
repo_AppStream                                       created by dnf
  config-manager from file:///repo/AppStream
repo_BaseOS                                          created by dnf
  config-manager from file:///repo/BaseOS
```

Using dnf

At this point, you should have operational repositories, so it is time to start using them. To use repositories, you need the **dnf** command. This command enables you to perform several tasks on the repositories. Table 9-3 provides an overview of common **dnf** tasks.

Table 9-3 Common **dnf** Tasks

Task	Explanation
search	Search packages for a string that occurs in the package name or summary.
search all	Search packages for a string that occurs in the package name, summary, or description.
[**what**]**provides */name**	Perform a deep search in the package to look for specific files within the package.
info	Provide more information about the package.
install	Install the package.
remove	Remove the package.
list [**all** | **installed**]	List all or installed packages.
group list	List package groups.
group install	Install all packages from a group.
update	Update packages specified.
clean all	Remove all stored metadata.

Using dnf to Find Software Packages

To install packages with **dnf**, you first need to know the name of the package. The **dnf search** command can help you with that. When you use **dnf search**, it first gets in touch with the online repositories (which might take a minute), after which it downloads the most recent repository metadata to the local machine. Then, **dnf search** looks in the package name and description for the string you have been looking for. If this doesn't give the expected result, try using **dnf search all**, which performs a deeper search in the package description as well. In Example 9-4, you can see what the result looks like after using **dnf search user**.

Example 9-4 dnf search Sample Output

```
[root@server1 ~]# dnf search user
Updating Subscription Management repositories.
Unable to read consumer identity

This system is not registered with an entitlement server. You can use
  subscription-manager to register.

Last metadata expiration check: 0:01:45 ago on Wed 14 Sep 2022
  10:52:12 AM CEST.
=========================================================== Name & Summary
  Matched: user ===========================================================
gnome-user-docs.noarch : GNOME User Documentation
libuser.x86_64 : A user and group account administration library
libuser.i686 : A user and group account administration library
perl-User-pwent.noarch : By-name interface to Perl built-in user name
  resolver
usermode.x86_64 : Tools for certain user account management tasks
usermode-gtk.x86_64 : Graphical tools for certain user account
  management tasks
userspace-rcu.x86_64 : RCU (read-copy-update) implementation in
  user-space
userspace-rcu.i686 : RCU (read-copy-update) implementation in
  user-space
util-linux-user.x86_64 : libuser based util-linux utilities
xdg-user-dirs.x86_64 : Handles user special directories
=================================================================== Name
  Matched: user ===========================================================
anaconda-user-help.noarch : Content for the Anaconda built-in help
  system
gnome-shell-extension-user-theme.noarch : Support for custom themes in
  GNOME Shell
xdg-user-dirs-gtk.x86_64 : Gnome integration of special directories
================================================================ Summary
  Matched: user ===========================================================
NetworkManager.x86_64 : Network connection manager and user
  applications
PackageKit-command-not-found.x86_64 : Ask the user to install command
  line programs automatically
accountsservice.x86_64 : D-Bus interfaces for querying and
  manipulating user account information
anaconda-gui.x86_64 : Graphical user interface for the Anaconda
  installer...
```

Because the **dnf search** command looks in the package name and summary only, it often does not show what you need. In some cases you might need to find a package that contains a specific file. To do this, the **dnf whatprovides** command or **dnf provides** command will help you. (There is no functional difference between these two commands, and there's even a third option that does exactly the same: **dnf wp**.) To make it clear that you are looking for packages containing a specific file, you need to specify the filename as */filename, or use the full pathname to the file you want to use. So if you need to look for the package containing the file Containerfile, for example, use **dnf whatprovides */Containerfile**. It will show the name of the package as a result.

Getting More Information About Packages

Before you install a package, it is a good idea to get some more information about the package. Because the **dnf** command was developed to be intuitive, it is almost possible to guess how that works. Just use **dnf info**, followed by the name of the package. In Example 9-5, you see what this looks like for the nmap package (which, by the way, is a very useful tool). It is a network sniffer that allows you to find ports that are open on other hosts. Just use **nmap 192.168.4.100** to give it a try, but be aware that some network administrators really do not like nmap and might consider this a hostile attack.

Example 9-5 Sample Output of **dnf info nmap**

```
[root@server1 ~]# dnf info nmap
Updating Subscription Management repositories.
Unable to read consumer identity
This system is not registered with an entitlement server. You can use
subscription-manager to register.
Last metadata expiration check: 0:04:47 ago on Wed 14 Sep 2022
10:52:12 AM CEST.
Available Packages
Name         : nmap
Epoch        : 3
Version      : 7.91
Release      : 10.el9
Architecture : x86_64
Size         : 5.6 M
Source       : nmap-7.91-10.el9.src.rpm
Repository   : repo_AppStream
```

```
Summary         : Network exploration tool and security scanner
URL             : http://nmap.org/
License         : Nmap
Description     : Nmap is a utility for network exploration or security
  auditing.  It supports
                : ping scanning (determine which hosts are up), many
  port scanning techniques
                : (determine what services the hosts are offering), and
  TCP/IP fingerprinting
                : (remote host operating system identification). Nmap
  also offers flexible target
                : and port specification, decoy scanning, determination
  of TCP sequence
                : predictability characteristics, reverse-identd
  scanning, and more. In addition
                : to the classic command-line nmap executable, the Nmap
  suite includes a flexible
                : data transfer, redirection, and debugging tool (netcat
  utility ncat), a utility
                : for comparing scan results (ndiff), and a packet
  generation and response
                : analysis tool (nping).
```

Installing and Removing Software Packages

If after looking at the **dnf info** output you are happy with the package, the next step is to install it. As with anything else you are doing with **dnf**, it is not hard to guess how to do that: use **dnf install nmap**. When used in this way, the **dnf** command asks for confirmation. If when you type the **dnf install** command you are sure about what you are doing, you might as well use the **-y** option, which passes a "yes" to the confirmation prompt that **dnf** normally issues. Example 9-6 shows what the result looks like.

Example 9-6 Installing Software with **dnf**

```
[root@server1 ~]# dnf install nmap
Updating Subscription Management repositories.
Unable to read consumer identity

This system is not registered with an entitlement server. You can use
  subscription-manager to register.

Last metadata expiration check: 0:05:58 ago on Wed 14 Sep 2022
  10:52:12 AM CEST.
```

```
Dependencies resolved.
==========================================================================
==========================================================================
 Package                        Architecture                      Version
Repository                                 Size
==========================================================================
==========================================================================
Installing:
 nmap                           x86_64                      3:7.91-10.el9
repo_AppStream                           5.6 M
Transaction Summary
==========================================================================
==========================================================================
Install  1 Package

Total size: 5.6 M
Installed size: 24 M
Is this ok [y/N]: y
Downloading Packages:
Running transaction check
Transaction check succeeded.
Running transaction test
Transaction test succeeded.
Running transaction
  Preparing        :
1/1
  Installing       : nmap-3:7.91-10.el9.x86_64
1/1
  Running scriptlet: nmap-3:7.91-10.el9.x86_64
1/1
  Verifying        : nmap-3:7.91-10.el9.x86_64
1/1
Installed products updated.

Installed:
  nmap-3:7.91-10.el9.x86_64

Complete!
```

In Example 9-6, you can see that **dnf** starts by analyzing what is going to be installed. Once that is clear, it gives an overview of the package that is going to be installed, including its dependencies. Then, the package itself is installed to the system.

To remove software packages from a machine, use the **dnf remove** command. This command also does a dependency analysis, which means that it will remove not only the selected package but also all packages that depend on it. This may sometimes lead to a long list of software packages that are going to be removed. To avoid unpleasant surprises, you should never use **dnf remove** with the **-y** option.

NOTE Some packages are protected. Therefore, you cannot easily remove them. If **dnf remove** encounters protected packages, it refuses to remove them.

Showing Lists of Packages

When working with **dnf**, you may also use the **dnf list** command to show lists of packages. Used without arguments, **dnf list** shows a list of all software packages that are available, including the repository they were installed from—assuming that the package has been installed. If a repository name is shown, the package is available in that specific repository. If @anaconda is listed, the package has already been installed on this system. Example 9-7 shows the partial output of the **dnf list** command.

Example 9-7 Partial Output of the **dnf list** Command

```
[root@server3 ~]# dnf list | less
Updating Subscription Management repositories.
Unable to read consumer identity

This system is not registered with an entitlement server. You can use
subscription-manager to register.

Last metadata expiration check: 0:12:17 ago on Wed 14 Sep 2022
10:52:12 AM CEST.
Installed Packages
ModemManager.x86_64                1.18.2-3.el9          @anaconda
ModemManager-glib.x86_64           1.18.2-3.el9          @anaconda
```

```
NetworkManager.x86_64                      1:1.36.0-4.el9_0     @anaconda
NetworkManager-adsl.x86_64                 1:1.36.0-4.el9_0     @anaconda
NetworkManager-bluetooth.x86_64            1:1.36.0-4.el9_0     @anaconda
NetworkManager-config-server.noarch        1:1.36.0-4.el9_0     @anaconda
NetworkManager-libnm.x86_64                1:1.36.0-4.el9_0     @anaconda
NetworkManager-team.x86_64                 1:1.36.0-4.el9_0     @anaconda
NetworkManager-tui.x86_64                  1:1.36.0-4.el9_0     @anaconda
NetworkManager-wifi.x86_64                 1:1.36.0-4.el9_0     @anaconda
NetworkManager-wwan.x86_64                 1:1.36.0-4.el9_0     @anaconda
PackageKit.x86_64                          1.2.4-2.el9          @AppStream
PackageKit-command-not-found.x86_64        1.2.4-2.el9          @AppStream
PackageKit-glib.x86_64                     1.2.4-2.el9          @AppStream
PackageKit-gstreamer-plugin.x86_64         1.2.4-2.el9          @AppStream
PackageKit-gtk3-module.x86_64              1.2.4-2.el9          @AppStream
abattis-cantarell-fonts.noarch             0.301-4.el9          @AppStream
accountsservice.x86_64                     0.6.55-10.el9        @AppStream
accountsservice-libs.x86_64                0.6.55-10.el9        @AppStream
...
```

If you only want to see which packages are installed on your server, you can use the **dnf list installed** command. The **dnf list** command can also prove useful when used with the name of a specific package as its argument. For instance, type **dnf list kernel** to show which version of the kernel is actually installed and which version is available as the most recent version in the repositories, which is particularly useful if your system is using online repositories and you want to check if a newer version of the package is available. Example 9-8 shows the result of this command, taken from a registered RHEL 9 system.

Example 9-8 Use **dnf list *packagename*** for Information About Installed and Available Versions

```
[root@localhost ~]# dnf list kernel
Updating Subscription Management repositories.
Last metadata expiration check: 0:04:09 ago on Wed 14 Sep 2022
11:02:40 AM CEST.
Installed Packages
```

```
kernel.x86_64
5.14.0-70.13.1.el9_0
@anaconda
Available Packages
kernel.x86_64
5.14.0-70.22.1.el9_0
rhel-9-for-x86_64-baseos-rpms
```

Updating Packages

One of the major benefits of working with **dnf** repositories is that repositories make it easy to update packages. The repository maintainer is responsible for copying updated packages to the repositories. The index in the repository always contains the current version of a package in the repository. On the local machine also, a database is available with the current versions of the packages that are used. When you use the **dnf update** command, current versions of packages that are installed are compared to the version of these packages in the repositories. As shown in Example 9-9, **dnf** next shows an overview of updatable packages. From this overview, type **y** to install the updates.

Notice that while updating packages the old version of the package is replaced with a newer version of the package. There is one exception, which is for the kernel package. Even if you are using the **dnf update kernel** command, the kernel package is not updated, but the newer kernel is installed in addition to the old kernel, so that while booting you can select the kernel that you want to use. This is useful if the new kernel won't work because of hardware compatibility issues. In that case, you can interrupt the GRUB 2 boot process (see Chapter 17, "Managing and Understanding the Boot Procedure," for more details) to start the older kernel.

Example 9-9 Using **dnf update**

```
[root@localhost ~]# dnf update kernel
Updating Subscription Management repositories.
Last metadata expiration check: 0:06:25 ago on Wed 14 Sep 2022
11:02:40 AM CEST.
================================================================
Dependencies resolved.
 Package                    Architecture                  Version
Repository                                          Size
================================================================
Installing:
 kernel                              x86_64
5.14.0-70.22.1.el9_0                     rhel-9-for-x86_64-baseos-rpms
595 k
```

```
Installing dependencies:
 kernel-core                           x86_64
5.14.0-70.22.1.el9_0                        rhel-9-for-x86_64-baseos-rpms
34 M
 kernel-modules                        x86_64
5.14.0-70.22.1.el9_0                        rhel-9-for-x86_64-baseos-rpms
21 M
Transaction Summary
=====================================================================
Install  3 Packages

Total download size: 56 M
Installed size: 93 M
Is this ok [y/N]:
```

Working with dnf Package Groups

While managing specific services on a Linux machine, you often need several different packages. If, for instance, you want to make your machine a virtualization host, you need the KVM packages, but also all supporting packages such as qemu, libvirt, and the client packages. Or while configuring your server as a web server, you need to install additional packages like PHP as well in many cases.

To make it easier to manage specific functionality, instead of specific packages, you can work with package groups as well. A ***package group*** is defined in the repository, and **dnf** offers the group management commands to work with these groups. For an overview of all current groups, use **dnf group list**. This shows output as in Example 9-10.

> **TIP** The name of the command is **dnf group**, but there are aliases that ensure that **dnf groups** and even commands like **dnf groupinstall** are also working. So, you can use any of these commands.

Example 9-10 Showing Available **dnf** Groups

```
[root@localhost ~]# dnf group list
Updating Subscription Management repositories.
Last metadata expiration check: 0:11:10 ago on Wed 14 Sep 2022
11:02:40 AM CEST.
Available Environment Groups:
   Server
   Minimal Install
   Workstation
```

```
    Virtualization Host
    Custom Operating System
Installed Environment Groups:
    Server with GUI
Installed Groups:
    Container Management
    Headless Management
Available Groups:
    .NET Development
    Console Internet Tools
    RPM Development Tools
    Scientific Support
    Legacy UNIX Compatibility
    Network Servers
    Graphical Administration Tools
    Development Tools
    Security Tools
    Smart Card Support
    System Tools
```

Notice that some **dnf** groups are not listed by default. To show those as well, type **dnf group list hidden**. You see that the list of groups that is displayed is considerably longer. The difference is that **dnf group list** shows environment groups, which contain basic functionality. Within an environment group, different subgroups can be used; these are displayed only when using **dnf group list hidden**.

To get information about packages available in a group, you use **dnf group info**. Because group names normally contain spaces, do not forget to put the entire group name between quotes. So, type **dnf group info "Container Management"** to see what is in the Container Management group. As you can see in Example 9-11, this command shows mandatory items and optional items in the group. The items can be groups and individual packages.

Example 9-11 Showing Group Contents with **dnf group info**

```
[root@localhost ~]# dnf group info "Container Management"
Updating Subscription Management repositories.
Last metadata expiration check: 0:12:49 ago on Wed 14 Sep 2022
11:02:40 AM CEST.
Group: Container Management
 Description: Tools for managing Linux containers
```

```
Mandatory Packages:
  buildah
  containernetworking-plugins
  podman
Optional Packages:
  python3-psutil
  toolbox
```

Using dnf History

While you're working with **dnf**, all actions are registered. You can use the **dnf history** command to get an overview of all actions that have been issued. From the history file, it is possible to undo specific actions; use **dnf history undo** followed by the number of the specific action you want to undo.

In Example 9-12, you see the result of the **dnf history** command, where every action has its own ID.

Example 9-12 Showing Past **dnf** Actions Using **dnf history**

```
[root@localhost ~]# dnf history
Updating Subscription Management repositories.
ID     | Command line
| Date and time     | Action(s)      | Altered
----------------------------------------------------------------------
----------------------------------------------------------------------
------------------------
     2 | install nmap
| 2022-09-14 10:45 | Install        |    1 <
     1 |
```

As you can see, action number 2 altered one package and was used to install packages. To undo this action completely, type **dnf history undo 2**. In Exercise 9-2, you apply some of the most useful **dnf** commands for common package management tasks, as discussed previously.

Exercise 9-2 Using dnf for Package Management

1. Type **dnf repolist** to show a list of the current repositories that your system is using.
2. Type **dnf search seinfo**. This will give no matching result.
3. Type **dnf provides seinfo**. The command shows that the setools-console-<*version*> package contains this file.
4. Install this package using **dnf install -y setools-console**. Depending on your current configuration, you might notice that quite a few dependencies have to be installed also.
5. Type **dnf list setools-console**. You see that the package is listed as installed.
6. Type **dnf history** and note the number of the last **dnf** command you used.
7. Type **dnf history undo <*nn*>** (where **<*nn*>** is replaced with the number that you found in step 6). This undoes the last action, so it removes the package you just installed.
8. Repeat the **dnf list setools-console** command. The package is now listed as available but not as installed.

Managing Package Modules

Up to Red Hat Enterprise Linux 7, all packages were offered in one repository. This made package version management challenging, as Red Hat has always maintained the philosophy that major versions of packages should not be changed during a distribution lifetime. The issue is that changing a major version of any package often involves changing dependencies as well, and if that happens, it is very difficult to guarantee that all packages are installed with the right version. As a result of adhering to this philosophy, Red Hat was not able to introduce Python 3 during the RHEL 7 lifetime. The current Python 2 version that was included in RHEL 7, however, became deprecated, and customers had a hard time understanding this.

To offer a higher level of flexibility, with the introduction of RHEL 8, Red Hat introduced two different repositories. The BaseOS repository is for core operating system packages, and all packages in this repository will not change their major version during the distribution lifetime. The Application Stream (AppStream) repository contains other packages that may change their major version during the distribution lifetime. Important applications like Python are provided as AppStream packages, to ensure that if a new major version becomes available during the distribution lifetime, this major version can be included.

Understanding dnf Modules

In the AppStream repository, content with varying life cycles is provided. This content may be provided as traditional RPM packages, but also as modules. A ***module*** describes a set of RPM packages that belong together, and adds features to package management. Typically, modules are organized around a specific version of an application, and in a module you'll find module packages, together with all of the dependencies for that specific version.

Each module can have one or more application streams. A ***stream*** contains one specific version, and updates are provided for a specific stream. By using streams, different versions of packages can be offered through the same repositories. When you're working with modules that have different streams, only one stream can be enabled at the same time. This allows users to select the package version that is needed in their environment.

Modules can also have one or more profiles. A ***profile*** is a list of packages that are installed together for a particular use case. You may find, for instance, a minimal profile, a default profile, a server profile, and many more. While you're working with modules, you may select which profile you want to use. Table 9-4 provides an overview of key terminology when working with modules.

Table 9-4 dnf Module Terminology

Item	Explanation
RPM	The default package format. Contains files, as well as metadata that describes how to install the files. Optionally may contain pre- and post-installation scripts as well.
Module	A delivery mechanism to install RPM packages. In a module, different versions and profiles can be provided.
Application stream	A specific version of the module.
Profile	A collection of packages that are installed together for a particular use case.

Managing Modules

The **dnf** command in RHEL 9 supports working with modules using the **dnf module** command. To find out which modules are available, you may want to start with the **dnf module list** command. You can see its sample output in Example 9-13.

NOTE In RHEL 9.0 no modules are provided. It is expected that in future updates modules will be provided. To show the working of the **dnf module** command, all examples are taken from CentOS Stream.

Example 9-13 Showing **dnf** Modules with **dnf module list**

```
[root@localhost ~]# dnf module list
Last metadata expiration check: 2:51:45 ago on Wed 14 Sep 2022
08:39:28 AM CEST.
CentOS Stream 9 - AppStream
Name                Stream        Profiles
Summary
maven               3.8           common [d]
Java project management and project comprehension tool
nodejs              18            common [d], development, minimal, s2i
Javascript runtime
php                 8.1           common [d], devel, minimal          PHP
scripting language
ruby                3.1           common [d]                          An
interpreter of object-oriented scripting language
Hint: [d]efault, [e]nabled, [x]disabled, [i]nstalled
```

In the list of modules, you can see whether or not the module is installed and whether or not a specific stream is enabled. To list specific streams for a module, use the **dnf module list *modulename*** command. For instance, use **dnf module list maven** to get details about streams that are available for the Maven module, as shown in Example 9-14.

Example 9-14 Showing Details About **dnf** Modules with **dnf module list**

```
[root@localhost ~]# dnf module list maven
Last metadata expiration check: 2:53:36 ago on Wed 14 Sep 2022
08:39:28 AM CEST.
CentOS Stream 9 - AppStream
Name                     Stream                     Profiles
Summary
maven                    3.8                        common [d]        Java
project management and project comprehension tool


Hint: [d]efault, [e]nabled, [x]disabled, [i]nstalled
```

After you find out which module streams are available, the next step is to get information about specific profiles. You can use **dnf module info** to obtain this information. For instance, use **dnf module info php** to get more information about the php module. This will provide information for profiles that are available in all the module streams. To find profile information for a specific stream, you can provide the stream version as an argument. For instance, use **dnf module info php:8.1** (see Example 9-15).

Example 9-15 Showing Information About **dnf** Modules with **dnf module list**

```
[
root@localhost ~]# dnf module info php:8.1
Last metadata expiration check: 2:55:06 ago on Wed 14 Sep 2022
08:39:28 AM CEST.
Name             : php
Stream           : 8.1
Version          : 920220706080036
Context          : 9
Architecture     : x86_64
Profiles         : common [d], devel, minimal
Default profiles : common
Repo             : appstream
Summary          : PHP scripting language
Description      : php 8.1 module
Requires         :
Artifacts        : apcu-panel-0:5.1.21-1.module_el9+137+d73770a9.
                   noarch
                 : php-0:8.1.8-1.module_el9+158+97f99411.src
                 : php-0:8.1.8-1.module_el9+158+97f99411.x86_64
                 : php-bcmath-0:8.1.8-1.module_el9+158+97f99411.x86_64
                 : php-bcmath-debuginfo-0:8.1.8-1.module_el9+158+
                   97f99411.x86_64
                 : php-cli-0:8.1.8-1.module_el9+158+97f99411.x86_64
                 : php-cli-debuginfo-0:8.1.8-1.module_el9+158+
                   97f99411.x86_64
                 : php-common-0:8.1.8-1.module_el9+158+97f99411.x86_64
                 : php-common-debuginfo-0:8.1.8-
…
1.module_el9+158+97f99411.x86_64
                 : php-process-0:8.1.8-1.module_el9+158+97f99411.
                   x86_64
```

```
                    : php-process-debuginfo-0:8.1.8-1.module_el9+158+
                      97f99411.x86_64
                    : php-snmp-0:8.1.8-1.module_el9+158+97f99411.x86_64
                    : php-snmp-debuginfo-0:8.1.8-1.module_el9+158+
                      97f99411.x86_64
                    : php-soap-0:8.1.8-1.module_el9+158+97f99411.x86_64
                    : php-soap-debuginfo-0:8.1.8-1.module_el9+158+
                      97f99411.x86_64
                    : php-xml-0:8.1.8-1.module_el9+158+97f99411.x86_64
                    : php-xml-debuginfo-0:8.1.8-1.module_el9+158+
                      97f99411.x86_64

Hint: [d]efault, [e]nabled, [x]disabled, [i]nstalled, [a]ctive]
```

After you find module information, the next step is to enable a module stream and install modules. Every module has a default module stream, providing access to a specific version. If that version is what you need, you don't have to enable anything. If you want to work with a different version, you should start by enabling the corresponding module stream. For example, type **dnf module enable php:8.1** to enable that specific version.

Enabling a module stream before starting to work with a specific module is not mandatory. If you just use **dnf module install** to install packages from a module, packages from the default module stream will be installed. You can also switch between application stream versions. If, for instance, you are now on php:8.1 and you want to change to php:8.2, you just have to type **dnf module install php:8.2**. This will disable the old stream and enable the new stream. After doing this, to ensure that all dependent packages that are not in the module itself are updated as well, type **dnf distro-sync** to finalize the procedure.

Managing Software Packages with rpm

Once upon a time, repositories did not exist, and the **rpm** command was used to install package files after they had been downloaded. That worked, but there was one major issue: the ***dependency hell***. Because RPM packages have always focused on specific functionality, to install specific software, a collection of RPM packages was normally required. Therefore, a "missing dependency" message was often issued while users were trying to install RPM packages, which meant that to install the selected package, other packages needed to be installed first. Sometimes a whole chain of dependencies needed to be installed to finally get the desired functionality. That did not make working with RPM packages a joyful experience.

On modern RHEL systems, repositories are used, and packages are installed using **dnf**. The **dnf** command considers all package dependencies and tries to look them up in the currently available repositories. On a RHEL system configured to get updates from Red Hat, or on a CentOS system where consistent repositories are used, the result is that package installation nowadays is without problems and the **rpm** command no longer is used for software installation.

Even after downloading an RPM package file, you do not need to use the **rpm -Uvh** ***packagename*** command to install it (even if it still works). A much better alternative is **dnf install** ***packagename***, which installs the package and also considers the repositories to resolve dependencies automatically. That does not mean the **rpm** command has become totally useless. You can still use it to query RPM packages.

> **TIP** On your system, two package databases are maintained: the **dnf** database and the RPM database. When you are installing packages through **dnf**, the **dnf** database is updated first, after which the updated information is synchronized to the RPM database. If you install packages using the **rpm** command, the update is written to the RPM database only and will not be updated to the **dnf** database, which is an important reason not to use the **rpm** command to install software packages.

Understanding RPM Filenames

When you're working with RPM packages directly, it makes sense to understand how the RPM filename is composed. A typical RPM filename looks like autofs-5.0.7-40.el7.x86_64.rpm. This name consists of several parts:

- **autofs:** The name of the actual package.
- **5.0.7:** The version of the package. This normally corresponds to the name of the package as it was released by the package creator.
- **-40:** The sub-version of the package.
- **el7:** The Red Hat version this package was created for.
- **x86_64:** The platform (32 bits or 64 bits) this package was created for.

Querying the RPM Database

The **rpm** command enables you to get much information about packages. Using RPM queries can be a really useful way to find out how software can be configured and used. To start, you can use the **rpm -qa** command. Like **dnf list installed**, this command shows a list of all software that is installed on the machine. Use **grep** on this command to find out specific package names. To perform queries on RPM packages, you just need the name and not the version information.

After finding the package about which you want more information, you can start with some generic queries to find out what is in the package. In the following examples, I assume that you are using RPM queries on the nmap RPM package. To start, type **rpm -qi nmap** to get a description of the package. This will perform a query of a package that is already installed on your system, and it will query the package database to get more details about it.

The next step is to use **rpm -ql nmap**, which shows a list of all files that are in the package. On some packages, the result can be a really long list of filenames that is not particularly useful. To get more specific information, use **rpm -qd nmap**, which shows all documentation available for the package, or **rpm -qc nmap**, which shows all configuration files in the package.

Using RPM queries can really help in finding out more useful information about packages. The only thing that you need to know is the RPM package name that a specific file belongs to. To find this, use **rpm -qf**, followed by the specific filename you are looking for. Use, for instance, **rpm -qf /bin/ls** to find the name of the RPM package the **ls** command comes from. In upcoming Exercise 9-3, you'll see how useful it can be to use RPM queries in this way.

Querying RPM Package Files

RPM queries by default are used on the RPM database, and what you are querying are installed RPM packages. It sometimes makes sense to query an RPM package file before actually installing it. To do this, you need to add the **-p** option to the query, because without the **-p** option, you will be querying the database, not the package file. Also, when querying a package file, you need to refer to the complete filename, including the version number and all other information that you do not have to use when querying the RPM database. As an example, the **rpm -qp --scripts httpd-2.4.6-19.el7.centos.x86_64.rpm** command queries the specific RPM file to see whether it contains scripts.

A query option that needs special attention is **--scripts**, which queries an RPM package or package file to see which scripts it contains (if any). This option is especially important when combined with the **-p** option, to find out whether a package file that you are going to install includes any scripts.

When you install RPM packages, you do so as root. Before installing an RPM package from an unknown source, you need to make sure that it does not include any rogue scripts. If you do not, you risk installing malware on your computer without even knowing it.

Table 9-5 describes the most important RPM querying options.

Table 9-5 Common RPM Query Commands

Command	Description
rpm -qf	Uses a filename as its argument to find the specific RPM package a file belongs to.
rpm -ql	Uses the RPM database to provide a list of files in the RPM package.
rpm -qi	Uses the RPM database to provide package information (equivalent to **yum info**).
rpm -qd	Uses the RPM database to show all documentation that is available in the package.
rpm -qc	Uses the RPM database to show all configuration files that are available in the package.
rpm -q --scripts	Uses the RPM database to show scripts that are used in the package. This is particularly useful if combined with the **-p** option.
rpm -qp ***<pkg>***	The **-p** option is used with all the previously listed options to query individual RPM package files instead of the RPM package database. Using this option before installation helps you find out what is actually in the package before it is installed.
rpm -qR	Shows dependencies for a specific package.
rpm -V	Shows which parts of a specific package have been changed since installation.
rpm -Va	Verifies all installed packages and shows which parts of the package have been changed since installation. This is an easy and convenient way to do a package integrity check.
rpm -qa	Lists all packages that are installed on this server.

Using repoquery

While **rpm -qp** provides useful tools to query packages before installation, there is a slight problem with this command: It works only on RPM package files, and it cannot query files directly from the repositories. If you want to query packages from the repositories before they have been installed, you need **repoquery**. This binary is not installed by default, so make sure to install the **dnf-utils** RPM package to use it.

The **repoquery** command is pretty similar to the **rpm -q** command and uses many similar options. There is just one significant option missing: **--scripts**. A simple solution is to make sure that you are using trusted repositories only, to prevent installing software that contains dangerous script code.

If you need to thoroughly analyze what an RPM package is doing when it is installed, you can download it to your machine, which allows you to use the **rpm -qp --scripts** command on the package. To download a package from the repository to the local directory, you can use the **yumdownloader** command, which comes from the **yum-utils** package.

Now that you have learned all about RPM querying options, you can practice these newly acquired skills in Exercise 9-3 to get more information about software that is installed on your RHEL system.

Exercise 9-3 Using RPM Queries

1. To practice working with **rpm**, we need a package. It doesn't really matter which package that is. Type **dnf install -y dnsmasq** (you may get a message that the package is already installed).
2. Type **which dnsmasq**. This command gives the complete pathname of the **dnsmasq** command.
3. Type **rpm -qf $(which dnsmasq)**. This does an RPM file query on the result of the **which dnsmasq** command; you learn more about this technique in Chapter 19, "An Introduction to Automation with Bash Shell Scripting."
4. Now that you know that the dnsmasq binary comes from the dnsmasq package, use **rpm -qi dnsmasq** to show more information about the package.
5. The information that is shown with **rpm -qi** is useful, but it does not give the details that are needed to start working with the software in the package. Use **rpm -ql dnsmasq** to show a list of all files in the package.
6. Use **rpm -qd dnsmasq** to show the available documentation. Notice that this command reveals that there is a man page, but there is also a doc.html file and a setup.html file in the /usr/share/doc/dnsmasq-version directory. Open these files with your browser to get more information about the use of dnsmasq.
7. Type **rpm -qc dnsmasq** to see which configuration files are used by dnsmasq.
8. After installation, it does not make much sense, but it is always good to know which scripts are executed when a package is installed. Use **rpm -q --scripts dnsmasq** to show the script code that can be executed from this RPM.

TIP Working with RPM queries is a valuable skill on the RHCSA exam. If you know how to handle queries, you can find all relevant configuration files and the documentation.

Summary

In this chapter, you learned how to work with software on Red Hat Enterprise Linux. You learned how to use **dnf** to manage software packages coming from repositories. You also learned how to use the **rpm** command to perform queries on the packages on your system. Make sure that you master these essential skills well; they are key to getting things done on Red Hat Enterprise Linux.

Exam Preparation Tasks

As mentioned in the section "How to Use This Book" in the Introduction, you have several choices for exam preparation: the end-of-chapter labs; the memory tables in Appendix C; Chapter 27, "Final Preparation"; and the practice exams.

Review All Key Topics

Review the most important topics in the chapter, noted with the Key Topic icon in the margin of the page. Table 9-6 lists a reference for these key topics and the page number on which each is found.

Table 9-6 Key Topics for Chapter 9

Key Topic Element	Description	Page
Table 9-3	Common **dnf** Tasks	206
List	RPM package name components	222
Table 9-5	Common RPM Query Commands	224

Complete Tables and Lists from Memory

Print a copy of Appendix C, "Memory Tables" (found on the companion website), or at least the section for this chapter, and complete the tables and lists from memory. Appendix D, "Memory Tables Answer Key," includes completed tables and lists to check your work.

Define Key Terms

Define the following key terms from this chapter and check your answers in the glossary:

package, **dnf**, Red Hat Package Manager (RPM), repository, dependency Application Stream (AppStream), package group, module, stream, profile, dependency hell

Review Questions

The questions that follow are meant to help you test your knowledge of concepts and terminology and the breadth of your knowledge. You can find the answers to these questions in Appendix A.

1. You have a directory containing a collection of RPM packages and want to make that directory a repository. Which command enables you to do that?
2. What needs to be in the repository file to point to a repository on http://server.example.com/repo?
3. You have just configured a new repository to be used on your RHEL computer. Which command enables you to verify that the repository is indeed available?
4. Which command enables you to search the RPM package containing the file useradd?
5. Which two commands do you need to use to show the name of the **dnf** group that contains security tools and shows what is in that group?
6. Which command do you use to ensure that all PHP-related packages are going to be installed using the older version 7.1, without actually installing anything yet?
7. You want to make sure that an RPM package that you have downloaded does not contain any dangerous script code. Which command enables you to do so?
8. Which command reveals all documentation in an RPM package?
9. Which command shows the RPM package a file comes from?
10. Which command enables you to query software from the repository?

End-of-Chapter Lab

In this end-of-chapter lab, you use some of the essential RHEL package management skills. All assignments can be done on one server.

Lab 9.1

1. Copy some RPM files from the installation disk to the /myrepo directory. Make this directory a repository and make sure that your server is using this repository.
2. List the repositories currently in use on your server.
3. Search for the package that contains the cache-only DNS name server. Do not install it yet.
4. Perform an extensive query of the package so that you know before you install it which files it contains, which dependencies it has, and where to find the documentation and configuration.
5. Check whether the RPM package contains any scripts. You may download it, but you may not install it yet; you want to know which scripts are in a package before actually installing it, right?
6. Install the package you found in step 3.
7. Undo the installation.

The following topics are covered in this chapter:

- Introducing Process Management
- Managing Shell Jobs
- Using Common Command-Line Tools for Process Management
- Using **top** to Manage Processes
- Using **tuned** to Optimize Performance

The following RHCSA exam objectives are covered in this chapter:

- Identify CPU/memory-intensive processes and kill processes
- Adjust process scheduling
- Manage tuning profiles

CHAPTER 10

Managing Processes

Process management is an important task for a Linux administrator. In this chapter, you learn what you need to know to manage processes from a perspective of the daily operation of a server. You learn how to work with shell jobs and generic processes. You also are introduced to system performance optimization using **tuned**.

"Do I Know This Already?" Quiz

The "Do I Know This Already?" quiz enables you to assess whether you should read this entire chapter thoroughly or jump to the "Exam Preparation Tasks" section. If you are in doubt about your answers to these questions or your own assessment of your knowledge of the topics, read the entire chapter. Table 10-1 lists the major headings in this chapter and their corresponding "Do I Know This Already?" quiz questions. You can find the answers in Appendix A, "Answers to the 'Do I Know This Already?' Quizzes and Review Questions."

Table 10-1 "Do I Know This Already?" Section-to-Question Mapping

Foundation Topics Section	Questions
Introducing Process Management	1
Managing Shell Jobs	2–3
Using Common Command-Line Tools for Process Management	4–8
Using **top** to Manage Processes	9
Using **tuned** to Optimize Performance	10

1. Which of the following are not generally considered a type of process? (Choose two.)
    a. A shell job
    b. A cron job
    c. A daemon
    d. A thread

2. Which of the following can be used to move a job to the background?
   a. Press &
   b. Press Ctrl-Z and then type **bg**
   c. Press Ctrl-D and then type **bg**
   d. Press Ctrl-Z, followed by **&**

3. Which key combination enables you to cancel a current interactive shell job?
   a. Ctrl-C
   b. Ctrl-D
   c. Ctrl-Z
   d. Ctrl-Break

4. Which of the following statements are true about threads? (Choose two.)
   a. Threads cannot be managed individually by an administrator.
   b. Multithreaded processes can make the working of processes more efficient.
   c. Threads can be used only on supported platforms.
   d. Using multiple processes is more efficient, in general, than using multiple threads.

5. Which of the following commands is most appropriate if you're looking for detailed information about the command and how it was started?
   a. **ps ef**
   b. **ps aux**
   c. **ps**
   d. **ps fax**

6. Of the following **nice** values, which will increase the priority of the selected process?
   a. 100
   b. 20
   c. -19
   d. -100

7. Which of the following shows correct syntax to change the priority for the current process with PID 1234?
   a. **nice -n 5 1234**
   b. **renice 5 1234**
   c. **renice 5 -p 1234**
   d. **nice 5 -p 1234**

8. Which of the following commands cannot be used to send signals to processes?
   a. **kill**
   b. **mkill**
   c. **pkill**
   d. **killall**

9. Which of the following commands would you use from **top** to change the priority of a process?
   a. **r**
   b. **n**
   c. **c**
   d. **k**

10. Which of the following commands will set the current performance profile to powersave?
    a. **tuneadm profile set powersave**
    b. **tuned-adm profile powersave**
    c. **tuneadm profile --set powersave**
    d. **tuned-adm profile --set powersave**

Foundation Topics

Introducing Process Management

For everything that happens on a Linux server, a process is started. For that reason, process management is among the key skills that an administrator has to master. To do this efficiently, you need to know which type of ***process*** you are dealing with. A major distinction can be made between three process types:

- *Shell jobs* are commands started from the command line. They are associated with the shell that was current when the process was started. Shell jobs are also referred to as *interactive processes*.
- *Daemons* are processes that provide services. They normally are started when a computer is booted and often (but certainly not in all cases) run with root privileges.
- *Kernel threads* are a part of the Linux kernel. You cannot manage them using common tools, but for monitoring of performance on a system, it's important to keep an eye on them.

When a process is started, it can use multiple threads. A ***thread*** is a task started by a process and that a dedicated CPU can service. The Linux shell does not offer tools to manage individual threads. Thread management should be taken care of from within the command.

If you want to manage a process efficiently, it is paramount that you know what type of process you are dealing with. Shell jobs require a different approach than the processes that are automatically started when a computer boots.

Managing Shell Jobs

When a user types a command, a shell ***job*** is started. If no particular measures have been taken, the job is started as a ***foreground process***, occupying the terminal it was started from until it has finished its work. As a Linux administrator, you need to know how to start shell jobs as foreground processes or as ***background processes*** and what you can do to manage shell jobs.

Running Jobs in the Foreground and Background

By default, any executed command is started as a foreground job. That means that you cannot do anything on the terminal where the command was started until it is done. For many commands, that does not really matter because the command often takes a little while to complete, after which it returns access to the shell from which it was started. Sometimes it might prove useful to start commands in the background. This makes sense for processes that do not require user interaction and take significant time to finish. A process that does require user interaction will not be able to get that when running in the background, and for that reason will typically stall when moved to the background. You can take two different approaches to run a process in the background.

If you know that a job will take a long time to complete, you can start it with an **&** behind it. This command immediately starts the job in the background to make room for other tasks to be started from the command line. To move the last job that was started in the background back as a foreground job, use the **fg** command. This command immediately, and with no further questions, brings the last job back to the foreground. If multiple jobs are currently running in the background, you can move a job back to the foreground by adding its job ID, as shown by the **jobs** command.

A job might sometimes have been started that takes (much) longer than predicted. If that happens, you can use Ctrl-Z to temporarily stop the job. This does not remove the job from memory; it just pauses the job so that it can be managed. Once the job is paused, you can continue it as a background job by using the **bg** command. An alternative key sequence that you can use to manage shell jobs is Ctrl-C. This key combination stops the current job and removes it from memory.

A related key combination is Ctrl-D, which sends the End Of File (EOF) character to the current job. The result is that the job stops waiting for further input so that it can complete what it was currently doing. The result of pressing Ctrl-D is sometimes similar to the result of pressing Ctrl-C, but there is a difference. When Ctrl-C is used, the job is just canceled, and nothing is closed properly. When Ctrl-D is used, the job stops waiting for further input and next terminates, which often is just what is needed to complete in a proper way.

Managing Shell Jobs

When you're moving jobs between the foreground and background, it may be useful to have an overview of all current jobs. To get such an overview, use the **jobs** command. As you can see in Table 10-2, this command gives an overview of all jobs currently running as a background job, including the job number assigned to the job when starting it in the background. These job numbers can be used as an argument to the **fg** and **bg** commands to perform job management tasks. In Exercise 10-1, you learn how to perform common job management tasks from the shell.

Table 10-2 Job Management Overview

Command	Use
& (used at the end of a command line)	Starts the command immediately in the background.
Ctrl-Z	Stops the job temporarily so that it can be managed. For instance, it can be moved to the background.
Ctrl-D	Sends the EOF character to the current job to indicate that it should stop waiting for further input.
Ctrl-C	Can be used to cancel the current interactive job.
bg	Continues the job that has just been frozen using Ctrl-Z in the background.
fg	Brings back to the foreground the last job that was moved to background execution.
jobs	Shows which jobs are currently running from this shell. Displays job numbers that can be used as an argument to the commands **bg** and **fg**.

Exercise 10-1 Managing Jobs

1. Open a root shell and type the following commands:

```
sleep 3600 &
dd if=/dev/zero of=/dev/null &
sleep 7200
```

2. Because you started the last command with no **&** after the command, you have to wait 2 hours before you get back control of the shell. Press Ctrl-Z to stop the command.
3. Type **jobs**. You will see the three jobs that you just started. The first two of them have the Running state, and the last job currently is in the Stopped state.
4. Type **bg 3** to continue running job 3 in the background. Note that because it was started as the last job, you did not really have to add the number 3.
5. Type **fg 1** to move job 1 to the foreground.
6. Press Ctrl-C to cancel job number 1 and type **jobs** to confirm that it is now gone.
7. Use the same approach to cancel jobs 2 and 3 also.
8. Open a second terminal on your server.

9. From that second terminal, type **dd if=/dev/zero of=/dev/null &**
10. Type **exit** to close the second terminal.
11. From the other terminal, start **top**. You will see that the **dd** job is still running. It should show on **top** of the list of running processes. From **top**, press **k** to kill the **dd** job. It will prompt for a PID to kill; make sure to enter the PID of the process you want to terminate, and then press Enter to apply default values.

NOTE You learned how to manage interactive shell jobs in this section. Note that all of these jobs are processes as well. As the user who started the job, you can also manage it. In the next section, you learn how to use process management to manage jobs started by other users.

Understanding Parent–Child Relations

When a process is started from a shell, it becomes a child process of that shell. In process management, the parent–child relationship between processes is very important. The parent is needed to manage the child. For that reason, all processes started from a shell are terminated when that shell is stopped. This also offers an easy way to terminate processes no longer needed.

Processes started in the background will not be killed when the parent shell from which they were started is killed. To terminate these processes, you need to use the **kill** command, as described later in this chapter.

NOTE In earlier versions of the Bash shell, background processes were also killed when the shell they were started from was terminated. To prevent that, the process could be started with the **nohup** command in front of it. Using **nohup** for this purpose is no longer needed in RHEL 9. If a parent process is killed while the child process still is active, the child process becomes a child of **systemd** instead.

Using Common Command-Line Tools for Process Management

On a Linux server, many processes are usually running. On an average server or desktop computer, there are often more than 100 active processes. With so many processes being active, things may go wrong. If that happens, it is good to know how noninteractive processes can be stopped or how the priority of these processes can be adjusted to make more system resources available for other processes.

Understanding Processes and Threads

Tasks on Linux are typically started as processes. One process can start several worker threads. Working with threads makes sense, because if the process is very busy, the threads can be handled by different CPUs or CPU cores available in the machine. As a Linux administrator, you cannot manage individual threads; you can manage processes, though. It is the programmer of the multithreaded application that has to define how threads relate to one another.

Before we talk about different ways to manage processes, it is good to know that there are two different types of background processes: kernel threads and daemon processes. *Kernel threads* are a part of the Linux kernel, and each of them is started with its own ***process identification number (PID)***. When managing processes, you can easily recognize the kernel processes because they have a name that is between square brackets. Example 10-1 shows a list of a few processes as output of the command **ps aux | head** (discussed later in this chapter), in which you can see a couple of kernel threads.

As an administrator, you need to know that kernel threads cannot be managed. You cannot adjust their priority; neither is it possible to kill them, except by taking the entire machine down.

Example 10-1 Showing Kernel Threads with **ps aux**

```
[root@server3 ~]# ps aux | head
USER   PID %CPU %MEM          VSZ    RSS TTY  STAT     START  TIME
  COMMAND
root     1  0.0  0.4 252864 7792 ?   Ss     08:25   0:02    /usr/lib/
  systemd/systemd --switched-root --system --deserialize 17
root     2  0.0  0.0      0     0 ?   S    08:25   0:00   [kthreadd]
root     3  0.0  0.0      0     0 ?   I<    08:25   0:00   [rcu_gp]
root     4  0.0  0.0      0     0 ?   I<    08:25   0:00   [rcu_par_gp]
root     6  0.0  0.0      0     0 ?   I<    08:25   0:00   [kworker/0:
  0H-kblockd]
root     8  0.0  0.0      0     0 ?   I<    08:25   0:00  [mm_percpu_wq]
root     9  0.0  0.0      0     0 ?     S    08:25   0:00  [ksoftirqd/0]
root    10  0.0  0.0      0     0 ?   I     08:25   0:00   [rcu_sched]
root    11  0.0  0.0      0     0 ?     S    08:25   0:00  [migration/0]
```

Using ps to Get Process Information

The most common command to get an overview of currently running processes is **ps**. If used without any arguments, the **ps** command shows only those processes that have been started by the current user. You can use many different options to display different process properties. If you are looking for a short summary of the active processes, use **ps aux** (as you saw in Example 10-1). If you are looking for not only the name of the process but also the exact command that was used to start the process, use **ps -ef** (see Example 10-2). Alternative ways to use **ps** exist as well, such as the command **ps fax**, which shows hierarchical relationships between parent and child processes (see Example 10-3).

Example 10-2 Using **ps -ef** to See the Exact Command Used to Start Processes

```
[root@server3 ~]# ps -ef
UID          PID     PPID  C STIME TTY          TIME      CMD
root        1       0   0 08:25 ?        00:00:02  /usr/lib/systemd/systemd
  --switched-root --system --deserialize  17
...
root   34948       2   0 12:16 ?        00:00:00      [kworker/0:1-events]
root   34971    1030   0 12:17 ?        00:00:00         sshd: root [priv]
root   34975    34971   0 12:17 ?        00:00:00   sshd: root@pts/2
root   34976    34975   0 12:17 pts/2     00:00:00   -bash
root   35034        1   0 12:17 pts/2     00:00:00   sleep 3600
root   35062        2   0 12:20 ?        00:00:00      [kworker/u256:2]
root   35064        2   0 12:20 ?        00:00:00   [kworker/0:3-cgroup_
  destroy]
root   35067        2   0 12:20 ?        00:00:00      [kworker/1:2-events_
  freezable_power_]
root   35087      939   0 12:21 ?        00:00:00   sleep 60
root   35088    33127   0 12:22 pts/1     00:00:00     ps -ef
```

NOTE For many commands, options need to start with a hyphen. For some commands, this is not the case and using the hyphen is optional. The **ps** command is one of these commands, due to historic reasons. In the old times of UNIX, there were two main flavors: the System V flavor, in which using hyphens before options was mandatory, and the BSD flavor, in which using hyphens was optional. The **ps** command is based on both of these flavors, and for that reason some options don't have to start with a hyphen.

Example 10-3 Using **ps fax** to Show Parent-Child Relationships Between Processes

```
[root@server3 ~]# ps fax
      PID TTY      STAT   TIME   COMMAND
        2 ?        S      0:00  [kthreadd]
        3 ?        I<     0:00  \_ [rcu_gp]
        4 ?        I<     0:00  \_ [rcu_par_gp]
...
  2460 ?        Ssl    0:00   \_ /usr/bin/pulseaudio --daemonize=no
  2465 ?        Ssl    0:00   \_ /usr/bin/dbus-daemon
  --session--address=systemd: --nofork --nopidfile --systemd-activation --
  2561 ?        Ssl    0:00   \_ /usr/libexec/at-spi-bus-launcher
  2566 ?        Sl     0:00   |   \_ /usr/bin/dbus-daemon --config-
    file=/usr/share/defaults/at-spi2/ accessibility.conf --nofork
  2569 ?        Sl     0:00   \_ /usr/libexec/at-spi2-registryd
    --use-gnome-session
  2589 ?        Ssl    0:00   \_ /usr/libexec/xdg-permission-store
  2594 ?        Sl     0:00   \_ /usr/libexec/ibus-portal
  2704 ?        Sl     0:00   \_ /usr/libexec/dconf-service
  2587 ?        Sl     0:00   /usr/libexec/ibus-x11 --kill-daemon
  2758 ?        Sl     0:00   /usr/bin/gnome-keyring-daemon --daemonize
    --login
  2908 tty3     Sl     0:00   /usr/libexec/ibus-x11 --kill-daemon
  2936 ?        Ssl    0:00   /usr/libexec/geoclue
  3102 tty3     Sl+    0:00   /usr/libexec/gsd-printer
  3173 tty3     Sl+    0:12   /usr/bin/vmtoolsd -n vmusr
  3378 ?        Ssl    0:00   /usr/libexec/fwupd/fwupd
  3440 ?        Ss     0:00   gpg-agent --homedir /var/lib/fwupd/gnupg
  --use-standard-socket --daemon
  3455 ?        S      0:00   /usr/libexec/platform-python /usr/
    libexec/rhsmd
 33093 ?        Ss     0:00   /usr/lib/systemd/systemd --user
  33105 ?        S      0:00   \_ (sd-pam)
  33117 ?        S<sl   0:00   \_ /usr/bin/pulseaudio --daemonize=no
 33123 ?        Ssl    0:00   \_ /usr/bin/dbus-daemon --session
  --address=systemd: --nofork   --nopidfile --systemd-activation --
 35034 pts/2    S      0:00   sleep 3600
```

An important piece of information to get out of the **ps** command is the PID. Many tasks require the PID to operate, and that is why a command like **ps aux | grep dd**, which will show process details about **dd**, including its PID, is quite common. An alternative way to get the same result is to use the **pgrep** command. Use **pgrep dd** to get a list of all PIDs that have a name containing the string “dd”.

Understanding Process Priorities

On modern Linux systems, cgroups are used to allocate system resources. In cgroups, three system areas, the so-called *slices*, are defined:

- **system:** This is where all systemd-managed processes are running.
- **user:** This is where all user processes (including root processes) are running.
- **machine:** This optional slice is used for virtual machines and containers.

By default, all slices have the same CPUWeight. That means that CPU capacity is equally divided if there is high demand. All processes in the system slice get as much CPU cycles as all processes in the user slice, and that can result in surprising behavior. Within a slice, process priority can be managed by using **nice** and **renice**.

Exploring Relations Between Slices

As mentioned before, by default all processes in the system slice get as many CPU cycles as all processes in the user slice. You won't get any questions about this on the RHCSA exam, but as it may lead to surprising situations, it's good to know how this works anyway. Apply the following procedure to discover what the result can be.

Step 1. Open a root shell and clone the course git repository: **git clone https://github.com/sandervanvugt/rhcsa**

Step 2. Use **cp rhcsa/stress* /etc/systemd/system**

Step 3. Type **systemctl daemon-reload** to ensure that systemd catches the new files.

Step 4. Type **systemctl start stress1**, followed by **systemctl start stress2**

Step 5. Use **top** to monitor CPU usage of the processes. You'll see that there are two very active **dd** processes, which each get about 50 percent of all CPU capacity. Keep the **top** screen open.

Step 6. Open a terminal, and as a non-root user, type **while true; do true; done**

Step 7. Observe what is happening in **top**. If you have a single-core system, you will see that both **dd** processes get 50 percent of all CPU cycles, and the user bash process that was just started also gets 50 percent of all CPU cycles. This proves that one very busy user process can have dramatic consequences for the system processes.

Step 8. If in the previous step you don't see the described behavior, type **1** in the **top** interface. This will show a line for each CPU core on your system. You should see multiple CPU cores.

Step 9. To temporarily shut down a CPU core, use the command **echo 0 > /sys/bus/cpu/devices/cpu1/online**. Repeat this command for each CPU, except for cpu0.

Step 10. To enable any CPU core you've just disabled, use either **echo 1 > /sys/bus/cpu/devices/cpu1/online** or **reboot**.

Step 11. Use **killall dd** to make sure all **dd** processes are terminated.

As you've just seen, the standard configuration of cgroup slices can lead to unexpected results. If you don't like this behavior, you can increase the priority of the system slice. Use **systemctl set-property system.slice CPUWeight=800** to set the CPUWeight of all processes in the system slices eight times as high as all processes in the user slice.

Managing Process Priorities

When Linux processes are started, they are started with a specific priority. By default, all regular processes are equal and are started with the same priority, which is the priority number 20, as shown by utilities like **top**. In some cases, it is useful to change the default priority that was assigned to the process when it was started. You can do that using the **nice** and **renice** commands. Use ***nice*** if you want to start a process with an adjusted priority. Use **renice** to change the priority for a currently active process. Alternatively, you can use the **r** command from the **top** utility to change the priority of a currently running process.

Changing process priority may make sense in two different scenarios. Suppose, for example, that you are about to start a backup job that does not necessarily have to finish fast. Typically, backup jobs are rather resource intensive, so you might want to start the backup job in a way that does not annoy other users too much, by lowering its priority.

Another example is where you are about to start a very important calculation job. To ensure that it is handled as fast as possible, you might want to give it an increased priority, taking away CPU time from other processes.

On earlier Linux versions, it could be dangerous to increase the priority of one job too much, because of the risk that other processes (including vital kernel processes) might be blocked out completely. On current Linux kernels, that risk is minimized for these reasons:

- Modern Linux kernels differentiate between essential kernel threads that are started as real-time processes and normal user processes. Increasing the priority of a user process will never be able to block out kernel threads or other processes that were started as real-time processes.

- Modern computers often have multiple CPU cores. A single-threaded process that is running with the highest priority will never be able to get beyond the boundaries of the CPU it is running on.
- As you've read before, processes are running in slices, and by default, each slice can claim as many CPU cycles as each other slice.

When using **nice** or **renice** to adjust process priority, you can select from values ranging from –20 to 19. The default niceness of a process is set to 0 (which results in the priority value of 20). By applying a negative niceness, you increase the priority. Use a positive niceness to decrease the priority. It is a good idea not to use the ultimate values immediately. Instead, use increments of 5 and see how it affects the application.

TIP Do not set process priority to –20; it risks blocking other processes from getting served.

Let's take a look at examples of how to use **nice** and **renice**:

1. Run the command **nice -n 5 dd if=/dev/zero of=/dev/null &** to an infinite I/O-intensive job, but with an adjusted niceness so that some room remains for other processes as well.
2. Use **ps aux | grep dd** to find the PID of the **dd** command that you just started. The PID is in the second column of the command output.
3. Use **renice -n 10 -p 1234** (assuming that 1234 is the PID you just found).
4. Use **top** to verify the adjusted process priority and stop the **dd** process you just started.

Note that regular users can only decrease the priority of a running process. You must be root to give processes increased priority by using negative **nice** values.

Sending Signals to Processes with kill, killall, and pkill

Before you start to think about using the ***kill*** command or sending other ***signals*** to processes, it is good to know that Linux processes have a hierarchical relationship. Every process has a parent process, and as long as it lives, the parent process is responsible for the child processes it has created. In older versions of Linux, killing a parent process would also kill all of its child processes. In RHEL 9, if you kill a parent process, all of its child processes become children of the systemd process.

The Linux kernel allows many signals to be sent to processes. Use **man 7 signal** for a complete overview of all the available signals. Three of these signals work for all processes:

- The signal SIGTERM (15) is used to ask a process to stop.
- The signal SIGKILL (9) is used to force a process to stop.
- The SIGHUP (1) signal is used to hang up a process. The effect is that the process will reread its configuration files, which makes this a useful signal to use after making modifications to a process configuration file.

To send a signal to a process, you use the **kill** command. The most common use is the need to stop a process, which you can do by using the **kill** command followed by the PID of the process. This sends the SIGTERM signal to the process, which normally causes the process to cease its activity and close all open files.

Sometimes the **kill** command does not work because the process you want to kill can ignore it. In that case, you can use **kill -9** to send the SIGKILL signal to the process. Because the SIGKILL signal cannot be ignored, it forces the process to stop, but you also risk losing data while using this command. In general, it is a bad idea to use **kill -9**:

- You risk losing data.
- Your system may become unstable if other processes depend on the process you have just killed.

TIP Use **kill -l** to show a list of available signals that can be used with **kill**.

There are some commands that are related to kill: **killall** and **pkill**. The **pkill** command is a bit easier to use because it takes the name rather than the PID of the process as an argument. You can use the **killall** command if multiple processes using the same name need to be killed simultaneously. However, it is recommended to use **kill**, followed by the exact PID of processes you want to stop, because otherwise you risk terminating processes that didn't need to be killed anyway.

Using **killall** was particularly common when Linux environments were multiprocessing instead of multithreading. In a multiprocessing environment where a server starts several commands, all with the same name, it is not easy to stop these commands one by one based on their individual PID. Using **killall** enables you to terminate all these processes simultaneously.

In a multithreaded environment, the urge to use **killall** is weaker. Because there is often just one process that is generating several threads, all these threads are terminated anyway by stopping the process that started them. You still can use **killall**, though, to terminate lots of processes with the same name that have been started on your server. In Exercise 10-2, you practice using **ps**, **nice**, **kill**, and related utilities to manage processes.

Exercise 10-2 Managing Processes from the Command Line

1. Open a root shell. From this shell, type **dd if=/dev/zero of=/dev/null &**. Repeat this command three times.
2. Type **ps aux | grep dd**. This command shows all lines of output that have the letters *dd* in them; you will see more than just the **dd** processes, but that should not really matter. The processes you just started are listed last.
3. Use the PID of one of the **dd** processes to adjust the niceness, using **renice -n 5 <*PID*>**.
4. Type **ps fax | grep -B5 dd**. The **-B5** option shows the matching lines, including the five lines before that. Because **ps fax** shows hierarchical relationships between processes, you should also find the shell and its PID from which all the **dd** processes were started.
5. Find the PID of the shell from which the **dd** processes were started and type **kill -9 <*PID*>**, replacing **<*PID*>** with the PID of the shell you just found. Because the **dd** processes were started as background processes, they are not killed when their parent shell is killed. Instead, they have been moved up and are now children of the systemd process.
6. Use **killall** to kill all remaining **dd** processes.

Killing Zombies

Zombies are processes with a special state. Zombie processes are processes that have completed execution but are still listed in the process table. You can check if you have zombies using **ps aux | grep defunct**. Although zombies are harmless, it is annoying to have them, and you may want to do something to clean them up.

The issue with zombies is that you cannot kill them in the way that works for normal processes. Rebooting your system is a solution, but doing so is a bit too much for processes that aren't really causing any harm. Fortunately, in recent RHEL systems you can often—not in all cases—get rid of zombies by applying the following procedure:

Step 1. Make sure you have cloned the books git repository, using **git clone https://github.com/sandervanvugt/rhcsa**.

Step 2. Enter the rhcsa directory, using **cd rhcsa**, and use **./zombie** to start the demo zombie process.

Step 3. Use **ps aux | grep zombie** to verify the zombie is running. You should see two processes, one being the parent that is responsible for the zombie, the other one being the zombie itself.

Step 4. Use **kill <childpid>**, in which **<childpid>** is replaced with the actual PID of the child processes you've found in step 3. Notice that this fails.

Step 5. use **kill -SIGCHLD <parentpid>**. This will tell the parent process to remove its child processes. Now the zombie will get adopted by systemd, and after a few seconds it will be removed.

Step 6. If the zombie wasn't killed by this procedure, use **kill -9** to kill the parent process.

Using top to Manage Processes

A convenient tool to manage processes is **top**. For common process management tasks, **top** is great because it gives an overview of the most active processes currently running (hence the name **top**). This enables you to easily find processes that might need attention. From **top**, you can also perform common process management tasks, such as adjusting the current process priority and killing processes. Figure 10-1 shows the interface that appears when you start **top**.

```
top - 12:54:15 up 35 min,  1 user,  load average: 0.00, 0.00, 0.00
Tasks: 307 total,   1 running, 305 sleeping,   0 stopped,   1 zombie
%Cpu(s):  0.2 us,  0.2 sy,  0.0 ni, 99.5 id,  0.0 wa,  0.2 hi,  0.0 si,  0.0 st
MiB Mem :   3696.9 total,   1734.8 free,   1243.2 used,    718.8 buff/cache
MiB Swap:   2048.0 total,   2048.0 free,      0.0 used.   2168.0 avail Mem

    PID USER      PR  NI    VIRT    RES    SHR S  %CPU  %MEM     TIME+ COMMAND
   5776 root      20   0  462240  71844  28208 S   0.3   1.9   0:01.38 rhsm-service
   6669 root      20   0  226052   4484   3604 R   0.3   0.1   0:00.03 top
      1 root      20   0  171760  16088  10360 S   0.0   0.4   0:01.04 systemd
      2 root      20   0       0      0      0 S   0.0   0.0   0:00.01 kthreadd
      3 root       0 -20       0      0      0 I   0.0   0.0   0:00.00 rcu_gp
      4 root       0 -20       0      0      0 I   0.0   0.0   0:00.00 rcu_par_gp
      6 root       0 -20       0      0      0 I   0.0   0.0   0:00.00 kworker/0:0H-events_highpri
      9 root       0 -20       0      0      0 I   0.0   0.0   0:00.00 mm_percpu_wq
     10 root      20   0       0      0      0 S   0.0   0.0   0:00.00 rcu_tasks_kthre
     11 root      20   0       0      0      0 S   0.0   0.0   0:00.00 rcu_tasks_rude_
     12 root      20   0       0      0      0 S   0.0   0.0   0:00.00 rcu_tasks_trace
     13 root      20   0       0      0      0 S   0.0   0.0   0:00.01 ksoftirqd/0
     14 root      20   0       0      0      0 I   0.0   0.0   0:00.09 rcu_preempt
     15 root      rt   0       0      0      0 S   0.0   0.0   0:00.01 migration/0
     16 root      20   0       0      0      0 S   0.0   0.0   0:00.00 cpuhp/0
     17 root      20   0       0      0      0 S   0.0   0.0   0:00.00 cpuhp/1
     18 root      rt   0       0      0      0 S   0.0   0.0   0:00.18 migration/1
     19 root      20   0       0      0      0 S   0.0   0.0   0:00.16 ksoftirqd/1
     21 root       0 -20       0      0      0 I   0.0   0.0   0:00.00 kworker/1:0H-events_highpri
     24 root      20   0       0      0      0 S   0.0   0.0   0:00.00 kdevtmpfs
     25 root       0 -20       0      0      0 I   0.0   0.0   0:00.00 netns
     26 root       0 -20       0      0      0 I   0.0   0.0   0:00.00 inet_frag_wq
     27 root      20   0       0      0      0 S   0.0   0.0   0:00.00 kauditd
     29 root      20   0       0      0      0 S   0.0   0.0   0:00.00 khungtaskd
     30 root      20   0       0      0      0 S   0.0   0.0   0:00.00 oom_reaper
     31 root       0 -20       0      0      0 I   0.0   0.0   0:00.00 writeback
     32 root      20   0       0      0      0 S   0.0   0.0   0:00.07 kcompactd0
     33 root      25   5       0      0      0 S   0.0   0.0   0:00.00 ksmd
```

Figure 10-1 Using **top** Makes Process Management Easy

Among the information that you can conveniently obtain from the **top** utility is the process state. Table 10-3 provides an overview of the different process states that you may observe.

Table 10-3 Linux Process States Overview

State	Meaning
Running (R)	The process is currently active and using CPU time, or in the queue of runnable processes waiting to get services.
Sleeping (S)	The process is waiting for an event to complete.
Uninterruptible sleep (D)	The process is in a sleep state that cannot be stopped. This usually happens while a process is waiting for I/O. This state is also known as blocking state.
Stopped (T)	The process has been stopped, which typically has happened to an interactive shell process, using the Ctrl-Z key sequence.
Zombie (Z)	The process has been stopped but could not be removed by its parent, which has put it in an unmanageable state.

Now that you know how to use the **kill** and **nice** commands from the command line, using the same functionality from **top** is even easier. From **top**, type **k**; **top** then prompts for the PID of the process you want to send a signal to. By default, the most active process is selected. After you enter the PID, **top** asks which signal you want to send. By default, signal 15 for SIGTERM is used. However, if you want to insist on a bit more, you can type **9** for SIGKILL. Now press Enter to terminate the process.

To renice a running process from **top**, type **r**. You are first prompted for the PID of the process you want to renice. After entering the PID, you are prompted for the **nice** value you want to use. Enter a positive value to decrease process priority or a negative value to increase process priority.

Another important parameter you can get from **top** is the load average. The load average is expressed as the number of processes that are in a runnable state (R) or in a blocking state (D). Processes are in a runnable state if they currently are running, or waiting to be serviced. Processes are in a blocking state if they are waiting for I/O. The load average is shown for the last 1, 5, and 15 minutes, and you can see the current values in the upper-right corner of the **top** screen. Alternatively, you can use the **uptime** command to show current load average statistics (see Example 10-4).

Example 10-4 Using **uptime** for Information About Load Average

```
[root@server3 ~]# uptime
 12:43:03 up  4:17,  3 users,  load average: 4.90, 0.98, 0.19
```

As a rule of thumb, the load average should not be higher than the number of CPU cores in your system. You can find out the number of CPU cores in your system by using the **lscpu** command. If the load average over a longer period is higher than the number of CPUs in your system, you may have a performance problem. In Exercise 10-3 you investigate the load average statistics and learn how to manage load average.

Exercise 10-3 Managing Load Average

1. Open a root shell. From this shell, type **dd if=/dev/zero of=/dev/null &**. Repeat this command three times.
2. Type **top** and observe the current load average. After a few seconds, use **q** to quit **top**.
3. From the command line, type **uptime**. You should see the numbers that are shown as the load average is slowly increasing.
4. Type **lscpu** and look for the number of CPU(s). Also look for the Core(s) per CPU parameter so that you can calculate the total number of CPU cores.
5. Use **killall dd** to kill all **dd** processes.

Using tuned to Optimize Performance

To offer the best possible performance right from the start, RHEL 9 comes with **tuned**. It offers a daemon that monitors system activity and provides some profiles. In the ***profiles***, an administrator can automatically tune a system for best possible latency, throughput, or power consumption.

Based on the properties of an installed system, a ***tuned*** profile is selected automatically at installation, and after installation it's possible to manually change the current profile. Administrators can also change settings in a **tuned** profile. Table 10-4 gives an overview of the most important default profiles.

Table 10-4 tuned Profile Overview

Profile	Use
balanced	The best compromise between power usage and performance
desktop	Based on the balanced profile, but tuned for better response to interactive applications
latency-performance	Tuned for maximum throughput
network-latency	Based on latency-performance, but with additional options to reduce network latency
network-throughput	Based on throughput-performance, optimizes older CPUs for streaming content
powersave	Tunes for maximum power saving
throughput-performance	Tunes for maximum throughput
virtual-guest	Optimizes Linux for running as a virtual machine
virtual-host	Optimizes Linux for use as a KVM host

It is relatively easy to create custom profiles. Also, when you're installing specific packages, profiles may be added. So you may find that some additional performance profiles exist on your server.

To manage the performance profile, the **tuned-adm** command is provided. It talks to the **tuned** daemon, so before you can use it, run **systemctl enable --now tuned** to start the **tuned** daemon. Next, use **tuned-adm** active to find out which profile currently is selected. For an overview of profiles available on your server, type **tuned-adm list**. To select another profile, type **tuned-adm profile profile-name**. The **tuned** service can also recommend a **tuned** profile for your system: use **tuned-adm recommend**. In Exercise 10-4 you can practice working with **tuned**.

Exercise 10-4 Using tuned

1. Use **dnf -y install tuned** to ensure that **tuned** is installed. (It probably already is.)
2. Type **systemctl status tuned** to check whether **tuned** currently is running. If it is not, use **systemctl enable --now tuned**.
3. Type **tuned-adm active** to see which profile currently is used.
4. Type **tuned-adm recommend** to see which **tuned** profile is recommended.
5. To select and activate the **throughput-performance** profile, type **tuned-adm profile throughput-performance**.

Summary

Managing processes is a common task for a Linux system administrator. In this chapter, you learned how to look up specific processes and how to change their priority using **nice** and **kill**. You also learned how to use **tuned** to select the performance profile that best matches your server's workload.

Exam Preparation Tasks

As mentioned in the section "How to Use This Book" in the Introduction, you have several choices for exam preparation: the end-of-chapter labs; the memory tables in Appendix C; Chapter 27, "Final Preparation"; and the practice exams.

Review All Key Topics

Review the most important topics in the chapter, noted with the Key Topic icon in the margin of the page. Table 10-5 lists a reference for these key topics and the page number on which each is found.

Table 10-5 Key Topics for Chapter 10

Key Topic Element	Description	Page
Table 10-2	Job Management Overview	236
List	Essential signals overview	244
Table 10-3	Linux Process States Overview	247

Complete Tables and Lists from Memory

Print a copy of Appendix C, "Memory Tables" (found on the companion website), or at least the section for this chapter, and complete the tables and lists from memory. Appendix D, "Memory Tables Answer Key," includes completed tables and lists to check your work.

Define Key Terms

Define the following key terms from this chapter and check your answers in the glossary:

process, thread, job, foreground process, background process, process identification number (PID), **nice**, **kill**, signal, zombie, profile, **tuned**

Review Questions

The questions that follow are meant to help you test your knowledge of concepts and terminology and the breadth of your knowledge. You can find the answers to these questions in Appendix A.

1. Which command gives an overview of all current shell jobs?
2. How do you stop the current shell job to continue running it in the background?
3. Which keystroke combination can you use to cancel the current shell job?
4. A user is asking you to cancel one of the jobs he has started. You cannot access the shell that user currently is working from. What can you do to cancel his job anyway?
5. Which command would you use to show parent–child relationships between processes?
6. Which command enables you to change the priority of PID 1234 to a higher priority?
7. On your system, 20 **dd** processes are currently running. What is the easiest way to stop all of them?
8. Which command enables you to stop the command with the name **mycommand**?
9. Which command do you use from **top** to kill a process?
10. What is required to select a performance profile that best matches your system needs?

End-of-Chapter Lab

In this end-of-chapter lab, you apply some of the most important process management tasks. Use the tools that you find the most convenient to perform these labs.

Lab 10.1

1. Launch the command **dd if=/dev/zero of=/dev/null** three times as a background job.
2. Increase the priority of one of these commands using the **nice** value **-5**. Change the priority of the same process again, but this time use the value **-15**. Observe the difference.
3. Kill all the **dd** processes you just started.
4. Ensure that **tuned** is installed and active, and set the throughput-performance profile.

The following topics are covered in this chapter:

- Understanding Systemd
- Managing Units Through Systemd

The following RHCSA exam objectives are covered in this chapter:

- Start, stop, and check the status of network services
- Start and stop services and configure services to automatically start at boot

CHAPTER 11

Working with Systemd

In this chapter, you learn about Systemd, which is the system and service manager used on RHEL since RHEL 7. You discover all the things that Systemd can do, and after you have a good general understanding, you learn how to work with Systemd services. Systemd is also involved in booting your system in a desired state, which is called a *target*. That topic is covered in Chapter 17, "Managing and Understanding the Boot Procedure."

"Do I Know This Already?" Quiz

The "Do I Know This Already?" quiz enables you to assess whether you should read this entire chapter thoroughly or jump to the "Exam Preparation Tasks" section. If you are in doubt about your answers to these questions or your own assessment of your knowledge of the topics, read the entire chapter. Table 11-1 lists the major headings in this chapter and their corresponding "Do I Know This Already?" quiz questions. You can find the answers in Appendix A, "Answers to the 'Do I Know This Already?' Quizzes and Review Questions."

Table 11-1 "Do I Know This Already?" Section-to-Question Mapping

Foundation Topics Section	Questions
Understanding Systemd	1–5
Managing Units Through Systemd	6–10

1. Which command shows all service unit files on your system that are currently loaded?
   a. **systemctl -t service**
   b. **systemctl -t service --all**
   c. **systemctl --list-services**
   d. **systemctl --show-units | grep services**

2. Which statement about Systemd wants is *not* true?
   a. You can create wants by using the **systemctl enable** command.
   b. The target to which a specific want applies is agnostic of the associated wants.
   c. Wants are always administered in the /usr/lib/systemd/system directory.
   d. Each service knows to which target it wants to be added.
3. What is the best solution to avoid conflicts between incompatible units?
   a. Nothing; the unit files have defined for themselves which units they are not compatible with.
   b. Disable the service using **systemctl disable**.
   c. Unmask the service using **systemctl unmask**.
   d. Mask the service using **systemctl mask**.
4. Which of the following is not a valid status for Systemd services?
   a. Active(running)
   b. Active(exited)
   c. Active(waiting)
   d. Running(dead)
5. Which of the following statements is *not* true about socket units?
   a. A socket unit requires a service unit with the same name.
   b. Socket units can listen on ports and activate services only when activity occurs on a port.
   c. Socket units cannot contain the name of the associated binary that should be started.
   d. Socket units may react upon path activity.
6. Which of the following is not a valid Systemd unit type?
   a. service
   b. udev
   c. mount
   d. socket

7. You want to find out which other Systemd units have dependencies to a specific unit. Which command would you use?
    a. **systemd list-dependencies --reverse**
    b. **systemctl list-dependencies --reverse**
    c. **systemctl status my.unit --show-deps**
    d. **systemd status my.unit --show-deps -r**

8. How do you change the default editor that Systemd uses to **vim**?
    a. **export EDITOR=vim**
    b. **export SYSTEMD_EDITOR=vim**
    c. **export EDITOR=/bin/vim**
    d. **export SYSTEMD_EDITOR=/bin/vim**

9. Which of the following keywords should you use to define a Systemd dependency if you want to ensure that the boot procedure doesn't fail if the dependency fails?
    a. Required
    b. Requisite
    c. Before
    d. Wants

10. Which of the following is *not* a valid command while working with units in **systemctl**?
    a. **systemctl unit start**
    b. **systemctl status -l unit**
    c. **systemctl mask unit**
    d. **systemctl disable unit**

Foundation Topics

Understanding Systemd

Systemd is the part of Red Hat Enterprise Linux that is responsible for starting not only services but also a variety of other items. In this chapter, you learn how Systemd is organized and what items are started from Systemd.

To describe it in a generic way, the Systemd system and service manager is used to start stuff. The stuff is referred to as ***units***. Units can be many things. One of the most important unit types is the service. Typically, services are processes that provide specific functionality and allow connections from external clients coming in, such as the SSH service, the Apache web service, and many more. Apart from service, other unit types exist, such as socket, mount, and target. To display a list of available units, type **systemctl -t help** (see Example 11-1).

Example 11-1 Unit Types in Systemd

```
[root@server1 ~]# systemctl -t help
Available unit types:
service
socket
target
device
mount
automount
swap
timer
path
slice
scope
```

Understanding Systemd Unit Locations

The major benefit of working with Systemd, as compared to previous methods Red Hat used for managing services, is that it provides a uniform interface to start units. This interface is defined in the unit file. Unit files can occur in three locations:

- **/usr/lib/systemd/system:** Contains default unit files that have been installed from RPM packages. You should never edit these files directly.

- **/etc/systemd/system:** Contains custom unit files. It may also contain files that have been written by an administrator or generated by the **systemctl edit** command.
- **/run/systemd/system:** Contains unit files that have been generated automatically.

If a unit file exists in more than one of these locations, units in the /run directory have highest precedence and will overwrite any settings that were defined elsewhere. Units in /etc/systemd/system have second highest precedence, and units in /usr/lib/systemd/system come last.

Understanding Systemd Service Units

Probably the most important unit type is the service unit. It is used to start processes. You can start any type of process by using a service unit, including daemon processes and commands.

Example 11-2 shows a service unit file, vsftpd.service, for the Very Secure FTP service.

Example 11-2 A Service Unit File

```
[Unit]
Description=Vsftpd ftp daemon
After=network.target

[Service]
Type=forking
ExecStart=/usr/sbin/vsftpd /etc/vsftpd/vsftpd.conf

[Install]
WantedBy=multi-user.target
```

You can see from this unit file example that unit files are relatively easy to understand. Systemd *service* unit files typically consist of the following three sections (other types of unit files have different sections):

- **[Unit]** Describes the unit and defines dependencies. This section also contains the important **After** statement and optionally the **Before** statement. These statements define dependencies between different units, and they relate to the perspective of this unit. The **Before** statement indicates that this unit should be started before the unit that is specified. The **After** statement indicates that this unit should be started after the unit that is specified.

- **[Service]** Describes how to start and stop the service and request status installation. Normally, you can expect an ExecStart line, which indicates how to start the unit, or an ExecStop line, which indicates how to stop the unit. Note the **Type** option, which is used to specify how the process should start. The **forking** type is commonly used by daemon processes, but you can also use other types, such as **oneshot** and **simple**, which will start any command from a Systemd unit. See **man 5 systemd.service** for more details.
- **[Install]** Indicates in which target this unit has to be started. The section "Understanding Systemd Target Units" a bit later in this chapter explains how to work with targets. This section is optional, but units that don't have an [Install] section cannot be started automatically.

Understanding Systemd Mount Units

A mount unit specifies how a file system can be mounted on a specific directory. Mount units are an alternative for mounting file systems through /etc/fstab, about which you'll learn more in Chapter 14 "Managing Storage." Example 11-3 shows a mount unit file, tmp.mount.

Example 11-3 A Mount Unit File

```
[root@server1 ~]# cat /usr/lib/systemd/system/tmp.mount
[Unit]
Description=Temporary Directory /tmp
Documentation=https://systemd.io/TEMPORARY_DIRECTORIES
Documentation=man:file-hierarchy(7)
Documentation=https://www.freedesktop.org/wiki/Software/systemd/
  APIFileSystems
ConditionPathIsSymbolicLink=!/tmp
DefaultDependencies=no
Conflicts=umount.target
Before=local-fs.target umount.target
After=swap.target

[Mount]
What=tmpfs
Where=/tmp
Type=tmpfs
Options=mode=1777,strictatime,nosuid,nodev,size=50%,nr_inodes=1m

# Make 'systemctl enable tmp.mount' work:
[Install]
WantedBy=local-fs.target
```

The tmp.mount unit file in Example 11-3 shows some interesting additional configuration options in its sections:

- **[Unit]** The **Conflicts** statement is used to list units that cannot be used together with this unit. Use this statement for mutually exclusive units.
- **[Mount]** This section defines exactly where the mount has to be performed. Here you see the arguments that are typically used in any **mount** command.

Understanding Systemd Socket Units

Another type of unit that is interesting to look at is the socket. A socket creates a method for applications to communicate with one another. A socket may be defined as a file but also as a port on which Systemd will be listening for incoming connections. That way, a service doesn't have to run continuously but instead will start only if a connection is coming in on the socket that is specified. Every socket needs a corresponding service file. Example 11-4 shows what the cockpit.socket file looks like; notice that this file requires a service file with the name cockpit.service.

Example 11-4 A Socket Unit File

```
[Unit]
Description=Cockpit Web Service Socket
Documentation=man:cockpit-ws(8)
Wants=cockpit-motd.service

[Socket]
ListenStream=9090
ExecStartPost=-/usr/share/cockpit/motd/update-motd '' localhost
ExecStartPost=-/bin/ln -snf active.motd /run/cockpit/motd
ExecStopPost=-/bin/ln -snf /usr/share/cockpit/motd/inactive.motd /run/
  cockpit/motd

[Install]
WantedBy=sockets.target
```

The important option in Example 11-4 is **ListenStream**. This option defines the TCP port that Systemd should be listening to for incoming connections. Sockets can also be created for UDP ports, in which case you would use **ListenDatagram** instead of **ListenStream**.

Understanding Systemd Target Units

The unit files are used to build the functionality that is needed on your server. To make it possible to load them in the right order and at the right moment, you use a specific type of unit: the target unit. A simple definition of a ***target*** unit is "a group of units." Some targets are used to define the state a server should be started in. As such, target units are comparable to the runlevels used in earlier versions of RHEL.

Other targets are just a group of services that make it easy to manage not only individual units but also all the units that are required to get specific functionality. The sound.target is an example of such a target; you can use it to easily start or stop all units that are required to enable sound on a system.

Targets by themselves can have dependencies on other targets. These dependencies are defined in the target unit. An example of such a dependency relation is the basic.target. This target defines all the units that should always be started. You can use the **systemctl list-dependencies** command for an overview of any existing dependencies.

Example 11-5 shows the definition of a target unit file, multi-user.target, which defines the normal operational state of a RHEL server.

Example 11-5 A Target Unit File

```
[Unit]
Description=Multi-User System
Documentation=man:systemd.special(7)
Requires=basic.target
Conflicts=rescue.service rescue.target
After=basic.target rescue.service rescue.target
AllowIsolate=yes
```

You can see that by itself the target unit does not contain any information about the units that it should start. It just defines what it requires and which services and targets it cannot coexist with. It also defines load ordering, by using the **After** statement in the [Unit] section. The target file does not contain any information about the units that should be included; that is defined in the [Install] section of the different unit files.

When administrators use the **systemctl enable** command, to ensure that a unit is automatically started while booting, the [Install] section of that unit is considered to determine to which target the unit should be added.

When you add a unit to a target, under the hood a symbolic link is created in the target directory in /etc/systemd/system. If, for instance, you enabled the vsftpd service to be automatically started, you'll find that a symbolic link /etc/systemd/system/multi-user.target/wants/vsftpd.service has been added, pointing to the unit file in /usr/lib/systemd/system/vsftpd.service and thus ensuring that the unit will automatically be started. In Systemd terminology, this symbolic link is known as a ***want***, as it defines what the target wants to start when it is processed.

Managing Units Through Systemd

Managing the current state of Systemd units is an important task for RHEL administrators. Managing units means not only managing their current state but also changing options used by the different units.

Managing Systemd units starts with starting and stopping units. As an administrator, you use the **systemctl** command to do that. In Exercise 11-1, you start, stop, and manage a unit. After you configure a unit so that it can be started without problems, you need to make sure that it restarts automatically upon reboot. You do this by enabling or disabling the unit.

TIP The **systemctl** command has a large number of options, which may appear overwhelming at first sight, but there's no need to be overwhelmed. Just ensure that the **bash-completion** package is installed and use Tab completion on the **systemctl** command, which provides easy access to all of the available options.

Exercise 11-1 Managing Units with systemctl

1. From a root shell, type **dnf -y install vsftpd** to install the Very Secure FTP service.
2. Type **systemctl start vsftpd** to activate the FTP server on your machine.
3. Type **systemctl status vsftpd** to get output like that shown in Example 11-6, where you can see that the vsftpd service is currently operational. In the Loaded line, you can also see that the service is currently disabled, which means that it will not be activated on a system restart. The vendor preset also shows as disabled, which means that, by default, after installation this unit will not automatically be enabled.
4. Type **systemctl enable vsftpd** to create a symbolic link in the wants directory for the multiuser target to ensure that the service is automatically started after a restart.
5. Type **systemctl status vsftpd** again. You'll see that the unit file has changed from being disabled to enabled.

Example 11-6 Requesting Current Unit Status with **systemctl status**

```
[root@server1 system]# systemctl status vsftpd
● vsftpd.service - Vsftpd ftp daemon
     Loaded: loaded (/usr/lib/systemd/system/vsftpd.service; enabled;
  vendor preset: disabled)
     Active: active (running) since Thu 2022-09-15 08:42:50 CEST; 6s
   ago
    Process: 33967 ExecStart=/usr/sbin/vsftpd /etc/vsftpd/vsftpd.conf
  (code=exited, status=0/SUCCESS)
   Main PID: 33968 (vsftpd)
      Tasks: 1 (limit: 23272)
     Memory: 708.0K
        CPU: 2ms
     CGroup: /system.slice/vsftpd.service
             └─33968 /usr/sbin/vsftpd /etc/vsftpd/vsftpd.conf

Sep 15 08:42:50 server1.example.com systemd[1]: Starting Vsftpd ftp
  daemon...
Sep 15 08:42:50 server1.example.com systemd[1]: Started Vsftpd ftp
  daemon. .
```

When requesting the current status of a Systemd unit as in Example 11-6, you can see different kinds of information about it. Table 11-2 shows the different kinds of information that you can get about unit files when using the **systemctl status** command.

Table 11-2 Systemd Status Overview

Status	Description
Loaded	The unit file has been processed and the unit is active.
Active(running)	The unit is running with one or more active processes.
Active(exited)	The unit has successfully completed a one-time run.
Active(waiting)	The unit is running and waiting for an event.
Inactive(dead)	The unit is not running.
Enabled	The unit will be started at boot time.
Disabled	The unit will not be started at boot time.
Static	The unit cannot be enabled but may be started by another unit automatically.

As an administrator, you also often need to get a current overview of the current status of Systemd unit files. Different commands, some of which are shown in Table 11-3, can help you get this insight.

Table 11-3 systemctl Unit Overview Commands

Command	Description
systemctl -t service	Shows only service units
systemctl list-units -t service	Shows all active service units (same result as the previous command)
systemctl list-units -t service --all	Shows inactive service units as well as active service units
systemctl --failed -t service	Shows all services that have failed
systemctl status -l your.service	Shows detailed status information about services

Managing Dependencies

In general, there are two ways to manage Systemd dependencies:

- Unit types such as socket, timer, and path are directly related to a service unit. Systemd can make the connection because the first part of the name is the same: cockpit.socket works with cockpit.service. Accessing either of these unit types will automatically trigger the service type.
- Dependencies can be defined within the unit, using keywords like **Requires**, **Requisite**, **After**, and **Before**.

As an administrator, you can request a list of unit dependencies. Type **systemctl list-dependencies** followed by a unit name to find out which dependencies it has; add the **--reverse** option to find out which units are required for this unit to be started. Example 11-7 shows an example of this command.

Example 11-7 Showing Unit Dependencies

```
[root@server1 ~]# systemctl list-dependencies vsftpd
  vsftpd.service
└─system.slice
└─basic.target
  ├─alsa-restore.service
  ├─alsa-state.service
  ├─firewalld.service
```

```
├─microcode.service
├─rhel-autorelabel-mark.service
├─rhel-autorelabel.service
├─rhel-configure.service
├─rhel-dmesg.service
├─rhel-loadmodules.service
├─paths.target
├─slices.target
│ ├─-.slice
│ ├─system.slice
├─sockets.target
│ ├─avahi-daemon.socket
│ ├─cups.socket
│ ├─dbus.socket
│ ├─dm-event.socket
│ ├─iscsid.socket
│ ├─iscsiuio.socket
│ ├─lvm2-lvmetad.socket
│ ├─rpcbind.socket
│ ├─systemd-initctl.socket
│ ├─systemd-journald.socket
│ ├─systemd-shutdownd.socket
│ ├─systemd-udevd-control.socket
│ ├─systemd-udevd-kernel.socket
├─sysinit.target
│ ├─dev-hugepages.mount
│ ├─dev-mqueue.mount
│ ├─dmraid-activation.service
│ ├─iscsi.service
```

To ensure accurate dependency management, you can use different keywords in the [Unit] section of a unit:

- **Requires:** If this unit loads, units listed here will load also. If one of the other units is deactivated, this unit will also be deactivated.
- **Requisite:** If the unit listed here is not already loaded, this unit will fail.
- **Wants:** This unit wants to load the units that are listed here, but it will not fail if any of the listed units fail.
- **Before:** This unit will start before the unit specified with **Before**.
- **After:** This unit will start after the unit specified with **After**.

In upcoming Exercise 11-2 you learn how to use these options to manage unit dependency relations.

Managing Unit Options

When working with Systemd unit files, you risk getting overwhelmed by its many options. Every unit file can be configured with different options. To figure out which options are available for a specific unit, use the **systemctl show** command. For instance, the **systemctl show sshd** command shows all Systemd options that can be configured in the sshd.service unit, including their current default values. Example 11-8 shows the output of this command.

Example 11-8 Showing Available Options with **systemctl show**

```
[root@server1 ~]# systemctl show | head -20
Id=sshd.service
Names=sshd.service
Requires=basic.target
Wants=sshd-keygen.service system.slice
WantedBy=multi-user.target
ConsistsOf=sshd-keygen.service
Conflicts=shutdown.target
ConflictedBy=sshd.socket
Before=shutdown.target multi-user.target
After=network.target sshd-keygen.service systemd-journald.socket
  basic.target system.slice
Description=OpenSSH server daemon
LoadState=loaded
ActiveState=active
SubState=running
FragmentPath=/usr/lib/systemd/system/sshd.service
UnitFileState=enabled
InactiveExitTimestamp=Sat 2015-05-02 11:06:02 EDT
InactiveExitTimestampMonotonic=2596332166
ActiveEnterTimestamp=Sat 2015-05-02 11:06:02 EDT
ActiveEnterTimestampMonotonic=2596332166
ActiveExitTimestamp=Sat 2015-05-02 11:05:22 EDT
ActiveExitTimestampMonotonic=2559916100
InactiveEnterTimestamp=Sat 2015-05-02 11:06:02 EDT
```

When changing unit files to apply options, you need to make sure that the changes are written to /etc/systemd/system, which is the location where custom unit files should be created. The recommended way to do so is to use the **systemctl edit** command. This command creates a subdirectory in /etc/systemd/system for the service that you are editing; for example, if you use **systemctl edit sshd.service**, you get a directory with the name /etc/systemd/systemd/sshd.service.d in which a file with the name override.conf is created. All settings that are applied in this file overwrite any existing settings in the service file in /usr/lib/systemd/system. In Exercise 11-2 you learn how to apply changes to Systemd units.

TIP By default, Systemd uses the **nano** editor. Not everybody likes that very much (including me). If you want **vim** to be used instead of **nano**, edit the /root/.bash_profile file to include the following line: **export SYSTEMD_EDITOR="/bin/vim"** and add this line to the ~/.bashrc file. After you log in again, **vim** will be used as the default editor. If you would rather use /bin/vim as the default editor for all commands that need an external editor (including systemctl), you may also include **export EDITOR="/bin/vim"** instead.

Exercise 11-2 Changing Unit Configuration

1. From a root shell, type **dnf -y install httpd** to install the Apache web server package.
2. Use **systemctl cat httpd.service** to show the current configuration of the unit file that starts the Apache web server.
3. Type **systemctl show httpd.service** to get an overview of available configuration options for this unit file.
4. Type **export SYSTEMD_EDITOR=/bin/vim** to ensure you use **vim** as the default editor for the duration of this session. (Optionally, add this line to ~/.bashrc to make it persistent.)
5. Use **systemctl edit httpd.service** to change the default configuration, and add a [Service] section that includes the **Restart=always** and **RestartSec=5s** lines.
6. Enter **systemctl daemon-reload** to ensure that Systemd picks up the new configuration.
7. Type **systemctl start httpd** to start the httpd service and **systemctl status sshd** to verify that the sshd service is indeed running.

8. Use **killall httpd** to kill the httpd process.
9. Type **systemctl status httpd** and then repeat after 5 seconds. You'll notice that the httpd process gets automatically restarted.

Summary

In this chapter you learned how to work with Systemd. You read how to manage Systemd service state and how to change different options in Systemd. In the next chapter you'll learn how to schedule tasks using the cron and at services.

Exam Preparation Tasks

As mentioned in the section "How to Use This Book" in the Introduction, you have several choices for exam preparation: the end-of-chapter labs; the memory tables in Appendix C; Chapter 27, "Final Preparation"; and the practice exams.

Review All Key Topics

Review the most important topics in the chapter, noted with the Key Topic icon in the margin of the page. Table 11-4 lists a reference for these key topics and the page numbers on which each is found.

Table 11-4 Key Topics for Chapter 11

Key Topic Element	Description	Page Number
Example 11-1	Unit Types in Systemd	256
List	Three sections of a Systemd unit file	257
Section	Understanding Systemd Target Units	260
Exercise 11-1	Managing Units with **systemctl**	261
Table 11-3	**systemctl** Unit Overview Commands	263

Complete Tables and Lists from Memory

Print a copy of Appendix C, "Memory Tables" (found on the companion website), or at least the section for this chapter, and complete the tables and lists from memory. Appendix D, "Memory Tables Answer Key," includes completed tables and lists to check your work.

Define Key Terms

Define the following key terms from this chapter and check your answers in the glossary:

Systemd, unit, target, want

Review Questions

The questions that follow are meant to help you test your knowledge of concepts and terminology and the breadth of your knowledge. You can find the answers to these questions in Appendix A.

1. What is a unit?
2. Which command should you use to show all service units that are currently loaded?
3. How do you create a want for a service?
4. How do you change the default editor for **systemctl**?
5. Which directory contains custom Systemd unit files?
6. What should you include to ensure that a unit file will automatically load another unit file?
7. Which command shows available configuration options for the httpd.service unit?
8. Which command shows all dependencies for a specific unit?
9. What does it mean if **systemctl status** shows that a unit is dead?
10. How do you create a Systemd override file?

End-of-Chapter Lab

You have now learned how to work with Systemd. Before you continue, it is a good idea to work on a lab that helps ensure you can apply the skills that you acquired in this chapter.

Lab 11.1

1. Install the vsftpd and httpd services.
2. Set the default **systemctl** editor to **vim**.
3. Edit the httpd.service unit file such that starting httpd will always auto-start vsftpd. Edit the httpd service such that after failure it will automatically start again in 10 seconds.

The following topics are covered in this chapter:

- Understanding Task Scheduling Options in RHEL
- Using Systemd Timers
- Configuring cron to Automate Recurring Tasks
- Configuring at to Schedule Future Tasks

The following RHCSA exam objective is covered in this chapter:

- Schedule tasks using at and cron

Scheduling Tasks

On a Linux server it is important that certain tasks run at certain times. This can be done by using the at and cron services, which can be configured to run tasks in the future. The at service is for executing future tasks once only, and the cron service is for executing recurring regular tasks. Apart from these services, which have been around in all previous versions of RHEL, Systemd is providing timer units that can be used as an alternative. In this chapter you learn how to configure both cron and at, as well as Systemd timers.

"Do I Know This Already?" Quiz

The "Do I Know This Already?" quiz enables you to assess whether you should read this entire chapter thoroughly or jump to the "Exam Preparation Tasks" section. If you are in doubt about your answers to these questions or your own assessment of your knowledge of the topics, read the entire chapter. Table 12-1 lists the major headings in this chapter and their corresponding "Do I Know This Already?" quiz questions. You can find the answers in Appendix A, "Answers to the 'Do I Know This Already?' Quizzes and Review Questions."

Table 12-1 "Do I Know This Already?" Section-to-Question Mapping

Foundation Topics Section	Questions
Understanding Task Scheduling Options in RHEL	1
Using Systemd Timers	2–4
Configuring cron to Automate Recurring Tasks	5–8
Configuring at to Schedule Future Tasks	9–10

1. What is the default solution for scheduling recurring jobs in RHEL 9?
   a. Systemd timers
   b. cron
   c. anacron
   d. at

2. How do you configure a timer to start at a specific time?
   a. Use a cron-style starting time notation in the [Timer] section.
   b. Use OnCalendar in the [Timer] section.
   c. Use OnTime in the [Timer] section.
   d. Schedule it through cron.

3. You want a timer to be started 1 minute after starting of the Systemd service. Which option do you use?
   a. OnCalendar
   b. OnUnitActiveSec
   c. OnBootSec
   d. OnStartupSec

4. You want a systemd user unit to be started 2 minutes after the user has logged in. Which of the following would you use?
   a. OnCalendar
   b. OnUserLogin
   c. OnUserActiveSec
   d. OnStartupSec

5. Which of the following would run a cron task Sunday at 11 a.m.?
   a. *** 11 7 * ***
   b. **0 11 * 7 ***
   c. **0 11 * * 7**
   d. **11 0 * 7 ***

6. Which of the following launches a job every 5 minutes from Monday through Friday?
   a. ***/5 * * * 1-5**
   b. ***/5 * 1-5 * ***
   c. **0/5 * * * 1-5**
   d. **0/5 * 1-5 * ***

7. How do you create a cron job for a specific user?
   a. Log in as that user and type **crontab -e** to open the cron editor.
   b. Open the crontab file in the user home directory and add what you want to add.
   c. As root, type **crontab -e username**.
   d. As root, type **crontab -u username -e**.
8. Which of the following is not a recommended way to specify jobs that should be executed with cron?
   a. Modify /etc/crontab.
   b. Put the jobs in separate scripts in /etc/cron.d.
   c. Use **crontab -e** to create user-specific cron jobs.
   d. Put scripts in /etc/cron.{hourly|daily|weekly|monthly} for automatic execution.
9. After you enter commands in the at shell, which command enables you to close the at shell?
   a. Ctrl-V
   b. Ctrl-D
   c. **exit**
   d. **:wq**
10. Which command enables you to see current at jobs scheduled for execution?
   a. **atrm**
   b. **atls**
   c. **atq**
   d. **at**

Foundation Topics

Understanding Task Scheduling Options in RHEL

RHEL 9 offers different solutions for scheduling tasks:

- Systemd timers are now the default solution to ensure that specific tasks are started at specific moments.
- **cron** is the legacy scheduler service. It is still supported and responsible for scheduling a few services.
- **st** is used to schedule an occasional user job for future execution.

Using Systemd Timers

Since its initial appearance in RHEL 7, systemd has been replacing many services. Since the release of RHEL 9 it is also responsible for scheduling tasks. It is now the primary mechanism to do so, which means that if ever you are trying to find out how future tasks are executed, you should consider systemd timers first.

A systemd ***timer*** is always used together with a service file, and the names should match. For example, the logrotate.timer file is used to modify the logrotate.service file. The service unit defines *how* the service should be started, and the timer defines *when* it will be started. If you need a service to be started by a timer, you enable the timer, not the service. Example 12-1 shows what the logrotate.timer file looks like.

Example 12-1 Sample Timer Contents

```
[root@server1 system]# systemctl cat logrotate.timer
# /usr/lib/systemd/system/logrotate.timer
[Unit]
Description=Daily rotation of log files
Documentation=man:logrotate(8) man:logrotate.conf(5)

[Timer]
OnCalendar=daily
AccuracySec=1h
Persistent=true

[Install]
WantedBy=timers.target
```

To define how the timer should be started, the timer unit contains a [Timer] section. In the code in Example 12-1, you can see that it lists three options:

- **OnCalendar:** Describes when the timer should execute. In this case it is set to daily, which ensures daily execution.
- **AccuracySec:** Indicates a time window within which the timer should execute. In Example 12-1 it is set to 1 hour. If the timer needs to be executed at a more specific time, it is common to set it to a lower value. Use 1us for the best accuracy.
- **Persistent:** A modifier to OnCalendar=daily, it specifies that the last execution time should be stored on disk, so that the next time it executes is exactly one day later.

In systemd timers, different options can be used to indicate when the related service should be started. Table 12-2 lists the most important options.

Table 12-2 Timing Options in Systemd Timers

Option	Use
OnActiveSec	Defines a timer relative to the moment the timer is activated.
OnBootSec	Defines a timer relative to when the machine was booted.
OnStartupSec	Specifies a time relative to when the service manager was started. In most cases this is the same as OnBootSec, but not when systemd user units are used.
OnUnitActiveSec	Defines a timer relative to when the unit that the timer activates was last activated.
OnCalendar	Defines timers based on calendar event expressions, such as daily. See **man systemd.time** for more details.

In Exercise 12-1 you'll learn how to explore how systemd timers are organized.

Exercise 12-1: Using Systemd Timers

1. Use **systemctl list-units -t timer** to show a list of all timers.
2. Type **systemctl list-unit-files logrotate.***, which should show there is a logrotate.service and a logrotate.timer.
3. Enter **systemctl cat logrotate.service** to verify the contents of the logrotate.service unit file. Notice that it doesn't have an [Install] section.

4. Use **systemctl status logrotate.service**, which will show it marked as triggered by the logrotate.timer.
5. Use **systemctl status logrotate.timer** to verify the status of the related timer.
6. Install the sysstat package, using **dnf install -y sysstat**.
7. Verify the unit files that were added from this package, using **systemctl list-unit-files sysstat***.
8. Type **systemctl cat sysstat-collect.timer** to show what the sysstat-collect timer is doing. You'll see the line OnCalendar=*:00/10, which ensures that it will run every 10 minutes.

Configuring cron to Automate Recurring Tasks

Task scheduling has been common on Linux for a long time, and in the past the **crond** service was the primary tool to schedule tasks.

The ***crond*** service consists of two major components. First is the cron daemon **crond**, which in RHEL 9 is also started as a systemd service. This daemon looks every minute to see whether there is work to do. Second, this work to do is defined in the cron configuration, which consists of multiple files working together to provide the right information to the right service at the right time. In this section, you learn how to configure cron.

EXAM TIP Even if systemd timers are now the default solution for running recurring tasks, cron is still available. Make sure you master both for purposes of preparing for the RHCSA exam!

Managing the crond Service

The **crond** service is started by default on every RHEL system. Managing the **crond** service itself is easy: it does not need much management. Where other services need to be reloaded or restarted to activate changes to their configuration, this is not needed by **crond**. The **crond** daemon wakes up every minute and checks its configuration to see whether anything needs to be started.

To monitor the current status of the **crond** service, you can use the **systemctl status crond** command. Example 12-2 shows the output of this command.

Example 12-2 Monitoring the Current State of the crond Service

```
[root@localhost ~]# systemctl status crond
● crond.service - Command Scheduler
     Loaded: loaded (/usr/lib/systemd/system/crond.service; enabled;
vendor preset: enabled)
     Active: active (running) since Mon 2022-11-21 12:19:12 CET; 1h
  21min ago
    Main PID: 1169 (crond)
       Tasks: 2 (limit: 23284)
      Memory: 1.5M
         CPU: 66ms
      CGroup: /system.slice/crond.service
              ├─1169 /usr/sbin/crond -n
              └─6689 /usr/sbin/anacron -s
Nov 21 13:01:01 localhost.localdomain anacron[6689]: Will run job
  'cron.daily' in 12 min.
Nov 21 13:01:01 localhost.localdomain anacron[6689]: Will run job
  'cron.weekly' in 32 min.
Nov 21 13:01:01 localhost.localdomain anacron[6689]: Will run job
  'cron.monthly' in 52 min.
Nov 21 13:01:01 localhost.localdomain anacron[6689]: Jobs will be
  executed sequentially
Nov 21 13:01:01 localhost.localdomain run-parts[6691]: (/etc/cron.
  hourly) finished 0anacron
Nov 21 13:01:01 localhost.localdomain CROND[6675]: (root) CMDEND
  (run-parts /etc/cron.hourly)
Nov 21 13:13:01 localhost.localdomain anacron[6689]: Job 'cron.daily'
  started
Nov 21 13:13:01 localhost.localdomain anacron[6689]: Job 'cron.daily'
  terminated
Nov 21 13:33:01 localhost.localdomain anacron[6689]: Job 'cron.weekly'
  started
Nov 21 13:33:01 localhost.localdomain anacron[6689]: Job 'cron.weekly'
  terminated
```

The most significant part of the output of the **systemctl status crond** command is in the beginning, which indicates that the cron service is loaded and enabled. The fact that the service is enabled means that it will automatically be started whenever this service is restarting. The last part of the command output shows current status information. Through the journald service, the **systemctl** command can find out what is actually happening to the **crond** service.

Understanding cron Timing

When scheduling services through cron, you need to specify when exactly the services need to be started. In the crontab configuration (which is explained in more depth in the next section), you use a time string to indicate when tasks should be started. Table 12-3 shows the time and date fields used (in the order specified).

Table 12-3 cron Time and Date Fields

Field	Values
minute	0–59
hour	0–23
day of month	1–31
month	1–12 (or month names)
day of week	0–7 (Sunday is 0 or 7), or day names

In any of these fields, you can use an * as a wildcard to refer to any value. Ranges of numbers are allowed, as are lists and patterns. Some examples are listed next:

- *** 11 * * *** Every minute between 11:00 and 11:59 (probably not what you want)
- **0 11 * * 1-5** Every day at 11 a.m. on weekdays only
- **0 7-18 * * 1-5** Every hour at the top of the hour between 7 a.m. and 6 p.m. on weekdays
- **0 */2 2 12 5** Every two hours on the hour on December 2 and every Friday in December

> **TIP** You don't need to remember all this; **man 5 crontab** shows all possible constructions.

Managing cron Configuration Files

The main configuration file for cron is /etc/crontab, but you will not change this file directly. It does give you a convenient overview, though, of some time specifications that can be used in cron. It also sets environment variables that are used by the commands that are executed through cron (see Example 12-3). To make modifications to the cron jobs, there are other locations where cron jobs should be specified.

Example 12-3 /etc/crontab Sample Content

```
[root@server2 ~]# cat /etc/crontab
SHELL=/bin/bash
PATH=/sbin:/bin:/usr/sbin:/usr/bin
MAILTO=root

# For details see man 4 crontabs

# Example of job definition:
# .---------------- minute (0 - 59)
# |  .------------- hour (0 - 23)
# |  |  .---------- day of month (1 - 31)
# |  |  |  .------- month (1 - 12) OR jan,feb,mar,apr ...
# |  |  |  |  .---- day of week (0 - 6) (Sunday=0 or 7) OR
sun,mon,tue,wed,thu,fri,sat
# |  |  |  |  |
# *  *  *  *  * user-name command to be executed
```

Instead of modifying /etc/crontab, different cron configuration files are used:

- cron files in /etc/cron.d
- Scripts in /etc/cron.hourly, cron.daily, cron.weekly, and cron.monthly
- User-specific files that are created with **crontab -e**

In this section, you get an overview of these locations.

NOTE If you want to experiment with how cron works, you should allow for a sufficient amount of time for the job to be executed. The **crond** service reads its configuration every minute, after which new jobs can be scheduled for execution on the next minute. So, if you want to make sure your job is executed as fast as possible, allow for a safe margin of three minutes between the moment you save the cron configuration and the execution time.

To start, cron jobs can be started for specific users. To create a user-specific cron job, type **crontab -e** after logging in as that user, or as root type **crontab -e -u username**. These user-specific cron jobs are the most common way for scheduling additional jobs through cron.

When you are using **crontab -e**, the default editor opens and creates a temporary file. After you edit the cron configuration, the temporary file is moved to its final location in the directory /var/spool/cron. In this directory, a file is created for each user. These files should never be edited directly! When the file is saved by **crontab -e**, it is activated automatically.

Whereas in the early days of RHEL the /etc/crontab file was modified directly, on RHEL 9 you do not do that anymore. If you want to add cron jobs, you add these to the /etc/cron.d directory. Just put a file in that directory (the exact name does not really matter) and make sure that it meets the syntax of a typical cron job. In Example 12-4, you can see an example of the /etc/cron.d/0hourly.cron file, which takes care of running hourly jobs through cron.

Example 12-4 Example cron Jobs in /etc/cron.d

```
[root@server1 cron.d]# ls
0hourly
[root@server1 cron.d]# cat 0hourly
# Run the hourly jobs
SHELL=/bin/bash
PATH=/sbin:/bin:/usr/sbin:/usr/bin
MAILTO=root
01 * * * * root run-parts /etc/cron.hourly
```

This example starts by setting environment variables. These are the environment variables that should be considered while running this specific job. On the last line the job itself is defined. The first part of this definition specifies when the job should run. In this case it will run 1 minute after each hour, each day of the month, each month, and each day of the week. The job will be executed as the root user, and the job itself involves the **run-parts** command, which is responsible for running the scripted cron jobs in /etc/cron.hourly.

The last way to schedule cron jobs is through the following directories:

- /etc/cron.hourly
- /etc/cron.daily
- /etc/cron.weekly
- /etc/cron.monthly

In these directories, you typically find scripts (not files that meet the crontab syntax requirements) that are put in there from RPM package files. When opening these scripts, notice that no information is included about the time when the command should be executed. The reason is that the exact time of execution does not really matter. The only thing that does matter is that the job is launched once an hour, once a day, a week, or a month, and **anacron** is taking care of everything else.

Understanding the Purpose of anacron

To ensure regular execution of the job, cron uses the ***anacron*** service. This service takes care of starting the hourly, daily, weekly, and monthly cron jobs, no matter at which exact time. To determine how this should be done, anacron uses the /etc/anacrontab file. Example 12-5 shows the contents of the /etc/anacrontab file, which is used to specify how anacron jobs should be executed.

Example 12-5 anacrontab Configuration

```
[root@server1 spool]# cat /etc/anacrontab
# /etc/anacrontab: configuration file for anacron

# See anacron(8) and anacrontab(5) for details.

SHELL=/bin/sh
PATH=/sbin:/bin:/usr/sbin:/usr/bin
MAILTO=root
# the maximal random delay added to the base delay of the jobs
RANDOM_DELAY=45
# the jobs will be started during the following hours only
START_HOURS_RANGE=3-22

#period in days  delay in minutes job-identifier     command
1        5    cron.daily             nice run-parts  /etc/cron.daily
7        25    cron.weekly            nice run-parts  /etc/cron.weekly
@monthly 45 cron.monthly           nice run-parts  /etc/cron.monthly
```

In /etc/anacrontab, the jobs to be executed are specified in lines that contain four fields, as shown in Example 12-5. The first field specifies the frequency of job execution, expressed in days. The second field specifies how long anacron waits before executing the job, which is followed by the third field that contains a job identifier. The fourth field specifies the command that should be executed.

TIP Although it's useful to know how anacron works, it typically is not a service that is configured directly. The need to configure services through anacron is taken away by the /etc/cron.hourly, cron.daily, cron.weekly, and cron.monthly files.

NOTE It is not easy to get an overview of the cron jobs actually scheduled for execution. There is no single command that would show all currently scheduled cron jobs. The **crontab -l** command does list cron jobs, but only for the current user account.

Managing cron Security

By default, all users can enter cron jobs. It is possible to limit which user is allowed to schedule cron jobs by using the /etc/cron.allow and /etc/cron.deny configuration files. If the cron.allow file exists, a user must be listed in it to be allowed to use cron. If the /etc/cron.deny file exists, a user must not be listed in it to be allowed to set up cron jobs. Both files should not exist on the same system at the same time. Only root can use cron if neither file exists.

In Exercise 12-2, you apply some of the cron basics and schedule cron jobs using different mechanisms.

Exercise 12-2 Running Scheduled Tasks Through cron

1. Open a root shell. Type **cat /etc/crontab** to get an impression of the contents of the /etc/crontab configuration file.
2. Type **crontab -e**. This opens an editor interface that by default uses **vi** as its editor. Add the following line:

```
0 2 * * 1-5 logger message from root
```

3. Use the **vi** command **:wq!** to close the editing session and write changes.
4. Type **cd /etc/cron.hourly**. In this directory, create a script file with the name **eachhour** that contains the following line:

```
logger This message is written at $(date)
```

5. Use **chmod +x eachhour** to make the script executable; if you fail to make it executable, it will not work.
6. Enter the directory /etc/crond.d and in this directory create a file with the name **eachhour**. Put the following contents in the file:

```
11 * * * * root logger This message is written from /etc/cron.d
```

7. Save the modifications to the configuration file and continue to the next section. (For optimal effect, perform step 8 after a couple of hours.)
8. After a couple of hours, type **grep written /var/log/messages** and read the messages to verify correct cron operations.

Configuring at to Schedule Future Tasks

Whereas cron is used to schedule jobs that need to be executed on a regular basis, the atd service is available for services that need to be executed only once. On RHEL 9, the atd service is available by default, so all that you need to do is schedule jobs.

To run a job through the atd service, you would use the **at** command, followed by the time the job needs to be executed. This can be a specific time, as in **at 14:00**, but it can also be a time indication like **at teatime** or **at noon**. After you type this, the ***at*** shell opens. From this shell, you can type several commands that will be executed at the specific time that is mentioned. After entering the commands, press Ctrl-D to quit the at shell.

After scheduling jobs with at, you can use the **atq** command (*q* for *queue*) to get an overview of all jobs currently scheduled. It is also possible to remove current at jobs. To do this, use the **atrm** command, optionally followed by the number of the at job that you want to remove. In Exercise 12-3, you learn how to work with at to schedule jobs for execution at a specific time.

TIP The **batch** command works like **at**, but it's a bit more sophisticated. When using **batch**, you can specify that a job is started only when system performance parameters allow. Typically, that is when system load is lower than 0.8. This value is a bit low on modern multi-CPU systems, which is why the load value can be specified manually when starting **atd**, using the **-l** command-line option. Use, for instance, **atd -l 3.0** to make sure that no batch job is started when the system load is higher than 3.0.

Exercise 12-3 Scheduling Jobs with at

1. Type **systemctl status atd**. In the line that starts with Loaded:, this command should show you that the service is currently loaded and enabled, which means that it is ready to start receiving jobs.
2. Type **at 15:00** (or replace with any time near to the time at which you are working on this exercise).
3. Type **logger message from at**. Press Ctrl-D to close the at shell.
4. Type **atq** to verify that the job has indeed been scheduled.

Summary

In this chapter, you learned how to schedule jobs for future execution. RHEL 9 provides three solutions to do so: systemd timers have become the default solution, the legacy cron service is still around, and at can be used to schedule deferred user tasks.

Exam Preparation Tasks

As mentioned in the section "How to Use This Book" in the Introduction, you have several choices for exam preparation: the end-of-chapter labs; the memory tables in Appendix C; Chapter 27, "Final Preparation"; and the practice exams.

Review All Key Topics

Review the most important topics in the chapter, noted with the Key Topic icon in the margin of the page. Table 12-4 lists a reference for these key topics and the page number on which each is found.

Table 12-4 Key Topics for Chapter 12

Key Topic Element	Description	Page
Table 12-2	Timing Options in Systemd Timers	275
Table 12-3	cron Time and Date Fields	278
List	crontab time indicators examples	278
List	Methods to enter crontab information	279

Define Key Terms

Define the following key terms from this chapter and check your answers in the glossary:

timer, crond, anacron, at

Review Questions

The questions that follow are meant to help you test your knowledge of concepts and terminology and the breadth of your knowledge. You can find the answers to these questions in Appendix A.

1. Where do you configure a cron job that needs to be executed once every two weeks?
2. How do you configure a service to be started 5 minutes after your system has started?
3. You have enabled a systemd service unit file to be started by a timer, but it doesn't work. What should you check?

4. What is the easiest way to start a service every 7 hours?
5. How do you match a specific timer to a specific service?
6. Which command enables you to schedule a cron job for user lisa?
7. How do you specify that user boris is never allowed to schedule jobs through cron?
8. You need to make sure that a job is executed every day, even if the server at execution time is temporarily unavailable. How do you do this?
9. Which service must be running to schedule at jobs?
10. Which command enables you to find out whether any current at jobs are scheduled for execution?

End-of-Chapter Lab

In this end-of-chapter lab, you work on at jobs and on cron jobs.

Lab 12.1

1. Create a cron job that performs an update of all software on your computer every evening at 11 p.m.
2. Schedule your machine to be rebooted at 3 a.m. tomorrow morning.
3. Use a systemd timer to start the vsftpd service five minutes after your system has started.

The following topics are covered in this chapter:

- Understanding System Logging
- Working with systemd-journald
- Configuring rsyslogd
- Rotating Log Files

The following RHCSA exam objectives are covered in this chapter:

- Locate and interpret system log files and journals
- Preserve system journals

CHAPTER 13

Configuring Logging

Analyzing log files is an important system administrator task. If anything goes wrong on a Linux system, the answer is often in the log files. On RHEL 9, two different log systems are used, and it is important to know which information can be found where. This chapter teaches you all about it. You learn how to read log files, how to configure rsyslogd and journald, and how to set up your system for log rotation so that you can prevent your disks from being completely filled up by services that are logging too enthusiastically.

"Do I Know This Already?" Quiz

The "Do I Know This Already?" quiz enables you to assess whether you should read this entire chapter thoroughly or jump to the "Exam Preparation Tasks" section. If you are in doubt about your answers to these questions or your own assessment of your knowledge of the topics, read the entire chapter. Table 13-1 lists the major headings in this chapter and their corresponding "Do I Know This Already?" quiz questions. You can find the answers in Appendix A, "Answers to the 'Do I Know This Already?' Quizzes and Review Questions."

Table 13-1 "Do I Know This Already?" Section-to-Question Mapping

Foundation Topics Section	Questions
Understanding System Logging	1–3
Working with systemd-journald	4–6
Configuring rsyslogd	7–9
Rotating Log Files	10

1. Which of the following statements about systemd-journald is *not* true?
   a. systemd-journald logs kernel messages.
   b. systemd-journald writes to the journal, which by default does not persist between boots.

   c. systemd-journald is a replacement of rsyslogd.
   d. To read files from the systemd journal, you use the **journalctl** command.

2. Which log would you read to find messages related to authentication errors?
   a. /var/log/messages
   b. /var/log/lastlog
   c. /var/log/audit/audit.log
   d. /var/log/secure

3. Which log would you read to find information that relates to SELinux events?
   a. /var/log/messages
   b. /var/log/lastlog
   c. /var/log/audit/audit.log
   d. /var/log/secure

4. Which directory is used to store the systemd journal persistently?
   a. /var/log/journal
   b. /var/run/journal
   c. /run/log
   d. /run/log/journal

5. What do you need to do to make the systemd journal persistent?
   a. Create the directory /var/log/journal.
   b. Open /etc/sysconfig/journal and set the PERSISTENT option to **yes**.
   c. Open the /etc/systemd/journald.conf file and set the PERSISTENT option to **yes**.
   d. Create the /var/log/journal file and set appropriate permissions.

6. After making the systemd journal persistent, what should you do to immediately activate this change?
   a. Reboot your server.
   b. Nothing, it will be picked up automatically.
   c. Use systemctl daemon-reload.
   d. Use systemctl restart systemd-journal-flush.

7. What is the name of the rsyslogd configuration file?
   a. /etc/rsyslog.conf
   b. /etc/sysconfig/rsyslogd.conf
   c. /etc/sysconfig/rsyslog.conf
   d. /etc/rsyslog.d/rsyslogd.conf

8. In the rsyslog.conf file, which of the following destinations refers to a specific rsyslogd module?
   a. -/var/log/maillog
   b. /var/log/messages
   c. :omusrmsg:*
   d. *

9. Which facility is the best solution if you want to configure the Apache web server to log messages through rsyslog?
   a. daemon
   b. apache
   c. syslog
   d. local0-7

10. You want to maximize the file size of a log file to 10 MB. Where do you configure this?
    a. Create a file in /etc/logrotate.d and specify the maximal size in that file.
    b. Put the maximal size in the logrotate cron job.
    c. Configure the destination with the maximal size option.
    d. This cannot be done.

Foundation Topics

Understanding System Logging

Most services used on a Linux server write information to log files. This information can be written to different destinations, and there are multiple solutions to find the relevant information in system logs. No fewer than three different approaches can be used by services to write log information:

- **Systemd-journald:** With the introduction of Systemd, the journald log service systemd-journald has been introduced also. This service is tightly integrated with Systemd, which allows administrators to read detailed information from the journal while monitoring service status using the **systemctl status** command or the **journalctl** command. Systemd-journald is the default solution for logging in RHEL 9.
- **Direct write:** Some services write logging information directly to the log files—even some important services such as the Apache web server and the Samba file server. This approach to logging is not recommended.
- **rsyslogd:** rsyslogd is the enhancement of syslogd, a service that takes care of managing centralized log files. syslogd has been around for a long time. Even if systemd-journald is now the default for logging, rsyslogd provides features not offered by systemd-journald, and for that reason it is still offered on RHEL 9. Also, rsyslogd is still configured to work as it did in older versions of RHEL, which means that you can still use the log files it generates to get the log information you need.

Understanding the Role of systemd-journald and rsyslogd

On RHEL 9, ***systemd-journald*** provides an advanced log management system. It collects messages from the kernel, the entire boot procedure, and services and writes these messages to an event journal. This event journal is stored in a binary format, and you can query it by using the **journalctl** command. The **journalctl** command enables you to access a deep level of detail about messages that are logged, as it is an integrated part of Systemd and, as such, receives all messages that have been generated by Systemd units.

Because the journal that is written by systemd-journald is not persistent between reboots, messages are also forwarded to the rsyslogd service, which writes the messages to different files in the /var/log directory. ***rsyslogd*** also offers features that do not exist in journald, such as centralized logging and filtering messages by using modules. Numerous modules are available to enhance rsyslog logging, such as output modules that allow administrators to store messages in a database. As the rsyslogd advanced features are used a lot, RHEL 9 still offers rsyslogd for logging as an addition to systemd-journald.

Systemd-journald is tightly integrated with systemd; therefore, it logs everything that your server is doing. rsyslogd adds some services to it. In particular, it takes care of writing log information to specific files (that will be persistent between reboots), and it allows you to configure remote logging and log servers.

Apart from rsyslogd and systemd-journald, there is the auditd service. This service provides auditing, an in-depth trace of what specific services, processes, or users have been doing. Configuration of auditing is beyond the scope of the RHCSA exam, but you'll notice that SELinux, for instance, logs detailed messages to the auditd service.

To get more information about what has been happening on a machine running RHEL, administrators have to take three approaches:

- Use the **journalctl** command to get more detailed information from the journal.
- Use the **systemctl status <unit>** command to get a short overview of the most recent significant events that have been logged by Systemd units through systemd-journald. This command shows the status of services, as well as the most recent log entries that have been written. Example 13-1 shows some status log messages that have been logged for this service.
- Monitor the files in /var/log that are written by rsyslogd.

Example 13-1 Using **systemctl status** to Show Relevant Log Information

```
[root@server1 ~]# systemctl status sshd -l
   sshd.service - OpenSSH server daemon
   Loaded: loaded (/usr/lib/systemd/system/sshd.service; enabled;
  vendor preset: enabled)
   Active: active (running) since Sat 2019-06-08 03:34:56 EDT;  55min
  ago
     Docs:                 man:sshd(8)
                    man:sshd_config(5)
 Main PID: 1055 (sshd)
    Tasks: 1 (limit: 11363)
   Memory: 5.5M
   Cgroup: /system.slice/sshd.service
```

```
             └─1055 /usr/sbin/sshd -D -oCiphers=aes256-gcm@openssh.com,
   chacha20-poly1305@openssh.com,ae>

Jun 08 03:34:56 server1.example.com systemd[1]: Starting OpenSSH
   server daemon...
Jun 08 03:34:56 server1.example.com sshd[1055]: Server listening on
   0.0.0.0 port 22.
Jun 08 03:34:56 server1.example.com sshd[1055]: Server listening on ::
   port 22.
Jun 08 03:34:56 server1.example.com systemd[1]: Started OpenSSH server
   daemon.
Jun 08 03:57:38 server1.example.com sshd[3368]: Accepted password for
   root from 192.168.4.1 port 5470>
Jun 08 03:57:38 server1.example.com sshd[3368]: pam_
   unix(sshd:session):session opened for user root
```

Reading Log Files

Apart from the messages that are written by systemd-journald to the journal and which can be read using the ***journalctl*** command, on a Linux system you'll also find different log files in the directory /var/log. Most of the files in this directory are managed by rsyslogd, but some of the files are created directly by specific services. You can read these files by using a pager utility such as **less**.

The exact number of files in the /var/log directory will change, depending on the configuration of a server and the services that are running on that server. Some files, however, do exist on most occasions, and as an administrator, you should know which files they are and what content can be expected in these files. Table 13-2 provides an overview of some of the standard files that are created in this directory.

Table 13-2 System Log Files Overview

Log File	Explanation
/var/log/messages	This is the most commonly used log file; it is the generic log file where most messages are written to.
/var/log/dmesg	Contains kernel log messages.
/var/log/secure	Contains authentication-related messages. Look here to see which authentication errors have occurred on a server.
/var/log/boot.log	Contains messages that are related to system startup.
/var/log/audit/audit.log	Contains audit messages. SELinux writes to this file.
/var/log/maillog	Contains mail-related messages.
/var/log/httpd/	Contains log files that are written by the Apache web server (if it is installed). Notice that Apache writes messages to these files directly and not through rsyslog.

Understanding Log File Contents

As an administrator, you need to be able to interpret the contents of log files. For example, Example 13-2 shows partial content from the /var/log/messages file.

Example 13-2 /var/log/messages Sample Content

```
[root@localhost ~]# tail -10 /var/log/messages
Jan 26 09:45:06 localhost systemd[1590]: Reached target Exit the
  Session.
Jan 26 09:45:06 localhost systemd[1]: user@42.service: Deactivated
  successfully.
Jan 26 09:45:06 localhost systemd[1]: Stopped User Manager for UID 42.
Jan 26 09:45:06 localhost systemd[1]: Stopping User Runtime Directory
  /run/user/42...
Jan 26 09:45:06 localhost systemd[1]: run-user-42.mount: Deactivated
  successfully.
Jan 26 09:45:06 localhost systemd[1]: user-runtime-dir@42.service:
  Deactivated successfully.
Jan 26 09:45:06 localhost systemd[1]: Stopped User Runtime Directory
  /run/user/42.
Jan 26 09:45:06 localhost systemd[1]: Removed slice User Slice of
  UID 42.
Jan 26 09:45:06 localhost systemd[1]: user-42.slice: Consumed 3.786s
  CPU time.
Jan 26 09:45:15 localhost systemd[1]: fprintd.service: Deactivated
  successfully..
```

As you can see in Example 13-2, each line that is logged has specific elements:

- **Date and time:** Every log message starts with a timestamp. For filtering purposes, the timestamp is written as military time.
- **Host:** The host the message originated from. This is relevant because rsyslogd can be configured to handle remote logging as well.
- **Service or process name and PID:** The name of the service or process that generated the message.
- **Message content:** The content of the message, which contains the exact message that has been logged.

To read the content of a log file, you can use a pager utility, like **less**, or you can live monitor what is happening in the log file, as described in the next section.

Live Log File Monitoring

When you are configuring services on Linux, it might be useful to see in real time what is happening. You could, for example, open two terminal sessions at the same time. In one terminal session, you configure and test the service. In the other terminal session, you see in real time what is happening. The **tail -f <logfile>** command shows in real time which lines are added to the log file. Exercise 13-1 in the following section shows a small example in which **tail -f** is used. When you're monitoring a log file with **tail -f**, the trace remains open until you press Ctrl-C to close it.

Using logger

Most services write information to the log files all by themselves or through rsyslogd. The **logger** command enables users to write messages to rsyslog from the command line or a script. Using this command is simple. Just type **logger**, followed by the message you want to write to the logs. The **logger** utility, in this way, offers a convenient solution to write messages from scripts. This allows you to have a script write to syslog if something goes wrong.

When using **logger**, you can also specify the priority and facility to log to. The command **logger -p kern.err hello** writes **hello** to the kernel facility, for example, using the error priority (priority and facility are discussed in more detail later in this chapter). This option enables you to test the working of specific rsyslog facilities. In Exercise 13-1, you use **tail -f** to monitor a log file in real time and use **logger** to write log messages to a log file.

Exercise 13-1 Using Live Log Monitoring and logger

1. Open a root shell.
2. From the root shell, type **tail -f /var/log/messages**.
3. Open a second terminal window. In this terminal window, type **su - student** to open a subshell as user student.
4. Type **su -** to open a root shell, but enter the wrong password.
5. Look at the file /var/log/messages. You see an error message was logged here.
6. From the student shell, type **logger hello**. You'll see the message appearing in the /var/log/messages file in real time.
7. In the **tail -f** terminal, press Ctrl-C to stop tracing the messages file.
8. Type **tail -20 /var/log/secure**. This shows the last 20 lines in /var/log/secure, which also shows the messages that the **su -** password errors have generated previously.

Working with systemd-journald

The systemd-journald service stores log messages in the journal, a binary file that is temporarily stored in the file /run/log/journal. This file can be examined using the **journalctl** command.

Using journalctl to Find Events

The easiest way to use **journalctl** is by just typing the command. It shows that recent events have been written to the journal since your server last started. The result of this command is shown in the **less** pager, and by default you'll see the beginning of the journal. Because the journal is written from the moment your server boots, the start of the output shows boot-related log messages. If you want to see the last messages that have been logged, you can use **journalctl -f**, which shows the last lines of the messages where new log lines are automatically added. You can also type **journalctl** and use (uppercase) **G** to go to the end of the journal. Also note that the search options / and ? work in the **journalctl** output. Example 13-3 shows a partial result of this command.

Example 13-3 Watching Log Information Generated by systemd-journald

```
-- Logs begin at Sat 2019-06-08 04:45:34 EDT, end at Sat 2019-06-08
   04:56:11 EDT. --
Jun 08 04:45:34 server1.example.com kernel: Linux version 4.18.0-80.
   el8.x86_64 (mockbuild@x86-vm-08.b>
Jun 08 04:45:34 server1.example.com kernel: Command line: BOOT_
   IMAGE=(hd0,msdos1)/vmlinuz-4.18.0-80.e>
Jun 08 04:45:34 server1.example.com kernel: Disabled fast string
   operations
Jun 08 04:45:34 server1.example.com kernel: x86/fpu: Supporting XSAVE
   feature 0x001: 'x87 floating po>
Jun 08 04:45:34 server1.example.com kernel: x86/fpu: Supporting XSAVE
   feature 0x002: 'SSE registers'
Jun 08 04:45:34 server1.example.com kernel: x86/fpu: Supporting XSAVE
   feature 0x004: 'AVX registers'
Jun 08 04:45:34 server1.example.com kernel: x86/fpu: Supporting XSAVE
   feature 0x008: 'MPX bounds regi>
Jun 08 04:45:34 server1.example.com kernel: x86/fpu: Supporting XSAVE
   feature 0x010: 'MPX CSR'
Jun 08 04:45:34 server1.example.com kernel: x86/fpu: xstate_offset[2]:
   576, xstate_sizes[2]:  256
Jun 08 04:45:34 server1.example.com kernel: x86/fpu: xstate_offset[3]:
   832, xstate_sizes[3]:   64
Jun 08 04:45:34 server1.example.com kernel: x86/fpu: xstate_offset[4]:
   896, xstate_sizes[4]:   64
Jun 08 04:45:34 server1.example.com kernel: x86/fpu: Enabled xstate
   features 0x1f, context size is 96>
```

What makes **journalctl** a flexible command is that its many filtering options allow you to show exactly what you need. Exercise 13-2 shows some of the most interesting options.

Exercise 13-2 Discovering journalctl

1. Type **journalctl**. You'll see the content of the journal since your server last started, starting at the beginning of the journal. The content is shown in **less**, so you can use common **less** commands to walk through the file.
2. Type **q** to quit the pager. Now type **journalctl --no-pager**. This shows the contents of the journal without using a pager.
3. Type **journalctl -f**. This opens the live view mode of **journalctl**, which allows you to see new messages scrolling by in real time. Press Ctrl-C to interrupt.
4. Type **journalctl**, press the Spacebar, and then press the Tab key twice. When prompted to view all possibilities, type **y** and then press the Enter key. This shows specific options that can be used for filtering. Type, for instance, **journalctl _UID=1000** to show messages that have been logged for your student user account.
5. Type **journalctl -n 20**. The **-n 20** option displays the last 20 lines of the journal (just like **tail -n 20**).
6. Type **journalctl -p err**. This command shows errors only.
7. If you want to view journal messages that have been written in a specific time period, you can use the **--since** and **--until** commands. Both options take the time parameter in the format YYYY-MM-DD hh:mm:ss. Also, you can use **yesterday**, **today**, and **tomorrow** as parameters. So, type **journalctl --since yesterday** to show all messages that have been written since yesterday.
8. **journalctl** allows you to combine different options, as well. So, if you want to show all messages with a priority error that have been written since yesterday, use **journalctl --since yesterday -p err**.
9. If you need as much detail as possible, use **journalctl -o verbose**. This shows different options that are used when writing to the journal (see Example 13-4). All these options can be used to tell the **journalctl** command which specific information you are looking for. Type, for instance, **journalctl _SYSTEMD_UNIT=sshd.service** to show more information about the sshd Systemd unit.
10. Type **journalctl --dmesg**. This shows kernel-related messages only. Not many people use this command, as the **dmesg** command gives the exact same result.

In the preceding exercise, you typed **journalctl -o verbose** to show verbose output. Example 13-4 shows an example of the **verbose** output. As you can see, this provides detailed information for all items that have been logged, including the PID, the ID of the associated user and group account, the command that is associated, and more. This verbose information may help you in debugging specific Systemd units.

Example 13-4 Showing Detailed Log Information with **journalctl -o verbose**

```
[root@server1 ~]# journalctl _SYSTEMD_UNIT=sshd.service -o verbose
-- Logs begin at Sat 2019-06-08 04:45:34 EDT, end at Sat 2019-06-08
05:01:40 EDT. --
Sat 2019-06-08 04:45:52.633752 EDT [s=53e57e2481434e078e8306367dc5645c
  ;i=898;b=f35bb68348284f9ead79c3>
    _BOOT_ID=f35bb68348284f9ead79c3c6750adfa1
    _MACHINE_ID=5aa095b495ed458d934c54a88078c165
    _HOSTNAME=server1.example.com
    PRIORITY=6
    _UID=0
    _GID=0
    _SYSTEMD_SLICE=system.slice
    _CAP_EFFECTIVE=3fffffffff
    _TRANSPORT=syslog
    SYSLOG_FACILITY=10
    SYSLOG_IDENTIFIER=sshd
    SYSLOG_PID=1211
    MESSAGE=Server listening on 0.0.0.0 port 22.
    _PID=1211
    _COMM=sshd
    _EXE=/usr/sbin/sshd
    _CMDLINE=/usr/sbin/sshd -D -oCiphers=aes256-gcm@openssh.com,
  chacha20-poly1305@openssh.com,aes256->
    _SELINUX_CONTEXT=system_u:system_r:sshd_t:s0-s0:c0.c1023
    _SYSTEMD_CGROUP=/system.slice/sshd.service
    _SYSTEMD_UNIT=sshd.service
    _SYSTEMD_INVOCATION_ID=728a7dfecd7d436387dcd6e319c208c7
    _SOURCE_REALTIME_TIMESTAMP=1559983552633752
Sat 2019-06-08 04:45:52.634696 EDT [s=53e57e2481434e078e8306367dc5645c
  ;i=899;b=f35bb68348284f9ead79c3>
    _BOOT_ID=f35bb68348284f9ead79c3c6750adfa1
lines 1-26
```

There are some more interesting options to use with the **journalctl** command. The **-b** option shows a boot log, which includes just the messages that were generated while booting. The **-x** option adds explanation to the information that is shown. This explanation makes it easier to interpret specific messages. You should also consider the **-u** option, which allows you to see messages that have been logged for a specific systemd unit only. Use, for instance, **journalctl -u sshd** to see all messages that have been logged for the sshd service. Table 13-3 provides an overview of the most interesting **journalctl** options.

Table 13-3 Most Useful **journalctl** Options

Option	Use
-f	Shows the bottom of the journal and live adds new messages that are generated
-b	Shows the boot log
-x	Adds additional explanation to the logged items
-u	Used to filter log messages for a specific unit only
-p	Allows for filtering of messages with a specific priority

Preserving the Systemd Journal

By default, the journal is stored in the file /run/log/journal. The entire /run directory is used for current process status information only, which means that the journal is cleared when the system reboots. To make the journal persistent between system restarts, you should create a directory /var/log/journal.

Storing the journal permanently requires the Storage=auto parameter in /etc/systemd/journald.conf, which is set by default. This parameter can have different values:

- **Storage=auto** The journal will be written on disk if the directory /var/log/journal exists.
- **Storage=volatile** The journal will be stored only in the /run/log/journal directory.
- **Storage=persistent** The journal will be stored on disk in the directory /var/log/journal. This directory will be created automatically if it doesn't exist.
- **Storage=none** No data will be stored, but forwarding to other targets such as the kernel log buffer or syslog will still work.

Even when the journal is written to the permanent file in /var/log/journal, that does not mean that the journal is kept forever. The journal has built-in ***log rotation*** that will be used monthly. Also, the journal is limited to a maximum size of 10 percent of the size of the file system that it is on, and it will stop growing if less than 15 percent of the file system is still free. If that happens, the oldest messages from the journal are dropped automatically to make room for newer messages. To change these settings, you can modify the file /etc/systemd/journald.conf, as shown in Example 13-5 (along with other parameters you can set).

Example 13-5 Setting journald Parameters Through /etc/systemd/journald.conf

```
[Journal]
#Storage=auto
#Compress=yes
#Seal=yes
#SplitMode=uid
#SyncIntervalSec=5m
#RateLimitIntervalSec=30s
#RateLimitBurst=10000
#SystemMaxUse=
#SystemKeepFree=
#SystemMaxFileSize=
#SystemMaxFiles=100
#RuntimeMaxUse=
#RuntimeKeepFree=
#RuntimeMaxFileSize=
#RuntimeMaxFiles=100
#MaxRetentionSec=
#MaxFileSec=1month
#ForwardToSyslog=no
#ForwardToKMsg=no
#ForwardToConsole=no
#ForwardToWall=yes
#TTYPath=/dev/console
#MaxLevelStore=debug
#MaxLevelSyslog=debug
```

Making the systemd journal permanent is not hard to do. Exercise 13-3 shows how to proceed.

Exercise 13-3 Making the systemd Journal Persistent

1. Open a root shell and type **mkdir /var/log/journal**.
2. Before journald can write the journal to this directory, you have to set ownership. Type **chown root:systemd-journal /var/log/journal**, followed by **chmod 2755 /var/log/journal**.
3. Use **systemctl restart systemd-journal-flush** to reload the new systemd-journald parameters.
4. The Systemd journal is now persistent across reboots.

Configuring rsyslogd

To make sure that the information that needs to be logged is written to the location where you want to find it, you can configure the rsyslogd service through the /etc/rsyslog.conf file and optional drop-in files in /etc/rsyslog.d. In the /etc/rsyslog.conf file, you find different sections that allow you to specify where and how information should be written.

Understanding rsyslogd Configuration Files

Like many other services on RHEL, the configuration for rsyslogd is not defined in just one configuration file. The /etc/rsyslog.conf file is the central location where rsyslogd is configured. From this file, the content of the directory /etc/rsyslog.d is included. This directory can be populated by installing RPM packages on a server. When looking for specific log configuration, make sure to always consider the contents of this directory also.

Understanding rsyslog.conf Sections

The rsyslog.conf file is used to specify what should be logged and where it should be logged. To do this, you'll find different sections in the rsyslog.conf file:

- **#### MODULES ####:** rsyslogd is modular. Modules are included to enhance the supported features in rsyslogd.
- **#### GLOBAL DIRECTIVES ####:** This section is used to specify global parameters, such as the location where auxiliary files are written or the default timestamp format.
- **#### RULES ####:** This is the most important part of the rsyslog.conf file. It contains the rules that specify what information should be logged to which destination.

Understanding Facilities, Priorities, and Log Destinations

To specify what information should be logged to which destination, rsyslogd uses facilities, priorities, and destinations:

- A ***facility*** specifies a category of information that is logged. rsyslogd uses a fixed list of facilities, which cannot be extended. This is because of backward compatibility with the legacy syslog service.
- A ***priority*** is used to define the severity of the message that needs to be logged. When you specify a priority, by default all messages with that priority and all higher priorities are logged.
- A ***destination*** defines where the message should be written. Typical destinations are files, but rsyslog modules can be used as a destination as well, to allow further processing through a rsyslogd module.

Example 13-6 shows the RULES section in rsyslog.

Example 13-6 The RULES Section in rsyslog.conf

```
#### RULES ####

# Log all kernel messages to the console.
# Logging much else clutters up the screen.
#kern.*                                        /dev/console

# Log anything (except mail) of level info or higher.
# Do not log private authentication messages!
*.info;mail.none;authpriv.none;cron.none      /var/log/messages

# The authpriv file has restricted access.
authpriv.*                                             /var/log/secure

# Log all the mail messages in one place.
mail.*                                         -/var/log/maillog


# Log cron stuff
cron.*                                         /var/log/cron

# Everybody gets emergency messages
*.emerg                                        :omusrmsg:*

# Save news errors of level crit and higher in a special file.
uucp,news.crit                                          /var/log/spooler
```

In Example 13-6, you can see how different facilities and priorities are used to define locations where information can be logged. The available facilities and priorities are fixed and cannot be added to. Table 13-4 shows which facilities are available, and Table 13-5 shows a list of all priorities.

When you specify a destination, a file is often used. If the filename starts with a hyphen (as in -/var/log/maillog), the log messages will not be immediately committed to the file but instead will be buffered to make writes more efficient. Device files can also be used, such as /dev/console. If this device is used, messages are written in real time to the console. On modern servers, this often does not make sense, because administrators often log in remotely and do not see what is happening on the server console.

Table 13-4 rsyslogd Facilities

Facility	Used by
auth/authpriv	Messages related to authentication.
cron	Messages generated by the **crond** service.
daemon	Generic facility that can be used for nonspecified daemons.
kern	Kernel messages.
lpr	Messages generated through the legacy lpd print system.
mail	Email-related messages.
mark	Special facility that can be used to write a marker periodically.
news	Messages generated by the NNTP news system.
security	Same as auth/authpriv. Should not be used anymore.
syslog	Messages generated by the syslog system.
user	Messages generated in user space.
uucp	Messages generated by the legacy UUCP system.
local0-7	Messages generated by services that are configured by any of the local0 through local7 facilities.

The syslog facilities were defined in the 1980s, and to guarantee backward compatibility, no new facilities can be added. The result is that some facilities still exist that basically serve no purpose anymore, and some services that have become relevant at a later stage do not have their own facility. As a solution, two specific facility types can be used. The daemon facility is a generic facility that can be used by any daemon. In addition, the local0 through local7 facilities can be used.

If services that do not have their own rsyslogd facility need to write log messages to a specific log file anyway, these services can be configured to use any of the local0 through local7 facilities. You next have to configure the services to use these facilities as well. The procedure you follow to do that is specific to the service you are using. Then you need to add a rule to the rsyslog.conf file to send messages that come in through that facility to a specific log file.

To determine which types of messages should be logged, you can use different severities in rsyslog.conf lines. These severities are the syslog priorities. Table 13-5 provides an overview of the available priorities in ascending order.

Table 13-5 rsyslogd Priorities

Priority	Description
debug	Debug messages that will give as much information as possible about service operation.
info	Informational messages about normal service operation.
notice	Informational messages about items that might become an issue later.
warning (warn)	Something is suboptimal, but there is no real error yet.
error (err)	A noncritical error has occurred.
crit	A critical error has occurred.
alert	Message used when the availability of the service is about to be discontinued.
emerg (panic)	Message generated when the availability of the service is discontinued.

When a specific priority is used, all messages with that priority and higher are logged according to the specifications used in that specific rule. If you need to configure logging in a detailed way, where messages with different priorities are sent to different files, you can specify the priority with an equal sign (=) in front of it, as in the following line, which will write all cron messages with only the debug priority to a specific file with the name /var/log/cron.debug. The - in front of the line specifies to buffer writes so that information is logged in a more efficient way.

```
cron.=debug -/var/log/cron.debug
```

> **TIP** You don't need to learn the names of rsyslogd facilities and priorities by heart. They are all listed in **man 5 rsyslog.conf**. On the exam, you have access to the man pages, so this information will be easily accessible.

Exercise 13-4 shows how to change rsyslog.conf. You configure the Apache service to log messages through syslog, and you create a rule that logs debug messages to a specific log file.

Exercise 13-4 Changing rsyslog.conf Rules

1. By default, the Apache service does not log through rsyslog but keeps its own logging. You are going to change that. To start, type **dnf install -y httpd** to ensure that the Apache service is installed.
2. After installing the Apache service, open its configuration file /etc/httpd/conf/httpd.conf and verify it has the following line:

```
ErrorLog    syslog:local1
```

3. Type **systemctl restart httpd**.
4. Create a line in the /etc/rsyslog.conf file that will send all messages that it receives for facility local1 (which is now used by the httpd service) to the file /var/log/httpd-error.log. To do this, include the following line in the #### RULES #### section of the file:

```
local1.error          /var/log/httpd-error.log
```

5. Tell rsyslogd to reload its configuration, by using **systemctl restart rsyslog**.
6. All Apache error messages will now be written to the httpd-error.log file.
7. From the Firefox browser, go to http://localhost/index.html. Because no index.html page exists yet, this will be written to the error log.
8. Create a snap-in file that logs debug messages to a specific file as well. To do this, type **echo "*.debug /var/log/messages-debug" /etc/rsyslog.d/debug.conf**.
9. Again, restart rsyslogd using **systemctl restart rsyslog**.
10. Use the command **tail -f /var/log/messages-debug** to open a trace on the newly created file.
11. From a second terminal, type **logger -p daemon.debug "Daemon Debug Message"**. You'll see the debug message passing by.
12. Press Ctrl-C to close the debug log file.

Rotating Log Files

To prevent syslog messages from filling up your system completely, you can rotate the log messages. That means that when a certain threshold has been reached, the old log file is closed and a new log file is opened. The logrotate utility is started periodically to take care of rotating log files.

When a log file is rotated, the old log file is typically copied to a file that has the rotation date in it. So, if /var/log/messages is rotated on June 8, 2023, the rotated filename will be /var/log/messages-20230608. As a default, four old log files are kept on the system. Files older than that period are removed from the system automatically.

WARNING Log files that have been rotated are not stored anywhere; they are just gone. If your company policy requires you to be able to access information about events that have happened more than five weeks ago, for example, you should either back up log files or configure a centralized log server where logrotate keeps rotated messages for a significantly longer period.

The default settings for log rotation are kept in the file /etc/logrotate.conf (see Example 13-7).

Example 13-7 /etc/logrotate.conf Sample Content

```
[root@server1 cron.d]# cat /etc/logrotate.conf
# see "man logrotate" for details

# global options do not affect preceding include directives

# rotate log files weekly
weekly

# keep 4 weeks worth of backlogs
rotate 4

# create new (empty) log files after rotating old ones
create

# use date as a suffix of the rotated file
dateext

# uncomment this if you want your log files compressed
#compress

# packages drop log rotation information into this directory
include /etc/logrotate.d

# system-specific logs may be also be configured here.
```

The most significant settings used in this configuration file tell logrotate to rotate files on a weekly basis and keep four old versions of the file. You can obtain more information about other parameters in this file through the **man logrotate** command.

If specific files need specific settings, you can create a configuration file for that file in /etc/logrotate.d. The settings for that specific file overwrite the default settings in /etc/logrotate.conf. You will find that different files exist in this directory already to take care of some of the configuration files.

Summary

In this chapter, you learned how to configure logging. You read how the rsyslogd and journald services are used on RHEL to keep log information, and you learned how to manage logs that are written by these services. You also learned how to configure log rotation and make the journal persistent.

Exam Preparation Tasks

As mentioned in the section "How to Use This Book" in the Introduction, you have several choices for exam preparation: the end-of-chapter labs; the memory tables in Appendix C; Chapter 27, "Final Preparation"; and the practice exams.

Review All Key Topics

Review the most important topics in the chapter, noted with the Key Topic icon in the margin of the page. Table 13-6 lists a reference for these key topics and the page number on which each is found.

Table 13-6 Key Topics for Chapter 13

Key Topic Element	Description	Page
Paragraph	systemd-journald explanation	290
Paragraph	rsyslogd explanation	290
Table 13-2	System Log Files Overview	292
Table 13-3	Most Useful **journalctl** Options	298
Exercise 13-3	Making the systemd Journal Persistent	300
Table 13-4	rsyslogd Facilities	302
Table 13-5	rsyslogd Priorities	303

Complete Tables and Lists from Memory

Print a copy of Appendix C, "Memory Tables" (found on the companion website), or at least the section for this chapter, and complete the tables and lists from memory. Appendix D, "Memory Tables Answer Key," includes completed tables and lists to check your work.

Define Key Terms

Define the following key terms from this chapter and check your answers in the glossary:

systemd-journald, rsyslogd, **journalctl**, log rotation, facility, priority, destination

Review Questions

The questions that follow are meant to help you test your knowledge of concepts and terminology and the breadth of your knowledge. You can find the answers to these questions in Appendix A.

1. Which file is used to configure rsyslogd?
2. Which log file contains messages related to authentication?
3. If you do not configure anything, how long will it take for log files to be rotated away?
4. Which command enables you to log a message from the command line to the user facility, using the notice priority?
5. Which line would you add to write all messages with a priority of info to the file /var/log/messages.info?
6. Which configuration file enables you to allow the journal to grow beyond its default size restrictions?
7. Which command allows you to check the systemd journal for boot messages, where an explanation is included?

8. Which command enables you to see all journald messages that have been written for PID 1 between 9:00 a.m. and 3:00 p.m.?
9. Which command do you use to see all messages that have been logged for the sshd service?
10. Which procedure enables you to make the systemd journal persistent?

End-of-Chapter Lab

You have now learned how to work with logging on Red Hat Enterprise Linux 9 and know how to configure rsyslogd and journald. You can now complete the end-of-chapter lab to reinforce these newly acquired skills.

Lab 13.1

1. Configure the journal to be persistent across system reboots.
2. Make a configuration file that writes all messages with an info priority to the file /var/log/messages.info.
3. Configure logrotate to keep ten old versions of log files.

The following topics are covered in this chapter:

- Understanding MBR and GPT Partitions
- Managing Partitions and File Systems
- Mounting File Systems

The following RHCSA exam objectives are covered in this chapter:

- List, create, delete partitions on MBR and GPT disks
- Configure systems to mount file systems at boot by universally unique ID (UUID) or label
- Add new partitions and logical volumes, and swap to a system non-destructively
- Create, mount, unmount, and use vfat, ext4, and xfs file systems

CHAPTER 14

Managing Storage

Working with storage is an important task for a Linux administrator. In this chapter, you acquire the first set of essential storage skills. You learn how to create and manage partitions, format them with the file system you need to use, and mount these file systems.

"Do I Know This Already?" Quiz

The "Do I Know This Already?" quiz enables you to assess whether you should read this entire chapter thoroughly or jump to the "Exam Preparation Tasks" section. If you are in doubt about your answers to these questions or your own assessment of your knowledge of the topics, read the entire chapter. Table 14-1 lists the major headings in this chapter and their corresponding "Do I Know This Already?" quiz questions. You can find the answers in Appendix A, "Answers to the 'Do I Know This Already?' Quizzes and Review Questions."

Table 14-1 "Do I Know This Already?" Section-to-Question Mapping

Foundation Topics Section	Questions
Understanding MBR and GPT Partitions	1–2
Managing Partitions and File Systems	3–6
Mounting File Systems	7–10

1. Which of the following is *not* an advantage of using a GUID partition table over using an MBR partition table?
    a. Access time to a directory is quicker.
    b. A total amount of 8 ZiB can be addressed by a partition.
    c. With GUID partitions, a backup copy of the partition table is created automatically.
    d. There can be up to 128 partitions in total.

2. Which of the following statements about GPT partitions is not true?
   a. You can easily convert an existing MBR disk to GPT by using **gdisk**.
   b. You can use **fdisk** to write a GPT disk label.
   c. Partition types in GPT are four characters instead of two characters.
   d. GPT partitions can be created on MBR as well as EFI systems.

3. Which partition type is commonly used to create a swap partition?
   a. 81
   b. 82
   c. 83
   d. 8e

4. What is the default disk device name you would expect to see in KVM virtual machines?
   a. /dev/sda
   b. /dev/hda
   c. /dev/vda
   d. /dev/xsda

5. Which of the following statements is *not* true?
   a. You should not ever use **gdisk** on an MBR disk.
   b. **fdisk** offers support to manage GPT partitions as well.
   c. Depending on your needs, you can create MBR and GPT partitions on the same disk.
   d. If your server boots from EFI, you must use GPT partitions.

6. Which of the following file systems is used as the default in RHEL 9?
   a. Ext4
   b. XFS
   c. btrfs
   d. Ext3

7. Which command enables you to find current UUIDs set to the file systems on your server?
   a. **mount**
   b. **df -h**
   c. **lsblk**
   d. **blkid**

8. What would you put in the device column of /etc/fstab to mount a file system based on its unique ID 42f419c4-633f-4ed7-b161-519a4dadd3da?
   a. 42f419c4-633f-4ed7-b161-519a4dadd3da
   b. /dev/42f419c4-633f-4ed7-b161-519a4dadd3da
   c. ID=42f419c4-633f-4ed7-b161-519a4dadd3da
   d. UUID=42f419c4-633f-4ed7-b161-519a4dadd3da

9. Which command can you use to verify the contents of /etc/fstab before booting?
   a. **fsck --fstab**
   b. **findmnt --verify**
   c. **mount -a**
   d. **reboot**

10. While creating a systemd mount unit file, different elements are required. Which of the following is not one of them?
    a. The mount unit filename corresponds to the mount point.
    b. An [Install] section is included to set the default runlevel.
    c. A **what** statement is included to indicate what should be mounted.
    d. A **where** statement is included to indicate where the device should be mounted.

Foundation Topics

Understanding MBR and GPT Partitions

To use a hard drive, it needs to have ***partitions***. Some operating systems install everything to one partition, while other operating systems such as Linux normally have several partitions on one hard disk. Using more than one partition on a system makes sense for multiple reasons:

- It's easier to distinguish between different types of data.
- Specific mount options can be used to enhance security or performance.
- It's easier to create a backup strategy where only relevant portions of the OS are backed up.
- If one partition accidentally fills up completely, the other partitions still are usable and your system might not crash immediately.

NOTE Instead of using multiple different partitions, you can also use LVM logical volumes or Stratis file systems. Managing logical volumes and Stratis file systems is covered in Chapter 15, "Managing Advanced Storage."

On recent versions of RHEL, two different partitioning schemes are available. Before creating your first partition, you should understand these schemes.

Understanding the MBR Partitioning Scheme

When the personal computer was invented in the early 1980s, a system was needed to define hard disk layout. This system became known as the ***Master Boot Record (MBR)*** partitioning scheme. While booting a computer, the ***Basic Input/Output System (BIOS)*** was loaded to access hardware devices. From the BIOS, the bootable disk device was read, and on this bootable device, the MBR was allocated. The MBR contains all that is needed to start a computer, including a boot loader and a partition table.

When hard disks first came out for PCs in the early 1980s, users could have different operating systems on them. Some of these included MS-DOS/PC-DOS, PC/IX (IBM's UNIX for 8086 PCs), CPM86, and MPM86. The disk would be partitioned in such a way that each operating system installed got a part of the disk. One of the partitions would be made active, meaning the code in the boot sector in the MBR would read the first sector of that active partition and run the code. That code would then load the rest of the OS. This explains why four partitions were deemed "enough."

The MBR was defined as the first 512 bytes on a computer hard drive, and in the MBR an operating system boot loader (such as GRUB 2; see Chapter 17, "Managing and Understanding the Boot Procedure") was present, as well as a partition table. The size that was used for the partition table was relatively small, just 64 bytes, with the result that in the MBR no more than four partitions could be created. Since partition size data was stored in 32-bit values, and a default sector size of 512 bytes was used, the maximum size that could be used by a partition was limited to 2 TiB (hardly a problem in the early 1980s).

In the MBR, just four partitions could be created. Because many PC operating systems needed more than four partitions, a solution was found to go beyond the number of four. In the MBR, one partition could be created as an ***extended partition***, as opposed to the other partitions that were created as ***primary partitions***. Within the extended partition, multiple ***logical partitions*** could be created to reach a total number of 15 partitions that could be addressed by the Linux kernel.

Understanding the Need for GPT Partitioning

Current computer hard drives have become too big to be addressed by MBR partitions. That is one of the main reasons why a new partitioning scheme was needed. This partitioning scheme is the ***GUID Partition Table (GPT)***. On computers that are using the new ***Unified Extensible Firmware Interface (UEFI)*** as a replacement for the old BIOS system, GPT partitions are the only way to address disks. Also, older computer systems that are using BIOS instead of UEFI can be configured with globally unique ID (GUID) partitions, which is necessary if a disk with a size bigger than 2 TiB needs to be addressed.

Using GUID offers many benefits:

- The maximum partition size is 8 zebibyte (ZiB), which is 1024 × 1024 × 1024 × 1024 gibibytes.
- In GPT, up to a maximum number of 128 partitions can be created.
- The 2-TiB limit no longer exists.
- Because space that is available to store partitions is much bigger than 64 bytes, which was used in MBR, there is no longer a need to distinguish between primary, extended, and logical partitions.
- GPT uses a 128-bit GUID to identify partitions.

- A backup copy of the GUID partition table is created by default at the end of the disk, which eliminates the single point of failure that exists on MBR partition tables.

Understanding Storage Measurement Units

When talking about storage, we use different measurement units. In some cases, units like megabyte (MB) are used. In other cases, units like mebibyte (MiB) are used. The difference between these two is that a megabyte is a multiple of 1,000, and a mebibyte is a multiple of 1,024. In computers, it makes sense to talk about multiples of 1,024 because that is how computers address items. However, confusion was created when hardware vendors a long time ago started referring to megabytes instead of mebibytes.

In the early days of computing, the difference was not that important. The difference between a kilobyte (KB) and a kibibyte (KiB) is just 24 bytes. The bigger the numbers grow, the bigger the difference becomes. A gigabyte, for instance, is 1,000 × 1,000 × 1,000 bytes, so 1,000,000,000 bytes, whereas a gibibyte is 1,024 × 1,024 × 1,024 bytes, which makes a total of 1,073,741,824 bytes, which is over 70 MB larger than 1 GB.

On current Linux distributions, the binary numbers (MiB, not MB) have become the standard. In Table 14-2, you can see an overview of the values that are used.

In the past, KB, MB, and so on were used both in decimal and binary situations; sometimes they were even mixed. For example, 1-Mbps line speed is one million bits per second. The once famous "1.44 MB" floppy disk was really 1,440,000 bytes in size (80 tracks × 2 heads × 9 sectors × 512-byte sectors), creating a mixed meaning of MB: 1.44 × (decimal K) × (binary K).

Table 14-2 Disk Size Specifications

Symbol	Name	Value	Symbol	Name	Value
KB	Kilobyte	1000^1	KiB	Kibibyte	1024^1
MB	Megabyte	1000^2	MiB	Mebibyte	1024^2
GB	Gigabyte	1000^3	GiB	Gibibyte	1024^3
TB	Terabyte	1000^4	TiB	Tebibyte	1024^4
PB	Petabyte	1000^5	PiB	Pebibyte	1024^5
EB	Exabyte	1000^6	EiB	Exbibyte	1024^6
ZB	Zettabyte	1000^7	ZiB	Zebibyte	1024^7
YB	Yottabyte	1000^8	YiB	Yobibyte	1024^8

Managing Partitions and File Systems

As discussed in the previous section, two different types of partitions can be used on RHEL. To match the different partition types, there are also two different partitioning utilities. The **fdisk** utility has been around for a long time and can be used to create and manage MBR as well as GPT partitions. The **gdisk** utility is used to create GPT partitions. In this section, you learn how to use both.

Apart from **fdisk** and **gdisk**, there are other partitioning utilities as well, of which **parted** is probably the most important. Some people like it, as it is relatively easy to use, but at the same time it hides some of the more advanced features. For that reason, this chapter focuses on working with **fdisk** and **gdisk** and introduces **parted** only briefly.

For both MBR and GPT partitions, you need to specify the name of the disk device as an argument. Use the **lsblk** command to print a list of all disk devices available on your system. Table 14-3 shows the most common disk device names that you work with on RHEL.

Table 14-3 Common Disk Device Types

Device Name	Description
/dev/sda	A hard disk that uses the SCSI driver. Used for SCSI and SATA disk devices. Common on physical servers but also in VMware virtual machines.
/dev/nvme0n1	The first hard disk on an NVM Express (NVMe) interface. NVMe is a server-grade method to address advanced SSD devices. Note at the end of the device name that the first disk in this case is referred to as *n1* instead of *a* (as is common with the other types).
/dev/hda	The (legacy) IDE disk device type. You will seldom see this device type on modern computers.
/dev/vda	A disk in a KVM virtual machine that uses the virtio disk driver. This is the common disk device type for KVM virtual machines.
/dev/xvda	A disk in a Xen virtual machine that uses the Xen virtual disk driver. You see this when installing RHEL as a virtual machine in Xen virtualization. RHEL 9 cannot be used as a Xen hypervisor, but you might see RHEL 9 virtual machines on top of the Xen hypervisor using these disk types.

As you can see in Table 14-3, almost all disk device names end with the letter *a*. The reason is that it is the first disk that was found in your server. The second SCSI disk, for instance, would have the name /dev/sdb. If many disks are installed in a server, you can have up to /dev/sdz and even beyond. After /dev/sdz, the kernel continues creating devices with names like /dev/sdaa and /dev/sdab. Notice that on NVMe devices, numbers are used instead of letters. So the first NVMe disk is nvme0n1, the second NVMe disk is nvme0n2, and so on.

Creating MBR Partitions with fdisk

To create an MBR disk partition, you have to apply a multiple-step procedure, as shown in Exercise 14-1.

Exercise 14-1 Creating MBR Partitions with fdisk

This exercise has been written to use an installation of RHEL that contains an unused disk. You can easily add a second disk to your environment. This can be a virtual disk that is added through your virtualization program, or a USB flash drive if you're working on a physical installation. In that case, make sure to replace the device names in this exercise with the device names that match your hardware.

1. Open a root shell and type **lsblk**. This lists the block devices that are available.
2. Open a root shell and run the **fdisk** command. This command needs as its argument the name of the disk device where you want to create the partition. This exercise uses /dev/sdb. Change that, if needed, according to your hardware.

```
[root@server1 ~]# fdisk /dev/sdb

Welcome to fdisk (util-linux 2.37.4).

Changes will remain in memory only, until you decide to write
  them.

Be careful before using the write command.


Device does not contain a recognized partition table.

Created a new DOS disklabel with disk identifier 0x2c00c707.

Command (m for help):
```

3. Before you do anything, it is a good idea to check how much disk space you have available. Press **p** to see an overview of current disk allocation:

```
Command (m for help): p

Disk /dev/sdb: 20 GiB, 21474836480 bytes, 41943040 sectors

Disk model: VMware Virtual S

Units: sectors of 1 * 512 = 512 bytes

Sector size (logical/physical): 512 bytes / 512 bytes

Disklabel type: dos

Disk identifier: 0x2c00c707
```

In the output of this command, in particular look for the total number of sectors and the last sector that is currently used. If the last partition does not end on the last sector, you have available space to create a new partition. In this case, that shouldn't be an issue because you are supposed to use a new disk in this exercise.

4. Type **n** to add a new partition:

```
Command (m for help): n
Partition type
   p   primary (0 primary, 0 extended, 4 free)
   e   extended (container for logical partitions)
Select (default p):
```

5. Press **p** to create a primary partition. Accept the partition number that is now suggested, which should be /dev/sdb1.
6. Specify the first sector on disk that the new partition will start on. The first available sector is suggested by default, so press Enter to accept.
7. Type **+1G** to make this a 1-GiB partition. If you were to just press Enter, the last sector available on disk would be suggested. If you were to use that, after this exercise you would not have any disk space left to create additional partitions or logical volumes, so you should use another last sector. To use another last sector, you can do one of the following:

   - Enter the number of the last sector you want to use.
   - Enter **+number** to create a partition that sizes a specific number of sectors.
   - Enter **+number(K,M,G)** to specify the size you want to assign to the partition in KiB, MiB, or GiB.

```
Command (m for help): n
Partition type
   p   primary (0 primary, 0 extended, 4 free)
   e   extended (container for logical partitions)
Select (default p): p
Partition number (1-4, default 1):
I/O size (minimum/optimal): 512 bytes / 512 bytes
First sector (2048-41943039, default 2048):
Last sector, +/-sectors or +/-size{K,M,G,T,P} (2048-41943039,
  default 41943039): +1G
Created a new partition 1 of type 'Linux' and of size 1 GiB
```

After you enter the partition's ending boundary, **fdisk** will show a confirmation.

8. At this point, you can define the partition type. By default, a Linux partition type is used. If you want the partition to be of any other partition type, use **t** to change it. For this exercise there is no need to change the partition type. Common partition types include the following:
   - **82:** Linux swap
   - **83:** Linux
   - **8e:** Linux LVM
9. If you are happy with the modifications, press **w** to write them to disk and exit **fdisk**.
10. Type **lsblk** to verify that the new partition has been created successfully.

Using Extended and Logical Partitions on MBR

In the previous procedure, you learned how to add a primary partition. If three MBR partitions have been created already, there is room for one more primary partition, after which the partition table is completely filled up. If you want to go beyond four partitions on an MBR disk, you have to create an extended partition. Following that, you can create logical partitions within the extended partition.

Using logical partitions does allow you to go beyond the limitation of four partitions in the MBR; there is a disadvantage as well, though. All logical partitions exist within the extended partition. If something goes wrong with the extended partition, you have a problem with all logical partitions existing within it as well. If you need more than four separate storage allocation units, you might be better off using LVM instead of logical partitions. If you're on a completely new disk, you might just want to create GPT partitions instead. In Exercise 14-2 you learn how to work with extended and logical partitions.

NOTE An extended partition is used only for the purpose of creating logical partitions. You cannot create file systems directly on an extended partition!

Exercise 14-2 Creating Logical Partitions

1. In a root shell, type **fdisk /dev/sdb** to open the **fdisk** interface.
2. Type **n** to create a new partition. To create a logical partition, when **fdisk** prompts which partition type you want to create, enter **e**. This allows you to create an extended partition, which is necessary to later add logical partitions.

```
Command (m for help): n

Partition type
```

```
    p   primary (1 primary, 0 extended, 3 free)
    e   extended (container for logical partitions)
Select (default p): e
```

3. If the extended partition is the fourth partition that you are writing to the MBR, it will also be the last partition that can be added to the MBR. For that reason, it should fill the rest of your computer's hard disk. Press Enter to accept the default first sector and press Enter again when **fdisk** prompts for the last sector (even if this is not the fourth partition yet).

```
Select (default p): e
Partition number (2-4, default 2):
First sector (2099200-41943039, default 2099200):
Last sector, +/-sectors or +/-size{K,M,G,T,P} (2099200-41943039,
default 41943039):

Created a new partition 2 of type 'Extended' and of size 19 GiB.
```

4. Now that the extended partition has been created, you can create a logical partition within it. Still from the **fdisk** interface, press **n** again. Because all of the space in the drive has been allocated to partitions, the utility will by default suggest adding a logical partition with partition number 5.

```
Command (m for help): n
All space for primary partitions is in use.
Adding logical partition 5
First sector (2101248-41943039, default 2101248):
```

5. Press Enter to accept the default first sector. When asked for the last sector, enter **+1G**:

```
First sector (2101248-41943039, default 2101248):
Last sector, +/-sectors or +/-size{K,M,G,T,P} (2101248-41943039,
default 41943039): +1G

Created a new partition 5 of type 'Linux' and of size 1 GiB.
```

6. Now that the logical partition has been created, enter **w** to write the changes to disk and quit **fdisk**.

TIP In some cases, **fdisk** will print a message after writing the partitions to disk, stating that it could not update the partition table. If that happens, you can try using the **partprobe** command to manually update the partition table. Use **lsblk** to verify that it now is visible. If this is not the case, use **reboot** to restart your system.

Creating GPT Partitions with gdisk

If a disk is configured with a GUID Partition Table (GPT), or if it is a new disk that does not contain anything yet and has a size that goes beyond 2 TiB, you need to create GUID partitions. The easiest way to do so is by using the **gdisk** utility. This utility has a lot of similarities with **fdisk** but also has some differences.

Notice that you can only decide which type of partition table to create when initializing an unused disk. Once either MBR or GPT partitions have been created on a disk, you cannot change its type. The preferred utility for creating GPT partitions is **gdisk**. Alternatively, after starting **fdisk** on a new disk, you can use the **g** command to initialize a GPT. Exercise 14-3 shows how to create partitions in **gdisk** on a disk that doesn't have any partitions yet.

WARNING! Do not ever use **gdisk** on a disk that has been formatted with **fdisk** and already contains **fdisk** partitions. **gdisk** will detect that an MBR is present, and it will convert this to a GPT (see the following code listing). Your computer most likely will not be able to boot after doing this! When you see the following message, use **q** to quit **gdisk** immediately, without saving anything!

```
[root@server1 ~]# gdisk /dev/sda
GPT fdisk (gdisk) version 1.0.7


Partition table scan:
  MBR: MBR only
  BSD: not present
  APM: not present
  GPT: not present
****************************************************************
Found invalid GPT and valid MBR; converting MBR to GPT format
in memory. THIS OPERATION IS POTENTIALLY DESTRUCTIVE! Exit by
typing 'q' if you don't want to convert your MBR partitions
to GPT format!
****************************************************************
```

```
Warning! Secondary partition table overlaps the last partition by
33 blocks!
You will need to delete this partition or resize it in another
utility.
Command (? for help):
```

To save you the hassle of going through this, I verified it does what it says. After converting an MBR to a GPT, your machine will not start anymore.

Exercise 14-3 Creating GPT Partitions with gdisk

To apply the procedure in this exercise, you need a new disk device. Do *not* use a disk that contains data that you want to keep, because this exercise will delete all data on it. If you are using this exercise on a virtual machine, you may add the new disk through the virtualization software. If you are working on a physical machine, you can use a USB thumb drive as a disk device for this exercise. Note that this exercise works perfectly on a computer that starts from BIOS and not EFI; all you need is a dedicated disk device.

1. To create a partition with **gdisk**, open a root shell and type **gdisk /dev/sdc**. (Replace /dev/sdc with the exact device name used on your computer.) **gdisk** will try to detect the current layout of the disk, and if it detects nothing, it will create the GPT and associated disk layout.

```
[root@server1 ~]# gdisk /dev/sdc
GPT fdisk (gdisk) version 1.0.7

Partition table scan:
  MBR: not present
  BSD: not present
  APM: not present
  GPT: not present

Creating new GPT entries in memory.

Command (? for help):
```

2. Type **n** to enter a new partition. You can choose any partition number between 1 and 128, but it is wise to accept the default partition number that is suggested.

```
Command (? for help): n
Partition number (1-128, default 1): 1
```

3. You now are asked to enter the first sector. By default, the first sector that is available on disk will be used, but you can specify an offset as well. This does not make sense, so just press Enter to accept the default first sector that is proposed.

```
First sector (34-2097118, default = 2048) or {+-}size{KMGTP}:
```

4. When asked for the last sector, by default the last sector that is available on disk is proposed (which would create a partition that fills the entire hard disk). You can specify a different last sector, or specify the disk size using **+**, the size, and KMGTP. So to create a 1-GiB disk partition, use **+1G**.

```
Partition number (1-128, default 1): 1

First sector (34-41943006, default = 2048) or {+-}size{KMGTP}:

Last sector (2048-41943006, default = 41943006) or {+-}
size{KMGTP}: +1G

Current type is 8300 (Linux filesystem)

Hex code or GUID (L to show codes, Enter = 8300):
```

5. You now are asked to set the partition type. If you do not do anything, the partition type is set to 8300, which is the Linux file system partition type. Other options are available as well. You can press **l** to show a list of available partition types.

```
Current type is 'Linux filesystem'

Hex code or GUID (L to show codes, Enter = 8300): l

0700 Microsoft basic data  0c01 Microsoft reserved  2700 Windows
  RE

3000 ONIE boot              3001 ONIE config           3900 Plan 9

4100 PowerPC PReP boot      4200 Windows LDM data      4201 Windows
   LDM       metadata

4202 Windows Storage Spac  7501 IBM GPFS              7f00 ChromeOS
  kernel

7f01 ChromeOS root          7f02 ChromeOS reserved     8200 Linux
   swap

8300 Linux filesystem       8301 Linux reserved        8302 Linux
  / home

8303 Linux x86 root (/)     8304 Linux x86-64 root (/  8305 Linux
   ARM64          root (/)
```

```
8306 Linux /srv              8307 Linux ARM32 root (/)  8400 Intel
  Rapid          Start
8e00 Linux LVM               a000 Android bootloader    a001 Android
   bootloader 2
a002 Android boot            a003 Android recovery      a004 Android
  misc
a005 Android metadata        a006 Android system        a007 Android
   cache
a008 Android data            a009 Android persistent    a00a Android
  factory
a00b Android fastboot/ter    a00c Android OEM           a500 FreeBSD
   disklabel
a501 FreeBSD boot            a502 FreeBSD swap          a503 FreeBSD
   UFS
a504 FreeBSD ZFS             a505 FreeBSD Vinum/RAID    a580 Midnight
  BSD data
a581 Midnight BSD boot       a582 Midnight BSD swap     a583 Midnight
   BSD UFS
a584 Midnight BSD ZFS        a585 Midnight BSD Vinum    a600 OpenBSD
   disklabel
a800 Apple UFS               a901 NetBSD swap           a902 NetBSD
   FFS
a903 NetBSD LFS              a904 NetBSD concatenated   a905 NetBSD
   encrypted
a906 NetBSD RAID             ab00 Recovery HD           af00 Apple
   HFS/HFS+
af01 Apple RAID              af02 Apple RAID offline    af03 Apple
  label
```

The relevant partition types are as follows:

- **8200:** Linux swap
- **8300:** Linux file system
- **8e00:** Linux LVM

Notice that these are the same partition types as the ones that are used in MBR, with two 0s added to the IDs. You can also just press Enter to accept the default partition type 8300.

6. The partition is now created (but not yet written to disk). Press **p** to show an overview, which allows you to verify that this is really what you want to use.

```
Command (? for help): p
Disk /dev/sdc: 41943040 sectors, 20.0 GiB
Model: VMware Virtual S
Sector size (logical/physical): 512/512 bytes
Disk identifier (GUID): 49433C2B-16A9-4EA4-9D79-285E3AF7D133
Partition table holds up to 128 entries
Main partition table begins at sector 2 and ends at sector 33
First usable sector is 34, last usable sector is 41943006
Partitions will be aligned on 2048-sector boundaries
Total free space is 39845821 sectors (19.0 GiB)

Number  Start (sector)    End (sector)  Size       Code  Name
   1            2048         2099199   1024.0 MiB  8300  Linux
filesystem

Command (? for help):
```

7. If you are satisfied with the current partitioning, press **w** to write changes to disk and commit. This gives a warning which you can safely ignore by typing **Y**, after which the new partition table is written to the GUID partition table.

```
Command (? for help): w


Final checks complete. About to write GPT data. THIS WILL
OVERWRITE EXISTING
PARTITIONS!!


Do you want to proceed? (Y/N): Y
OK; writing new GUID partition table (GPT) to /dev/sdc.


The operation has completed successfully.
```

8. If at this point you get an error message indicating that the partition table is in use, type **partprobe** to update the kernel partition table.

Creating GPT Partitions with parted

As previously mentioned, apart from **fdisk** and **gdisk**, the **parted** utility can be used to create partitions. Because it lacks support for advanced features, I have focused on **fdisk** and **gdisk**, but I'd like to give you a quick overview of working with **parted**.

To use **parted**, you need to know that it has an interactive shell in which you can work with its different options. Exercise 14-4 guides you through the procedure of creating partitions using **parted**. This exercise assumes you have a new and unused disk device /dev/sdd available.

Exercise 14-4 Creating Partitions with parted

You need a new disk to work with this procedure. This exercise assumes that the new disk name is /dev/sdd.

1. From a root shell, type **parted /dev/sdd**. This opens the interactive **parted** shell.
2. Type **help** to get an overview of available commands.
3. Type **print**. You will see a message about an unrecognized disk label.
4. Type **mklabel** and press Enter. **parted** will now prompt for a disk label type. Press the Tab key twice to see a list of available disk label types. From the list, select **gpt** and press Enter.
5. Type **mkpart**. The utility prompts for a partition name. Type **part1** (the partition name doesn't really matter).
6. Now the utility prompts for a file system type. This is a very confusing option, because it suggests that you are setting a file system type here, but that is not the case. Also, when using Tab completion, you'll see a list of file systems that you've probably never used before. In fact, you could just press Enter to accept the default suggestion of ext2, as the setting isn't used anyway, but I suggest using a file system type that comes close to what you're going to use on the partition. So type **xfs** and press Enter to continue.
7. Now you are prompted for a start location. You can specify the start location as a number of blocks, or an offset from the start of the device. Notice that you can type 1M to specify the start of the partition at 1 megabyte, or type 1 MiB to have it start at 1 MiB. This is confusing, so make sure you specify the appropriate value here. At this point, type **1MiB** and press Enter.
8. Type **1GiB** to specify the end of the partition. After doing so, type **print** to print the current partition table, and type **quit** to quit the utility and commit your changes.
9. Type **lsblk** to verify the new partition has been created. It should show as /dev/sdd1.
10. Use **mkfs.ext4 /dev/sdd1** to format this partition with the Ext4 file system.

Creating File Systems

At this point, you know how to create partitions. A partition all by itself is not very useful. It only becomes useful if you decide to do something with it. That often means that you have to put a file system on top of it. In this section, you learn how to do that.

Different file systems can be used on RHEL 9. Table 14-4 provides an overview of the most common file systems.

Table 14-4 File System Overview

File System	Description
XFS	The default file system in RHEL 9.
Ext4	The default file system in previous versions of RHEL; still available and supported in RHEL 9.
Ext3	The previous version of Ext4. On RHEL 9, there is no need to use Ext3 anymore.
Ext2	A very basic file system that was developed in the early 1990s. There is no need to use this file system on RHEL 9 anymore.
BtrFS	A relatively new file system that is not supported in RHEL 9.
NTFS	A Windows-compatible file system that is not supported on RHEL 9.
VFAT	A file system that offers compatibility with Windows and macOS and is the functional equivalent of the FAT32 file system. Useful on USB thumb drives that exchange data with other computers but not on a server's hard disks.

To format a partition with one of the supported file systems, you can use the **mkfs** command, using the option **-t** to specify which specific file system to use. Alternatively, you can use one of the file system–specific tools such as mkfs.ext4 to format an Ext4 file system.

> **NOTE** If you use **mkfs** without any further specification of which file system you want to format, an Ext2 file system will be formatted. This is probably not what you want to use, so do not forget to specify which file system you want to use.

To format a partition with the default XFS file system, use the command **mkfs.xfs**. Example 14-1 shows the output of this command.

Example 14-1 Formatting a File System with XFS

```
[root@server1 ~]# mkfs.xfs /dev/sdb1
meta-data=/dev/sdb1              isize=512    agcount=4, agsize=65536 blks
         =                       sectsz=512   attr=2, projid32bit=1
         =                       crc=1        finobt=1, sparse=1, rmapbt=0
         =                       reflink=1    bigtime=1 inobtcount=1
data     =                       bsize=4096   blocks=262144, imaxpct=25
         =                       sunit=0      swidth=0 blks
naming   =version 2              bsize=4096   ascii-ci=0, ftype=1
log      =internal log           bsize=4096   blocks=2560, version=2
         =                       sectsz=512   sunit=0 blks, lazy-count=1
realtime =none                   extsz=4096   blocks=0, rtextents=0
```

In Exercise 14-5, you create a file system on the previously created partition /dev/sdb1.

Exercise 14-5 Creating a File System

In Exercise 14-1, you created a partition /dev/sdb1. In this exercise, you format it with an XFS file system. This exercise has one step only.

1. From a root shell, type **mkfs.xfs /dev/sdb1**

Changing File System Properties

When working with file systems, you can manage some properties as well. File system properties are specific for the file system you are using, so you work with different properties and different tools for the different file systems.

Managing Ext4 File System Properties

The generic tool for managing Ext4 file system properties is **tune2fs**. This tool was developed a long time ago for the Ext2 file system and is compatible with Ext3 and Ext4 also. When you're managing Ext4 file system properties, **tune2fs -l** is a nice command to start with. Example 14-2 presents the output of this command where different file system properties are shown. Notice that you first have to create an Ext4 file system, using **mkfs.ext4**, before you can use **tune2fs**.

Example 14-2 Showing File System Properties with **tune2fs -l**

```
[root@server1 ~]# tune2fs -l /dev/sdd1
tune2fs 1.46.5 (30-Dec-2021)
Filesystem volume name:   <none>
Last mounted on:          <not available>
Filesystem UUID:          5d34b37c-5d32-4790-8364-d22a8b8f88db
Filesystem magic number:  0xEF53
Filesystem revision #:    1 (dynamic)
Filesystem features:      has_journal ext_attr resize_inode dir_index
filetype extent 64bit flex_bg sparse_super large_file huge_file dir_
nlink extra_isize metadata_csum
Filesystem flags:         signed_directory_hash
Default mount options:    user_xattr acl
Filesystem state:         clean
Errors behavior:          Continue
Filesystem OS type:       Linux
Inode count:              65536
Block count:              262144
Reserved block count:     13107
Overhead clusters:        12949
Free blocks:              249189
Free inodes:              65525
First block:              0
Block size:               4096
Fragment size:            4096
Group descriptor size:    64
Reserved GDT blocks:      127
Blocks per group:         32768
Fragments per group:      32768
Inodes per group:         8192
Inode blocks per group:   512
Flex block group size:    16
Filesystem created:       Thu Sep 15 11:56:26 2022
Last mount time:          n/a
Last write time:          Thu Sep 15 11:56:26 2022
Mount count:              0
Maximum mount count:      -1
Last checked:             Thu Sep 15 11:56:26 2022
Check interval:           0 (<none>)
Lifetime writes:          533 kB
```

```
Reserved blocks uid:       0 (user root)
Reserved blocks gid:       0 (group root)
First inode:               11
Inode size:                256
Required extra isize:      32
Desired extra isize:       32
Journal inode:             8
Default directory hash:    half_md4
Directory Hash Seed:       ba256a6f-1ebe-4d68-8ff3-7a26064235bf
Journal backup:            inode blocks
Checksum type:             crc32c
Checksum:                  0x49ee65b4
```

As you can see, the **tune2fs -l** command shows many file system properties. One interesting property is the file system label, which shows as the Filesystem volume name. Labels are used to set a unique name for a file system, which allows the file system to be mounted in a consistent way, even if the underlying device name changes. Also interesting are the file system features and default ***mount*** options.

To change any of the default file system options, you can use the **tune2fs** command with other parameters. Some common usage examples are listed here:

- Use **tune2fs -o** to set default file system mount options. When set to the file system, the option does not have to be specified while mounting through /etc/fstab anymore. Use, for instance, **tune2fs -o acl,user_xattr** to switch on access control lists and user-extended attributes. Use a **^** in front of the option to switch it off again, as in **tune2fs -o ^acl,user_xattr**.
- Ext file systems also come with file system features that may be enabled as a default. To switch on a file system feature, use **tune2fs -O** followed by the feature. To turn a feature off, use a **^** in front of the feature name.
- Use **tune2fs -L** to set a label on the file system. As described in the section "Mounting File Systems" later in this chapter, you can use a file system label to mount a file system based on its name instead of the device name. Instead of **tune2fs -L**, the **e2label** command enables you to set a label on the file system.

Managing XFS File System Properties

The XFS file system is a completely different file system, and for that reason also has a completely different set of tools to manage its properties. It does not allow you to set file system attributes within the file system metadata. You can, however, change some XFS properties, using the **xfs_admin** command. For instance, use **xfs_admin -L mylabel** to set the file system label to mylabel.

Adding Swap Partitions

You use most of the partitions on a Linux server for regular file systems. On Linux, swap space is normally allocated on a disk device. That can be a partition or an LVM logical volume (discussed in Chapter 15). In case of an emergency, you can even use a file to extend the available swap space.

Using swap on Linux is a convenient way to improve Linux kernel memory usage. If a shortage of physical RAM occurs, non-recently used memory pages can be moved to swap, which makes more RAM available for programs that need access to memory pages. Most Linux servers for that reason are configured with a certain amount of swap. If swap starts being used intensively, you could be in trouble, though, and that is why swap usage should be closely monitored.

Sometimes, allocating more swap space makes sense. If a shortage of memory occurs, this shortage can be alleviated by allocating more swap space in some situations. This is done through a procedure where first a partition is created with the swap partition type, and then this partition is formatted as swap. Exercise 14-6 describes how to do this.

Exercise 14-6 Creating a Swap Partition

1. Type **fdisk /dev/sdb** to open your disk in **fdisk**.
2. Press **n** to add a new partition. Specify start cylinder and size to create a 1-GiB partition.
3. Type **t** to change the partition type. If you are using **fdisk**, type **swap** to set the swap partition type to 82. If you are using **gdisk**, use partition type **8200**. Press **w** to write and exit.
4. Use **mkswap** to format the partition as swap space. Use, for instance, **mkswap /dev/sdb6** if the partition you have just created is /dev/sdb6.
5. Type **free -m**. You see the amount of swap space that is currently allocated. This does not include the swap space you have just created, as it still needs to be activated.
6. Use **swapon** to switch on the newly allocated swap space. If, for instance, the swap device you have just created is /dev/sdb6, use **swapon /dev/sdb6** to activate the swap space.

7. Type **free -m** again. You see that the new swap space has been added to your server.
8. Open the file /etc/fstab with an editor and, on the last line, add the following to ensure the swap space is also available after a reboot: **/dev/sdb6 none swap defaults 0 0**

Adding Swap Files

If you do not have free disk space to create a swap partition and you do need to add swap space urgently, you can use a swap file as well. From a performance perspective, it does not even make that much difference if a swap file is used instead of a swap device such as a partition or a logical volume, and it may help you fulfill an urgent need in a timely manner.

To add a swap file, you need to create the file first. The **dd if=/dev/zero of=/swapfile bs=1M count=100** command would add 100 blocks with a size of 1 MiB from the /dev/zero device (which generates 0s) to the /swapfile file. The result is a 100-MiB file that can be configured as swap. To do so, you can follow the same procedure as for swap partitions. First use **mkswap /swapfile** to mark the file as a swap file, and then use **swapon /swapfile** to activate it. Also, put it in the /etc/fstab file so that it will be initialized automatically, using a line that looks as follows:

```
/swapfile  none swap  defaults  0 0
```

Mounting File Systems

Just creating a partition and putting a file system on it is not enough to start using it. To use a partition, you have to mount it as well. By mounting a partition (or better, the file system on it), you make its contents accessible through a specific directory.

To mount a file system, some information is needed:

- **What to mount:** This information is mandatory and specifies the name of the device that needs to be mounted.
- **Where to mount it:** This is also mandatory information that specifies the directory on which the device should be mounted.
- **What file system to mount:** Optionally, you can specify the file system type. In most cases, this is not necessary. The **mount** command will detect which file system is used on the device and make sure the correct driver is used.

- **Mount options:** Many mount options can be used when mounting a device. Using options is optional and depends on the needs you may have for the file system.

Manually Mounting File Systems

To manually mount a file system, you use the **mount** command. To disconnect a mounted file system, you use the ***umount*** command. Using these commands is relatively easy. To mount the file system that is on /dev/sdb5 on the directory /mnt, for example, use the following command:

```
mount /dev/sdb5 /mnt
```

To disconnect the mount, you can use **umount** with either the name of the device or the name of the mount point you want to disconnect. So, both of the following commands will work:

```
umount /dev/sdb5
umount /mnt
```

Using Device Names, UUIDs, or Disk Labels

To mount a device, you can use the name of the device, as in the command **mount /dev/sdb5 /mnt**. If your server is used in an environment where a dynamic storage topology is used, this is not always the best approach. You may today have a storage device /dev/sdb5, which after changes in the storage topology can be /dev/sdc5 after the next reboot of your server. This is why on a default RHEL 9 installation, ***universally unique IDs (UUIDs)*** are used instead of device names.

Every file system by default has a UUID associated with it—not just file systems that are used to store files but also special file systems such as the swap file system. You can use the **blkid** command to get an overview of the current file systems on your system and the UUID that is used by that file system.

Before the use of UUIDs was common, file systems were often configured to work with ***labels***, which can be set using the **e2label** command, the **xfs_admin -L** command, or, while creating the file system, the **mkfs.xxxx -L** command. This has become more uncommon in recent Linux versions. If a file system has a label, the **blkid** command will also show it. In Example 14-3 you can see an example of **blkid** output.

Example 14-3 Using **blkid** to Find Current File System UUIDs

```
[root@server1 ~]# blkid
/dev/mapper/rhel-swap: UUID="3f377db9-7a25-4456-bdd4-0bac9aa50515"
  TYPE="swap"
/dev/sdd1: PARTLABEL="part1" PARTUUID="97ddf1cb-6f5e-407e-a9d1-
  e4345862283d"
/dev/sdb5: UUID="5d34b37c-5d32-4790-8364-d22a8b8f88db" BLOCK_
  SIZE="4096" TYPE="ext4" PARTUUID="e049881b-05"
/dev/sdb1: UUID="1e6b3b75-3454-4e03-b5a9-81e5fa1f0ccd" BLOCK_
  SIZE="512" TYPE="xfs" PARTUUID="e049881b-01"
/dev/sdb6: UUID="b7ada118-3586-4b22-90db-451d821f1fcf" TYPE="swap"
  PARTUUID="e049881b-06"
/dev/sr0: BLOCK_SIZE="2048" UUID="2022-04-19-20-42-48-00" LABEL="RHEL-
  9-0-0-BaseOS-x86_64" TYPE="iso9660" PTUUID="3a60e52f" PTTYPE="dos"
/dev/mapper/rhel-root: UUID="1e9d930d-4c05-4c91-9bca-a1b13b45ee24"
  BLOCK_SIZE="512" TYPE="xfs"
/dev/sdc1: PARTLABEL="Linux filesystem"
  PARTUUID="c021ce85-8a1b-461a-b27f-d911e2ede649"
/dev/sda2: UUID="bKb2nd-kGTl-voHS-h8Gj-AjTD-fORt-X53K9A" TYPE="LVM2_
  member" PARTUUID="908faf3e-02"
/dev/sda1: UUID="6c2b4028-1dcb-44cb-b5b7-c8e52352b06c" BLOCK_
  SIZE="512" TYPE="xfs" PARTUUID="908faf3e-01"
```

To mount a file system based on a UUID, you use **UUID=nnnnn** instead of the device name. So if you want to mount /dev/sdb5 from Example 14-3 based on its UUID, the command becomes as follows:

```
mount UUID="5d34b37c-5d32-4790-8364-d22a8b8f88db" /mnt
```

Manually mounting devices using the UUID is not exactly easier. If mounts are automated as discussed in the next section, however, using UUIDs instead of device names does make sense.

To mount a file system using a label, you use the **mount LABEL=labelname** command. For example, use **mount LABEL=mylabel /mnt** to temporarily mount the file system with the name mylabel on the /mnt directory.

Automating File System Mounts Through /etc/fstab

Normally, you do not want to be mounting file systems manually. Once you are happy with them, it is a good idea to have them mounted automatically. The classical way to do this is through the /etc/***fstab*** file. Example 14-4 shows what the contents of this file may look like.

Example 14-4 Sample /etc/fstab File Contents

```
[root@server1 ~]# cat /etc/fstab
#
# /etc/fstab
# Created by anaconda on Thu Sep  1 12:06:40 2022
#
# Accessible filesystems, by reference, are maintained under '/dev/
  disk/'.
# See man pages fstab(5), findfs(8), mount(8) and/or blkid(8) for more
   info.
#
# After editing this file, run 'systemctl daemon-reload' to update
   systemd
# units generated from this file.
#
/dev/mapper/rhel-root   /                       xfs     defaults        0 0
UUID=6c2b4028-1dcb-44cb-b5b7-c8e52352b06c /boot                   xfs
   defaults        0 0.
/dev/mapper/rhel-swap   none                    swap    defaults        0 0
/dev/sr0                  /repo                 iso9660 defaults        0 0
```

In the /etc/fstab file, everything is specified to mount the file system automatically. For this purpose, every line has six fields, as summarized in Table 14-5.

Table 14-5 /etc/fstab Fields

Field	Description
Device	The device that must be mounted. A device name, UUID, or label can be used.
Mount Point	The directory or kernel interface where the device needs to be mounted.
File System	The file system type.
Mount Options	Mount options.
Dump Support	Use 1 to enable support to back up using the **dump** utility. This may be necessary for some backup solutions.
Automatic Check	This field specifies whether the file system should be checked automatically when booting. Use 0 to disable automated check, 1 if this is the root file system and it has to be checked automatically, and 2 for all other file systems that need automatic checking while booting. Network file systems should have this option set to 0.

Based on what has previously been discussed about the **mount** command, you should have no problem understanding the Device, Mount Point, and File System fields in /etc/fstab. Notice that in the mount point not all file systems use a directory name. Some system devices such as swap are not mounted on a directory, but on a kernel interface. It is easy to recognize when a kernel interface is used; its name does not start with a / (and does not exist in the file system on your server).

The Mount Options field defines specific mount options that can be used. If no specific options are required, this line will just read "defaults." To offer specific functionality, a large number of mount options can be specified here. Table 14-6 gives an overview of some of the more common mount options.

Table 14-6 Common Mount Options

Option	Use
auto / noauto	Mounts/does not mount the file system automatically.
acl	Adds support for file system access control lists (see Chapter 7, "Permissions Management").
user_xattr	Adds support for user-extended attributes (see Chapter 7).
ro	Mounts the file system in read-only mode.
atime / noatime	Disables/enables access time modifications.
noexec / exec	Denies/allows execution of program files from the file system.

The fifth column of /etc/fstab specifies support for the **dump** utility, which was developed a long time ago to create file system backups. On modern file systems this option is not needed, which is why you will see it set to 0 in most cases.

The last column indicates if the file system integrity needs to be checked while booting. Enter a 0 if you do not want to check the file system at all, a 1 if this is the root file system that needs to be checked before anything else, and a 2 if this is a non-root file system that needs to be checked while booting. Because file system consistency is checked in another way, this option is now commonly set to the value 0.

After adding mounts to /etc/fstab, it's a good idea to check that you didn't make any errors. If /etc/fstab contains errors, you won't be able to boot your system anymore, and on the RHCSA exam the result could be that you fail the exam. The following options can be used to verify /etc/fstab contents:

- **findmnt --verify** Verifies /etc/fstab syntax and alerts you if anything is incorrect.
- **mount -a** Mounts all file systems that have a line in /etc/fstab and are not currently mounted.

In Exercise 14-7, you learn how to mount partitions through /etc/fstab by mounting the XFS-formatted partition /dev/sdb5 that you created in previous exercises.

Exercise 14-7 Mounting Partitions Through /etc/fstab

1. From a root shell, type **blkid**. Use the mouse to copy the UUID="nnnn" part for /dev/sdb5.
2. Type **mkdir -p /mounts/data** to create a mount point for this partition.
3. Open /etc/fstab in an editor and add the following line:

```
UUID="nnnn"    /mounts/data    xfs    defaults 0 0
```

4. Before you attempt an automatic mount while rebooting, it is a good idea to test the configuration. Type **mount -a**. This command mounts everything that is specified in /etc/fstab and that has not been mounted already.
5. Type **df -h** to verify that the partition has been mounted correctly.

Using Systemd Mounts

The /etc/fstab file has been used to automate mounts since the earliest days of UNIX. In recent RHEL versions it is used as an input file to create systemd mounts, as ultimately systemd is responsible for mounting file systems. You can find the files generated by /etc/fstab in the directory /run/systemd/generator. In Example 14-5 you can see what its contents may look like.

Example 14-5 Sample Systemd Mount File

```
[root@server1 ~]# cat /run/systemd/generator/repo.mount
# Automatically generated by systemd-fstab-generator

[Unit]
Documentation=man:fstab(5) man:systemd-fstab-generator(8)
SourcePath=/etc/fstab
Before=local-fs.target
After=blockdev@dev-sr0.target

[Mount]
What=/dev/sr0
Where=/repo
Type=iso9660
```

As mounts are taken care of by systemd, you could also choose to mount your file systems this way. To do so, you need to create a mount file in /etc/systemd/system, meeting the following requirements:

- The name of the file corresponds to the directory where you want to mount its device. So if you want to mount on /data, the file is data.mount.
- The file contains a [Mount] section that has the lines What, Where, and Type.
- The file has an [Install] section, containing WantedBy=some.target. Without this section the mount cannot be enabled.

In Exercise 14-8 you'll create a mount file for the /dev/sdc1 device that was previously created.

Exercise 14-8 Creating a Systemd Mount File

1. Use **mkfs.ext4 /dev/sdc1** to format /dev/sdc1 with an Ext4 file system.
2. Type **mkdir /exercise** to create the mount point
3. Use **vim /etc/systemd/system/exercise.mount** and give the file the following contents:

```
[Unit]
Before=local-fs.target

[Mount]
What=/dev/sdc1
Where=/exercise
Type=ext4

[Install]
WantedBy=multi-user.target
```

4. Use **systemctl enable --now exercise.mount** to enable and start the mount unit.
5. Type **mount | grep exercise** to verify the mount was created.
6. Use **systemctl status exercise.mount** to verify the unit file.

Summary

In this important chapter, you learned how to work with partitions and file systems on RHEL 9. You learned how to create partitions for MBR and GPT disks and how to put a file system on top of the partition. You also learned how to mount these partitions manually and automatically through /etc/fstab or by using systemd unit files.

Exam Preparation Tasks

As mentioned in the section "How to Use This Book" in the Introduction, you have several choices for exam preparation: the end-of-chapter labs; the memory tables in Appendix C; Chapter 27, "Final Preparation"; and the practice exams.

Review All Key Topics

Review the most important topics in the chapter, noted with the Key Topic icon in the margin of the page. Table 14-7 lists a reference for these key topics and the page numbers on which each is found.

Table 14-7 Key Topics for Chapter 14

Key Topic Element	Description	Page
Table 14-2	Disk Size Specifications	316
Table 14-3	Common Disk Device Types	317
Table 14-4	File System Overview	328
Table 14-5	/etc/fstab Fields	336
Table 14-6	Common Mount Options	337

Complete Tables and Lists from Memory

Print a copy of Appendix C, "Memory Tables" (found on the companion website), or at least the section for this chapter, and complete the tables and lists from memory. Appendix D, "Memory Tables Answer Key," includes completed tables and lists to check your work.

Define Key Terms

Define the following key terms from this chapter and check your answers in the glossary:

partition, Master Boot Record (MBR), Basic Input/Output System (BIOS), extended partition, primary partition, logical partition, GUID Partition Table (GPT), Unified Extensible Firmware Interface (UEFI), XFS, Ext4, Ext3, Ext2, BtrFS, VFAT, **mount, umount**, universally unique ID (UUID), label, fstab

Review Questions

The questions that follow use an open-ended format that is meant to help you test your knowledge of concepts and terminology and the breadth of your knowledge. You can find the answers to these questions in Appendix A.

1. Which tool do you use to create GUID partitions?
2. Which tool do you use to create MBR partitions?
3. What is the default file system on RHEL 9?
4. What is the name of the file that is used to automatically mount partitions while booting?
5. Which mount option do you use if you want a file system not to be mounted automatically while booting?
6. Which command enables you to format a partition that has type 82 with the appropriate file system?
7. You have just added a couple of partitions for automatic mounting while booting. How can you safely test if this is going to work without actually rebooting?
8. Which file system is created if you use the **mkfs** command without any file system specification?
9. How do you format an Ext4 partition?
10. How do you find UUIDs for all devices on your computer?

End-of-Chapter Lab

To perform this end-of-chapter lab, you'll need to add a new and unused disk device. Create this new disk device using the virtualization software you're using, or by adding an empty USB thumb drive.

Lab 14.1

1. Add two partitions to your server. Create both partitions with a size of 100 MiB. One of these partitions must be configured as swap space; the other partition must be formatted with an Ext4 file system.
2. Configure your server to automatically mount these partitions. Mount the Ext4 partition on /mounts/data and mount the swap partition as swap space.
3. Reboot your server and verify that all is mounted correctly. In case of problems, read Chapter 18, "Essential Troubleshooting Skills," for tips on how to troubleshoot.

The following topics are covered in this chapter:

- Understanding LVM
- Creating LVM Logical Volumes
- Resizing LVM Logical Volumes
- Configuring Stratis

The following RHCSA exam objectives are covered in this chapter:

- Create and remove physical volumes
- Assign physical volumes to volume groups
- Create and delete logical volumes
- Extend existing logical volumes

CHAPTER 15

Managing Advanced Storage

In Chapter 14, "Managing Storage," you learned how to manage partitions on a hard disk. Creating multiple partitions on a disk is useful because it enables you to keep different data types in separate partitions, but it does not offer the flexibility that the advanced storage solutions offer. In this chapter, you learn how to work with advanced storage solutions, including Logical Volume Manager (LVM) and Stratis.

"Do I Know This Already?" Quiz

The "Do I Know This Already?" quiz enables you to assess whether you should read this entire chapter thoroughly or jump to the "Exam Preparation Tasks" section. If you are in doubt about your answers to these questions or your own assessment of your knowledge of the topics, read the entire chapter. Table 15-1 lists the major headings in this chapter and their corresponding "Do I Know This Already?" quiz questions. You can find the answers in Appendix A, "Answers to the 'Do I Know This Already?' Quizzes and Review Questions."

Table 15-1 "Do I Know This Already?" Section-to-Question Mapping

Foundation Topics Section	Questions
Understanding LVM	1–2
Creating LVM Logical Volumes	3–5
Resizing LVM Logical Volumes	6–8
Configuring Stratis	9–10

1. Which of the following is not a standard component in an LVM setup?
   a. Logical volume
   b. File system
   c. Volume group
   d. Physical volume

2. Which of the following is not an LVM feature?
   a. Volume resizing
   b. Hot replacement of failing disk
   c. Copy on write
   d. Snapshots

3. Which partition type do you need on a GPT partition to mark it with the LVM partition type?
   a. 83
   b. 8e
   c. 8300
   d. 8e00

4. Which of the following commands shows correctly how to create a logical volume that uses 50% of available disk space in the volume group?
   a. **vgadd -n lvdata -l +50%FREE vgdata**
   b. **lvcreate lvdata -l 50%FREE vgdata**
   c. **lvcreate -n lvdata -l 50%FREE vgdata**
   d. **lvadd -n lvdata -l 50% FREE /dev/vgdata**

5. Which commands show an overview of available physical volumes? (Choose two.)
   a. **pvshow**
   b. **pvdisplay**
   c. **pvs**
   d. **pvlist**

6. Which statement about resizing LVM logical volumes is *not* true?
   a. The Ext4 file system can be increased and decreased in size.
   b. Use **lvextend** with the **-r** option to automatically resize the file system.
   c. The XFS file system cannot be resized.
   d. To increase the size of a logical volume, you need allocatable space in the volume group.

7. You want to remove the physical volume /dev/sdd2 from the volume group vgdata. Which of the following statements about the removal procedure is *not* true?
   a. The file system must support shrinking.
   b. You need the amount of used extents on /dev/sdd2 to be available on remaining devices.
   c. Before you can use **vgreduce**, you have to move used extents to the remaining volumes.
   d. Use **pvmove** to move used extents.

8. You have extended the size of a logical volume without extending the XFS file system it contains. Which of the following solutions can you use to fix it?
   a. Use **lvresize** again, but this time with the **-r** option. The command will resize just the file system.
   b. Bring the logical volume back to its original size and then use **lvresize -r** again.
   c. Use **fsresize** to resize the file system later.
   d. Use **xfs_growfs** to grow the file system to the size available in the logical volume.

9. How much storage is used in a Stratis file system for metadata storage?
   a. 527 MiB
   b. 1 GiB
   c. 4 MiB
   d. 4 GiB

10. Which of the following lines correctly shows how a Stratis file system should be mounted through /etc/fstab?
    a. **UUID=abcd /stratis xfs defaults 0 0**
    b. **/dev/stratis/stratis1 /stratis xfs defaults,x-systemd.requires= stratis.service 0 0**
    c. **UUID=abcd /stratis xfs defaults,x-systemd.requires=stratis.service 0 0**
    d. **/dev/stratis/stratis1 /stratis xfs defaults 0 0**

Foundation Topics

Understanding LVM

In the early days of Linux servers, storage was handled by creating partitions on disks. Even if this approach does work, there are some disadvantages, the most important of which is that partitions are inflexible. That is why the Logical Volume Manager was introduced. Whereas it is not possible to dynamically grow a partition that is running out of disk space, this is possible when working with LVM. LVM offers many other advantages as well, which you learn about in this chapter.

LVM Architecture

In the LVM architecture, several layers can be distinguished. On the lowest layer, the storage devices are used. These can be any storage devices, such as complete disks, partitions, logical units (LUNs) on a storage-area network (SAN), and whatever else is made possible in modern storage topologies. In this chapter you learn how to use partitions as physical volumes, which is recommended practice. By using partitions instead of complete disk devices, it is easy for other tools to recognize that some storage has already been configured on the block device, which makes it less likely that misconfigurations are going to occur.

The storage devices need to be flagged as physical volumes, which makes them usable in an LVM environment and makes them usable by other utilities trying to gain access to the logical volume. A storage device that is a physical volume can be added to the volume group, which is the abstraction of all available storage. The "abstraction" means that the volume group is not something that is fixed, but it can be resized when needed, which makes it possible to add more space on the volume group level when volumes are running out of disk space. The idea is simple: If you are running out of disk space on a logical volume, you take available disk space from the volume group. And if there is no available disk space in the volume group, you just add it by adding a physical volume.

On top of the volume group are the logical volumes. Logical volumes do not act on disks directly but get their disk space from available disk space in the volume group. That means that a logical volume may consist of available storage from multiple physical volumes, which adds an important layer of additional flexibility to the storage configuration.

NOTE It is a good idea to avoid logical volumes from spanning multiple physical volumes; if one of the physical volumes breaks, all files on the LVM file system will become inaccessible.

The actual file systems are created on the logical volumes. Because the logical volumes are flexible with regard to size, that makes the file systems flexible as well. If a file system is running out of disk space, it is relatively easy to extend the file system or to reduce it if the file system allows that. Note that in order to resize file systems when logical volumes are resized, the file systems must offer support for that.

Figure 15-1 gives an overview of the LVM architecture.

Key Topic

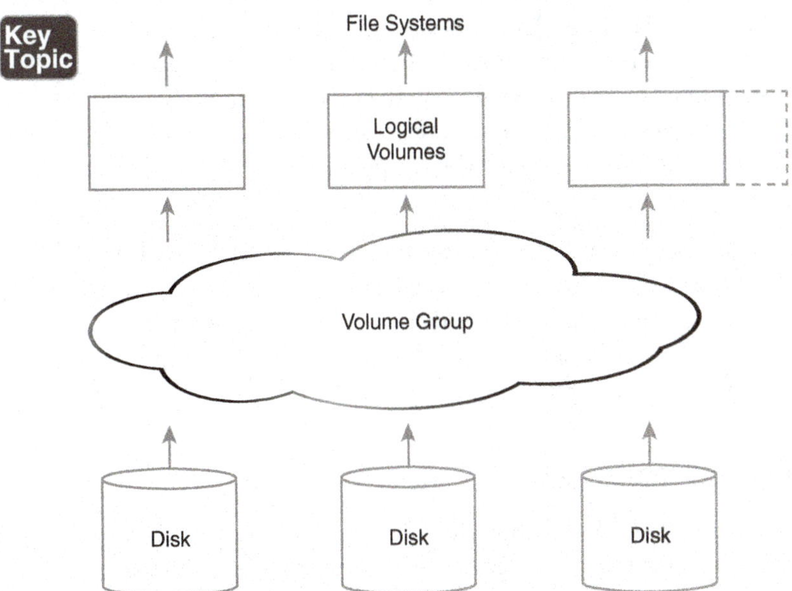

Figure 15-1 LVM Architecture Overview

LVM Features

There are several reasons why LVM is great. The most important reason is that LVM offers a flexible solution for managing storage. Volumes are no longer bound to the restrictions of physical hard drives. If additional storage space is needed, the volume group can easily be extended by adding a new physical volume, so that disk space can be added to the logical volumes. It is also possible to reduce the size of a logical volume, but only if the file system that was created on that volume supports the feature of reducing the size of the file system. Ext4 supports growing and shrinking; XFS size can only be increased.

Another important reason why administrators like using LVM is the support for snapshots. A ***snapshot*** keeps the current state of a logical volume and can be used to revert to a previous situation or to make a backup of the file system on the logical volume if the volume is open. Using snapshots is essential in backup strategies.

LVM snapshots are created by copying the logical volume administrative data (the metadata) that describes the current state of files to a snapshot volume. As long as nothing changes, from the LVM snapshot metadata the original blocks in the original volume are addressed. When blocks are modified, the blocks containing the previous state of the file are copied over to the snapshot volume, which for that reason will grow. Using this method ensures that, by accessing an LVM snapshot volume, the exact state of the files as they were when the snapshot was created can be accessed. Because the snapshot will grow when files on the original volume change, when planning for snapshots, you should make sure that a sufficient amount of disk space is available. Also, snapshots are supposed to be temporary: once a snapshot has served its purpose, it can be removed.

A third important advantage of using LVM logical volumes is the option to replace failing hardware easily. If a hard disk is failing, data can be moved within the volume group (through the **pvmove** command), the failing disk can then be removed from the volume group, and a new hard disk can be added dynamically, without requiring any downtime for the logical volume itself.

Creating LVM Logical Volumes

Creating LVM logical volumes involves creating the three layers in the LVM architecture. You first have to convert physical devices, such as disks or partitions, into physical volumes (PVs); then you need to create the volume group (VG) and assign PVs to it. As the last step, you need to create the logical volume (LV) itself. In this section, you learn what is involved in creating these three layers.

Different utilities exist for creating LVM logical volumes. This chapter focuses on using the command-line utilities. They are relatively easy to use, and they are available in all environments (whether you are running a graphical interface or not).

TIP You absolutely do not need to memorize the commands discussed in this chapter for the RHCSA exam. All you really need to remember are **pv**, **vg**, and **lv**. Open a command line, type **pv**, and press the Tab key twice. This will show all commands that start with *pv*, which are all commands that are used for managing physical volumes. After you have found the command you need, run this command with the **--help** option. This shows a usage summary that lists everything you must do to create the element you need. Example 15-1 shows an example of the **pvcreate --help** command (which is explained in the next subsection).

Example 15-1 Requesting Help for the **pvcreate** Command

```
[root@server1 ~]# pvcreate --help
  pvcreate - Initialize physical volume(s) for use by LVM

  pvcreate PV ...
        [ -f|--force ]
        [ -M|--metadatatype lvm2 ]
        [ -u|--uuid String ]
        [ -Z|--zero y|n ]
        [    --dataalignment Size[k|UNIT] ]
        [    --dataalignmentoffset Size[k|UNIT] ]
        [    --bootloaderareasize Size[m|UNIT] ]
        [    --labelsector Number ]
        [    --pvmetadatacopies 0|1|2 ]
        [    --metadatasize Size[m|UNIT] ]
        [    --metadataignore y|n ]
        [    --norestorefile ]
        [    --setphysicalvolumesize Size[m|UNIT] ]
        [    --reportformat basic|json ]
        [    --restorefile String ]
        [ COMMON_OPTIONS ]

  Common options for lvm:
        [ -d|--debug ]
        [ -h|--help ]
        [ -q|--quiet ]
        [ -v|--verbose ]
        [ -y|--yes ]
        [ -t|--test ]
        [    --commandprofile String ]
        [    --config String ]
        [    --driverloaded y|n ]
        [    --nolocking ]
        [    --lockopt String ]
        [    --longhelp ]
        [    --profile String ]
        [    --version ]
        [    --devicesfile String ]
        [    --devices PV ]
        [    --nohints ]
        [    --journal String ]

  Use --longhelp to show all options and advanced commands.
```

Creating the Physical Volumes

Before you can use the LVM tools to create ***physical volumes (PVs)***, you should create a partition marked as the LVM partition type. This is basically the same procedure as described in Chapter 14, with the only difference being that before writing changes to disk, you need to change the partition type.

In **fdisk** and **gdisk**, you can use **t** from the menu to change the type. If you are using an MBR disk, the partition type is 8e. If you are using a GUID disk, use the partition type 8e00. In **fdisk** you can also just type **lvm** as the partition type to use, as the RHEL 9 version of **fdisk** supports using aliases. If you are using **parted** to create partitions, you need to use the **set *n* lvm on** command from within the **parted** interface (where *n* is the number of the partition you want to mark for use with LVM).

After creating the partition and flagging it as an LVM partition type, you need to use **pvcreate** to mark it as a physical volume. This writes some metadata to the partition, which allows it to be used in a volume group. The entire procedure is summarized in Exercise 15-1, in which you create a physical volume. Also see Example 15-2 for an overview of this procedure.

Exercise 15-1 Creating a Physical Volume

To do this exercise, you need a hard disk that has free (unpartitioned) disk space available. The recommended method to make disk space available is to add a new hard disk in your virtual machine environment. In this exercise, I use a clean /dev/sdd device to create the partition. You may have to change the device name to match your configuration.

1. Open a root shell and type **fdisk /dev/sdd**
2. Type **p**. This will show the current partition table layout. There should be none at this point.
3. Type **g** to create a GPT partition table.
4. Type **n** to create a new partition. Press Enter when asked for the partition number, as well as when asked for the first sector.
5. When prompted for the last sector, type **+1G** to create a 1-GiB partition.
6. Type **t** to change the partition type. As you only have one partition at the moment, this partition is automatically selected. When prompted for the partition type, enter **lvm**.
7. Press **p** to verify the partition was created successfully.

8. Repeat this procedure to create three other 1-GiB LVM partitions for future use.
9. Press **w** to write the new partitions to disk and quit **fdisk**.
10. Use the **lsblk** command to verify that the new partitions were created successfully.
11. Type **pvcreate /dev/sdd1** to mark the new partition as an LVM physical volume (see Example 15-3).
12. Type **pvs** to verify that the physical volume was created successfully.

Example 15-2 Creating an LVM Partition in **fdisk**

```
[root@
[root@server1 ~]# fdisk /dev/sdd

Welcome to fdisk (util-linux 2.37.4).
Changes will remain in memory only, until you decide to write them.
Be careful before using the write command.



Command (m for help): g
Created a new GPT disklabel (GUID:
  3BCE8E49-EFDF-9144-ACD5-290F4FCCDA07).

Command (m for help): n
Partition number (1-128, default 1):
First sector (2048-41943006, default 2048):
Last sector, +/-sectors or +/-size{K,M,G,T,P} (2048-41943006, default
  41943006): +1G

Created a new partition 1 of type 'Linux filesystem' and of size 1
GiB.

Command (m for help): t
Selected partition 1
Partition type or alias (type L to list all): lvm
Changed type of partition 'Linux filesystem' to 'Linux LVM'.

Command (m for help): p
Disk /dev/sdd: 20 GiB, 21474836480 bytes, 41943040 sectors
Disk model: VMware Virtual S
```

```
Units: sectors of 1 * 512 = 512 bytes
Sector size (logical/physical): 512 bytes / 512 bytes
I/O size (minimum/optimal): 512 bytes / 512 bytes
Disklabel type: gpt
Disk identifier: 3BCE8E49-EFDF-9144-ACD5-290F4FCCDA07

Device      Start     End Sectors Size Type
/dev/sdd1    2048 2099199 2097152   1G Linux LVM

Command (m for help): w
The partition table has been altered.
Calling ioctl() to re-read partition table.
Syncing disks.
```

Example 15-3 Verifying the Physical Volume

```
[root@server1 ~]# pvcreate /dev/sdd1
  Physical volume "/dev/sdd1" successfully created.
[root@server1 ~]# pvs
  PV         VG   Fmt  Attr PSize   PFree
  /dev/sda2  rhel lvm2 a--  <19.00g    0
  /dev/sdd1       lvm2 ---    1.00g 1.00g
```

As an alternative to the **pvs** command, which shows a summary of the physical volumes and their attributes, you can use the **pvdisplay** command to show more details. Example 15-4 shows an example of the output of this command.

Example 15-4 Sample **pvdisplay** Command Output

```
[root@server1 ~]# pvdisplay /dev/sdd1
  "/dev/sdd1" is a new physical volume of "1.00 GiB"
  --- NEW Physical volume ---
  PV Name               /dev/sdd1
  VG Name
  PV Size               1.00 GiB
  Allocatable           NO
  PE Size               0
  Total PE              0
  Free PE               0
  Allocated PE          0
  PV UUID               cjdhpJ-bRh9-fg3B-KlPh-XQzD-unXV-ycVK36
```

If you want a compact overview of the current storage configuration on your server, you might also like the **lsblk** command. As shown in Example 15-5, this command gives a hierarchical overview of which disks and partitions are used in what LVM volume groups and logical volumes.

Example 15-5 Using **lsblk** for a Compact Overview of the Current Storage Configuration

```
[root@server1 ~]# lsblk
NAME            MAJ:MIN RM SIZE RO TYPE MOUNTPOINTS
sda               8:0    0  20G  0 disk
├─sda1            8:1    0   1G  0 part /boot
└─sda2            8:2    0  19G  0 part
  ├─rhel-root   253:0    0  17G  0 lvm  /
  └─rhel-swap   253:1    0   2G  0 lvm  [SWAP]
sdb               8:16   0  20G  0 disk
├─sdb1            8:17   0   1G  0 part
├─sdb2            8:18   0   1K  0 part
├─sdb5            8:21   0   1G  0 part
└─sdb6            8:22   0   1G  0 part
sdc               8:32   0  20G  0 disk
└─sdc1            8:33   0   1G  0 part /exercise
sdd               8:48   0  20G  0 disk
└─sdd1            8:49   0   1G  0 part
sr0              11:0    1   8G  0 rom  /repo
nvme0n1         259:0    0  20G  0 disk
```

Creating the Volume Groups

Now that the physical volume has been created, you can assign it to a ***volume group (VG)***. It is possible to add a physical volume to an existing volume group (which is discussed later in this chapter), but here you learn how to create a new volume group and add the physical volume to it. This is a simple one-command procedure. Just type **vgcreate** followed by the name of the volume group you want to create and the name of the physical device you want to add to it. So, if the physical volume name is /dev/sdd1, the complete command is **vgcreate vgdata /dev/sdd1**. You are completely free in your choice of name for the volume group. I like to start all volume group names with *vg*, which makes it easy to find the volume groups if there are many, but you are free to choose anything you like.

Between the previous section and the preceding paragraph, you have learned how to create a volume group in a two-step procedure where you first create the physical volume with the **pvcreate** command and then add the volume group using the **vgcreate** command. You can do this in a one-step procedure as well (where using a separate **pvcreate** command will not be necessary).

The one-step procedure is particularly useful for adding a complete disk device). If you want to add the disk /dev/sdc, for instance, just type **vgcreate vgdata /dev/sdc** to create a volume group vgdata that contains the /dev/sdc device. When you are doing this to add a device that has not been marked as a physical volume yet, the **vgcreate** utility will automatically flag it as a physical volume so that you can see it while using the **pvs** command.

When you're creating volume groups, a physical extent size is used. The ***physical extent*** size defines the size of the building blocks used to create logical volumes. A logical volume always has a size that is a multiple of the physical extent size. If you need to create huge logical volumes, it is more efficient to use a big physical extent size. If you do not specify anything, a default extent size of 4 MiB is used. The physical extent size is always specified as a multiple of 2 MiB, with a maximum size of 128 MiB. Use the **vgcreate -s** option to specify the physical extent size you want to use.

NOTE When you're working with LVM, you need to consider the physical extent size. This is the size of the basic building blocks used in the LVM configuration. When you're working with an ext4 file system, logical extents are used. The extent sizes on LVM are in no way related to the extent sizes that are used on the file systems.

After creating the volume group, you can request details about the volume group using the **vgs** command for a short summary, or the **vgdisplay** command to get more information. Example 15-6 shows an example of the output of the **vgdisplay** command.

Example 15-6 Showing Current Volume Group Properties

```
[root@server1 ~]# vgdisplay vgdata
  --- Volume group ---
  VG Name               vgdata
  System ID
  Format                lvm2
  Metadata Areas        1
```

```
Metadata Sequence No  1
VG Access             read/write
VG Status             resizable
MAX LV                0
Cur LV                0
Open LV               0
Max PV                0
Cur PV                1
Act PV                1
VG Size               1020.00 MiB
PE Size               4.00 MiB
Total PE              255
Alloc PE / Size       0 / 0
Free  PE / Size       255 / 1020.00 MiB
VG UUID               KrzkCo-QUFs-quJm-Z6pM-qMh0-ZchJ-c677c2
```

Creating the Logical Volumes and File Systems

Now that the volume group has been created, you can start creating one or more ***logical volumes (LVs)*** from it. This procedure is slightly more complicated than the creation of physical volumes or volume groups because there are more choices to be made. While creating the logical volume, you must specify a volume name and a size.

The volume size can be specified as an absolute value using the **-L** option. Use, for instance, **-L 5G** to create an LVM volume with a 5-GiB size. Alternatively, you can use relative sizes with the **-l** option. For instance, use **-l 50%FREE** to use half of all available disk space. You can also use the **-l** option to specify the number of extents that you want the logical volume to be. You'll further need to specify the name of the volume group that the logical volume is assigned to, and optionally (but highly recommended), you can use **-n** to specify the name of the logical volume. For instance, use **lvcreate -n lvdata -l 100 vgdata** to create a logical volume with the name lvdata and a size of 100 extents and add that to the vgdata volume group. Once the logical volume has been created, you can use the **mkfs** utility to create a file system on top of it.

Understanding LVM Device Naming

Now that the logical volume has been created, you can start using it. To do this, you need to know the device name. LVM volume device names can be addressed in multiple ways. The simple method is to address the device as /dev/vgname/lvname.

So, for example, if you have created a volume with the name lvdata, which gets its available disk space from the vgdata volume group, the device name would be /dev/vgdata/lvdata, which is in fact a symbolic link to the device mapper name (which is explained next).

For naming LVM volumes, another system plays a role: device mapper. The ***device mapper*** (abbreviated as dm) is a generic interface that the Linux kernel uses to address storage devices. The device mapper is used by multiple device types, such as LVM volumes, but also by software RAID and advanced network storage devices such as multipath devices.

Device mapper devices are generated on detection and use names that are generated while booting, like /dev/dm-0 and /dev/dm-1. To make these devices easier to access, the device mapper creates symbolic links in the /dev/mapper directory that point to these meaningless device names. The symbolic links follow the naming structure /dev/mapper/vgname-lvname.

So, the device /dev/vgdata/lvdata would also be known as /dev/mapper/vgdata-lvdata. When working with LVM logical volumes, you can use either of these device names. Example 15-7 shows an overview of the different LVM device names as provided by the device mapper. In Exercise 15-2, you learn how to create a volume group and logical volumes.

Example 15-7 LVM Device Name Overview

```
[root@server1 ~]# ls -l /dev/mapper/vgdata-lvdata /dev/vgdata/lvdata
lrwxrwxrwx. 1 root root 7 Sep 16 11:34 /dev/mapper/vgdata-lvdata ->
  ../dm-2
lrwxrwxrwx. 1 root root 7 Sep 16 11:34 /dev/vgdata/lvdata -> ../dm-2
```

Exercise 15-2 Creating the Volume Group and Logical Volumes

In Exercise 15-1, you created a physical volume. In this exercise, you continue working on that physical volume and assign it to a volume group. Then you add a logical volume from that volume group. You can work on this exercise only after successful completion of Exercise 15-1.

1. Open a root shell. Type **pvs** to verify the availability of physical volumes on your machine. You should see the /dev/sdd1 physical volume that was created previously.
2. Type **vgcreate vgdata /dev/sdd1**. This will create the volume group with the physical volume assigned to it.

3. Type **vgs** to verify that the volume group was created successfully. Also type **pvs**. Notice that this command now shows the name of the physical volumes, with the names of the volume groups they are assigned to.
4. Type **lvcreate -n lvdata -l 50%FREE vgdata**. This creates an LVM logical volume with the name lvdata, which will use 50% of available disk space in the vgdata volume group.
5. Type **lvs** to verify that the volume was added successfully.
6. At this point, you are ready to create a file system on top of the logical volume. Type **mkfs.ext4 /dev/vgdata/lvdata** to create the file system.
7. Type **mkdir /files** to create a folder on which the volume can be mounted.
8. Add the following line to the bottom of /etc/fstab:

```
/dev/vgdata/lvdata /files ext4 defaults 0 0
```

9. Type **mount -a** to verify that the mount works and mount the file system.
10. Use **lsblk** to verify that the partition was mounted successfully.

Table 15-2 summarizes the relevant commands for creating logical volumes.

Table 15-2 LVM Management Essential Commands

Command	Explanation
pvcreate	Creates physical volumes
pvs	Shows a summary of available physical volumes
pvdisplay	Shows a list of physical volumes and their properties
pvremove	Removes the physical volume signature from a block device
vgcreate	Creates volume groups
vgs	Shows a summary of available volume groups
vgdisplay	Shows a detailed list of volume groups and their properties
vgremove	Removes a volume group
lvcreate	Creates logical volumes
lvs	Shows a summary of all available logical volumes
lvdisplay	Shows a detailed list of available logical volumes and their properties
lvremove	Removes a logical volume

Resizing LVM Logical Volumes

One of the major benefits of using LVM is that LVM volumes are easy to resize, which is very useful if your file system is running out of available disk space. If the XFS file system is used, a volume can be increased, but not decreased, in size. Other file systems such as Ext4 support decreasing the file system size also. You can decrease an Ext4 file system offline only, which means that you need to unmount it before you can resize it. In this section, you learn how to increase the size of an LVM logical volume. To increase the size of a logical volume, you need to have disk space available in the volume group, so we address that first.

Resizing Volume Groups

The most important feature of LVM flexibility lies in the fact that it is so easy to resize the volume groups and the logical volumes that are using disk space from the volume groups. The **vgextend** command is used to add storage to a volume group, and the **vgreduce** command is used to take physical volumes out of a volume group. The procedure to add storage to a volume group is relatively easy:

1. Make sure that a physical volume or device is available to be added to the volume group.
2. Use **vgextend** to extend the volume group. The new disk space will show immediately in the volume group.

After extending a volume group, you can use the **vgs** command to verify that a physical volume has been added to the volume group. In Example 15-8, you can see that the vgdata VG contains two physical volumes, as indicated in the #PV column.

Example 15-8 Verifying VG Resize Operations with **vgs**

```
[root@server1 ~]# vgs
  VG      #PV  #LV  #SN   Attr     VSize      VFree
  centos    1    2    0   wz--n-   <19.00g    0
  vgdata    2    1    0   wz--n-   1020.00m   512.00m
```

Resizing Logical Volumes and File Systems

Like volume groups can be extended with the **vgextend** command, logical volumes can be extended with the **lvextend** command. This command has a very useful option **-r** to take care of extending the file systems on the logical volume at the same time; it is recommended to use this option and not the alternative approach that separately extends the logical volumes and the file systems on top of the logical volumes. Most file system resizing operations can be done online if the file system needs to be extended without unmounting it.

To grow the logical volume size, use **lvextend** or **lvresize**, followed by the **-r** option to resize the file system used on it. Then specify the size you want the resized volume to be. The easiest and most intuitive way to do that is by using **-L** followed by a + sign and the amount of disk space you want to add, as in **lvresize -L +1G -r /dev/vgdata/lvdata**. An alternative way to resize the logical volume is by using the **-l** option. This option is followed either by the number of extents that are added to the logical volume or by the absolute or relative percentage of extents in the volume group that will be used. You can, for example, use the following commands to resize the logical volume:

- **lvresize -r -l 75%VG /dev/vgdata/lvdata** Resizes the logical volume so that it will take 75% of the total disk space in the volume group. Notice that if currently the logical volume is using more than 75% of the volume group disk space, this command will try to reduce the logical volume size!
- **lvresize -r -l +75%VG /dev/vgdata/lvdata** Tries to add 75% of the total size of the volume group to the logical volume. This will work only if currently at least 75% of the volume group is unused. (Notice the difference with the previous command.)
- **lvresize -r -l +75%FREE /dev/vgdata/lvdata** Adds 75% of all free disk space to the logical volume.
- **lvresize -r -l 75%FREE /dev/vgdata/lvdata** Resizes the logical volume to a total size that equals 75% of the amount of free disk space, which may result in an attempt to reduce the logical volume size. (Notice the difference with the previous command.)

A ***logical extent*** is the logical building block used when creating logical volumes, and it maps to a physical extent, the size of which can be specified when creating a volume group. All resize operations need to match complete logical extents. You will sometimes notice that the resize size is rounded up or down to the logical extent size. You can also specify the number of logical extents that need to be added or removed directly by using the **-l** option with the **lvresize** command.

As you can see, resizing a logical volume has many options, and you need to take care to use the right options because it is easy to make a mistake! In Exercise 15-3, you learn how to resize logical volumes and the file systems used on top of them.

NOTE The size of an XFS file system cannot be decreased; it can only be increased. If you need a file system that can be shrunk in size, use Ext4, not XFS.

Exercise 15-3 Resizing Logical Volumes

In Exercises 15-1 and 15-2, you created a physical volume, volume group, and logical volume. In this exercise, you extend the size of the logical volume and the file system used on top of it.

1. Type **pvs** and **vgs** to show the current physical volume and volume group configuration.
2. Use **lsblk** to verify that you have an unused partition available that can be added to the volume group. In Exercise 15-1 you created the partition /dev/sdd2 for this purpose.
3. Type **vgextend vgdata /dev/sdd2** to extend vgdata with the total size of the /dev/sdd2 device.
4. Type **vgs** to verify that the available volume group size has increased.
5. Type **lvs** to verify the current size of the logical volume lvdata.
6. Type **df -h** to verify the current size of the file system on lvdata.
7. Type **lvextend -r -l +50%FREE /dev/vgdata/lvdata** to extend lvdata with 50% of all available disk space in the volume group.
8. Type **lvs** and **df -h** again to verify that the added disk space has become available.

Reducing Volume Groups

If a volume group consists of multiple PVs, a PV can be removed from the VG if the remaining PVs have sufficient free space to allocate the extents it currently uses. This procedure will not work if the remaining PVs are fully used already. Removing a PV from a VG is a two-step procedure. First, use **pvmove** to move used extents from the PV that you want to remove to any of the remaining volumes. Next, use **vgreduce** to complete the PV removal. In Exercise 15-4 you can practice this.

Exercise 15-4 Removing a VG from a PV

1. Use **fdisk** to create two partitions with a size of 2 GiB each, and set the type to **lvm**. In the remainder of this exercise, I'll assume you're using the partitions /dev/sdd3 and dev/sdd4 for this purpose.
2. Use **vgcreate vgdemo /dev/sdd3** to create a volume group.
3. Type **lvcreate -L 1G -n lvdemo /dev/vgdemo** to create a logical volume with a size of 1 GiB. Notice that it is essential not to use all of the available disk space!
4. Type **vgextend vgdemo /dev/sdd4** to extend the volume group.
5. Use **pvs** to verify extent usage on /dev/sdd3 and /dev/sdd4. You should see that sdd3 is using about half of its extents, and all extents on /dev/sdd4 are still unused.
6. Now type **lvextend -L +500M /dev/vgdemo/lvdemo /dev/sdd4** to grow the lvdemo logical volume. Notice that you have to add /dev/sdd4 to ensure that free extents will be taken from the sdd4 device.
7. Type **pvs** to verify current extent usage on the devices.
8. Create a file system, using **mkfs.ext4 /dev/vgdemo/lvdemo**
9. Temporarily mount the logical volume, using **mount /dev/vgdemo/lvdemo /mnt**
10. Use **df -h** to verify disk space usage.
11. Use **dd if=/dev/zero of=/mnt/bigfile bs=1M count=1100**. The size ensures that file data is on both PVs.
12. Now you can prepare sdd4 for removal. As a first step, you need to move all extents it uses to unused extents on sdd1. Type the following to do so: **pvmove -v /dev/sdd4 /dev/sdd3**. This can take a minute or two to complete.
13. Type **pvs**, which will show that /dev/sdd4 is now unused.
14. At this point you can remove the unused physical volume, using **vgreduce vgdemo /dev/sdd4**

Configuring Stratis

In RHEL 9, Red Hat is offering Stratis as an advanced storage solution. ***Stratis*** is a so-called *volume-managing file system*, and it introduces advanced storage features that were not available prior to RHEL 8. By doing so, Red Hat intends to offer an alternative to the Btrfs and ZFS file systems that are used in other environments. The following features are offered by Stratis:

- **Thin provisioning:** This feature enables a Stratis file system to present itself to users as much bigger than it really is. This is useful in many environments, such as virtual desktops, where each user may see 20 GiB of available storage in total although a much lower amount is actually provisioned to each user.

- **Snapshots:** A Stratis **snapshot** allows users to take a "picture" of the current state of a file system. This snapshot makes it easy to revert to the previous state of a file system, rolling back any changes that have been made.
- **Cache tier:** Cache tier is a Ceph storage feature that ensures that data can be stored physically closer to the Ceph client, which makes data access faster.
- **Programmatic API:** The programmatic API ensures that storage can easily be configured and modified through API access. This is particularly interesting in cloud environments, where setting up storage directly from cloud-native applications is extremely useful.
- **Monitoring and repair:** Whereas older file systems need tools like **fsck** to verify the integrity of the file system, Stratis has built-in features to monitor the health of the file system and repair it if necessary.

Understanding Stratis Architecture

The lowest layer in the Stratis architecture is the *pool*. From a functional perspective, the Stratis pool is comparable to an LVM volume group. A pool represents all the available storage and consists of one or more storage devices, which in a Stratis environment are referred to as *blockdev*. These block devices may not be thin provisioned at the underlying hardware level. Stratis creates a /dev/stratis/poolname directory for each pool.

From the Stratis pool, XFS file systems are created. Note that Stratis only works with XFS, and the XFS file system it uses is integrated with the Stratis volume. When a file system is created, no size is specified, and each file system can grow up to the size of all the available storage space in the pool. Stratis file systems are always thin provisioned. The thin volume automatically grows as more data is added to the file system.

Creating Stratis Storage

Creating Stratis volumes is a multistep process. This section provides a high-level overview, and then Exercise 15-5 in the following section guides you through the procedure. You start by creating a pool. Once the pool has been added, you can create file systems from it. Before you begin, make sure that the block devices you're going to use in Stratis have a minimal size of 5 GiB. Each Stratis file system occupies a minimum of 527 MiB of disk space, even if no data has been copied to the file system.

1. Install the Stratis software using **dnf** by installing the **stratis-cli** and **stratisd** packages.
2. Start and enable the user-space daemon, using **systemctl enable --now stratisd**.
3. Once the daemon is running, use the **stratis pool create** command to create the pool that you want to work with. For instance, use **stratis pool create mypool /dev/sde** to create a pool that is based on the block device /dev/sdd. You can add additional block devices later, using **stratis pool add-data *poolname blockdevname***, as in **stratis pool add-data mypool /dev/sde**.
4. Once you have created the pool, add a file system using **stratis fs create *poolname fsname***.
5. To verify that all was created successfully, use the **stratis fs list** command.
6. After creating the file system, you can mount it. To mount a Stratis file system through /etc/fstab, you *must* use the UUID; using the device name is not supported. Also, when mounting the Stratis volume through /etc/fstab, include the mount option **x-systemd.requires=stratisd.service** to ensure that the Systemd waits to activate this device until the stratisd service is loaded. Without this option you won't be able to boot your system anymore.

Managing Stratis

After creating the Stratis file system, you can perform several different management tasks. To start with, you can dynamically extend the pool, using **stratis pool add-data**. Also, you need to monitor Stratis volumes using Stratis-specific tools, as the traditional Linux tools cannot handle the thin-provisioned volumes. The following commands are available:

- **stratis blockdev:** Shows information about all block devices that are used for Stratis.
- **stratis pool:** Gives information about Stratis pools. Note in particular the Physical Used parameter, which should not come too close to the Physical Size parameter.
- **stratis filesystem:** Enables you to monitor individual file systems.

Another Stratis feature that you may want to manage is the snapshot. A snapshot contains the state of the file system at the moment the snapshot was created. After creation, the snapshot can be modified. It's also good to know that the snapshot and its origin are not linked, which allows the snapshot to live longer than the file system it was created from. This is fundamentally different from, for instance, LVM snapshots, which cannot stay alive if the volume they are linked to is removed.

In Exercise 15-5, you set up an environment with Stratis volumes.

Exercise 15-5 Managing Stratis Volumes

You need one dedicated disk with a minimal size of 5 GiB to perform the steps in this exercise. In this exercise, the disk name /dev/sde is used as an example. Replace this name with the disk device name that is presented on your hardware.

1. Type **dnf install stratisd stratis-cli** to install all the required packages.
2. Type **systemctl enable --now stratisd** to enable the Stratis daemon.
3. Type **stratis pool create mypool /dev/sde** to add the entire disk /dev/sde to the storage pool.
4. Type **stratis pool list** to verify successful creation of the pool.
5. Type **stratis fs create mypool stratis1** to create the first Stratis file system. Note that you don't have to specify a file system size.
6. Type **stratis fs list** to verify the creation of the file system.
7. Type **mkdir /stratis1** to create a mount point for the Stratis file system.
8. Type **stratis fs list** to find the Stratis volume UUID.
9. Add the following line to /etc/fstab to enable the volume to be mounted automatically. Make sure to use the UUID name that is used by your Stratis file system.

   ```
   UUID=xxx /stratis1 xfs defaults,x-systemd.requires=stratisd.
   service   0 0
   ```

10. Type **mount -a** to mount the Stratis volume. Use the **mount** command to verify that this procedure worked successfully.
11. Type **cp /etc/[a-f]* /stratis1** to copy some files to the Stratis volume.
12. Type **stratis filesystem snapshot mypool stratis1 stratis1-snap** to create a snapshot of the volume you just created. Note that this command may take up to a minute to complete.
13. Type **stratis filesystem list** to get statistics about current file system usage.
14. Type **rm -f /stratis1/a*** to remove all files that have a name starting with *a*.
15. Type **mount /dev/stratis/mypool/stratis1-snap /mnt** and verify that the files whose names start with *a* are still available in the /mnt directory.
16. Reboot your server. After reboot, verify that the Stratis volume is still automatically mounted.

Summary

In this chapter, you learned how to work with advanced storage on RHEL 9. First, you read how LVM is used to bring flexibility to storage. By using LVM, you get the advantages of volumes that can be resized easily and multidevice logical volumes. Next, you were introduced to Stratis, the volume-managing file system. Stratis brings next-generation storage features to RHEL 9, and by default creates thin-provisioned file systems.

Exam Preparation Tasks

As mentioned in the section "How to Use This Book" in the Introduction, you have several choices for exam preparation: the end-of-chapter labs; the memory tables in Appendix C; Chapter 27, "Final Preparation"; and the practice exams.

Review All Key Topics

Review the most important topics in the chapter, noted with the Key Topic icon in the margin of the page. Table 15-3 lists a reference for these key topics and the page number on which each is found.

Table 15-3 Key Topics for Chapter 15

Key Topic Element	Description	Page
Figure 15-1	LVM Architecture Overview	347
Table 15-2	LVM Management Essential Commands	357
List	LVM **lvresize** commands	359

Complete Tables and Lists from Memory

Print a copy of Appendix C, "Memory Tables" (found on the companion website), or at least the section for this chapter, and complete the tables and lists from memory. Appendix D, "Memory Tables Answer Key," includes completed tables and lists to check your work.

Define Key Terms

Define the following key terms from this chapter and check your answers in the glossary:

snapshot, physical volume (PV), volume group (VG), physical extent, logical volume (LV), device mapper, logical extent, Stratis

Review Questions

The questions that follow are meant to help you test your knowledge of concepts and terminology and the breadth of your knowledge. You can find the answers to these questions in Appendix A.

1. Which partition type is used on a GUID partition that needs to be used in LVM?
2. Which command enables you to create a volume group with the name vgroup that contains the physical device /dev/sdb3 and uses a physical extent size of 4 MiB?
3. Which command shows a short summary of the physical volumes on your system as well as the volume group to which these belong?
4. What do you need to do to add an entire hard disk /dev/sdd to the volume group vgroup?
5. Which command enables you to create a logical volume lvvol1 with a size of 6 MiB?
6. Which command enables you to add 100 MB to the logical volume lvvol1, assuming that the disk space is available in the volume group?
7. Which two commands do you use to remove a physical volume from a volume group?
8. When working with Stratis, what line would you add to /etc/fstab to mount the Stratis volume?
9. Which command do you use to create a Stratis pool that is based on the block device /dev/sdd?
10. How do you format a Stratis volume with the Ext4 file system?

End-of-Chapter Labs

To complete the following end-of-chapter labs, you need a dedicated disk device. Either use a USB thumb drive or add a new virtual disk to your virtual environment before starting.

Lab 15.1

1. Create a 500-MB logical volume named **lvgroup**. Format it with the XFS file system and mount it persistently on /groups. Reboot your server to verify that the mount works.

2. After rebooting, add another 250 MB to the lvgroup volume that you just created. Verify that the file system resizes as well while resizing the volume.
3. Verify that the volume extension was successful.

Lab 15.2

1. Create a Stratis pool with a size of 5 GiB. In this pool, create two Stratis file systems and ensure that they are automatically mounted.
2. Add an additional block device to the Stratis pool and verify that the size of the pool was successfully extended.
3. Ensure that the new Stratis device is automatically mounted on the directory /stratis while rebooting.

The following topics are covered in this chapter:

- Understanding the Role of the Linux Kernel
- Working with Kernel Modules
- Upgrading the Linux Kernel

CHAPTER 16

Basic Kernel Management

The Linux kernel is the heart of the Linux operating system. It takes care of many things, including hardware management. In this chapter, you learn all you need to know about the Linux kernel from an RHCSA perspective. In fact, you even learn a bit more. The topics covered in this chapter are *not* included in the current RHCSA exam objectives, but any serious Linux administrator should be able to deal with issues related to the kernel, so I address them in this chapter.

"Do I Know This Already?" Quiz

The "Do I Know This Already?" quiz enables you to assess whether you should read this entire chapter thoroughly or jump to the "Exam Preparation Tasks" section. If you are in doubt about your answers to these questions or your own assessment of your knowledge of the topics, read the entire chapter. Table 16-1 lists the major headings in this chapter and their corresponding "Do I Know This Already?" quiz questions. You can find the answers in Appendix A, "Answers to the 'Do I Know This Already?' Quizzes and Review Questions."

Table 16-1 "Do I Know This Already?" Section-to-Question Mapping

Foundation Topics Section	Questions
Understanding the Role of the Linux Kernel	1–4
Working with Kernel Modules	5–9
Upgrading the Linux Kernel	10

1. What causes a tainted kernel?
    a. A kernel driver that is not available as an open source driver
    b. A driver that was developed for a different operating system but has been ported to Linux
    c. A driver that has failed
    d. An unsupported driver

2. Which command shows kernel events since booting?
    a. **logger**
    b. **dmesg**
    c. **klogd**
    d. **journald**

3. Which command enables you to find the actual version of the kernel that is used?
    a. **uname -r**
    b. **uname -v**
    c. **procinfo -k**
    d. **procinfo -l**

4. Which command shows the current version of RHEL you are using?
    a. **uname -r**
    b. **cat /proc/rhel-version**
    c. **cat /etc/redhat-release**
    d. **uname -k**

5. What is the name of the process that helps the kernel to initialize hardware devices properly?
    a. **systemd-udevd**
    b. **hwinit**
    c. **udev**
    d. **udevd**

6. Where does your system find the default rules that are used for initializing new hardware devices?
    a. /etc/udev/rules.d
    b. /usr/lib/udev/rules.d
    c. /usr/lib/udev.d/rules
    d. /etc/udev.d/rules

7. Which command should you use to unload a kernel module, including all of its dependencies?
   a. **rmmod**
   b. **insmod -r**
   c. **modprobe -r**
   d. **modprobe**

8. Which command enables you to see whether the appropriate kernel modules have been loaded for hardware in your server?
   a. **lsmod**
   b. **modprobe -l**
   c. **lspci -k**
   d. **lspci**

9. Where do you specify a kernel module parameter to make it persistent?
   a. /etc/modules.conf
   b. /etc/modprobe.conf
   c. /etc/modprobe.d/somefilename
   d. /usr/lib/modprobe.d/somefilename

10. Which statements about updating the kernel are *not* true?
    a. The **dnf update kernel** command will install a new kernel and not update it.
    b. The **dnf install kernel** command will install a new kernel and keep the old kernel.
    c. The kernel package should be set as a **dnf**-protected package to ensure that after an update the old kernel is still available.
    d. After you have installed a new kernel version, you must run the **grub2-mkconfig** command to modify the GRUB 2 boot menu so that it shows the old kernel and the newly installed kernel.

Foundation Topics

Understanding the Role of the Linux Kernel

The Linux kernel is the heart of the operating system. It is the layer between the user who works with Linux from a shell environment and the hardware that is available in the computer on which the user is working. The ***kernel*** manages the I/O instructions it receives from the software and translates them into the processing instructions that are executed by the central processing unit and other hardware in the computer. The kernel also takes care of handling essential operating system tasks. One example of such a task is the scheduler that makes sure any processes that are started on the operating system are handled by the CPU.

Understanding the Use of Kernel Threads and Drivers

The operating system tasks that are performed by the kernel are implemented by different kernel threads. Kernel threads are easily recognized with a command like **ps aux**. The kernel thread names are listed between square brackets (see Example 16-1).

Example 16-1 Listing Kernel Threads with **ps aux**

```
[root@server1 ~]# ps aux | head -n 20
USER     PID %CPU %MEM    VSZ   RSS TTY    STAT    START   TIME COMMAND
root     1    1.8  0.6   52980  6812 ?      Ss    11:44   0:02 /usr/lib/
systemd/systemd --switched-root --system --deserialize 23
root     2    0.0  0.0      0     0 ?     S    11:44   0:00  [kthreadd]
root     3    0.0  0.0      0     0 ?     S    11:44   0:00  [ksoftirqd/0]
root     4    0.0  0.0      0     0 ?     S    11:44   0:00  [kworker/0:0]
root     5    0.0  0.0      0     0 ?     S<   11:44   0:00  [kworker/0:0H]
root     6    0.0  0.0      0     0 ?     S    11:44   0:00  [kworker/u128:0]
root     7    0.1  0.0      0     0 ?     S    11:44   0:00  [migration/0]
root     8    0.0  0.0      0     0 ?     S    11:44   0:00  [rcu_bh]
root     9    0.0  0.0      0     0 ?     S    11:44   0:00  [rcuob/0]
root     10   0.0  0.0      0     0 ?     S    11:44   0:00  [rcuob/1]
root     11   0.0  0.0      0     0 ?     S    11:44   0:00  [rcuob/2]
root     12   0.0  0.0      0     0 ?     S    11:44   0:00  [rcuob/3]
root     13   0.0  0.0      0     0 ?     S    11:44   0:00  [rcuob/4]
root     14   0.0  0.0      0     0 ?     S    11:44   0:00  [rcuob/5]
root     15   0.0  0.0      0     0 ?     S    11:44   0:00  [rcuob/6]
root     16   0.0  0.0      0     0 ?     S    11:44   0:00  [rcuob/7]
root     17   0.0  0.0      0     0 ?     S    11:44   0:00  [rcuob/8]
root     18   0.0  0.0      0     0 ?     S    11:44   0:00  [rcuob/9]
root     19   0.0  0.0      0     0 ?     S    11:44   0:00  [rcuob/10]
```

Another important task of the Linux kernel is hardware initialization. To make sure that this hardware can be used, the Linux kernel uses drivers. Every piece of hardware contains specific features, and to use these features, a driver must be loaded. The Linux kernel is modular, and drivers are loaded as kernel modules, which you'll read more about later in this chapter.

In some cases, the availability of drivers is an issue because hardware manufacturers are not always willing to provide open source drivers that can be integrated well with the Linux kernel. That can result in a driver that does not provide all the functionality that is provided by the hardware.

If a manufacturer is not willing to provide open source drivers, an alternative is to work with closed source drivers. Although these make it possible to use the hardware in Linux, the solution is not ideal. Because a driver performs privileged instructions within the kernel space, a badly functioning driver may crash the entire kernel. If this happens with an open source driver, the Linux kernel community can help debug the problem and make sure that the issue is fixed. If it happens with a closed source driver, the Linux kernel community cannot do anything. But, a proprietary driver may provide access to features that are not provided by its open source equivalent.

To make it easy to see whether a kernel is using closed source drivers, the concept of the tainted kernel is used. A ***tainted kernel*** is a kernel that contains closed source drivers. The concept of tainted kernels helps in troubleshooting drivers. If your RHEL kernel appears to be tainted, Red Hat support can identify it as a tainted kernel and recognize which driver is tainting it. To fix the problem, Red Hat might ask you to take out the driver that is making it a tainted kernel.

Analyzing What the Kernel Is Doing

To help analyze what the kernel is doing, the Linux operating systems provide some tools:

- The **dmesg** utility
- The /proc file system
- The **uname** utility

The first utility to consider if you require detailed information about the kernel activity is ***dmesg***. This utility shows the contents of the kernel ring buffer, an area of memory where the Linux kernel keeps its recent log messages. An alternative method to get access to the same information in the kernel ring buffer is the **journalctl --dmesg** command, which is equivalent to **journalctl -k**. In Example 16-2, you can see a part of the result of the **dmesg** command.

Example 16-2 Analyzing Kernel Activity Using **dmesg**

```
[    8.153928] sd 0:0:0:0: Attached scsi generic sg0 type 0
[    8.154289] sd 0:0:1:0: Attached scsi generic sg1 type 0
[    8.154330] sd 0:0:2:0: Attached scsi generic sg2 type 0
[    8.154360] sd 0:0:3:0: Attached scsi generic sg3 type 0
[    8.154421] sr 4:0:0:0: Attached scsi generic sg4 type 5
[    8.729016] ip_tables: (C) 2000-2006 Netfilter Core Team
[    8.850599] nf_conntrack version 0.5.0 (7897 buckets, 31588 max)
[    8.939613] ip6_tables: (C) 2000-2006 Netfilter Core Team
[    9.160092] Ebtables v2.0 registered
[    9.203710] Bridge firewalling registered
[    9.586603] IPv6: ADDRCONF(NETDEV_UP): eno16777736: link is not ready
[    9.587520] e1000: eno16777736 NIC Link is Up 1000 Mbps Full Duplex,
  Flow Control: None
[    9.589066] IPv6: ADDRCONF(NETDEV_CHANGE): eno16777736: link becomes
  ready
[   10.689365] Rounding down aligned max_sectors from 4294967295 to
  4294967288
[ 5158.470480] Adjusting tsc more than 11% (6940512 vs 6913395)
[21766.132181] e1000: eno16777736 NIC Link is Down
[21770.391597] e1000: eno16777736 NIC Link is Up 1000 Mbps Full
  Duplex, Flow Control: None
[21780.434547] e1000: eno16777736 NIC Link is Down
```

In the **dmesg** output, all kernel-related messages are shown. Each message starts with a time indicator that shows at which specific second the event was logged. This time indicator is relative to the start of the kernel, which allows you to see exactly how many seconds have passed between the start of the kernel and a particular event. (Notice that the **journalctl -k** and **journalctl --dmesg** commands show clock time, instead of time that is relative to the start of the kernel.) This time indicator gives a clear indication of what has been happening and at which time it has happened.

Another valuable source of information is the /proc file system. The ***/proc*** file system is an interface to the Linux kernel, and it contains files with detailed status information about what is happening on your server. Many of the performance-related tools mine the /proc file system for more information.

As an administrator, you will find that some of the files in /proc are very readable and contain status information about the CPU, memory, mounts, and more. Take a look, for instance, at /proc/meminfo, which gives detailed information about each memory segment and what exactly is happening in these memory segments.

A last useful source of information is the **uname** command. This command gives different kinds of information about your operating system. Type, for instance, **uname -a** for an overview of all relevant parameters of **uname -r** to see which kernel version currently is used. This information also shows when you are using the **hostnamectl status** command, which shows useful additional information as well (see Example 16-3).

TIP On some occasions, you might need to know specific information about the RHEL version you are using. To get that information, run the **cat /etc/redhat-release** command and review its output; it will tell you which Red Hat version you are using and which update level is applied.

Example 16-3 Getting More Information About the System

```
[root@server1 ~]# hostnamectl status
 Static hostname: server1.example.com
       Icon name: computer-vm
         Chassis: vm ¬
      Machine ID: d04b1233036748edbcf73adc926c98e3
         Boot ID: 21e4e2e53648413dbe7975f64f570e51
  Virtualization: vmware
Operating System: Red Hat Enterprise Linux 9.0 (Plow)
     CPE OS Name: cpe:/o:redhat:enterprise_linux:9::baseos
          Kernel: Linux 5.14.0-70.13.1.el9_0.x86_64
    Architecture: x86-64
 Hardware Vendor: VMware, Inc.
  Hardware Model: VMware Virtual Platform
```

Working with Kernel Modules

In the old days of Linux, kernels had to be compiled to include all drivers that were required to support computer hardware. Other specific functionality needed to be compiled into the kernel as well. Since the release of Linux kernel 2.0 in 1996, kernels are no longer compiled but modular. A modular kernel consists of a relatively small core kernel and provides driver support through ***modules*** that are loaded when required. Modular kernels are very efficient, as they include only those modules that really are needed.

TIP A kernel module implements specific kernel functionality. Kernel modules are used to load drivers that allow proper communications with hardware devices, but are not limited to loading hardware drivers alone. For example, file system support is loaded as modules. Other kernel features can be loaded as modules as well.

Understanding Hardware Initialization

The loading of drivers is an automated process that roughly goes like this:

1. During boot, the kernel probes available hardware.
2. Upon detection of a hardware component, the **systemd-udevd** process takes care of loading the appropriate driver and making the hardware device available.
3. To decide how the devices are initialized, **systemd-udevd** reads rules files in /usr/lib/udev/rules.d. These are system-provided rules files that should not be modified.
4. After processing the system-provided udev rules files, **systemd-udevd** goes to the /etc/udev/rules.d directory to read any custom rules if these are available.
5. As a result, required kernel modules are loaded automatically, and status about the kernel modules and associated hardware is written to the sysfs file system, which is mounted on the /sys directory. The Linux kernel uses this pseudo file system to track hardware-related settings.

The **systemd-udevd** process is not a one-time-only process; it continuously monitors plugging and unplugging of new hardware devices. To get an impression of how this works, as root you can type the command **udevadm monitor**. This lists all events that are processed while activating new hardware devices. For instance, if you plug in a USB device while this command is active, you can see exactly what's happening. Press Ctrl-C to close the **udevadm monitor** output.

Example 16-4 shows output of the **udevadm monitor** command. In this command, you can see how features that are offered by the hardware are discovered automatically by the kernel and systemd-udevd working together. Each phase of the hardware probing is concluded by the creation of a file in the /sys file system. Once the hardware has been fully initialized, you can also see that some kernel modules are loaded.

NOTE Although useful to know, hardware initialization is not included in the current RHCSA objectives.

Example 16-4 Output of the **udevadm monitor** Command

```
[root@server2 ~]# udevadm monitor
monitor will print the received events for:
UDEV - the event which udev sends out after rule processing
KERNEL - the kernel uevent

KERNEL[132406.831270] add
  /devices/pci0000:00/0000:00:11.0/0000:02:04.0/usb1/1-1 (usb)
KERNEL[132406.974110] add
  /devices/pci0000:00/0000:00:11.0/0000:02:04.0/usb1/1-1/1-1:1.0 (usb)
UDEV [132406.988182] add
  /devices/pci0000:00/0000:00:11.0/0000:02:04.0/usb1/1-1 (usb)
KERNEL[132406.999249] add /module/usb_storage (module)
UDEV [132407.001203] add /module/usb_storage (module)
KERNEL[132407.002559] add
  /devices/pci0000:00/0000:00:11.0/0000:02:04.0/usb1/1-1/1-1:1.0/
  host33 (scsi)
UDEV [132407.002575] add
  /devices/pci0000:00/0000:00:11.0/0000:02:04.0/usb1/1-1/1-1:1.0 (usb)
KERNEL[132407.002583] add
  /devices/pci0000:00/0000:00:11.0/0000:02:04.0/usb1/1-1/1-1:1.0/
  host33/scsi_host/host33 (scsi_host)
KERNEL[132407.002590] add /bus/usb/drivers/usb-storage (drivers)
UDEV [132407.004479] add /bus/usb/drivers/usb-storage (drivers)
UDEV [132407.005798] add
  /devices/pci0000:00/0000:00:11.0/0000:02:04.0/usb1/1-1/1-1:1.0/
  host33 (scsi)
UDEV [132407.007385] add
  /devices/pci0000:00/0000:00:11.0/0000:02:04.0/usb1/1-1/1-1:1.0/
  host33/scsi_host/host33 (scsi_host)
KERNEL[132408.008331] add
  /devices/pci0000:00/0000:00:11.0/0000:02:04.0/usb1/1-1/1-1:1.0/
  host33/target33:0:0 (scsi)
KERNEL[132408.008355] add
  /devices/pci0000:00/0000:00:11.0/0000:02:04.0/usb1/1-1/1-1:1.0/
  host33/target33:0:0/33:0:0:0 (scsi)
...
KERNEL[132409.381930] add        /module/fat (module)
KERNEL[132409.381951] add        /kernel/slab/fat_cache (slab)
KERNEL[132409.381958] add        /kernel/slab/fat_inode_cache (slab)
KERNEL[132409.381964] add        /module/vfat (module)
UDEV  [132409.385090] add        /module/fat (module)
UDEV  [132409.385107] add        /kernel/slab/fat_cache (slab)
UDEV  [132409.385113] add        /kernel/slab/fat_inode_cache (slab)
UDEV  [132409.386110] add        /module/vfat (module)
```

Managing Kernel Modules

Linux kernel modules normally are loaded automatically for the devices that need them, but you will on rare occasions have to load the appropriate kernel modules manually. A few commands are used for manual management of kernel modules. Table 16-2 provides an overview.

An alternative method of loading kernel modules is through the /etc/modules-load.d directory. In this directory, you can create files to load modules automatically that are not already loaded by the systemd-udevd method. For default modules that should always be loaded, this directory has a counterpart in /usr/lib/modules-load.d.

Key Topic

Table 16-2 Linux Kernel Module Management Overview

Command	Use
lsmod	Lists currently loaded kernel modules
modinfo	Displays information about kernel modules
modprobe	Loads kernel modules, including all of their dependencies
modprobe -r	Unloads kernel modules, considering kernel module dependencies

The first command to use when working with kernel modules is **lsmod**. This command lists all kernel modules that currently are used, including the modules by which this specific module is used. Example 16-5 shows the output of the first ten lines of the **lsmod** command.

Example 16-5 Listing Loaded Modules with **lsmod**

```
[root@server1 ~]# lsmod | head
Module                  Size  Used by
nls_utf8               16384  1
isofs                  45056  1
fuse                  126976  3
rfcomm                 90112  6
xt_CHECKSUM            16384  1
ipt_MASQUERADE         16384  1
xt_conntrack           16384  1
ipt_REJECT             16384  1
nft_counter            16384  16
```

TIP Many Linux commands show their output in different columns, and it is not always clear which column is used to show which kind of information. Most of these commands have a header line on the first line of command output. So, if in the output of any command you are not sure what you are seeing, pipe the output of the command through **head** to see whether there is a header file, or pipe the command output to **less**, which allows you to page up to the first line of command output easily.

If you want to have more information about a specific kernel module, you can use the **modinfo** command. This gives complete information about specific kernel modules, including two interesting sections: the alias and the parms. A module alias is another name that can also be used to address the module. The parms lines refer to parameters that can be set while loading the module. (In the section "Managing Kernel Module Parameters" later in this chapter, you learn how to work with kernel module parameters.) Example 16-6 shows partial output of the **modinfo e1000** command.

Example 16-6 Showing Module Information with **modinfo**

```
[root@server1 ~]# modinfo e1000
filename:        /lib/modules/5.14.0-70.13.1.el9_0.x86_64/kernel/
  drivers/net/ethernet/intel/e1000/e1000.ko.xz
license:         GPL v2
description:     Intel(R) PRO/1000 Network Driver
author:          Intel Corporation, <linux.nics@intel.com>
rhelversion:     9.0
srcversion:      55BD0A50779C0A80232DEDD
alias:           pci:v00008086d00002E6Esv*sd*bc*sc*i*
alias:           pci:v00008086d000010B5sv*sd*bc*sc*i*
alias:           pci:v00008086d00001099sv*sd*bc*sc*i*
...
depends:
retpoline:       Y
intree:          Y
name:            e1000
vermagic:        5.14.0-70.13.1.el9_0.x86_64 SMP preempt mod_unload
  modversions
sig_id:          PKCS#7
signer:          Red Hat Enterprise Linux kernel signing key
```

```
sig_key:         41:63:79:65:D6:4F:EC:E6:A4:AB:67:F7:77:10:AD:65:DC:C3
   :CA:C6
sig_hashalgo:    sha256
signature:
…
parm:            TxDescriptors:Number of transmit descriptors (array
    of int)
parm:            RxDescriptors:Number of receive descriptors (array of
int)
parm:            Speed:Speed setting (array of int)
parm:            Duplex:Duplex setting (array of int)
parm:            AutoNeg:Advertised auto-negotiation setting (array of
    int)
parm:            FlowControl:Flow Control setting (array of int)
parm:            XsumRX:Disable or enable Receive Checksum offload
   (array of int)
parm:            TxIntDelay:Transmit Interrupt Delay (array of int)
parm:            TxAbsIntDelay:Transmit Absolute Interrupt Delay
   (array of int)
parm:            RxIntDelay:Receive Interrupt Delay (array of int)
parm:            RxAbsIntDelay:Receive Absolute Interrupt Delay (array
    of int)
parm:            InterruptThrottleRate:Interrupt Throttling Rate
   (array of int)
parm:            SmartPowerDownEnable:Enable PHY smart power down
   (array of int)
parm:            copybreak:Maximum size of packet that is copied to a
   new buffer on receive (uint)
parm:            debug:Debug level (0=none,...,16=all) (int) (int)
```

To manually load and unload modules, you can use the **modprobe** and **modprobe -r** commands. On earlier Linux versions, you may have used the **insmod** and **rmmod** commands. These should no longer be used because they do not load kernel module dependencies. In Exercise 16-1, you learn how to manage kernel modules using these commands.

Exercise 16-1 Managing Kernel Modules from the Command Line

1. Open a root shell and type **lsmod | less**. This shows all kernel modules currently loaded.
2. Type **modprobe vfat** to load the vfat kernel module.
3. Verify that the module is loaded by using the **lsmod | grep vfat** command. You can see that the module is loaded, as well as some of its dependencies.

4. Type **modinfo vfat** to get information about the vfat kernel module. Notice that it does not have any parameters.
5. Type **modprobe -r vfat** to unload the vfat kernel module again.
6. Type **modprobe -r xfs** to try to unload the xfs kernel module. Notice that you get an error message because the kernel module currently is in use.

Checking Driver Availability for Hardware Devices

On modern Linux servers, many hardware devices are supported. On occasion, you might find that some devices are not supported properly because their modules are not currently loaded. The best way to find out whether this is the case for your hardware is by using the **lspci** command. If used without arguments, it shows all hardware devices that have been detected on the PCI bus. A very useful argument is **-k**, which lists all kernel modules that are used for the PCI devices that were detected. Example 16-7 shows sample output of the **lspci -k** command.

Example 16-7 Checking Kernel Module Availability

```
[root@server1 ~]# lspci -k | head
00:00.0 Host bridge: Intel Corporation 440BX/ZX/DX - 82443BX/ZX/DX
  Host bridge (rev 01)
        Subsystem: VMware Virtual Machine Chipset
        Kernel driver in use: agpgart-intel
00:01.0 PCI bridge: Intel Corporation 440BX/ZX/DX - 82443BX/ZX/DX AGP
  bridge (rev 01)
00:07.0 ISA bridge: Intel Corporation 82371AB/EB/MB PIIX4 ISA (rev 08)
        Subsystem: VMware Virtual Machine Chipset
00:07.1 IDE interface: Intel Corporation 82371AB/EB/MB PIIX4 IDE (rev
  01)
        Subsystem: VMware Virtual Machine Chipset
        Kernel driver in use: ata_piix
        Kernel modules: ata_piix, ata_generic
00:07.3 Bridge: Intel Corporation 82371AB/EB/MB PIIX4 ACPI (rev 08)
        Subsystem: VMware Virtual Machine Chipset
        Kernel modules: i2c_piix4
00:07.7 System peripheral: VMware Virtual Machine Communication
  Interface (rev 10)
        Subsystem: VMware Virtual Machine Communication Interface
        Kernel driver in use: vmw_vmci
        Kernel modules: vmw_vmci
```

```
00:0f.0 VGA compatible controller: VMware SVGA II Adapter
        Subsystem: VMware SVGA II Adapter
        Kernel driver in use: vmwgfx
        Kernel modules: vmwgfx
00:10.0 SCSI storage controller: LSI Logic / Symbios Logic 53c1030
  PCI-X Fusion-MPT Dual Ultra320 SCSI (rev 01)
        Subsystem: VMware LSI Logic Parallel SCSI Controller
        Kernel driver in use: mptspi
        Kernel modules: mptspi
00:11.0 PCI bridge: VMware PCI bridge (rev 02)
00:15.0 PCI bridge: VMware PCI Express Root Port (rev 01)
        Kernel driver in use: pcieport
```

If you discover that PCI devices were found for which no kernel modules could be loaded, you are probably dealing with a device that is not supported. You can try to find a closed source kernel module, but you should realize that doing so might endanger the stability of your kernel. A much better approach is to check with your hardware vendor that Linux is fully supported before you purchase specific hardware.

Managing Kernel Module Parameters

Occasionally, you might want to load kernel modules with specific parameters. To do so, you first need to find out which parameter you want to use. If you have found the parameter you want to use, you can load it manually, specifying the name of the parameter followed by the value that you want to assign. To make this an automated procedure, you can create a file in the /etc/modprobe.d directory, where the module is loaded, including the parameter you want to be loaded. In Exercise 16-2 you see how to do this using the cdrom kernel module.

Exercise 16-2 Loading Kernel Modules with Parameters

1. Type **lsmod | grep cdrom**. If you have used the optical drive in your computer, this module should be loaded, and it should indicate that it is used by the sr_mod module.
2. Type **modprobe -r cdrom**. This will not work because the module is in use by the sr_mod module.
3. Type **modprobe -r sr_mod; modprobe -r cdrom**. This should unload both modules, but it will most likely fail. (It won't fail if currently no optical device is mounted.)

4. Type **umount /dev/sr0** to unmount the mounted cdrom file system and use **modprobe -r sr_mod**. This should now work.
5. Type **modinfo cdrom**. This shows information about the cdrom module, including the parameters that it supports. One of these is the **debug** parameter, which supports a Boolean as its value.
6. Type **modprobe cdrom debug=1**. This loads the cdrom module with the **debug** parameter set to on.
7. Type **dmesg**. For some kernel modules, load information is written to the kernel ring buffer, which can be displayed using the **dmesg** command. Unfortunately, this is not the case for the cdrom kernel module.
8. Create a file with the name /etc/modprobe.d/cdrom.conf and give it the following contents:

```
options cdrom debug=1
```

This enables the parameter every time the cdrom kernel module loads.

Upgrading the Linux Kernel

From time to time, you need to upgrade the Linux kernel. When you upgrade the Linux kernel, a new version of the kernel is installed and used as the default kernel. The old version of the kernel file will still be available, though. This ensures that your computer can still boot if the new kernel includes nonsupported functionality. To install a new version of the kernel, you can use the command **dnf upgrade kernel**. The **dnf install kernel** command also works. Both commands install the new kernel beside the old kernel.

The kernel files for the last four kernels that you have installed on your server will be kept in the /boot directory. The GRUB 2 boot loader automatically picks up all kernels that it finds in this directory. This allows you to select an older kernel version while booting, which is useful if the newly installed kernel doesn't boot correctly.

Summary

In this chapter, you learned how to work with the Linux kernel. You learned that the Linux kernel is modular and how working with kernel modules is important. You also learned how to manage kernel modules and how kernel modules are managed automatically while working with new hardware.

Exam Preparation Tasks

As mentioned in the section "How to Use This Book" in the Introduction, you have several choices for exam preparation: the end-of-chapter labs; the memory tables in Appendix C; Chapter 27, "Final Preparation"; and the practice exams.

Review All Key Topics

Review the most important topics in the chapter, noted with the Key Topic icon in the margin of the page. Table 16-3 lists a reference for these key topics and the page number on which each is found.

Table 16-3 Key Topics for Chapter 16

Key Topic Element	Description	Page
List	Overview of kernel-related tools	373
Table 16-2	Linux Kernel Module Management Overview	378

Complete Tables and Lists from Memory

Print a copy of Appendix C, "Memory Tables" (found on the companion website), or at least the section for this chapter, and complete the tables and lists from memory. Appendix D, "Memory Tables Answer Key," includes completed tables and lists to check your work.

Define Key Terms

Define the following key terms from this chapter and check your answers in the glossary:

kernel, tainted kernel, **dmesg**, /proc, module

Review Questions

The questions that follow are meant to help you test your knowledge of concepts and terminology and the breadth of your knowledge. You can find the answers to these questions in Appendix A.

1. Which command shows the current version of the kernel that is used on your computer?
2. Where do you find current version information about your RHEL installation?

3. Which command shows a list of kernel modules that currently are loaded?
4. Which command enables you to discover kernel module parameters?
5. How do you unload a kernel module?
6. What can you do if you get an error message while trying to unload a kernel module?
7. How do you find which kernel module parameters are supported?
8. Where do you specify kernel module parameters that should be used persistently?
9. Assuming that the cdrom module has a parameter **debug**, which must be set to 1 to enable debug mode, which line would you include in the file that will automatically load that module?
10. How do you install a new version of the kernel?

End-of-Chapter Lab

In the end-of-chapter lab, you install a new version of the kernel and work with kernel modules.

Lab 16.1

1. Find out whether a new version of the kernel is available. If so, install it and reboot your computer so that it is used.
2. Use the appropriate command to show recent events that have been logged by the kernel.
3. Locate the kernel module that is used by your network card. Find out whether it has options. Try loading one of these kernel module options manually; if that succeeds, take the required measures to load this option persistently.

The following topics are covered in this chapter:

- Managing Systemd Targets
- Working with GRUB 2

The following RHCSA exam objectives are covered in this chapter:

- Configure systems to boot into a specific target automatically
- Modify the system bootloader

CHAPTER 17

Managing and Understanding the Boot Procedure

In this chapter, you learn how the boot procedure on Red Hat Enterprise Linux is organized. In the first part of this chapter, you learn about Systemd targets and how you can use them to boot your Linux system into a specific state. The second part of this chapter discusses GRUB2 and how to apply changes to the GRUB 2 boot loader. Troubleshooting is not a topic in this chapter; it is covered in Chapter 18, "Essential Troubleshooting Skills."

"Do I Know This Already?" Quiz

The "Do I Know This Already?" quiz enables you to assess whether you should read this entire chapter thoroughly or jump to the "Exam Preparation Tasks" section. If you are in doubt about your answers to these questions or your own assessment of your knowledge of the topics, read the entire chapter. Table 17-1 lists the major headings in this chapter and their corresponding "Do I Know This Already?" quiz questions. You can find the answers in Appendix A, "Answers to the 'Do I Know This Already?' Quizzes and Review Questions."

Table 17-1 "Do I Know This Already?" Section-to-Question Mapping

Foundation Topics Section	Questions
Managing Systemd Targets	1–7
Working with GRUB 2	8–10

1. Which of the following is the most efficient way to define a system want?
   a. Use the **systemctl enable** command.
   b. Define the want in the unit file [Service] section.
   c. Create a symbolic link in the /usr/lib/system/system directory.
   d. Create a symbolic link in the unit wants directory in the /etc/system/system directory.

2. Which target is considered the normal target for servers to start in?
   a. graphical.target
   b. server.target
   c. multi-user.target
   d. default.target

3. Which of the following is *not* an example of a systemd target?
   a. rescue.target
   b. restart.target
   c. multi-user.target
   d. graphical.target

4. Where do you define which target a unit should be started in if it is enabled?
   a. The target unit file
   b. The wants directory
   c. The systemctl.conf file
   d. The [Install] section in the unit file

5. To allow targets to be isolated, you need a specific statement in the target unit file. Which of the following describes that statement?
   a. AllowIsolate
   b. Isolate
   c. SetIsolate
   d. Isolated

6. An administrator wants to change the current multi-user.target to the rescue.target. Which of the following should the admin do?
   a. Use the **systemctl isolate rescue.target** command.
   b. Use the **systemctl start rescue.target** command.
   c. Restart the system, and from the GRUB boot prompt specify that rescue.target should be started.
   d. Use the **systemctl enable rescue.target --now** command.

7. To which legacy System V runlevel does multi-user.target correspond?
    a. 2
    b. 3
    c. 4
    d. 5

8. What is the name of the file where you should apply changes to the GRUB 2 configuration?
    a. /boot/grub/menu.lst
    b. /boot/grub2/grub.cfg
    c. /etc/sysconfig/grub
    d. /etc/default/grub

9. After applying changes to the GRUB 2 configuration, you need to write those changes. Which of the following commands will do that for you?
    a. **grub2 -o /boot/grub/grub.cfg**
    b. **grub2-mkconfig > /boot/grub2/grub.cfg**
    c. **grub2 > /boot/grub2/grub.cfg**
    d. **grub2-install > /boot/grub2/grub.cfg**

10. What is the name of the GRUB2 configuration file that is generated on a UEFI system?
    a. /boot/efi/redhat/grub.cfg
    b. /boot/efi/EFI/redhat/grub.cfg
    c. /boot/EFI/grub.cfg
    d. /boot/EFI/efi/grub.cfg

Foundation Topics

Managing Systemd Targets

Systemd is the service in Red Hat Enterprise Linux 9 that is responsible for starting all kinds of things. Systemd goes way beyond starting services; other items are started from Systemd as well. In Chapter 11, "Working with Systemd," you learned about the Systemd fundamentals; this chapter looks at how Systemd targets are used to boot your system into a specific state.

Understanding Systemd Targets

A systemd *target* is basically just a group of units that belong together. Some targets are just that and nothing else, whereas other targets can be used to define the state a system is booting in, because these targets have one specific property that regular targets don't have: they can be isolated. Isolatable targets contain everything a system needs to boot or change its current state. Four targets can be used while booting:

- **emergency.target:** In this target only a minimal number of units are started, just enough to fix your system if something is seriously wrong. You'll find that it is quite minimal, as some important units are not started.
- **rescue.target:** This target starts all units that are required to get a fully operational Linux system. It doesn't start nonessential services though.
- **multi-user.target:** This target is often used as the default target a system starts in. It starts everything that is needed for full system functionality and is commonly used on servers.
- **graphical.target:** This target also is commonly used. It starts all units that are needed for full functionality, as well as a graphical interface.

Working with Targets

Working with targets may seem complicated, but it is not. It drills down to three common tasks:

- Adding units to be automatically started
- Setting a default target
- Running a nondefault target to enter troubleshooting mode

In Chapter 11 you learned how to use the **systemctl enable** and **systemctl disable** commands to add services to or remove services from targets. In this chapter you learn how to set a default target and how to run a nondefault target to enter troubleshooting mode. But first let's take a closer look at the working of targets under the hood.

Understanding Target Units

Behind a target there is some configuration. This configuration consists of two parts:

- The target unit file
- The "wants" directory, which contains references to all unit files that need to be loaded when entering a specific target

Targets by themselves can have ***dependencies*** to other targets, which are defined in the target ***unit*** file. Example 17-1 shows the definition of the multi-user.target file, which defines the normal operational state of a RHEL server.

Example 17-1 The multi-user.target File

```
[root@localhost ~]# systemctl cat multi-user.target
# /usr/lib/systemd/system/multi-user.target
#  SPDX-License-Identifier: LGPL-2.1+
#
#  This file is part of systemd.
#
#  systemd is free software; you can redistribute it and/or modify it
#  under the terms of the GNU Lesser General Public License as
  published by
#  the Free Software Foundation; either version 2.1 of the License,
  or
#  (at your option) any later version.

[Unit]
Description=Multi-User System
Documentation=man:systemd.special(7)
Requires=basic.target
Conflicts=rescue.service rescue.target
After=basic.target rescue.service rescue.target
AllowIsolate=yes
```

You can see that by itself the target unit does not contain much. It just defines what it requires and which services and targets it cannot coexist with. It also defines load ordering, by using the **After** statement in the [Unit] section. The target file does not contain any information about the units that should be included; that is, in the individual unit files and the wants (explained in the upcoming section "Understanding Wants").

Systemd targets look a bit like runlevels used in older versions of RHEL, but targets are more than that. A target is a group of units, and there are multiple different targets. Some targets, such as the multi-user.target and the graphical.target, define a specific state that the system needs to enter. Other targets just bundle a group of units together, such as the nfs.target and the sound.target. These targets are included from other targets, such as multi-user.target or graphical.target.

Understanding Wants

Understanding the concept of a want simply requires understanding the verb *want* in the English language, as in "I want a cookie." ***Wants*** in Systemd define which units Systemd wants when starting a specific target. Wants are created when Systemd units are enabled using **systemctl enable**, and this happens by creating a symbolic link in the /etc/systemd/system directory. In this directory, you'll find a subdirectory for every target, containing wants as symbolic links to specific services that are to be started. The multi-user.target, for instance, contains its wants in /etc/systemd/system/multi-user.target.wants/.

Managing Systemd Targets

As an administrator, you need to make sure that the required services are started when your server boots. To do this, use the **systemctl enable** and **systemctl disable** commands. You do not have to think about the specific target a service has to be started in. Through the [Install] section in the service unit file, the services know for themselves in which targets they need to be started, and a want is created automatically in that target when the service is enabled. The following procedure walks you through the steps of enabling a service:

1. Type **dnf install -y vsftpd**, followed by **systemctl status vsftpd**. If the service has not yet been enabled, the Loaded line will show that it currently is disabled:

```
[root@server202 ~]# systemctl status vsftpd
vsftpd.service - Vsftpd ftp daemon
    Loaded: loaded (/usr/lib/systemd/system/vsftpd.service; disabled)
    Active: inactive (dead)
```

2. Type **ls /etc/systemd/system/multi-user.target.wants**. You'll see symbolic links that are taking care of starting the different services on your machine. You can also see that the vsftpd.service link does not exist.
3. Type **systemctl enable vsftpd**. The command shows you that it is creating a symbolic link for the file /usr/lib/systemd/system/vsftpd.service to the directory /etc/systemd/system/multi-user.target.wants. So basically, when you enable a Systemd unit file, in the background a symbolic link is created.

TIP On the RHCSA exam, you are likely to enable a couple of services. It is a good idea to read through the exam questions, identify the services that need to be enabled, and enable them all at once to make sure that they are started automatically when you restart. This prevents your being so focused on configuring the service that you completely forget to enable it as well.

Isolating Targets

As already discussed, on Systemd machines there are several targets. You also know that a target is a collection of units. Some of those targets have a special role because they can be isolated. These are also the targets that you can set as the targets to get into after system start.

By isolating a target, you start that target with all of its dependencies. Only targets that have the **isolate** option enabled can be isolated. We'll explore the **systemctl isolate** command later in this section. Before doing that, let's take a look at the default targets on your computer.

To get a list of all targets currently loaded, type **systemctl --type=target**. You'll see a list of all the targets currently active. If your server is running a graphical environment, this will include all the dependencies required to install the graphical. target also. However, this list shows only the active targets, not all the targets. Type **systemctl -t target --all** for an overview of all targets that exist on your computer. You'll now see inactive targets also (see Example 17-2).

Example 17-2 Showing System Targets

```
root@localhost ~]# systemctl --type=target --all
  UNIT                        LOAD                ACTIVE   SUB
DESCRIPTION
  basic.target             loaded                        active
active Basic System
  bluetooth.target                            loaded
active                    active Bluetooth
  cryptsetup.target                           loaded
active                    active Local Encrypted  Volumes
  dbus.target                                          not-found
inactive                     dead                dbus.target
  emergency.target                            loaded
inactive       dead                Emergency Mode
  getty-pre.target                            loaded
active                    active Login Prompts  (Pre)
  getty.target                          loaded                  active
active Login Prompts
 graphical.target             loaded                     active
active Graphical   Interface
  initrd-fs.target            loaded                     inactive
dead              Initrd File   Systems
  initrd-root-device.target  loaded                          inactive
dead    Initrd Root    Device
  initrd-root-fs.target             loaded                     inactive
dead              Initrd Root File    System
  initrd-switch-root.target loaded                inactive      dead
Switch Root
  initrd.target                              loaded
inactive        dead   Initrd Default  Target
  local-fs-pre.target                               loaded
active      active Local File   Systems (Pre)
  local-fs.target                              loaded
active    active Local File   Systems
  multi-user.target                                loaded
active      active Multi-User  System
  network-online.target                          loaded
active       active Network is  Online
  network-pre.target                               loaded
active       active Network (Pre)
  network.target                              loaded
active       active Network
  nfs-client.target             loaded                    active
active NFS client  services
  nss-lookup.target            loaded                    inactive
dead                    Host and Network  Name Lookups
```

```
  nss-user-lookup.target                loaded              active
active User and Group  Name Lookups
  paths.target                     loaded                   active
active Paths
  remote-fs-pre.target             loaded                   active
active Remote File   Systems (Pre)
  remote-fs.target              loaded                 active
active Remote File   Systems
  rescue.target                                 loaded
inactive      dead                Rescue Mode
  rpc_pipefs.target               loaded                  active
active                rpc_pipefs.  target
  rpcbind.target             loaded       active       active
RPC Port Mapper
  shutdown.target              loaded                 inactive
dead                Shutdown
  slices.target                   loaded     active    active
Slices
  sockets.target                  loaded     active    active
Sockets
  sound.target                      loaded     active    active
Sound Card
  sshd-keygen.target                 loaded     active    active
sshd-keygen.  target
  swap.target                         loaded     active    active
Swap  sysinit.target                 loaded     active    active
System   Initialization
```

Of the targets on your system, a few have an important role because they can be started (isolated) to determine the state your server starts in. These are also the targets that can be set as the default targets. These targets also roughly correspond to runlevels used on earlier versions of RHEL. These are the following targets:

poweroff.target	runlevel 0
rescue.target	runlevel 1
multi-user.target	runlevel 3
graphical.target	runlevel 5
reboot.target	runlevel 6

If you look at the contents of each of these targets, you'll also see that they contain the AllowIsolate=yes line. That means that you can switch the current state of your computer to either one of these targets using the **systemctl isolate** command. Exercise 17-1 shows you how to do this.

Exercise 17-1 Isolating Targets

1. From a root shell, go to the directory /usr/lib/systemd/system. Type **grep Isolate *.target**. This command shows a list of all targets that allow isolation.
2. Type **systemctl isolate rescue.target**. This command switches your computer to rescue.target. You need to type the root password on the console of your server to log in.
3. Type **systemctl isolate reboot.target**. This command restarts your computer.

Setting the Default Target

Setting the default target is an easy procedure that can be accomplished from the command line. Type **systemctl get-default** to see the current default target and use **systemctl set-default** to set the desired default target.

To set the graphical.target as the default target, you need to make sure that the required packages are installed. If this is not the case, you can use the **dnf group list** command to show a list of all RPM package groups. The "server with GUI" package group applies. Use **dnf group install "server with gui"** to install all GUI packages on a server where they have not been installed yet.

Working with GRUB 2

The GRUB 2 boot loader is one of the first things that needs to be working well to boot a Linux server. As an administrator, you will sometimes need to apply modifications to the GRUB 2 boot loader configuration. This section explains how to do so. The RHEL 9 boot procedure is discussed in more detail in Chapter 18, where troubleshooting topics are covered as well.

Understanding GRUB 2

The GRUB 2 ***boot loader*** makes sure that you can boot Linux. ***GRUB*** 2 is installed in the boot sector of your server's hard drive and is configured to load a Linux kernel and the initramfs:

- The ***kernel*** is the heart of the operating system, allowing users to interact with the hardware that is installed in the server.
- The ***initramfs*** contains drivers that are needed to start your server. It contains a mini file system that is mounted during boot. In it are kernel modules that are needed during the rest of the boot process (for example, the LVM modules and SCSI modules for accessing disks that are not supported by default).

Normally, GRUB 2 works just fine and does not need much maintenance. In some cases, though, you might have to change its configuration. To apply changes to the GRUB 2 configuration, the starting point is the /etc/default/grub file, which has options that tell GRUB what to do and how to do it. Example 17-3 shows the contents of this file after an installation with default settings of RHEL 9.

Example 17-3 Contents of the /etc/default/grub File

```
[root@localhost ~]# cat /etc/default/grub
GRUB_TIMEOUT=5
GRUB_DISTRIBUTOR="$(sed 's, release .*$,,g' /etc/system-release)"
GRUB_DEFAULT=saved
GRUB_DISABLE_SUBMENU=true
GRUB_TERMINAL_OUTPUT="console"
GRUB_CMDLINE_LINUX="crashkernel=auto resume=/dev/mapper/rhel-swap
  rd.lvm.lv=rhel/root rd.lvm.lv=rhel/swap rhgb quiet"
GRUB_DISABLE_RECOVERY="true"
GRUB_ENABLE_BLSCFG=true
```

As you can see, the /etc/default/grub file does not contain much information. The most important part that it configures is the GRUB_CMDLINE_LINUX option. This line contains boot arguments for the kernel on your server.

TIP For the RHCSA exam, make sure that you understand the contents of the /etc/default/grub file. That is the most important part of the GRUB 2 configuration anyway.

Apart from the configuration in /etc/default/grub, there are a few configuration files in /etc/grub.d. In these files, you'll find rather complicated shell code that tells GRUB what to load and how to load it. You typically do not have to modify these files. You also do not need to modify anything if you want the capability to select from different kernels while booting. GRUB 2 picks up new kernels automatically and adds them to the boot menu automatically, so nothing has to be added manually.

Understanding GRUB 2 Configuration Files

Based on the configuration files mentioned previously, the main configuration file is created. If your system is a BIOS system, the name of the file is /boot/grub2/grub.cfg. On a UEFI system the file is written to /boot/efi/EFI/redhat/grub.cfg on RHEL and /boot/efi/EFI/centos/grub.cfg on CentOS. After making modifications to the GRUB 2 configuration, you'll need to regenerate the relevant configuration file with the **grub2-mkconfig** command, which is why you should know the name of the file that applies to your system architecture. Do *not* edit it, as this file is automatically generated.

Modifying Default GRUB 2 Boot Options

To apply modifications to the GRUB 2 boot loader, the file /etc/default/grub is your entry point. The most important line in this file is GRUB_CMDLINE_LINUX, which defines how the Linux kernel should be started. In this line, you can apply permanent fixes to the GRUB 2 configuration. Some likely candidates for removal are the options **rhgb** and **quiet**. These options tell the kernel to hide all output while booting. That is nice to hide confusing messages for end users, but if you are a server administrator, you probably just want to remove these options so that you can see what happens while booting.

TIP On the exam, you want to know immediately if something does not work out well. To accomplish this, it is a good idea to remove the **rhgb** and **quiet** boot options. Without these you will not have to guess why your server takes a long time after a restart; you'll just be able to see.

Another interesting parameter is GRUB_TIMEOUT. This defines the amount of time your server waits for you to access the GRUB 2 boot menu before it continues booting automatically. If your server runs on physical hardware that takes a long time to get through the BIOS checks, it may be interesting to increase this time a bit so that you have more time to access the boot menu.

While working with GRUB 2, you need to know a bit about kernel boot arguments. There are many of them, and most of them you'll never use, but it is good to know where you can find them. Type **man 7 bootparam** for a man page that contains an excellent description of all boot parameters that you may use while starting the kernel.

To write the modified configuration to the appropriate files, you use the **grub2-mkconfig** command and redirect its output to the appropriate configuration file. On a BIOS system, the command would be **grub2-mkconfig -o /boot/grub2/grub.cfg** and on a UEFI system the command would be **grub2-mkconfig -o /boot/efi/EFI/redhat/grub.cfg**.

In Exercise 17-2, you learn how to apply modifications to the GRUB 2 configuration and write them to the /boot/grub2/grub.cfg configuration file.

TIP You should know how to apply changes to the GRUB configuration, but you should also know that the default GRUB 2 configuration works fine as it is for almost all computers. So, you will probably never have to apply any changes at all!

Exercise 17-2 Applying Modifications to GRUB 2

1. Open the file /etc/default/grub with an editor and remove the **rhgb** and **quiet** options from the GRUB_CMDLINE_LINUX line.
2. From the same file, set the GRUB_TIMEOUT parameter to 10 seconds. Save changes to the file and close the editor.
3. From the command line, type **grub2-mkconfig > /boot/grub2/grub.cfg** to write the changes to GRUB 2. (Note that instead of using the redirector **>** to write changes to the grub.cfg file, you could use the **-o** option. Both methods have the same result.)
4. Reboot and verify that while booting you see boot messages scrolling by.

Summary

In this chapter you learned how Systemd and GRUB 2 are used to bring your server into the exact state you desire at the end of the boot procedure. You also learned how Systemd is organized, and how units can be configured for automatic start with the use of targets. Finally, you read how to apply changes to the default GRUB 2 boot loader. In the next chapter, you learn how to troubleshoot the boot procedure and fix some common problems.

Exam Preparation Tasks

As mentioned in the section "How to Use This Book" in the Introduction, you have several choices for exam preparation: the end-of-chapter labs; the memory tables in Appendix C; Chapter 27, "Final Preparation"; and the practice exams.

Review All Key Topics

Review the most important topics in the chapter, noted with the Key Topic icon in the margin of the page. Table 17-2 lists a reference for these key topics and the page number on which each is found.

Table 17-2 Key Topics for Chapter 17

Key Topic Element	Description	Page
Section	Understanding Target Units	391
Section	Managing Systemd Targets	392
Exercise 17-1	Isolating Targets	396
List	Explanation of the role of kernel and initramfs	396
Example 17-3	Contents of the /etc/default/grub File	397
Exercise 17-2	Applying Modifications to GRUB 2	399

Define Key Terms

Define the following key terms from this chapter and check your answers in the glossary:

Systemd, target, dependency, unit, want, boot loader, GRUB, kernel, initramfs

Review Questions

The questions that follow are meant to help you test your knowledge of concepts and terminology and the breadth of your knowledge. You can find the answers to these questions in Appendix A.

1. What is a unit?
2. Which command enables you to make sure that a target is no longer eligible for automatic start on system boot?
3. Which configuration file should you modify to apply common changes to GRUB 2?
4. Which command should you use to show all service units that are currently loaded?
5. How do you create a want for a service?
6. How do you switch the current operational target to the rescue.target?
7. Why can it happen that you get the message that a target cannot be isolated?
8. You want to shut down a Systemd service, but before doing that you want to know which other units have dependencies to this service. Which command would you use?
9. What is the name of the GRUB 2 configuration file where you apply changes to GRUB 2?
10. After applying changes to the GRUB 2 configuration, which command should you run?

End-of-Chapter Labs

You have now learned how to work with Systemd targets and the GRUB 2 boot loader. Before you continue, it is a good idea to work on some labs that help you ensure that you can apply the skills that you acquired in this chapter.

Lab 17.1

1. Set the default target to multi-user.target.
2. Reboot to verify this is working as expected.

Lab 17.2

1. Change your GRUB 2 boot configuration so that you will see boot messages upon startup.

The following topics are covered in this chapter:

- Understanding the RHEL 9 Boot Procedure
- Passing Kernel Boot Arguments
- Using a Rescue Disk
- Fixing Common Issues

The following RHCSA exam objectives are covered in this chapter:

- Boot systems into different targets manually
- Interrupt the boot process in order to gain access to a system

CHAPTER 18

Essential Troubleshooting Skills

In Chapter 17, "Managing and Understanding the Boot Procedure," you learned how a RHEL 9 server boots and which role the boot loader GRUB 2 and Systemd play in that process. In this chapter, you learn what you can do when common problems occur while booting your server. This chapter teaches general approaches that help to fix some of the most common problems that may occur while booting. Make sure to master the topics discussed in this chapter well; they might save your (professional) life one day!

"Do I Know This Already?" Quiz

The "Do I Know This Already?" quiz enables you to assess whether you should read this entire chapter thoroughly or jump to the "Exam Preparation Tasks" section. If you are in doubt about your answers to these questions or your own assessment of your knowledge of the topics, read the entire chapter. Table 18-1 lists the major headings in this chapter and their corresponding "Do I Know This Already?" quiz questions. You can find the answers in Appendix A, "Answers to the 'Do I Know This Already?' Quizzes and Review Questions."

Table 18-1 "Do I Know This Already?" Section-to-Question Mapping

Foundation Topics Section	Questions
Understanding the RHEL 9 Boot Procedure	1
Passing Kernel Boot Arguments	2–6
Using a Rescue Disk	7
Fixing Common Issues	8–10

1. Which of the following comes first in the Red Hat Enterprise Linux 9 boot procedure?
   a. Systemd
   b. Kernel
   c. GRUB 2
   d. Initramfs

2. You have just entered a kernel argument on the GRUB 2 boot prompt. Pressing which key(s) enables you to start with this boot argument?
   a. ZZ
   b. Ctrl-X
   c. Esc
   d. Enter

3. Your initramfs seems faulty and cannot initialize the LVM volumes on your disk. Which configuration file should you check for options that are used?
   a. /etc/dracut.d/dracut.conf
   b. /etc/dracut.conf
   c. /etc/sysconfig/dracut
   d. /etc/mkinitrd.conf

4. You do not have the root password and want to reset it. Which kernel argument offers the recommended way to reset it?
   a. **init=/bin/bash**
   b. **init=/bin/sh**
   c. **systemd.unit=emergency.target**
   d. **rd.break**

5. You want to see exactly what is happening on system boot. Which two boot options should you remove from the GRUB 2 boot prompt? (Choose two.)
   a. **rhgb**
   b. **logo**
   c. **quiet**
   d. **silent**

6. You want to enter the most minimal troubleshooting mode where as few services as possible are loaded. Which boot argument should you use?
   a. **systemd.unit=break.target**
   b. **systemd.unit=emergency.target**
   c. **systemd.unit=rescue.target**
   d. **1**

7. Which of the following situations can be resolved only by using a rescue disk?
   a. The kernel stops loading.
   b. The initramfs stops loading.
   c. You never get to a GRUB 2 boot prompt.
   d. You are prompted to enter the root password for maintenance mode.

8. You have entered a troubleshooting mode, and disk access is read-only. What should you do?
   a. Restart the troubleshooting mode and pass the **rw** boot option to the kernel.
   b. Use the **rd.break** boot argument to manually start into the initramfs mode.
   c. Use **mount -o remount,rw /**
   d. Use **mount /**

9. Your server shows a blinking cursor only while booting. No GRUB 2 menu is available. What is the first step in troubleshooting this issue?
   a. From a rescue disk, try the **Boot from local disk** option.
   b. Start a rescue environment and reinstall GRUB.
   c. Start a rescue environment and re-create the initramfs.
   d. Use the **rd.break** boot argument.

10. After resetting the root password from an environment that was started with the **init=/bin/bash** kernel boot argument, how can you restart the system normally?
    a. **reboot**
    b. **systemctl isolate multi-user.target**
    c. **exec /usr/lib/systemd/system**
    d. **exit**

Foundation Topics

Understanding the RHEL 9 Boot Procedure

To fix boot issues, it is essential to have a good understanding of the boot procedure. If an issue occurs during boot, you need to be able to judge in which phase of the boot procedure the issue occurs so that you can select the appropriate tool to fix the issue.

The following steps summarize how the boot procedure happens on Linux:

1. **Performing POST:** The machine is powered on. From the system firmware, which can be the modern Universal Extended Firmware Interface (UEFI) or the classical Basic Input/Output System (BIOS), the Power-On Self-Test (POST) is executed, and the hardware that is required to start the system is initialized.
2. **Selecting the bootable device:** Either from the UEFI boot firmware or from the BIOS, a bootable device is located.
3. **Loading the boot loader:** From the bootable device, a boot loader is located. On RHEL, this is usually GRUB 2.
4. **Loading the kernel:** The boot loader may present a boot menu to the user or can be configured to automatically start a default operating system. To load Linux, the kernel is loaded together with the initramfs. The ***initramfs*** contains kernel modules for all hardware that is required to boot, as well as the initial scripts required to proceed to the next stage of booting. On RHEL 9, the initramfs contains a complete operational system (which may be used for troubleshooting purposes).
5. **Starting /sbin/init:** Once the kernel is loaded into memory, the first of all processes is loaded, but still from the initramfs. This is the /sbin/init process, which on RHEL is linked to Systemd. The **systemd-udevd** daemon is loaded as well to take care of further hardware initialization. All this is still happening from the initramfs image.
6. **Processing initrd.target:** The Systemd process executes all units from the initrd.target, which prepares a minimal operating environment, where the root file system on disk is mounted on the /sysroot directory. At this point, enough is loaded to pass to the system installation that was written to the hard drive.
7. **Switching to the root file system:** The system switches to the root file system that is on disk and at this point can load the Systemd process from disk as well.

8. **Running the default target:** Systemd looks for the default target to execute and runs all of its units. In this process, a login screen is presented, and the user can authenticate. Note that the login prompt can be prompted before all Systemd unit files have been loaded successfully. So, seeing a login prompt does not necessarily mean that your server is fully operational yet; services may still be loaded in the background.

In each of the phases listed, issues may occur because of misconfiguration or other problems. Table 18-2 summarizes where a specific phase is configured and what you can do to troubleshoot if something goes wrong.

> **TIP** Troubleshooting has always been a part of the RHCSA exam. If you encounter an issue, make sure that you can identify in which phase of the boot procedure it occurs and what you can do to fix it.

Table 18-2 Boot Phase Configuration and Troubleshooting Overview

Boot Phase	Configuring It	Fixing It
POST	Hardware configuration (F2, Esc, F10, or another key).	Replace hardware.
Selecting the bootable device	BIOS/UEFI configuration or hardware boot menu.	Replace hardware or use rescue system.
Loading the boot loader	**grub2-install** and edits to /etc/defaults/grub.	Use the GRUB boot prompt and edits to /etc/defaults/grub, followed by **grub2-mkconfig**
Loading the kernel	Edits to the GRUB configuration and /etc/ dracut.conf.	Use the GRUB boot prompt and edits to /etc/defaults/grub, followed by **grub2-mkconfig**
Starting /sbin/init	Compiled into initramfs.	Use the **init =** kernel boot argument, **rd.break** kernel boot argument.
Processing initrd.target	Compiled into initramfs.	Use the **dracut** command. (You won't often have to troubleshoot this.)
Switch to the root file system	Edits to the /etc/fstab file.	Apply edits to the /etc/fstab file.
Running the default target	Using **systemctl set-default** to create the /etc/systemd/system/default.target symbolic link.	Start the rescue.target as a kernel boot argument.

In the next section you learn how to apply the different troubleshooting techniques described in this table.

Passing Kernel Boot Arguments

If your server does not boot normally, the ***GRUB*** boot prompt offers a convenient way to stop the boot procedure and pass specific options to the kernel while booting. In this section, you learn how to access the boot prompt and how to pass specific boot arguments to the kernel while booting.

Accessing the Boot Prompt

When your server boots, you briefly see the GRUB 2 menu. Look fast because it will last for only a few seconds. From this boot menu you can type **e** to enter a mode where you can edit commands, or **c** to enter a full GRUB command prompt, as shown in Figure 18-1. To pass boot options to a starting kernel, use **e**.

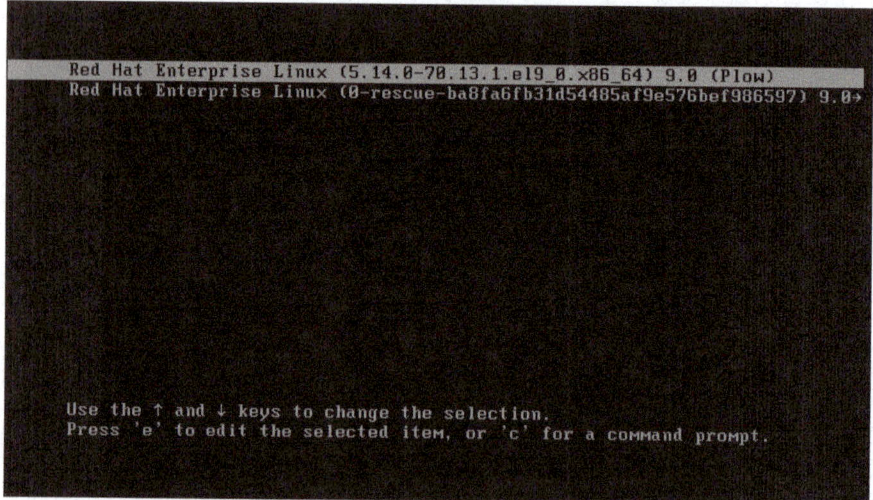

Figure 18-1 Entering the GRUB Boot Prompt

After passing an **e** to the GRUB boot menu, you'll see the interface that is shown in Figure 18-2. From this interface, scroll down to locate the section that begins with linux ($root)/vmlinuz followed by a lot of arguments. This is the line that tells GRUB how to start a kernel, and by default it looks like this:

```
linux ($root)/vmlinuz-{versionnumber].el9.x86_64 root=/dev/mapper/
rhel-root   ro crash kernel=[options] resume=/dev/mapper/rhel-swap
rd.lvm.lv=rhel/  root rd.lvm.lv=rhel/swap rhgb quiet
```

```
load_video
set gfxpayload=keep
insmod gzio
linux ($root)/vmlinuz-5.14.0-70.13.1.el9_0.x86_64 root=/dev/mapper/rhel-root r\
o crashkernel=1G-4G:192M,4G-64G:256M,64G-:512M resume=/dev/mapper/rhel-swap rd\
.lvm.lv=rhel/root rd.lvm.lv=rhel/swap rhgb quiet
initrd ($root)/initramfs-5.14.0-70.13.1.el9_0.x86_64.img




     Press Ctrl-x to start, Ctrl-c for a command prompt or Escape to
     discard edits and return to the menu. Pressing Tab lists
     possible completions.
```

Figure 18-2 Enter Boot Arguments on the Line That Starts with linux

To start, it is a good idea to remove the **rhgb** and **quiet** parts from this line; these arguments hide boot messages for you, and typically you do want to see what is happening while booting. In the next section you learn about some troubleshooting options that you can enter from the GRUB boot prompt.

After entering the boot options you want to use, press Ctrl-X to start the kernel with these options. Notice that these options are used one time only and are not persistent. To make them persistent, you must modify the contents of the /etc/default/grub configuration file and use **grub2-mkconfig -o /boot/grub2/grub.cfg** to apply the modification. (Refer to Chapter 17 for more details about this procedure.)

Starting a Troubleshooting Target

If you encounter trouble when booting your server, you have several options that you can enter on the GRUB 2 boot prompt:

- **rd.break:** This stops the boot procedure while still in the initramfs stage. Your system will still be in the initramfs stage of booting, which means that the root file system is not mounted on / yet. You'll have to provide the root password to enter this mode.
- **init=/bin/sh or init=/bin/bash:** This specifies that a shell should be started immediately after loading the kernel and initrd. This option provides the earliest possible access to a running system. You won't have to enter the root password, but notice that only the root file system is mounted and it is still read-only. Read more about this option in the section "Resetting the Root Password" later in this chapter.

- **systemd.unit=emergency.target:** This enters a mode that loads a bare minimum number of Systemd units. It requires a root password. To see that only a very limited number of unit files have been loaded, you can type the **systemctl list-units** command.
- **systemd.unit=rescue.target:** This starts some more Systemd units to bring you in a more complete operational mode. It does require a root password. To see that only a very limited number of unit files have been loaded, you can type the **systemctl list-units** command.

In Exercise 18-1, you learn how to enter the troubleshooting targets. The other modes listed here are discussed in the following sections.

Exercise 18-1 Exploring Troubleshooting Targets

1. (Re)start your computer. When the GRUB menu shows, select the first line in the menu and press **e**.
2. Scroll down to the line that starts with linux $(root)/vmlinuz. At the end of this line, type **systemd.unit=rescue.target**. Also remove the options **rhgb quit** from this line. Press Ctrl-X to boot with these modifications.
3. Enter the root password when you are prompted for it.
4. Type **systemctl list-units**. This shows all unit files that are currently loaded. You can see that a basic system environment has been loaded.
5. Type **systemctl show-environment**. This shows current shell environment variables.
6. Type **systemctl reboot** to reboot your machine.
7. When the GRUB menu appears, press **e** again to enter the editor mode. At the end of the line that loads the kernel, type **systemd.unit=emergency.target**. Press Ctrl-X to boot with this option.
8. When prompted for it, enter the root password to log in.
9. After successful login, type **systemctl list-units**. Notice that the number of unit files loaded is reduced to a bare minimum.
10. Type **reboot** to restart your system into the default target.

Using a Rescue Disk

If you are lucky when you encounter trouble, you'll still be able to boot from hard disk. If you are a bit less lucky, you'll just see a blinking cursor on a system that does not boot at all. If that happens, you need a rescue disk. The default rescue image for Red Hat Enterprise Linux is on the installation disk. When booting from the installation disk, you'll see a Troubleshooting menu item. Select this item to get access to the options you need to repair your machine.

Restoring System Access Using a Rescue Disk

After selecting the Troubleshooting option, you are presented with the following options, as shown in Figure 18-3:

- **Install Red Hat Enterprise Linux 9 in Basic Graphics Mode:** This option reinstalls your machine. Do not use it unless you want to troubleshoot a situation where a normal installation does not work and you need a basic graphics mode. Normally, you should never need to use this option to troubleshoot a broken installation.
- **Rescue a Red Hat Enterprise Linux System:** This is the most flexible rescue system. In Exercise 18-2, you can explore it in detail. This should be the first option of choice when using a rescue disk.
- **Run a Memory Test:** Run this option if you encounter memory errors. It allows you to mark bad memory chips so that your machine can boot normally.
- **Boot from Local Drive:** If you cannot boot from GRUB on your hard disk, try this option first. It offers a boot loader that tries to install from your machine's hard drive, and as such is the least intrusive option available.

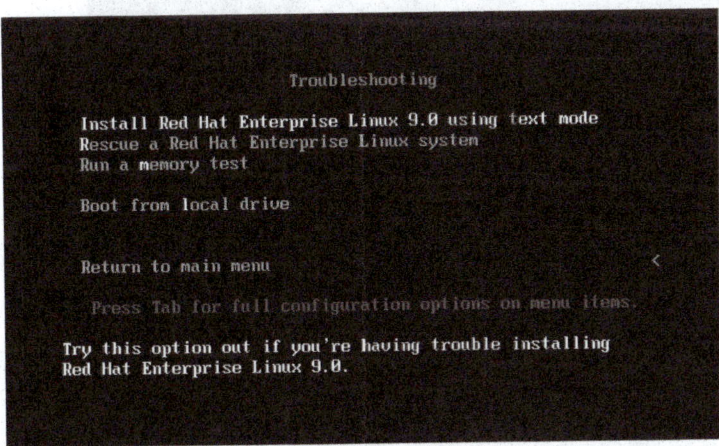

Figure 18-3 Starting from a Rescue Disk

After starting a rescue system, you usually need to enable full access to the on-disk installation. Typically, the rescue disk detects your installation and mounts it on the /mnt/sysimage directory. To fix access to the configuration files and their default locations as they should be available on disk, use the **chroot /mnt/sysimage** command to make the contents of this directory your actual working environment. If you do not use this **chroot** command, many utilities will not work, because if they write to a configuration file, it will be the version that exists on the read-only disk. Using the **chroot** command ensures that all path references to configuration files are correct.

In Exercise 18-2, you learn how to use the Rescue a Red Hat Enterprise Linux System option to troubleshoot a system that does not boot anymore.

Exercise 18-2 Using the Rescue Option

1. Restart your server from the installation disk. Select the **Troubleshooting** menu option.
2. From the Troubleshooting menu, select **Rescue a Red Hat Enterprise Linux System**. This prompts you to press Enter to start the installation. Do not worry; this option does not overwrite your current configuration, it just loads a rescue system.
3. The rescue system now prompts you that it will try to find an installed Linux system and mount on /mnt/sysimage. Press 1 to accept the **Continue** option (see Figure 18-4).

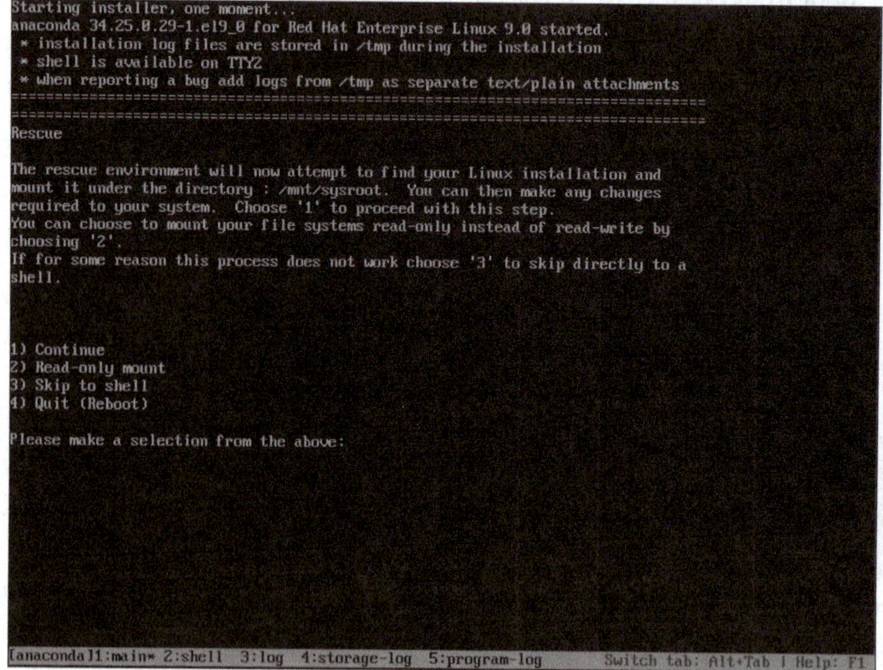

Figure 18-4 The Rescue System Looks for an Installed System Image and Mounts It for You

4. If a valid Red Hat installation was found, you are prompted that your system has been mounted under /mnt/sysimage. At this point, you can press Enter to access the rescue shell.
5. Your Linux installation at this point is accessible through the /mnt/sysimage directory. Type **chroot /mnt/sysimage**. At this point, you have access to your root file system and you can access all tools that you need to repair access to your system.
6. Type **exit** to quit the **chroot** environment, and type **reboot** to restart your machine in a normal mode.

Reinstalling GRUB Using a Rescue Disk

One of the common reasons you might need to start a rescue disk is that the GRUB 2 boot loader breaks. If that happens, you might need to reinstall it. After you have restored access to your server using a rescue disk, reinstalling GRUB 2 is not hard to do and consists of two steps:

- Make sure that you have made the contents of the /mnt/sysimage directory available to your current working environment, using **chroot** as described before.
- Use the **grub2-install** command, followed by the name of the device on which you want to reinstall GRUB 2. So on a KVM virtual machine, the command to use is **grub2-install /dev/vda**, and on a physical server or a VMware or Virtual Box virtual machine, it is **grub2-install /dev/sda**.

Re-creating the Initramfs Using a Rescue Disk

Occasionally, the initramfs image may get damaged as well. If this happens, you cannot boot your server into normal operational mode. To repair the initramfs image after booting into the rescue environment, you can use the ***dracut*** command. If used with no arguments, this command creates a new initramfs for the kernel currently loaded.

Alternatively, you can use the **dracut** command with several options to make an initramfs for specific kernel environments. The **dracut** configuration is dispersed over different locations:

- /usr/lib/dracut/dracut.conf.d/*.conf contains the system default configuration files.
- /etc/dracut.conf.d contains custom dracut configuration files.

- /etc/dracut.conf is now deprecated and should not be used anymore. Put your configuration in files in /etc/dracut.conf.d/ instead.

> **TIP** According to the RHCSA objectives, you should not have to work with a rescue disk on the exam. However, as a Linux administrator, you should expect the unexpected, which is why it is a good idea to ensure that you can handle common as well as less common troubleshooting scenarios.

Fixing Common Issues

In one small chapter such as this, it is not possible to consider all the possible problems one might encounter when working with Linux. There are some problems, though, that are more likely to occur than others. In this section you learn about some of the more common problems.

Reinstalling GRUB 2

Boot loader code does not disappear just like that, but on occasion it can happen that the GRUB 2 boot code gets damaged. In that case, you should know how to reinstall GRUB 2. The exact approach depends on whether your server is still in a bootable state. If it is, reinstalling GRUB 2 is fairly easy. Just type **grub2-install** followed by the name of the device to which you want to install it. The command has many different options to fine-tune what exactly will be installed, but you probably will not need them because, by default, the command installs everything you need to make your system bootable again.

Reinstalling GRUB 2 becomes a little bit more complicated if your machine is in a nonbootable state. If that happens, you first need to start a rescue system and restore access to your server from the rescue system. (See Exercise 18-2 for the exact procedure for how to do that.) After mounting your server's file systems on /mnt/sysimage and using **chroot /mnt/sysimage** to make the mounted system image your root image, reinstalling is as easy as described previously: just run **grub2-install** to install GRUB 2 to the desired installation device. So, if you are in a KVM virtual machine, run **grub2-install /dev/vda**, and if you are on a physical disk, run **grub2-install /dev/sda**.

Fixing the Initramfs

In rare cases, the initramfs might get damaged. If you analyze the boot procedure carefully, you will learn that you have a problem with the initramfs because you'll never see the root file system getting mounted on the root directory, nor will you see any Systemd units getting started. If you suspect that you are having a problem with the initramfs, it is easy to re-create it. To re-create it using all default settings (which is fine in most cases), you can just run the **dracut --force** command. (Without **--force**, the command will refuse to overwrite your existing initramfs.)

Recovering from File System Issues

If you make a misconfiguration to your file system mounts, the boot procedure may just end with the message "Give root password for maintenance." This message is, in particular, generated by the **fsck** command that is trying to verify the integrity of the file systems in /etc/fstab while booting. If **fsck** fails, manual intervention is required that may result in this message during boot. Make sure that you know what to do when this happens to you!

TIP Make sure to master this topic very well. File system–related topics have a heavy weight in the RHCSA objectives, and it is likely that you will need to create partitions and/or logical volumes and put them in /etc/fstab for automatic mounting. That also makes it likely that something will go wrong, and if that happens on the exam, you'd better make sure that you know how to fix it!

If a device is referred to that does not exist, or if there is an error in the UUID that is used to mount the device, for example, Systemd waits first to see whether the device comes back by itself. If that does not happen, it gives the message "Give root password for maintenance" (see Figure 18-5). If that happens, you should by all means first enter the root password. Then you can type **journalctl -xb** as suggested to see whether relevant messages providing information about what is wrong are written to the journal boot log. If the problem is file system oriented, type **mount -o remount,rw /** to make sure the root file system is mounted read/write and analyze what is wrong in the /etc/fstab file and fix it.

```
[  OK  ] Listening on Load/Save RF Kill Switch Status /dev/rfkill Watch.
         Starting Load/Save RF Kill Switch Status...
[  OK  ] Started Load/Save RF Kill Switch Status.
[  OK  ] Started /usr/sbin/lvm vgchange -aay --autoactivation event vgdata.
[  OK  ] Finished Wait for udev To Complete Device Initialization.
[  OK  ] Reached target Preparation for Local File Systems.
         Mounting /exercise...
         Mounting /repo...
[  OK  ] Mounted /repo.
[  OK  ] Mounted /exercise.
[ TIME ] Timed out waiting for device /dev/disk/by-uuid/6c2b4028-1dcb-44cb-b5b7-c8e52352b06.
[DEPEND] Dependency failed for /boot.
[DEPEND] Dependency failed for Local File Systems.
[DEPEND] Dependency failed for Mark the need to relabel after reboot.
[  OK  ] Stopped Forward Password Requests to Wall Directory Watch.
[  OK  ] Reached target Timer Units.
[  OK  ] Reached target Sound Card.
[  OK  ] Reached target Bluetooth Support.
         Starting Restore /run/initramfs on shutdown...
[  OK  ] Reached target Preparation for Network.
[  OK  ] Reached target Network.
[  OK  ] Reached target User and Group Name Lookups.
[  OK  ] Reached target Network is Online.
[  OK  ] Reached target Path Units.
[  OK  ] Reached target Socket Units.
[  OK  ] Started Emergency Shell.
[  OK  ] Reached target Emergency Mode.
[  OK  ] Reached target Preparation for Remote File Systems.
[  OK  ] Reached target Remote File Systems.
         Starting Crash recovery kernel arming...
         Starting Tell Plymouth To Write Out Runtime Data...
         Starting Create Volatile Files and Directories...
[  OK  ] Finished Restore /run/initramfs on shutdown.
[  OK  ] Finished Tell Plymouth To Write Out Runtime Data.
[  OK  ] Finished Create Volatile Files and Directories.
         Starting Security Auditing Service...
[FAILED] Failed to start Crash recovery kernel arming.
See 'systemctl status kdump.service' for details.
[  OK  ] Started Security Auditing Service.
         Starting Record System Boot/Shutdown in UTMP...
[  OK  ] Finished Record System Boot/Shutdown in UTMP.
         Starting Record Runlevel Change in UTMP...
[  OK  ] Finished Record Runlevel Change in UTMP.
You are in emergency mode. After logging in, type "journalctl -xb" to view
system logs, "systemctl reboot" to reboot, "systemctl default" or "exit"
to boot into default mode.
Give root password for maintenance
(or press Control-D to continue):
```

Figure 18-5 If You See This, You Normally Have an /etc/fstab Issue

Resetting the Root Password

A common scenario for a Linux administrator is that the root password has gone missing. If that happens, you need to reset it. The only way to do that is by booting into minimal mode, which allows you to log in without entering a password. To do so, follow these steps:

1. On system boot, press **e** when the GRUB 2 boot menu is shown.
2. Enter **init=/bin/bash** as a boot argument to the line that loads the kernel and press Ctrl-X to boot with this option.
3. Once a root shell is opened, type **mount -o remount,rw /** to get read/write access to the root filesystem.
4. Now you can enter **passwd** and set the new password for the user root.

5. Because at this very early boot stage SELinux has not been activated yet, the context type on /etc/shadow will be messed up. Type **touch /.autorelabel** to create the autorelabel file in the root directory. This will make sure that while rebooting the SELinux security labels are set correctly.

6. Type **exec /usr/lib/systemd/systemd** to replace /bin/bash (which is the current PID 1) with Systemd. This will start your system the normal way. Notice that you cannot use the **reboot** command, as /bin/bash is currently PID 1 and the **reboot** command requires Systemd as the PID 1.

7. Verify that you can log in as the root user after rebooting.

In the previous procedure you changed the root password from an init=/bin/bash shell. Getting out of an init=/bin/bash environment is a bit special, as Systemd is not currently loaded. Because of this, you cannot just use the **reboot** command to restart, as **reboot** invokes Systemd. Typing **exit** is also not an option, as you would exit from the PID 1 and leave the kernel with no PID 1. Therefore, you have to manually start Systemd.

In this special environment where bash is PID 1, you cannot just type **/usr/lib/systemd/system** to start Systemd. That is because typing a command normally creates a child process to the current process—a process generically known as "forking." In this case that doesn't work, as Systemd needs to be PID 1. The solution that was used in the previous procedure was to use **exec /usr/lib/systemd/system**. Whereas ***fork*** will create a child process to the current process, ***exec*** replaces the current process with the command that is started this way. This allows Systemd to be started as PID 1, and that's exactly what is needed in this scenario.

Summary

In this chapter, you learned how to troubleshoot the Red Hat Enterprise Linux 9 boot procedure. You learned in general what happens when a server boots and at which specific points you can interfere to fix things that go wrong. You also learned what to do in some specific cases. Make sure that you know these procedures well; you are likely to encounter them on the exam.

Exam Preparation Tasks

As mentioned in the section "How to Use This Book" in the Introduction, you have several choices for exam preparation: the end-of-chapter labs; the memory tables in Appendix C; Chapter 27, "Final Preparation"; and the practice exams.

Review All Key Topics

Review the most important topics in the chapter, noted with the Key Topic icon in the margin of the page. Table 18-3 lists a reference for these key topics and the page number on which each is found.

Table 18-3 Key Topics for Chapter 18

Key Topic Element	Description	Page
List	Summary of phases processed while booting	406
Table 18-2	Boot Phase Configuration and Troubleshooting Overview	407
List	Summary of relevant GRUB 2 boot options for troubleshooting	409
Section	Resetting the Root Password	416

Complete Tables and Lists from Memory

Print a copy of Appendix C, "Memory Tables" (found on the companion website), or at least the section for this chapter, and complete the tables and lists from memory. Appendix D, "Memory Tables Answer Key," includes completed tables and lists to check your work.

Define Key Terms

Define the following key terms from this chapter and check your answers in the glossary:

initramfs, GRUB, **dracut**, **fork**, **exec**

Review Questions

The questions that follow are meant to help you test your knowledge of concepts and terminology and the breadth of your knowledge. You can find the answers to these questions in Appendix A.

1. Which key do you need to press to enter the GRUB boot menu editor mode?
2. During startup, the boot procedure is not completed and the server asks for the root password instead. What is likely to be the reason for this?

3. You want to enter troubleshooting mode, but you do not know the root password. Which argument would you pass to the kernel to enter a mode that provides access to most of the machine's functionality?
4. You start your server and nothing happens. You just see a blinking cursor and that's all. What is the first step to troubleshoot this issue?
5. You want to find out which units are available in a specific troubleshooting environment. Which command would you use?
6. You have just changed the root password from the init=/bin/bash environment. What should you do to start your system the normal way now?
7. How do you ensure that after resetting the root password all files are provided with the right SELinux context label?
8. You are in troubleshooting mode, and you cannot write any file to the root file system. The root file system was mounted correctly. What can you do to make it writable again?
9. You have applied changes to the GRUB 2 boot loader and want to save them. How do you do that?
10. You do not know the root password on a machine where you want to enter the most minimal troubleshooting mode. Which GRUB 2 boot argument would you use?

End-of-Chapter Lab

Lab 18.1 shows you how to troubleshoot some common problems.

Lab 18.1

1. Restart your server and change the root password from the appropriate troubleshooting mode.
2. In /etc/fstab, change one of the device names so that on the next reboot the file system on it cannot be mounted. Restart and fix the issue that you encounter.
3. Use a rescue disk to bring your server up in full troubleshooting mode from the rescue disk.
4. Re-create the initramfs.

The following topics are covered in this chapter:

- Understanding Shell Scripting Core Elements
- Using Variables and Input
- Using Conditional Loops

The following RHCSA exam objectives are covered in this chapter:

- Conditionally execute code (use of if, test, [], etc.)
- Using Looping constructs (for, etc.) to process file and command line input
- Process script inputs ($1, $2, etc.)
- Process output of shell commands within a script

An Introduction to Automation with Bash Shell Scripting

Shell scripting is a science all by itself. You do not learn about all the nuts and bolts related to this science in this chapter, however. Instead, you learn how to apply basic shell scripting elements, which allows you to write a simple shell script and analyze what is happening in a shell script.

"Do I Know This Already?" Quiz

The "Do I Know This Already?" quiz enables you to assess whether you should read this entire chapter thoroughly or jump to the "Exam Preparation Tasks" section. If you are in doubt about your answers to these questions or your own assessment of your knowledge of the topics, read the entire chapter. Table 19-1 lists the major headings in this chapter and their corresponding "Do I Know This Already?" quiz questions. You can find the answers in Appendix A, "Answers to the 'Do I Know This Already?' Quizzes and Review Questions."

Table 19-1 "Do I Know This Already?" Section-to-Question Mapping

Foundation Topics Section	Questions
Understanding Shell Scripting Core Elements	1–2
Using Variables and Input	3–5
Using Conditional Loops	6–10

1. Which line should every Bash shell script start with?
   a. **/bin/bash**
   b. **#!/bin/bash**
   c. **!#/bin/bash**
   d. **!/bin/bash**

2. What is the purpose of the **exit 0** command that can be used at the end of a script?
   a. It informs the parent shell that the script executed without any problems.
   b. It makes sure the script can be stopped properly.
   c. It is required only if a **for** loop has been used to close the **for** loop structure.
   d. It is used to terminate a conditional structure in the script.

3. How do you stop a script to allow a user to provide input?
   a. **pause**
   b. **break**
   c. **read**
   d. **stop**

4. Which line stores the value of the first argument that was provided when starting a script in the variable NAME?
   a. **NAME = $1**
   b. **$1 = NAME**
   c. **NAME = $@**
   d. **NAME=$1**

5. What is the best way to distinguish between different arguments that have been passed into a shell script?
   a. **$?**
   b. **$#**
   c. **$***
   d. **$@**

6. What is used to close an **if** loop?
   a. **end**
   b. **exit**
   c. **stop**
   d. **fi**

7. What is missing in the following script at the position of the dots?

```
if [ -f $1 ]
then
     echo "$1 is a file"
..... [ -d $1 ]
then
       echo "$1 is a directory"
else
      echo "I do not know what \$1 is"
fi
```

   a. **else**
   b. **if**
   c. **elif**
   d. **or**

8. What is missing in the following script at the position of the dots?

```
for (( counter=100; counter>1; counter-- )); .......
          echo $counter
done
exit 0
```

   a. **in**
   b. **do**
   c. **run**
   d. **start**

9. Which command is used to send a message with the subject "error" to the user root if something didn't work out in a script?
   a. **mail error root**
   b. **mail -s error root**
   c. **mail -s error root .**
   d. **mail -s error root < .**

10. In a **case** statement, it is a good idea to include a line that applies to all other situations. Which of the following would do that?
   a. ***)**
   b. *****
   c. **else**
   d. **or**

Foundation Topics

Understanding Shell Scripting Core Elements

Basically, a shell script is a list of commands that is sequentially executed, with some optional scripting logic in it that allows code to be executed under specific conditions only. To understand complex shell scripts, let's start by looking at a very basic script, shown in Example 19-1.

Example 19-1 Basic Script

```
#!/bin/bash
#
# This is a script that greets the world
# Usage: ./hello

clear
echo hello world

exit 0
```

This basic script contains a few elements that should be used in all scripts. To start, there is the ***shebang***. This is the line #!/bin/bash. When a script is started from a ***parent shell*** environment, it opens a subshell. In this ***subshell***, different commands are executed. These commands can be interpreted in any way, and to make it clear how they should be interpreted, the shebang is used. In this case, the shebang makes clear that the script is a Bash shell script. Other shells can be specified as well. For instance, if your script contains Perl code, the shebang should be #!/usr/bin/perl.

It is good practice to start a script with a shebang; if it is omitted, the script code will be executed by the shell that is used in the parent shell as well. Because your scripts may also be executed by, for instance, users of ksh, using a shebang to call /bin/bash as a subshell is important to avoid confusion.

Right after the shebang, there is a part that explains what the script is about. It is a good idea in every script to include a few comment lines. In a short script, it is often obvious what the script is doing. If the script is becoming longer, and as more people get involved in writing and maintaining the script, it will often become less clear what the writer of the script intended to do. To avoid that situation, make sure that you include comment lines, starting with a #. Include them not only in the beginning of the script but also at the start of every subsection of the script. Comments will surely be helpful if you read your script a few months later and don't remember exactly what you were trying to do while creating it! You can also use comments within lines. No matter in which position the # is used, everything from the # until the end of the line is comment text.

Next is the body of the script. In Example 19-1, the body is just a simple script containing a few commands that are sequentially executed. The body may grow as the script develops.

At the end of the script, I included the statement **exit 0**. An **exit** statement tells the parent shell whether the script was successful. A 0 means that it was successful, and anything else means that the script has encountered a problem. The exit status of the last command in the script is the exit status of the script itself, unless the **exit** command is used at the end of the script. But it is good to know that you can work with **exit** to inform the parent shell how it all went. To request the exit status of the last command, from the parent shell, use the **echo $?** command. This request can be useful to determine whether and why something didn't work out.

After writing a script, make sure that it can be executed. The most common way to do this is to apply the execute permission to it. So, if the name of the script is hello, use **chmod +x hello** to make it executable. The script can also be executed as an argument of the **bash** command, for instance. Use **bash hello** to run the hello script. If started as an argument of the **bash** command, the script does not need to be executable.

You can basically store the script anywhere you like, but if you are going to store it in a location that is not included in the $PATH, you need to execute it with a ./ in front of the script name. So, just typing **hello** is not enough to run your script; type **./hello** to run it. Note that ./ is also required if you want to run the script from the current directory, because on Linux the current directory is not included in the $PATH variable. Or put it in a standard directory that is included in the $PATH variable, like /usr/local/bin. In Exercise 19-1 you apply these skills and write a simple shell script.

Exercise 19-1 Writing a Simple Shell Script

1. Use **vim** to create a script with the name **hello** in your home directory.
2. Give this script the contents that you see in Example 19-1 and close it.
3. Use **./hello** to try to execute it. You'll get a "permission denied" error message.
4. Type **chmod +x hello** and try to execute it again. You'll see that it now works.

Using Variables and Input

Linux Bash scripts are much more than just a list of sequentially executed commands. One of the nice things about scripts is that they can work with variables and input to make the script flexible. In this section, you learn how to work with variables and input.

Using Positional Parameters

When starting a script, you can use arguments. An *argument* is anything that you put behind the script command while starting it. Arguments can be used to make a script more flexible. Take, for instance, the **useradd lisa** command. In this example, the command is **useradd**, and the argument **lisa** specifies what needs to be done. In this case, a user with the name **lisa** has to be created. In this example, **lisa** is the argument to the command **useradd**. In a script, the first argument is referred to as **$1**, the second argument is referred to as **$2**, and so on. The script in Example 19-2 shows how an argument can be used. Go ahead and try it using any arguments you want to use!

Example 19-2 Script That Uses Arguments

```
#!/bin/bash
# run this script with a few arguments
echo The first argument is $1
echo The second argument is $2
echo the third argument is $3
```

If you tried to run the sample code from Example 19-2, you might have noticed that its contents are not perfect. If you use three arguments while using the script, it will work perfectly. If you use only two arguments, the third echo will print with no value for $3. If you use four arguments, the fourth value (which would be stored in $4) will never be used. So, if you want to use arguments, you'll be better off using a more flexible approach. Example 19-3 shows a script that uses a more flexible approach.

Example 19-3 Script That Uses Arguments in a Flexible Way

```
#!/bin/bash
# run this script with a few arguments
echo you have entered $# arguments
for i in $@
do
  echo $i
done
exit 0
```

In Example 19-3, two new items that relate to the arguments are introduced:

- $# is a counter that shows how many arguments were used when starting the script.
- $@ refers to all arguments that were used when starting the script.

To evaluate the arguments that were used when starting this script, you can use a conditional loop with **for**. In conditional loops with **for**, commands are executed as long as the condition is true. In this script, the condition is **for i in $@**, which means "for each argument." Each time the script goes through the loop, a value from the $@ variable is assigned to the $i variable. So, as long as there are arguments, the body of the script is executed. The body of a **for** loop always starts with **do** and is closed with **done**, and between these two, the commands that need to be executed are listed. So, the script in Example 19-3 will use **echo** to show the value of each argument and stop when no more arguments are available. In Exercise 19-2, you can try this for yourself by writing a script that works with positional parameters.

Exercise 19-2 Working with Positional Parameters

1. Open an editor, create a script named **ex192a**, and copy the contents from Example 19-2 into this script.
2. Save the script and make it executable.
3. Run the **./ex192a a b c** command. You'll see that three lines are echoed.
4. Run the **./ex192a a b c d e f** command. You'll see that three lines are still echoed.
5. Open an editor to create the script **ex192** and copy the contents from Example 19-3 into this script.
6. Save the script and make it executable.
7. Run the **./ex192 a b c d e** command. You'll see that five lines are echoed.
8. Run the **./ex192** command without arguments. You'll see that the command does not echo any arguments, but it does indicate that zero arguments are entered.

Working with Variables

A ***variable*** is a label that is used to refer to a specific location in memory that contains a specific value. Variables can be defined statically by using NAME=value or can be defined in a dynamic way. There are two solutions to define a variable dynamically:

- Use **read** in the script to ask the user who runs the script for input.
- Use command substitution to use the result of a command and assign that result to a variable. For example, the **date +%d-%m-%y** command shows the

current date in day-month-year format. To assign that date to a variable in a script, you could use the **TODAY=$(date +%d-%m-%y)** command.

In command substitution, you just have to enclose in parentheses the command whose result you want to use, with a dollar sign preceding the opening parenthesis. As an alternative to this notation, you can use backquotes. So the **TODAY=`date +%d-%m-%y`** command would do exactly the same.

In the previous section about positional parameters, you learned how to provide arguments when starting a script. In some cases, a more efficient approach is to ask for information when you find out that something essential is missing. The script in Example 19-4 shows how to do this using **read**.

Example 19-4 Script That Uses the **read** Command

```
#!/bin/bash
if [ -z $1 ]; then
          echo enter a name
          read NAME
else
          NAME=$1
fi
echo you have entered the text $NAME
exit 0
```

In Example 19-4, an **if ... then ... else ... fi** statement is used to check whether the argument **$1** exists. This is done by using the **test** command, which can be written in either of two ways: **test** or **[...]**. In Example 19-4, the line **if [-z $1]** executes to see if the test **-z $1** is true. The **-z test** checks whether $1 is nonexistent. Stated otherwise, the line **if [-z $1]** checks whether $1 is empty; if so, it means that no argument was provided when starting this script. If this is the case, the commands after the **then** statement are executed. Notice that when you're writing the **test** command with the square brackets, it is essential to include one space after the opening bracket and one space before the closing bracket; without these spaces, the command will not work.

Notice that the **then** statement immediately follows the **test** command. This is possible because a semicolon is used (;). A semicolon is a command separator and can replace a new line in a script. In the **then** statement, two commands are executed: an **echo** command that displays a message onscreen and a **read** command. The **read** command stops the script so that user input can be processed and stored in the variable NAME. So, the line **read NAME** puts all user input in the variable NAME, which will be used later in the script.

In Example 19-4, the next part is introduced by the **else** statement. The commands after the **else** statement are executed in all other cases, which in this case means "if an argument was provided." If that is the case, the variable NAME is defined and the current value of $1 is assigned to it.

Notice how the variable is defined: directly after the name of the variable there is an = sign, which is followed by $1. Notice that you should never use spaces when defining variables.

Then, the **if** loop is closed with a **fi** statement. Once the **if** loop has been completed, you know for sure that the variable NAME is defined and has a value. The last line of the script reads the value of the variable NAME and displays this value to STDOUT via the **echo** command. Notice that to request the current value of a variable, the script refers to the variable name, preceded by a $ sign.

In Exercise 19-3, you can practice working with input.

Exercise 19-3 Working with Input

1. Open an editor and create a script with the name **ex193**. Enter the contents of Example 19-4 in this script.
2. Write the script to disk and use **chmod +x ex193** to make it executable.
3. Run the script using **./ex193** and no further arguments. You'll see that it prompts for input.
4. Run the script using **hello** as its argument. It will echo "you have entered the text hello" to the STDOUT.

Using Conditional Loops

As you have already seen, you can use ***conditional loops*** in a script. These conditional loops are executed only if a certain condition is true. In Bash the following conditional loops are often used:

- **if ... then ... else:** Used to execute code if a specific condition is true
- **for:** Used to execute commands for a range of values
- **while:** Used to execute code as long as a specific condition is true
- **until:** Used to execute code until a specific condition is true
- **case:** Used to evaluate specific values, where beforehand a limited number of values is expected

Working with if ... then ... else

The **if ... then ... else** construction is common to evaluate specific conditions. You already saw an example with it in Example 19-4. This conditional loop is often used together with the **test** command, which you saw in action earlier to check whether a file exists. This command enables you to do many other things as well, such as compare files, compare integers, and much more.

> **TIP** Look at the man page of the **test** command.

The basic construction with **if** is **if ... then ... fi**. This construction evaluates one single condition, as in the following example:

```
if [ -z $1 ]
then
        echo no value provided
fi
```

In Example 19-4 you saw how two conditions can be evaluated by including **else** in the statement. Example 19-5 shows how multiple conditions can be evaluated by contracting **else** with **if** to become **elif**. This construction is useful if many different values need to be checked. In Example 19-5 note that multiple **test** commands are used as well.

Example 19-5 Script with **if ... then ... else**

```
#!/bin/bash
# run this script with one argument
# the goal is to find out if the argument is a file or a directory
if [ -f $1 ]
then
        echo "$1 is a file"
elif [ -d $1 ]
then
        echo "$1 is a directory"
else
        echo "I do not know what \$1 is"
fi
exit 0
```

Also note the use of the backslash (\) in Example 19-5. This character informs the shell that it should not interpret the following character, which is known as *escaping* the character. Obviously, if you wanted the value of **$1** to be printed instead of the string **$1**, you would need to remove the ****.

Using || and &&

Instead of writing full **if ... then** statements, you can use the logical operators || and &&. || is a logical **OR** and will execute the second part of the statement only if the first part is not true; **&&** is the logical **AND** and will execute the second part of the statement only if the first part is true. Consider these two one-liners:

```
[ -z $1 ] && echo no argument provided
ping -c 1 10.0.0.20 2>/dev/null || echo node is not available
```

In the first example, a test is performed (using the alternative **test** command syntax) to see whether $1 is empty. If that test is true (which basically means that the **test** command exits with the exit code 0), the second command is executed.

In the second example, a **ping** command is used to check the availability of a host. The logical OR is used in this example to echo the text "node is not available" in case the **ping** command was not successful. You'll often find that instead of fully written **if ... then** statements, the **&&** and || constructions are used. In Exercise 19-4 you can practice some **if ... then ... else** skills, using either **if ... then ... else** or && and ||.

Exercise 19-4 Using if ... then ... else

In this exercise, you work on a script that checks if the argument is a file, a directory, or neither.

1. Start an editor and create a script using **filechk** as the name.
2. Copy the contents from Example 19-5 to this script.
3. Run a couple of tests with it, such as

```
./filechk /etc/hosts
./filechk /usr
./filechk non-existing-file
```

Applying for

The **for** conditional provides an excellent solution for processing ranges of data. In Example 19-6, you can see the first script with **for**, where a range is defined and processed as long as there are unprocessed values in that range.

Example 19-6 Script with **for**

```
#!/bin/bash
#
for (( COUNTER=100; COUNTER>1; COUNTER-- )); do
          echo $COUNTER
done
exit 0
```

A **for** conditional statement always starts with **for**, which is followed by the condition that needs to be checked. Then comes **do**, which is followed by the commands that need to be executed if the condition is true, and the conditional statement is closed with **done**.

In Example 19-6, you can see that the condition is a range of numbers assigned to the variable COUNTER. The variable first is initialized with a value of 100, and as long as the value is higher than 1, in each ***iteration***, 1 is subtracted. As long as the condition is true, the value of the $COUNTER variable is displayed, using the **echo** commands.

Example 19-7 shows one of my favorite one-liners with **for**. The range is defined this time as a series of numbers, starting with 100 and moving up to 104.

Example 19-7 One-Liner with **for**

```
for i in {100..104}; do ping -c 1 192.168.4.$i >/dev/null && echo
  192.168.4.$i is up; done
```

Notice how the range is defined: You specify the first number, followed by two dots and closed with the last number in the range. With **for i in**, each of these numbers is assigned to the variable **i**. For each of these numbers, a **ping** command is executed, where the option **-c 1** makes sure that only one ping request is sent.

In this **ping** command, it is not the result that counts, which is why the result is redirected to the /dev/null device. Based on the exit status of the **ping** command, the part behind the **&&** is executed. So, if the host could be reached, a line is echoed indicating that it is up.

Understanding while and until

Whereas the **for** statement that you just read about is useful to work through ranges of items, the **while** statement is useful if you want to monitor something like the availability of a process. In Example 19-8 you can see how **while** is used to monitor process activity.

Example 19-8 Monitoring Processes with **while**

```
#!/bin/bash
#
# usage: monitor <processname>
while ps aux | grep $1 | grep -v grep > ~/output.txt
do
        sleep 5
done

clear
echo your process has stopped
logger $1 is no longer present
```

The script in Example 19-8 consists of two parts. First, there is the **while** loop. Second, there is everything that needs to be executed when the **while** loop no longer evaluates to true. The core of the **while** loop is the **ps** command, which is grepped for the occurrence of $1. Notice the use of **grep -v grep**, which excludes lines containing the **grep** command from the result. Keep in mind that the **ps** command will include all running commands, including the **grep** command that the output of the **ps** command is piped to. This can result in a false positive match. The results of the **ps aux** command are redirected to the file ~/output.txt. That makes it possible to read the results later from ~/output.txt if that is needed, but they do not show by default.

The commands that need to be executed if the statement evaluates to true follow after the **while** statements. In this case, the command is **sleep 5**, which will basically pause the script for 5 seconds. As long as the **while** command evaluates to true, it keeps on running. If it does no longer (which in this case means that the process is no longer available), it stops and the commands that follow the **while** loop can be executed.

The counterpart of **while** is **until**, which opens an iteration that lasts until the condition is true. In Example 19-9, **until** is used to filter the output of the **users** command for the occurrence of $1, which would be a username. Until this command is true, the iteration continues. When the username is found in the output of **users**, the iteration closes and the commands after the **until** loop are executed.

Example 19-9 Monitoring User Login with **until**

```
#!/bin/bash
#
until users | grep $1 > /dev/null
do
     echo $1 is not logged in yet
     sleep 5
done
echo $1 has just logged in
```

Understanding case

The last of the important iteration loops is **case**. The **case** statement is used to evaluate a number of expected values. The **case** statement in particular is important in Linux startup scripts that were used to start services in previous versions of RHEL. In a **case** statement, you define every specific argument that you expect, which is followed by the command that needs to be executed if that argument was used.

In Example 19-10, you can see the blueprint of the **case** statement that was used in the service scripts in earlier versions of RHEL to start almost any service. This statement works on $1, which is the name of a startup script. Following the name of the script, the user can type **start**, **stop**, **restart**, and so on.

Example 19-10 Evaluating Specific Cases with **case**

```
case "$1" in
    start)
              start;;
    stop)
    rm -f $lockfile
    stop;;
    restart)
              restart;;
    reload)
              reload;;
    status)
              status
              ;;
    *)
              echo "Usage: $0 (start|stop|restart|reload|status) "
              ;;
esac
```

The **case** statement has a few particularities. To start, the generic syntax is **case *item-to-evaluate* in**. This syntax is followed by a list of all possible values that need to be evaluated. Each item is closed with a closing parenthesis. This) is followed by a list of commands that need to be executed if a specific argument was used. The list of commands is closed with a double semicolon. This ;; can be used directly after the last command, and it can be used on a separate line. Also notice that the *) refers to all other options not previously specified. It is a "catchall" statement. The **case** statement is closed by an **esac** statement.

Notice that the evaluations in **case** are performed in order. When the first match is made, the **case** statement will not evaluate anything else. Within the evaluation, wildcard-like patterns can be used. This shows in the *) evaluation, which matches everything. But you also could use evaluations like start|Start|START) to match the use of a different case.

Bash Shell Script Debugging

When a script does not do what you expect it to do, debugging the script is useful. Try starting it as an argument to the **bash -x** command. This command shows you line by line what the script is trying to do and also shows you specific errors if it does not work. Example 19-11 shows a script using **bash -x** where it becomes immediately clear that the **grep** command does not know what it is expected to do; the reason is that it is missing an argument to work on.

Example 19-11 Using **bash -x** to Debug Scripts

```
[root@server1 ~]# bash -x 319.sh
+ grep
Usage: grep [OPTION]... PATTERN [FILE]...
Try 'grep --help' for more information.
+ users
+ echo is not logged in yet
is not logged in yet
+ sleep 5
```

Summary

In this chapter you learned how to write shell scripts. You also worked through a few examples and are now familiar with some of the basic elements that are required to create a successful script.

Exam Preparation Tasks

As mentioned in the section "How to Use This Book" in the Introduction, you have several choices for exam preparation: the end-of-chapter labs; the memory tables in Appendix C; Chapter 27, "Final Preparation"; and the practice exams.

Review All Key Topics

Review the most important topics in the chapter, noted with the Key Topic icon in the margin of the page. Table 19-2 lists a reference for these key topics and the page number on which each is found.

Table 19-2 Key Topics for Chapter 19

Key Topic Element	Description	Page
Paragraph	Definition of variable	427
List	Dynamically defining variables	427
List	Conditional loops overview	429

Define Key Terms

Define the following key terms from this chapter and check your answers in the glossary:

shebang, parent shell, subshell, variable, conditional loop, OR, AND, iteration

Review Questions

The questions that follow are meant to help you test your knowledge of concepts and terminology and the breadth of your knowledge. You can find the answers to these questions in Appendix A.

1. What is the effect if a script does *not* start with a shebang?
2. How can you check if a variable VAR has no value?
3. What would you use in a script to count the number of arguments that have been used?
4. What would you use to refer to all arguments that have been used when starting the script?
5. How do you process user input in a script?

6. What is the simplest way to test whether a file exists and execute the **echo "file does not exist"** command if it does not?
7. Which test would you perform to find out if an item is a file or a directory?
8. Which construction would you use to evaluate a range of items?
9. How do you close an **elif** statement in a script?
10. In a **case** statement, you evaluate a range of items. For each of these items, you execute one or more commands. What do you need to use after the last command to close the specific item?

End-of-Chapter Lab

In this end-of-chapter lab, you apply your scripting skills to write two simple scripts.

Lab 19.1

1. Write a script that works with arguments. If the argument **one** is used, the script should create a file named /tmp/one. If the argument **two** is used, the script should send a message containing the subject "two" to the root user.
2. Write a countdown script. The script should use one argument (and not more than one). This argument specifies the number of minutes to count down. It should start with that number of minutes and count down second by second, writing the text "there are nn seconds remaining" at every iteration. Use **sleep** to define the seconds. When there is no more time left, the script should echo "time is over" and quit.

The following topics are covered in this chapter:

- Hardening the SSH Server
- Using Other Useful sshd Options
- Configuring Key-Based Authentication with Passphrases

The following RHCSA exam objective is covered in this chapter:

- Configure key-based authentication for SSH

Configuring SSH

Secure Shell (SSH) is among the most important utilities that system administrators use. In Chapter 5, "Connecting to Red Hat Enterprise Linux 9," you learned how to use SSH to connect to a server using a password or key-based authentication. In this chapter, you learn about some of the more advanced configuration settings.

"Do I Know This Already?" Quiz

The "Do I Know This Already?" quiz enables you to assess whether you should read this entire chapter thoroughly or jump to the "Exam Preparation Tasks" section. If you are in doubt about your answers to these questions or your own assessment of your knowledge of the topics, read the entire chapter. Table 20-1 lists the major headings in this chapter and their corresponding "Do I Know This Already?" quiz questions. You can find the answers in Appendix A, "Answers to the 'Do I Know This Already?' Quizzes and Review Questions."

Table 20-1 "Do I Know This Already?" Section-to-Question Mapping

Foundation Topics Section	Questions
Hardening the SSH Server	1–5
Using Other Useful sshd Options	6–8, 10
Configuring Key-Based Authentication with Passphrases	9

1. Which of the following is *not* a common approach to prevent brute-force attacks against SSH servers?
    a. Disable X11 forwarding
    b. Have SSH listening on a nondefault port
    c. Disable password login
    d. Allow specific users only to log in

2. Which of the following successfully limits SSH server access to users bob and lisa only?
   a. **LimitUsers bob,lisa**
   b. **AllowedUsers bob lisa**
   c. **AllowUsers bob lisa**
   d. **AllowedUsers bob,lisa**

3. Which of the following commands must be used to provide nondefault port 2022 with the correct SELinux label?
   a. **semanage ports -m -t ssh_port_t -p 2022**
   b. **semanage port -m -t ssh_port_t -p tcp 2022**
   c. **semanage ports -a -t sshd_port_t -p tcp 2022**
   d. **semanage port -a -t ssh_port_t -p tcp 2022**

4. Which of the following descriptions is correct for the MaxAuthTries option?
   a. After reaching the number of attempts specified here, the account will be locked.
   b. This option specifies the maximum number of login attempts. After reaching half the number specified here, additional failures are logged.
   c. After reaching the number of attempts specified here, the IP address where the login attempts come from is blocked.
   d. The number specified here indicates the maximum number of login attempts per minute.

5. Which log file do you analyze to get information about failed SSH login attempts?
   a. /var/log/auth
   b. /var/log/authentication
   c. /var/log/messages
   d. /var/log/secure

6. SSH login in your test environment takes a long time. Which of the following options could be most likely responsible for the connection time problems?
   a. UseLogin
   b. GSSAPIAuthentication
   c. UseDNS
   d. TCPKeepAlive

7. Which of the following options is *not* used to keep SSH connections alive?
   a. TCPKeepAlive
   b. ClientAliveInterval
   c. ClientAliveCountMax
   d. UseDNS

8. Which file on an SSH client computer needs to be added to set the ServerKeepAliveInterval for an individual user?
   a. ~/.ssh/ssh_config
   b. ~/.ssh/config
   c. /etc/ssh/config
   d. /etc/ssh/ssh_config

9. Assuming that a passphrase-protected public/private key pair has already been created, how do you configure your session so that you have to enter the passphrase once only?
   a. Copy the passphrase to the ~/.ssh/passphrase file.
   b. Run **ssh-add /bin/bash** followed by **ssh-agent**.
   c. Run **ssh-agent /bin/bash** followed by **ssh-add**.
   d. This is not possible; you must enter the passphrase each time a connection is created.

10. The MaxSessions option can be used to tune the maximum number of sessions that can be open at the same time. Which value does it have by default?
   a. 10
   b. 25
   c. 100
   d. 1000

Foundation Topics

Hardening the SSH Server

SSH is an important and convenient solution that helps you establish remote ***connections*** to servers. It is also a dangerous solution. If your SSH server is visible directly from the Internet, you can be sure that sooner or later an intruder will try to connect to your server, intending to do harm.

Dictionary attacks are common against an SSH server. In a dictionary attack, the attacker uses common passwords (the dictionary) that are used to try repeated log-ins. The attacker uses the fact that SSH servers usually offer their services on port 22 and that still too many Linux servers have a root account that is allowed to log in over SSH. Based on that information, it is easy for an attacker to try to log in as root just by guessing the password. If the password uses limited complexity, and no additional security measures have been taken, sooner or later the intruder will be able to connect. Fortunately, you can take some measures to protect SSH servers against these kinds of attacks:

- Disable root login
- Disable password login
- Configure a nondefault port for SSH to listen on
- Allow specific users only to log in on SSH

In the following subsections, you learn what is involved in changing these options.

Limiting Root Access

In past versions of RHEL, the root user was allowed to log in, locally as well as remotely, through SSH. In RHEL 9 this has been fixed. The RHEL 9 installer now has an option not to set a password for the root user, which disables root login. Also, by default the root user is not allowed to log in through SSH. This is accomplished by the option **PermitRootLogin prohibit-password**, which is set by default. This option allows the root user to log in only if the user has a valid public/private-key pair, and it is recommended not to change this.

Even if root login to SSH is disabled, it's still possible to perform remote administration tasks. To do so, you'll first have to log in remotely as a non-root user, using a command like **ssh student@remoteserver**. Once the session to the remote server has been established, use **sudo -i** to open a root shell if you're using a sudo-enabled user, or **su -** for non-sudo-enabled users. This is also the procedure to follow if no root password has been set.

Configuring Alternative Ports

Many security problems on Linux servers start with a port scan issued by the attacker. Scanning all of the 65,535 ports that can potentially be listening takes a lot of time, but most port scans focus on known ports only, and SSH port 22 is always among the first ports scanned. Do not underestimate the risk of port scans. On several occasions, I found that an SSH port listening at port 22 was discovered within an hour after installation of the server.

To protect against port scans, you can configure your SSH server to listen on another port. By default, the sshd_config file contains the line Port 22 that tells SSH to listen on privileged port 22. To have SSH listen on another port, you must change port 22 to something else. Different ports can be used. You can choose to use a completely random port like 2022, but it can also be handy to configure SSH to listen on port 443.

Port 443 by default is assigned to web servers using Transport Layer Security (TLS) to offer encryption. If the users who want to access the SSH server are normally behind a proxy that allows traffic to ports 80 and 443 only, it may make sense to configure SSH to listen on port 443. You should realize, though, that by doing so port 443 cannot be used by your web server anymore; a port can be assigned to one service at a time only! So, do this only on a machine where you are not planning to run a TLS-enabled web server!

TIP To avoid being locked out of your server after making a change to the SSH listening port while being connected remotely, it is a good idea to open two sessions to your SSH server. Use one session to apply changes and test, and use the other session to keep your current connection option. Active sessions will not be disconnected after restarting the SSH server (unless you fail to restart the SSH server successfully).

Modifying SELinux to Allow for Port Changes

After changing the SSH port, you also need to configure SELinux to allow for this change. (See Chapter 22, "Managing SELinux," for more details about SELinux.) Network ports are labeled with SELinux security labels to prevent services from accessing ports where they should not go. To allow a service to connect to a nondefault port, you need to use **semanage port** to change the label on the target port. Before doing so, it is a good idea to check whether the port already has a label. You can do this by using the **semanage port -l** command.

If the port does not have a security label set yet, use **-a** to add a label to the port. If a security label has been set already, use **-m** to modify the current security label. Use, for instance, the command **semanage port -a -t ssh_port_t -p tcp 2022** to label port 2022 for access by sshd. If you want to relabel a port that already was in use by another service, you have to use **semanage port -m** to modify the current port assignment. This is needed if, for instance, you want SSH to be able to bind to port 443.

Limiting User Access

You can find many options for sshd by just browsing through the sshd_config file. One of the most interesting options to use is AllowUsers. This option takes a space-separated list of all users that will be allowed login through SSH. Notice that this is a powerful option, limiting login to only these users and excluding all other users, including the root user.

When you use the AllowUsers parameter, carefully consider which username you want to allow or deny access. In a scripted brute-force attack, intruders normally also try common usernames such as admin, Administrator, and jsmith. It is easy to add a layer of security by selecting an uncommon username. Notice the following about the AllowUsers parameter:

- The AllowUsers option by default does not appear anywhere in the default /etc/ssh/sshd_config file.
- The AllowUsers option is a better option than PermitRootLogin because it is more restrictive than just denying root to log in.
- If the AllowUsers option does not specify root, you can still become root by using **su -** or **sudo -i** after making a connection as a normal user.

A parameter that looks promising, but is misleading, is MaxAuthTries. You might think that this option locks access to the SSH login prompt after a maximum number of failed login attempts. Such functionality proves useful when connecting to a local server (of which configuration can easily be changed if so required), but on an SSH server with Internet access, it is a rather dangerous option, making it easy to perform a denial-of-service attack on the server. An intruder would only have to run a script that tries to log in as a specific user to block access for that user for an amount of time. That is why MaxAuthTries does not do what you might think it would do. It just starts logging failed login attempts after half the number of successful login attempts specified here.

Still, the MaxAuthTries option is useful. For analyzing security events related to your SSH server, it is not that interesting to know when a user by accident has typed a wrong password one or two times. It becomes interesting only after multiple failed attempts. The higher the number of attempts, the more likely it is that an intruder is trying to get in. SSH writes log information about failed login attempts to the AUTHPRIV syslog facility. By default, this facility is configured to write information about login failures to /var/log/secure.

In Exercise 20-1, you apply the common SSH options that have been discussed so far.

Exercise 20-1 Configuring SSH Security Options

In this exercise, the sshd process should be configured on server1. Use a second server, server2, to test access to server1.

1. Open a root shell on server1, and from there, open the sshd configuration file /etc/ssh/sshd_config in an editor.
2. Find the Port line, and below that line add the line **Port 2022**. This tells the sshd process that it should bind to two different ports, which ensures that you can still open SSH sessions even if you have made an error.
3. Add the line **AllowUsers student** to the SSH configuration file as well.
4. Save changes to the configuration file and restart sshd, using **systemctl restart sshd**. You will see an error message.
5. Type **systemctl status -l sshd**. You'll see a "permission denied" error for SSH trying to connect to port 2022.
6. Type **semanage port -a -t ssh_port_t -p tcp 2022** to apply the correct SELinux label to port 2022.
7. Open the firewall for port 2022 also, using **firewall-cmd --add-port=2022/tcp**, followed by **firewall-cmd --add-port=2022/tcp --permanent**
8. Type **systemctl status -l sshd** again. You'll see that the sshd process is now listening on two ports.
9. Try to log in to your SSH server from your other server, using **ssh -p 2022 student@server1**. After the user shell has opened, type **su -** to get root access.

Using Other Useful sshd Options

Apart from the security-related options, there are some useful miscellaneous options that you can use to streamline SSH performance. In the next two subsections, you read about some of the most significant of these options.

Session Options

To start with, there is the UseDNS option. This option is on by default and instructs the SSH server to look up the remote hostname and check with DNS that the resolved hostname for the remote host maps back to the same IP address. Although this option has some security benefits, it also involves a significant performance penalty. If client connections are slow, make sure to set it to no, to switch off client hostname verification completely.

Another session-related option is MaxSessions. This option specifies the maximum number of sessions that can be opened from one IP address simultaneously. If you are expecting multiple users to use the same IP address to log in to your SSH server, you might need to increase this option beyond its default value of 10.

Connection Keepalive Options

TCP connections in general are a relatively scarce resource, which is why connections that are not used for some time normally time out. You can use a few options to keep inactive connections alive for a longer period of time.

The TCPKeepAlive option is used to monitor whether the client is still available. Using this option (which is on by default) ensures that the connection is released for any machine that is inactive for a certain period of time. If used by itself, however, it might lead to a situation where unused connections are released as well, which is why it makes sense to use the ClientAliveInterval option. This option sets an interval, in seconds, after which the server sends a packet to the client if no activity has been detected. The ClientAliveCountMax parameter specifies how many of these packets should be sent. If ClientAliveInterval is set to 30, and ClientAliveCountMax is set to 10, for instance, inactive connections are kept alive for about five minutes. It is a good idea to set this to match the amount of time you want to keep inactive connections open.

The ClientAliveInterval and ClientAliveCountMax options can be specified on a server only. There is a client-side equivalent to these options also. If you cannot change the configuration of the SSH server, use the ServerAliveInterval and ServerAliveCountMax options to initiate connection keepalive traffic from the client machine. These options are set in the /etc/ssh/ssh_config file if they need to be applied for all users on that machine, or in ~/.ssh/config if applied for individual users.

Table 20-2 provides an overview of the most useful SSH options.

Table 20-2 Most Useful sshd Configuration Options

Option	Use
Port	Defines the TCP listening port.
PermitRootLogin	Indicates whether to allow or disallow root login.
MaxAuthTries	Specifies the maximum number of authentication tries. After reaching half of this number, failures are logged to syslog.
MaxSessions	Indicates the maximum number of sessions that can be open from one IP address.
AllowUsers	Specifies a space-separated list of users who are allowed to connect to the server.
PasswordAuthentication	Specifies whether to allow password authentication. This option is on by default.
TCPKeepAlive	Specifies whether or not to clean up inactive TCP connections.
ClientAliveInterval	Specifies the interval, in seconds, that packets are sent to the client to figure out if the client is still alive.
ClientAliveCountMax	Specifies the number of client alive packets that need to be sent.
UseDNS	If on, uses DNS name lookup to match incoming IP addresses to names.
ServerAliveInterval	Specifies the interval, in seconds, at which a client sends a packet to a server to keep connections alive.
ServerAliveCountMax	Specifies the maximum number of packets a client sends to a server to keep connections alive.

Configuring Key-Based Authentication with Passphrases

By default, password authentication is allowed on RHEL SSH servers. If a public/private key pair is used, as explained in Chapter 5, this key pair is used first. If you want to allow public/private key-based authentication only and disable password-based authentication completely, set the PasswordAuthentication option to no.

When you use public/private keys, a passphrase can be used. Using a ***passphrase*** makes the key pair stronger. Not only does an intruder have to get access to the private key, but when he does, he must also know the passphrase to use the key. This is why for establishing client/server connections with public/private keys, it is recommended to use passphrases. Without further configuration, the use of passphrases would mean that users have to enter the passphrase every time before a connection can be created, and that is inconvenient.

To make working with passphrases a bit less complicated, you can cache the passphrase for a session. To do this, you need the **ssh-agent** and **ssh-add** commands. Assuming that the public/private key pair has already been created, this is an easy three-step procedure:

Step 1. Type **ssh-agent /bin/bash** to start the agent for the current (Bash) shell.

Step 2. Type **ssh-add** to add the passphrase for the current user's private key. The key is now cached.

Step 3. Connect to the remote server. Notice that there is no longer a need to enter the passphrase.

This procedure needs to be repeated for all new sessions that are created.

Summary

In this chapter, you learned how to configure the SSH server with advanced options. You also learned how to set security options for sshd and how to set specific client options that help in keeping connections alive for a longer period.

Exam Preparation Tasks

As mentioned in the section "How to Use This Book" in the Introduction, you have several choices for exam preparation: the end-of-chapter labs; the memory tables in Appendix C; Chapter 27, "Final Preparation"; and the practice exams.

Review All Key Topics

Review the most important topic in the chapter, noted with the Key Topic icon in the margin of the page. Table 20-3 lists a reference for this key topic and the page number on which it is found.

Table 20-3 Key Topic for Chapter 20

Key Topic Element	Description	Page
Table 20-2	Most Useful sshd Configuration Options	447

Complete Tables and Lists from Memory

Print a copy of Appendix C, "Memory Tables" (found on the companion website), or at least the section for this chapter, and complete the tables and lists from memory. Appendix D, "Memory Tables Answer Key," includes completed tables and lists to check your work.

Define Key Terms

Define the following key terms from this chapter and check your answers in the glossary:

connection, passphrase

Review Questions

The questions that follow are meant to help you test your knowledge of concepts and terminology and the breadth of your knowledge. You can find the answers to these questions in Appendix A.

1. Which two commands do you need to cache the passphrase that is set on your private key?
2. You want to disallow root login and only allow user lisa to log in to your server. How would you do that?
3. How do you configure your SSH server to listen on two different ports?
4. What is the name of the main SSH configuration file?
5. When configuring a cache to store the passphrase for your key, where will this passphrase be stored?
6. What is the name of the file that contains SSH client settings for all users?
7. Which setting should you use to set the maximum number of concurrent SSH sessions to 10?
8. How do you configure SELinux to allow SSH to bind to port 2022?
9. How do you configure the firewall on the SSH server to allow incoming connections to port 2022?
10. Which setting could you use if you experience long timeouts while trying to establish an SSH connection?

End-of-Chapter Lab

In this end-of-chapter lab, you configure SSH for enhanced security and optimized connection settings. Use server1 to set up the SSH server, and use server2 as the SSH client.

Lab 20.1

1. Configure your SSH server in such a way that inactive sessions will be kept open for at least one hour.
2. Secure your SSH server so that it listens on port 2022 only and that only user lisa is allowed to log in.
3. Test the settings from server2. Make sure that the firewall as well as SELinux are configured to support your settings.

The following topics are covered in this chapter:

- Configuring a Basic Apache Server
- Understanding Apache Configuration Files
- Creating Apache Virtual Hosts

Managing Apache HTTP Services

This chapter discusses a subject that is not listed in the RHCSA objectives. However, for a Red Hat server administrator, it is important to know how to deal with the Apache web service. In Chapter 22, "Managing SELinux," you'll learn how to configure SELinux. To learn about SELinux, it is convenient to also know a bit about services that can be secured with SELinux, which is why it is useful to know how to configure an Apache server. Also, in Chapter 11, "Working with Systemd," you learned how to work with services in an RHEL environment. Knowing how to configure a common service like the Apache web service will surely help you to do so. That is why this chapter explains Apache web server basics.

"Do I Know This Already?" Quiz

The "Do I Know This Already?" quiz enables you to assess whether you should read this entire chapter thoroughly or jump to the "Exam Preparation Tasks" section. If you are in doubt about your answers to these questions or your own assessment of your knowledge of the topics, read the entire chapter. Table 21-1 lists the major headings in this chapter and their corresponding "Do I Know This Already?" quiz questions. You can find the answers in Appendix A, "Answers to the 'Do I Know This Already?' Quizzes and Review Questions."

Table 21-1 "Do I Know This Already?" Section-to-Question Mapping

Foundation Topics Section	Questions
Configuring a Basic Apache Server	1–4
Understanding Apache Configuration Files	5–7
Creating Apache Virtual Hosts	8–10

1. Which command installs the software packages that are needed to configure an Apache web server?
   a. **dnf install httpd**
   b. **dnf install web-server**
   c. **dnf install apache**
   d. **dnf install apache2**

2. What is the name of the main Apache configuration file?
   a. /etc/httpd/conf/httpd.conf
   b. /etc/httpd/httpd.conf
   c. /etc/apache2/apache.conf
   d. /etc/httpd/default-server.conf

3. Which parameter in the Apache configuration file is used to specify where Apache will serve its documents from?
   a. ServerRoot
   b. ServerDocuments
   c. DocumentRoot
   d. DocumentIndex

4. Which parameter in the main Apache configuration file defines the location where the Apache process looks for its configuration files?
   a. ServerRoot
   b. ServerDocuments
   c. DocumentRoot
   d. DocumentIndex

5. Which directory contains the main Apache configuration file?
   a. /etc/httpd
   b. /etc/httpd/conf
   c. /etc/httpd/conf.d
   d. /etc/httpd/conf.modules.d

6. Which directory contains the configuration files for the different Apache modules?
   a. /etc/httpd
   b. /etc/httpd/conf
   c. /etc/httpd/conf.d
   d. /etc/httpd/conf.modules.d

7. Which directory is used to drop configuration files that are installed from RPMs?
   a. /etc/httpd
   b. /etc/httpd/conf
   c. /etc/httpd/conf.d
   d. /etc/httpd/conf.modules.d

8. Which virtual host type allows you to run multiple virtual hosts on the same IP address?
   a. Name-based
   b. IP-based
   c. Configuration-based
   d. Default

9. Which line is used to start the definition of a virtual host that listens on port 80 of all IP addresses on the current server?
   a. <VirtualHost *:80>
   b. <VirtualHost *>
   c. <NameHost *:80
   d. <NameHost *>

10. Which of the following statements about virtual hosts is *not* true?
    a. When virtual hosts are offered through an httpd process, the default configuration no longer works.
    b. The names of virtual hosts must be resolvable through /etc/hosts or DNS.
    c. To use virtual hosts, the mod_virt package must be installed.
    d. Virtual host configurations can be specified in httpd.conf.

Foundation Topics

Configuring a Basic Apache Server

Configuring a basic Apache server is not hard to do. It consists of a few easy steps:

Step 1. Install the required software.

Step 2. Identify the main configuration file.

Step 3. Create some web server content.

Installing the Required Software

The Apache server is provided through some different software packages. The basic package is httpd, which contains everything that is needed for an operational but basic web server. There are some additional packages, as well. Use **dnf group install "Basic Web Server"** to install all relevant packages in one command.

Identifying the Main Configuration File

The configuration of the Apache web server goes through different configuration files. The section "Understanding Apache Configuration Files" later in this chapter provides an overview of the way these files are organized. The main Apache configuration file is /etc/httpd/conf/httpd.conf. In this file, many parameters are specified. The most important parameter to understand for setting up a basic web server is the ***DocumentRoot*** parameter. This parameter specifies the default location where the Apache web server looks for its contents.

Another important configuration parameter is the ServerRoot. This defines the default directory where Apache will look for its configuration files. By default, the /etc/httpd directory is used for this purpose, but alternative directories can be used as well. Many other configuration files are referenced in the httpd.conf file, a portion of which is shown in Example 21-1. The use of additional configuration files makes it easy for applications to install drop-in files that will be included by the Apache server from RPM packages. The names of all these configuration files are relative to the ServerRoot /etc/httpd.

Example 21-1 Partial Contents of the /etc/httpd/conf/httpd.conf Configuration File

```
[root@localhost ~]# grep -v '#' /etc/httpd/conf/httpd.conf

ServerRoot "/etc/httpd"

Listen 80

Include conf.modules.d/*.conf

User apache
Group apache

ServerAdmin root@localhost

<Directory />
    AllowOverride none
    Require all denied
</Directory>

DocumentRoot "/var/www/html"

<Directory "/var/www">
    AllowOverride None
    Require all granted
</Directory>

<Directory "/var/www/html">
    Options Indexes FollowSymLinks

    AllowOverride None

    Require all granted
</Directory>

<IfModule dir_module>
    DirectoryIndex index.html
</IfModule>

<Files ".ht*">
    Require all denied
</Files>
```

```
ErrorLog "logs/error_log"

LogLevel warn

<IfModule log_config_module>
    LogFormat "%h %l %u %t \"%r\" %>s %b \"%{Referer}i\" \"%
  {User-Agent}i\"" combined
    LogFormat "%h %l %u %t \"%r\" %>s %b" common

    <IfModule logio_module>
      LogFormat "%h %l %u %t \"%r\" %>s %b \"%{Referer}i\" \"%
  {User-Agent}i\" %I %O" combinedio
    </IfModule>



    CustomLog "logs/access_log" combined
</IfModule>

<IfModule alias_module>



    ScriptAlias /cgi-bin/ "/var/www/cgi-bin/"

</IfModule>

<Directory "/var/www/cgi-bin">
    AllowOverride None
    Options None
    Require all granted
</Directory>

<IfModule mime_module>
    TypesConfig /etc/mime.types

    AddType application/x-compress .Z
    AddType application/x-gzip .gz .tgz



    AddType text/html .shtml
    AddOutputFilter INCLUDES .shtml
</IfModule>
AddDefaultCharset UTF-8
```

```
<IfModule mime_magic_module>
    MIMEMagicFile conf/magic
</IfModule>

EnableSendfile on
IncludeOptional conf.d/*.conf
```

Creating Web Server Content

After identifying the web server DocumentRoot, you know all you need to know to configure a basic web server. The Apache web server by default looks for a file with the name index.html and will present the contents of that document to clients using a browser to access the web server. It suffices to configure this file with very basic contents; just a line like "Welcome to my web server" will do.

To test the web server, you can launch a browser. The Firefox browser is installed by default on all graphical installations of RHEL 9. If your server does not run a graphical interface, use **dnf install curl** to work with Apache from the command line.

In Exercise 21-1, you learn how to set up a basic Apache web server—nothing fancy, just enough to get you going and test web server functionality.

Exercise 21-1 Setting Up a Basic Web Server

1. Type **dnf install httpd**
2. Open the main Apache configuration file with an editor, and look up the line that starts with DocumentRoot. This line identifies the location where the Apache server will look for the contents it will service. Confirm that it is set to /var/www/html.
3. In the directory /var/www/html, create a file with the name **index.html**. In this file, type the following: **Welcome to my web server**.
4. To start and enable the web server, type **systemctl enable --now httpd**. This starts the web server and makes sure that it starts automatically after restarting the server. Use **systemctl status httpd** to check that the web server is up and running. In Example 21-2 you can see what the result of this command should look like.
5. Type **dnf install curl** to install the elinks text-based browser. Type **curl http://localhost** to connect to the web server and verify it is working.

Example 21-2 Verifying the Availability of the Apache Web Server with **systemctl status**

```
[root@localhost ~]# systemctl status httpd
   httpd.service - The Apache HTTP Server
   Loaded: loaded (/usr/lib/systemd/system/httpd.service; enabled;
  vendor preset: disabled)
   Active: active (running) since Fri 2022-07-05 03:06:02 EDT; 2s ago
     Docs: man:httpd.service(8)
   Main PID: 4540 (httpd)
   Status: "Started, listening on: port 443, port 80"
    Tasks: 213 (limit: 11222)
   Memory: 24.2M
   CGroup: /system.slice/httpd.service
           |-4540 /usr/sbin/httpd -DFOREGROUND
           |-4542 /usr/sbin/httpd -DFOREGROUND
           |-4543 /usr/sbin/httpd -DFOREGROUND
           |-4544 /usr/sbin/httpd -DFOREGROUND
           |-4545 /usr/sbin/httpd -DFOREGROUND

Jul 05 03:06:02 localhost.localdomain systemd[1]: Starting The Apache
  HTTP Server...
Jul 05 03:06:02 localhost.localdomain httpd[4540]: AH00558: httpd:
  Could not reliably determine the server'>
Jul 05 03:06:02 localhost.localdomain httpd[4540]: Server configured,
  listening on: port 443, port 80
Jul 05 03:06:02 localhost.localdomain systemd[1]: Started The Apache
  HTTP Server.
```

Understanding Apache Configuration Files

A default installation of the Apache web server creates a relatively complex configuration tree in the /etc/httpd directory. Example 21-3 shows the default contents of this directory. The contents of this directory may differ on your server if additional software has been installed. Apache is modular, and upon installation of additional Apache modules, different configuration files might be installed here.

Example 21-3 Default Contents of the /etc/httpd Directory

```
[root@server1 httpd]# ls -l
total 8
drwxr-xr-x. 2 root root 35 Feb 23 03:12 conf
drwxr-xr-x. 2 root root 4096 Feb 25 12:41 conf.d
drwxr-xr-x. 2 root root 4096 Feb 25 12:41 conf.modules.d
lrwxrwxrwx. 1 root root 19 Feb 17 13:26 logs -> ../../var/log/httpd
lrwxrwxrwx. 1 root root 29 Feb 17 13:26 modules -> ../../usr/lib64/
  httpd/modules
lrwxrwxrwx. 1 root root 10 Feb 17 13:26 run -> /run/httpd
```

The first thing you notice is the presence of three symbolic links to logs, modules, and a run directory. These are created to allow Apache to be started in a chroot environment.

A ***chroot*** environment provides a fake root directory. This is a directory in the file system that is presented as the root directory for the process that is running in the chroot environment. This is done for security reasons: processes that are running in a chroot environment can access files in that chroot environment only, which decreases the risk of security incidents occurring when intruders manage to get a login shell using the web server identity and try walking through the file system to do unauthorized things.

The main configuration files for the Apache web server are in the /etc/httpd/conf directory. To start, the httpd.conf file contains the most important configuration parameters. Apart from that, there is a file with the name magic. This file is used by the browser to interpret how the contents of the web server should be displayed. It makes sure that the web server content is shown correctly in different browsers.

The /etc/httpd/conf.d directory contains files that are included in the Apache configuration. Files are added by the line Include conf.d/*.conf in the httpd.conf file. This directory can be used by RPMs that include Apache drop-in files. As is the case for the ServerRoot, this approach makes it possible to add configuration files that define the different web pages without changing the contents of the /etc/httpd/conf/httpd.conf file.

The last configuration directory is /etc/httpd/conf.modules.d. Apache is a modular web server. Therefore, the functionality of the Apache web server can easily be extended by adding additional modules that enable many different features. If modules are used, they can use their own module-specific configuration files, which will be dropped in the /etc/httpd/conf.modules.d directory. Again, the purpose of this approach is to keep the configuration in /etc/httpd/conf/httpd.conf as clean as possible and to make sure that module-specific configuration is not overwritten if the Apache generic configuration is updated.

Creating Apache Virtual Hosts

Many companies host more than one website. Fortunately, it is not necessary to install a new Apache server for every website that you want to run. Apache can be configured to work with virtual hosts. A ***virtual host*** is a distinct Apache configuration file or section that is created for a unique hostname. When you're working with virtual hosts, the procedure to access the host is roughly like the following:

1. The client starts a session to a specific virtual host, normally by starting a browser and entering the URL to the website the client wants to use.
2. DNS helps resolve the IP address of the virtual host, which is the IP address of the Apache server that can host different virtual hosts.
3. The Apache process receives requests for all the virtual hosts it is hosting.
4. The Apache process reads the HTTP header of each request to analyze which virtual host this request needs to be forwarded to.
5. Apache reads the specific virtual host configuration file to find which document root is used by this specific virtual host.
6. The request is forwarded to the appropriate contents file in that specific document root.

When you're working with virtual hosts, there are a few things to be aware of:

- If your Apache server is configured for virtual hosts, all servers it is hosting should be handled by virtual hosts. To create a catch-all entry for all HTTP requests that are directed to this host but that do not have a specific virtual host file, you can create a virtual host for _default_:80. If you don't do that, packets that successfully arrive on your server via DNS name resolution but don't find a matching virtual host are sent to the virtual host whose configuration the Apache process finds first. That leads to unpredicted results.
- Name-based virtual hosting is the most common solution. In this solution, virtual hosts use different names but the same IP address.
- IP-based virtual hosts are less common but are required if the name of a web server must be resolved to a unique IP address. IP-based virtual hosts do require several IP addresses on the same machine and are common in configurations where the Apache server uses TLS to secure connections.

Configuring virtual hosts is not an RHCSA objective, but it is useful to know how to configure them as a Linux administrator. Therefore, Exercise 21-2 walks you through the procedure.

Exercise 21-2 Configuring Apache Virtual Hosts

In this exercise, you create two virtual hosts. To set up virtual hosts, you first set up name resolution, after which you create the virtual hosts' configuration. Because SELinux has not been discussed yet, you temporarily switch off SELinux.

> **NOTE** I later tell you that you should never switch off SELinux. For once, I make an exception to this important security rule. To focus on what needs to be done on the Apache web server, it is easier to focus just on Apache and not to configure SELinux as well.

1. On both server1 and server2, open the file /etc/hosts with an editor and add two lines that make it possible to resolve the names of the virtual host you are going to create to the IP address of the virtual machine:

```
192.168.4.210 server1.example.com server1
192.168.4.220 server2.example.com server2
192.168.4.210 account.example.com account
192.168.4.210 sales.example.com sales
```

2. On server1, open a root shell and add the following to the /etc/httpd/conf/httpd.conf file. (You can leave all other settings as they are.)

```
<Directory /www/docs>
        Require all granted
        AllowOverride None
</Directory>
```

3. On server1, open a root shell and create a configuration file with the name **account.example.com.conf** in the directory /etc/httpd/conf.d. Give this file the following content:

```
<VirtualHost *:80>
        ServerAdmin webmaster@account.example.com
        DocumentRoot /www/docs/account.example.com
        ServerName account.example.com
        ErrorLog logs/account.example.com-error_log
        CustomLog logs/account.example.com-access_log common
</VirtualHost>
```

4. Close the configuration file, and from the root shell type **mkdir -p /www/docs/account.example.com**
5. Create a file with the name **index.html** in the account document root, and make sure its contents reads as follows: Welcome to account.
6. Temporarily switch off SELinux using **setenforce 0**.

7. Use **systemctl restart httpd** to restart the Apache web server.
8. Use **curl http://account.example.com**. You should now see the account welcome page. (You may have to install curl, using **dnf install -y curl**.)
9. Back on the root shell, copy the /etc/httpd/conf.d/account.example.com.conf file to a file with the name /etc/httpd/conf.d/sales.example.com.conf.
10. Open the sales.example.com.conf file in **vi**, and use the **vi** command **:%s/account/sales/g**. This should replace all instances of "account" with "sales."
11. Create the **/www/docs/sales.example.com** document root, and create a file **index.html** in it, containing the text "Welcome to the sales server."
12. Restart httpd and verify that both the account and the sales servers are accessible.

Summary

In this chapter, you learned about Apache basics. The information in this chapter helps you configure a basic Apache web server, which helps with testing advanced topics like firewall configuration or SELinux configuration that are covered in subsequent chapters.

Exam Preparation Tasks

As mentioned in the section "How to Use This Book" in the Introduction, you have several choices for exam preparation: the end-of-chapter labs; the memory tables in Appendix C; Chapter 27, "Final Preparation"; and the practice exams.

Review All Key Topics

Review the most important topics in the chapter, noted with the Key Topic icon in the margin of the page. Table 21-2 lists a reference for these key topics and the page number on which each is found.

Table 21-2 Key Topics for Chapter 21

Key Topic Element	Description	Page
Paragraph	chroot environment explanation	461
List	Virtual host explanation	462

Define Key Terms

Define the following key terms from this chapter and check your answers in the glossary:

DocumentRoot, chroot, virtual host

Review Questions

The questions that follow are meant to help you test your knowledge of concepts and terminology and the breadth of your knowledge. You can find the answers to these questions in Appendix A.

1. Which **dnf** group can be used to install Apache and relevant related packages?
2. How do you enable the httpd service to be started automatically when booting?
3. What is the default location where RPMs can drop plug-in configuration files that should be considered by the Apache server?
4. Which command enables you to test a web server from a server that does not offer a graphical interface?
5. What is the name of the default Apache configuration file?
6. Which directory is used as the default Apache document root?
7. Which file does the Apache process look for by default in the document root?
8. Which command enables you to see whether the Apache web server is currently running?
9. Which location is preferable for storing virtual host configuration files?
10. Names of configuration files and directories in the main Apache configuration file are relative to the ServerRoot. To which directory is the ServerRoot set by default?

End-of-Chapter Lab

In this end-of-chapter lab, you install and configure a basic Apache web server.

Lab 21.1

1. Install the required packages that allow you to run a basic web server. Make sure that the web server process is started automatically when your server reboots. Do *not* use a virtual server.
2. Use **curl** to make sure the web server presents a default page showing "Welcome to my web server."
3. Type **dnf install httpd-manual** to install the Apache documentation.
4. Use a browser to test access to the /manual web page on your server.

The following topics are covered in this chapter:

- Understanding SELinux Working Modes
- Understanding Context Settings and the Policy
- Restoring Default File Contexts
- Managing Port Access
- Using Boolean Settings to Modify SELinux Settings
- Diagnosing and Addressing SELinux Policy Violations

The following RHCSA exam objectives are covered in this chapter:

- Set enforcing and permissive modes for SELinux
- List and identify SELinux file and process context
- Restore default file contexts
- Use Boolean settings to modify system SELinux settings
- Diagnose and address routine SELinux policy violations
- Manage SELinux port labels

CHAPTER 22

Managing SELinux

Since the earliest days of Linux, file permissions have been the standard method of securing Linux systems. In some cases, file permissions are just not enough to secure a server fully. Let's take a look at an example:

> One morning I found out that my server was hacked. An intruder had broken through a bad script on my web server and had obtained shell access as the httpd user—this was possible due to a bug in the shell code that I was using. Using this file access, the intruder managed to create thousands of little PHP scripts that were involved in a massive DDoS attack.

From a security perspective, it is interesting that nothing really was wrong with the security settings on this server. All permissions were set in a decent way, and the httpd user, like any other user on a Linux server, does have permissions to create files in /var/tmp, as in /tmp. So, what would have been a good solution to prevent this kind of problem?

You could, of course, argue that the administrator of the web server should have been doing a better job and should have been watching what the scripts on the server were doing. But that is not how Linux servers are normally used. The Linux server administrator does not necessarily have in-depth knowledge of the internals of all the applications running on the Linux server, and the application administrator does not understand enough about Linux to ensure that something like this can never happen.

Another solution is to apply further security measures. For instance, this specific situation would have been prevented if the permission to run program files from the /tmp and /var/tmp directory had been taken away by using the **noexec mount** option. But even if that would have worked for this specific situation, it is not a good overall security solution that prevents applications from doing things they are not supposed to be doing. Basically, Linux just needs a default security solution that covers all settings.

That is why SELinux was invented. SELinux provides mandatory access control to a Linux server, where every system call is denied unless it has been specifically allowed. This chapter explains how to use SELinux to make sure that serious security incidents will never happen on your server.

TIP By any means, make sure that at the end of the exam SELinux is working on your server. If it is not, it will cost you many points!

"Do I Know This Already?" Quiz

The "Do I Know This Already?" quiz enables you to assess whether you should read this entire chapter thoroughly or jump to the "Exam Preparation Tasks" section. If you are in doubt about your answers to these questions or your own assessment of your knowledge of the topics, read the entire chapter. Table 22-1 lists the major headings in this chapter and their corresponding "Do I Know This Already?" quiz questions. You can find the answers in Appendix A, "Answers to the 'Do I Know This Already?' Quizzes and Review Questions."

Table 22-1 "Do I Know This Already?" Section-to-Question Mapping

Foundation Topics Section	Questions
Understanding SELinux Working Modes	1–2
Understanding Context Settings and the Policy	3–5
Restoring Default File Contexts	6
Managing Port Access	7
Using Boolean Settings to Modify SELinux Settings	8
Diagnosing and Addressing SELinux Policy Violations	9–10

1. Which of the following allows you to set SELinux in disabled mode in RHEL 9?
   a. From a root shell, use **setenforce 0**
   b. Use the GRUB kernel boot argument **selinux=0**
   c. Set **selinux=disabled** in /etc/sysconfig/selinux
   d. Remove the SELinux packages using **dnf remove selinux**

2. Which of the following commands enable you to see the current SELinux mode? (Choose two.)
   a. **sestatus**
   b. **lsmode**
   c. **semode**
   d. **getenforce**

3. Which of the following items in the context label is the most significant for SELinux system administration tasks?
   a. Type
   b. User
   c. Role
   d. Mission

4. Which command-line switch is used with many commands to display SELinux-related information?
   a. **-S**
   b. **-X**
   c. **-Z**
   d. **-D**

5. Which of the following commands should be used to set the context type of the directory /web to httpd_sys_content_t?
   a. **chcon -t httpd_sys_content_t /web**
   b. **semanage -t httpd_sys_content_t "/web(/.*)?"**
   c. **semanage fcontext -t httpd_sys_content_t "/web(/.*)?"**
   d. **semanage fcontext -a -t httpd_sys_content_t "/web(/.*)?"**

6. Which command must you run to ensure that a file has the appropriate SELinux context after moving the file to another location?
   a. **reboot**
   b. **restorecon /new/filename**
   c. **chcon**
   d. **restorecon -R /etc/selinux -v**

7. While setting a port context using **semanage port -a -t ssh_port_t -p tcp 443**, you get an error message telling you that the port is already defined. Which of the following statements is true?
   a. You cannot change a default port setting like 443, as it is used already for https.
   b. You have already issued the command earlier.
   c. You need to use **-m** to modify the port context, not **-a** to add it.
   d. The syntax you use is incorrect.

8. Which command enables you to change a Boolean in a way that it survives a reboot?
   a. **chcon boolean -P**
   b. **setsebool -P**
   c. **setsebool**
   d. **semanage boolean**
9. Which file contains all the information you need to troubleshoot SELinux messages?
   a. /var/log/audit/audit.log
   b. /var/log/selinux/selinux.log
   c. /var/log/messages
   d. /var/log/selinux.log
10. You want to grep the audit log for SELinux log messages. Which of the following strings should you use **grep** on?
    a. selinux
    b. deny
    c. violation
    d. AVC

Foundation Topics

Understanding SELinux Working Modes

If SELinux is enabled and nothing else has been configured, all system calls are denied. To specify what exactly is allowed, a policy is used. In this policy, rules define which source domain is allowed to access which target domain. The source domain is the object that is trying to access something. Typically, this is a process or a user. The target domain is the object that is accessed. Typically, that is a file, a directory, or a network port. To define exactly what is allowed, context labels are used. Using these labels is the essence of SELinux because these labels are used to define access rules. Table 22-2 summarizes the most important SELinux building blocks.

Table 22-2 SELinux Core Elements

Element	Use
Policy	A collection of rules that define which source has access to which target.
Source domain	The object that is trying to access a target. Typically a user or a process.
Target domain	The thing that a source domain is trying to access. Typically a file or a port.
Context	A security label that is used to categorize objects in SELinux.
Rule	A specific part of the policy that determines which source domain has which access permissions to which target domain.
Label	Also referred to as context label, defined to determine which source domain has access to which target domain.

On a Linux system, you can choose to enable or disable SELinux. When SELinux is enabled, kernel support for SELinux is loaded, and some applications that are SELinux aware change their behavior, because specific libraries are used on a system that has SELinux enabled. If SELinux is disabled, no SELinux activity happens at all. Changing between SELinux enabled mode and SELinux disabled mode requires a reboot of your system. The reason is that SELinux is a feature that is deeply interwoven with the Linux kernel.

If on a system SELinux is enabled, you can select to put SELinux in enforcing mode or in permissive mode. In ***enforcing*** mode, SELinux is fully operational and enforcing all SELinux rules in the policy. If SELinux is in permissive mode, all SELinux-related activity is logged, but no access is blocked. This makes SELinux permissive mode an excellent mode to do troubleshooting, but it also makes your system temporarily insecure. ***Permissive*** mode is also a great way to do something and see the result from an SELinux perspective by analyzing the messages that are written to /var/log/audit/audit.log. That can help in building new and more efficient policies.

To set the default SELinux mode while booting, use the file /etc/sysconfig/selinux. Example 22-1 shows the content of this file.

Example 22-1 Content of the /etc/sysconfig/selinux File

```
[root@server1 ~]# cat /etc/sysconfig/selinux

# This file controls the state of SELinux on the system.
# SELINUX= can take one of these three values:
#     enforcing - SELinux security policy is enforced.
#     permissive - SELinux prints warnings instead of enforcing.
#     disabled - No SELinux policy is loaded.
# See also:

# https://docs.fedoraproject.org/en-US/quick-docs/getting-started-
  with-selinux/#getting-started-with-selinux-selinux-states-and-modes
#
# NOTE: In earlier Fedora kernel builds, SELINUX=disabled would also
# fully disable SELinux during boot. If you need a system with
  SELinux
# fully disabled instead of SELinux running with no policy loaded,
  you
# need to pass selinux=0 to the kernel command line. You can use
  grubby
# to persistently set the bootloader to boot with selinux=0:
#
#    grubby --update-kernel ALL --args selinux=0
#
# To revert back to SELinux enabled:
#
#    grubby --update-kernel ALL --remove-args selinux
#
SELINUX=enforcing
# SELINUXTYPE= can take one of these three values:
#     targeted - Targeted processes are protected,
#     minimum - Modification of targeted policy. Only selected
  processes are protected.
#     mls - Multi Level Security protection.
SELINUXTYPE=targeted
```

As you can see, in this file, which is read while booting, you can choose to put SELinux in enforcing or permissive mode. On older versions of RHEL, it was possible to define disabled mode as a default; in RHEL 9 this can no longer be done. To put SELinux in disabled mode, use the GRUB kernel boot argument **selinux=0**. You can also set permissive mode from the GRUB shell, by passing the kernel boot option **enforcing=0**.

On a server that currently has SELinux enabled, you can use the **getenforce** command to see whether SELinux currently is in enforcing mode or in permissive mode. To switch between permissive mode and enforcing mode, you can use **setenforce**. The command **setenforce 0** temporarily puts SELinux in permissive mode, and **setenforce 1** puts SELinux temporarily in enforcing mode. To change the default mode persistently, you need to write it to /etc/sysconfig/selinux, or change GRUB kernel boot arguments.

Another useful command is **sestatus**. If used with the option **-v**, this command shows detailed information about the current status of SELinux on a server. Example 22-2 shows the output of the **sestatus -v** command. It not only shows you which parts of SELinux are enabled but also shows the current version of the policy that is loaded and the context labels for some critical parts of the system.

Example 22-2 Using **sestatus -v** to Get Detailed Information About the Current Protection Status

```
[root@server1 ~]# sestatus -v
SELinux status:                 enabled
SELinuxfs mount:                /sys/fs/selinux
SELinux root directory:         /etc/selinux
Loaded policy name:             targeted
Current mode:                   enforcing
Mode from config file:          enforcing
Policy MLS status:              enabled
Policy deny_unknown status:     allowed
Memory protection checking:     actual (secure)
Max kernel policy version:      33

Process contexts:
Current context:                unconfined_u:unconfined_r:unconfined_
  t:s0-s0:c0.c1023
Init context:                   system_u:system_r:init_t:s0
/usr/sbin/sshd                  system_u:system_r:sshd_t:s0-s0:c0.
  c1023
```

```
File contexts:
Controlling terminal:          unconfined_u:object_r:user_devpts_t:s0
/etc/passwd                    system_u:object_r:passwd_file_t:s0
/etc/shadow                    system_u:object_r:shadow_t:s0
/bin/bash                      system_u:object_r:shell_exec_t:s0
/bin/login                     system_u:object_r:login_exec_t:s0
/bin/sh                        system_u:object_r:bin_t:s0 ->
  system_u:object_r:shell_exec_t:s0
/sbin/agetty                   system_u:object_r:getty_exec_t:s0
/sbin/init                     system_u:object_r:bin_t:s0 ->
  system_u:object_r:init_exec_t:s0
/usr/sbin/sshd                 system_u:object_r:sshd_exec_t:s0
```

In Exercise 22-1, you practice working with the different modes.

Exercise 22-1 Manipulating SELinux Modes

1. Open a root console on your server and type **getenforce**. You'll normally see that SELinux is in enforcing mode. If the output of **getenforce** shows Disabled, edit the /etc/default/grub file and add the argument **selinux=1** to the line that starts the Linux kernel (it is the line that starts with the word **linux**). Then save the file and use the command **grub2-mkconfig -o /boot/grub2/grub.cfg** and reboot the system before you continue.
2. Type **setenforce 0** and type **getenforce** again. SELinux now switches to permissive mode.
3. Type **setenforce 1** and verify that SELinux is back to enforcing mode.
4. Type **sestatus -v** and read current status information about SELinux.

Note that on real Red Hat servers, SELinux on occasion is set to be disabled. Putting SELinux in disabled mode certainly makes it easier for administrators to run their applications. However, it also makes the server much less secure. Often, ignorance of the system administrator is the only reason SELinux is put in disabled mode. If an application vendor tells you that the application is supported only if SELinux is disabled, that often simply means the application vendor has no knowledge about SELinux. Advanced administrators can use **sepolicy generate** to allow almost any application to run in an environment where SELinux is enabled.

A fully enforcing system is especially important if your server is accessed directly by users from the Internet. If your server cannot be reached directly from the Internet and is in a safe internal network, having SELinux enabled is not strictly necessary (but I recommend always keeping it in enforcing mode anyway). On the RHCSA exam, however, you must make sure that SELinux is enabled and fully protecting your server.

Understanding Context Settings and the Policy

Context settings are an important part of SELinux operations. The context is a label that can be applied to different objects:

- Files and directories
- Ports
- Processes
- Users

Context labels define the nature of the object, and SELinux rules are created to match context labels of source objects (often referred to as source domains) to the context labels of target objects (referred to as target domains). So, setting correct context labels is a very important skill for system administrators. You learn how to do that later in this chapter.

> **NOTE** Managing SELinux context labels is a key skill for securing systems with SELinux. It is not listed in the RHCSA exam objectives though. Nevertheless, I'll give you a decent explanation of how context labels work, because a mismatch of context labels can create lots of SELinux-related problems.

Monitoring Current Context Labels

To see current context settings on the objects in the previous bulleted list, many commands offer support for the **-Z** option. In Example 22-3, you see how **ls -Z** shows context settings for some directories in the / file system. Other commands also support the **-Z** option to show current context label settings. Some examples are **ps Zaux**, which shows a list of all processes, including their context label, and **ss -Ztul**, which shows all network ports and the current context label associated with each port.

Example 22-3 Displaying Context Labels on Files with **ls -Z**

```
[root@server1 /]# ls -Z
      system_u:object_r:bin_t:s0 bin     unconfined_u:object_r:
  default_t:s0 repo
      system_u:object_r:boot_t:s0 boot      system_u:object_r:admin_
  home_t:s0 root
    system_u:object_r:device_t:s0 dev         system_u:object_r:var_
  run_t:s0 run
      system_u:object_r:etc_t:s0 etc      system_u:object_r:bin_t:
  s0 sbin
  system_u:object_r:unlabeled_t:s0 files
  system_u:object_r:var_t:  s0 srv
  system_u:object_r:home_root_t:s0 home
  system_u:object_r:root_t:  s0 stratis
      system_u:object_r:lib_t:s0 lib     system_u:object_r:unlabeled_
  t:s0 stratis1
      system_u:object_r:lib_t:s0 lib64      system_u:object_r:sysfs_t:
   s0 sys
      system_u:object_r:mnt_t:s0 media      system_u:object_r:tmp_t:
  s0 tmp
      system_u:object_r:mnt_t:s0 mnt      system_u:object_r:usr_t:
  s0 usr
      system_u:object_r:usr_t:s0 opt      system_u:object_r:var_t:
  s0 var
     system_u:object_r:proc_t:s0 proc       system_u:object_r:
  unlabeled_t:s0 vdo1
```

Every context label always consists of three different parts:

- **User:** The user can be recognized by _u in the context label; it is set to system_u on most directories in Example 22-3. SELinux users are not the same as Linux users, and they are not important on the RHCSA exam.
- **Role:** The role can be recognized by _r in the context label. In Example 22-3, most objects are labeled with the object_r role. In advanced SELinux management, specific SELinux users can be assigned permissions to specific SELinux roles. For the RHCSA exam, you do not have to know how to configure roles.
- **Type:** The type context can be recognized by _t in the context label. In Example 22-3, you can see that a wide variety of context types are applied to the directories in the / file system. Make sure that you know how to work with context types, because they are what the RHCSA exam expects you to know.

TIP Just to make sure that you are focusing on the parts that really matter on the RHCSA exam, you need to work with context types only. You can safely ignore the user and role parts of the context label.

Setting Context Types

As an administrator, you need to know how to set ***context types*** on target domains. If currently your application is not working as expected, you can often make it work correctly by setting the appropriate context on the target domain. In RHCSA, this is the key SELinux skill that you should master.

You can set context types on files and directories and other objects such as network ports. Let's focus on that task first.

There are two commands to set context type:

- **semanage:** This is the command you want to use. The **semanage** command writes the new context to the SELinux policy, from which it is applied to the file system.
- **chcon:** This command is for use in specific cases only and normally should be avoided. The **chcon** command writes the new context to the file system and not to the policy. Everything that is applied with **chcon** is overwritten when the file system is relabeled, or the original context is restored from the policy to the file system. Do *not* use this command!

NOTE You might want to know why I bother mentioning **chcon** if you should not use it. Well, you'll see the **chcon** command still being referred to in older documentation, which might give the impression that it is a useful command. It is not, because if your file system is relabeled, all changes applied with **chcon** are lost. File system relabeling actions can take you by surprise if you are new to SELinux, and you will fail your exam if by accident file system relabeling happens on a file system where you have applied SELinux context with **chcon**. So, I repeat: do *not* use it.

TIP The **semanage** command may not be installed by default. Fortunately, you can type **dnf whatprovides */semanage** to find the policycoreutils-python-utils RPM package containing **semanage** and then install it. Do not learn the names of all relevant RPMs by heart; just remember **dnf whatprovides**. It will find any RPM you need. See Chapter 9, "Managing Software," for more information about the use of the **dnf** command and package management in general.

To set context using **semanage**, you first need to find the appropriate context (a topic covered in more depth in the next section, "Finding the Context Type You Need"). An easy way to find the appropriate context is by looking at the default context settings on already-existing items. If you want to change the context for a custom web server DocumentRoot, for example, type **ls -Z /var/www** to see the context settings that are set on the default web server DocumentRoot:

```
[root@server1 /]# ls -Z /var/www
drwxr-xr-x. root root system_u:object_r:httpd_sys_script_exec_t:s0
cgi-bin
drwxr-xr-x. root root system_u:object_r:httpd_sys_content_t:s0 html
```

As you can see, the context settings on /var/www/html are set to httpd_sys_content_t. (As a reminder, we're looking only at the context type because the user and role are for advanced use only.) To set this context type to any new directory that you want to use as the DocumentRoot, use the following command:

```
semanage fcontext -a -t httpd_sys_content_t "/mydir(/.*)?"
```

In this command, the option **-a** is used to add a context type. This is what you need to do for all directories that you have created manually. Then you use **-t** to change the context type (as opposed to user and role). The last part of the command is a regular expression, which is used to refer to the directory /mydir and anything that might exist below this directory.

Setting the context in this way is not enough, though, because you'll write it only to the policy and not to the file system. To complete the command, you need to apply the policy setting to the file system, as follows:

```
restorecon -R -v /mydir
```

You'll see that the new context is now applied, which allows the httpd process to access the directory.

TIP The **semanage** command is not the easiest command to remember. Fortunately, it has some excellent man pages. Type **man semanage** and use **G** to go all the way down to the bottom of the man page. You'll now see the "See Also" section, which mentions **semanage-fcontext**, which is about managing file context with **semanage**. Open this man page using **man semanage-fcontext**, type **/example**, and you'll see some pretty examples that mention exactly what you need to know (see Example 22-4).

Example 22-4 semanage fcontext Usage Example from the man Page

```
EXAMPLE
       remember to run restorecon after you set the file context
       Add file-context for everything under /web
       # semanage fcontext -a -t httpd_sys_content_t "/web(/.*)?"
       # restorecon -R -v /web

       Substitute /home1 with /home when setting file context
       # semanage fcontext -a -e /home /home1
       # restorecon -R -v /home1

       For home directories under top level directory, for example
         /disk6/home,
       execute the following commands.
       # semanage fcontext -a -t home_root_t "/disk6"
       # semanage fcontext -a -e /home /disk6/home
       # restorecon -R -v /disk6

SEE ALSO
       selinux (8), semanage (8)
AUTHOR
       This man page was written by Daniel Walsh <dwalsh@redhat.com>
                            20130617       semanage-fcontext(8)
```

Now it is time for an exercise. In Exercise 22-2, you learn how to change the DocumentRoot for the Apache web server and label the new DocumentRoot in the right way.

Exercise 22-2 Setting a Context Label on a Nondefault Apache DocumentRoot

1. Open a root shell and type **dnf install httpd curl -y**.
2. Still from the root shell, type **mkdir /web**.
3. Type **vim /web/index.html** and put the following contents in the file: **welcome to my web server**.
4. Type **vim /etc/httpd/conf/httpd.conf** to open the Apache configuration file and find the **DocumentRoot** parameter. Change it so that it reads **DocumentRoot "/web"**.
5. In the same httpd.conf configuration file, add the following section, as without this section it will be Apache and not SELinux blocking access to the new DocumentRoot:

```
<Directory "/web">
    AllowOverride None
```

```
    Require all granted
&lt;/Directory&gt;
```

6. Type **systemctl enable --now httpd** to start and enable the httpd service. Note that if the httpd service was already running, you'll need to use **systemctl restart httpd** to restart it so that it can pick up the changes you've made to the httpd.conf configuration file.
7. Type **curl http://localhost**. You'll see the default Red Hat web page and not the contents of the index.html file you have just created.
8. Type **setenforce 0** to switch SELinux to permissive mode.
9. Repeat step 7. You'll now get access to your custom web page, which proves that SELinux was doing something to block access.
10. Type **semanage fcontext -a -t httpd_sys_content_t "/web(/.*)?"** to apply the new context label to /web.
11. Type **restorecon -R -v /web**. The **-v** (verbose) option ensures that you see what is happening and that you will see the new context being applied to /web.
12. Set SELinux back in enforcing mode, using **setenforce 1**.
13. Type **curl http://localhost**. You'll get access to your custom web page because SELinux now allows access to it.

Finding the Context Type You Need

One of the challenging parts of setting SELinux contexts is finding the context you need. Roughly, there are three approaches:

- Look at the default environment.
- Read the configuration files.
- Use **man -k _selinux** to find SELinux-specific man pages for your service.

The most powerful way of getting the SELinux information you need is by using **man -k _selinux**, which searches the database of man pages for those that match _selinux in the name or description of the man page. On RHEL 9, however, these man pages are not installed by default. To install them, you need to install the selinux-policy-doc package. In Exercise 22-3 you'll learn how to do this and use the SELinux man pages.

Exercise 22-3 Installing SELinux-Specific Man Pages

1. Type **man -k _selinux**. You'll probably see just one or two man pages.
2. Type **dnf search selinux**. This will show several packages, including the selinux-policy-doc package.
3. Install this package by using **dnf install selinux-policy-doc**
4. Type **man -k _selinux**. You should now see a long list of man pages.
5. In case that **man -k _selinux** does not show a list of man pages, type **mandb** to update the database that contains names and descriptions of all man pages that are installed.
6. Once the **mandb** command has finished (this can take a minute), type **man -k _selinux**. You'll now see a long list of man pages scrolling by.
7. Type **man -k _selinux | grep http** to find the man pages that documents SELinux settings for the httpd service and scroll through it. Notice that it is a complete list of all that you can do with SELinux on the httpd service.

Restoring Default File Contexts

In the previous section, you learned how to apply context types using **semanage**. You also applied the context settings from the policy to the file system using **restorecon**. The **restorecon** command is a useful command because in the policy the default settings are defined for most files and directories on your computer. If the wrong context setting is ever applied, you just have to type **restorecon** to reapply it from the policy to the file system.

Using **restorecon** this way can be useful to fix problems on new files. Before explaining how to do it, let's take a look at how new context settings are applied:

- If a new file is created, it inherits the context settings from the parent directory.
- If a file is copied to a directory, this is considered a new file, so it inherits the context settings from the parent directory.
- If a file is moved, or copied while keeping its properties (by using **cp -a**), the original context settings of the file are applied.

Especially the latter of these three situations is easily fixed by using **restorecon**. Exercise 22-4 simulates this problem, and you fix it using **restorecon**.

It is also possible to relabel the entire file system. Doing so applies all context settings as defined in the policy to the file system. Because the policy should always be leading and contain correct context settings, relabeling a file system may be a good idea. To relabel the file system, you can either use the command **restorecon -Rv /** or create a file with the name **/.autorelabel**. If the /.autorelabel file exists, the next time your server is restarted, the file system will automatically be relabeled. Once the file system has been relabeled, the file /.autorelabel will be removed. Using /.autorelabel is a good idea if you're not sure that current context labels are consistent with the SELinux policy settings.

A relabeling action sometimes occurs spontaneously. If while troubleshooting a server you have started the server in a mode where SELinux is disabled, and you have applied modifications to the file system, SELinux will detect that the file system has changed without SELinux monitoring it. This will result in an automatic relabeling of the entire file system. Note that on a large file system, relabeling the file system can take a significant amount of time; on a minimal system such as the one that is used on the RHCSA exam, a complete file system relabeling should be done in less than 2 minutes.

Exercise 22-4 Using restorecon to Relabel Files

1. From a root shell, type **ls -Z /etc/hosts**. You'll see the file has the net_conf_t context label.
2. Type **cp /etc/hosts ~** to copy the file to the root home directory. Because copying is considered the creation of a new file, the context setting on the ~/hosts file is set as admin_home_t. Use **ls -Z ~/hosts** to verify this.
3. Type **mv ~/hosts /etc** and confirm that you want to overwrite the existing file.
4. Type **ls -Z /etc/hosts** to confirm that the context type is still set to admin_home_t.
5. Type **restorecon -v /etc/hosts** to reapply the correct context type. The **-v** option shows you what is happening.
6. Type **touch /.autorelabel** and restart your server. While restarting, make sure to press the Escape key so that you'll see boot messages. You'll see that the file system is automatically relabeled.

Managing Port Access

Managing file context is a key skill on the exam, but it is not the only skill that matters. When services are configured to listen on a nondefault port, you'll need to set the appropriate context on the port or access will be denied.

To set a port label, use **semanage port**. If, for instance, you want your Apache web server to offer services on port 8008, use **semanage port -a -t http_port_t -p tcp 8008**. After changing the port label, you don't have to run the **restorecon** utility—the change will be effective immediately. In Exercise 22-5 you'll learn how to change a port label.

Exercise 22-5 Changing Port Labels

1. From a root shell, type **vim /etc/httpd/conf/httpd.conf**. Look up the line that starts with Listen and change it so that it reads **Listen 82**.
2. Use **systemctl restart httpd** to restart the Apache server with this new setting. You will see an error message.
3. Type **systemctl status httpd**. The log messages show "Permission denied … could not bind to address 0.0.0.0:82."
4. Use **setenforce 0** to set SELinux to permissive mode and **systemctl restart httpd** to restart Apache. It will now work, so you have confirmed that the problems are caused by SELinux.
5. Type **setenforce 1** to switch back to enforcing mode.
6. Type **semanage port -a -t http_port_t -p tcp 82** to apply the correct port label.
7. Use **systemctl restart httpd**. It will now restart without any issues.

Using Boolean Settings to Modify SELinux Settings

The SELinux policy includes many rules. Some of these rules allow specific activity, whereas other rules deny that activity. Changing rules is not always easy, and that is why SELinux Booleans are provided to easily change the behavior of a rule. By applying a Boolean, multiple rules are changed to allow or deny specific behavior.

An example of a Boolean is ftpd_anon_write, which by default is set to off. That means that even if you have configured your FTP server to allow anonymous writes, the Boolean will still deny it, and the anonymous user cannot upload any files. If a Boolean denies specific activity, it will always be denied, regardless of the setting in the configuration file. The opposite is also true though: if the Boolean allows activity but it is not enabled in the configuration file, it will still not work.

To get a list of Booleans on your system, type **getsebool -a**. If you are looking for Booleans that are set for a specific service, use **grep** to filter down the results. In Example 22-5, you can see how this command is used to show current Booleans that match FTP.

An alternative way to show current Boolean settings is by using the **semanage boolean -l** command. This command provides some more details, because it shows the current Boolean setting and the default Boolean setting.

Example 22-5 Displaying Boolean Settings

```
root@server1 ~]# getsebool -a | grep ftp
ftp_home_dir --> off
ftpd_anon_write --> off
ftpd_connect_all_unreserved --> off
ftpd_connect_db --> off
ftpd_full_access --> off
ftpd_use_cifs --> off
ftpd_use_fusefs --> off
ftpd_use_nfs --> off
ftpd_use_passive_mode --> off
httpd_can_connect_ftp --> off
httpd_enable_ftp_server --> off
sftpd_anon_write --> off
sftpd_enable_homedirs --> off
sftpd_full_access --> off
sftpd_write_ssh_home --> off
tftp_anon_write --> off
tftp_home_dir --> off
```

To change a Boolean, you can use **setsebool.** If you want to switch the ftpd_anon_write Boolean to allow anonymous writes, for example, use **setsebool ftpd_anon_write on.** This changes the runtime value of the Boolean but does not change it permanently. To apply permanent changes to a Boolean, use **setsebool -P**. Notice that this takes longer, because parts of the policy need to be recompiled to apply the modification. In Exercise 22-6, you apply these commands to see how Booleans are working.

Exercise 22-6 Working with SELinux Booleans

1. From a root shell, type **getsebool -a | grep ftp.** You'll see the ftpd_anon_write Boolean, with its current value set to off.
2. Type **setsebool ftpd_anon_write on.** This changes the value in the runtime.
3. Type **getsebool ftpd_anon_write.** It shows the value of the Boolean as on.

4. Type **semanage boolean -l | grep ftpd_anon**. Notice that this command shows the runtime configuration set to on, but the permanent setting is still set to off.
5. Use **setsebool -P ftpd_anon_write on** to switch the runtime and the default setting for the Boolean to on.
6. Repeat **semanage boolean -l | grep ftpd_anon**. Notice that it is now set to on, on.

Diagnosing and Addressing SELinux Policy Violations

Configuring a system with SELinux can be a challenging task. To make it easier to understand what is happening, SELinux logs everything it is doing. The primary source to get logging information is the ***audit log***, which is in /var/log/audit/audit.log. SELinux messages are logged with type=AVC in the audit log. So, to see what SELinux is doing, you can use the command **grep AVC /var/log/audit/audit.log**. If SELinux messages have been logged, this command shows a result as in Example 22-6.

Example 22-6 Getting SELinux Messages from audit.log

```
[root@server1 ~]# grep AVC /var/log/audit/audit.log | grep http
type=AVC msg=audit(1559986797.093:185): avc:  denied  { getattr } for
  pid=32939 comm="httpd" path="/web/index.html" dev="dm-0"
  ino=35321780 scontext=system_u:system_r:httpd_t:s0
  tcontext=unconfined_u:object_r:default_t:s0 tclass=file permissive=0
type=AVC msg=audit(1559986797.093:186): avc:  denied  { getattr } for
  pid=32939 comm="httpd" path="/web/index.html" dev="dm-0"
  ino=35321780 scontext=system_u:system_r:httpd_t:s0
  tcontext=unconfined_u:object_r:default_t:s0 tclass=file permissive=0
type=AVC msg=audit(1559986815.360:188): avc:  denied  { getattr } for
  pid=32939 comm="httpd" path="/web/index.html" dev="dm-0"
  ino=35321780 scontext=system_u:system_r:httpd_t:s0
  tcontext=unconfined_u:object_r:default_t:s0 tclass=file permissive=0
type=AVC msg=audit(1559986815.360:189): avc:  denied  { getattr } for
  pid=32939 comm="httpd" path="/web/index.html" dev="dm-0"
  ino=35321780 scontext=system_u:system_r:httpd_t:s0
  tcontext=unconfined_u:object_r:default_t:s0 tclass=file permissive=0
type=AVC msg=audit(1559986883.549:192): avc:  denied  { getattr } for
  pid=33214 comm="httpd" path="/web/index.html" dev="dm-0"
  ino=35321780 scontext=system_u:system_r:httpd_t:s0
  tcontext=unconfined_u:object_r:default_t:s0 tclass=file permissive=0
```

```
type=AVC msg=audit(1559986883.550:193): avc:  denied  { getattr } for
  pid=33214 comm="httpd" path="/web/index.html" dev="dm-0" ino=35321780
  scontext=system_u:system_r:httpd_t:s0   tcontext=unconfined_u:object
  _r:default_t:s0 tclass=file permissive=0
type=AVC msg=audit(1559986927.406:197): avc:  denied  { getattr } for
  pid=33214 comm="httpd" path="/web/index.html" dev="dm-0"
  ino=35321780 scontext=system_u:system_r:httpd_t:s0
  tcontext=unconfined_u:object_r:default_t:s0 tclass=file permissive=1
type=AVC msg=audit(1559986927.406:198): avc:  denied  { read } for
  pid=33214 comm="httpd" name="index.html" dev="dm-0" ino=35321780 sco
  ntext=system_u:system_r:httpd_t:s0   tcontext=unconfined_u:object_r:
default_t:s0 tclass=file permissive=1
type=AVC msg=audit(1559986927.406:198): avc:  denied  { open } for
  pid=33214 comm="httpd" path="/web/index.html" dev="dm-0"
  ino=35321780 scontext=system_u:system_r:httpd_t:s0
  tcontext=unconfined_u:object_r:default_t:s0 tclass=file permissive=1
type=AVC msg=audit(1559986927.406:199): avc:  denied  { map } for
  pid=33214 comm="httpd" path="/web/index.html" dev="dm-0"
  ino=35321780 scontext=system_u:system_r:httpd_t:s0 tcontext=unconfin
  ed_u:object_r:default_t:s0 tclass=file permissive=1
```

At first sight, the SELinux log messages look complicated. If you look a bit closer, though, they are not that hard to understand. Let's take a closer look at the last line in the log file:

```
type=AVC msg=audit(1559986927.406:199): avc:  denied  { map } for
pid=33214 comm="httpd" path="/web/index.html" dev="dm-0"   ino=35321780
scontext=system_u:system_r:httpd_t:s0 tcontext=  unconfined_u:object_
r:default_t:s0 tclass=file permissive=1
```

The first relevant part in this line is the text avc: denied { map }. That means that a map request was denied, so some process has tried to read attributes of a file and that was denied, because it is a policy violation. Following that message, we can see comm=httpd, which means that the command trying to issue the getattr request was httpd, and we can see path="web/index.html", which is the file that this process has tried to access.

In the last part of the log line, we can get information about the source context and the target context. The ***source context*** (which is the context setting of the **httpd** command) is set to http_t, and the ***target context*** (which is the context setting of the /web/index.html file) is set to default_t. And apparently, SELinux did not like that too much. So, to fix this, you would have to relabel the file, as discussed earlier in the chapter.

Making SELinux Analyzing Easier

Based on the information you find in the audit.log, you may be able to decide what you need to do to fix the problem. Because the information in the audit.log is not easy to understand, the **sealert** command is offered to provide simplified messages about SELinux-related events. You may need to install sealert by using dnf -y install setroubleshoot-server. After installing it, it is a good idea to restart your server to make sure that all processes that are involved are restarted correctly. The next time an SELinux message is written to the audit log, an easier-to-understand message is written to the systemd journal. Example 22-7 shows an output example.

Example 22-7 **sealert** Makes Analyzing SELinux Logs Easier

```
[root@server1 ~]# journalctl | grep sealert
Oct 26 08:21:42 server1.example.com setroubleshoot[36518]: SELinux
  is preventing /usr/sbin/httpd from name_bind access on the tcp_
  socket port 82. For complete SELinux messages run: sealert -l
  fde99ca7-d84d-4956-beec-aa55d0a68044
Oct 26 08:21:43 server1.example.com setroubleshoot[36518]: SELinux
  is preventing /usr/sbin/httpd from name_bind access on the tcp_
  socket port 82. For complete SELinux messages run: sealert -l
  fde99ca7-d84d-4956-beec-aa55d0a68044
```

To get more details, you should run the command that is suggested. This will get information from the SELinux event database, including suggestions on how to fix the problem. Example 22-8 shows the first lines of the output for the command that is suggested in Example 22-7.

Example 22-8 Exploring **sealert** Messages

```
[root@server1 ~]# sealert -l fde99ca7-d84d-4956-beec-aa55d0a68044
SELinux is preventing /usr/sbin/httpd from name_bind access on the
tcp_socket port 82.

*****  Plugin bind_ports (99.5 confidence) suggests   ***************
If you want to allow /usr/sbin/httpd to bind to network port 82
Then you need to modify the port type.
Do
# semanage port -a -t PORT_TYPE -p tcp 82
    where PORT_TYPE is one of the following: http_cache_port_t, http_
  port_t, jboss_management_port_t, jboss_messaging_port_t, ntop_
  port_t, puppet_port_t.
*****  Plugin catchall (1.49 confidence) suggests   *****************
```

```
If you believe that httpd should be allowed name_bind access on the
port 82 tcp_socket by default.
Then you should report this as a bug.
You can generate a local policy module to allow this access.
Do
allow this access for now by executing:
# ausearch -c 'httpd' --raw | audit2allow -M my-httpd
# semodule -X 300 -i my-httpd.pp

Additional Information:
```

The useful thing about **sealert** is that it tries to analyze what has happened and, based on the analysis, suggests what you need to do to fix the problem. The not-so-useful part is that in some cases, hundreds of possible context types are shown, and the administrator has to choose the right one. So, if you do not know what you are doing, you risk getting completely lost. In other cases the output will be very useful, as is the case for the output in Example 22-8, which is suggesting to run the **semanage port** command to fix the issue.

When working with **sealert**, you can see that different plug-ins are called, and every plug-in has a confidence score. If, as in the example in Example 22-8, one plug-in has a 99.5% confidence score, while the other has only a 1.49% confidence score, it may be obvious that the former approach is what you should choose. Unfortunately, however, it is not always that readable.

TIP If you are not sure what SELinux is trying to tell you, install the setroubleshoot-server package and analyze what **sealert** shows. The information that is shown by **sealert** is often a lot more readable. Sometimes it will not help you at all, whereas sometimes the information can prove quite helpful.

Summary

This chapter provided an RHCSA-level introduction to SELinux. You learned why SELinux is needed for security and how SELinux uses context as the main feature to apply security. You also learned how to set the default SELinux mode and how to analyze in case things go wrong.

Exam Preparation Tasks

As mentioned in the section "How to Use This Book" in the Introduction, you have several choices for exam preparation: the end-of-chapter labs; the memory tables in Appendix C; Chapter 27, "Final Preparation"; and the practice exams.

Review All Key Topics

Review the most important topics in the chapter, noted with the Key Topic icon in the margin of the page. Table 22-3 lists a reference for these key topics and the page number on which each is found.

Table 22-3 Key Topics for Chapter 22

Key Topic Element	Description	Page
Table 22-2	SELinux Core Elements	473
List	Elements a context label can be applied to	477
List	Three parts of a context label	478
List	How new context settings are applied	483

Complete Tables and Lists from Memory

Print a copy of Appendix C, "Memory Tables" (found on the companion website), or at least the section for this chapter, and complete the tables and lists from memory. Appendix D, "Memory Tables Answer Key," includes completed tables and lists to check your work.

Define Key Terms

Define the following key terms from this chapter and check your answers in the glossary:

policy, context, enforcing, permissive, context type, audit log, source context, target context

Review Questions

The questions that follow are meant to help you test your knowledge of concepts and terminology and the breadth of your knowledge. You can find the answers to these questions in Appendix A.

1. You want to put SELinux temporarily in permissive mode. Which command do you use?
2. You need a list of all available Booleans. Which command do you use?
3. You do not see any service-specific SELinux man page. What solution do you need to apply?
4. What is the name of the package you need to install to get easy-to-read SELinux log messages in the audit log?
5. What commands do you need to run to apply the httpd_sys_content_t context type to the directory /web?
6. When would you use the **chcon** command?
7. Which file do you need to change if you want to completely disable SELinux?
8. Where does SELinux log all of its messages?
9. You have no clue which context types are available for the ftp service. What command enables you to get more specific information?
10. Your service does not work as expected, and you want to know whether it is due to SELinux or something else. What is the easiest way to find out?

End-of-Chapter Lab

You have now learned how SELinux works. To practice managing this essential service, work through this end-of-chapter lab about SELinux.

Lab 22.1

1. Change the Apache document root to **/web**. In this directory, create a file with the name **index.html** and give it the content **welcome to my web server**. Restart the httpd process and try to access the web server. This will not work. Fix the problem.

2. In the home directory of the user root, create a file with the name **hosts** and give it the following content:

```
192.168.4.200 labipa.example.com
192.168.4.210 server1.example.com
192.168.4.220 server2.example.com
```

3. Move the file to the /etc directory and do what is necessary to give this file the correct context.

The following topics are covered in this chapter:

- Understanding Linux Firewalling
- Working with Firewalld

The following RHCSA exam objective is covered in this chapter:

- Configure firewall settings using firewall-cmd/firewalld

CHAPTER 23

Configuring a Firewall

If a server is connected to the Internet, it needs to be protected against unauthorized access. SELinux is one part of this protection, as discussed in Chapter 22, "Managing SELinux," and a firewall is the second part. The Linux kernel implements firewalling via the netfilter framework. To configure which packets are allowed and which are not, Firewalld is the default solution in RHEL 9. In this chapter, you learn how a basic Firewalld configuration is created in an RHEL 9 environment.

"Do I Know This Already?" Quiz

The "Do I Know This Already?" quiz enables you to assess whether you should read this entire chapter thoroughly or jump to the "Exam Preparation Tasks" section. If you are in doubt about your answers to these questions or your own assessment of your knowledge of the topics, read the entire chapter. Table 23-1 lists the major headings in this chapter and their corresponding "Do I Know This Already?" quiz questions. You can find the answers in Appendix A, "Answers to the 'Do I Know This Already?' Quizzes and Review Questions."

Table 23-1 "Do I Know This Already?" Section-to-Question Mapping

Foundation Topics Section	Questions
Understanding Linux Firewalling	1–3, 7
Working with Firewalld	4–6, 8–10

1. Which of the following is not a standard Firewalld zone?
   a. untrusted
   b. trusted
   c. external
   d. internal

2. Which of the following is the name of the firewalling service as implemented in the Linux kernel?
   a. iptables
   b. firewalld
   c. netfilter
   d. firewall-mod

3. Which of the following is *not* an advantage of Firewalld?
   a. Rules can be modified through DBus.
   b. It has an easy-to-use command-line interface.
   c. It has an easy-to-use graphical interface.
   d. It can be used to manage the iptables service.

4. Which command enables you to list all available Firewalld services?
   a. **firewall-cmd --list-services**
   b. **firewall-cmd --list-all**
   c. **firewall-cmd --get-services**
   d. **firewall-cmd --show-services**

5. What is the name of the GUI tool that enables you to easily manage Firewalld configurations?
   a. **system-config-firewall**
   b. **firewall-gtk**
   c. **firewall-config**
   d. **firewall-gui**

6. Which of the following shows the correct syntax for adding a port persistently to the current Firewalld configuration?
   a. **firewall-cmd --addport=2022/tcp --permanent**
   b. **firewall-cmd --add-port=2022/tcp --permanent**
   c. **firewall-cmd --addport=2022/tcp --persistent**
   d. **firewall-cmd --add port=2022/tcp --persistent**

7. Which zone should you use for an interface that is on a network where you need minimal firewall protection because every other computer on that same network is trusted?
   a. trusted
   b. home
   c. work
   d. private
8. Which of the following statements is true about the **--permanent** command-line option when used with **firewall-cmd**?
   a. Configuration that is added using **--permanent** is activated immediately and will be activated automatically after (re)starting Firewalld.
   b. Configuration that is added using **--permanent** is activated immediately.
   c. Configuration that is added using **--permanent** is not activated immediately and can be activated only by using **systemctl restart firewalld**.
   d. To activate configuration that has been added with the **--permanent** option, you need to reload the firewall configuration by using **firewall-cmd --reload**.
9. Which command enables you to get an overview of all the current firewall configurations for all zones?
   a. **firewall-cmd --show-current**
   b. **firewall-cmd --list-all**
   c. **firewall-cmd --list-current**
   d. **firewall-cmd --show-all**
10. How can you easily write the current runtime configuration to the permanent configuration?
    a. When using **firewall-cmd**, add the **--permanent** option to all commands.
    b. Only write the permanent configuration, and use **systemctl restart firewalld** to activate the permanent configuration in the runtime as well.
    c. Manually edit the firewalld zone file.
    d. Write all options to the runtime configuration, and then use the **firewall-cmd --runtime-to-permanent** command to add these options to the persistent configuration.

Foundation Topics

Understanding Linux Firewalling

You can use a ***firewall*** to limit traffic coming in to a server or going out of the server. Firewalling is implemented in the Linux kernel by means of the netfilter subsystem. ***Netfilter*** allows kernel modules to inspect every incoming, outgoing, or forwarded packet and act upon such a packet by either allowing it or blocking it. So, the kernel firewall allows for inspection of incoming packets, outgoing packets, and packets that are traversing from one interface to another if the RHEL server is providing routing functionality.

Understanding Previous Solutions

To interact with netfilter, different solutions can be used. On earlier versions of Red Hat Enterprise Linux, ***iptables*** was the default solution to configure netfilter packet filtering. This solution worked with the command-line utility **iptables**, which provided a sophisticated and detailed way of defining firewall rules, but that also was challenging to use for the occasional administrator because of the complicated syntax of **iptables** commands and because the ordering rules could become relatively complex.

The iptables service is no longer offered in RHEL. It has been replaced with ***nftables***, a newer solution with more advanced options than the ones offered by iptables. The **nft** command-line tool offers an advanced interface to write rules directly to nftables.

Understanding Firewalld

Firewalld is a system service that can configure firewall rules by using different interfaces. Administrators can manage rules in a Firewalld environment, but even more important is that applications can request ports to be opened using the DBus messaging system, which means that rules can be added or removed without any direct action required of the system administrator, which allows applications to address the firewall from user space.

Firewalld was developed as a completely new solution for managing Linux firewalls. It uses the firewalld service to manage the netfilter firewall configuration and the **firewall-cmd** command-line utility.

Understanding Firewalld Zones

Firewalld makes firewall management easier by working with zones. A ***zone*** is a collection of rules that are applied to incoming packets matching a specific source address or network interface. Firewalld applies to incoming packets only by default, and no filtering happens on outgoing packets.

The use of zones is particularly important on servers that have multiple interfaces. On such servers, zones allow administrators to easily assign a specific set of rules. On servers that have just one network interface, you might very well need just one zone, which is the default zone. Every packet that comes into a system is analyzed for its source address, and based on that source address, Firewalld analyzes whether or not the packet belongs to a specific zone. If not, the zone for the incoming network interface is used. If no specific zone is available, the packet is handled by the settings in the default zone.

Firewalld works with some default zones. Table 23-2 describes these default zones.

Table 23-2 Firewalld Default Zones

Zone Name	Default Settings
block	Incoming network connections are rejected with an "icmp-host-prohibited" message. Only network connections that were initiated on this system are allowed.
dmz	For use on computers in the demilitarized zone. Only selected incoming connections are accepted, and limited access to the internal network is allowed.
drop	Any incoming packets are dropped and there is no reply.
external	For use on external networks with masquerading (Network Address Translation [NAT]) enabled, used especially on routers. Only selected incoming connections are accepted.
home	For use with home networks. Most computers on the same network are trusted, and only selected incoming connections are accepted.
internal	For use in internal networks. Most computers on the same network are trusted, and only selected incoming connections are accepted.
public	For use in public areas. Other computers in the same network are not trusted, and limited connections are accepted. This is the default zone for all newly created network interfaces.
trusted	All network connections are accepted.
work	For use in work areas. Most computers on the same network are trusted, and only selected incoming connections are accepted.

Understanding Firewalld Services

The second key element while working with Firewalld is the service. Note that a service in Firewalld is *not* the same as a service in Systemd; a Firewalld ***service*** specifies what exactly should be accepted as incoming and outgoing traffic in the firewall. It typically includes ports to be opened, as well as supporting kernel modules that should be loaded. Behind all services are XML files that define the service; these files can be found in the /usr/lib/firewalld/services directory.

In Firewalld, many default services are defined, which allows administrators to easily allow or deny access to specific ports on a server. Behind each service is a configuration file that explains which UDP or TCP ports are involved and, if so required, which kernel modules must be loaded. To get a list of all services available on your computer, you can use the command **firewall-cmd --get-services** (see Example 23-1).

Example 23-1 Use **firewall-cmd --get-services** for a List of All Available Services

```
[root@server1 ~]# firewall-cmd --get-services
RH-Satellite-6 RH-Satellite-6-capsule amanda-client amanda-k5-client
amqp amqps apcupsd audit bacula bacula-client bb bgp bitcoin bitcoin-
rpc bitcoin-testnet bitcoin-testnet-rpc bittorrent-lsd ceph ceph-
mon cfengine cockpit collectd condor-collector ctdb dhcp dhcpv6
dhcpv6-client distcc dns dns-over-tls docker-registry docker-swarm
dropbox-lansync elasticsearch etcd-client etcd-server finger foreman
foreman-proxy freeipa-4 freeipa-ldap freeipa-ldaps freeipa-replication
freeipa-trust ftp galera ganglia-client ganglia-master git grafana gre
high-availability http https imap imaps ipp ipp-client ipsec irc ircs
iscsi-target isns jenkins kadmin kdeconnect kerberos kibana klogin
kpasswd kprop kshell kube-api kube-apiserver kube-control-plane kube-
controller-manager kube-scheduler kubelet-worker ldap ldaps libvirt
libvirt-tls lightning-network llmnr managesieve matrix mdns memcache
minidlna mongodb mosh mountd mqtt mqtt-tls ms-wbt mssql murmur mysql
nbd netbios-ns nfs nfs3 nmea-0183 nrpe ntp nut openvpn ovirt-imageio
ovirt-storageconsole ovirt-vmconsole plex pmcd pmproxy pmwebapi
pmwebapis pop3 pop3s postgresql privoxy prometheus proxy-dhcp ptp
pulseaudio puppetmaster quassel radius rdp redis redis-sentinel rpc-
bind rquotad rsh rsyncd rtsp salt-master samba samba-client samba-dc
sane sip sips slp smtp smtp-submission smtps snmp snmptrap spideroak-
lansync spotify-sync squid ssdp ssh steam-streaming svdrp svn
syncthing syncthing-gui synergy syslog syslog-tls telnet tentacle tftp
tile38 tinc tor-socks transmission-client upnp-client vdsm vnc-server
wbem-http wbem-https wireguard wsman wsmans xdmcp xmpp-bosh xmpp-
client xmpp-local xmpp-server zabbix-agent zabbix-server
```

In essence, what it comes down to when working with Firewalld is that the right services need to be added to the right zones. In special cases, the configuration may be enhanced with more specific settings. In the next section, you learn which tools you can use for that purpose.

To add your own services, custom service XML files can be added to the /etc/firewalld/services directory and will automatically be picked up after restarting the Firewalld service.

Example 23-2 shows what the contents of a service file look like.

Example 23-2 Contents of the ftp.xml Service File

```
[root@server1 services]# cat ftp.xml
<?xml version="1.0" encoding="utf-8"?>
<service>
  <short>FTP</short>
  <description>FTP is a protocol used for remote file transfer. If
  you plan to make your FTP
server publicly available, enable this option. You need the vsftpd
  package installed for this
option to be useful.</description>
  <port protocol="tcp" port="21"/>
  <module name="nf_conntrack_ftp"/>
</service>
```

Working with Firewalld

In this section, you learn how to configure a firewall with the Firewalld command-line interface tool, **firewall-cmd**. The Firewalld service also offers a GUI version of this tool, **firewall-config**, but the RHCSA exam objectives list only **firewall-cmd**, so this section focuses on working from the command line.

When working with either of these tools, be aware of where exactly modifications are made. Both tools work with an in-memory state of the configuration in addition to an on-disk state (permanent state) of the configuration. While using either of these tools, make sure to commit changes to disk before proceeding.

The **firewall-cmd** tool is an easily accessible tool that enables administrators to change the runtime configuration of the firewall and to write this configuration to disk. Before learning all the options available with this versatile command, in Exercise 23-1 you work with some of the most important options **firewall-cmd** offers.

Exercise 23-1 Managing the Firewall with firewall-cmd

1. Open a root shell. Type **firewall-cmd --get-default-zone**. This shows the current default zone, which is set to public.
2. To see which zones are available, type **firewall-cmd --get-zones**.
3. Show the services that are available on your server by typing **firewall-cmd --get-services**. Notice that the **firewall-cmd --get** options show what is available on your server, so basically you can use **firewall-cmd --get-<item>** to request information about a specific item.
4. To see which services are available in the current zone, type **firewall-cmd --list-services**. You'll see a short list containing a Dynamic Host Configuration Protocol (DHCP) client as well as Secure Shell (SSH) and the Cockpit web-based management interface. In the public zone only a limited number of services are enabled by default.
5. Type **firewall-cmd --list-all**. Look at the output and compare the output to the result of **firewall-cmd --list-all --zone=public**. Both commands show a complete overview of the current firewall configuration, as shown in Example 23-3. Notice that you see much more than just the zone and the services that are configured in that zone; you also see information about the interfaces and more advanced items.

Example 23-3 Showing Current Firewall Configuration

```
[root@server1 ~]# firewall-cmd --list-all
public (active)
  target: default
  icmp-block-inversion: no
  interfaces: ens160
  sources:
  services: cockpit dhcpv6-client ssh
  ports:
  protocols:
  masquerade: no
  forward-ports:
  source-ports:
  icmp-blocks:
  rich rules:
```

6. Type **firewall-cmd --add-service=vnc-server** to open VNC server access in the firewall. Verify using **firewall-cmd --list-all**.
7. Type **systemctl restart firewalld** and repeat **firewall-cmd --list-all**. Notice that the vnc-server service is no longer listed; the reason is that the previous command has added the service to the runtime configuration but not to the persistent configuration.
8. Add the vnc-server service again, but make it permanent this time, using **firewall-cmd --add-service vnc-server --permanent**.
9. Type **firewall-cmd --list-all** again to verify. You'll see that VNC server service is not listed. Services that have been added to the on-disk configuration are not added automatically to the runtime configuration. Type **firewall-cmd --reload** to reload the on-disk configuration into the runtime configuration.
10. Type **firewall-cmd --add-port=2020/tcp --permanent**, followed by **firewall-cmd --reload**. Verify using **firewall-cmd --list-all**. You'll see that a port has now been added to the Firewalld configuration.

TIP On the exam, work with services as much as possible. Only use specific ports if no services contain the ports that you want to open.

In the preceding exercise, you worked with zones and services and you learned how to add services and ports to the default zone. You should work with services as much as possible; adding individual ports is not recommended practice. You have also learned how working with runtime as well as permanent configuration can be inefficient. An alternative approach exists: just write all your configuration to runtime, and next use **firewall-cmd --runtime-to-permanent** to make the runtime configuration permanent.

The **firewall-cmd** interface offers many more options. Table 23-3 describes some of the most important command-line options.

Table 23-3 Common **firewall-cmd** Options

firewall-cmd Option	Explanation
--get-zones	Lists all available zones
--get-default-zone	Shows the zone currently set as the default zone
--set-default-zone=<*ZONE*>	Changes the default zone
--get-services	Shows all available services

--list-services	Shows services currently in use
--add-service=<*service-name*> [--zone=<*ZONE*>]	Adds a service to the current default zone or the zone that is specified
--remove-service=<*service-name*>	Removes a service from the configuration
--list-all-zones	Shows configuration for all zones
--add-port=<port/protocol> [--zone=<*ZONE*>]	Adds a port and protocol
--remove-port=<port/protocol> [--zone=<*ZONE*>]	Removes a port from the configuration
--add-interface=<*INTERFACE*> [--zone=<*ZONE*>]	Adds an interface to the default zone or a specific zone that is specified
--remove-interface=<*INTERFACE*> [--zone=<*ZONE*>]	Removes an interface from a specific zone
--add-source=<*ipaddress/netmask*> [--zone=<*ZONE*>]	Adds a specific IP address
--remove-source=<*ipaddress/netmask*> [--zone=<*ZONE*>]	Removes an IP address from the configuration
--permanent	Writes configuration to disk and not to runtime
--runtime-to-permanent	Adds the current runtime configuration to the permanent configuration
--reload	Reloads the on-disk configuration

Summary

In this chapter, you learned how to set up a basic firewall environment, where Firewalld services are added to Firewalld zones to allow access to specific services on your computer. You also learned how to set up a base firewall by using the **firewall-cmd** command-line tool.

Exam Preparation Tasks

As mentioned in the section "How to Use This Book" in the Introduction, you have several choices for exam preparation: the end-of-chapter labs; the memory tables in Appendix C; Chapter 27, "Final Preparation"; and the practice exams.

Review All Key Topics

Review the most important topics in the chapter, noted with the Key Topic icon in the margin of the page. Table 23-4 lists a reference for these key topics and the page number on which each is found.

Table 23-4 Key Topics for Chapter 23

Key Topic Element	Description	Page
Paragraph	Introduces firewalling in the Linux kernel	498
Paragraph	Introduces netfilter as opposed to other firewalling tools	498
Paragraph	Introduces how Firewalld zones are used	499
Table 23-2	Firewalld Default Zones	499
Section	Understanding Firewalld Services	500
Table 23-3	Common **firewall-cmd** Options	503

Complete Tables and Lists from Memory

Print a copy of Appendix C, "Memory Tables" (found on the companion website), or at least the section for this chapter, and complete the tables and lists from memory. Appendix D, "Memory Tables Answer Key," includes completed tables and lists to check your work.

Define Key Terms

Define the following key terms from this chapter and check your answers in the glossary:

firewall, netfilter, iptables, nftables, firewalld, zone, service

Review Questions

The questions that follow are meant to help you test your knowledge of concepts and terminology and the breadth of your knowledge. You can find the answers to these questions in Appendix A.

1. Which service should be running before you try to create a firewall configuration with **firewall-config**?
2. Which command adds UDP port 2345 to the firewall configuration in the default zone?

3. Which command enables you to list all firewall configurations in all zones?
4. Which command enables you to remove the vnc-server service from the current firewall configuration?
5. Which **firewall-cmd** command enables you to activate a new configuration that has been added with the **--permanent** option?
6. Which **firewall-cmd** option enables you to verify that a new configuration has been added to the current zone and is now active?
7. Which command enables you to add the interface eno1 to the public zone?
8. If you add a new interface to the firewall configuration while no zone is specified, which zone will it be added to?
9. Which command enables you to add the source IP address 192.168.0.0/24 to the default zone?
10. Which command enables you to list all services that are currently available in Firewalld?

End-of-Chapter Lab

You have now learned how to work with Firewalld on a Red Hat Enterprise Linux 9 server. Make sure to master these skills by working through this end-of-chapter lab.

Lab 23.1

1. Create a firewall configuration that allows access to the following services that may be running on your server:
   - web
   - ftp
   - ssh
2. Make sure the configuration is persistent and will be activated after a restart of your server.

The following topics are covered in this chapter:

- Using NFS Services
- Mounting Remote File Systems Through fstab
- Using Automount to Mount Remote File Systems

The following RHCSA exam objectives are covered in this chapter:

- Mount and unmount network file systems using NFS
- Configure autofs

Accessing Network Storage

The RHCSA exam requires that you know how to access network storage. This encompasses different topics. In this chapter we discuss accessing network storage that has been provided through NFS. You learn how to mount network storage through the fstab file, as well as how to automatically mount this storage on demand using automount.

"Do I Know This Already?" Quiz

The "Do I Know This Already?" quiz enables you to assess whether you should read this entire chapter thoroughly or jump to the "Exam Preparation Tasks" section. If you are in doubt about your answers to these questions or your own assessment of your knowledge of the topics, read the entire chapter. Table 24-1 lists the major headings in this chapter and their corresponding "Do I Know This Already?" quiz questions. You can find the answers in Appendix A, "Answers to the 'Do I Know This Already?' Quizzes and Review Questions."

Table 24-1 "Do I Know This Already?" Section-to-Question Mapping

Foundation Topics Section	Questions
Using NFS Services	1–5
Mounting Remote File Systems Through fstab	6
Using Automount to Mount Remote File Systems	7–10

1. Which command should you use to list shares offered by an NFS server?
   a. **lsmount**
   b. **showmount -e**
   c. **lsexport**
   d. **showexport**

2. Which of the following is not a feature in NFSv4?

   a. Integration with Active Directory

   b. Kerberized security

   c. Services offered on TCP port 2049

   d. The root mount

3. What is the name of the package that needs to be installed to mount NFS shares on an NFS client?

   a. nfs-client

   b. nfs-tools

   c. nfs-utils

   d. nfs

4. You type the command **showmount -e** to display available mounts on an NFS server, but you do not get any result. Which of the following is the most likely explanation?

   a. The NFS client software is not running.

   b. You are using a UID that does not exist on the server.

   c. SELinux is not configured properly.

   d. The firewall does not allow **showmount** traffic.

5. What is the name of the systemd service that provides NFS shares?

   a. **nfs.service**

   b. **nfs-kernel-server.service**

   c. **nfs-server.service**

   d. **netmount.service**

6. Which mount option needs to be used in /etc/fstab to mount NFS shares successfully?

   a. **_netdev**

   b. **_netfs**

   c. **none**

   d. **nfs**

7. Which of the following is not a required step in configuring automount?
   a. Identify the name of the automount directory in /etc/auto.master.
   b. Create an indirect file in /etc/auto.something.
   c. Start and enable the autofs service.
   d. On the local mount point, set the appropriate permissions.

8. Assuming that the name of the directory you want automount to monitor is /myfiles, what is the recommended name for the corresponding configuration file?
   a. /etc/automount/auto.myfiles
   b. /etc/auto.myfiles
   c. /etc/myfiles.auto
   d. There is no recommended name.

9. Which of the following lines correctly identifies the syntax of a wildcard automount configuration that uses the NFS protocol?
   a. &. -rw server:/homes/*
   b. &. rw. server:/homes/*
   c. * -rw server:/homes/&
   d. * rw. server:/homes/&

10. What is the name of the service that automount uses?
    a. autofs
    b. automount
    c. autofiles
    d. auto

Foundation Topics

Using NFS Services

In previous chapters, you learned how to work with local file systems and mount them into the file system structure. In this chapter, you learn how to work with network file systems. The classic network file system is the ***Network File System (NFS)***. It is a protocol that was developed for UNIX by Sun in the early 1980s, and it has been available on Linux forever. Its purpose is to make it possible to mount remote file systems into the local file system hierarchy.

Understanding NFS Security

When NFS was developed in the 1980s, it was often used together with Network Information Service (NIS), a solution that provides a network-based authentication server. With the use of NIS, all servers connected to NIS used the same user accounts, and security was dealt with by the NIS server. The only thing that needed to be configured on the NFS server was host access. So, NFS security by default was limited to allowing and restricting specific hosts to access it.

Since the 1990s, NIS is not often used any more. NFS, however, continues to be a very popular service, primarily because it is fast and easy to configure. Without NIS, the feature that provided user-based security has been removed, and that may make NFS seem to be an unsecure solution. Let's look at an example: Imagine that on server1, user linda has UID 1001. On server2, which is the NFS server, UID 1001 is used by user bob. After successfully connecting from server1 to server2, server1 user linda would have the same access to server2 resources as user bob. This obviously is an undesired situation.

To prevent situations like this from happening, you should use NFS together with a centralized authentication service. Commonly, a combination of the Lightweight Directory Access Protocol (LDAP) and Kerberos is used to provide this functionality. Configuration and integration of NFS with LDAP and Kerberos are not included in the RHCSA exam objectives, and for that reason will not be covered here.

RHEL NFS Versions

On Red Hat Enterprise Linux, NFS 4 is the default version of NFS. If when making an NFS mount the NFS server offers a previous version of NFS, the client falls automatically back to that version. From a client, you can also force a specific NFS version to be used for the mount, by using the **mount** option **nfsvers**

This technique can prove useful if you are connecting to a server or a device that offers NFS 3 only. Fortunately, this type of server or device is increasingly uncommon nowadays.

Setting Up NFS

Setting up an NFS server is not a part of the RHCSA exam. However, to practice your NFS-based skills, it's useful to set up your own NFS test server. To do so, you need to go through a few tasks:

1. Create a local directory you want to share.
2. Edit the /etc/exports file to define the NFS share.
3. Start the NFS server.
4. Configure your firewall to allow incoming NFS traffic.

Exercise 24-1 guides you through these steps.

Exercise 24-1 Offering an NFS Share

You need a second server to do this exercise. A RHEL server that was installed using the minimal server installation pattern is sufficient. This exercise assumes that a server with the name server2.example.com is available to offer these services.

1. Type **mkdir -p /nfsdata /users/user1 /users/user2** to create some local directories that are going to be shared.
2. Copy some random files to this directory, using **cp /etc/[a-c]* /nfsdata**.
3. Use **vim** to create the **/etc/exports** file and give it the following contents:

```
/nfsdata    *(rw,no_root_squash)
/users      *(rw,no_root_squash)
```

4. Type **dnf install -y nfs-utils** to install the required packages.
5. Type **systemctl enable --now nfs-server** to start and enable the NFS server.
6. Type **firewall-cmd --add-service nfs --permanent** to add the nfs service. Also type **firewall-cmd --add-service rpc-bind --permanent** and **firewall-cmd --add-service mountd --permanent** to add the bind and mountd services.
7. To make the newly added services effective at this point, type **firewall-cmd --reload**.

Mounting the NFS Share

To mount an NFS share, you first need to find the names of the shares. This information can be provided by the administrator, but it is also possible to find out yourself. To discover which shares are available, you have multiple options:

- If NFSv4 is used on the server, you can use a root mount. That means that you just mount the root directory of the NFS server, and under the mount point you'll only see the shares that you have access to.
- Use the **showmount -e nfsserver** command to find out which shares are available.

You'll practice mounting NFS shares in Exercise 24-2.

WARNING The **showmount** command may have issues with NFSv4 servers that are behind a firewall. The reason is that **showmount** relies on the portmapper service, which uses random UDP ports while making a connection, and the firewalld nfs service opens port 2049 only, which does not allow portmapper traffic. If the firewall is set up correctly, the mountd and rpc-bind services need to be added to the firewall as well. It is very well possible that shares have been set up correctly on the server, but you cannot see them because **showmount** does not get through the firewall. If you suspect that this is the case, use the NFS root mount, or just try mounting the NFS share as explained in Exercise 24-2.

Exercise 24-2 Mounting an NFS Share

1. On server1, type **dnf install -y nfs-utils** to install the RPM package that contains the **showmount** utility.
2. Type **showmount -e server2.example.com** to see all exports available from server2.
3. On server1, type **mount server2.example.com:/ /mnt**. (Note the space between the slashes in the command.) This performs an NFSv4 pseudo root mount of all NFS shares.
4. Type **mount | grep server2** to verify the mount has succeeded.
5. Still on server1, type **ls /mnt**. This shows the subdirectories data and home, which correspond to the mounts offered by the NFS server.

Mounting Remote File Systems Through fstab

You now know how to manually mount NFS file systems from the command line. If a file system needs to be available persistently, you need to use a different solution. Mounts can be automated either by using the /etc/fstab file or by using the autofs service. In this section, you learn how to make the mount through /etc/fstab. This is a convenient solution if you need the remote file system to be available permanently.

Mounting NFS Shares Through fstab

As you learned in earlier chapters, the /etc/fstab file is used to mount file systems that need to be mounted automatically when a server restarts. Only the user root can add mounts to this configuration file, thus providing shares that will be available for all users. The /etc/fstab file can be used to mount the NFS file system as well as other network-based file systems such as Samba. To mount an NFS file system through /etc/fstab, make sure that the following line is included:

```
server1:/share /nfs/mount/point nfs  sync  0 0
```

When making an NFS mount through fstab, you have a few options to consider:

- In the first column, you need to specify the server and share name. Use a colon after the name of the server to identify the mount as an NFS share.
- The second column has the directory where you want to mount the NFS share; this is not different from a regular mount.
- The third column contains the NFS file system type.
- The fourth column is used to specify mount options and includes the sync option. This ensures that modified files are committed to the remote file system immediately and are not placed in write buffers first (which would increase the risk of data getting lost). On older versions of RHEL, this column should include the _netdev option to ensure that this mount is only done after the network services are running. Because of better dependency handling, using this option is no longer required.
- The fifth column contains a zero, which means that no backup support through the **dump** utility is requested.
- The sixth column also contains a zero, to indicate that no **fsck** has to be performed on this file system while booting to check the integrity of the file system. The integrity of the file system would need to be checked on the server, not on the client.

Using Automount to Mount Remote File Systems

As an alternative to using /etc/fstab, you can configure automount to mount the share automatically. *Automount* can be used for SMB as well as NFS mounts, and the big difference is that mounts through automount are affected on demand and not by default. So, using automount ensures that no file systems are mounted that are not really needed.

On RHEL 9 there are two solutions for offering automount services. First, there is the old **autofs** service, which has been around for a long time. Second, systemd provides automount unit files, which are used together with mount unit files to ensure that a mount is done only when the corresponding directory is mounted. For purposes of the RHEL 9 RHCSA exam, you do not have to know about systemd automount, because only autofs is covered. The main reason is that autofs offers wildcard mounts, a feature that is not supported by systemd automount.

Understanding Automount

Automount is implemented by the autofs service that takes care of mounting a share when an attempt is made to access it. That means it is mounted on demand and that it does not have to be mounted permanently. An important benefit of using automount is that it works completely in user space and, contrary to mounts that are made through the **mount** command, no root permissions are required.

Defining Mounts in Automount

In automount, mounts are defined through a two-step procedure. First, you need to edit the master configuration file /etc/auto.master. In this directory you identify the mount point (for instance, /nfsdata). Next, and on the same line, you identify the name of the secondary file, as all further configuration happens in this secondary file. The line you create could look as follows:

```
/nfsdata     /etc/auto.nfsdata
```

In the secondary file you put the name of the subdirectory that will be created in the mount point directory as a relative filename. For instance, you start the line with **files**, to mount /nfsdata/files. After the name of the subdirectory, you specify NFS mount options, as well as the server and share name to access the NFS share. This line could look as follows:

```
files    -rw    server2:/nfsdata
```

Configuring Automount for NFS

Configuring an automount solution is a multistep procedure. To show how it works, Exercise 24-3 lists all steps involved. Follow the steps in this exercise to see for yourself how to configure automount.

Exercise 24-3 Configuring Direct and Indirect Maps to Mount NFS Shares

This exercise is performed on server1. It uses the NFS shares provided by server2 that you created in Exercise 24-1.

1. Type **dnf install -y autofs** to install the autofs package.
2. Type **showmount -e server2.example.com**, which shows you NFS exports offered by server2.
3. Type **vim /etc/auto.master** and add the following line:

```
/nfsdata /etc/auto.nfsdata
```

4. Type **vim /etc/auto.nfsdata** and add the following line:

```
files -rw server2:/nfsdata
```

5. Type **systemctl enable --now autofs** to start and enable the autofs service.
6. Type **ls /**; notice that there is no /nfsdata directory.
7. Type **cd /nfsdata/files** to get access to the /nfsdata directory.
8. Type **mount** and notice the last three lines in the mount output, created by the autofs service.

Using Wildcards in Automount

In Exercise 24-3, you learned how to perform automounts based on fixed directory names. In some cases, this is not very useful, and you are better off using wildcards. This is, for example, the case for automounting home directories. By using a wildcard, automount tries to mount a share that matches the name of the directory that is accessed.

With home directories, a very helpful solution is to have the home directory of a specific user automounted when that user logs in. This allows administrators to store home directories on a central NFS server, instead of on individual workstations. So, for example, if user linda logs in, she gets access to the NFS exported directory /home/linda, and when user anna logs in, she gets access to /home/anna. Using wildcards in automount offers an excellent tool to do this.

To create a wildcard mount, you will use lines like *** -rw server2:/users/&**. In this line, the * represents the local mount point, which in this case represents anything, and the & represents the matching item on the remote server.

Obviously, you could also choose to export the /home directory and mount just the /home directory, but that increases the risk that user anna gets access to user linda's home directory. For that reason, using a wildcard mount is a much cleaner solution, as demonstrated in Exercise 24-4.

Exercise 24-4 Configuring Wildcard Mounts

This exercise is performed on server1. It uses the NFS shares that are provided by server2, which you created in Exercise 24-1. On server2, the directory /users is exported, which simulates an NFS server that exports home directories. You are going to configure a wildcard mount, such that when /users/user1 is accessed, that exact directory is mounted, and when /users/user2 is accessed, that directory is mounted.

1. Open the file /etc/auto.master and make sure it includes the following line:

```
/users     /etc/auto.users
```

2. Create the file **/etc/auto.users** and give it the following contents:

```
*     -rw     server2:/users/&
```

3. Type **systemctl restart autofs** to restart the autofs service.
4. Type **cd /users/user1** to get access to the NFS export /users/user1 on the server2 server.

Summary

In this chapter you learned how to mount remote file systems and how to configure automount. You first learned how to manually mount an NFS file system from the command line. Then you learned how these mounts can be automated through /etc/fstab or automount.

Exam Preparation Tasks

As mentioned in the section "How to Use This Book" in the Introduction, you have several choices for exam preparation: the end-of-chapter labs; the memory tables in Appendix C; Chapter 27, "Final Preparation"; and the practice exams.

Review All Key Topics

Review the most important topic in the chapter, noted with the Key Topic icon in the margin of the page. Table 24-2 lists a reference for this key topic and the page number on which it is found.

Table 24-2 Key Topic for Chapter 24

Key Topic Element	Description	Page
List	Options to consider when making an NFS mount through fstab	515

Define Key Terms

Define the following key terms from this chapter and check your answers in the glossary:

Network File System (NFS), automount

Review Questions

The questions that follow are meant to help you test your knowledge of concepts and terminology and the breadth of your knowledge. You can find the answers to these questions in Appendix A.

1. On your NFS server, you have verified that the nfs service is active, and the firewall allows access to TCP port 2049. A client uses **showmount** against your server but doesn't see any exports. What is the most likely explanation?
2. Which command enables you to show available NFS mounts on server1?
3. Which command enables you to mount an NFS share that is available on server1:/share?
4. How would you mount all NFS shares that are provided by **nfsserver** on the directory /shares?
5. Which additional mount option is required in /etc/fstab to ensure that NFS shares are only mounted after the network services have been started?
6. Which option should you include in /etc/fstab to ensure that changes to the mounted file system are written to the NFS server immediately?

7. Which autofs feature is not supported by systemd automount?
8. What is the name of the main automount configuration file?
9. What is the name of the service that implements automount?
10. Which ports do you need to open in the firewall of the automount client?

End-of-Chapter Lab

In this chapter, you learned how to mount remote file systems and automate those mounts using /etc/fstab or automount. In this end-of-chapter lab, you practice these skills in a way that is similar to how you need to perform them on the exam.

Lab 24.1

1. Set up an NFS server that shares the /home directory on server2.
2. Configure server1 to access the NFS-shared home directory using automount. You need to do this using wildcard automount.

The following topics are covered in this chapter:

- Understanding Local Time
- Using Network Time Protocol
- Managing Time on Red Hat Enterprise Linux

The following RHCSA exam objective is covered in this chapter:

- Configure time service clients

Configuring Time Services

An increasing number of services offered through Linux servers depend on the correct configuration of time on the server. Think of services such as database synchronization, Kerberos authentication, and more. In this chapter, you learn how time is configured on a Linux server.

"Do I Know This Already?" Quiz

The "Do I Know This Already?" quiz enables you to assess whether you should read this entire chapter thoroughly or jump to the "Exam Preparation Tasks" section. If you are in doubt about your answers to these questions or your own assessment of your knowledge of the topics, read the entire chapter. Table 25-1 lists the major headings in this chapter and their corresponding "Do I Know This Already?" quiz questions. You can find the answers in Appendix A, "Answers to the 'Do I Know This Already?' Quizzes and Review Questions."

Table 25-1 "Do I Know This Already?" Section-to-Question Mapping

Foundation Topics Section	Questions
Understanding Local Time	1–2
Using Network Time Protocol	4–5
Managing Time on Red Hat Enterprise Linux	3, 6–10

1. When a system is started, where does it initially get the system time?
    a. NTP
    b. Software time
    c. The hardware clock
    d. Network time

2. Which of the following statements is *not* true about local time?
   a. Local time is the current time in the current time zone.
   b. In local time, DST is considered.
   c. System time typically should correspond to the current local time.
   d. Hardware time typically corresponds to the current local time.

3. Which is the recommended command in RHEL 9 to set the local time zone?
   a. **hwclock**
   b. **tz**
   c. **date**
   d. **timedatectl**

4. Which clock type would you recommend on a server that is *not* connected to any other server but needs to be configured with the most accurate time possible?
   a. RTC
   b. UTC
   c. An atomic clock
   d. NTP

5. Which configuration file contains the default list of NTP servers that should be contacted on RHEL 9?
   a. /etc/ntp/ntp.conf
   b. /etc/ntp.conf
   c. /etc/chrony/chronyd.conf
   d. /etc/chrony.conf

6. Which of the following shows correct syntax to set the current system time to 9:30 p.m.?
   a. **date 9:30**
   b. **date --set 9.30 PM**
   c. **date -s 21:30**
   d. **date 2130**

7. Which command correctly translates epoch time into human time?
   a. **date --date '@1420987251'**
   b. **time --date '$1420987251'**
   c. **time --date '#1420987251'**
   d. **time --date '1420987251'**

8. Which command do you use to set the system time to the current hardware time?
   a. **hwclock --hctosys**
   b. **hwclock --systohc**
   c. **date --set-hc**
   d. **ntpdate**

9. Which command enables you to show current information that includes the local time, hardware time, and the time zone the system is in?
   a. **timedatectl --all**
   b. **timedatectl --tz**
   c. **timedatectl -ht**
   d. **timedatectl**

10. Which command can you use to verify that a time client that is running the chrony service has successfully synchronized?
    a. **timedatectl**
    b. **chronyc sources**
    c. **systemctl chrony status**
    d. **chronyc status**

Foundation Topics

Understanding Local Time

When a Linux server boots, the hardware clock, also referred to as the ***real-time clock (RTC)***, is read. This clock typically resides in the computer hardware, and the time it defines is known as ***hardware time***. Generally, the hardware clock is an integrated circuit on the system board that is completely independent of the current state of the operating system and keeps running even when the computer is shut down, as long as the mainboard battery or power supply feeds it. From the hardware clock, the system gets its initial time setting.

The time on the hardware clock on Linux servers is usually set to ***Coordinated Universal Time (UTC)***. UTC is a time that is the same everywhere on the planet, and based on UTC, the current local time is calculated. (Later in this chapter you learn how this works.)

System time is maintained by the operating system. Once the system has booted, the system clock is completely independent of the hardware clock. Therefore, when system time is changed, the new system time is not automatically synchronized with the hardware clock.

System time maintained by the operating system is kept in UTC. Applications running on the server convert system time into local time. Local time is the actual time in the current time zone. In local time, daylight saving time (DST) is considered so that it always shows an accurate time for that system. Table 25-2 gives an overview of the different concepts that play a role in Linux time.

Table 25-2 Understanding Linux Time

Concept	Explanation
Hardware clock	The hardware clock that resides on the main card of a computer system
Real-time clock	Same as the hardware clock
System time	The time that is maintained by the operating system
Software clock	Similar to system time
Coordinated Universal Time (UTC)	A worldwide standard time
Daylight saving time	Calculation that is made to change time automatically when DST changes occur
Local time	The time that corresponds to the time in the current time zone

Using Network Time Protocol

As you learned, the current system time is based on a hardware clock. This hardware clock is typically a part of the computer's motherboard, and it might be unreliable. Because of its potential unreliability, it is a good idea to use time from a more reliable source. Generally speaking, two solutions are available.

One option is to buy a more reliable hardware clock. This may be, for instance, a very accurate atomic clock connected directly to your computer. When such a very reliable clock is used, an increased accuracy of the system time is guaranteed. Using an external hardware clock is a common solution to guarantee that datacenter time is maintained, even if the connection to external networks for ***time synchronization*** temporarily is not available.

Another and more common solution is to configure your server to use ***Network Time Protocol (NTP)***. NTP is a method of maintaining system time that is provided through NTP servers on the Internet. It is an easy solution to provide an accurate time to servers, because most servers are connected to the Internet anyway.

To determine which Internet NTP server should be used, the concept of stratum is used. The ***stratum*** defines the reliability of an NTP time source, and the lower the stratum, the more reliable it is. Typically, Internet time servers use stratum 1 or 2. When configuring local time servers, you can use a higher stratum number to configure the local time server as a backup, except that it will never be used when Internet time is available.

It is good practice, for example, to set stratum 5 on a local time server with a very reliable hardware clock and stratum 8 on a local time server that is not very reliable. A setting of stratum 10 can be used for the local clock on every node that uses NTP time. This enables the server to still have synchronized time when no external connection is available. Stratum 15 is used by clocks that want to indicate they should not be used for time synchronization.

Setting up a server to use NTP time on RHEL 9 is easy if the server is already connected to the Internet. If this is the case, the /etc/chrony.conf file is configured with a standard list of NTP servers on the Internet that should be contacted. The only thing the administrator has to do is switch on NTP, by using **timedatectl set-ntp 1**.

Managing Time on Red Hat Enterprise Linux

Different commands are involved in managing time on Red Hat Enterprise Linux. Table 25-3 provides an overview.

Table 25-3 Commands Related to RHEL 9 Time Management

Command	Short Description
date	Manages local time
hwclock	Manages hardware time
timedatectl	Developed to manage all aspects of time on RHEL 9

On a Linux system, time is calculated as an offset of epoch time. ***Epoch time*** is the number of seconds since January 1, 1970, in UTC. In some logs (such as /var/log/audit/audit.log), you'll find timestamps in epoch time and not in human time. To convert such an epoch timestamp to human time, you can use the **--date** option, followed by the epoch string, starting with an @:

```
date --date '@1420987251'
```

The use of epoch time also creates a potential timing problem on Linux. On a 32-bit system, the number of seconds that can be counted in the field that is reserved for time notation will be exceeded in 2037. (Try setting the time to somewhere in 2050 if you are on a 32-bit kernel; it will not work.) However, 64-bit systems can address time until far into the twenty-second century.

Using date

The **date** command enables you to manage the system time. You can also use it to show the current time in different formats. Some common usage examples of **date** are listed here:

- **date:** Shows the current system time
- **date +%d-%m-%y:** Shows the current system day of month, month, and year
- **date -s 16:03:** Sets the current time to 3 minutes past 4 p.m.

Using hwclock

The **date** command enables you to set and show the current system time. Using the **date** command will not change the hardware time that is used on your system. To manage hardware time, you can use the **hwclock** command. The **hwclock** command has many options, some of which are of particular interest:

- **hwclock --systohc:** Synchronizes current system time to the hardware clock
- **hwclock --hctosys:** Synchronizes current hardware time to the system clock

Using timedatectl

A command that was introduced in RHEL 7 that enables you to manage many aspects of time is **timedatectl**. As shown in Example 25-1, when used without any arguments, this command shows detailed information about the current time and date. It also displays the time zone your system is in, in addition to information about the use of NTP ***network time*** and information about the use of DST.

Example 25-1 Using **timedatectl** to Get Detailed Information About Current Time Settings

```
[root@server1 ~]# timedatectl
               Local time: Mon 2019-06-10 08:27:57 EDT
           Universal time: Mon 2019-06-10 12:27:57 UTC
                 RTC time: Mon 2019-06-10 12:27:57
                Time zone: America/New_York (EDT, -0400)
System clock synchronized: yes
              NTP service: active
          RTC in local TZ: no
```

The **timedatectl** command works with commands to perform time operations. Table 25-4 provides an overview of the relevant commands.

Table 25-4 **timedatectl** Command Overview

Command	Explanation
status	Shows the current time settings
set-time TIME	Sets the current time
set-timezone ZONE	Sets the current time zone
list-timezone	Shows a list of all time zones
set-local-rtc [0|1]	Controls whether the RTC (hardware clock) is in local time
set-ntp [0|1]	Controls whether NTP is enabled

The **timedatectl** command was developed as a generic solution to manage time on RHEL. It has some functions that are offered through other commands, but the purpose of the command is that eventually it will replace other commands used for managing time and date settings. When **timedatectl** is used to switch on NTP time, it talks to the **chronyd** process. Exercise 25-1 walks you through some common options to manage time on a RHEL 9 server.

Exercise 25-1 Managing Local Time

1. Open a root shell and type **date**.
2. Type **hwclock** and see whether it shows approximately the same time as **date** in step 1.
3. Type **timedatectl status** to show current time settings.
4. Type **timedatectl list-timezones** to show a list of all time zone definitions.
5. Type **timedatectl set-timezone Europe/Amsterdam** to set the current time zone to Amsterdam.
6. Type **timedatectl show** and note the differences with the previous output.
7. Type **timedatectl set-ntp 1** to switch on NTP use. You might see the error "failed to issue method call." If you get this message, type **dnf -y install chrony** and try again.
8. Open the configuration file /etc/chrony.conf and look up the server lines. These are used to specify the servers that should be used for NTP time synchronization.
9. Type **systemctl status chronyd** and verify that the chrony service is started and enabled. If this is not the case, use **systemctl start chronyd; systemctl enable chronyd** to make sure that it is operational.
10. Type **systemctl status -l chronyd** and read the status information. Example 25-2 shows you what the output of the command should look like.

Example 25-2 Monitoring Current Time Synchronization Status

```
[root@server1 ~]# systemctl status -l chronyd
   chronyd.service - NTP client/server
         Loaded: loaded (/usr/lib/systemd/system/chronyd.service;
  enabled; vendor preset: enabled)
        Active: active (running) since Mon 2019-06-10 05:22:30 EDT;
  3h 8min ago
       Docs: man:chronyd(8)
           man:chrony.conf(5)
        Main PID: 1062 (chronyd)
        Tasks: 1 (limit: 11365)
        Memory: 1.5M
        CGroup: /system.slice/chronyd.service
            └─1062 /usr/sbin/chronyd
```

```
Jun 10 07:21:04 server1.example.com chronyd[1062]: Selected source
  5.200.6.34
Jun 10 07:28:40 server1.example.com chronyd[1062]: Selected source
  213.154.236.182
Jun 10 07:28:42 server1.example.com chronyd[1062]: Source
  149.210.142.45 replaced with 195.242.98.57
Jun 10 07:43:51 server1.example.com chronyd[1062]: Selected source
  5.200.6.34
Jun 10 07:53:35 server1.example.com chronyd[1062]: Selected source
  195.242.98.57
Jun 10 08:16:24 server1.example.com chronyd[1062]: Forward time jump
  detected!
Jun 10 08:16:24 server1.example.com chronyd[1062]: Can't synchronise:
  no selectable sources
Jun 10 08:20:44 server1.example.com chronyd[1062]: Selected source
  213.154.236.182
Jun 10 08:22:57 server1.example.com chronyd[1062]: Source
  195.242.98.57 replaced with 195.191.113.251
Jun 10 08:25:05 server1.example.com chronyd[1062]: Selected source
  5.200.6.34
```

Managing Time Zone Settings

Between Linux servers, time is normally communicated in UTC. This allows servers across different time zones to use the same time settings, which makes managing time in large organizations a lot easier. To make it easier for end users, though, the local time must also be set. To do this, you need to select the appropriate time zone.

On Red Hat Enterprise Linux 9, you have three approaches to setting the correct local time zone:

- Go to the directory /usr/share/zoneinfo, where you'll find different subdirectories containing files for each time zone that has been defined. To set the local time zone on a server, you can create a symbolic link with the name /etc/localtime to the time zone file that is involved. If you want to set local time to Los Angeles time, for instance, use **ln -sf /usr/share/zoneinfo/America/Los_Angeles /etc/localtime**.
- Use the **tzselect** utility. This tool starts the interface shown in Example 25-3, from which the appropriate region and locale can be selected.
- Use **timedatectl** to set the time zone information; this is the recommended method.

Example 25-3 Selecting the Time Zone Using **tzselect**

```
[root@localhost ~]# tzselect
Please identify a location so that time zone rules can be set
  correctly.
Please select a continent, ocean, "coord", or "TZ".
 1) Africa
 2) Americas
 3) Antarctica
 4) Asia
 5) Atlantic Ocean
 6) Australia
 7) Europe
 8) Indian Ocean
 9) Pacific Ocean
10) coord - I want to use geographical coordinates.
11) TZ - I want to specify the time zone using the Posix TZ format.
#? 1
Please select a country whose clocks agree with yours.
 1) Algeria                  20) Gambia          39) Sao Tome & Principe
 2) Angola                   21) Ghana           40) Senegal
 3) Benin                    22) Guinea          41) Sierra Leone
 4) Botswana                 23) Guinea-Bissau   42) Somalia
 5) Burkina Faso             24) Kenya           43) South Africa
 6) Burundi                  25) Lesotho         44) South Sudan
 7) Côte d'Ivoire            26) Liberia         45) Spain
 8) Cameroon                 27) Libya           46) St Helena
 9) Central African Rep.     28) Madagascar      47) Sudan
10) Chad                     29) Malawi          48) Swaziland
11) Comoros                  30) Mali            49) Tanzania
12) Congo (Dem. Rep.)        31) Mauritania      50) Togo
13) Congo (Rep.)             32) Mayotte         51) Tunisia
14) Djibouti                 33) Morocco         52) Uganda
15) Egypt                    34) Mozambique      53) Western Sahara
16) Equatorial Guinea        35) Namibia         54) Zambia
17) Eritrea                  36) Niger           55) Zimbabwe
18) Ethiopia                 37) Nigeria
19) Gabon                    38) Rwanda
#? 54
```

```
The following information has been given:

        Zambia
        Central Africa Time

Therefore TZ='Africa/Maputo' will be used.
Selected time is now: Mon Jul 22 12:03:41 CAT 2019.
Universal Time is now: Mon Jul 22 10:03:41 UTC 2019.
Is the above information OK?
1) Yes
2) No
#? 1

You can make this change permanent for yourself by appending the line
  TZ='Africa/Maputo'; export TZ to the file '.profile' in your home
  directory; then log out and log in again.

Here is that TZ value again, this time on standard output so that you
  can use the /usr/bin/tzselect command in shell scripts: Africa/Maputo
```

Configuring Time Service Clients

By default, the **chrony** service is configured to get the right time from the Internet. As a default configuration, the highly reliable time servers from pool.ntp.org are used to synchronize time. However, in a corporate environment it is not always desirable for time clients to go out to the Internet, and local time services should be used instead. This can be configured by making a simple modification to the chrony.conf configuration file.

By default, the chrony.conf configuration file contains the line pool 2.rhel.pool.ntp.org. If you comment out this line by putting a pound sign in front of it and add the line server yourtimeserver.example.com, your time server will be used instead of the servers in pool.ntp.org. Exercise 25-2 explains how to make this modification. Notice that this exercise requires access to two servers, in which server1 is configured as the time server and server2 is configured as the time client.

Exercise 25-2 Configuring an NTP Time Client

1. On server1, open a root shell and use **vim /etc/chrony.conf** to edit the chrony main configuration file.
2. Disable the line pool 2.rhel.pool.ntp.org by putting a # sign in front of it.
3. Include the line **allow 192.168.0.0/16** to allow access from all clients that use a local IP address starting with 192.168.
4. Also include the line **local stratum 8**. This ensures that the local time server is going to advertise itself with a stratum of 8, which means it will be used by clients, but only if no Internet time servers are available. Next, close the configuration file.
5. Use **systemctl restart chronyd** to restart the chrony process with the new settings.
6. Still on server1, type **firewall-cmd --add-service ntp --permanent**, followed by **firewall-cmd --reload**. This opens the firewall for time services.
7. Open a root shell on server2.
8. On server2, open the configuration file /etc/chrony.conf and disable the line **pool 2.rhel.pool.ntp.org**.
9. Add the line server **server1.example.com**. Make sure that name resolution to server1.example.com is configured, and if not, use the IP address of server1 instead.
10. Type **systemctl restart chronyd** to restart the chrony service with the new settings.
11. On server2, type the command **chronyc sources**. It should show the name or IP address of server1, the stratum of 8 that is advertised, and a synchronization status indicating that server2 has successfully synchronized its time.

Summary

In this chapter, you learned how time works on Linux. You read how your operating system can get its time by using hardware time, system time, and local time. You also learned how to manage time using the **date, hwclock**, and **timedatectl** commands.

Exam Preparation Tasks

As mentioned in the section "How to Use This Book" in the Introduction, you have several choices for exam preparation: the end-of-chapter labs; the memory tables in Appendix C; Chapter 27, "Final Preparation"; and the practice exams.

Review All Key Topics

Review the most important topics in the chapter, noted with the Key Topic icon in the margin of the page. Table 25-5 lists a reference for these key topics and the page number on which each is found.

Table 25-5 Key Topics for Chapter 25

Key Topic Element	Description	Page
Paragraph	Definition of hardware time	526
Paragraph	Definition of system time	526
Table 25-2	Understanding Linux Time	526
Paragraph	Using NTP time	527
Table 25-3	Commands Related to RHEL 9 Time Management	528
Paragraph	Explanation of epoch time	528
Table 25-4	**timedatectl** Command Overview	529

Complete Tables and Lists from Memory

Print a copy of Appendix C, "Memory Tables" (found on the companion website), or at least the section for this chapter, and complete the tables and lists from memory. Appendix D, "Memory Tables Answer Key," includes completed tables and lists to check your work.

Define Key Terms

Define the following key terms from this chapter and check your answers in the glossary:

real-time clock (RTC), hardware time, Coordinated Universal Time (UTC), system time, time synchronization, Network Time Protocol (NTP), stratum, epoch time, network time

Review Questions

The questions that follow are meant to help you test your knowledge of concepts and terminology and the breadth of your knowledge. You can find the answers to these questions in Appendix A.

1. Which command enables you to set the system time to 4:24 p.m.?
2. Which command sets hardware time to the current system time?
3. Which command enables you to show epoch time as human-readable time?
4. Which command enables you to synchronize the system clock with hardware time?
5. Which service is used to manage NTP time on RHEL 9?
6. Which command enables you to use NTP time on your server?
7. Which configuration file contains the list of NTP servers to be used?
8. Which command enables you to list time zones?
9. Which command enables you to set the current time zone?
10. How do you use chrony to set system time?

End-of-Chapter Lab

In this chapter, you learned how to manage time on Linux servers. Because it is very important to ensure that a server uses the correct time, you can now practice some of the most essential skills you have acquired in this chapter.

Lab 25.1

1. Compare the current hardware time to the system time. If there is a difference, make sure to synchronize time.
2. Set the time zone to correspond to the current time in Boston (USA East Coast).

The following topics are covered in this chapter:

- Understanding Containers
- Running a Container
- Working with Container Images
- Managing Containers
- Managing Container Storage
- Running Containers as Systemd Services

The following RHCSA exam objectives are covered in this chapter:

- Find and retrieve container images from a remote registry
- Inspect container images
- Perform container management using commands such as podman and skopeo
- Build a container from a Containerfile
- Perform basic container management such as running, starting, stopping, and listing running containers
- Run a service inside a container
- Configure a container to start automatically as a systemd service
- Attach persistent storage to a container

Managing Containers

Containers have revolutionized datacenter IT. Where services not so long ago were running directly on top of the server operating system, nowadays services are often offered as containers. Red Hat Enterprise Linux 9 includes a complete platform to run containers. In this chapter you learn how to work with them.

"Do I Know This Already?" Quiz

The "Do I Know This Already?" quiz enables you to assess whether you should read this entire chapter thoroughly or jump to the "Exam Preparation Tasks" section. If you are in doubt about your answers to these questions or your own assessment of your knowledge of the topics, read the entire chapter. Table 26-1 lists the major headings in this chapter and their corresponding "Do I Know This Already?" quiz questions. You can find the answers in Appendix A, "Answers to the 'Do I Know This Already?' Quizzes and Review Questions."

Table 26-1 "Do I Know This Already?" Section-to-Question Mapping

Foundation Topics Section	Questions
Understanding Containers	1, 2
Running a Container	3, 4
Working with Container Images	5, 6
Managing Containers	7
Managing Container Storage	8, 9
Running Containers as Systemd Services	10

1. The success of containers depends on different Linux features. Which of the following is not one of them?
   a. Cgroups
   b. Semaphores
   c. Namespaces
   d. SELinux

2. What is the name of the Red Hat solution to add enterprise features such as scalability and availability to containers?
   a. OpenStack
   b. OpenShift
   c. Kubernetes
   d. JBoss

3. How do you detach from a running container without shutting it down?
   a. **exit**
   b. **quit**
   c. **detach**
   d. Ctrl-P, Ctrl-Q

4. Which command will run an application container in the background?
   a. **podman run nginx**
   b. **podman run -d nginx**
   c. **podman run --background nginx**
   d. **podman run -it nginx**

5. Which command do you use to inspect images that have not yet been pulled to your local system?
   a. **podman inspect**
   b. **buildah inspect**
   c. **skopeo inspect**
   d. **docker inspect**

6. Which command do you use for an overview of the registries currently in use?
   a. **podman info**
   b. **podman status**
   c. **podman search**
   d. **podman registries**

7. There are many ways to figure out whether a container needs any environment variables. Which of the following can you use?

   a. Use **podman inspect** to inspect the image that you want to run. Within the image, you'll often find usage information.

   b. Use **podman run** to run the container. If environment variables are required, it will fail. You can next use **podman logs** to inspect messages that have been logged to STDOUT.

   c. Read the documentation provided in the container registry.

   d. All of the above.

8. Which SELinux context type must be set on host directories that you want to expose as persistent storage in the container using bind mounts?

   a. **container_t**

   b. **container_file_t**

   c. **container_storage_t**

   d. **public_content_rw_t**

9. Which of the following commands shows correct syntax to automatically set the correct SELinux context type on a host directory that should be exposed as persistent storage inside a container?

   a. **podman run --name mynginx -v /opt/nginx:/var/lib/nginx nginx**

   b. **podman run --name mynginx --bind /opt/nginx:/var/lib/nginx nginx**

   c. **podman run --name mynginx -v /opt/nginx:/var/lib/nginx:Z nginx**

   d. **podman run --name mynginx --bind /opt/nginx:/var/lib/nginx:Z nginx**

10. What is needed to ensure that a container that user anna has created can be started as a systemd service at system start, not just when user anna is logging in?

    a. Configure the container as a systemd service.

    b. Use **loginctl enable-linger anna** to enable the linger feature for user anna.

    c. Use **systemctl enable-linger anna** to enable the linger feature for user anna.

    d. Just use **systemctl --user enable** to enable the container.

Foundation Topics

Understanding Containers

In the past decade, containers have revolutionized the way services are offered. Where not so long ago physical or virtual servers were installed to offer application access, this is now done by using containers. But what exactly is a container? Let's start with an easy conceptual description: a ***container*** is just a fancy way to run an application based on a container image that contains all dependencies required to run that application.

To install a noncontainerized application on a server, the server administrator must make sure that not only the application is installed but also all the other software dependencies required by the application. This includes, for instance, the right (supported) version of the underlying operating system. This makes it difficult for application developers, who need to provide many versions of their applications to support all current operating systems.

A container is a complete package that runs on top of the ***container engine***, an integrated part of the host operating system. A container is comparable to an application on your smartphone: you get the complete application package from the smartphone's app store and install it on your phone.

To use a container, you run the container from the container image. This container image is found in the container ***registry***, which can be compared to the app store that hosts smartphone applications. The result is the container, which is the runnable instance of the container image.

To run containers, you need a host operating system that includes a container engine, as well as some tools used to manage the containers. On versions of RHEL prior to RHEL 8, this was supported by Docker. Docker delivered the container engine as well as the tools to manage the containers. In RHEL 8, Red Hat replaced Docker with a new solution, which is still used on RHEL 9: ***CRI-o*** is the container engine, and Red Hat offers three main tools to manage the containers:

- **podman:** The main tool, used to start, stop, and manage containers
- **buildah:** A specialized tool that helps you create custom images
- **skopeo:** A tool that is used for managing and testing container images

Container Host Requirements

Sometimes it is said that containers are Linux, and that is true. This is because containers rely heavily on features that are offered by the Linux kernel, including the following:

- Namespaces for isolation between processes
- Control groups for resource management
- SELinux for security

Let's explore each of these features. To start with, containers need namespaces. A ***namespace*** provides isolation for system resources. To best understand what namespaces are like, let's look at the chroot jail, a feature that was introduced in the 1990s. A chroot jail is a security feature that presents the contents of a directory as if it is the root directory of your system, so the process that runs in a chroot jail can't see anything but the contents of that directory.

Chroot jails are important for security. When a process is restricted to just the contents of a chroot jail, there is no risk of it accessing other parts of the operating system. However, to make sure this works, all the dependencies required to run the process must be present in the chroot jail.

Chroot jails still exist, but the functionality is now leveraged and is a part of what is called the mount namespace. Here's an overview of it and some of the other namespaces (note that new namespaces may be added in the future as well):

- **Mount:** The mount namespace is equivalent to the chroot namespace. The contents of a directory are presented in such a way that no other directories can be accessed.
- **Process:** A process namespace makes sure that processes running in this namespace cannot reach or connect to processes in other namespaces.
- **Network:** Network namespaces can be compared to VLAN. Nodes connected to a specific network namespace cannot see what is happening in other network namespaces, and contact to other namespaces is possible only through routers.
- **User:** The user namespace can be used to separate user IDs and group IDs between namespaces. As a result, user accounts are specific to each namespace, and a user who is available in one namespace may not be available in another namespace.
- **Interprocess communication (ipc):** Interprocess communication is what processes use to connect to one another, and these namespaces ensure that connection can be made only to processes in the same namespace.

In containers, almost all of the namespaces are implemented to ensure that the container is a perfectly isolated environment. Only the network namespace is not enabled by default, to ensure that communication between containers is not restricted by default.

The second important Linux component that is required for running containers is the control group, or cgroup. Cgroups are a kernel feature that enables resource access limitation. By default, there is no restriction to the amount of memory or the number of CPU cycles a process can access. Cgroups make it possible to create that limitation in such a way that each container has strictly limited access to available resources.

The last important pillar of containers is implemented on RHEL by using SELinux. As you've learned elsewhere in this book, SELinux secures access by using resource labels. On RHEL, a specific context label is added to ensure that containers can access only the resources they need access to and nothing else.

Containers on RHEL 9

Since its launch in 2014, ***Docker*** has been the leading solution for running containers. Up to RHEL 7, Docker was the default container stack used on Red Hat Enterprise Linux. As previously mentioned, with the release of RHEL 8, Red Hat decided to discontinue Docker support and offer its own stack. This stack is based on the CRI-o container runtime and uses Podman as the main tool to run containers. The new solution offers a few advantages over the Docker solution:

- In Podman, containers can be started by ordinary users that do not need any elevated privileges. This is called the *rootless container*.
- When users start containers, the containers run in a user namespace where they are strictly isolated and not accessible to other users.
- Podman containers run on top of the lightweight CRI-o container runtime, without needing any daemon to do their work.

An important benefit of using Podman is the rootless container. On RHEL 8 and 9, rootless containers are started by non-root users and don't require root privileges. This makes running containers much more secure, but it also does come with some challenges. Rootless containers cannot access any components on the host operating system that require root access. For example, rootless containers do not have an IP address (because it requires root privileges to allocate an IP address) and can bind only to a nonprivileged TCP or UDP port. Also, if the rootless container needs access to host-based storage, the user who runs the container must be owner of the directory that provides the storage.

Container Orchestration

The solutions for running containers that are discussed in this chapter are all about running standalone containers on top of a single host. If that host goes down, you don't have any running containers left anymore. When containers are used to run mission-critical services, additional features are needed. They include the following:

- Easy connection to a wide range of external storage types
- Secure access to sensitive data
- Decoupling, such that site-specific data is strictly separated from the code inside the container environment
- Scalability, such that when the workload increases, additional instances can easily be added
- Availability, ensuring that the outage of a container host doesn't result in container unavailability

To implement these features, Kubernetes has developed itself as the industry standard. ***Kubernetes*** is open source and, currently, it is the only solution that matters for adding enterprise features to containers. Red Hat has its own Kubernetes distribution, which is called ***OpenShift***. For building a scalable, flexible, and reliable infrastructure based on containers, you should investigate the options offered by either Kubernetes or OpenShift. These topics are outside the scope of the RHCSA exam and for that reason will not be discussed further here.

Running a Container

To get familiar with containers, let's start by running some. To get full access to all tools that RHEL is offering for running containers, you should start by installing the appropriate software. You can do this by using **sudo dnf install container-tools**. After installing this software, you can start running your first container by using **podman run**, which does not require any root privileges. You can use this command with many arguments; the only argument that is really required, however, is the name of the image that you want to run. As we discuss later, the ***image*** is fetched from one of the container registries that is configured by default. To run your first container, use the command **podman run nginx**. This will try to start the **nginx** image from one of the known registries. You can see the result of running this command in Example 26-1.

Example 26-1 Podman May Prompt Which Registry You Want to Use

```
[root@server1 ~]# podman run nginx
? Please select an image:
    registry.fedoraproject.org/nginx:latest
    registry.access.redhat.com/nginx:latest
    registry.centos.org/nginx:latest
    quay.io/nginx:latest
    docker.io/library/nginx:latest
```

While using **podman run**, it may not be clear from which registry the image you want to run should be started. If that is the case, the **podman** command will prompt to make a choice from one of the available registries, as can be seen in Example 26-1. This can be avoided by including the complete registry name of the image: if you use **podman run docker.io/library/nginx**, Podman knows it needs to fetch the image from the docker.io registry. Example 26-2 shows how this works out.

Example 26-2 Running Your First Container with **podman run nginx**

```
[root@server1 ~]# podman run docker.io/librarynginx
Resolved "nginx" as an alias (/var/cache/containers/short-name-
  aliases.conf)
Trying to pull docker.io/library/nginx:latest...
Getting image source signatures
Copying blob eef26ceb3309 done
Copying blob 71689475aec2 done
Copying blob 8e3ed6a9e43a done
Copying blob f88a23025338 done
Copying blob 0df440342e26 done
Copying blob e9995326b091 done
Copying config 76c69feac3 done
Writing manifest to image destination
Storing signatures
/docker-entrypoint.sh: /docker-entrypoint.d/ is not empty, will
  attempt to perform configuration
/docker-entrypoint.sh: Looking for shell scripts in /
  docker-entrypoint.d/
/docker-entrypoint.sh: Launching /docker-entrypoint.d/10-listen-on-
  ipv6-by-default.sh
10-listen-on-ipv6-by-default.sh: info: Getting the checksum of /etc/
  nginx/conf.d/default.conf
10-listen-on-ipv6-by-default.sh: info: Enabled listen on IPv6 in /etc/
  nginx/conf.d/default.conf
/docker-entrypoint.sh: Launching /docker-entrypoint.d/20-envsubst-on-
  templates.sh
```

```
/docker-entrypoint.sh: Launching /docker-entrypoint.d/30-tune-worker-
  processes.sh
/docker-entrypoint.sh: Configuration complete; ready for start up
2022/10/31 07:27:27 [notice] 1#1: using the "epoll" event method
2022/10/31 07:27:27 [notice] 1#1: nginx/1.23.2
2022/10/31 07:27:27 [notice] 1#1: built by gcc 10.2.1 20210110 (Debian
  10.2.1-6)
2022/10/31 07:27:27 [notice] 1#1: OS: Linux 5.14.0-70.13.1.el9_0.x86_64
2022/10/31 07:27:27 [notice] 1#1: getrlimit(RLIMIT_NOFILE):
  1048576:1048576
2022/10/31 07:27:27 [notice] 1#1: start worker processes
2022/10/31 07:27:27 [notice] 1#1: start worker process 24
2022/10/31 07:27:27 [notice] 1#1: start worker process 25
```

As you can see in Example 26-2, when running the container, Podman starts by fetching the container image from the registry you want to use. Container images typically consist of multiple layers, which is why you can see that different blobs are copied. When the image file is available on your local server, the nginx container is started. As you will also notice, the container runs in the foreground. Use Ctrl-C to terminate the container.

You typically want to run containers in detached mode (which runs the container in the background) or in a mode where you have access to the container console. You can run a container in detached mode by using **podman run -d nginx**. Notice that all options that modify the **podman** command (**podman run** in this case) need to be placed behind the **podman** command and not after the name of the image.

When you run a container in detached mode, it really runs like a daemon in the background. Alternatively, you can run the container in interactive TTY mode. In this mode, you get access to the container TTY and from there can work within the container. However, this makes sense only if the container is configured to start a shell as its default command. If it does not, you may have to add /bin/sh to the container image, so that it starts a shell instead of its default command.

Let's have a look at how this works:

Step 1. To start the nginx image in interactive TTY mode, use the command **podman run -it nginx**.

Step 2. You are now connected to a TTY in which you only have access to the nginx process output. That doesn't make sense, so use Ctrl-C to get out.

Step 3. Now start the container using **podman run -it nginx /bin/sh**. This will start the **/bin/sh** command, instead of the container default command, which will give you access to a shell. After starting the container in this way, you have access to the TTY, and all the commands that you enter are entered in the container and not on the host operating system.

TIP Container images are normally created as minimal environments, and for that reason you may not be able to run a bash shell. That's why in the previous example we used **/bin/sh**. This is a minimal shell, and no matter which container image you use, it will always be there.

When you're running in interactive mode, there are two ways to get out of it:

- Use **exit** to exit the TTY mode. If you started the container using **podman run -it nginx /bin/sh**, this will stop the container. That's because the **exit** command stops the primary container command, and once that is stopped the container has no reason to be around anymore.
- Use Ctrl-P, Ctrl-Q to detach. This approach ensures that in all cases the container keeps on running in the background in detached mode. That may not always be very useful though. If like in the previous example you've started the nginx image with **/bin/sh** as the default command (instead of the nginx service), keeping it around might not make much sense because it isn't providing any functionality anyway.

To get an overview of currently running containers, you can use the **podman ps** command. This will show you only containers that are currently running. If a container has been started but has already been stopped, you won't see it. If you also want to see containers that have been running but are now inactive, use **podman ps -a**. In Example 26-3 you can see the output of the **podman ps -a** command.

Example 26-3 podman ps -a Output

```
student@podman ~]$ podman ps -a
CONTAINER ID  IMAGE        COMMAND     CREATED          STATUS
PORTS            NAMES
1f6426109d3f  docker.io/      sh          6 minutes ago  Exited (0) 6
  minutes ago  adoring_
              library/
feynman
              busybox: latest
0fa670dc56fe  docker.io/      nginx -g    8 minutes ago  Up 8
  minutes              web1
              library/      daemon o...                   ago
              nginx:latest
15520f225787  docker.io/     nginx -g     32 minutes ago Exited (0)
  32 minutes ago peaceful_
              library/     daemon o...
visvesvaraya
              nginx:latest
```

Notice the various columns in the output of the **podman ps** command. Table 26-2 summarizes what these columns are used for.

Table 26-2 podman ps Output Columns Overview

Column	Use
CONTAINER_ID	The automatically generated container ID; often used in names of files created for this container.
IMAGE	The complete registry reference to the image used for this container.
COMMAND	The command that was started as the default command with this container.
CREATED	The identifier when the container was created.
STATUS	Current status.
PORTS	If applicable, ports configured or forwarded for this container.
NAMES	The name of this container. If no name was specified, a name will be automatically generated.

In Exercise 26-1 you can practice running containers and basic container management.

Exercise 26-1 Running Containers with podman

1. Use **sudo dnf install container-tools** to install the container software.
2. Type **podman ps -a** to get an overview of currently existing containers. Observe the STATUS field, where you can see whether the container currently is active.
3. Type **podman run -d nginx.** This command starts an nginx container in detached mode.
4. Type **podman ps** and observe the output. In the CONTAINER ID field, you'll see the unique ID that has been generated. Also observe the NAME field, where you'll see a name that has automatically been generated.
5. Type **podman run -it busybox**. This command runs the busybox cloud image, a minimized Linux distribution that is often used as the foundation for building custom containers.
6. Because the busybox container image was configured to run a shell as the default command, you'll get access to the shell that it is running. Type **ps aux** to see the processes running in this container namespace. Notice that the **ps** command works, which is not the case for all container images you may be using.
7. Type **exit** to close the busybox shell.

8. Type **podman ps**. You won't see the busybox container anymore because in the previous step you exited it.
9. Type **podman run -it busybox** once more, and when you have access to its interactive shell, press Ctrl-P, Ctrl-Q to detach.
10. Use **podman ps**. You'll notice the busybox container is still running. Look at the NAME column to find the name for the container that was automatically generated.
11. Use **podman attach <name>**, where <name> should be replaced with the name you found in the preceding step. This will reconnect you to the shell that is still waiting on the busybox container.
12. Use Ctrl-P, Ctrl-Q again to detach.
13. Type **podman stop <name>**. This will stop the busybox container.

TIP When you run non-root containers, the container files are copied to the ~/.local/share/containers/storage directory. Make sure you have enough storage space in the user home directory. With an average file size of about 60 MB for each container, disk space will be used fast!

Working with Container Images

The foundation of every container is the container image. The container is a running instance of the image, where while running it a writable layer is added to store changes made to the container. To work with images successfully, you need to know how to access container registries and how to find the appropriate image from these registries. Container images are created in the Docker format. The Docker format has become an important standard for defining container images, which is why you can run container images in Docker format without any problem in RHEL.

Using Registries

Container images are typically fetched from container registries, which are specified in the /etc/containers/registries.conf configuration file. A user who runs a rootless container can create a file ~/.config/containers/registries.conf. In case of conflict, settings in the user-specific file will override settings in the generic file.

In the registries.conf file, different registries are in use by default. Don't worry too much about the exact names of these registries, as they tend to change between different versions of RHEL. Among the registries, you'll find Red Hat registries that give access to licensed software. You need to enter your Red Hat credentials to access these registries. Also, the Docker registry is used. Docker hosts the biggest container registry currently available, containing more than 10,000,000 images, and adding the Docker registry as the last registry will increase your chances of finding the desired container image.

In the registries.conf file, all container registries are listed as unqualified-search-registries. This is because Red Hat recommends the complete image name (including the registry you want to use it from) to avoid ambiguity. So instead of using **podman run -d nginx**, use **podman run -d docker.io/library/nginx**.

To see which registries are currently used, you can use the **podman info** command. Apart from information about the registries that are used, this command also shows other useful information about your current environment. Example 26-4 shows what the output of this command might look like.

Example 26-4 Using **podman info** to Find Which Registries Are Used

```
[student@server1 ~]$ podman info | grep -A 10 registries
registries:
  search:
  - registry.fedoraproject.org
  - registry.access.redhat.com
  - registry.centos.org
  - quay.io
  - docker.io
store:
  configFile: /home/student/.config/containers/storage.conf
  containerStore:
    number: 0   OsArch: linux/amd64
  Version: 4.0.2
```

NOTE Much of what is happening in containerized environments is standardized in the Open Containers Initiative (OCI). All companies involved in containers are currently making a huge effort to make their containers OCI compliant. Because of this, you can use Docker images without any issues in a podman environment.

Finding Images

To find available images, you can use the **podman search** command. If you need to access images from one of the subscriber-only Red Hat registries as well, you need to log in to the registry first because the Red Hat registries are accessible only to users who have a valid Red Hat account. Use **podman login** to enter your current Red Hat username and password, which will give you access to these registries. To log in to a registry, you have to specify the name of the registry you want to log in to. For instance, use **podman login registry.access.redhat.com** to log in to that specific registry.

After enabling access to the Red Hat registries that you want to use, use **podman search** to find the images you need. Example 26-5 shows the partial result of the **podman search mariadb** command output.

Example 26-5 podman search mariadb Partial Result

```
INDEX        NAME                    DESCRIPTION
  STARS    OFFICIAL    AUTOMATED
docker.io  docker.io/panubo/    MariaDB Galera Cluster          23
  [OK]
           mariadb-galera
docker.io  docker.io/demyx/     Non-root Docker image running   0
           mariadb              Alpine Linux a...
docker.io  docker.io/toughiq/   Dockerized Automated MariaDB    41
  [OK]
           mariadb-cluster      Galera Cluster ...
docker.io  docker.io/bianjp/    Lightweight MariaDB docker      15
  [OK]
           mariadb-alpine       image with Alpine...
docker.io  docker.io/           MariaDB relational database     2
  [OK]
           clearlinux/mariadb   management syste...
docker.io  docker.io/           Fast, simple, and lightweight   2
  [OK]
           jonbaldie/mariadb    MariaDB Docker...
docker.io  docker.io/           Docker MariaDB server w/        1
  [OK]
           tiredofit/mariadb    S6 Overlay, Zabbix ...
```

In the output of **podman search**, different fields are used to describe the images that were found. Table 26-3 gives an overview.

Table 26-3 podman search Output Fields

Field	Use
INDEX	The name of the registry where this image was found.
NAME	The full name of the image.
DESCRIPTION	A more verbose description. Use **--no-trunc** to see the complete description.
STARS	A community appreciation, expressed in stars.
OFFICIAL	Indicates whether this image was provided by the software vendor.
AUTOMATED	Indicates whether this image is automatically built.

You might notice that in some cases this **podman search** command gives a lot of results. To filter down the results a bit, you can use the **--filter** option. Use **podman search --filter is-official=true alpine** to see only alpine images that are created by the application vendor, for instance, or **podman search --filter stars=5 alpine** to show only alpine images that have been appreciated with at least five stars. Alpine is a common cloud image that is used a lot, because it is really small.

TIP While you're looking for images, search for the UBI images in the Red Hat registries. UBI stands for Universal Base Image, and it's the image that is used as the foundation for all of the Red Hat products.

Inspecting Images

Because images are provided by the open source community, it is important to get more information before you start using them. This allows you to investigate what exactly the image is doing. The best way to do so is to use the **skopeo inspect** command. The advantage of using **skopeo** to inspect images is that the inspection happens directly from the registry without any need to first pull the image.

Alternatively, you can inspect local images. To do so, use **podman inspect**. This command works only on images that are available on your local system but gives more detailed output than **skopeo inspect**. Use **podman images** for a list of images that are locally available, and use **podman pull** to pull an image first. Example 26-6 shows a partial result of the **podman inspect** command.

Example 26-6 Using **podman inspect** to Verify Image Contents

```
student@podman ~]$ podman inspect busybox
[
    {
        "Id":
"6858809bf669cc5da7cb6af83d0fae838284d12e1be0182f92f6bd96559873e3",
        "Digest": "sha256:d366a4665ab44f0648d7a00ae3fae139d55e32f9712c
  67accd604bb55df9d05a",
        "RepoTags": [
            "docker.io/library/busybox:latest"
        ],
        "RepoDigests": [
"docker.io/library/busybox@sha256:2ca5e69e244d2da7368f7088ea3ad0653c3ce
  7aaccd0b8823d11b0d5de956002",
"docker.io/library/busybox@sha256:d366a4665ab44f0648d7a00ae3fae139d55e3
  2f9712c67accd604bb55df9d05a"
        ],
       "Parent": "",
        "Comment": "",
        "Created": "2020-09-09T01:38:02.334927351Z",
        "Config": {
            "Env": [
"PATH=/usr/local/sbin:/usr/local/bin:/usr/sbin:/usr/bin:/sbin:/bin"
            ],
            "Cmd": [
                "sh"
            ]
        },
        "Version": "18.09.7",
        "Author": "",
        "Architecture": "amd64",
        "Os": "linux",
        "Size": 1454611,
        "VirtualSize": 1454611,
        "GraphDriver": {
            "Name": "overlay",
            "Data": {
                "UpperDir": "/home/student/.
local/share/containers/storage/overlay/
be8b8b42328a15af9dd6af4cba85821aad30adde28d249d1ea03c74690530d1c/diff",
               "WorkDir": "/home/student/.
local/share/containers/storage/overlay/
be8b8b42328a15af9dd6af4cba85821aad30adde28d249d1ea03c74690530d1c/work"
```

```
            }
        },
        "RootFS": {
            "Type": "layers",
            "Layers": [
"sha256:be8b8b42328a15af9dd6af4cba85821aad30adde28d249d1ea03c74690530
  d1c"
            ]
        },
        "Labels": null,
        "Annotations": {},
        "ManifestType": "application/vnd.docker.distribution.manifest.
  v2+json",
        "User": "",
        "History": [
            {
                "created": "2020-09-09T01:38:02.18459328Z",
                "created_by": "/bin/sh -c #(nop) ADD file:72be520892
  d0a903df801c6425de761264d7c1bc7984d5cf285d778147826586 in / "
            },
            {
                "created": "2020-09-09T01:38:02.334927351Z",
                "created_by": "/bin/sh -c #(nop)  CMD [\"sh\"]",
                "empty_layer": true
            }
        ]
    }
]
```


When you use **podman inspect**, the most interesting information that you should be looking for is the command (Cmd). This is the command that the image runs by default when it is started as a container. Remember: a container is just a fancy way to start an application, and the Cmd line will tell you which application that is.

TIP To run a container, you can use **podman run**. This command first pulls the image, stores it on your local system, and then runs the container. You can also use **podman pull** first to store the image without running it, and after pulling it, you can still run it. This second method is more secure because it allows you to inspect the contents of the image before running it.

Performing Image Housekeeping

For every container that you have ever started, an image is downloaded and stored locally. To prevent your system from filling up, you might want to do a bit of housekeeping every now and then. To remove container images, use the **podman rmi** command. Notice that this command works only if the container is no longer in use. If **podman rmi** gives an error message, ensure that the container has been stopped and removed first. Exercise 26-2 shows how to manage your container images.

Exercise 26-2 Managing Container Images

1. Type **podman info | grep -A 10 registries** to check which registries are currently used.
2. Use **podman login registry.access.redhat.com** and enter your Red Hat account credentials to ensure full access to the Red Hat registries.
3. Use **podman search registry.access.redhat.com/ubi** to search only in registry.access.redhat.com for all the UBI images.
4. Use **skopeo inspect docker://registry.access.redhat.com/ubi9** to show information about the container image. Do you see which command is started by default by this image? (Notice that this information is not revealed using **skopeo**.)
5. Now use **podman pull registry.access.redhat.com/ubi9** to pull the image.
6. Type **podman images** to verify the image is now locally available.
7. Type **podman inspect registry.access.redhat.com/ubi9** and look for the command that is started by default by this image. You used **skopeo inspect** in step 4, whereas now you're using **podman inspect**, which shows more details.

Building Images from a Containerfile

Container images provide an easy way to distribute applications. While using containers, application developers no longer have to provide an installer file that runs on all common operating systems. They just have to build a container image, which will run on any OCI-compliant container engine, no matter if that is Docker or Podman.

To build container images, generic system images are commonly used, to which specific applications are added. To make building images easy, Docker introduced the Dockerfile, which in Podman is standardized as the Containerfile. In a Containerfile, different instructions can be used to build custom images, using the **podman build** command. In Example 26-7 you'll find a simple example of Containerfile contents.

Example 26-7 Example Containerfile Contents

```
FROM registry.access.redhat.com/ubi8/ubi:latest
RUN dnf install nmap
CMD ["/usr/sbin/nmap", "-sn", "192.168.29.0/24"] [
```

In a Containerfile you may have different lines defining exactly what needs to be done. Table 26-4 outlines the common Containerfile directives.

TIP On the RHCSA exam, you'll only need to work with an existing Containerfile; you won't have to create one yourself.

Table 26-4 Common Containerfile Directives

Directive	Use
FROM	Identifies the base image to use
RUN	Specifies commands to run in the base image while building the custom image
CMD	Identifies the default command that should be started by the custom image

To build a custom container image based on a Containerfile, you use the **podman build -t imagename:tag .** command. In this command the dot at the end refers to the current directory. Replace it with the name of any other directory that may contain the Containerfile you want to use. The **-t** option is used to specify an image tag. The image tag consists of two parts: the name of the image, which is followed by a specific tag. This specific tag may be used to provide version information. To build a custom image based on the Containerfile in Example 26-7, you could, for instance, use the command **podman build -t mymap:1.0 .**. After building the custom image, use the **podman images** command to verify that it has been added. In Exercise 26-3 you can practice working with a Containerfile.

Exercise 26-3 Building Custom Images with a Containerfile

1. Use **mkdir exercise264; cd exercise264** to ensure that your Containerfile is going to be created in a custom directory.
2. Use an editor to create a Containerfile with the following contents:

   ```
   FROM docker.io/library/alpine
   RUN apk add nmap
   CMD ["nmap", "-sn", "172.16.0.0/24"]
   ```

3. Type **podman build -t alpmap:1.0 .**

4. Verify the image builds successfully. Once completed, use **podman images** to verify the image has been added.
5. Use **podman run alpmap:1.0** to run the image you've just created. If the **nmap** command gets stuck, use Ctrl-C to interrupt it.

In Exercise 26-3 you've created your own custom image based on the alpine image. Alpine is a common cloud image that is used a lot, because it is really small. Even if you're running your containerized applications on top of Red Hat, that doesn't mean that you have to use the UBI image, which is provided by Red Hat as a universal base image. If you want it to be small and efficient, better to use alpine instead.

Managing Containers

While working with containers, you need to be aware of a few operational management tasks:

- Managing container status
- Running commands in a container
- Managing container ports
- Managing container environment variables

In this section you learn how to perform these tasks.

Managing Container Status

You have already learned how **podman ps** shows a list of currently running containers and how you can extend this list to show containers that have been stopped by using **podman ps -a**. But let's talk about what brings a container to a stopped status.

To understand containers, you need to understand that they are just a fancy way to run an application. Containers run applications, including all of the application dependencies, but in the end, the purpose of a container is to run an application. In some cases, the application is a process that is meant to be running all the time. In other cases, the application is just a shell, or another command that runs, produces its result, and then exits, as you have seen in Exercise 26-3. Containers in the latter category are started, run the command, and then just stop because the command has been executed successfully, and there is nothing wrong with that.

Before we continue, let me explain where the potential confusion about the stopped status of containers comes from. Sometimes, a container is considered to be something like a virtual machine. If you start an Ubuntu virtual machine, for instance, it starts and will keep on running until somebody comes and decides to stop it. Containers are not virtual machines. Every container image is configured with a default command, and as just discussed, the container runs the default command and then exits, as it's done after running the command. Some containers, however, run services, which keep running all the time.

For those containers that do keep on running after starting them, you can use a few commands to stop and start them:

- **podman stop** sends a SIGTERM signal to the container. If that doesn't give any result after 10 seconds, a SIGKILL command is sent.
- **podman kill** immediately sends a SIGKILL command. In most cases, that's not necessary because **podman stop** will send a SIGKILL after 10 seconds.
- **podman restart** restarts a container that is currently running.

Also, don't forget that after stopping a container, it is still available on your local system. That availability is convenient because it allows you to easily restart a container and maintain access to modifications that have previously been applied and stored in the writable layer that has been added to the container image while running the container. If, however, you've been starting and stopping containers a lot and don't need to keep the container files around, use **podman rm** to remove those container files. Alternatively, use **podman run --rm** to run your container. This command ensures that after it is run, the container files are automatically cleaned up.

Running Commands in a Container

When a container starts, it executes the container entrypoint command. This is the default command that is specified to be started in the container image. In some cases, you may have to run other commands inside the container as well. To do so, you can use the **podman exec** command. This allows you to run a second command inside a container that has already been started, provided that this other command is available in the namespaced container file system (which often is a small file system that contains only essential utilities).

If a command is not available in a container image, you can install it, using the image operating system package installer. However, this doesn't make sense in many cases. Installing additional commands will only make the container image significantly bigger and, for that reason, slower. So, you're better off trying to use default facilities that are provided in the container image.

While running a command, you can run it as a one-shot-only command command. In that case, the command output is written to STDOUT. You can also use **podman exec** in interactive TTY mode to run several commands inside the container.

For example, you can use **podman exec mycontainer uname -r** to run the command and write its output to STDOUT, or **podman exec -it mycontainer /bin/bash** to open a Bash shell in the container and run several commands from there. In Exercise 26-4 you practice running commands in a container.

Exercise 26-4 Running Commands in a Container

1. Use **podman run -d --rm --name=web2 docker.io/library/nginx**
2. Type **podman ps** to verify that the web2 container is available.
3. Use **podman exec -it web2 /bin/bash** to open a Bash shell in the container.
4. Within the container shell, type **ps aux**. You will see that there is no **ps** command in the nginx container; the reason is that many containers come without even fundamental standard tools.
5. Type **ls /proc**, and notice that a few directories have a numeric name. These are the PID directories, and if you don't have access to the **ps** command, this is how you can find process information.
6. Each /proc/<PID> directory has a file with the name cdmline. Type **cat /proc/1/cmdline** to find that the nginx process has been started as PID 1 within the container.
7. Type **exit** to close the Bash shell you just opened on the container.
8. Type **podman ps** to confirm that the web2 container is still running. It should be running because the **exit** command you used in the preceding step only exited the Bash shell, not the primary command running inside the container.
9. On the container host, type **uname -r** to confirm the current kernel version. The el9 part of the kernel name indicates this is an Enterprise Linux kernel, which you'll see only on RHEL, CentOS, and related distributions.
10. Type **podman run -it docker.io/library/ubuntu**. This will run the latest Ubuntu image from the Docker registry and give access to a shell. Because the image has the shell set as the entrypoint command (the default command it should start), you don't need to specify the name of the shell as well.
11. Type **cat /etc/os-release** to confirm this really is an Ubuntu container.
12. Type **uname -r** to see the Enterprise Linux kernel that you saw previously in step 6. The reason is that containers really are all running on the same kernel, no matter which Linux distribution container you're running on top.
13. Type **exit** to close the interactive TTY. Does that command shut down the container?
14. Use **podman ps** to verify the Ubuntu container is no longer active. While using **exit** in step 13, you exited the entrypoint command running in the container, so there is now nothing else to be done.

Managing Container Ports

Rootless containers in podman run without a network address because a rootless container has insufficient privileges to allocate a network address. Root containers do get a dedicated IP address, but that's an IP address on an isolated network that cannot be accessed directly from external networks. In either case, to make the service running in the container accessible from the outside, you need to configure port forwarding, where a port on the container host is used to access a port in the container application. Notice that if you are running a rootless container, you can address only nonprivileged ports on the host: ports 1–1024 are accessible by the root user only.

TIP If you do want to run a container that has an IP address and can bind to a privileged port, you need to run a root container. Use **sudo podman run ...** to run root containers. If you run a root container, you also need to use **sudo podman ps** to verify that it is running. The root container is running in the root user namespace and therefore is not accessible or visible by ordinary users. The opposite is also true: if you type **sudo podman ps**, you'll only see root containers, not the rootless containers that have been started by users.

To run a container with port forwarding, you add the **-p** option to the **podman run** command. Use **podman run --name nginxport -d -p 8080:80 nginx** to run the nginx image as a container and make the nginx process accessible on host port 8080, which will be forwarded to the standard http port 80 on which nginx is offering its services. Don't forget to use **sudo firewall-cmd --add-port 8080/tcp --permanent; sudo firewall-cmd --reload** to open the port in the firewall as well afterward! After exposing a web server container on a host port, you can use **curl localhost:8080** to verify access. Exercise 26-5 guides you through this procedure.

Exercise 26-5 Managing Container Port Mappings

1. Type **podman run --name nginxport -d -p 8080:80 nginx** to run an nginx container and expose it on host port 8080.
2. Type **podman ps** to verify that the container has been started successfully with port forwarding enabled.
3. Use **sudo firewall-cmd --add-port 8080/tcp --permanent; sudo firewall-cmd --reload** to open this port in the firewall on the host operating system.
4. Type **curl localhost:8080** to verify that you get access to the default nginx welcome page.

Managing Container Environment Variables

Many containers can be started without providing any additional information. Some containers need further specification of how to do their work. This information is typically passed using environment variables. A well-known example where you have to pass environment variables to be able to run the container successfully is mariadb, the database service that needs at least to know the password for the root user that it is going to use.

If a container needs environment variables to do its work, there are a few ways to figure this out:

- Just run the container without any environment variables. It will immediately stop, and the main application will generate an error message. Use **podman logs** on your container to read the log for information on what went wrong.
- Use **podman inspect** to see whether there is a **usage** line in the container image that tells you how to run the container. This may not always work, as it depends on whether or not the image creator has included a **usage** line in the container image.

After you've found out how to run the container, run it, specifying the environment variables with the **-e** option. To run a mariadb instance, for example, you can use **podman run -d -e MYSQL_ROOT_PASSWORD=password -e MYSQL_USER=anna -e MYSQL_PASSWORD=password -e MYSQL_DATABASE=mydb -p 3306:3306 mariadb**. Exercise 26-6 guides you through the procedure of running a container using environment variables.

Exercise 26-6 Managing Container Environment Variables

1. Use **podman run docker.io/library/mariadb**. It will fail (and you will see an error message on the STDOUT).
2. Use **podman ps -a** to see the automatically generated name for the failing mariadb container.
3. Use **podman logs container_name** to see the Entrypoint application error log. Make sure to replace container_name with the name you found in step 2.
4. Use **podman inspect mariadb** and look for a **usage** line. You won't see any.
5. Use **podman search registry.redhat.io/rhel9/mariadb** to find the exact version number of the mariadb image in the RHEL registry.
6. Use **podman login registry.redhat.io** and provide valid credentials to log in.
7. Use **podman run registry.redhat.io/rhel9/mariadb-*nnn*** (make sure to replace *nnn* with the version number you found in step 5). It will also fail but will show

much more usage details on the STDOUT. The reason is that the Red Hat mariadb image is not the same as the image that was fetched from the Docker registry in the first step of this procedure.

8. Use **podman inspect registry.redhat.io/rhel9/mariadb-*nnn*** and in the command output search for the **usage** line. It will tell you exactly how to run the mariadb image.
9. According to the instructions that you found here, type **podman run -d -e MYSQL_USER=bob -e MYSQL_PASSWORD=password -e MYSQL_DATABASE=mydb -e MYSQL_ROOT_PASSWORD=password -p 3306:3306 registry.redhat.io/rhel9/mariadb-105**. (By the time you read this, the version number may be different, so make sure to check the version number of the image if you're experiencing a failure in running this command.)
10. Use **podman ps**. You will see the mariadb container has now been started successfully.

Managing Container Storage

When a container is started from an image, a writable layer is added to the container. The writable layer is ephemeral: modifications made to the container image are written to the writable layer, but when the container is removed, all modifications that have been applied in the container are removed also. So if you run an application in a container and want to make sure that modifications are stored persistently, you need to add persistent storage.

To add persistent storage to Podman containers, you bind-mount a directory on the host operating system into the container. A bind-mount is a specific type of mount, where a directory is mounted instead of a block device. Doing so ensures that the contents of the directory on the host operating system are accessible within the container. So, when files are written within the container to the bind-mounted directory, they are committed to the host operating system as well, which ensures that data will be available beyond the lifetime of the container. For more advanced storage, you should use an ***orchestration*** solution. When you use OpenShift or Kubernetes, it's easy to expose different types of cloud and datacenter storage to the containers.

To access a host directory from a container, it needs to be prepared:

- The host directory must be writable for the user account that runs the container.
- The appropriate SELinux context label must be set to container_file_t.

Obviously, the container_file_t context label can be set manually by a user who has administrator privileges, using **semanage fcontext -a -t container_file_t "/hostdir(/.*)?"; restorecon**. It can also be set automatically, but that works only if the user who runs the container is the owner of the directory. It is not enough if the user has write permissions on the directory! For an easy way to apply the right SELinux context, you should focus on the automatic solution.

To mount the volume, you use the **-v host_dir:container_dir** command. If the user running the container is owner, or the container is a root container, you can use **-v host_dir:container_dir:Z** as an alternative to setting the SELinux context automatically. So, to make sure that a mariadb database is started in a way that database files are stored on the host operating system, you use **podman run -d --name mydb -v /home/$(id -un)/dbfiles:/var/lib/mysql:Z -e MYSQL_USER=user -e MYSQL_PASSWORD=password -e MYSQL_DATABASE=mydatabase registry.redhat.io/rhel9/mariadb-105**. In Exercise 26-7 you can practice running containers with storage attached.

Exercise 26-7 Attaching Storage to Containers

1. Use **sudo mkdir /opt/dbfiles; sudo chmod o+w /opt/dbfiles** to create a directory on the host operating system.
2. Use **podman login registry.redhat.io** and provide valid credentials to log in.
3. Use **podman run -d --name mydbase -v /opt/dbfiles:/var/lib/mysql:Z -e MYSQL_USER=user -e MYSQL_PASSWORD=password -e MYSQL_DATABASE=mydbase registry.redhat.io/rhel9/mariadb-105**. The output of this command shows "operation not permitted."
4. Type **podman ps -a**. You'll see that starting the container has failed.
5. Use **podman logs mydbase** to investigate why it has failed. Because the error was not related to the container application, the logs don't show you anything; the problem is related to Linux permissions.
6. Remove the failed container by using **podman rm mydbase**.
7. Type **sudo chown $(id -un) /opt/dbfiles**.
8. Run the command shown in step 3 again. It will now be successful.
9. Use **ls -ldZ /opt/dbfiles**. You'll see that the container_file_t SELinux context has automatically been set.

To understand what is really happening while running rootless containers, it makes sense to investigate a bit more. Rootless containers are launched in a namespace. For each user, a namespace is created in which all containers are started. The namespace provides isolation, which allows the container inside the namespace to run as the root user, where this root-level access does not exist outside of the namespace. To make this work, inside the container namespace different UIDs are used than those used outside of the namespace.

To ensure that access is working correctly, UIDs are mapped between the namespace and the host OS. This UID mapping allows any UID inside the container namespace to be mapped to a valid UID on the container host. The **podman unshare** command can be used to run commands inside the container namespace, which in some cases is necessary to make sure the container is started the right way. To start with, as a non-root user, type **podman unshare cat /proc/self/uid_map**. This shows that the root user (UID 0) maps to the current user ID, which in Example 26-8 is shown as UID 1000.

Example 26-8 Using **podman unshare** to Show UID Mappings

```
[student@server1 ~]$ podman unshare cat /proc/self/uid_map
         0       1000          1
         1     100000      65536
```

If you want to set appropriate directory ownership on bind-mounted directories for rootless containers, additional work is required:

Step 1. Find the UID of the user that runs the container main application. In many cases **podman inspect imagename** will show this.

Step 2. Use **podman unshare chown nn:nn directoryname** to set the container UID as the owner of the directory on the host. Notice that this directory *must* be in the rootless user home directory, as otherwise it wouldn't be a part of the user namespace.

Step 3. Use **podman unshare /cat/proc/self/uid_map** to verify the user ID mapping.

Step 4. Verify that the mapped user is owner on the host by using **ls -ld ~/directoryname**.

In Exercise 26-8 you'll practice bind-mounting in rootless containers

Exercise 26-8 Bind Mounting in Rootless Containers

1. Make sure you're in a non-root shell.
2. Use **podman search mariadb | grep quay**. The images in quay.io are optimized for use in Red Hat environments, and most of them are rootless by nature.

3. Type **podman run -d --name mydb -e MYSQL_ROOT_PASSWORD=password quay.io/centos7/mariadb-103-centos7**
4. Use **podman exec mydb grep mysql /etc/passwd** to verify the UID of the mysql user, which is set to 27.
5. Use **podman stop mydb; podman rm mydb**, as you'll now have to set up the storage environment with the right permissions before starting the container again.
6. Type **mkdir ~/mydb**
7. Use **podman unshare chown 27:27 mydb** to set appropriate permissions inside the user namespace.
8. Check the UID mapping by typing **podman unshare cat /proc/self/uid_map**
9. Use **ls -ld mydb** to verify the directory owner UID that is used in the host OS. At this point the UIDs are set correctly.
10. Type **podman run -d --name mydb -e MYSQL_ROOT_PASSWORD=password -v /home/student/mydb:/var/lib/mysql:Z quay.io/centos7/mariadb-103-centos7** to start the rootless mariadb container.
11. Use **ls -Z mydb** to verify the database files have been created successfully.

Running Containers as Systemd Services

As containers are becoming increasingly common as the way to start services, a way is needed to start them automatically. When you're using Kubernetes or OpenShift to orchestrate container usage, this is easy: the orchestration platform ensures that the container is started automatically, unless you decide this is not desired behavior. On a standalone platform where containers are running rootless containers, systemd is needed to autostart containers.

In systemd, services are easily started and enabled with root permissions using commands like **systemctl enable --now myservice.service**. If no root permissions are available, you need to use **systemctl --user**. The **--user** option allows users to run the common systemd commands, but in user space only. This works for any service that can run without root permissions; for instance, use **systemctl --user start myservice.service** to start the myservice service.

By default, when **systemctl --user** is used, services can be automatically started only when a user session is started. To define an exception to that, you can use the **loginctl** session manager, which is part of the systemd solution to enable ***linger*** for a specific user account. If you use **loginctl enable-linger myuser**, you enable this for the user myuser. When linger is enabled, systemd services that are enabled for that specific user will be started on system start, not only when the user is logging in.

The next step is to generate a systemd unit file to start containers. Obviously, you can write these files yourself, but a much easier way is to use **podman generate systemd --name mycontainer --files** to do so. Note that this container file must be generated in the ~/.config/systemd/user/ directory, so you have to create that directory and change to it before running the **podman generate** command.

The **podman generate systemd** command assumes that a container with the name mycontainer has already been created and will result in a unit file that can be enabled using **systemctl --user enable container-mycontainer.service**. In Example 26-9 you can see what such a unit file looks like.

Example 26-9 Podman Autogenerated Container Service File

```
[student@server1 ~]$ cat container-wbe2.service
# container-wbe2.service
# autogenerated by Podman 4.0.2
# Mon Oct 31 10:35:47 CET 2022

[Unit]
Description=Podman container-wbe2.service
Documentation=man:podman-generate-systemd(1)
Wants=network-online.target
After=network-online.target
RequiresMountsFor=/run/user/1000/containers

[Service]
Environment=PODMAN_SYSTEMD_UNIT=%n
Restart=on-failure
TimeoutStopSec=70
ExecStart=/usr/bin/podman start wbe2
ExecStop=/usr/bin/podman stop -t 10 wbe2
ExecStopPost=/usr/bin/podman stop -t 10 wbe2
PIDFile=/run/user/1000/containers/overlay-containers/2a7fe7b225bdbbfd3b
  3deb6488b9c57400530b2e77310fd3294b6d08b8dc630b/userdata/conmon.pid
Type=forking

[Install]
WantedBy=default.target
```

In Exercise 26-9 you can practice working with Podman autogenerated systemd unit files.

Exercise 26-9 Running Containers as Systemd Services

1. Use **sudo useradd linda** to create user linda.
2. Use **sudo passwd linda** to set the password for user linda.
3. Type **sudo loginctl enable-linger linda** to enable the linger feature for user linda.
4. Use **ssh linda@localhost** to log in. The procedure doesn't work from a **su** or **sudo** environment.
5. Type **mkdir -p ~/.config/systemd/user; cd ~/.config/systemd/user** to create and activate the directory where the systemd user files will be created.
6. Use **podman run -d --name mynginx -p 8081:80 nginx** to start an nginx pod.
7. Type **podman ps** to verify the nginx pod has been started.
8. Create the systemd user files using **podman generate systemd --name mynginx --files**.
9. A systemd unit file with the name container-mynginx.service is created.
10. Type **systemctl --user daemon-reload** to ensure that systemd picks up the changes.
11. Use **systemctl --user enable container-mynginx.service** to enable the systemd user service. (Do *not* try to start it, because it has already been started!)
12. Type **systemctl --user status container-mynginx.service** to verify the service has the state of enabled.
13. Reboot your server, and after rebooting, open a shell as your regular non-root user.
14. Type **ps faux | grep -A3 -B3 mynginx** to show that the mynginx container has successfully been started and is running as user linda.

Summary

In this chapter you learned about containers. First, you learned how containers really come forth from the Linux operating system and then learned all that is needed to run containers. This includes managing images, managing containers and container storage, as well as running containers as systemd services.

Exam Preparation Tasks

As mentioned in the section "How to Use This Book" in the Introduction, you have several choices for exam preparation: the end-of-chapter labs; the memory tables in Appendix C; Chapter 27, "Final Preparation"; and the practice exams.

Review All Key Topics

Review the most important topics in the chapter, noted with the Key Topic icon in the margin of the page. Table 26-5 lists a reference for these key topics and the page numbers on which each is found.

Table 26-5 Key Topics for Chapter 26

Key Topic Element	Description	Page
List	Three main tools to manage containers	542
List	Essential Linux kernel features for containers	543
List	Commands to manage container state	559
List	Finding information about variables to use	562
List	Preparing host storage	563

Complete Tables and Lists from Memory

There are no memory tables or lists in this chapter.

Define Key Terms

Define the following key terms from this chapter and check your answers in the glossary:

container, container engine, registry, CRI-o, namespace, Docker, Kubernetes, OpenShift, image, orchestration, linger

Review Questions

The questions that follow are meant to help you test your knowledge of concepts and terminology and the breadth of your knowledge. You can find the answers to these questions in Appendix A.

1. What is the name of the tool that Red Hat includes with RHEL 9 to work with container images without having to download them from the registry first?

2. What are the three Linux features that are needed in container environments?
3. What is the name of the container engine on RHEL 9?
4. Which file defines the registries that are currently used?
5. After you start a container, using **podman run ubuntu**, executing **podman ps** doesn't show it as running. What is happening?
6. What do you need to do to start a rootless container that bind-mounts a directory in the home directory of the current user account?
7. How can you find the default command that a container image will use when started?
8. How do you start an Ubuntu-based container that prints the contents of /etc/os-release and then exits?
9. What do you need to do to run a podman nginx container in such a way that host port 82 forwards traffic to container port 80?
10. Which command do you use to generate a systemd unit file for the container with the name nginx?

End-of-Chapter Lab

At this point you should be familiar with running containers in a RHEL environment. You can now complete the end-of-chapter lab to reinforce these newly acquired skills.

Lab 26.1

1. Ensure that you have logged in to get access to the Red Hat container registries.
2. Download the mariadb container image to the local computer.
3. Start the mariadb container, meeting the following requirements:
   - The container must be accessible at port 3206.
   - The MYSQL_ROOT_PASSWORD must be set to "password"
   - A database with the name mydb is created.
   - A bind-mounted directory is accessible: the directory /opt/mariadb on the host must be mapped to /var/lib/mysql in the container.
4. Configure systemd to automatically start the container as a user systemd unit upon (re)start of the computer.

## CHAPTER 27

Final Preparation

Congratulations! You made it through the book, and now it's time to finish getting ready for the RHCSA exam. This chapter helps you get ready to take and pass the exam. In this chapter, you learn more about the exam process and how to register for the exam. You also get some useful tips that will help you avoid some common pitfalls while taking the exam.

General Tips

In this section, you get some general tips about the exam. You learn how to verify your exam readiness, how to register for the exam, and what to do on the exam.

Verifying Your Readiness

Register for the exam only when you think that you are ready to pass it. This book contains a lot of material to help you verify your exam readiness. To start with, you should be able to answer all the "Do I Know This Already?" quiz questions, which you find at the beginning of each chapter. You should also have completed all the exercises in the chapters successfully, as well as the end-of-chapter labs. The labs are the first real way of testing your readiness because the questions are formulated similarly to the real exam questions, providing a good way to gauge whether you are ready for the exam.

Registering for the Exam

There are three ways of taking the RHCSA exam. You can take it as a kiosk exam provided in a testing center, as part of a Red Hat training course, or as a home exam. The option to take the exam from home has made it much easier for candidates around the world to get certified, and has become the most common way to take the exam.

A kiosk exam is administered in a test center on an individual basis, where you work through the exam tasks on a kiosk computer. This computer is monitored remotely through multiple cameras while you work on the exam tasks. The good thing about a kiosk exam is that you schedule the exam for a time and place that is convenient to you. This also applies to the home exam.

The home exam can be taken from the convenience of your own house. You do need to be able to work in a quiet room without interruptions, and your desk must be clear of everything but your computer. You also need a valid ID and one internal as well as an external web cam to register and take the home exam. You will be monitored through these connected web cams, and you'll use them to show your ID and the room in which you are taking the exam before starting the exam. To start the home exam, you'll have to download and run the Red Hat exam environment on your laptop, which will enable you to log in securely to the remote exam environment. This environment runs completely from a USB thumb drive, so you won't install anything on your own computer.

The third option to take the exam is as a part of a Red Hat training course in a classroom. Red Hat offers five-day courses to prepare for the RHCSA exam. The last day of such a course is dedicated to taking the exam, and you and your fellow students will work on the exam, which is administered by a local proctor, in a classroom.

You can register to take the exam either through Redhat.com (following the links under the Services & support tab) or through a training company. Either way, you take the same exam. It might be easier, though, to get a discount by booking through a local training company. Booking through Red Hat will be faster normally, as you have direct access to Red Hat.

On Exam Day

Make sure to bring appropriate identification to the exam or to have it handy for a home exam. To be allowed to take the exam, you need an approved government ID. Normally, a passport or driver's license will do; other types of proof may be accepted in your country as well. Do not forget it; without ID, you will not be allowed to take the exam.

Also, make sure you are on time. For an exam in a test center, it is a good idea to arrive 30 minutes before the exam's scheduled starting time. If you are late, you will normally be allowed to sit for the exam, but you will not get extra time. So, just make sure that you are on time. If you're taking a home exam, I advise you to start the exam environment 30 minutes before the scheduled exam time. It will take a while for the environment to load completely.

After proving your identity, you are introduced to the exam environment. Because of the nondisclosure agreement that every test-taker signs with Red Hat, I cannot tell you in detail what the exam environment looks like. I can tell you, though, that there will be an environment that consists of one or more servers that you can access from a graphical desktop environment that runs Red Hat Linux. There is also a list of tasks that you must perform. Work your way through the tasks, reading all carefully and thoroughly, and you will pass the exam if you have prepared well.

During the Exam

The tasks that you have to work on during the exam are not necessarily presented in the most logical order. Therefore, it is a good idea to start reading through all the tasks before you start working on the first assignment. While reading through all the tasks, you can decide which is the best order to create the configurations needed. Determine the best possible order for yourself, because it may not be obvious.

You have 2 hours and 30 minutes to work through all the exam assignments. Expect about 17 assignments; you might see a bit more or less.

Another very important tip is to read carefully, a skill that not many people have been taught well. IT administrators are very skilled in scanning web pages to retrieve the information that they need. That skill will not help you on the exam. Reading skills do. I cannot stress that enough. I estimate that 40% of all people who fail the exam do so because they do not read the exam questions carefully. (They scan instead.) So, let me give you some tips on how to read the exam questions:

- If English is not your native language, you can switch the language that questions are presented in. Maybe the English-language question is not clear to you, but the question translated in another language is. So, if in doubt, read the translation as well.
- Because the questions are originally written in English—the default language and the preference of most exam candidates—they tend to be perfect in that form, because Red Hat applies a tremendous effort to make them perfect. Red Hat must rely on translators to ensure the questions are translated correctly, so the quality of the English-language questions is the best. You are free to use translated questions, but you should use the English-language questions as your primary source.
- To make sure that you do not miss anything, make a task list for each question. You have scratch paper with you during the exam. Use it to make a short list of tasks that you have to accomplish, and work on them one by one. This approach helps you concentrate on what the exam question is actually asking.
- After you have worked on all assignments, take a short break. (You are allowed to take a break during the exam.) When you return, read all questions again to make sure that you did not miss anything. Taking a short break is important; it allows you to distance yourself from the exam, after which you should read the questions as if it is the first time that you have seen them.

Another important part of the exam is the order in which you work on the assignments. Regardless of the specific exam content, some topics need to be addressed before other topics. Make sure that you deal with those topics first. If you do not, it will make it more difficult or even impossible to complete the other assignments. Roughly speaking, here is the order in which you should work on the exam topics:

1. Make sure that your server boots and you have root access to it.
2. Configure networking in the way it is supposed to work.
3. Configure any repositories that you need.
4. Install and enable all services that need to be up and running at the end of the exam.
5. Work on all storage-related tasks.
6. Create all required user and group accounts.
7. Set permissions.
8. Make sure SELinux is working and configured as required.
9. Work on everything else.

The third thing that you need to know about the exam is that you should reboot at least a couple of times. A successful reboot allows you to verify that everything is working up to the moment you have rebooted. Before rebooting, it is a good idea to remove the rhgb and quiet options from the GRUB boot loader. Removing them allows you to see what actually happens and makes troubleshooting a lot easier.

Do not reboot only at the end of the exam, because if at that moment you encounter an issue, you might not have enough time to fix it. You should at least make sure to reboot after working on all storage-related assignments.

The Nondisclosure Agreement

The RHCSA certification is the most sought-after certification that currently exists in IT. It represents a real value because it demonstrates that the person who has passed the RHCSA exam is able to work through a list of realistic assignments and complete the job successfully. It is in everybody's interest to help maintain this high value of the RHCSA certification. The nondisclosure agreement (NDA) is an important part of that.

The RHCSA exam requires demonstrating real skills because the content of the exam is not publicly available. Please help keep these exams valuable by not talking about questions that you have seen on the exam. Anyone who knows before the exam which questions will be asked will have an easier exam than you had, which means that the value of the certification will diminish and will make your effort less valuable. So, please help protect what you have worked so hard for and do not talk about exam content to anyone.

Also, you should realize that there is a penalty for disclosing exam questions after you have signed the NDA. You will lose your certification if you have passed the exam, or you will become barred from retaking it if you did not pass.

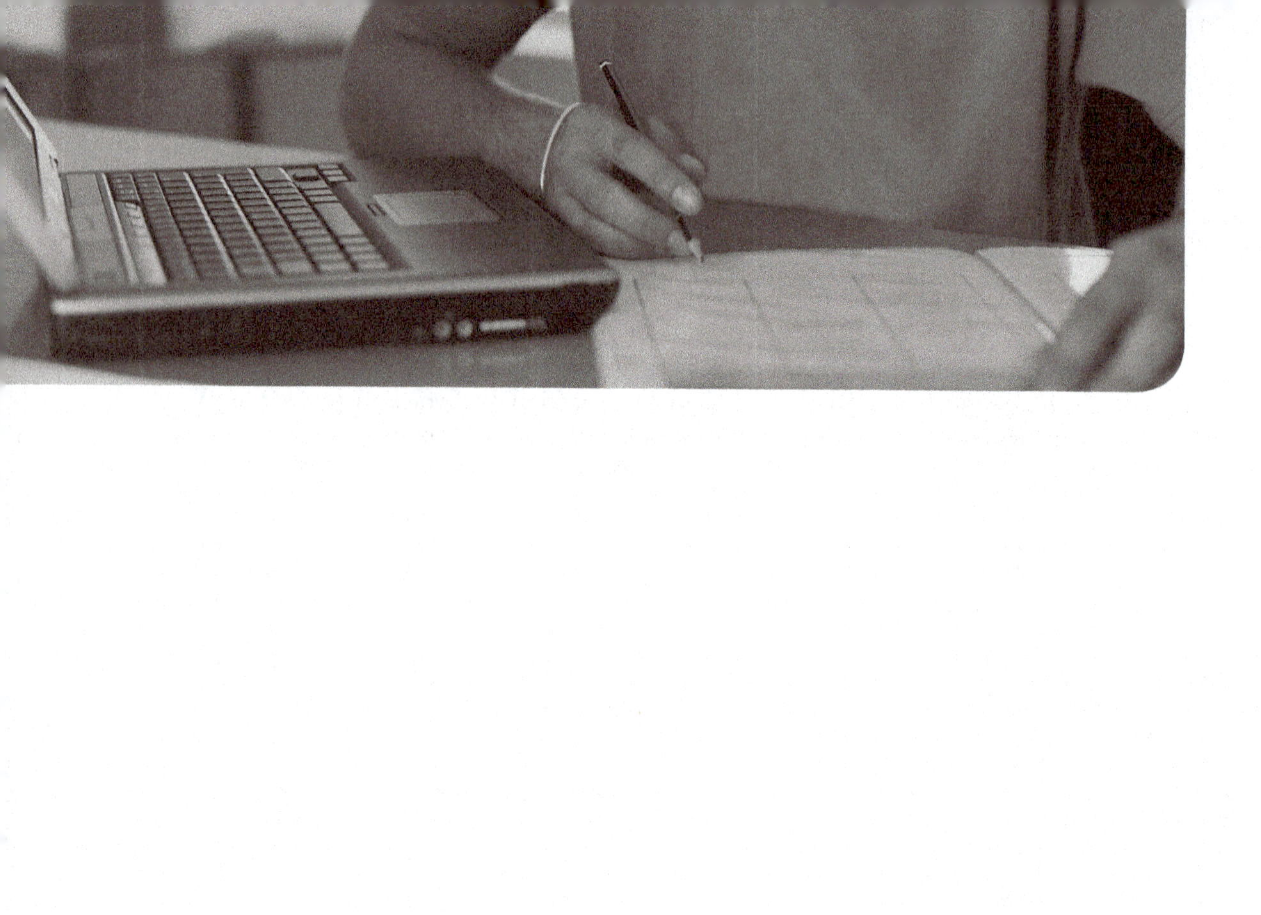

Theoretical Pre-Assessment Exam

This chapter provides an RHCSA theoretical pre-assessment exam to help you determine what you know and what you do not know. This theoretical exam is provided so that you can assess your skills and determine the best route forward for studying for the exam.

The RHCSA exam is a 100% practical exam. You work on actual configuration tasks, and you must deliver a working configuration at the end of the exam. Therefore, passing this practical exam requires that you have a working knowledge of RHEL 9. This chapter helps you check whether you have the requisite knowledge.

In the following pre-exam theoretical exam, you are asked how you would approach some essential tasks. The purpose is to check for yourself whether you are on the right track. You do not have to provide a detailed step-by-step procedure. You just need to know what needs to be done. For instance, if the question asks how to set the appropriate SELinux context type on a nondefault web server document root, you know what you need to do if you say "check the semanage-fcontext man page." If you do not have the answers to any of these questions, you know that you need to do additional studying on those topics.

In this theoretical pre-assessment exam, some key elements are covered. This test is *not* 100% comprehensive; it just focuses on some of the most essential skills.

1. You need to create a shared group environment where members of the group sales can easily share permissions with one another. Which approach would you suggest?
2. You need to change the hostname of the computer to something else and do it persistently. How would you do that?
3. On your disk, you have to create a logical volume with a size of 500 MB and the name my_lv. You do not have LVM volumes yet. List the steps to take to create the logical volume and mount it as an Ext4 file system on the /data directory. Also ensure that the extent size this logical volume uses is 8 MiB.

4. While booting, your server gives an error and shows "Enter root password for maintenance mode." What is the most likely explanation for this problem?
5. You need to access a repository that is available on ftp://server.example.com/pub/repofiles. How would you do this?
6. You need to schedule a command to be executed automatically every day at midnight as user bob. How would you do that?
7. How do you create a user who is not allowed to log in?
8. You have configured your web server to listen at port 8082, and now it doesn't start anymore. How do you troubleshoot?
9. You have access to the server console, but you do not have the root password to log in to that server. Describe step by step what you would do to get access to the server by changing the password of user root.
10. How do you configure a server to use the best performance profile?
11. You need to install the RPM package that contains the file sealert, but you have no clue what the name of this package is. What is the best way to find the package name?
12. You need to locate all files containing the text "root" in the /etc directory. How would you do that?
13. You are trying to find relevant man pages that match the keyword user. You type **man -k user** but get the "nothing appropriate" message. How can you fix this?
14. How do you add a user to a new secondary group with the name sales without modifying the existing (secondary) group assignments?
15. How would you create a 5-GiB Stratis volume with the name stratisdata and mount it automatically on /stratisdata?
16. How would you configure time synchronization, such that your server is synchronizing time with server10.example.com?
17. How do you set up automount in such a way that any user who accesses their home directory in /home/ldapusers will automatically mount the matching directory from nfsserver:/home/ldapuser/?

RHCSA Practice Exam A

General Notes

Here are some tips to ensure your exam starts with a clean environment:

- You do not need external servers or resources.
- Do *not* register or connect to external repositories.
- Install a new VM according to the instructions in each practice exam.
- No sample solutions are provided for these practice exams. On the real exam, you need to be able to verify the solutions for yourself as well.
- You should be able to complete each exam within two hours.

After applying these tips, you're ready to get started. Good luck!

1. Install a RHEL 9 virtual machine that meets the following requirements:
   - 2 GB of RAM
   - 20 GB of disk space using default partitioning
   - One additional 20-GB disk that does not have any partitions installed
   - Server with GUI installation pattern
2. Create user **student** with password **password**, and user **root** with password **password**.
3. Configure your system to automatically mount the ISO of the installation disk on the directory **/repo**. Configure your system to remove this loop-mounted ISO as the only repository that is used for installation. Do *not* register your system with **subscription-manager**, and remove all references to external repositories that may already exist.
4. Reboot your server. Assume that you don't know the root password, and use the appropriate mode to enter a root shell that doesn't require a password. Set the root password to **mypassword**.
5. Set default values for new users. Set the default password validity to 90 days, and set the first UID that is used for new users to 2000.

6. Create users **edwin** and **santos** and make them members of the group **livingopensource** as a secondary group membership. Also, create users **serene** and **alex** and make them members of the group **operations** as a secondary group. Ensure that user santos has UID 1234 and cannot start an interactive shell.
7. Create shared group directories **/groups/livingopensource** and **/groups/operations**, and make sure the groups meet the following requirements:
   - Members of the group livingopensource have full access to their directory.
   - Members of the group operations have full access to their directory.
   - New files that are created in the group directory are group owned by the group owner of the parent directory.
   - Others have no access to the group directories.
8. Create a 2-GiB volume group with the name **myvg**, using 8-MiB physical extents. In this volume group, create a 500-MiB logical volume with the name **mydata,** and mount it persistently on the directory /mydata.
9. Find all files that are owned by user edwin and copy them to the directory/rootedwinfiles.
10. Schedule a task that runs the command **touch /etc/motd** every day from Monday through Friday at 2 a.m.
11. Add a new 10-GiB virtual disk to your virtual machine. On this disk, add a Stratis volume and mount it persistently.
12. Create user **bob** and set this user's shell so that this user can only change the password and cannot do anything else.
13. Install the vsftpd service and ensure that it is started automatically at reboot.
14. Create a container that runs an HTTP server. Ensure that it mounts the host directory /httproot on the directory /var/www/html.
15. Configure this container such that it is automatically started on system boot as a system user service.
16. Create a directory with the name **/users** and ensure it contains the subdirectories **linda** and **anna**. Export this directory by using an NFS server.
17. Create users **linda** and **anna** and set their home directories to /home/users/linda and /home/users/anna. Make sure that while these users access their home directory, autofs is used to mount the NFS shares /users/linda and /users/anna from the same server.

RHCSA Practice Exam B

General Notes

Here are some tips to ensure your exam starts with a clean environment:

- You do not need external servers or resources.
- Do not register or connect to external repositories.
- Install a new VM according to the instructions in each practice exam.
- No sample solutions are provided for these practice exams. On the real exam, you need to be able to verify the solutions for yourself as well.
- You should be able to complete each exam within two hours.

After applying these tips, you're ready to get started. Good luck!

1. Install a RHEL 9 virtual machine that meets the following requirements:
   - 2 GB of RAM
   - 20 GB of disk space using default partitioning
   - One additional 20-GB disk that does not have partitions installed
   - Server with GUI installation pattern
2. Create user **student** with password **password**, and user **root** with password **password**.
3. Configure your system to automatically mount the ISO of the installation disk on the directory **/repo**. Configure your system to remove this loop-mounted ISO as the only repository that is used for installation. Do *not* register your system with **subscription-manager**, and remove all references to external repositories that may already exist.
4. Create a 1-GB partition on /dev/sdb. Format it with the vfat file system. Mount it persistently on the directory /mydata, using the label **mylabel**.
5. Set default values for new users. Ensure that an empty file with the name **NEWFILE** is copied to the home directory of each new user that is created.

6. Create users **laura** and **linda** and make them members of the group **livingopensource** as a secondary group membership. Also, create users **lisa** and **lori** and make them members of the group **operations** as a secondary group.
7. Create shared group directories **/groups/livingopensource** and **/groups/operations** and make sure these groups meet the following requirements:
   - Members of the group livingopensource have full access to their directory.
   - Members of the group operations have full access to their directory.
   - Users should be allowed to delete only their own files.
   - Others should have no access to any of the directories.
8. Create a 2-GiB swap partition and mount it persistently.
9. Resize the LVM logical volume that contains the root file system and add 1 GiB. Perform all tasks necessary to do so.
10. Find all files that are owned by user linda and copy them to the file /tmp/lindafiles/.
11. Create user **vicky** with the custom UID **2008**.
12. Install a web server and ensure that it is started automatically.
13. Configure a container that runs the docker.io/library/mysql:latest image and ensure it meets the following conditions
    - It runs as a rootless container in the user linda account.
    - It is configured to use the mysql root password **password**.
    - It bind mounts the host directory /home/student/mysql to the container directory /var/lib/mysql.
    - It automatically starts through a systemd job, where it is not needed for user linda to log in.

Answers to the "Do I Know This Already?" Quizzes and Review Questions

Answers to the "Do I Know This Already?" Quizzes

Chapter 1

1. A and B. Fedora is an experimental/enthusiast version containing many components that may or may not make it into the RHEL distribution tree and onto the RHCSA exam. CentOS Stream is also not an optimal choice, as it continuously evolves.
2. D. All RHEL software updates are made available in CentOS as well. For the rest, CentOS Stream is an unsupported platform.
3. A. In particular, when working with virtual machines, you'll be happy to have a GUI at your disposal.
4. C. XFS is used as the default file system. When Red Hat decided which file system to use as the default file system, Btrfs was not stable enough yet.
5. A. The size of an XFS file system cannot be reduced.
6. C. The Fedora project tries to make a stable distribution as well. There are many Fedora users around the globe who use it as a production distribution.
7. D. The Troubleshoot an Existing Installation option is available when booting from disk, not on the Installation Summary screen.
8. D. You are allowed to use an unsecure password; you just have to confirm it twice.
9. D. Language settings can be changed after installation. This is done easily through the Settings option in the graphical interface.
10. B. Even if it makes sense having /var on a dedicated partition, this is not part of a default installation.

Chapter 2

1. B. You first must redirect the standard output to a file, and then **2>&1** is used to specify that errors are to be treated in the same way.
2. B. /etc/bashrc is processed when a subshell is started, and it is included while starting a login shell as well.
3. C. On Linux, the current directory is not set in the **$PATH** variable.
4. D. A pipe (|) is used to process the output of the first command and use it as input of the second command.
5. D. The command **history -c** removes the in-memory state from the history file of current history. That doesn't just remove the line that contains the password, but everything. Use **history -d <number>** to remove a line with a specific number.
6. D. Ctrl-X is not a valid history command.
7. D. Bash completion works for commands, files, variables, and other names if configuration for that has been added (like hostnames for the SSH command).
8. A. You need the command **:%s/old/new/g** to replace all instances of *old* with *new*. % means that it must be applied on the entire file. **s** stands for substitute. The **g** option is used to apply the command to not only the first occurrence in a line (which is the default behavior) but all occurrences in the line.
9. B. The /etc/motd file contains messages that are displayed after user login on a terminal session. If you want to show a message before users log in, edit the /etc/issue file.
10. C. The **man -k** command uses a database to find the keywords you are looking for. On RHEL 9, this database is updated with the **mandb** command. On older versions of RHEL (prior to RHEL 7), the **makewhatis** command was used instead.

Chapter 3

1. D. /run is the default location where temporary files are created. Notice that these can also be created in the /tmp directory, but within /run a directory structure is created to ensure each process has its own environment that is not accessible by other processes, and that makes /run more secure.
2. C. The /var directory is used on Linux to store files that may grow unexpectedly.
3. B, C, and D. The **nodev** option specifies that the mount cannot be used to access device files. With **noexec**, executable files cannot be started from the mount, and **nosuid** denies the use of the SUID permission.
4. C. The **df -h** command shows mounted devices and the amount of disk space currently in use on these devices. The **-T** option helps in recognizing real file systems (as opposed to kernel interfaces) because it shows the file system type as well.

5. C. The option **-a** shows hidden files, **-l** gives a long listing, **-r** reverts the sorting so that newest files are shown last, and **-t** sorts on modification time, which by default shows newest files first.
6. C. To copy hidden files as well as regular files, you need to put a **.** after the name of the directory the files are in. Answer A copies hidden files as well, but it creates a subdirectory $USER in the current directory.
7. A. The **mv** command enables you to move files and rename files.
8. D. In hard links, no difference exists between the first hard link and subsequent hard links.
9. C. The option **-s** is used to create a symbolic link. While creating a link, you first have to specify the source, and next you specify the destination.
10. D. Use the option **-u** to update an existing tar archive.

Chapter 4

1. A. The **head** command by default shows the first ten lines in a text file.
2. D. The **wc** command shows the number of lines, words, and characters in a file.
3. D. When you use **less**, the G key brings you to the end of the current file.
4. A. The **-d** option is used to specify the field delimiter that needs to be used to distinguish different fields in files while using **cut**.
5. A. The **sort** command can sort files or command output based on specific keys. If no specific key is mentioned, sorting happens based on fields. The option **-k3** will therefore sort the third field in the output of the **ps aux** command.
6. D. When used in a regular expression, the ^ sign in front of the text you are looking for indicates that the text has to be at the beginning of the line.
7. A. The ? regular expression is used to refer to zero or one of the previous characters. This makes the previous character optional, which can be useful. If the regular expression is **colou?r**, for example, you would get a match on *color* as well as *colour*.
8. D. + is used to indicate the preceding character should occur one or more times. Notice that this is an extended regular expression and most tools need additional options to work with extended regular expressions.
9. D. The **awk** command first needs to know which field separator should be used. This is specified with the **-F :** option. Then, it needs to specify a string that it should look for, which is **/user/**. To indicate that the fourth field of a matching file should be printed, you need to include the **{ print $4 }** command.
10. B. Use **grep -v** to exclude from the results lines containing the regular expression.

Chapter 5

1. B. The console is the screen you are working from. On the console, a terminal is started as the working environment. In the terminal, a shell is operational to interpret the commands you are typing.
2. A. The console is the screen you are working from. On the console, a terminal is started as the working environment. In the terminal, a shell is operational to interpret the commands you are typing.
3. C. The console is the screen you are working from. On the console, a terminal is started as the working environment. In the terminal, a shell is operational to interpret the commands you are typing.
4. B. The six virtual consoles that are available on Linux by default are numbered /dev/tty1 through /dev/tty6. The device /dev/pts/6 is used to refer to the sixth pseudo terminal, which is created by opening six terminal windows in a graphical environment.
5. A and C. A pseudo terminal device is created when opening new terminals using SSH or from the graphical interface.
6. D. Typically, a server reboot is necessary only after making changes to the kernel and kernel modules that are in use. Changing the network configuration does not normally require a reboot, because it is possible to just restart the network service.
7. C. Windows has no native support for SSH. You need to install PuTTY or similar software to remotely connect to Linux using SSH.
8. D. Key fingerprints of hosts that you have previously connected to are stored in your home directory, in the subdirectory .ssh in a file with the name known_hosts.
9. C. The **ForwardX11** option in the /etc/ssh/ssh_config file enables support for graphical applications through SSH.
10. C. To initiate key-based remote authentication, you should copy the public key to the remote server. The most convenient way to do so is using the **ssh-copy-id** command.

Chapter 6

1. A and D. The RHEL 9 installation program offers an option to set no password for user root, which will effectively disable the root user account. If you want to allow root user login, it's wise not to allow this user to log in. You cannot delete the root user, as it is required for much system functionality.
2. D. In the sudo configuration file, all members of the group wheel by default get access to all administrator tasks.

3. B. To define an exception, the exception is listed after the generic command and not before. Notice that answer C may also be working, but depends on the current PATH setting and for that reason should not be used in this way.
4. C. To use pipes in the sudo shell, the entire command must be executed as an argument to the **sh -c** command. Answer D might look correct as well, but it is not, because the **grep** command is not executed with sudo privileges.
5. C. The file /etc/default/useradd is read for default settings when new user accounts are created. Notice that it only includes some settings, including the name of the default home directory. Most user-related settings are in /etc/login.defs.
6. A. The **chage -l** command enables you to manage password properties.
7. B. There is no file /etc/.profile.
8. A. The **vigr** command creates a copy of the /etc/group file so that changes can be applied safely.
9. C and D. The **id** and **groups** commands show a list of all groups a user is a member of.
10. C. If a file /etc/nologin exists, only the user root will be allowed to log in. To display an optional message to users trying to log in, the message can be included in /etc/nologin.txt.

Chapter 7

1. C. The **newgrp** command is used to set the effective primary group, which will affect default group ownership on new files until the current shell session is ended. The **chgrp** command is used to set the group owner of an existing file; **chgrp** is not related to any user account, and it affects newly created files only.
2. A. The **find / -user linda** command searches all files that are owned by user linda. Notice that **find** also has a **-uid** option that allows you to locate files based on a specific UID setting. This does not allow you to search files based on a username, but it will let you find files based on the UID of a specific user.
3. C. **chgrp myfile sales** does not set group ownership for the file myfile. The order in this command is wrong; **chgrp** first needs the name of the group, followed by the name of the owner that needs to be set.
4. C. When used in relative mode, the three digits are used to specify user, group, and others permissions. The value 6 is used to apply read and write.
5. D. The essence to the answer is the use of uppercase X, also known as "special X." This changes the permission on the directory, but not on files.

6. C. The **chmod g+s /dir** command adds (+) the SGID permission to /dir; **chmod u+s /dir** adds SUID to the directory; **chmod g-s /dir** removes the SGID permission; and the 1 in **chmod 1770 /dir** would set the sticky bit and not SGID.
7. D. The **passwd** command needs the SUID permission to be set, to make it possible to write changes to the /etc/shadow file.
8. A. The root user needs a higher level of security, and for that reason has a different umask than regular users.
9. C. The umask 027 will give all permissions to the file owner, read permissions to the group, and no permissions to others.
10. C. The **lsattr** command shows current attribute settings to files. The **ls** command is not capable of showing file attributes, and the other commands that are listed do not exist.

Chapter 8

1. D. Based on the /26 subnet mask, the networks are 192.168.4.0, 192.168.4.64, 192.168.4.128, and 192.168.4.192. That means that IP addresses II, III, and IV belong to the same network.
2. B. The 169.254.0.0 network address does not belong to the private address ranges, which are 10.0.0.0/8, 172.16.0.0/12, and 192.168.0.0/16. The address 169.254.0.0 is from the APIPA range. This is a range of IP addresses that can be automatically self-assigned by a client that is trying to reach an unreachable DHCP server.
3. A, B, or C. On RHEL 9, network device names are generated automatically, and the exact name you'll get depends on the information that is revealed by the kernel driver in use. If no specific information is revealed by the driver, the legacy name eth0 is used.
4. D. Use of the **ifconfig** command is deprecated; use the **ip** command instead. The **ip addr show** command shows information about the state of the interface as well as the current IP address assignment.
5. A. The network service no longer exists in RHEL 9.
6. B. The nmcli-examples man page was created to make working with the long commands in **nmcli** a bit easier. Note that **nmcli** also has excellent command-line completion features.
7. C. On RHEL 9, nmtui is the default utility to set and modify the network interface.
8. D. When the connection is added, you use **ip4** and **gw4** (without a *v*).

9. A. You should not set the DNS servers directly in /etc/resolv.conf, because that file is automatically written by the NetworkManager service.
10. C. The name of the configuration file that contains the hostname is /etc/hostname. You should use **hostnamectl** to change its contents.

Chapter 9

1. D. The gpgcheck= line indicates whether to check the integrity of packages in the repository using a GPG key. Although useful, this capability is not mandatory in all cases.
2. B. If a RHEL system is not registered with Red Hat, no repositories are available. This is important to realize for the RHCSA exam, because it means that you need to connect to a repository before you can install anything.
3. C. Use baseurl to specify which URL to use. If the URL is based on the local file system, it uses the URI file:// followed by the path on the local file system, which in this case is /repo. This explains why there are three slashes in the baseurl.
4. A, D. GPG package signing is used to set a checksum on packages so that altered packages can easily be recognized. The main purpose of signing packages is to make it easy to protect packages on Internet repositories. For internal repositories that cannot be accessed by Internet users, the need to add GPG package signatures is less urgent. If you access a signed repository for the first time, the **dnf** command will query to import the GPG key.
5. C, D. Both the commands **dnf provides** and **dnf whatprovides** can be used to search for files within a specific package. While using **dnf whatprovides**, the file pattern must be specified as */filename or as a full path.
6. B. The dnf module application stream allows for working with different versions of user space software side by side.
7. C. To install a specific profile from a dnf module application stream, add the profile name to the application stream version using a /.
8. A. The **dnf install** command installs individually downloaded RPM files while looking for package dependencies in the current repositories. This is better than using **rpm -ivh**, which does not consider the **dnf** repositories. In earlier versions of RHEL, the **dnf localinstall** command was used to install packages that were downloaded to the local file system, but this command is now deprecated.
9. C. Use the **rpm -qf** command to find which RPM package a specific file comes from.

10. C. The **--scripts** option checks whether there are scripts in an RPM package. If you want to query the package file and not the database of installed RPMs, you need to add the **-p** option to the **-q** option, which is used to perform RPM queries.

Chapter 10

1. B and D. There are two different types of processes that each request a different management approach. These are shell jobs and daemons. A cron job and a thread are subdivisions of these generic categories.
2. B. The Ctrl-Z command temporarily freezes a current job, after which the **bg** command can be used to resume that job in the background.
3. A. The Ctrl-C command cancels the current job. Ctrl-D sends the EOF character to the current job, which can result in a stop if this allows the job to complete properly. The difference with Ctrl-C is that the job is canceled with no regard to what it was doing. The Ctrl-Z keystroke freezes the job.
4. A and B. Individual threads cannot be managed by an administrator. Using threads makes working in a multi-CPU environment more efficient because one process cannot be running on multiple CPUs simultaneously, unless the process is using threads.
5. A. The **ps ef** command shows all processes, including the exact command that was used to start them.
6. C. To increase process priority, you need a negative nice value. Note that -20 is the lowest value that can be used.
7. C. Use the **renice** command to change priority for currently running processes. To refer to the process you want to renice, use the **-p** option.
8. B. **mkill** is not a current command to send signals to processes.
9. A. To change the process priority from **top**, use **r** for renice.
10. B. To set the tuned performance profile, use **tuned-adm profile**, followed by the name of the profile you want to set.

Chapter 11

1. A. The **-t service** argument shows all currently loaded services only.
2. C. Wants are specific to a particular system and for that reason are managed through /etc/systemd/system (not /usr/lib/systemd/system).
3. D. Masking a service makes it impossible to enable it.
4. D. Running(dead) is not a valid status for systemd services. You see Inactive(dead) for units that currently are not active.

5. D. Socket units monitor socket activity, which may consist of a file being accessed or a network port being accessed. They do not monitor PATH activity. This is done by the path unit type.
6. B. udev is not a valid systemd unit type (device is a valid unit type though). All others are.
7. B. Answers A and B are very similar, but answer A uses the wrong command. You have to use the **systemctl** command, not the **systemd** command.
8. C and D. The SYSTEMD_EDITOR variable defines which editor to use. You need to set a full path name for this editor. Alternatively, you can use the EDITOR variable to set the default editor for all commands that need to be able to use an editor.
9. D. The Wants dependency type defines that a specific unit is wanted, without setting a hard requirement.
10. A. The word order is wrong. It should be **systemctl start unit**, not **systemctl unit start**.

Chapter 12

1. A. In RHEL 9 systemd timers are used as the default solution for scheduling future jobs.
2. B. To specify a starting time using systemd timers, use OnCalendar.
3. D. Use OnStartupSec to specify that a timer should run at a specific time after starting systemd.
4. D. In user systemd services, you use OnStartupSec to specify that a service should be started a specific time after the user systemd service has been started.
5. C. The fields in cron timing are minute, hour, day of month, month, and day of week. Answer C matches this pattern to run the task on the seventh day of the week at 11 a.m.
6. A. To launch a job from Monday through Friday, you should use **1-5** in the last part of the time indicator. The minute indicator ***/5** will launch the job every 5 minutes.
7. A and D. You cannot modify user cron files directly, but have to go through the crontab editor. This editor is started with the **crontab -e** command. As the root user, you can use **crontab -u <username> -e** to edit a specific user crontab.
8. A. The /etc/crontab file should not be edited directly, but only by using input files that are stored in either the user environment or in /etc/cron.*/ directories.

9. B. The Ctrl-D key sequence sends the end-of-file (EOF) character to the at shell and closes it.
10. C. The **atq** command queries the at service and provides an overview of jobs currently scheduled for execution.

Chapter 13

1. C. system-journald is not a replacement of rsyslogd. It is an additional service that logs information to the journal. In RHEL 9, they are integrated to work together to provide you with the logging information you need.
2. D. Most messages are written to the /var/log/messages file, but authentication-related messages are written to /var/log/secure. Check the contents of /etc/rsyslog.conf and look for authpriv to find out what exactly is happening for this facility.
3. C. SELinux events are logged through the audit service, which maintains its log in /var/log/audit/audit.log.
4. D. If systemd-journald has been configured for persistent storage of the journal, the journal is stored in /var/log/journal. Note that by default the systemd journal is not stored persistently.
5. D. To make the systemd journal persistent, you have to create a directory /var/log/journal and ensure it has the appropriate permissions.
6. D. The **systemd-journal-flush** service will update the systemd journal to use its current settings.
7. A. The rsyslogd configuration file is /etc/rsyslog.conf.
8. C. rsyslogd destinations often are files. For further processing, however, log information can be sent to an rsyslogd module. If this is the case, the name of the module is referred to as :modulename:.
9. D. The local facilities local0 through local7 can be used to configure services that do not use rsyslog by default to send messages to a specific rsyslog destination, which needs to be further configured in the rsyslog.conf file.
10. A. The logrotate service can rotate files based on the maximal file size. The recommended way to configure this is to drop a file in /etc/logrotate.d containing parameters for this specific file.

Chapter 14

1. A. Using GUI partition tables offers many advantages, but it does not make access to a directory faster.
2. A. There is no easy way to change MBR partitions to GPT.
3. B. Partition type 82 is normally used to create Linux partitions.

4. C. KVM virtual machines use the virtio driver to address hard disks. This driver generates the device /dev/vda as the first disk device.
5. C. A disk can have one partition table only. For that reason, it is not possible to have MBR and GPT partitions on the same disk.
6. B. XFS is used as the default file system; partitions can still be formatted with other file systems, like Ext4.
7. D. The **blkid** command shows all file systems, their UUID, and if applicable, their label.
8. D. To mount a file system based on its UUID, use UUID=nnnn in the /etc/fstab device column.
9. B. The best option to verify the content of /etc/fstab is to use the **findmnt --verify** command. This command will complain about errors in lines, regardless of the current mounted state of a device. The **mount -a** command can also be helpful, but it only works on devices that are not currently mounted.
10. B. Although convenient, having an [Install] section is only required if you want to enable the mount unit file.

Chapter 15

1. B. It is common to create a file system on top of a logical volume, but this is not a requirement. For instance, a logical volume can be used as a device that is presented as a disk device for a virtual machine.
2. C. Copy on write is a feature that is offered by modern file systems, such as Btrfs. It copies the original blocks a file was using before creating a new file, which allows users to easily revert to a previous state of the file. Copy on write is not an LVM feature.
3. D. On a GPT disk, LVM partitions must be flagged with the partition type 8e00.
4. C. The **lvcreate** command is used to create logical volumes. Use **-n <name>** to specify the name. The option **-l 50%FREE** will assign 50% of available disk space, and **vgdata** is the volume group it will be assigned from.
5. B and C. The **pvdisplay** command is used to show extensive information about physical volumes. The **pvs** command shows a summary of essential physical volume properties only.
6. C. You can increase the size of an XFS file system, but it cannot be decreased.
7. A. Reducing a volume group doesn't always involve reducing the logical volumes it contains as well, which means that you may be able to reduce the volume group without reducing the logical volumes, and in that case file system shrinking is not required.

8. D. You can always grow the file system later, using file system–specific tools.
9. A. To write metadata, each Stratis volume requires 527 MiB of storage.
10. C. You need to mount Stratis volumes using the UUID and not the device name. Also, the option **x-systemd.requires=stratisd.service** needs to be included to ensure that the stratisd.service is loaded before systemd tries to mount the Stratis volume.

Chapter 16

1. A. A tainted kernel is caused by drivers that are not available as open source drivers. Using these may have an impact on the stability of the Linux operating system, which is why it is good to have an option to recognize them easily.
2. B. The **dmesg** utility shows the contents of the kernel ring buffer. This is the area of memory where the Linux kernel logs information to, so it gives a clear overview of recent kernel events. Alternatively, use **journalctl -k**.
3. A. The **uname -r** command shows the current kernel version. The **uname -v** command gives information about the hardware in your computer, and the **procinfo** command does not exist.
4. C. The /etc/redhat-release version contains information about the current version of RHEL you are using, including the update level.
5. A. On a systemd-based operating system such as RHEL 9, the systemd-udevd process takes care of initializing new hardware devices.
6. B. Default rules for hardware initialization are in the directory /usr/lib/udev/rules.d; custom rules should be stored in /etc/udev/rules.d.
7. C. The **modprobe** command is the only command that should be used for managing kernel modules, as it considers kernel module dependencies as well. Use **modprobe** to load a kernel module and **modprobe -r** to unload it from memory.
8. C. The **lspci -k** command lists devices that are detected on the PCI bus and supporting kernel modules that have been loaded for those devices. Alternatively, **lspci -v** shows more verbose information about modules that are currently loaded.
9. C. The /etc/modprobe.d directory is used for files that create custom configurations. The files /etc/modules.conf and modprobe.conf were used for this purpose in the past. On RHEL 9, kernel module parameters are passed through /usr/lib/modprobe.d if they are used for operating system–managed permanent parameters.
10. C and D. Kernels are not updated, they are installed. You can use either **dnf update kernel** or **yum install kernel** to do so. There are no additional requirements, which makes answers C and D false.

Chapter 17

1. A. The **systemctl enable** command creates a want for the current unit in the target that is listed in the [Install] section in the service unit file.
2. C. Servers typically don't run a graphical interface and will start the multi-user. target.
3. B. There is no restart.target.
4. D. Unit files contain an [Install] section that is used to specify in which target the unit should be started.
5. A. The required statement is **AllowIsolate**. All other statements mentioned here are invalid.
6. A. To switch from a target with more unit files to a target with fewer unit files, use **systemctl isolate**.
7. B. The multi-user.target corresponds roughly to runlevel 3 as used in a System V environment.
8. D. Changes to GRUB 2 need to be applied to /etc/default/grub, not to /boot/grub2/grub.cfg. The /boot/grub2/grub.cfg file cannot be edited directly; you have to apply changes to /etc/default/grub and run the **grub2-mkconfig** command to write them to the appropriate configuration file.
9. B. The **grub2-mkconfig** command enables you to regenerate the GRUB 2 configuration. The result, by default, is echoed to the screen. Use redirection to write it to a file.
10. B. The /boot/efi/EFI/redhat/grub.cfg file is used to store the GRUB 2 bootloader on a UEFI system.

Chapter 18

1. C. During the boot procedure, the GRUB 2 boot loader gets loaded first. From here, the kernel with the associated initramfs is loaded. Once that has completed, systemd can be loaded.
2. B. The Ctrl-X key sequence leaves the GRUB 2 shell and continues booting.
3. B. The /etc/dracut.conf file is used for managing the initramfs file system.
4. A and B. The **init=/bin/bash** GRUB 2 boot option allows you to open a root shell without having to enter a password. **init=/bin/sh** will do the same.
5. A and C. The **rhgb** and **quiet** boot options make it impossible to see what is happening while booting.
6. B. The emergency.target systemd target gives just a root shell and not much more than that. All other options that are mentioned also include the loading of several systemd unit files.

7. C. If you do not get to a GRUB 2 boot prompt, you cannot select an alternate startup mechanism. This situation requires you to use a rescue disk so that GRUB can be reinstalled. If the kernel or initramfs cannot load successfully, you might need to use a rescue disk also, but in many cases an alternate kernel is provided by default.
8. C. The **mount -o remount,rw /** option remounts the / file system in read/write mode.
9. A. Because the error occurs before the GRUB 2 menu is loaded, the only option to fix this is to use a rescue disk.
10. C. When you enter the Linux system with the **init=/bin/bash** kernel boot option, you don't have systemd. As answers A and B need systemd, they won't work. Also, the **exit** command won't work, as it will close the current shell and leave you with no working environment. The only option that does work is **exec /usr/lib/systemd/system**, which replaces the current bash shell with systemd.

Chapter 19

1. B. The first line of a Bash shell script contains the *shebang*, which defines the subshell that should be used for executing the script code.
2. A. The **exit 0** statement at the end of a script is an optional one to inform the parent shell that the script code was executed successfully.
3. C. The **read** statement stops a script, which allows a user to provide input. If **read** is used with a variable name as its argument, the user input is stored in this variable.
4. D. The first argument is referred to as $1. To store $1 in a variable with the name, use the command **NAME=$1**. Make sure that no spaces are included, which is why answer A is incorrect.
5. D. Both **$@** and **$*** can be used to refer to all arguments that were provided when starting a script, but **$@** is the preferred method because it enables the script to distinguish between the different individual arguments, whereas **$*** refers to all the provided arguments as one entity.
6. D. A conditional loop that is started with **if** is closed with **fi**.
7. C. If within an **if** loop a new conditional check is opened, this conditional check is started with **elif**.
8. B. After the condition is started in a **for** loop, **do** is used to start the commands that need to be started when the condition is true.
9. D. The **mail** command needs its subject specified with the **-s** option. The **mail** command normally waits until a dot is entered on an empty line to start

sending the message. This dot can be fed to the **mail** command using STDIN redirection, using <.

10. A. In a **case** statement, the different options are proposed with a) behind them. ***)** refers to all other options (not specified in the script).

Chapter 20

1. A. X11 forwarding applies to sessions that have already been authorized. Disabling it does not protect against brute-force attacks.
2. C. The **AllowUsers** parameter can be used to restrict SSH access to specific users only.
3. D. To change the port on which SSH is listening in SELinux, the port must be allowed as well. To do so, use **semanage port**. The context type needs to be set to **ssh_port_t**.
4. B. The MaxAuthTries setting starts logging failed login attempts after half the number of attempts specified here.
5. D. Login-related settings are logged to /var/log/secure.
6. C. SSH is trying to do a reverse lookup of the DNS name belonging to a target IP address. If faulty DNS configuration is used, this will take a long time.
7. D. The UseDNS option has nothing to do with SSH session keepalive.
8. A. SSH client settings that apply to a specific user only can be stored in ~/.ssh/config.
9. C. The **ssh-agent** command adds an SSH credentials cache to a shell. Next, you need to run **ssh-add** to add a specific key to the cache.
10. A. By default, an SSH server can support ten sessions only.

Chapter 21

1. A. The httpd package contains the core components of the Apache web server. It can be installed using **yum install httpd**.
2. A. The default Apache configuration file is /etc/httpd/conf/httpd.conf.
3. C. The **DocumentRoot** parameter specifies where the Apache web server will look for its contents.
4. A. The **ServerRoot** parameter defines where Apache will look for its configuration files. All file references in the httpd.conf configuration file are relative to this directory.
5. B. The /etc/httpd/conf directory contains the main Apache configuration file httpd.conf.

6. D. The /etc/httpd/conf.modules.d directory contains configuration files that are used by specific Apache modules.
7. C. The /etc/httpd/conf.d directory is used by RPMs that can drop files in that directory without changing the contents of the main Apache configuration file.
8. A. The name-based virtual host is used as the default virtual host type. It allows multiple virtual hosts to be hosted on the same IP address.
9. A. The **VirtualHost** parameter is used to open a virtual host definition. * refers to all IP addresses, and **:80** defines the port it should listen on.
10. C. No additional packages need to be installed to enable virtual hosts. Virtual hosts are supported through the default httpd RPM package.

Chapter 22

1. B. In older versions of Red Hat, the file /etc/sysconfig/selinux could be modified to contain the setting **selinux=disabled.** In RHEL 9 you can start a system in disabled mode only by using the GRUB boot argument **selinux=0**.
2. A and D. The **getenforce** command is used to request the current SELinux mode. The **sestatus** command can be used also. It shows the current mode, and some additional security-related information as well.
3. A. For basic SELinux configuration, you need to make sure that the appropriate context type is set. User and role are for advanced use only.
4. C. The **-Z** option displays SELinux-related information and can be used with many commands.
5. D. This is the only command that provides correct usage information about **semanage**. Remember that **chcon** should be avoided at all times.
6. B. When you're moving a file, the original file context is moved with the file. To ensure that the file has the context that is appropriate for the new file location, you should use **restorecon** on it.
7. C. If a port has already been labeled, use **semanage port -m** to modify it.
8. B. To change Booleans, use **setsebool**; to make the change persistent, use **-P**.
9. A. SELinux messages are logged by auditd, which writes the log messages to /var/log/audit/audit.log. Only if **sealert** is installed are messages written to /var/log/messages as well, but that does not happen by default.
10. D. SELinux log messages in audit log always contain the text *avc*, which stands for access vector cache.

Chapter 23

1. A. On a default configuration, there is no untrusted zone in firewalld.
2. C. Netfilter is the name of the firewall implementation in the Linux kernel. Different toolsets exist to manage netfilter firewalls. Iptables has been the default management interface for a long time, and in Red Hat Enterprise Linux 7, firewalld was added as an alternative solution to manage firewalls.
3. D. Iptables is a legacy service and has been replaced with the nftables utility. Firewalld is used to provide an easy-to-use management interface for nftables.
4. C. The **firewall-cmd --get-services** command shows all services that are available in firewalld.
5. C. The name of the GUI tool that can be used to manage firewall configurations is **firewall-config**.
6. B. Answer B shows the correct syntax.
7. A. The trusted zone is provided for interfaces that need minimal protection.
8. D. Configuration that is added with the **--permanent** option is not activated immediately and needs either a restart of the firewalld service or the command **firewall-cmd --reload**.
9. B. The **--list-all** command without further options shows all configurations for all zones.
10. D. The **--runtime-to-permanent** option writes all current configuration to the permanent configuration. Although answer B would also work, answer D is preferred as it doesn't require you to restart the firewalld service.

Chapter 24

1. B. The **showmount** command can be used to get information about mounts. Use **showmount -e** to get a list of all mounts that have been exported.
2. A. NFSv4 does not offer straight integration with Active Directory. Similar functionality is provided by the option to use Kerberized security.
3. C. The nfs-utils package contains all that is needed to mount NFS shares.
4. D. **showmount** is using the NFS portmapper, which is using random UDP ports to make the connection. Portmapper traffic is not automatically allowed when the nfs service is added to the firewall because RPC ports that are needed by **showmount** are blocked by the firewall. Ensure that the rpc-bind and mountd services are added to the firewall to enable the **showmount** command to work as it should.
5. C. The Systemd nfs-server.service file is used to offer NFS services.

6. B. On older RHEL versions, the **_netdev** mount option needed to be specified in /etc/fstab to indicate that the network service is required before starting the NFS service. Because of improved dependency handling in systemd, on current RHEL no additional mount options are required.
7. D. You do not have to set permissions on the local file system for automount to be effective.
8. B. Each automounted directory should have a configuration file that has a name that matches the name of the automounted directory. For /myfiles, that would be /etc/auto.myfiles.
9. C. The first element is *, which refers to all directories that may be accessed in the local directory. The **&** matches this directory on the NFS share. The **-rw** option is used to specify NFS mount options.
10. A. Automount uses the autofs service.

Chapter 25

1. C. When booting, a server reads the hardware clock and sets the local time according to hardware time.
2. D. Hardware time on Linux servers typically is set to UTC, but local administrators may choose to make an exception to that general habit.
3. D. The **timedatectl** command, introduced as a new solution in RHEL 7, allows you to manage many aspects of time.
4. C. Atomic clocks can be used as a very accurate alternative to the normal hardware clock.
5. D. The /etc/chrony.conf file contains the default list of NTP servers that should be contacted on RHEL 9.
6. C. The **-s** option is used to set the current time, and to do so, military time format is the default.
7. A. To translate epoch time into human time, you need to put @ in front of the epoch time string.
8. A. Use **hwclock --hctosys** to synchronize system time with hardware time.
9. D. When used without arguments, **timedatectl** gives a complete overview of current time settings on your server.
10. B. The **chronyc sources** command will show all current synchronization sources, as well as the stratum that was obtained from these sources.

Chapter 26

1. B. Containers are implemented on top of Linux features like cgroups for resource allocation and limitation, namespaces for isolation, and SELinux for enhanced security.
2. B. Red Hat OpenShift provides a container orchestration platform that is based on Kubernetes.
3. D. From a running container, use Ctrl-P, Ctrl-Q to detach without exiting the primary container application.
4. B. When you're running a container, it runs in the foreground by default. To run it in detached mode, use **podman run -d**, which starts it in the background.
5. C. To inspect images that have not yet been pulled, you can use **skopeo inspect**. This command does not give as much result as **podman inspect** or **buildah inspect** after the image has been pulled.
6. A. The **podman info** command gives information about the complete podman working environment. It includes a list of registries currently in use.
7. D. If environment variables are required for starting a container, the environment variables to be used are well documented within the image, as well as in the documentation on the container registry. Alternatively, you may just run the container and read the container logs after it has failed.
8. B. The **container_file_t** SELinux context type must be set on the host directory that you want to bind-mount to make it available as storage inside the container.
9. C. To perform the bind mount, you must use the **-v** option with **podman run**. To automatically set correct SELinux context, you must use the **:Z** option right after the name of the directory within the container. Also, you must make sure that the user who runs this command is the owner of the directory on the host operating system.
10. B. After you enable a container with **systemctl --user enable**, the container service will be started when the user logs in. To have the container start when the system starts, enable the linger feature by using **loginctl enable-linger**.

Answers to the Review Questions

Chapter 1

1. You have different options. The recommended option is to use a free version of RHEL, as provided through developers.redhat.com. Alternatively, you can use Rocky Linux or AlmaLinux.
2. The network card might not be enabled. This is dependent on the environment that you're using. If the network card is enabled, you'll automatically obtain configuration from a DHCP server.
3. You need 1 GB of RAM to install a minimal system.
4. By default, updates and installation of additional software packages require Internet connectivity.
5. Use an ISO image to install a virtual machine on the computer.
6. It is easier to open two terminal windows side by side.
7. XFS is the default file system on RHEL 9.
8. You can install RHEL if you do not have Internet access. But you cannot register with RHN, so you will not have access to repositories after the installation has finished and you'll need to set up repository access manually.
9. Registering your RHEL 9 installation gives access to the RHEL repositories, so that software packages can be installed and updated.
10. Use the Minimal Install pattern if you have a very limited amount of disk space available.

Chapter 2

1. A variable is a placeholder that contains a specific value and that can be used in scripts to work with dynamic contents.
2. **man -k** enables you to find the correct man page based on keyword usage.
3. Change /etc/bashrc to ensure a variable is set for every shell that is started.
4. Use **pinfo** to read the information.
5. Bash stores its history in ~/.bash_history.
6. **mandb** updates the database that contains man keywords.
7. Use **+** to undo the last modification you have applied in **vim**.
8. Add **2> /dev/null** to a command to ensure that it doesn't show an error message.
9. Use **echo $PATH** to read the current contents of the **$PATH** variable.
10. Press Ctrl-R and type **dog**.

Chapter 3

1. /etc contains configuration files.
2. **ls -alt** displays a list of current directory contents, with the newest files listed first. (**-a** also shows files that have a name that starts with a dot.)
3. **mv myfile yourfile** renames myfile to yourfile.
4. **rm -rf /directory** wipes an entire directory structure, including all of its contents.
5. **ln -s /tmp ~** creates in your home directory a link to /tmp.
6. **cp /etc/[abc]* .** copies all files that have a name that starts with a, b, or c from the directory /etc to your current directory.
7. **ln -s /etc ~** creates in your home directory a link to /etc.
8. Use **rm symlink** to safely remove a symbolic link to a directory. If **rm** is aliased to **rm -i** and you do not want to answer yes for every individual file, use **\rm** instead.
9. **tar zcvf /tmp/etchome.tgz /etc /home** creates a compressed archive of /etc and /home and writes it to /tmp/etchome.tgz.
10. **tar xvf /tmp/etchome.tgz /etc/passwd** extracts /etc/passwd from /tmp/etchome.tgz.

Chapter 4

1. **ps aux | less** shows the results of **ps aux** in a way that is easily browsable.
2. **tail -n 5 ~/samplefile** shows the last five lines from ~/samplefile.
3. **wc ~/samplefile**. You might use **-w** to show only the number of words.
4. Press Ctrl-C to stop showing output.
5. **grep -v -e '^#' -e '^;' filename** excludes all lines that start with either a # or a ;.
6. Use + to match one or more of the preceding characters.
7. **grep -i text file** finds both *text* and *TEXT* in a file.
8. **grep -B 5 '^PATH' filename** shows all lines starting with *PATH* as well as the preceding five lines.
9. **sed -n 9p ~/samplefile** shows line 9 from ~/samplefile.
10. **sed -i 's/user/users/g' ~/samplefile** replaces the word *user* with the word *users* in ~/samplefile.

Chapter 5

1. Typically, the console is the main screen on a Linux server.
2. Press Ctrl-Alt-F2 to switch back from a text-based login prompt to current work on the GUI.
3. **w** or **who** shows all users who currently have a terminal session open to a Linux server.
4. /dev/pts/0 is the device name that is used by the first SSH session that is opened to a server where no GUI is operational.
5. **ssh -v** shows detailed information on what SSH is doing while logging in.
6. **ssh -X** initiates an SSH session with support for graphical applications.
7. ~/.ssh/config needs to be edited to modify SSH client settings.
8. **scp /etc/hosts lisa@server2:/tmp** copies the /etc/hosts file to the directory /tmp on server2 using the username lisa.
9. ~/.ssh/authorized_keys stores public keys for remote users who want to log in using key-based authentication.
10. **ssh-keygen** generates an SSH public/private key pair.

Chapter 6

1. timestamp_timeout, which can be set in the Default configuration in /etc/sudoers.
2. **sudo** is defined in /etc/sudoers.
3. Use **visudo** to modify a **sudo** configuration. Or even better, use an editor to create **sudo** configuration files in /etc/sudoers.d/
4. Use **pkexec visudo** to run the **visudo** command with **sudo** privileges.
5. Just one additional group membership is defined in /etc/group.
6. Making a user a member of the wheel group grants the user access to all admin commands through **sudo**.
7. Use **vigr** to modify the /etc/group file manually.
8. **passwd** and **chage** can be used to change user password information.
9. /etc/shadow stores user passwords.
10. /etc/group stores group accounts.

Chapter 7

1. **chown :groupname filename** or **chown .groupname filename** sets the group owner to a file.
2. **find / -user username** finds all files owned by a specific user.

3. **chmod -R 770 /data** applies read, write, and execute permissions to all files in /data for the user and group owners while setting no permissions for others.
4. In relative permission mode, use **chmod +x file** to add the execute permission to a file that you want to make executable.
5. Using **chmod g+s /directory** ensures that group ownership of all new files created in a directory is set to the group owner of that directory.
6. **chmod +t /directory** ensures that users can only delete files of which they are the owner or files that are in a directory of which they are the owner.
7. The **umask 027** should be used. The 7 in the third position indicates that no default permissions should be granted to "others."
8. You need to use the append only (a) extended attribute. Use **chattr +a <filename>** to set it.
9. Use **find / -perm +4000**. The **-perm** argument to **find** searches for permissions, and the permission mode you're looking for is 4 at the first position. By using a + and specifying the other permissions as a 0, you indicate that any other permissions may be allowed as well.
10. Attributes are not shown by the **ls** command. Use **lsattr** instead.

Chapter 8

1. 213.214.215.96 is the network address in 213.214.215.99/29.
2. **ip link show** shows link status and not the IP address.
3. The /etc/resolv.conf file is written automatically by NetworkManager. After restarting NetworkManager it will be rewritten, and locally applied changes will have disappeared.
4. /etc/hostname contains the hostname in RHEL 9.
5. **hostnamectl set-hostname** enables you to set the hostname easily.
6. NetworkManager stores the connections it creates in /etc/NetworkManager/
7. Change /etc/hosts to enable hostname resolution for a specific IP address.
8. Non-admin users can change NetworkManager settings according to the permissions that are set. Use **nmcli general permissions** for an overview of current permissions.
9. **systemctl status NetworkManager** verifies the service's current status.
10. **nmcli con mod "static" ipv4.addresses "10.0.0.20/24" 10.0.0.100** changes the current IP address and default gateway on your network connection.

Chapter 9

1. **createrepo** enables you to make a directory containing a collection of RPM packages a repository.
2. The line [some-label] name=some-name baseurl=http://server.example.com/repo needs to be in the repository file.
3. **dnf repolist** verifies that a repository is available.
4. **dnf provides */useradd** enables you to search the RPM package containing the file useradd.
5. Using **dnf group list** followed by **dnf group info "Security Tools"** shows the name and contents of the dnf group that contains security tools.
6. **dnf module enable php:5.1** ensures that all PHP-related packages are going to be installed using the older version 5.1, without actually installing anything yet.
7. **rpm -pq --scripts packagename** enables you to ensure that a downloaded RPM package does not contain dangerous script code.
8. **rpm -qd packagename** shows all documentation in an RPM package.
9. **rpm -qf /path/to/file** shows which RPM package a file comes from.
10. **repoquery** enables you to query software from the repository.

Chapter 10

1. **jobs** gives an overview of all current shell jobs.
2. Press Ctrl-Z and type **bg** to stop the current shell job to continue running it in the background.
3. Press Ctrl-C to cancel the current shell job.
4. Use process management tools such as **ps** and **kill** to cancel the job.
5. **ps fax** shows parent–child relationships between processes.
6. Use **renice -nn -p PID**, where **nn** is a value between –1 and –20. Notice that you need to be root in order to increase process priority.
7. **killall dd** stops all running processes.
8. **pkill mycommand** stops **mycommand**.
9. **k** is used to kill a process.
10. The **tuned** service must be running to select a performance profile.

Chapter 11

1. A unit is a thing that is started by systemd. There are different types of units, such as services, mounts, sockets, and many more.
2. Use **systemctl list-units** to show all service units that are currently loaded.
3. Creating a want for a service means that you'll mark it to be automatically started as system boot. You create a want for a service by using the **systemctl enable** command.
4. Set the **SYSTEMD_EDITOR** variable in /etc/profile to change the default editor for **systemctl**.
5. /etc/systemd/system/ contains custom systemd unit files.
6. Include **Requires** to ensure that a unit file will automatically load another unit file.
7. **systemctl show httpd** shows available configuration options for the httpd. service unit.
8. **systemctl list-dependencies --reverse** shows all dependencies for a specific unit.
9. **systemctl status** output indicating that a unit is dead is nothing serious; it simply means the service is currently not running.
10. Using **systemctl edit** on the unit that you want to modify creates a systemd override file.

Chapter 12

1. A cron job that needs to be executed once every two weeks is configured as a specific cron file in /etc/cron.d, or tied to a user account using **crontab -e -u** username.
2. Use a systemd timer that has the **OnBoot** option to specify how much time after system boot the corresponding service should be started.
3. If a service should be started by a timer, you have to enable the timer and not the service. Ensure this is what you've done.
4. Create a systemd timer that uses the OnUnitActive option to specify how much time after activation of a service it should be started again.
5. To match a timer to a service, you need to ensure they are using the same name. So to activate my.service, you need to create my.timer.
6. **crontab -e -u lisa** enables you to schedule a cron job for user lisa.
7. Create the file /etc/cron.deny and make sure that it includes username boris.
8. Specify the job in /etc/anacrontab and make sure that the anacron service is operational.

9. The atd service must be running to schedule at jobs; use **systemctl status atd** to verify.
10. Use **atq** to find out whether any current at jobs are scheduled for execution.

Chapter 13

1. /etc/rsyslog.conf is used to configure rsyslogd.
2. /var/log/secure contains messages related to authentication.
3. Log files are rotated away by default after five weeks (one week for the current file, and four weeks for old files).
4. **logger -p user.notice "some text"** logs a message from the command line to the user facility, using the notice priority.
5. Create a file in /etc/rsyslog.d. The name does not really matter. Give it the following contents: *.=info /var/log/messages.info.
6. You can configure the journal to grow beyond its default size restrictions in /etc/systemd/journald.conf.
7. **journalctl -xb** shows boot messages, including some explanation that makes interpreting them easier.
8. **journalctl _PID=1 --since 9:00:00 --until 15:00:00** shows all journald that have been written for PID 1 between 9:00 a.m. and 3:00 p.m.
9. Use **journalctl -u sshd** to see all messages that have been logged for the sshd service. Notice that you can see the last messages that have been logged for this service conveniently by using **systemctl status sshd**.
10. Making the systemd journal persistent requires the following four commands, in order: **mkdir /var/log/journal; chown root:systemd-journal /var/log/journal; chmod 2755 /var/log/journal; killall -USR1 systemd-journald**.

Chapter 14

1. Any tool. GPT can be managed using **fdisk**, **gdisk**, or **parted**.
2. **fdisk** or **parted** is used to create MBR partitions.
3. XFS is the default file system on RHEL 9.
4. /etc/fstab is used to automatically mount partitions while booting.
5. The **noauto** mount option is used to specify that a file system should not be mounted automatically while booting.
6. **mkswap** enables you to format a partition that has type 82 with the appropriate file system.

7. **mount -a** enables you to test, without actually rebooting, whether automatic mounting of the partitions while booting is going to work. Alternatively, use **findmnt --verify**.
8. Ext2 is created if you use the **mkfs** command without specifying a file system.
9. Use either **mkfs.ext4** or **mkfs -t ext4** to format an Ext4 partition.
10. Use **blkid** to find UUIDs for all devices on your computer.

Chapter 15

1. The 8e00 partition type is used on a GUID partition that needs to be used in LVM.
2. **vgcreate vggroup -s 4MiB /dev/sdb3** creates the specified volume group.
3. **pvs** shows a short summary of the physical volumes on your system as well as the volume group to which they belong.
4. Just type **vgextend vggroup /dev/sdd**. You do not have to do anything on the disk device itself.
5. Use **lvcreate -L 6M -n lvvol1 vgname**. Notice that this works only if you have created the volume group with a 2-MiB physical extent size.
6. **lvextend -L +100M /dev/vgname/lvvol1** adds 100 MB to the logical volume lvvol1.
7. First use **pvmove** to move used extents to the remaining PVs, next use **vgreduce** to remove the PV from the VG.
8. Add the line UUID=xxx /stratis1 xfs defaults,x-systemd.requires=stratisd.service 0 0 to /etc/fstab to mount the Stratis volume.
9. **stratis pool create mypool /dev/sdd** creates a Stratis pool that is based on the block device /dev/sdd.
10. You can't. Stratis comes with XFS by default and this cannot be changed.

Chapter 16

1. **uname -r** shows the current version of the kernel on a computer.
2. Current version information about your RHEL installation is found in /etc/redhat-release.
3. **lsmod** shows a list of currently loaded kernel modules.
4. **modinfo modulename** displays kernel module parameters.
5. **modprobe -r** unloads a kernel module.
6. Use **lsmod** to find out which other kernel modules currently need this kernel module and unload these kernel modules first. Note that this will not always work, especially if the considered hardware currently is in use.

7. Use **modinfo** to find which kernel module parameters are supported.
8. Create a file in /etc/modprobe.d and include the parameters using an **options** statement.
9. Include **options cdrom debug=1** in the file that will automatically load the cdrom module.
10. **yum upgrade kernel** installs a new version of the kernel.

Chapter 17

1. A unit is a thing that is started by systemd. There are different types of units, such as services, mounts, sockets, and many more.
2. Use **systemctl mask** to make sure that a target is no longer eligible for automatic start on system boot.
3. Modify /etc/default/grub to apply common changes to GRUB 2.
4. **systemctl --type=service** shows all service units that are currently loaded.
5. Create a want for a service by using **systemctl enable** on that service.
6. **systemctl isolate rescue.target** switches the current operational target to the rescue target.
7. There are two types of targets: targets that can run independently and targets that cannot. Check the target unit file to find out more about this and ensure the target is isolatable (which means it can run independently).
8. **systemctl list-dependencies --reverse** shows which other units have dependencies to a systemd service.
9. Apply changes to GRUB 2 in /etc/default/grub.
10. Run **grub2-mkconfig > /boot/grub2/grub.cfg** after applying changes to the GRUB 2 configuration.

Chapter 18

1. Press **e** to enter the GRUB boot menu editor mode.
2. An error in /etc/fstab prevents the **fsck** command on that file system from finishing successfully.
3. Pass **init=/bin/bash** to the Grub line that loads the kernel to start the procedure to reset the root password.
4. Start from a rescue system.
5. **systemctl list-units** shows which units are available in a specific troubleshooting environment.
6. Use **exec /usr/lib/systemd/system** to replace the bin/bash process with systemd.

7. **touch /.autorelabel** ensures that while rebooting, the SELinux context labels on all files are restored.
8. Use **mount -o remount,rw /** to make the root file system writable again.
9. **grub2-mkconfig -o /boot/grub2/grub.cfg** saves changes applied to the GRUB 2 boot loader.
10. **systemd.unit=emergency.target** enters the most minimal troubleshooting mode.

Chapter 19

1. The script will be interpreted by the same shell as the parent shell.
2. **test -z $VAR** or **[-z $VAR]** can be used to check whether a variable VAR has no value.
3. Use **$#** to count the number of arguments that have been used.
4. Use **$@** to refer to all arguments that have been used when starting the script.
5. Use **read SOMEVAR** to process user input in a script.
6. **[-f filename] || echo file does not exist** determines whether the file exists and, if not, executes the specified command.
7. **[-e filename]** can be used to determine whether an item is a file or a directory.
8. A **for** statement is typically used to evaluate a range of items.
9. You do not; it is a part of the **if** statement that is closed with **fi**.
10. Using ;; after the last command closes the specific item.

Chapter 20

1. Use **ssh-agent** and **ssh-add** to cache the passphrase that is set on your private key.
2. Use **AllowUsers lisa** to disallow root login and allow only user lisa to log in to your server.
3. Specify the **Port** line twice to configure your SSH server to listen on two different ports.
4. The main SSH configuration file is /etc/ssh/sshd_config.
5. The passphrase will be stored in a protected area in memory.
6. /etc/ssh/ssh_config contains SSH client settings for all users.
7. The **MaxSessions** parameter that manages this feature is already set to 10 as a default, so you don't need to change anything.
8. **semanage port -a -t ssh_port_t -p tcp 2022** configures SELinux to allow SSH to bind to port 2022.

9. **firewall-cmd –add-port 2022/tcp --permanent; firewall-cmd --reload** configure the firewall on the SSH server to allow incoming connections to port 2022.
10. Try **UseDNS**. This option, which is active by default, uses DNS to get the name of the target host for verification purposes.

Chapter 21

1. The Basic Web Server group contains useful Apache packages.
2. **systemctl enable --now httpd** starts the httpd service automatically when booting.
3. /etc/httpd/conf.d is the default location where RPMs can drop plug-in configuration files that should be considered by the Apache server.
4. **curl** enables you to test a web server from a server that does not offer a graphical interface.
5. /etc/httpd/conf/httpd.conf is the default Apache configuration file.
6. /var/www/html is used as the default Apache document root.
7. The Apache process looks for index.html.
8. Use either **systemctl status httpd** or **ps aux | grep http** to check whether the Apache web server is currently running.
9. /etc/httpd/conf.d is the preferred location for storing virtual host configuration files.
10. The ServerRoot is set by default to /etc/httpd.

Chapter 22

1. **setenforce 0** puts SELinux in permissive mode temporarily.
2. **getenforce -a** or **semanage boolean -l** provides a list of all available Booleans.
3. Install the RPM package that contains the man pages: **dnf install selinux-policy-doc**.
4. Install setroubleshoot-server to get easy-to-read SELinux log messages in the audit log.
5. Use **semanage fcontext -a -t httpd_sys_content_t "/web(/.*)?"** followed by **restorecon** to apply the httpd_sys_content_t context type to the directory /web.
6. Never!
7. Add the argument **selinux=0** to the line that configures the kernel in /etc/default/grub, and next use **grub2-mkconfig -o /boot/grub2/grub.cfg** to write the new boot loader configuration.
8. SELinux logs all of its messages in /var/log/audit/audit.log.

9. **man -k _selinux | grep ftp** shows which SELinux-related man pages are available for the FTP service, including ftpd_selinux. Read it for more information.
10. Use **setenforce 0** to temporarily switch SELinux to permissive mode and try again.

Chapter 23

1. firewalld should be running before you try to create a firewall configuration with **firewall-config**.
2. **firewall-cmd --add-port=2345/udp** adds UDP port 2345 to the firewall in the default zone.
3. **firewall-cmd --list-all-zones** lists all firewall configurations in all zones.
4. **firewall-cmd --remove-service=vnc-server** removes the vnc-server service from the current firewall configuration.
5. **--reload** activates a new configuration added with the **--permanent** option.
6. **--list-all** enables you to verify that a new configuration has been added to the current zone and is now active.
7. **firewall-cmd --add-interface=eno1 --zone=public** adds the interface eno1 to the public zone.
8. The new interface will be added to the default zone.
9. **firewall-cmd --permanent --add-source=192.168.0.0/24** adds the source IP address 192.168.0.0/24 to the default zone.
10. **firewall-cmd --get-services** lists all services that are currently available in firewalld.

Chapter 24

1. The **showmount** command needs the mountd and rpc-bind services to be opened in the firewall as well.
2. **showmount -e server1** shows available NFS mounts on server1. Note that the **showmount** command does not get through a firewall.
3. **mount [-t nfs] server1:/share /somewhere** mounts an NFS share that is available on server1:/share.
4. Use an NFS root mount: **mount nfsserver:/ /mnt**.
5. No additional options are needed, because of improved dependency handling in RHEL 9.
6. Include **sync** in /etc/fstab to ensure that changes to the mounted file system are written to the NFS server immediately.
7. Systemd automount cannot be used for wildcard mounts.

8. auto.master is the main automount configuration file.
9. autofs implements automount.
10. None. You'll have to open ports on the server, not on the client.

Chapter 25

1. **date -s 16:24** sets the system time to 4:24 p.m.
2. **hwclock --systohc** sets the hardware time to the current system time.
3. **date -d '@nnnnnnn'** shows epoch time as human-readable time.
4. **hwclock --hctosys** synchronizes the system clock with the hardware time.
5. chronyd is used to manage NTP time on RHEL 9.
6. **timedatectl set-ntp 1** enables you to use NTP time on your server.
7. /etc/chrony.conf contains the list of NTP servers to be used.
8. Either **timedatectl list-timezones** or **tzselect** can be used to list time zones.
9. **timedatectl set-timezone ZONE** is used to set the current time zone.
10. **timedatectl set-time TIME** is used to set the system time.

Chapter 26

1. RHEL 9 includes **skopeo** to work with container images.
2. Namespaces, cgroups, and SELinux are needed in container environments.
3. CRI-o is the container engine on RHEL 9.
4. The /etc/containers/registries.conf file defines the registries that are currently used.
5. In a container image, a default command is specified. When you start a container, the default command is executed. After executing the default command, the container stops. In generic system images like Ubuntu and Fedora, the default command is set to **/bin/bash**, so if you don't specify anything else, the container will immediately stop.
6. Find the UID used by the container, and use **podman unshare** to make that UID the owner of the directory you want to provide access to.
7. Use **podman inspect** on the image and look for the Cmd.
8. Use the **podman run ubuntu cat /etc/os-release** command.
9. You need to run it as a root container by using **sudo podman run -d -p82:80 nginx**. Next, you need to open the firewall by using **sudo firewall-cmd --add-port 82/tcp --permanent; sudo firewall-cmd --reload**.
10. Use the **podman generate systemd --name nginx --files** command.

Red Hat RHCSA 9 Cert Guide: EX200 Exam Updates

Over time, reader feedback allows Pearson to gauge which topics give our readers the most problems when taking the exams. To assist readers with those topics, the authors create new materials clarifying and expanding on those troublesome exam topics. As mentioned in the Introduction, the additional content about the exam is contained in a PDF on this book's companion website, at https://www.pearsonITcertification.com/title/9780138096274.

This appendix is intended to provide you with updated information if Red Hat, Inc. makes minor modifications to the exam upon which this book is based. When Red Hat, Inc. releases an entirely new exam, the changes are usually too extensive to provide in a simple update appendix. In those cases, you might need to consult the new edition of the book for the updated content. This appendix attempts to fill the void that occurs with any print book. In particular, this appendix does the following:

- Mentions technical items that might not have been mentioned elsewhere in the book
- Covers new topics if Red Hat, Inc. adds new content to the exam over time
- Provides a way to get up-to-the-minute current information about content for the exam

Always Get the Latest at the Book's Product Page

You are reading the version of this appendix that was available when your book was printed. However, given that the main purpose of this appendix is to be a living, changing document, it is important that you look for the latest version online at the book's companion website. To do so, follow these steps:

Step 1. Browse to www.pearsonITcertification.com/title/9780138096274.

Step 2. Click the Updates tab.

Step 3. If there is a new Appendix B document on the page, download the latest Appendix B document.

NOTE The downloaded document has a version number. Comparing the version of the print Appendix B (Version 1.0) with the latest online version of this appendix, you should do the following:

- **Same version:** Ignore the PDF that you downloaded from the companion website.
- **Website has a later version:** Ignore this Appendix B in your book and read only the latest version that you downloaded from the companion website.

Technical Content

The current Version 1.0 of this appendix does not contain additional technical coverage.

Glossary

$PATH A variable that contains a list of directories that are searched for executable files when a user enters a command.

. The current directory. Its value can be requested using the **pwd** command.

A

absolute filename A filename that is complete and starts with the name of the root directory, including all directories up to the current file or directory.

access control list (ACL) In Linux permissions, a system that makes it possible to grant permissions to more than one user and more than one group. Access control lists also allow administrators to set default permissions for specific directories.

Alma Linux Free open source alternative for Red Hat Enterprise Linux, which consists of the RHEL source code with all licensing removed.

anacron A service that ensures that vital cron jobs can be executed when the server is down at the moment that the job normally should be executed. Can be considered an extension to cron.

AND A logical construction that can be used in scripts. In an AND construction, the second command is executed only after successful execution of the first command.

application profile A collection of packages that may be used to install a specific version of software, according to a specific installation profile.

application stream A specific version of a dnf module that can be installed as such.

archiving A system that ensures that data can be properly backed up.

at A service that can be used to schedule future jobs for one-time execution.

attribute A property that can be set to a file or directory and that will be enforced no matter which user with access permission accesses the file. For instance, a file that has the immutable (**i**) attribute set cannot be deleted, not even by the root user. However, the root user does have the capability to change the attribute, which would allow the root user to delete the file anyway.

audit log The main log file in /var/log/audit/audit.log, which by default contains all messages that are logged by the auditd service.

auditd A service that runs by default on Red Hat Enterprise Linux and can be configured to log very detailed information about what is happening on RHEL. Auditing is complementary to system logging and can be used for compliancy reasons. On RHEL, the auditing system takes care of logging SELinux-related messages, which makes it a relatively important system.

autofs A service that takes care of automatically mounting file systems at the moment that a specific directory is accessed. This service is very useful to ensure the automatic mounting of home directories for users in a centralized user management system, as can be implemented by the LDAP service.

automount The process that is started by the autofs service. *See* autofs for more details.

B

background process A process that is running on a system without actively occupying a console. Processes can be started in the background by adding a & after the command that starts the process. *See also* foreground process.

backup A copy of important data, which can be restored if at any point in time the original data gets lost.

Bash The default shell that is used on Red Hat Enterprise Linux.

Basic Input/Output System (BIOS) The first software that is started when a computer starts on older IBM-compatible computers. Settings in the BIOS can be changed by using the BIOS setup program. *See also* Unified Extensible Firmware Interface (UEFI).

binary A numbering scheme that is based on bit values that can be on or off. Binary numbers are 0 and 1. Because binary numbers are difficult to use, decimal, hexadecimal, or octal numbers often are used.

BIOS *See* Basic Input/Output System.

boot loader Program that is started as the very first thing while starting a computer and that takes care of loading the operating system kernel and initramfs.

BtrFS A general-purpose Linux file system that is expected to become the default file system on Red Hat Enterprise Linux in a future release.

bzip2 A compression utility that can be used as an alternative to gzip.

C

cache In memory management, the area of memory where recently used files are stored. Cache is an important mechanism to speed up reads on servers.

capability A specific task that can be performed on Linux. User root has access to all capabilities; normal users have access to limited sets of capabilities only.

CentOS A Linux distribution that uses all Red Hat packages but has removed the Red Hat logo from all these packages to make it possible to distribute the software for free. CentOS is the best option for practicing for the RHCSA exam if you do not have access to RHEL.

certificate In PKI cryptography, contains the public key of the issuer of the certificate. This public key is signed with the certificate of a certificate authority, which guarantees its reliability.

certificate authority (CA) A commonly known organization that can be used to guarantee the reliability of PKI certificates. The certificate authority provides a certificate that can be used to sign public key certificates. Instead of using commonly known organizations, self-signed certificates can be used for internal purposes as well.

chrony The service that offers time synchronization services in Red Hat Enterprise Linux.

chroot An environment where a part of the file system is presented as if it were the root of the file system. Chroot is used as a security feature that hides part of the operating system that is not required by specific services.

CIFS *See* Common Internet File System.

cloud A computing platform that allows for flexible usage of hosted computing resources.

Common Internet File System (CIFS) The standardized version of the Microsoft Server Message Block (SMB) protocol, which is used to provide access to shared printers, files, and directories in a way that is compatible with Windows servers and clients. CIFS has become the de facto standard for file sharing in IT.

compression A technology that is used to reduce the size of files by analyzing redundant patterns and storing them more efficiently.

conditional loop In shell scripting, a set of commands that is executed only if a specific condition has been met.

connection (in network card configuration) A set of network configuration parameters that is associated to a network interface.

connection (in network communication) A session between two parties that has been initialized and will exist until the moment that the connection is tiered down.

console In Linux, the primary terminal where a user works. It is also a specific device with the name /dev/console.

container A ready-to-run application that is started from an image and includes all application dependencies.

container engine The code that allows containers to run on top of an operating system.

context In SELinux, a label that is used to define the security attributes of users, processes, ports, and directories. These contexts are used in the SELinux policy to define security rules.

context switch When the CPU switches from executing one task to executing another task.

context type In SELinux, a label that identifies the SELinux properties of users, ports, and processes.

Coordinated Universal Time (UTC) A time standard that is globally the same, no matter which specific time zone a user is in. UTC roughly corresponds to Greenwich Mean Time (GMT).

credentials file A file that can be used to mount CIFS file systems automatically from the /etc/fstab file. The credentials file is stored in a secure place, like the home directory of user root, and contains the username and password that are used to mount the remote file system.

CRI-o The default container engine on RHEL 9. Pronounced *CRY-o*.

cron A service that takes care of starting services repeatedly at specific times.

cryptography A technique used to protect data, often by converting information to an unreadable state, where keys are used to decipher the scrambled data. Cryptography is used not only to protect files while in transit but also to secure the authentication procedure.

D

deduplication A storage technology that analyzes data to be stored on disk and takes out duplicate patterns to allow for more efficient storage.

default route The route that is used by default to forward IP packets that have a destination on an external network.

dependency Generally, a situation where one item needs another item. Dependencies occur on multiple levels in Linux. In RPM package management, a dependency is a software package that needs to be present for another package to be installed. In Systemd, a dependency is a Systemd unit that must be loaded before another unit can be loaded.

dependency hell Situation where for package installation, other packages are needed, which by themselves could require dependencies as well. The problem of dependency hell has been fixed by the introduction of repository-based systems.

destination In rsyslog, the place where log messages should be sent by the logging system. Destinations are often files, but can also be input modules, output modules, users, or hosts.

device A peripheral that is attached to a computer to perform a specific task.

device file A file that is created in the /dev directory and that is used to represent and interact with a device.

device mapper A service that is used by the Linux kernel to communicate with storage devices. Device mapper is used by LVM, multipath, and other devices, but not by regular hard disks. Device files that are created by device mapper can be found in the /dev/mapper directory.

directory A folder in the file system that can be used to store files in an organized manner.

disabled mode The SELinux mode in which SELinux is completely deactivated.

distribution A Linux version that comes with its own installation program or which is ready for usage. Because Linux is a collection of different tools and other components, the Linux distribution gathers these tools and other components, may or may not enhance them, and distributes them so that users do not have to gather all the different components for themselves.

dmesg Utility that can be used to read the kernel ring buffer, which contains log messages that were generated by the Linux kernel.

dnf The new software manager that replaces the **yum** utility in RHEL 9.

Docker A common solution to run containers. Docker was the default container solution in RHEL 8 but is no longer supported and was replaced with CRI-o/podman in RHEL 9.

Domain Name System (DNS) The global system used to match logical server names to IP addresses.

dracut A utility used to generate the initramfs, an essential part of the Linux operating system that contains drivers and other vital files required to start a Linux system.

Dynamic Host Configuration Protocol (DHCP) A protocol used to ensure that hosts can obtain an IP address and related information automatically.

dynamic route A network route that is managed by an automatic routing protocol.

E

enforcing mode The SELinux mode where SELinux is fully operational and applies all restrictions that have been configured for a specific system.

environment The collection of settings that users or processes are using to do their work.

epoch time In Linux, the number of seconds that have passed since epoch (corresponds to midnight on January 1, 1970). Some utilities write epoch time instead of real clock time.

escaping In a shell environment, using special syntax to ensure that specific characters are not interpreted by the shell. Escaping may be necessary to show specific characters onscreen or to ensure that regular expression metacharacters are not interpreted by the bash shell first.

exec A system call that replaces the current process with another one. *See also* fork.

export In NFS, a directory that is shared on an NFS server to allow access to other servers.

Ext2, Ext3, and Ext4 Three different versions of the Ext file system. Up to RHEL 6, Ext4 was the default file system. It is now considered inadequate for modern storage needs, which is why Ext4 in RHEL 7 was replaced by XFS as the default file system.

extended partition A solution to create more than four partitions on an MBR disk. On MBR disks, a maximum of four partitions can be stored in the partition table. To make it possible to go beyond that number, one of the four partitions can be created as an extended partition. Within an extended partition, logical partitions can be created, which will perform just like regular partitions, allowing system administrators to create more partitions.

external command A command that exists as a file on disk.

F

facility In rsyslogd, the source where log information comes from. A strictly limited number of facilities have been defined in rsyslogd.

Fedora The free and open source Linux distribution that is sponsored by Red Hat. In Fedora, new features are provided and tested. Some of these features will be included in later releases of Red Hat Enterprise Linux.

FHS *See* Filesystem Hierarchy Standard.

file descriptor A pointer that is used by a Linux process to refer to files that are in use by the process.

file system A logical structure that is created on a storage device. In a Linux file system, inodes are used for file system administration, and the actual data is written to blocks. *See also* inode.

Filesystem Hierarchy Standard (FHS) A standard that defines which Linux directories should be used for which purpose. Read **man 7 file-hierarchy** for a specification of the FHS.

firewall A solution that can be used to filter packets on a network. Firewalls are used to ensure that only authorized traffic can reach a system. A firewall can be offered through the Linux kernel netfilter functionality but often is also offered as an appliance on the network.

firewalld The modern service (replacing iptables) that is used since RHEL 7 to implement firewalling based on the Linux kernel firewalling framework.

folder Also referred to as a directory, a structure in the file system used to organize files that belong together.

foreground process A process that is running on a system and occupies the console it is running on. Linux processes that are started by users can be started in the foreground or in the background. If a process has been started as a foreground process, no other processes can be started in the same terminal until it finishes or is moved to the background. *See also* background process.

fork A system call that starts a new process as a child of the current process. This is the default way commands are executed. *See also* exec.

fstab A configuration file that is used on Linux to mount file systems automatically when the system starts.

fully qualified domain name (FQDN) A complete DNS hostname that contains the name of the host (like myserver), as well as the DNS domain it is used in (like example.com).

G

GECOS A field in the /etc/passwd file that can be used to store personal data about a user on the Linux operating system. GECOS originally stood for General Electric Comprehensive Operating Supervisor.

globally unique ID (GUID) An identification number that consists of parts that ensure that it is globally unique.

GPT *See* GUID Partition Table.

group A collection of items. In user management, a group is used to assign permissions to multiple users simultaneously. In Linux, every user is a member of at least one group.

group owner The group that has been set as the owner of a file or a directory. On Linux, every file and directory has a user owner and a group owner. Group ownership is set when files are created, and unless configured otherwise, it is set to the primary group of the user who creates the file.

GRUB 2 The boot loader that is installed on most systems that need to start Linux. GRUB 2 provides a boot prompt from which different kernel boot options can be entered, which is useful if you need to troubleshoot the boot procedure.

GUID *See* globally unique ID.

GUID Partition Table (GPT) A modern solution to store partitions on a hard disk, as opposed to the older MBR partition table. In GUID partitions, a total of 128 partitions can be created, and no difference exists between primary, extended, and logical partitions anymore.

gzip One of the most common utilities that is used for compression and decompression of files on Linux.

H

hard link A name associated with an inode. Inodes are used to store Linux files. An inode contains the complete administration of the file, including the blocks in which the file is stored. A file that does not have at least one hard link is considered a deleted file. To increase file accessibility, more than one hard link can be created for an inode.

hardware time The time that is provided by computer hardware, typically the BIOS clock. When a Linux system boots, it sets the software time based on the hardware time. Because hardware time often is inaccurate, most Linux systems use the Network Time Protocol (NTP) to synchronize the system time with a reliable time source.

hexadecimal A 16-based numbering system that is based on groups of 4 bytes. Hexadecimal numbers start with the range 0 through 9, followed by A through F. Because hexadecimal is much more efficient in computer technology, hexadecimal numbers are often used. In IPv6, IP addresses are written as hexadecimal numbers.

hypervisor A piece of computer software, firmware, or hardware that creates and runs virtual machines. In Linux, KVM is used as the common hypervisor software.

I

image The read-only instance from which a container is started.

inheritance In permission management, the situation where new files that are created in a directory inherit the permission settings from the parent directory.

init The first process that is started once the Linux kernel and initramfs have been loaded. From the init process, all other processes are started. As of RHEL 7, the init process has been replaced by Systemd.

initramfs The initial RAM file system. Contains drivers and other files that are needed in the first stages of booting a Linux system. On Red Hat Enterprise Linux, the initramfs is generated during installation and can be manually re-created using the **dracut** utility.

inode A structure that contains the complete administration of a file. Every Linux file has an inode, and the inode contains all properties of the file but not the filename.

input module In rsyslog, a module that allows rsyslog to receive log messages from specific sources.

interface In Linux networking, the set of configuration parameters that can be activated for a specific device. Several interface configurations can exist for a device, but only one interface can be active at a time for a device.

internal command A command that is a part of the shell and does not exist as a file on disk.

Internet Protocol (IP) The primary communications protocol that is used by computers for communication. The Internet Protocol exists in two versions (IPv4 and IPv6). Apart from node addressing, it defines routing, which enables nodes to contact one another.

IP *See* Internet Protocol.

iptables An older solution to create firewall rules on the Linux operating system. It interfaces with the netfilter Linux kernel firewalling functionality and was the default solution to create software firewalls on earlier versions of RHEL. As of RHEL 7, iptables has been replaced by firewalld.

IPv4 Version 4 of the Internet protocol. It was developed in the 1970s and introduced in 1981. It allows a theoretical maximum of about 4 billion nodes to be addressed by using a 32-bit address space. It is still the most important IP version in use.

IPv6 Version 6 of the Internet protocol. It was developed in the 1990s to address the shortage in IPv6 addresses. It uses a 128-bit address space that allows for addressing 3,4e38 nodes and thus is considered a virtually unlimited address space.

iteration In shell scripting, one time of many that a conditional loop has been processed until the desired result has been reached.

J

job In a Linux shell, a task running in the current terminal. Jobs can be started in the foreground and in the background. Every job is also visible as a process.

journalctl The command used to manage systemd-journald.

journald *See* systemd-journald.

K

kernel The central component of the operating system. It manages I/O requests from software and translates them into data processing instructions for the hardware in the computer.

kernel ring buffer A part of memory where messages that are generated by the kernel are stored. The **dmesg** command enables you to read the contents of the kernel ring buffer.

kernel space The part of memory that is reserved for running privileged instructions. Kernel space is typically accessible by the operating system kernel, kernel extensions, and most device drivers. Applications normally run in user space, which ensures that a faulty application cannot crash the computer system.

Kernel-based Virtual Machine (KVM) The Linux kernel module that acts as a hypervisor and makes it possible to run virtual machines directly on top of the Linux kernel.

key-based login In SSH, login that uses public/private keys to prove the identity of the user who wants to log in. Key-based login is generally considered more secure than password-based login.

kill A command that can be used to send a signal to a Linux process. Many signals are defined (see **man 7 signal**), but only a few are commonly used, including SIGTERM and SIGKILL, both of which are used to stop processes.

Kubernetes The standard in container orchestration and also the foundation of Red Hat OpenShift.

KVM *See* Kernel-based Virtual Machine.

L

label A name that can be assigned to a file system. Using labels can be a good idea, because once a label is assigned, it will never be changed, which guarantees that the file system can still be mounted, even if other parameters such as the device name have changed. However, UUIDs are considered safer than labels because the chance of having a duplicate label by accident is much higher than the chance of having a duplicate UUID. *See also* universally unique ID (UUID).

line anchor In regular expressions, a character that refers to a specific position in a line.

linger The Systemd feature that is needed to start Systemd user units at system boot and not at user login.

Linux A UNIX-like operating system that consists of a kernel that was originally developed by Linus Torvalds (hence the name Linux). A current Linux operating system consists of a kernel and lots of open source tools that provide a complete operating system. Linux is packaged in the form of a distribution. Currently, Red Hat Enterprise Linux is among the most widely used Linux distributions.

log rotation A service that ensures that log files cannot grow too big. Log files are monitored according to specific parameters, such as a maximum age or size. Once this parameter is reached, the log file will be closed and a new log file will be opened. Old log files are kept for a limited period and will be removed, often after only a couple of weeks.

logical extent The building block that is used in LVM to create logical volumes. It normally has a size of a few megabytes that corresponds to the size of the physical extents that are used.

logical partition A partition that is created in an extended partition. *See also* extended partition.

logical volume In LVM, the entity on which a file system is created. Logical volumes are often used on RHEL because they offer important advantages, such as the option to dynamically resize the logical volume and the file system that it hosts.

Logical Volume Manager (LVM) The software that makes it possible to work with logical volumes.

login shell The shell that is opened directly after a user has logged in.

LVM *See* Logical Volume Manager.

M

masquerading A solution that enables a private IP address range that is not directly accessible from outside networks to be accessed by using one public IP address that is exposed on a router. This is also referred to as Network Address Translation (NAT).

Master Boot Record (MBR) On a BIOS system, the first 512 bytes on the primary hard disk. It contains a boot loader and a partition table that give access to the different partitions on the hard disk of that computer.

MBR *See* Master Boot Record.

module A piece of snap-in code. Modules are used by several systems on Linux, such as the kernel, GRUB 2, rsyslog, and more. Via modules, Linux components can be extended easily, and adding functionality does not require a total rewrite of the software.

module (in dnf) A collection of software packages that can be managed as one entity and can contain different versions of a software solution.

mount A connection that is made between a device and a directory. To access files on specific storage devices, the storage device needs to be mounted on a directory. This sets up the specified directory as the access point to files on the storage device. Mounts are typically organized by the system administrator and are not visible to end users.

multiplier In regular expressions, a character that indicates that multiples of the previous character are referred to.

N

namespace An isolated environment that is created by the Linux kernel and allows for running containers in complete isolation. Namespaces exist for multiple aspects of the operating system, including mounts, processes, users, and more.

netfilter The part of the Linux kernel that implements firewalling.

netmask *See* subnet mask.

Network Address Translation (NAT) *See* masquerading.

Network File System (NFS) A common UNIX solution to export physical file systems to other hosts on the network. The other hosts can mount the exported NFS directory in their local file system.

network time Time that is provided on the network.

Network Time Protocol (NTP) A standard that is used to provide reliable time to servers in a network. NTP on RHEL 9 is implemented by the chronyd service.

NFS *See* Network File System.

nftables The service that manages kernel firewalling. It is a replacement of the older iptables service.

nice A method to change the priority of Linux processes. A negative nice value will make the process more aggressive, giving it a higher priority (which is expressed by a lower priority number); a positive nice value will make a process less eager so that it gives priority to other processes.

NTP *See* Network Time Protocol.

O

octal A numbering scheme that uses the numbers 0 through 7 only. Used when working with Linux permissions using the **umask** setting or the **chmod** command.

OpenShift The Red Hat platform, based on Kubernetes, that is used for container orchestration.

OR A logical operation where the second command is executed only if the first command is not able to execute.

orchestration The technique that ensures containers can be offered in a scalable and redundant way in corporate environments.

output module In rsyslog, a module that is used to send log messages to a specific destination. Output modules make rsyslogd flexible and allow for the usage of log destinations that are not native to rsyslog.

ownership In file system permissions, the basis of the effective permissions that a user has. Every file has a user owner and a group owner assigned to it.

P

package A bundle that is used to distribute software. A package typically contains a compressed archive of files and metadata that includes instructions on how to install those files.

package group A group of packages that can be installed as such using the **dnf groups install** command.

package group (in dnf) A group of software packages that can be installed with a single command.

pager A program that can be used to browse page by page through a text file. The **less** utility provides one of the most common Linux pagers.

parent shell The environment from which a shell script or program is started. Processes or child scripts will inherit settings from the parent shell.

partition A subdivision of a hard disk on which a file system can be created to mount it into the directory structure.

passphrase Basically a password, but is supposed to be longer and more secure than a password.

password A token that is used in authentication. The password is a secret word that can be set by individual users and will be stored in an encrypted way.

path The complete reference to the location of a file.

permissions Attributes that can be set on files or directories to allow users or groups access to these files or directories.

permissive mode The SELinux mode where nothing is blocked but everything is logged in the audit log. This mode is typically used for troubleshooting SELinux issues.

physical extent The physical building block that is used when creating LVM physical volumes. Typically, the size is multiple megabytes.

physical volume The foundation building block of an LVM configuration. The physical volume typically corresponds to a partition or a complete disk device.

PID *See* process identification number.

pipe A structure that can be used to forward the output of one command to be used as input for another command.

policy *See* SELinux policy.

port A number that is used by a process to offer access to the process through a network connection.

port forwarding A firewalling technique where traffic that is coming in on a specific port is forwarded to another port that may be on the same host or on a different host.

Portable Operating System Interface (POSIX) A standard that was created to maintain compatibility between operating systems. The standard mainly applies to UNIX and guarantees that different flavors of Linux and UNIX are compatible with one another.

portmapper A Remote Procedure Call service that needs to run on systems that provide RPC services. Portmapper uses dynamic ports that do not correspond to specific TCP or UDP ports; the service will pick a UDP or TCP port that will be used as long as the process is active. When the process is restarted, chances are that different ports are used. They need to be mapped to fixed UDP and TCP ports in order to make it possible to open the firewall for these ports. Portmapper is still used by components of the NFS service.

POSIX *See* Portable Operating System Interface.

primary group The group that is listed in the group membership field for a user in /etc/passwd. Every Linux user is a member of a primary group. Apart from that, users can be made a member of secondary groups as well.

primary partition In MBR, one of a maximum of four partitions that can be created in the Master Boot Record. *See also* extended partition.

priority (in process handling) Specifies the importance of a process. Process priority is expressed with a number (which can be modified using **nice**). Processes with a lower priority number are serviced before processes with a higher priority number.

priority (in rsyslog) Used to specify the severity of a logged event. Based on the severity, specific actions can be taken.

private key In public/private key encryption, the key that is used to generate encrypted data.

privileged user *See* root.

proc A kernel interface that provides access to kernel information and kernel tunables. This interface is available through the /proc file system.

process A task that is running on a Linux machine. Roughly, a process corresponds to a program, although one program can start multiple processes.

process identification number (PID) A unique number that is used to identify a process running on a Linux system.

profile In **tuned**, a collection of performance settings that can easily be applied.

protocol A set of rules that is used in computing, such as in computer networking, to establish communications between two computers.

public key In cryptography, the key that is typically sent by a server to a client so that the client can send back encrypted data.

PV *See* physical volume.

Q

queue In process management, where processes wait before they can be executed.

R

real-time clock (RTC) The hardware clock that is installed on the computer motherboard.

reboot The procedure of stopping the computer and starting it again.

Red Hat Customer Portal The platform that Red Hat offers to provide patches for customers that have an active subscription. To provide these patches and updates, Red Hat Network provides the repositories that are needed for this purpose.

Red Hat Enterprise Linux (RHEL) The name of the software that Red Hat sells subscriptions for. It is available in a server edition and a desktop edition.

Red Hat Package Manager (RPM) The name for the package format that is used on RHEL for software packages and for the Package Management software. RPM has become the standard for package management on many other Linux distributions as well.

reference clock A clock that is used as a time source in an NTP time configuration. Typically, a reference clock is a highly reliable clock on the Internet, but it can be an internal clock on the computer's motherboard as well.

registry A location where container images are started from.

regular expression A search pattern that allows users to search text patterns in a flexible way. Not to be confused with shell metacharacters.

relative filename A filename that is relative to a directory that is not the root directory.

Remote Procedure Calls (RPC) A method for interprocess communication that allows a program to execute code in another address space. Remote Procedure Calls is an old protocol and as such is still used in the Network File System.

repository An installation source that contains installable packages and an index that contains information about the installable packages so that the installation program **dnf** can compare the version of packages currently installed with the version of packages available in the repository.

resident memory Memory pages that are in use by a program.

resolver The DNS client part that contains a list of DNS servers to contact to resolve DNS queries.

RHEL *See* Red Hat Enterprise Linux.

rich rules Rules in firewalld that allow the usage of a more complicated syntax so that more complex rules can be defined.

Rocky Linux Free open source alternative for Red Hat Enterprise Linux, which consists of the RHEL source code with all licensing removed.

root The privileged user account that is used for system administration tasks. User root has access to all capabilities, which means that permissions do not apply to user root and the root user account is virtually unlimited.

root directory The starting point of the file system hierarchy, noted as /.

RPC *See* Remote Procedure Calls.

RPM *See* Red Hat Package Manager.

rsyslogd The generic daemon that logs messages.

RTC *See* real-time clock.

S

Samba The name for the Linux service that implements the SMB protocol.

SAN *See* storage-area network.

scheduler The part of the Linux kernel that monitors the queue of runnable processes and allocates CPU time to these processes.

secondary group A group that a user is a member of but which membership is not defined in the /etc/passwd file. When new files are created, the secondary group will not automatically become the owner of those files.

Secure Shell (SSH) A solution that allows users to open a shell on a remote server where security is implemented by using public/private key cryptography.

Secure Sockets Layer (SSL) *See* Transport Layer Security (TLS).

SELinux A Linux kernel security module that provides a mechanism for supporting access control security policies.

SELinux Policy The collection of rules that is used to define SELinux security.

Server Message Block (SMB) An application-level protocol that is used to provide shared access to files, printers, and serial ports, which on Linux is implemented in the Samba server.

service (in firewalld) A configuration of firewall settings that is used to allow access to specific processes.

services (in Systemd) Processes that need to be started to provide specific functionality.

share A directory to which remote access is configured using a remote file system protocol such as NFS or CIFS.

shebang The characters used in a script to indicate which shell should be used for executing the code in the shell script. If no shebang is used, the script code will be interpreted by the parent shell, which may lead to errors in some cases. A shebang starts with a #, which is followed by a ! and the complete pathname of the shell, such as #!/bin/bash.

shell The environment from which commands can be executed. Bash is the default shell on Linux, but other shells exist as well.

shell metacharacters Characters such as *, ?, and [a-z] that allow users to refer to characters in filenames in a flexible way.

signal An instruction that can be sent to a process. Common signals exist, such as SIGTERM and SIGKILL, but the Linux kernel allows a total of 32 different signals to be used. To send a signal to a process, use the **kill** command.

SMB *See* Server Message Block.

snapshot A "photo" of the actual state of a file system.

software time *See* system time.

source context In SELinux, the context of the processes or users that initiate an action. A context in SELinux is a label that identifies allowed operations. Everything in an SELinux environment has a context.

SSH *See* Secure Shell.

standard error (STDERR) The default location where a program sends error messages.

standard input (STDIN) The default location where a program gets its input.

standard output (STDOUT) The default location where a program sends its regular output.

star A legacy extended version of **tar**, which offers support for extended attributes. Currently no longer required, as all of its functionality has been integrated in **tar**.

static route A route that is defined manually by a network administrator.

STDERR *See* standard error.

STDIN *See* standard input.

STDOUT *See* standard output.

storage-area network (SAN) A solution where disk devices are shared at a block level over the network. As such, they can be used in the same way as local disk devices on a Linux system. iSCSI and Fibre Channel are the common SAN protocols.

Stratis The new volume managing file system that was introduced in RHEL 8.

stratum In time synchronization, used to indicate the distance between a server and an authoritative Internet time source.

subnet mask A logical subdivision of an IP network.

subshell A shell that is started from another shell. Typically, a subshell is started by running a shell script.

symbolic link A special type of file that contains a reference to another file or directory in the form of an absolute or relative path.

sysfs The kernel interface that is mounted on the /sys directory and which is used to provide access to parameters that can be used for managing hardware settings.

system call A low-level operating system instruction.

system time The time that is maintained by the operating system. When a Linux system boots, system time is set to the current hardware time, and while the operating system is running, it is often synchronized using the Network Time Protocol (NTP).

Systemd The service manager on RHEL 9. Systemd is the very first process that starts after the kernel has loaded, and it takes care of starting all other processes and services on a Linux system.

systemd-journald The part of Systemd that takes care of logging information about events that have been happening. The introduction of journald ensures that information about all services can be logged, regardless of how the service itself is configured to deal with information that is to be logged.

T

tainted kernel A kernel in which unsupported kernel modules have been loaded.

tar The Tape Archiver; the default Linux utility that is used to create and extract backups.

target In Systemd, a collection of unit files that can be managed together.

target context The SELinux context that is set to a target object, such as a port, file, or directory.

terminal Originally, the screen that was used by a user to type commands on. On modern Linux systems, pseudo terminals can be used as a replacement. A pseudo terminal offers a shell window from which users enter the commands that need to be executed.

thin allocation In storage, an approach that enables the system to present more storage to the storage user than what is really available by using smart technologies to store data, like deduplication.

thread A thread is a subdivision of a process. Many processes are single threaded, which means that process is basically one entity that needs to be serviced. On a multicore or multi-CPU computer system, working with multithreaded processes makes sense. That way, the different cores can be used to handle the different threads, which allows a process to benefit from multicore or multithreaded environments.

time synchronization A system that ensures that multiple servers are using the exact same time. To accomplish time synchronization, it is common to use an external time server, as defined in the Network Time Protocol (NTP).

timer A Systemd unit type that can be used as an alternative to cron jobs and run units at a specific time.

timestamp An identifier that can be used on files, database records, and other types of data to identify when the last modification has been applied. Many services rely on timestamps. To ensure that timestamp-based systems work properly, time synchronization needs to be configured.

TLS *See* Transport Layer Security.

Transport Layer Security (TLS) A cryptographic protocol that is created to ensure secured communications over a computer network. In TLS, public and private keys are used, and certificates authenticate the counterparty. TLS was formerly known as SSL.

TTY A program that provides a virtual terminal on Linux. Every terminal still has a TTY name, which is either tty1-6 for virtual TTYs or /dev/pts/0-nn for pseudo terminals.

tuned A service on RHEL that enables administrators to easily apply performance settings by using profiles.

U

udev A service that works with the Linux kernel to initialize hardware.

UEFI *See* Unified Extensible Firmware Interface.

umask An octal value that defines the default permissions as a shell property.

umount The command that is used to decouple a file system from the directory on which it is mounted.

Unified Extensible Firmware Interface (UEFI) A replacement of the Basic Input/Output System used on older IBM-compatible computers as the first program that runs when the computer is started. UEFI is the layer between the operating system and the computer firmware.

unit An item that is managed by Systemd. Different types of units exist, including service, path, mount, and target units.

universally unique ID (UUID) An identification number consisting of a long random hexadecimal number that is globally unique.

unprivileged user A regular non-root user account to which access restrictions apply, as applied by permissions.

user An entity that is used on Linux to provide access to specific system resources. Users can be used to represent people, but many services also have a dedicated user account, which allows the service to run with the specific permissions that are needed for that service.

user space The area of memory that is accessible by application software that has been started with non-root privileges.

UTC *See* Coordinated Universal Time.

UUID *See* universally unique ID.

V

value The data that is assigned to a specific property, variable, or record.

variable A label that contains a specific value that can be changed dynamically. In scripting, variables are frequently used to allow the script to be flexible.

VFAT The Linux kernel driver that is used to access FAT-based file systems. FAT is a commonly used file system in Windows environments. The Linux VFAT driver allows usage of this file system.

VG *See* volume group.

virtual host In the Apache web server, a collection of configuration settings that is used to address a web server. What makes it a virtual host is that one installation of the Apache web server can be configured with multiple virtual hosts, which allows administrators to run multiple websites on one Apache server.

virtual memory The total amount of addressable memory. Virtual memory is called *virtual* memory because it does not refer to memory that really exists. Its only purpose is to make sure that Linux programs can set an address pointer that is unique and not in use by other programs.

volume group (VG) The abstraction layer that in Logical Volume Manager is used to represent all available storage presented by physical volumes from which logical volumes can be created.

W

want An indication for a Systemd unit file that it is supposed to be started from a specific Systemd target.

wildcard The * character, which in a shell environment refers to an unlimited number of any characters.

X

XFS A high-performance 64-bit file system that was created in 1993 by SGI and which in RHEL 9 is used as the default file system.

Xz A compression utility that can be used as an alternative to gzip or bzip2.

Y

Yellowdog Update, Modified The full name for Yum, the meta package handler that on older versions of RHEL was used to install packages from yum repositories. Now replaced with **dnf**.

Yum *See* Yellowdog Update, Modified.

Z

zombie A process that has lost contact with its parent and for that reason cannot be managed using regular tools.

zone In firewalld, a collection of one or more network interfaces that specific firewalld rules are associated with.

Index

Symbols

& (ampersand), 235, 431
* (asterisk), 61, 91–92, 278
\ (backslash), 430–431
#!/bin/bash, 424
^ (caret), 39
$ (dollar sign), 39
. (dot) regular expression, 91–92
= (equal sign), 41, 303
> (greater than symbol), 33
< (less than symbol), 33
&& (logical AND), 431
|| (logical OR), 431
!ls command (vim), 39
:%s/old/new/g command (vim), 39
| (pipe), 33–35, 431
+ (plus sign), 92
:q! command (vim), 38
? (question mark), 61, 92
(…) regular expression, 92
/ (root directory), 56
?text command (vim), 39
^text regular expression, 92
:w filename command (vim), 39
:wq command (vim), 38
\{1,3\} regular expression, 92
\{2\} regular expression, 92

A

a command (vim), 38
absolute filenames, 62–64
accounts
group
creating, 137–138
group properties, 138–139
primary, 137
secondary, 137
user
creating, 132–133, 136
default values, 134–135
normal accounts, 129–132
password properties, 135
system accounts, 129–132
user environment, 135–136
user properties, 134
AccuracySec option (systemd), 275
acl mount option, 337
addresses
broadcast, 172
IP (Internet Protocol), 170–173
MAC (media access control), 173
network
management of, 174
validation of, 175–178
administrators, setting, 16
alert priority, rsyslogd, 303
alias command, 31
aliases, 31
AllowUsers option (SSH), 444–445, 447
AlmaLinux, 8
ampersand (&), 235, 431
anacron service, 281
Apache server configuration
configuration files, 456–459, 460–461
content creation, 459–460
software installation, 456
virtual hosts, 456
Application Stream (AppStream) repository, 205–206
apropos command, 45
archives, 71–73
arguments, 30
asterisk (*), 61, 91, 92, 278
at command, 282–283
atd service, 282–283

atime mount option, 337
atq command, 283
audit log, 487–488
[auo] wildcard, 61
auth/authpriv facility, rsyslogd, 302
authentication, SSH (Secure Shell), 116–117, 447–448
auto mount option, 337
autofs service, 516
automation
  with crond service
    anacron, 281
    cron configuration files, 278–280
    cron time/date fields, 278
    management of, 276–277
    security, 282
  of file system mounts, 335–338
  with shell scripting
    conditional loops, 429–435
    core elements of, 424–425
    debugging, 435
    variables and input, 426–429
automount, mounting NFS (Network File System) shares from, 516–518
autorelabel file, 417
awk command, 94–96

B

background processes, 234–235
backslash (\), 430–431
balanced profile, 249
baseurl= option, repositories, 202
bash command, 425, 435
Bash shell. *See* shell
~/.bash_profile file, 41
~/.bashrc file, 41, 136
Basic Graphics Mode, 411
Basic Input/Output System (BIOS), 314, 315, 323, 406
batch command, 283
bg command, 235–237
binary notation, 172–173
bind-mounting in rootless containers, 565–566
/bin/sh, 547
BIOS (Basic Input/Output System), 314, 315, 323, 406
blkid command, 334, 338
block zone, firewalld, 499
blockdev, 362
Boolean settings, SELinux, 485–487
/boot directory, 56, 57–58
boot procedure
  GRUB 2 boot loader, 396–399
    boot options, 398–399
    components of, 396
    configuration files, 397–398
    reinstalling, 410–414
  overview of, 109–110
  Systemd targets, 390–396
    isolating, 393–396
    managing, 392–393
    showing list of, 393–396
    target units, 391–392
    types of, 390
    wants, 392
  troubleshooting
    boot phase configuration, 406–408
    boot prompt, accessing, 408–409
    file system issues, 415
    GRUB 2 reinstallation, 410–414
    initramfs, 415
    rescue disks, 410–414
    root password, resetting, 416–417
    troubleshooting targets, 409–410
boot prompt, accessing, 408–409
/boot/efi/EFI/centos/grub.cfg file, 397–398
/boot/efi/EFI/redhat/grub.cfg file, 397–398
/boot/grub2/grub.cfg file, 397–398
broadcast addresses, 172
BtrFS, 328
buildah, 542
bunzip2, 74
bzip2 command, 74

C

cache tier, 362
caret (^), 39
case loops, 434–435
cat command, 84, 85, 375
cd command, 62, 152
CentOS Stream, 7
Cert Guide environment, 9–10
chage command, 135

characters, counting, 88–89
chattr command, 160
chcon command, 479–480
chgrp command, 150
chmod command, 153–154, 156–158
chown command, 149–150
chrony service, 533–534
chronyd process, 529–530
chroot command, 411–413, 414
chroot environment, 461, 543
chvt command, 107
Classless Inter-Domain Routing (CIDR) notation, 171
ClientAliveCountMax option (SSH), 446, 447
ClientAliveInterval option (SSH), 446, 447
clients
  SSH options, 446–447
  time service, 533–534
clock. *See* time services
command line
  command-line completion, 37
  mounting NFS (Network File System) shares from, 514
command mode, vim, 38
commands. *See also individual commands*
  aliases, 31
  command-line completion, 37
  executing, 30–32
  help, 43
  internal/external, 31–32
  I/O redirection, 32–33
  pipes, 34–35
  running in containers, 559–560
  syntax for, 30
community distributions, 8
compression, file, 74–75
conditional loops, 429–435
  && (logical AND), 431
  || (logical OR), 431
  case, 434–435
  for, 431–432
  if...then...else, 430–431
  until, 432–434
  while, 432–434
configuration. *See also* configuration files; installation
  Apache server
    configuration files, 456–459, 460–461
    content creation, 459–460
    software installation, 456
    virtual hosts, 462–464
  boot procedure, 406–408
  firewalld
    firewall-cmd options, 501–504
    overview of, 498
    services, 500–501
    zones, 499
  GRUB 2 boot loader
    boot options, 398–399
    configuration files, 397–398
  network
    configuration files, 186–187
    hostnames, 187–189
    management with nmcli, 180–184, 190
    management with nmtui, 184–185, 190
    name resolution, 189–191
    permissions, 181
    validating, 175–180
  NFS (Network File System)
    automount, 516–518
    server setup, 513
    servers, 513
    shares, mounting, 514–518
  root password, 416–417
  rsyslogd, 300–304
    configuration files, 300
    facilities, priorities, and destinations, 301–303
    rules, changing, 304
  SSH (Secure Shell), 442–448
    connection keepalive options, 446–447
    hardening, 442–445
    key-based authentication, 447–448
    most useful options, 447
    passphrases, 447–448
    session options, 446
  Stratis, 361–364
  Systemd units, 266–267
  time services
    clients, 533–534
    local time, 526
    NTP (Network Time Protocol), 527
    time management commands, 527–531
    time zones, 531–533

configuration files
Apache, 456–459, 460–461
cron, 278–280
/etc/bashrc, 136
/etc/default/useradd, 134–135
/etc/group, 137–138
/etc/gshadow, 138
/etc/login.defs, 134–135
/etc/passwd, 129–130
/etc/profile, 136
/etc/shadow, 130–132
network, 186–187
rsyslogd, 300
shell environment, 41–43
Conflicts statement, 259
connection keepalive options (SSH), 446–447
consoles, local
booting/rebooting, 109–110
logging in to, 104–105
multiple terminals in
in graphical environment, 105–106
in nongraphical environment, 107–108
pseudo terminal devices, 108–109
shutting down, 109–110
terminals versus, 104
containerfiles, building images from, 556–558
containers
container images, 542
building from containerfiles, 556–558
finding, 552–553
inspecting, 553–555
managing, 556
registries, 542, 550–551
removing, 556
control group (cgroup), 544
environment variables, 561
host requirements for, 543–544
namespaces, 543–544
Open Containers Initiative (OCI), 551
orchestration, 545, 563, 566
overview of, 542
ports, 561
rootless, 544
running, 545–550
running commands in, 559–560
software solutions for, 542, 544–545
status of, 558–559
storage, 563–566
context settings, SELinux
context labels
monitoring, 477–478
setting, 481–482
context types
finding needed type, 482–483
setting, 479–481
overview of, 477
control group (cgroup), 544
Coordinated Universal Time (UTC), 526
cp command, 64–65
CREATE_HOME, 135
createrepo command, 204
CRI-o, 542, 544
crit priority, rsyslogd, 303
cron facility, rsyslogd, 302
crond service
anacron, 281
cron configuration files, 278–280
cron time/date fields, 278
management of, 276–277
running scheduled tasks through, 282
security, 282
cut command, 84, 87

D

daemons
crond
anacron, 281
cron configuration files, 278–280
cron time/date fields, 278
management of, 276–277
security, 282
definition of, 234
rsyslogd, 302
systemd-udevd, 376, 406
database, rpm, 222–223
date command, 528
date fields, cron, 278
daylight saving time (DST), 526
dd command (vim), 39
debug priority, rsyslogd, 303
debugging shell scripts, 435. *See also* troubleshooting
default file contexts, SELinux, 483–484

default permissions, 159–160
default shell, 133
default user account values, 134–135
dependencies
  repositories and, 198
  Systemd targets, 391–392
dependencies, Systemd, 263–265
dependency hell, 221
desktop profile, 249
destination, rsyslogd, 301–303
/dev directory, 56
/dev/hda, 317
device files, 33
device mapper, 356
device names
  file system, 334–335
  LVM (Logical Volume Manager), 355–356
/dev/mapper directory, 356
/dev/nvme0n1, 317
/dev/sda, 317
/dev/vda, 317
/dev/xvda, 317
df -Th command, 59–61
DHCP (Dynamic Host Configuration Protocol), 174
dictionary attacks, 442
directories. *See also individual directories*
  absolute versus relative pathnames in, 62–64
  copying, 64–65
  home, 133
  listing, 64
  moving, 65–66
  ownership
    changing, 149–150
    default, 150–151
    displaying, 148–149
  structure of, 61–62
  table of, 56–57
disk devices, 317–318
distributions, Red Hat Enterprise Linux (RHEL), 7–8
dmesg command, 373–375, 383
dmz zone, firewalld, 499
dnf command
  common dnf tasks, 206
  overview of, 198
  packages
    finding, 206–208
    installing/removing, 209–211
    listing, 211–213
    package groups, 214–216
    package modules, 217–221
    returning information about, 208–209
    updating, 213–214
  past actions, showing, 216–217
  repositories
    creating, 204–206
    options for, 202
    role of, 198–199
    security, 203–204
    specifying, 200–202
dnf config-manager tool, 201
dnf group install command, 206, 214, 396, 456
dnf group list command, 206, 214–216, 396
dnf history command, 216–217
dnf info command, 206, 208–209
dnf install command, 206, 209–211
dnf install curl command, 459, 464
dnf install httpd command, 459
dnf install kernel command, 383
dnf install vim-enhanced command, 38
dnf list command, 206, 211–213
dnf module command, 217–221
dnf module enable command, 221
dnf module install command, 221
dnf module list command, 217–221
dnf remove command, 206, 211
dnf search command, 206–208
dnf update command, 206, 213–214
dnf upgrade kernel command, 383
dnf whatprovides command, 208, 479
DNS (Domain Name Service), 189–191
Docker, 542, 544
DocumentRoot parameter, Apache, 456–459
dollar sign ($), 39
dot (.) regular expression, 91, 92
dracut command, 413, 415
drivers, kernel, 372–373
drop zone (firewalld), 499
DST (daylight saving time), 526

dump utility, 158, 337, 515
Dynamic Host Configuration Protocol (DHCP), 174

E

e2label command, 331, 334
echo command, 41, 428
editors
  vi, 38
  vim, 37–40
EFI (Extensible Firmware Interface), 57–58
else statement, 429
emergency.target, 390
emerg/panic priority, rsyslogd, 303
End Of File (EOF) character, 235
enforcing mode, SELinux, 473–475
engine, container, 542
env command, 40
ENV_PATH, 135
environment, shell, 135–136
  configuration files, 41–43
  definition of, 40
  variables, 40–41
environment variables
  container, 562–563
  shell, 40–41
EPEL (Extra Packages for Enterprise Linux) repositories, 199
epoch time, 528
equal sign (=), 41, 303
err/error priority, rsyslogd, 303
esac statement, 435
escaping, 91, 430–431
/etc directory, 56
/etc/anacrontab file, 281
/etc/bashrc file, 41, 136
/etc/containers/registries.conf file, 550–551
/etc/cron.allow file, 282
/etc/crontab file, 278–280
/etc/default/grub file, 396–397
/etc/default/useradd file, 134–135
/etc/fstab file, 335–338, 515
/etc/group file, 137–138
/etc/gshadow file, 138
/etc/httpd/conf/httpd.conf file, 456–459, 461
/etc/issue file, 42
/etc/login.defs file, 134–135
/etc/logrotate.conf file, 304–306
/etc/modprobe.d directory, 382
/etc/modules-load.d directory, 378
/etc/motd file, 42
/etc/NetworkManager/system-connections, 186
/etc/passwd file, 129–130
/etc/profile file, 41, 136
/etc/rsyslog.conf file, 300
/etc/rsyslog.d file, 300
/etc/shadow file, 130–132
/etc/sysconfig/network-scripts directory, 186
/etc/sysconfig/selinux file, 474–475
/etc/systemd/system directory, 257
/etc/yum.repos.d directory, 201
exabytes (EB), 316
exam, RHCSA
  exam day tips, 574–576
  nondisclosure agreement (NDA), 576–577
  practice exams, tips for, 581–582, 583–584
  registration for, 573–574
  theoretical pre-assessment exam, 579–580
  updates for, 617–618
  verifying readiness for, 573
exec command, 417
exec mount option, 337
execute permissions, 152–154
exit command, 36, 151, 425, 548
expressions, regular. *See* regular expressions
Ext2, 328
Ext3, 328
Ext4, 328, 329–331
extended partitions, 315, 320–322
extended regular expressions, 91–93
Extensible Firmware Interface (EFI), 57–58
external commands, 31–32
external zone (firewalld), 499

F

facilities, rsyslogd, 301–303
fdisk utility, 317, 318–322, 350–352
Fedora, 8
fg command, 235–237

file command, 73
file descriptors, 33
file systems. *See also* directories
- BtrFS, 328
- creating, 328–329
- /etc/bashrc, 331–332
- Ext2, 328
- Ext3, 328
- Ext4, 328, 329–331
- Filesystem Hierarchy Standard (FHS), 56–57
- mounting, 57–61
  - automating through /etc/fstab, 335–338
  - device names, 334–335
  - disk labels, 334–335
  - manually, 334
  - requirements for, 333–334
  - systemd mounts, 338–339
  - UUIDs, 334–335
- NFS
  - configuration, 513
  - history of, 512
  - security, 512
  - shares, mounting, 514–518
  - versions of, 512–513
- NTFS, 328
- swap files, 333
- troubleshooting, 415
- VFAT, 328
- volume-managing, 361
- XFS, 328, 331–332, 362

files. *See also* directories; log files
- absolute versus relative filenames, 62–64
- archives, 71–73
- compression of, 74–75
- configuration
  - Apache, 456–459, 460–461
  - cron, 278–280
  - /etc/bashrc, 136
  - /etc/default/useradd, 134–135
  - /etc/group, 137–138
  - /etc/gshadow, 138
  - /etc/login.defs, 134–135
  - /etc/passwd, 129–130
  - /etc/profile, 136
  - /etc/shadow, 130–132
  - GRUB 2 boot loader, 397–398
  - network, 186–187
  - rsyslogd, 300
  - shell environment, 41–43
- containerfiles, 556–558
- copying, 64–65, 114
- deleting, 66–67
- device, 33
- file descriptors, 33
- filtering
  - with cut command, 87
  - with sort command, 87–88
- hidden, 64
- links
  - creating, 69–70
  - definition of, 68
  - hard, 68, 71
  - removing, 70
  - symbolic (soft), 69, 71
- listing, 64
- moving, 65–66
- multi-user.target, 390, 391–392
- ownership
  - changing, 149–150
  - default, 150–151
  - displaying, 148–149
- rpm, 222, 223–224, 225
- secure file transfers, 115
- swap, 333
- synchronizing, 115
- Systemd, 257–258
- text
  - regular expressions, 89–96
  - text file-related tools, 84–89
- /usr/share/doc, 48–49
- wildcards and, 61

filtering text files
- with cut command, 87
- with sort command, 87–88

find command, 149
findmnt command, 59, 337
firewall-cmd command, 501–504
firewall-config command, 501
firewalls
- benefits of, 498
- firewalld
  - configuring, 501–504

overview of, 498
services, 500–501
zones, 499
folders. *See* directories
for loops, 431–432
foreground processes, 234–235
fork command, 417
forking, 258
forward slash (/), 56
FQDN (fully qualified domain name), 187
free -m command, 332
fsck command, 415
fstab file, 515
ftp.xml file, 501
fully qualified domain name (FQDN), 187

G

gdisk command, 317, 322–326, 350
getenforce command, 474–477
getent hosts command, 191
getsebool -a command, 484
gg command (vim), 39
gigabytes (GB), 316
GLOBAL DIRECTIVES #### section, rsyslog.conf, 300
gpasswd command, 151
GPG key, 203–204
gpgcheck= option, repositories, 202
gpgkey= option, repositories, 202
GPT (GUID Partition Table)
benefits of, 315–316
partitions
creating with gdisk, 322–326
creating with parted, 327
graphical applications, 113–114
graphical environments, multiple terminals in, 105–106
graphical.target, 390
greater than symbol (>), 33
grep command, 36, 93–94, 433, 484
group accounts
creating, 137–138
dnf package groups, 214–216
group properties, 138–139
primary groups, 137
secondary groups, 137
group ownership. *See* ownership, file/directory
groupadd command, 138
groupmems command, 139
groupmod command, 138–139
groups command, 151
GRUB 2 boot loader, 396–399
boot options, 398–399
components of, 396
configuration files, 397–398
reinstalling, 410–414
grub2-install command, 413, 414
grub2-mkconfig command, 397–398
gunzip utility, 74
gzip command, 74

H

halt command, 109–110
hard links, 68, 71
hardening, SSH (Secure Shell), 442–445
alternative port configuration, 443
root access, limiting, 442
SELinux, 443
hardware initialization, 376–377
hardware time, 526
head command, 84, 86
help
--help option, 43
/usr/share/doc documentation files, 48–49
hidden files, 64
history
Bash, 35–37
dnf, 216–217
history command, 35–37
home directories, 133
/home directory, 56, 58
home zone (firewalld), 499
host requirements, container, 543–544
hostnamectl set-hostname command, 187–188
hostnamectl status command, 187–188, 375
hostnames, 187–189
hosts, virtual, 170, 462–464
hwclock command, 528

I

i command (vim), 38
id command, 124
if…then…else loops, 430–431
if…then…else…fi statement, 428–429
ifconfig utility, 175
images, container
  building from containerfiles, 556–558
  finding, 552–553
  inspecting, 553–555
  managing, 556
  registries, 550–551
info command, 47–48
info priority, rsyslogd, 303
inheritance, 152
init=/bin/bash option, 409
init=/bin/sh option, 409
initramfs, 396, 406, 413, 415
initrd.target, 406
inodes, 68
input, shell scripting, 426–429
input mode, vim, 38
installation. *See also* configuration
  Apache server software, 456
  GRUB 2, 410–414
  Red Hat Enterprise Linux (RHEL)
    Cert Guide environment, 9–10
    repositories, 8
    setup requirements, 9
    software options, 7–8
    step-by-step process, 10–22
    subscriptions, 6–7
  SELinux man pages, 483
  software packages, 209–211
Installation Source option, 16
Installation Summary screen, 12–21
interactive processes. *See* shell jobs
interface management, 174
internal commands, 31–32
internal zone, firewalld, 499
interprocess communication (ipc), 543
I/O redirection, 32–33
IP (Internet Protocol) addresses, 170–173
  binary notation, 172–173
  IPv4 subnet masks, 171–172
  IPv6, 171
ip addr command, 175–178, 182
ip link command, 175–178
ip route command, 175–178
ip route show command, 178–179
iptables, 498
isolation of Systemd targets, 393–396
iteration. *See* loops, conditional

J

jails, chroot, 543
jobs. *See* shell jobs
jobs command, 235–237
journalctl command, 290–292, 295–298, 373–374, 415

K

KDUMP, 14
Kerberos, 512
kern facility, rsyslogd, 302
kernel. *See also* GRUB 2 boot loader
  analysis of, 373–375
  drivers, 372–373
  modules, 375–383
    checking availability of, 381–382
    definition of, 375
    dnf, 217–221
    hardware initialization, 376–377
    management of, 378–383
    parameters of, 382–383
  role of, 372–375
  tainted, 373
  threads, 234, 238, 372–373
  upgrading, 383
key-based authentication, 116–117, 203–204, 447–448
keyboard settings, 12–14
kibibytes (KiB), 316
kill command, 243–245
killall command, 243–245
kilobytes (KB), 316
Kubernetes, 545, 562
KVM, 9–10

L

[label] option, repositories, 202
labels
  file system, 334–335

- SELinux context labels
  - monitoring, 477–478
  - setting, 481–482
- language settings, 12
- latency-performance profile, 249
- LDAP (Lightweight Directory Access Protocol), 512
- less command, 84–85
- less than symbol (<), 33
- lid command, 139
- Lightweight Directory Access Protocol (LDAP), 512
- line anchors, 90
- lines, counting, 88–89
- linger feature, 541, 566–568
- links
  - creating, 69–70
  - definition of, 68
  - hard, 68, 71
  - removing, 70
  - symbolic (soft), 69, 71
- ListenDatagram, 259
- ListenStream, 259
- list-timezone command, 529
- live log ile monitoring, 294
- ln command, 69–70
- load averages, 247–248
- local consoles. *See* consoles, local
- local time, 526
- local0–7 facility, rsyslogd, 302
- ~/.local/share/containers/storage directory, 550
- log files, 487–488
  - audit, 487–488
  - contents of, 293
  - direct write, 290
  - live monitoring, 294
  - logger, 294
  - overview of, 290
  - reading, 292
  - rotating, 304–306
  - rsyslogd service, 290–292, 300–304
  - systemd-journald service
    - examining with journalctl, 295–298
    - role of, 290–292
    - systemd journal, preserving, 298–300
- logger, 294
- logical AND (&&), 431
- logical extent, 354, 359
- logical OR (||), 431
- logical partitions, 315, 320–322
- Logical Volume Manager. *See* LVM (Logical Volume Manager)
- logical volumes
  - creating, 348–349, 355, 356–357
  - resizing, 358–360
- loginctl session manager, 566–568
- logins, local console, 104–105
- logrotate command, 305
- loops, conditional, 429–435
  - case, 434–435
  - for, 431–432
  - if…then…else, 430–431
  - logical AND (&&), 431
  - logical OR (||), 431
  - until, 432–434
  - while, 432–434
- lpr facility, rsyslogd, 302
- ls command, 30, 34–35, 64, 69, 148–149, 477–478
- lsattr command, 161
- lsblk command, 317–318, 351, 353, 360
- lsmod command, 378
- lspci command, 381–382
- lv command, 348
- lvcreate command, 355, 357, 361
- lvdisplay command, 357
- lvextend command, 358–360
- LVM (Logical Volume Manager), 57–58
  - architecture, 346–347
  - benefits of, 346
  - device mapper, 356
  - device naming, 355–357
  - features, 347–348
  - logical extent, 354, 359
  - logical volumes
    - creating, 348–349, 355–357
    - resizing, 358–360
  - physical volumes, creating, 350–353
  - snapshots, 347–348
  - volume groups (VGs)
    - creating, 353–357
    - physical extent, 354
    - reducing, 360–361
    - resizing, 358
- lvremove command, 357

lvresize command, 358–360
lvs command, 357, 360

M

MAC (media access control) addresses, 173
mail facility, rsyslogd, 302
man command, 43–47, 398, 482–483
man logrotate command, 305
man pages, 44–47, 480, 483
man semanage command, 480
mandb command, 46
mark facility, rsyslogd, 302
Master Boot Record partitions. *See* MBR (Master Boot Record) partitions
MaxAuthTries option (SSH), 447
MaxSessions option (SSH), 447
MBR (Master Boot Record) partitions
  creating with fdisk, 318–320
  extended and logical partitions, 320–322
  overview of, 314–315
measurement units, storage, 316
mebibytes (MiB), 316
/media directory, 56
megabytes (MB), 316
memory tests, 411
Microsoft Hyper-V, 9–10
mirrorlist= option, repositories, 202
mkdir command, 62
mkfs command, 328–329, 355
mklabel command, 327
mkpart command, 327
mkswap command, 332–333
/mnt directory, 56
modes, SELinux, 473–477
modinfo command, 378–380, 383
modprobe command, 378–382
modules, 375–383
  checking availability of, 381–382
  definition of, 375
  dnf, 217–221
  hardware initialization, 376–377
  management of, 378–383
  parameters of, 382–383
MODULES #### section, rsyslog.conf, 300
more command, 85
MOTD_FILE, 134
mount command, 58–59, 333–338, 415, 512–513, 516
mount namespace, 543
mount units, Systemd, 258–259
mounting
  file systems
    automating through /etc/fstab, 335–338
    device names, 334–335
    disk labels, 334–335
    manually, 334
    requirements for, 333
    systemd mounts, 338–339
    UUIDs, 334–335
  NFS (Network File System) shares
    with automount, 516–518
    from command line, 514
    through /etc/fstab file, 515
multipliers in regular expressions, 91
multi-user.target file, 390–392
mv command, 65–66

N

name resolution, 189–191
name= option, repositories, 202
names, device
  file system, 334–335
  LVM (Logical Volume Manager), 355–356
namespaces, 543–544
nano editor, 266
NAT (Network Address Translation), 171
NDA (nondisclosure agreement), 576–577
netfilter, 498
netstat command, 179–180
Network Address Translation (NAT), 171
network addresses
  management of, 174
  validation of, 175–178
Network File System. *See* NFS (Network File System)
Network Information Service (NIS), 512
network masks, IPv4, 171–172
network namespace, 543
Network Time Protocol (NTP), 527
networking
  binary notation, 172–173

broadcast addresses, 172
configuration
configuration files, 186–187
hostnames, 187–189
management with nmcli, 180–184, 190
management with nmtui, 184–185, 190
name resolution, 189–191
permissions, 181
validating, 175–180
hostnames, 187–189
interface management, 174
IP (Internet Protocol) addresses, 170–173
binary notation, 172–173
IPv4 subnet masks, 171–172
IPv6, 171
MAC (media access control) addresses, 173
network addresses
management of, 174
validation of, 175–178
NetworkManager, 180
ports, 173, 179–180
protocols, 173
Red Hat Enterprise Linux (RHEL) installation settings, 20
network-latency profile, 249
NetworkManager, 180
network-throughput profile, 249
newgrp command, 150
news facility, rsyslogd, 302
NFS (Network File System)
history of, 512
security, 512
server setup, 513
shares, mounting
with automount, 516–518
from command line, 514
through /etc/fstab file, 515
versions of, 512–513
nfsvers= option (mount command), 512–513
nft command, 498
nftables, 498
nice command, 241–243
NIS (Network Information Service), 512
nmap command, 558
nmcli command, 182–184, 190
nm-connection-editor, 185
nmtui command, 184–185, 190
noatime mount option, 337
noauto mount option, 337
nodes, 170
noexec mount option, 337, 469
nohup command, 237
nondisclosure agreement (NDA), 576–577
nongraphical environments, multiple terminals in, 107–108
normal accounts, 129–132
notice priority, rsyslogd, 303
NTFS, 328
NTP (Network Time Protocol), 527
NVM Express (NVMe) interface, 317

O

o command (vim), 38
OnActiveSec option (systemd), 275
OnBootSec option (systemd), 275
OnCalendar option (systemd), 275
OnStartupSec option (systemd), 275
OnUnitActiveSec option (systemd), 275
Open Containers Initiative (OCI), 551
OpenShift, 545, 562
operators
logical AND (&&), 431
logical OR (||), 431
/opt directory, 56
options, command, 30
Oracle VM VirtualBox, 9–10
orchestration, container, 545, 563, 566
ownership, file/directory
changing, 149–150
default, 150–151
displaying, 148–149

P

p command (vim), 39
packages, software
managing with dnf, 213–214
common dnf tasks, 206
dnf history, 216–217
dnf package groups, 214–216
dnf package modules, 217–221
finding software packages with, 206–208
installing/removing packages with, 209–211

overview of, 198
returning package information with, 208–209
showing list of packages with, 211–213
updating packages with, 213–214
managing with rpm, 221–225
dependency hell, 221
overview of, 221–222
repoquery, 224–225
rpm database queries, 222–223
rpm filenames, 222
rpm package file queries, 223–225
Red Hat Enterprise Linux registration, 199
repositories
creating, 204–206
options for, 202
role of, 198–199
security, 203–204
specifying, 200–202
subscription management, 200
parent shell, 424
parent-child relationship, 237
parted command, 317, 327, 350
partitions
definition of, 314
disk device types, 317–318
extended, 315
GPT (GUID Partition Table)
benefits of, 315–316
creating with gdisk, 322–326
creating with parted, 327
logical, 315
MBR (Master Boot Record)
creating with fdisk, 318–320
extended and logical partitions, 320–322
overview of, 314–315
primary, 315
storage measurement units, 316
swap, 332–333
PASS_MAX_DAYS, 135
PASS_MIN_DAYS, 135
PASS_WARN_AGE, 135
passphrases, SSH (Secure Shell), 116–117, 447–448
passwd command, 135
PasswordAuthentication option (SSH), 447
passwords
Red Hat Enterprise Linux (RHEL) installation, 15
root password, resetting, 416–417
user accounts, 135
performance optimization, 248–249
permissions
attributes, user-extended, 160–161
default, 159–160
inheritance and, 152
network configuration, 181
read/write/execute, 152–154
set group ID (SGID), 155–159
set user ID (SUID), 155–159
sticky bit, 156–159
permissive mode, SELinux, 473–475
PermitRootLogin option, 447
PermitRootLogin prohibit-password option, 442
persistent modifier, 275
petabytes (PB), 316
pgrep command, 240
physical extent, 354
physical volumes, creating, 350–353
PID (process identification number), 238
pinfo command, 47–48
ping command, 431–432
pipe (|), 33–35, 431
pkexec command, 127
pkill command, 243–245
plus sign (+), 92
Podman, 542, 544
commands, running in container, 559–560
container environment variables, managing, 562–563
container images
building, 556–558
finding, 552–553
inspecting, 553–555
managing, 556
container ports, managing, 561
container status, managing, 558–559
container storage, managing, 563–564
containers, running, 545–550, 555, 566–568
registries, finding, 550–551
podman build command, 556–558

podman exec command, 559–560, 566
podman generate command, 567–568
podman generate systemd command, 567–568
podman info command, 550–551
podman inspect command, 553–555, 562–563
podman kill command, 559
podman login command, 552
podman logs command, 562–564
podman ps command, 548–550, 558–559
podman restart command, 559
podman rm command, 559
podman rmi command, 556
podman run command, 545–550, 555, 559, 561
podman search command, 552–553
podman stop command, 559
podman unshare command, 565
policy violations, SELinux, 487–490
PolicyKit, 127
pool, Stratis, 362–363
port access, SELinux, 484–485
Port option (SSH), 447
ports, 173
  container, 561
  SSH (Secure Shell), 443
  validation of, 179–180
positional parameters, 426–427
poweroff command, 109–110
Power-On Self-Test (POST), 406
powersave profile, 249
practice exams, tips for, 581–584
pre-assessment exam, 579–580
preparation
  for Red Hat Enterprise Linux (RHEL) installation
    Cert Guide environment, 9–10
    distributions, 7–8
    setup requirements, 9
    step-by-step process, 10–22
    subscriptions, 6–7
  for RHCSA exam
    exam day tips, 574–576
    nondisclosure agreement (NDA), 576–577
    registration, 573–574
    verifying readiness, 573
primary groups, 137
primary partitions, 315
priorities
  process, 241–243
    management of, 242–243
    overview of, 241
    relations between slices, 241–242
  rsyslogd, 301–303
private keys, 116
privileged users, 124
/proc directory, 56, 373–375
process identification number (PID), 238
process management
  command-line tools for
    kill command, 243–245
    killall command, 243–245
    nice command, 241–243
    pkill command, 243–245
    ps aux | head command, 238
    ps command, 239–240
    renice command, 241–243
    top command, 246–248
    tuned command, 248–249
  daemons, 234
  kernel threads, 234
  overview of, 234
  performance optimization, 248–249
  process priorities, 241–243
    management of, 242–243
    overview of, 241
    relations between slices, 241–242
  process states, 247
  process types, 238
  shell jobs, 234–237
    common job management tasks, 235–237
    definition of, 234
    parent-child relationship, 237
    running in foreground/background, 234–235
  signals, sending to processes, 243–245
  tuned profiles, 248–249
  zombies, 245–246
process namespace, 543
~/.profile file, 136
profiles
  dnf, 218

setting during Red Hat Enterprise Linux (RHEL) installation, 14
tuned, 248–249
programmatic API, 362
properties
Ext4 file systems, 329–331
group, 138–139
password, 135
user, 134
XFS file systems, 331–332
protocols, 173
ps aux command, 88, 238, 245–246, 372
ps command, 239–240
ps Zaux command, 477
pseudo terminal devices, 108–109
public keys, 116
public zone (firewalld), 499
pv command, 348
pvcreate command, 348, 350–352, 354, 357
pvdisplay command, 352–353, 357
pvmove command, 348, 360
pvremove command, 357
pvs command, 351–352, 356–357, 360
pwd command, 34, 62–63

Q

queries
repoquery, 224–225
rpm database, 222–223
rpm package files, 223–225
question mark (?), 61, 92
quiet option, GRUB 2 boot loader, 398

R

rd.break, 409
read command, 427–429
read permissions, 152–154
reading text files
with cat command, 85
with head and tail commands, 86
with less command, 84–85
real-time clock (RTC), 526
reboot command, 109–110, 417
rebooting system, 21–22, 109–110
Red Hat Customer Portal, 6–7, 198
Red Hat Enterprise Linux registration, 199
Red Hat Enterprise Linux (RHEL) installation
Cert Guide environment, 9–10
repositories, 8
setup requirements, 9
software options, 7–8
step-by-step process, 10–22
Begin Installation process, 21
Installation Summary screen, 12–21
Reboot System process, 21–22
Welcome to Red Hat Enterprise Linux 9.0 screen, 11
subscriptions, 6–7
Red Hat Enterprise Linux subscription management, 200
Red Hat Network (RHN), 7
Red Hat Package Manager (RPM), 198. *See also* rpm command
Red Hat Subscription Management (RHSM) tools, 199
redirection, I/O, 32–33
registration
of Red Hat Enterprise Linux, 199
for RHCSA exam, 573–574
registries, 542, 550–551
regular expressions, 89–96
awk command with, 94–96
definition of, 89
escaping in, 91
examples of, 89–90
extended, 91–93
grep command with, 93–94
line anchors, 90
wildcards and multipliers in, 91
relabeling action, SELinux, 484
relative filenames, 62–64
remote NFS shares, mounting
with automount, 516–518
through /etc/fstab file, 515
remote systems, accessing with SSH (Secure Shell), 110–113
renice command, 241–243
.repo files. *See* repositories
repoquery, 224–225
repositories, 8
Application Stream (AppStream) repository, 205–206
creating, 204–206

EPEL (Extra Packages for Enterprise Linux) repositories, 199
options for, 202
role of, 198–199
security, 203–204
specifying, 200–202
rescue disks, 410–414
rescue.target, 390
resizing
logical volumes, 358–360
volume groups (VGs), 358
restorecon command, 483–484
restoring SELinux default file contexts, 483–484
RHCSA exam. *See* exam, RHCSA
RHEL, 274
rhgb option, GRUB 2 boot loader, 398
rm command, 66, 70
rmdir command, 62
Rocky Linux, 8
root access, limiting, 442
root directory (/), 56
root password, 15, 416–417
root users (superusers), 124–125
rootless container, 544
routing, validation of, 179–180
rpm command, 221–225
dependency hell, 221
overview of, 221–222
repoquery, 224–225
rpm database queries, 222–223
rpm filenames, 222
rpm package file queries, 223–225
rsync command, 114–115
rsyslogd
configuration, 300–304
configuration files, 300
facilities, priorities, and destinations, 301–303
rules, changing, 304
role of, 290–292
RTC (real-time clock), 526
rules (rsyslogd), changing, 304
RULES #### section, rsyslog.conf, 300–301
/run directory, 56
/run/log/journal file, 298–300
Running (R) state, 247
run-parts command, 280
/run/systemd/system directory, 257

S

Samba, 515
/sbin/init, 406
scheduling
anacron service, 281
at command, 282–283
atd service, 282–283
batch command, 283
crond service
anacron, 281
cron configuration files, 278–280
cron time/date fields, 278
management of, 276–277
running scheduled tasks through, 282
security, 282
RHEL, 274
systemd timers, 274–276
scp command, 114
scripting, shell
conditional loops, 429–435
case, 434–435
for, 431–432
if...then...else, 430–431
logical AND (&&), 431
logical OR (||), 431
until, 432–434
while, 432–434
core elements of, 424–425
debugging, 435
variables and input, 426–429
sealert command, 489–490
secondary groups, 137–138
security
cron, 282
NFS (Network File System), 512
repositories, 203–204
rsyslogd, 302
security profiles, 14
SELinux, 463–464, 484, 544
Boolean settings, 485–487
context settings
context labels, monitoring, 477–478
context labels, setting, 481–482
context types, finding needed, 482–483

context types, setting, 479–481
overview of, 477
core elements of, 473
default file contexts, restoring, 483–484
man pages, installing, 483
overview of, 469
policy violations, 487–490
port access, managing, 484–485
relabeling action, 484
working modes, 473–477
semanage command, 443–445, 479–482, 484–486, 490, 564
sepolicy generate command, 476
Server with GUI option, 18
ServerAliveCountMax option (SSH), 447
ServerAliveInterval option (SSH), 447
ServerRoot parameter, Apache, 456–459
servers
Apache
software installation, 456–460
virtual hosts, 462–464
booting/rebooting, 109–110
shutting down, 109–110
session options, SSH (Secure Shell), 446
sestatus command, 475–477
set group ID (SGID) permissions, 155–159
set n lvm on command, 350
set user ID (SUID) permissions, 155–159
setenforce command, 474–477
set-local-rtc command, 529
set-ntp command, 529
setsebool command, 486
set-time command, 529
set-timezone command, 529
sftp command, 115
shares (NFS), mounting
with automount, 516–518
from command line, 514
through /etc/fstab file, 515
shebang, 424
shell
commands. *See also individual commands*
aliases, 31
command-line completion, 37
executing, 30–32
help, 43
internal/external, 31–32
I/O redirection, 32–33
pipes, 34–35
running in containers, 559–560
syntax for, 30
default, 133
definition of, 30
environment
configuration files, 41–43
definition of, 40
variables, 40–41. *See also individual variables*
help
--help option, 43
info/pinfo commands, 47–48
man pages, 44–47
/usr/share/doc documentation files, 48–49
history, 35–37
local console connections
booting/rebooting, 109–110
logging in to, 104–105
pseudo terminal devices, 108–109
shutting down, 109–110
switching between terminals, 105–108
terminals versus, 104
parent, 424
shell jobs, 234–237
common job management tasks, 235–237
definition of, 234
parent-child relationship, 237
running in foreground/background, 234–235
shell scripting
conditional loops, 429–435
core elements of, 424–425
debugging, 435
variables and input, 426–429
SSH (Secure Shell)
accessing remote systems with, 110–113
configuration, 442–448, 464
copying files in, 114
file synchronization, 115
graphical applications in, 113–114
key-based authentication for, 116–117, 447–448
passphrases, 460–461
secure file transfers, 115

secure file transfers in, 115
subshells, 41–42, 105, 424
wildcards, 61
shell jobs, 234–237
common job management tasks, 235–237
definition of, 234
parent-child relationship, 237
running in foreground/background, 234–235
showmount command, 514
shutting down system, 109–110
SIGKILL command, 559
SIGTERM signal, 559
skopeo, 542, 553
Sleeping (S) state, 247
slices, 241
management of, 242–243
overview of, 241
relations between, 241–242
snapshots
LVM (Logical Volume Manager), 347–348
Stratis, 362
socket units, Systemd, 259
soft links, 69, 71
software, Red Hat Enterprise Linux (RHEL), 7–8
software clock, 526
software management
with dnf
common dnf tasks, 206
dnf history, 216–217
dnf package groups, 214–216
dnf package modules, 217–221
finding software packages with, 206–208
installing/removing packages with, 209–211
overview of, 198
returning package information with, 208–209
showing list of packages with, 211–213
updating packages with, 213–214
Red Hat Enterprise Linux registration, 199
repositories
creating, 204–206
options for, 202
role of, 198–199
security, 203–204
specifying, 200–202
with rpm, 221–225
dependency hell, 221
overview of, 221–222
repoquery, 224–225
rpm database queries, 222–223
rpm filenames, 222
rpm package file queries, 223–225
subscription management, 200
Software Selection option, RHEL installation, 18
sort command, 84, 87–88
source context, 488
/srv directory, 56
ss command, 179–180, 477
SSH (Secure Shell)
accessing remote systems with, 110–113
configuration, 464
connection keepalive options, 446–447
hardening, 442–445
key-based authentication, 447–448
most useful options, 447
session options, 446
copying files in, 114
file synchronization, 115
graphical applications in, 113–114
key-based authentication for, 116–117, 447–448
passphrases, 460–461
secure file transfers in, 115
ssh command, 110–114
ssh-add command, 448
ssh-agent command, 448
ssh-keygen command, 117
st command, 274
star utility, 73
starting Red Hat Enterprise Linux (RHEL) installation, 21
states, process, 247
status, container, 558–559
status command, 529
STDERR, 32–33
STDIN, 32–33
STDOUT, 32–33
sticky bit, 156–159
Stopped (T) state, 247

storage. *See* containers; file systems; LVM (Logical Volume Manager); partitions; Stratis
Stratis, 361–364
  architecture, 362
  features of, 361–362
  management of, 363–364
  snapshots, 362
  volumes, creating, 362–363
stratis blockdev command, 363
stratis filesystem command, 363
stratis fs create command, 363
stratis fs list command, 363
stratis pool command, 363
stratum, 527
streams, dnf, 218
su command, 125–126
subnet masks, 172–173
subscription management, 200
subscription-manager tool, 199–201
subscriptions, Red Hat Enterprise Linux (RHEL), 6–7
subshells, 41–42, 105, 424
sudo command, 105, 126–128
sudo dnf install container-tools command, 545
sudo podman ps command, 561
sudo podman run command, 561
superusers, 124–125
swap files, 333
swap partitions, 332–333
swapon command, 332–333
symbolic links, 69, 71
synchronization, time, 527, 530–531
/sys directory, 56
syslog facility, rsyslogd, 302
system accounts, 129–132
system logging. *See* log files
system time, 526
systemctl command, 261–263, 275
systemctl disable command, 392–393
systemctl edit command, 266–267
systemctl enable command, 260–261, 363, 392–393, 459, 566–568
systemctl --failed -t service command, 263
systemctl get-default command, 396
systemctl halt command, 109–110
systemctl isolate command, 393–396
systemctl list-dependencies command, 260, 263
systemctl list-units command, 263, 275, 410
systemctl poweroff command, 109–110
systemctl reboot command, 109–110
systemctl restart autofs command, 518
systemctl restart httpd command, 464
systemctl set-default command, 396
systemctl show command, 265–267
systemctl start vsftpd command, 261
systemctl status command, 180, 261–263, 276–277, 290–292, 445, 459
systemctl -t help command, 256
systemctl -t service command, 263
systemctl --type=target command, 393–396
systemctl --user command, 566–568
Systemd, 109–110
  mounts, 338–339
  overview of, 256
  systemd-journald
    examining with journalctl, 295–298
    preserving, 298–300
    role of, 290–292
  targets, 390–396
    isolating, 393–396
    managing, 392–393
    showing list of, 393–396
    target units, 391–392
    types of, 390
    wants, 392
  timers, 274–276
  units
    changing configuration of, 266–267
    definition of, 256
    dependencies, 263–265
    displaying list of, 256
    locations, 256–257
    management of, 261–263
    mount, 258–259
    options for, 265–266
    socket, 259
    target, 260–261
    unit file, 257–258
systemd-udevd daemon, 376, 406
systemd.unit=emergency.target topion, 410
systemd.unit=rescue.target option, 410

T

tail command, 84, 86, 106, 294
tainted kernels, 373
tar command, 72–75
target context, 488
targets, Systemd, 390–396
  isolating, 393–396
  managing, 392–393
  showing list of, 393–396
  target units, 260–261, 391–392
  troubleshooting, 409–410
  types of, 390
  wants, 392
task scheduling. *See* scheduling
TCPKeepAlive option (SSH), 446, 447
terabytes (TB), 316
term command, 105
terminals, 107
  consoles versus, 104
  multiple
    in graphical environment, 105–106
    in nongraphical environment, 107–108
  pseudo terminal devices, 108–109
test command, 428, 431
/text command (vim), 39
text editors
  vi, 38
  vim, 37–40
text files
  regular expressions, 89–96
    awk command with, 94–96
    definition of, 89
    escaping in, 91
    examples of, 89–90
    extended, 91–93
    grep command with, 93–94
    line anchors, 90
    wildcards and multipliers in, 91
  text file-related tools
    cat, 85
    cut, 87
    head and tail commands, 86
    less, 84–85
    sort, 87–88
    table of, 84
    wc, 88–89
text$ regular expression, 92
text-processing tools
  awk, 94–96
  grep, 93–94
then statement, 428
theoretical pre-assessment exam, 579–580
thin provisioning, 361–362
threads, kernel, 234, 238, 372–373
throughput-performance profile, 249
time services
  client configuration, 533–534
  epoch time, 528
  local time, 526
  NTP (Network Time Protocol), 527
  RTC (real-time clock), 526
  system time, 526
  time management commands, 527–531
    date, 528
    hwclock, 528
    time, 32
    timedatectl, 529–530
  time synchronization, 527, 530–531
  time zone settings, 531–533
  time/date fields, 278
  time/date settings, 14–15
timedatectl command, 527, 529–533
timers, systemd, 274–276
TLS (Transport Layer Security), 443
/tmp directory, 57
top command, 246–248
touch /.autorelabel command, 417
Transport Layer Security (TLS), 443
troubleshooting
  boot issues
    boot phase configuration, 406–408
    boot prompt, accessing, 408–409
    file system issues, 415
    GRUB 2 reinstallation, 414
    initramfs, 415
    rescue disks, 410–414
    root password, resetting, 416–417
    troubleshooting targets, 409–410
  Red Hat Enterprise Linux (RHEL) installation, 10
  shell scripts, debugging, 435
trusted zone (firewalld), 499
tune2fs command, 329–331
tuned command, 248–249

type command, 31
tzselect utility, 531–533

U

u command (vim), 39
udevadm monitor command, 376–377
UEFI (Unified Extensible Firmware Interface), 315, 406
UID_MIN, 135
umask command, 159–160
umount command, 334
uname utility, 373–375
Unified Extensible Firmware Interface (UEFI), 315
Uninterruptible sleep (D) state, 247
units, Systemd
  changing configuration of, 266–267
  definition of, 256
  dependencies, 263–265
  displaying list of, 256
  locations, 256–257
  management of, 261–263
  mount, 258–259
  options for, 265–266
  socket, 259
  target, 260–261, 391–392
  unit file, 257–258
Universal Extended Firmware Interface (UEFI), 406
universally unique IDs (UUIDs), 334–335
UNIX, 512. *See also* NFS (Network File System)
unprivileged users, 124
until loops, 432–434
updates
  exam, 617–618
  software packages, 213–214
upgrades, Linux kernel, 383
uptime command, 247–248
UseDNS option (SSH), 447
user accounts, switching between, 125–126
User Creation option, RHEL installation, 16
user environment, 135–136
user facility, rsyslogd, 302
user management
  group accounts
    creating, 137–138
    group properties, 138–139
    primary groups, 137
    secondary groups, 137
  user accounts
    creating, 132–133, 136
    default values, 134–135
    normal accounts, 129–132
    password properties, 135
    system accounts, 129–132
    user environment, 135–136
    user properties, 134
  user types
    PolicyKit, 127
    privileged/unprivileged, 124
    root users (superusers), 124–125
    su command, 125–126
    sudo command, 126–128
    switching between, 125–126
user namespace, 543
user ownership. *See* ownership, file/directory
user_xattr mount option, 337
useradd command, 126, 132–133
userdel command, 132
user-extended attributes, 160–161
usermod command, 133–134, 138–139
/usr directory, 57, 58
/usr/lib/modules-load.d directory, 378
/usr/lib/systemd/system directory, 256
UTC (Coordinated Universal Time), 526
uucp facility, rsyslogd, 302
UUIDs (universally unique IDs), 334–335

V

v command (vim), 39
-v host_dir:container_dir command, 564
validation
  of network configuration, 175–180
    network addresses, 175–178
    network settings, 179–180
    ports and services, 179
    routing, 178–179
/var directory, 57, 58
variables, 40–41

$LANG, 40
$PATH, 31
container environment variables, 561
shell scripting, 426–429
defining, 427–429
positional parameters, 426–427
/var/log directory, 292–293
/var/log/audit/audit.log file, 487–488
Very Secure FTP service, 257
VFAT, 328
vg command, 348
vgcreate command, 353–354, 356–357, 361
vgdisplay command, 354–355, 357
vgextend command, 358, 360
vgreduce command, 358, 360–361
vgremove command, 357
vgs command, 354–355, 357–358, 360
vi editor, 38
vigr command, 132–133, 137–139
vim editor, 37–40
vimtutor command, 38
vipw command, 132–134
virtual hosts, Apache, 462–464
virtual terminals, 107–108
virtual-guest profile, 249
virtual-host profile, 249
visudo command, 127
VMware Workstation, 9–10
volume groups (VGs)
creating, 353–357
physical extent, 354
reducing, 360–361
resizing, 358
volume-managing file systems, 361. *See also* Stratis
volumes, Stratis, 362–363

W

wants, 260–261, 392
warning/warn priority, rsyslogd, 303
wc command, 88–89
we command, 84
Web server content, creating, 459–460
Welcome to Red Hat Enterprise Linux 9.0 screen, 11
which command, 31, 225
while loops, 432–434
whoami command, 126
wildcards, 61
in automount, 517–518
in regular expressions, 91
words, counting, 88–89
work zone (firewalld), 499
working modes, SELinux, 473–477
write permissions, 152–154

X

Xen virtual machine, 317
XFS file system, 328, 331–332, 362
xfs_admin command, 331–332, 334
xz utility, 74

Y

yottabytes (YB), 316
yumdownloader command, 225
yum-utils package, 225
yy command (vim), 39

Z

zettabytes (ZB), 316
zombies, 245–246, 247
zones, firewalld, 499

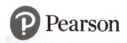